Nehru

THE MAKING OF INDIA

M. J. AKBAR

VIKING

VIKING

Published by the Penguin Group
27 Wrights Lane, London w8 5TZ, England
Viking Penguin Inc., 40 West 23rd Street, New York, New York 10010, USA
Penguin Books Australia Ltd, Ringwood, Victoria, Australia
Penguin Books Canada Ltd, 2801 John Street, Markham, Ontario, Canada L3R 1B4
Penguin Books (NZ) Ltd, 182–190 Wairau Road, Auckland 10, New Zealand

Penguin Books Ltd, Registered Offices: Harmondsworth, Middlesex, England

First published 1988
10 9 8 7 6 5 4 3

Printed in Great Britain by Richard Clay Ltd, Bungay, Suffolk
Filmset in 11/13 Sabon

A CIP catalogue record for this book is available from the British Library

ISBN 0–670–81699–X

Library of Congress Catalog Card No.: 88–50691

To
Mallika

Contents

Acknowledgements

Gandhi made him Prime Minister of India in 1947; the people endorsed the decision in the general elections of 1952. In 1955 the Cabinet awarded him the highest honour possible, the Bharat Ratna (Jewel of India) and by 1957 some Indians were seriously discussing the possibility that Jawaharlal Nehru was a prophet, the reincarnation of a *yogi* blessed with miraculous powers. A story appeared in newspapers that in January 1889, the 29-old-year Motilal, still childless and dearly desirous of a son – his first had died – went to the holy city of Rishikesh in the Himalayas along with Pandit Madan Mohan Malviya and Pandit Din Dayal Shastri. One evening they encountered a *yogi* who lived in a tree and practised penance there. Malviya told this famous *yogi* that Motilal wanted nothing more in this world than a son. The *yogi* took one look at Motilal and informed him that he was not destined to have one. Pandit Din Dayal intervened, quoting from the *shastras* to point out that if a *karmayogi* like him so desired, he could change destiny and award Motilal a boon. The *yogi* fell silent. He then thrice sprinkled water from his pot in front of Motilal, grew pale and told Motilal that he had taken away all the fruits of his penance of many lifetimes. The next day the *yogi* died. Ten months later Jawaharlal was born.

The agnostic visionary of modern India dismissed the story as myth – which became a Catch-22 denial because myth is precisely what people are far more ready to believe. The story was ascribed to Motilal and Malviya, and witnesses sprang to authenticate it by claiming they had heard it from the great men themselves. Belief is always more powerful than truth. In any case, what is beyond dispute is the extraordinary faith Motilal had in his son as a child of destiny. This is all the more surprising given the fact that perhaps the most remarkable aspect of Jawaharlal's childhood was how unremarkable it was. Far from displaying flashes of genius, the young Jawaharlal did not even seem to have the saving grace of ambition. But both his father, Motilal, and later his godfather, Gandhi, were convinced from early on that Jawaharlal was the man who would lead his country into freedom and then out of the grinding poverty and destructive strife that had chained India for so long. As much as any man could hope to do so, Jawaharlal honoured that awesome trust.

Nehru's horoscope, I have been informed by a gentleman who is good at these things, Prayaag Bandhopadhyay, shows that he was destined to have more fame than power – a most perceptive assessment. He was an idealist, and his ideas commanded an empire far larger than the India he ruled for eighteen years. He liked being called a philosopher–statesman in the Platonic mould, though he would hasten to add that his advice to philosophers was to cease philosophizing and get down to work. But behind whatever Jawaharlal did was an ideology, a pattern of ideas which he believed were in the best interests of not just his nation but also the world. Ved Mehta put it well in a piece in the *New Yorker* after his first meeting with the Prime Minister: Nehru, he wrote, was doing with India what a poet does with words. And he caught the essence of Jawaharlal: 'I feel I am confronting Sanskrit, Mughal and English India at the same time; he represents the three Indias with their extremes but without their contradictions . . . I feel the real secret of free India lies in the Prime Minister. His character reconciles the various Indias.' It was the alchemy of the Gandhi–Nehru idealism, of reconciling the contradictions which had crawled into the complex Indian psyche, that created modern India. Nehru's heart was filled with old-fashioned love; it was a vast reservoir of emotion for his country and its people, which burst often into words, actions, reactions. And Nehru's mind was steeped in new ideas – in science, in political theory and in a secular interpretation of history. As he said, he learned from books, not with an academic's purist passion but in order to serve the people better.

A life such as Jawaharlal Nehru's was bound to attract the attention of scribes, but there are many reasons for another biography – not the least of them being that there are actually fewer than people imagine. But there is one obvious question: is there anything more to say after S. Gopal's splendid and exhaustive three-volume study? The life of a great man is a fascinating labyrinth, and each author brings his own discoveries, the emphasis of his particular perceptions to such a subject. For me this book has been the fulcrum of a journey into my country's recent past, a search which had a personal significance, as I needed to know why the unity of India had been destroyed in the name of Islam. Through the prism of one man's life I discovered the illumination which enabled me to see the many dimensions of the philosophy of unity, as well as the nature of the struggle. For thirty years Nehru fought and suffered to make his country free and to keep his motherland united. In 1947 he achieved the first and failed in the second. The next seventeen years were devoted to preserving what was left, nourishing the flame of idealism in the teeth of dangerous storms and simultaneously building prosperity, brick by brick, grain by grain, in his war against the degrading poverty to which India had been reduced by imperialism and disunity.

It was about five years ago that I felt confident enough to propose this biography to Peter Mayer. Peter's affectionate generosity towards me prompted an immediate reply – yes. That was the easy part. It has been a long and difficult five years of work on this book, and it is obvious that it would never have been possible without the indulgence of my friends and the pampering of my colleagues. It has been my signal good fortune that I have friends who have tolerated my demands on them during the tense pregnancy which preceded publication. To Aveek and Arup Sarkar – well, they should be named the godfathers of this book. I can never forget all that they have done for me over so many years. I am even more grateful to a friend who is very dear to me, Shekhar

Bhatia – but I know he did it all for a brother. My heartfelt thanks go to all my fellow journalists on the *Telegraph*, who did all they could to reduce my daily professional burden. But there is one person to whom I am particularly beholden: Sunrita Sen joined me in an intricate search through books, newspapers, documents, and helped enormously in working out the puzzles hidden in the nooks and crannies of great events. I can never even hope to repay such an extravagant debt to this friend.

Sharada Prasad has, with now legendary silence, spent a long career at the centre of the most extraordinary drama as a close confidant of Mrs Indira Gandhi. He has also been a co-editor, along with Dr Gopal, of the Nehru papers, being published by the Jawaharlal Nehru Memorial Fund. In addition to many a quiet nudge along the way, Sharada has read the manuscript up to the partition period: my very grateful thanks for all his help. The venerable governor of Orissa, freedom fighter and historian B. N. Pande also read the early chapters: the guidance I received certainly bolstered my confidence. There are so many others who helped with books, encouragement, advice: P. D. Tandon, who was a journalist reporting from Anand Bhavan during the freedom movement; Bhola Chatterjee, who was an activist in the socialist revolt in Nepal; Akhilesh Mithal, in love with his city, Dilli, who spent a gentle winter's day recreating the ambience of Shahjahanabad; the vivacious Louise Nicholson, who cheered up a grey and dismal trip to Harrow in a season which the British, for some odd reason, insist on describing as summer. There are so many friends and acquaintances who helped in so very many ways that I am terrified of an unwarranted omission, but I can only plead with my vast number of unnamed benefactors to forgive me. Our librarians at Ananda Bazar, Shakti Das Roy and Tushar Sanyal, were absolutely wonderful; without their most generous help this work would have been impossible. I must add a very special thank you to Tarun Karmakar, who was absolutely splendid in his assistance in making the manuscript fit for an editor's eyes.

Which brings me to Peter Carson. It is difficult to convey quite how anxious an author can get when he finally offers his manuscript for a look outside his own closed world. Those who know him know that Peter may be kind, but he does not allow generosity to interfere noticeably with his judgement. When Peter nodded a twinkling approval, I celebrated. Over two books Peter has taught me a few things about writing – about pace and style and structure and the management of a concept. It was Peter, for instance, who suggested that I need not burden the book with cross-references to quotations; the sources, therefore, have been married with the text. It was Peter who provided the title of the book. After so many years and hundreds of thousands of words my mind had become numb; I just seemed unable to offer a reasonable title. Peter said it all during lunch on a sun-blessed London day: 'It is about the making of India, isn't it?' It is. Add to this the support, encouragement and affection I have received from Patrick Wright, and you have an author's dream situation. And most of all my thanks go to Zamir Ansari, who, of course, is a colleague in publishing but is also a beloved friend.

It is during phases such as work on a difficult book that one appreciates the true value of close friends. Our small circle in Calcutta has knitted itself into a warm group which, without much fuss, encouraged and supported me tremendously: Shekhar and Paakhi Bhatia, of course; Arup (who believed) and Leena Chowdhury; Bikash (who urged and urged) and Debjani Sinha; Ashish and Rani Mitra; Salloo and Nina Chowdhury; Sunil and Gita Gujral; Prakash and Sandhya Apte. A thank you – without fuss, with affection.

For more than five years now my children, Mukulika and Prayaag, have tolerated an absentee father. But perhaps they will understand when they read this book in a few years. Mukulika is now a beautiful little lady of eleven, and Prayaag a growing young man of six. Perhaps they will find their father's work of some benefit to their own lives: this is another gift of love to them. My wife Mallika has been the mature centre around which our family revolves: she has our love, though I am certain she wishes we would try her patience less. *Nehru: The Making of India* is dedicated to Mallika.

1 The Pandits

The only romantic thing about the Temple of Eighty-Four Bells (Chaurasi Ghanta) is the name. It is a rather undistinguished house of the Lord Shiva, the preferred deity of the Kashmiri Pandits who in the middle of the last century were the most notable residents of Bazar Sitaram, its lanes as narrow still as they were when built more than 350 years ago but infinitely more crowded. Winding, bustling, the air resonant with the cry of fruit and savoury vendors, the shops small and dark as if electricity had not yet reached them, the road still echoing to the clatter of a horse carriage or the heavy tread of a bullock cart, Bazar Sitaram is a commercial artery of the 'veritable heaven on earth' founded by the emperor who spent a lifetime infusing magic into stone, Abul Muzaffar Shahbuddin Muhammad Sahib-i-qiran-i-sani Shah Jahan, King of the World, Defender of the Faith and famous still in every corner of the earth as the builder of the Taj Mahal.

The city of Delhi is almost as old as the history of India. It precedes the age of the written record and enters the realm of a stronger belief: epic verse and legend. At the site of the ruins of the Purana Qila (the Old Fort) lay the fabled city of Indraprastha, or Inderpat (one of five *pats* or places, the others being Panipat, Sonepat, Tilpat and Baghpat), where the great war of Kuru Kshetra was fought between the Kurus and Pandavas, and was immortalized in the verse of the *Mahabharata*. Recent excavations have unearthed baked bricks and painted grey ware of the Epic Age: each layer of rubble reinforcing yet another legend. Like all political capitals, Delhi's fortunes swayed with the rise and fall of its temporal keepers. From the middle of the eleventh century begins Delhi's 'medieval period', and the monuments of its medieval kings still stand as witnesses to transitory glory. Here begins the age of the so-called Seven Cities; the seven bursts of construction by rajas and sultans in search of civilization. *Circa* 1050 came the First City: Qila Rai Pithora of the Tomar Rajput prince Raja Anangpal, who brought the Iron Pillar to Delhi. It was here that the faith in the Bell of Justice began –

any aggrieved person could summon the king by ringing the bell in those admittedly simpler times. Rai Pithora was lost by the last Rajput king of Delhi, Prithvi Raj III, to Shihab-ud-din Ghori, with whom started the reign of Muslim emperors that was finally broken in 1857: 1192–1857. The Second City of Delhi was built at Siri in 1303; the Third was the dream of the erratic genius Muhammad-bin-Tughlaq, who founded Tughlaqabad in 1321. The Fourth, in Jahanpanah, came in 1334; the Fifth, in 1354, at Ferozabad and Kotla; and the Sixth was built by the Mughal Humayun and Afghan Sher Shah, with its fort, Purana Qila, and the living-areas of Din-panah and Sher Shahabad, between 1530 and 1540. The Seventh City of Delhi was built around the Lal Qila, or the Red Fort, and the Jama Masjid (the Great Mosque) by Shah Jahan in 1648. (Each city, apart from Tughlaqabad, moved north, close to the coolness of the mountains and to the waters of the Yamuna.)

Five times in its medieval life Delhi was destroyed by punitive marauders who came to loot rather than rule, bar one exception. The Mughal, Timur, played havoc in 1398–9; the Persian, Nadir Shah, in 1739; the Afghan, Ahmad Shah Abdali, in 1757; the Rohilla, Ghulam Qadir Khan, in 1788. The exception was John Company (another name for the Honourable East India Company, founded in 1599), which ravaged and looted after the Indian Mutiny in 1857, but stayed on to repair and build what became the Eighth City – the work of Lutyens in the first quarter of this century, New Delhi. Delhi today is an amalgam of the city of Shah Jahan, the old Shahjahanabad whose walls were destroyed in the name of slum clearance in the 1950s, and New Delhi, with its House of Parliament, the Palace of the Viceroy (now Rashtrapati Bhavan), India Gate, sprawling old bungalows, depressing new flats and a rash of embassies trying to outdo one another in innovative architecture.

A 3.8-mile, 27-foot-high, 12-foot-thick stone wall encircled Shahjahanabad, built in 1651–8, topped by twenty-seven towers and broken by gates large and small, the prominent ones being Kashmiri, Mori, Kabuli, Lahori, Ajmeri, Turkomani, Akbarabadi and Masjid. And along the Yamuna river were the Raj Ghat, Qila Ghat and Nigambodh Ghat. During the long glory of Mughal power, the city of Shahjahanabad was a wonder to travellers like François Bernier, a physician, who described it as 'Qila-i-Mualla', the Court of the Exalted Fort. The most prosperous capital in Asia inevitably attracted artisans, business men, bureaucrats and fortune-seekers from all over: Armenia, Persia, Central Asia, Afghanistan, Kashmir. The Kashmiris had some historical advantages. A hundred years before the Emperor Akbar brought Kashmir into the Mughal Empire, the valley's ruler, Zain-ul-Abedin, had brought Persian to the Kashmiri court, and encouraged the Kashmiri Pandit community to join his government. The Pandit was a natural administrator. When Akbar made Persian the language of business in his empire, the Kashmiri Pandit was in a happy position to expand the range of his reach.

One of the first Pandits to emerge in the Mughal court was Sadanand Kaul, who was said to have been invited to the court by Akbar himself. He settled down in Agra and was part of Jahangir's entourage when he visited Kashmir. He survived into Shah Jahan's reign, had bestowed on him the title of Ghumkhuar and was granted a residence in Shahjahanabad. The Mughals loved Kashmir; its exquisite beauty was charm enough, but it was also nearer to their homeland north of the Pamirs. Dara Shikoh, the scholar-sufi son of Shah Jahan, lived for long spells in Kashmir and translated the *Upanishads* into Persian with the help of Pandits, including Janardhan Zutshi. The migration continued. Early in the eighteenth century Muhammad Shah Rangila made Jai Ram Bhan a raja. Some Kashmiri families, like the Bhans and Mullas, claim to have come to Delhi as early as the fourteenth century; and certainly pilgrimage must have taken a few of the devout Brahmins to Varanasi or Allahabad. But the court rather than the temple was the Kashmiri's preference. Surnames changed sometimes with changing roles: some Kauls became Bakshis after getting jobs in treasuries, and a Gurtoo became Bahadur ('Brave') after service in the imperial army. A Dar family adopted the title Shah, while Sapru is said to have originated from a compliment on proficiency in Persian – a conjunct of *sabiq* and *para* (from 'Farsi ka sabiq para', or a lesson well done). Nor were Kashmiris necessarily found lagging in the popular art of flattery, in particular bad poetry in praise of patrons. The rewards were considerable, including *jaghirs* and high appointments. Kashmiris became one of the most powerful factions of the court, as W. Irvine points out in *Later Mughals* (1971). All the competing migrants lived in the shadow of the fort, in close proximity to power. The Kashmiris chose the narrow lanes winding north-west from Turkman Gate, Bazar Sitaram: houses packed above shops, rich living next to middle class – the mansion of a Raja Kedar Nath or a Jiwan Ram Kaul 'Mohari' ('after coins') or a Ganga Ram Raina dominating an alley; the Shish Mahal of the Handoo family a stone's throw away from the mansion of the Haksars or the Saprus. The Pandits' literacy in Persian and their felicity in administration were the classic combination for court bureaucracy. Equally important was their sense that they were a bridge between the clashing perceptions, interests and demands of the two dominating communities of north India, the Hindus and the Muslims. By religion the Kashmiri Pandit was the epitome of the Hindu caste system, by temperament the epicure of Muslim-inspired civilization. He was both the Brahmin and the meat-eater, the man whom both Hindus and Muslims could trust.

Long years as the cultivated bureaucrat had also given the Kashmiri a fine nose for the shifting odours of power. Even as a Narain Das Okhal 'Zamir' enjoyed the status of a great Persian poet at the Mughal court, his brother Thakur Das became a *vakil* (court 'pleader') of John Company. The decline of Mughal power was gradual, but it could hardly be missed by the members of the Mughal caravan. Sayyid Ahmad Khan (later Sir Sayyid) captured the change in *Asar-al-Sanadid*, in this sharp description of the great imperial fort:

> It is said that the roof of the fort was originally entirely of silver but that since the reign of Farrukh Siyar it was removed and replaced by one of copper. Then under Muhammad Akbar II, the copper was removed and a wooden one substituted for it. Even the gold of the Sonehri Masjid was stripped and sold to finance Mughal decadence, being replaced by stone. Humayun's tomb was in ruins.

The ancestors of Jawaharlal Nehru came to Bazar Sitaram in what might, then, be called the Copper Age of Mughal decline. The generally accepted version of migration is the one offered by Jawaharlal himself in his *An Autobiography* (1930). The first six Mughal emperors spanned 180 years; but after the death of Aurangzeb in 1707 the next five came and went in only a dozen, four the victims of a relative or a courtier's knife. Of them, the longest survivor was Farrukh Siyar, who sat on the throne for six years from 1713 before his scheming ministers, the Sayyid brothers, dragged him out of his harem, imprisoned and then killed him. During this brief reign, writes Jawaharlal, Farrukh Siyar visited Kashmir, was entranced by the abilities of an eminent Sanskrit and Persian scholar, Raj Kaul, brought him back to Delhi around 1716 and gave him an estate beside a *nahar* (canal). Kashmiris, as we have noted, were quick to acquire names which might please the royal patron; what better homage could there be than turning the royal privilege into one's own name? And so Raj Kaul adopted the *takhallus* (title) Nehru. Eventually it was the Kaul which was eased out of the surname, and the Kaul-Nehrus became just Nehrus.

But there seems to be an element of convenience in this history; it may have more to do with exaggerated family stories Jawaharlal heard than with the truth. For one thing, there is no record of Farrukh Siyar ever having visited Kashmir; second, Nehru is not a name which a Kashmiri Pandit need acquire – it is one of the regular surnames of the caste, and it is easy enough to find Nehrus around either of the two villages in the valley from where the Nehrus are believed to have migrated, Noar, or Naru, in Badgam district and the other near the small town of Tral. Another claim says that the family came from the Rainwari area on the outskirts of Srinagar. (A famous family, as is well known, suddenly gets many ancestors.)

However, it is certain that the Nehrus were part of the Mughal court and had some zemindari rights over a few villages. But by the generation of Mausa Ram Kaul and Saheb Ram Kaul, Raj Kaul's grandsons, the inheritance had dissipated, perhaps in direct proportion to the decline of Mughal power. Mausa Ram's son, Lakshmi Narayan, shifted his loyalty and became the first *vakil* of the East India Company, which had acquired a formidable presence by now at the Mughal court. His son, Ganga Dhar, became a *kotwal* (chief constable) in the police at a very early age and held that job when the Mutiny reached Delhi in 1857. Ganga Dhar Nehru was only thirty. And it was that holocaust which, after a century and half, forced the descendants of Raj Kaul to leave the city which they had adopted.

From the 'feeble, cowardly and contemptible' Emperor Farrukh Siyar to the no less feeble, cowardly and contemptible Bahadur Shah Zafar, the Nehrus served as bureaucrats to the kingdom. Their fortunes vacillated with the uncertainties of the time; it was an age when emperors died of that very fatal epidemic called intrigue, and the court was a bedlam of climbers using every weapon known, from conspiracy to poetry, to usurp a little more from the collapsing treasury of a debilitated empire. Those aristocrats with any desire for calm kept away from Delhi; others, with more ambition, like the Marathas and Jats, extracted a heavy price in return for letting the Mughal façade remain; yet others, invaders from Persia, came, looted and returned. And slowly, from the east, the troops of John Company worked their way up, their *de facto* power transformed by degrees into *de jure* authority.

The last Great Mughal, Aurangzeb, died on 3 March 1707, with the confession of faith on his lips and the burden of pessimism in his heart. From his death-bed he wrote to his son Azam: 'I came alone and am going alone. I have not done well to the country and the people, and of the future there is no hope.' His three living sons, Muazzam, Muhammad Azam and Muhammad Kam Baksh, immediately began fulfilling their father's prophecy. By early 1708 Muazzam had killed his two brothers on two battlefields, Azam at Jajau near Agra in June 1707 and Kam Baksh near Hyderabad in 1709. Bahadur Shah, as he titled himself, might have maintained the empire, but he died of natural causes on 27 February 1712 – the last to die thus in a long while. His heir Jahandar Shah killed three brothers for the throne, then allowed his courtesan Lal Kumari to rule so that 'violence had full sway. It was a fine time for minstrels and singers and all the tribes of dancers and actors.' Using two powerful satraps, the Sayyid brothers, Farrukh Siyar strangled Jahandar Shah in the Red Fort in 1713; then the Sayyid brothers finished him in the same way. The brothers made and killed two more kings until Muhammad Shah brought a measure of stability. Stability, that is, for himself, not the empire. He dedicated himself completely to political inaction and pleasure. Every regional power helped itself to a part of the empire: Deccan went to Nizam-ul-Mulk; Awadh became semi-independent under Saadat Khan; Bengal went to Murshidabad and via Siraj-ud-Dowla to the English; the Marathas took west and central India; the Jats established their kingdom near Agra; the Rohillas founded Rohilkhand north of Ganga; the Sikhs took Punjab. Foreign invaders trooped in to loot the treasure of glorious generations, beginning with Nadir Shah. Within thirty years the achievements of two centuries had been squandered. In 1739 Nadir Shah entered Delhi in triumph and, infuriated at the sight of his dead soldiers who had been killed by some overambitious citizens, ordered a great massacre. He left with all the crown jewels including the Kohinoor and the Peacock Throne; a total of 15 crores of rupees in cash, jewels, 1,000 elephants, 7,000 horses, 10,000 camels, 500 builders and masons, 100 eunuchs and countless slaves. Looting India then became a bit of a habit. Ahmad Shah Abdali, who succeeded Nadir, did it constantly between 1748 and 1767.

In 1764 the Jats removed the silver roof from Rang Mahal, and in 1787 the Rohilla chief Ghulam Qadir Khan blinded Shah Alam II while his men dug the floors of the Red Fort in search of buried treasure. In 1788 the Maratha Scindias made the Mughal their protectorate, before Delhi passed into British control in 1803 after the Maratha wars. In the west Arthur Wellesley captured Ahmadnagar on 12 August, defeated Daulat Rao Scindia and Raghuji Bhonsle at Assaye, north of Aurangabad, on 23 September and completed the rout by 15 December. In the north Lord Lake captured Aligarh, Delhi and Agra, routing the Scindia's northern armies in September at Delhi and in Alwar in November. By the treaty of Surji-Arjungaon on 30 December, Scindia renounced all his claims on the Mughal emperor. Henceforth, that formality would remain with the British. The blind Shah Alam II was now under the control of the Company. As Sir Thomas Munro wrote: 'We are now the complete masters of India, and nothing can shake our power, if we take proper measures to confirm it.' The Grand Mughal was formally demoted by the British from emperor to king; a civilian colony was established within Shahjahanabad and a military cantonment beyond The Ridge. The administration was under a British Resident. There was peace. The blinded Shah Alam died (1803) in bed, a luxury few Mughal princes had experienced of late. So did Akbar Shah II, after thirty-one powerless years, in 1837. It was his successor Bahadur Shah II who, much against his will, was forced into an unexpected spasm of heroism before he died, writing beautiful if pathetic verse in a gaol in Burma, yearning for six yards of his motherland for a grave. He didn't get it.

The last flicker of an imperial flame lit more than 300 years before illuminated the country on 11 May 1857 when at about seven in the morning a party of mutineeers crossed the Yamuna on a bridge of boats. Simon Fraser, the commissioner, was in bed. Hutchinson, the collector, was already in court, dealing with a criminal case, along with police officer Mainuddin Hasan of the Paharganj police station. Captain Douglas, the British officer posted to Bahadur Shah's court, was receiving Munshi Jivanlal.

It was actually the Emperor who was the first to learn that a revolution was at the door; he could, literally, hear its clamour. He told Captain Douglas to go to the window and tell them to take their patriotism elsewhere. The last scion of the great Mughals had long since surrendered all pretensions. But the people of Delhi were in another mood that day. A rumour had swept the city that the Shah of Iran had called upon them to revolt and would come to help. Though the British quickly secured the Calcutta gate, the citizens threw open the Rajghat gate and let in the mutineers from across the river. The first casualty was Dr Chamanlal, an Indian Christian standing in front of his dispensary. The Emperor, in utter panic, appealed to the British to save him from patriotism. But there were no European troops in Delhi; the Sepoys, based in Rajpur, refused to obey their commander Brigadier Graves. Fraser, Douglas and Hutchinson were all to die soon, as were Jennings (the chaplain), his daughter Miss Jennings and her friend Miss Clifford. Two Anglo-Indian youths working in the telegraph office finally sent out the word which was to alert Punjab and the eventual saviour, Brigadier John Nicholson; they tapped an urgent message to Ambala, Lahore, Rawalpindi and Peshawar: 'The Sepoys have come in from Meerut and are burning everything – Mr Todd is dead, and we hear several Europeans. We must shut up.' That final touch of Indian English is classically authentic.

The Sepoys had been inspired by the tradition that Company rule would end in the 100th year after Plassey, but romance had no chance against British drill and discipline. History was against them. Even the Emperor's queen Begum Zeenat Mahal and his closest adviser Hakim Ahsanullah Khan were in league with the British. By 20 June the officers of John Nicholson's column were dining in 'the Elysium of the Dewan Khaas'. Captain Hodson ordered three princes, Mirza Moghul, Mirza Khizr Sultan and Mirza Abu Bakr, huddled in a bullock cart, to take off their clothes and then personally shot them dead. Twenty-one princes were hanged. Bahadur Shah opted for total silence; British sightseers would come to peer at this old man dressed in white, sitting crosslegged on a charpoy in the courtyard, while two attendants fanned him with peacock feathers, impotent emblems of sovereignty. When an English soldier came to look at this pathetic left-over, Bahadur Shah would bow and salaam and say, 'Bari khushee . . .' ('I am so happy . . .')

The Sikh soldiers with the Company found some justification for plunder in their famous popular prophecy that the Khalsa would reach Delhi one day. Among those they murdered were an uncle and a cousin of a man called Sayyid Ahmad Khan. Christian priests justified the butchery of Delhiites as proper retribution for the death of Mr Jennings, the chaplain. On 21 September, C. J. Griffiths found the streets 'deserted and silent, they resembled a city of the dead'. The poet Ghalib wrote: 'Here there is a vast ocean of blood before me; God alone knows what more I have still to behold.' Even as late as 31 October, Sir William Muir (lieutenant-governor, North-Western Province) received a report saying: 'Delhi is still standing in all its magnificence ... but the houses are desolate and plundered. The wretched inhabitants have been driven out to starve.'

One family to suffer this fate was the Nehrus. After 150 years of fluctuating fortunes, they were on the road, with nothing salvaged but their lives – and that too barely. It was, strangely, Ganga Dhar's belief in the English language which saved the family. He and his wife Jeorani, two sons, Bansi Dhar and Nand Lal, and two daughters, Patrani and Maharani, were among the countless refugees trudging towards Agra when suddenly they were stopped by British soldiers. Kashmiris are very fair, and the soldiers thought that one of the daughters was a kidnapped English girl. The consequences are not too difficult to imagine. But thanks to the fact that Ganga Dhar had taught his sons English they were able to communicate with the soldiers and convince them that they were mistaken. One of the more important things the British had done was to sanction a grant in 1823 to Delhi College (founded in 1792 near Ajmeri Gate to provide a conventional Islamic education) to begin classes in the English language. There were two Kashmiri Pandits, Mohan Lal and Ram Kishan Haksar, in that inaugural class of six. In 1843 Ganga Dhar Nehru joined the English classes himself, and from the very beginning of their education he put English on the curriculum of his two sons, Bansi Dhar and Nand Lal. This single act was to save the Nehrus, both physically and financially. Those who had learned Persian to serve the Mughals understood better than others that they would have to know English to serve the new master on the horizon.

Survival was a great struggle in Agra; and to compound the misery Ganga Dhar died at the very young age of thirty-four in 1861. Jeorani was shattered; worse, she was six months pregnant when her husband

died. On 6 May 1861 was born the first Nehru to become a national
hero of India, Motilal. Bansi Dhar got a job as a 'judgement-writer'
in the Sadr-Diwani-Adalat at Agra. He would to rise to subordinate
judge in the judicial service.

If English saved Bansi Dhar, then an Englishman rescued Nand
Lal. Principal Anderson of Agra College used his influence to put
Nand Lal on the payroll of Raja Fateh Singh, prince of a small state,
Khetri, in Rajasthan. Nand Lal began as a teacher, then became
private secretary and ended up as *diwan*, or prime minister, of the
state. The family enjoyed a life of comparative ease which the position
in Khetri brought. The growing and vivacious Motilal had the good
fortune of learning from Qazi Sadruddin, the tutor of Raja Fateh
Singh, and became proficient in Arabic and Persian even before he
entered his teens, when he went to Kanpur, where his brother Bansi
Dhar was posted, to join the local high school. Motilal's English was
a little awry, but he had no shortage of confidence. The twelve-year-
old wrote to H. Powell Esq., the headmaster:

> I respectfully beg to inform your honour that I am quite prepare for the
> examination of both classes i.e. 4th and 5th. Perhaps you know that
> when I informed to the Principal for my promotion in the 4th class, he
> refused and said, 'the other boys have also right as you have?' Therefore
> now, I wish to be promoted in the 4th class by my own power.

Motilal did not do very well after matriculation in Muir College at
Allahabad; but then academic achievement is not a family trait. The
teachers at Muir included scholars like Augustus Harrison, W. H.
Wright, Pandit Adityaram Bhattacharya and Maulvi Zakaullah.
Nand Lal served in Khetri till 1870, when his patron Raja Fateh
Singh died. The heir dropped his father's advisers, inevitably, and
Nand Lal returned to Agra, qualified as a lawyer and started practice
at the Sadr-Diwani-Adalat. When the High Court moved from Agra
to Allahabad in 1866, he followed. From the ruins of Delhi to hunger
in Agra to power in a tiny desert principality of Rajasthan to the
bourgeois comfort of a lawyer's life in Allahabad was the journey of
one lifetime. But from here the Nehrus were to radiate across the
subcontinent and then across the world, taking the name of Allahabad out of India's religious texts and into world history. The
British made Allahabad the capital of the North-Western Provinces

(as the United Provinces were called till 1901) in 1858, and the city acquired a university and the High Court, and automatically witnessed a revival.

Motilal was married in his teens, as was the norm. He had a son soon after, but both mother and son died in childbirth. He continued his education, but gave up the examination for a degree after sitting for the first paper, in the mistaken belief that he had done badly. Jawaharlal writes about his father's young days: 'He was looked upon as one of the leaders of the rowdy element in the college. He was attracted to Western dress and other Western ways at a time when it was uncommon for Indians to take to them except in big cities like Calcutta and Bombay.' Motilal now shifted to law and found a natural talent for it; he was first in the *vakils*' examination. In 1883 he started practice at Kanpur under a senior who was a family friend, Pandit Prithinath Chak. In 1886 he moved to Allahabad to join his elder brother; and the very first case he argued won him praise. Emotionally, Nand Lal embraced his younger brother in the court room itself. By then Motilal had been married again, to the beautiful Swarup Rani from Lahore, with her 'Dresden china perfection' (to quote the son's description). Their first child, a son, did not survive – the second child Motilal had lost. A sharper tragedy followed. In April 1887, at the still young age of forty-two, Nand Lal died, leaving behind his wife Nandrani, two daughters and five sons. Bansi Dhar's job forced him to live elsewhere, and quite suddenly 25-year-old Motilal was catapulted to the very crucial position in Indian society of head of the family. Within two years, the joy he had so often sought from fortune entered his life. At eleven-thirty at night on 14 November 1889 (the seventh day of Marghshirsh Badi 1946 by the Hindu Samvat calendar), Swarup Rani gave birth to a boy. And this child, Motilal's third son, by his second wife, survived.

Motilal called him Jawaharlal, a name which his son never quite liked.

2 Culture and Conflict in the Nineteenth Century

Perhaps the finest achievement of the Mughal Empire was the culture that it moulded. Dr Henny Sender has explained this very well in his essay on the Kashmiri Pandits (collected in R. E. Frykenberg, ed., *Delhi through the Ages*, 1986):

> The Mughals considered themselves Islamic rulers ... But their ruling ethos was non-communal and led to the emergence of a cross-communal service class. This was a development actively encouraged. Akbar's successors continued his tradition of drawing upon differentiated symbols of legitimacy to serve as Hindu *Maharajah* and *Padishah-i-Islam* simultaneously. Cleavages rested on class rather than religious lines; prevailing standards were aristocratic rather than communal. Among those who participated in the court culture, communalism was regarded as bad manners.

As the historian B. N. Pande put it in an essay: 'Destiny had ordained that the Mughals would play this unifying role. So strong was this tradition among the Mughals that even Aurangzeb could play the bigot only half-heartedly, and with considerable restraint.'

The great philosopher-king of Indian unity was Akbar, son of a Sunni father and a Shia mother, born in the house of a Hindu prince and brought up in the midst of Sufis. The intellectual reasoning and moral sentiments released by his concept of *din-e-Elahi* ('the religion of God') found their true apostle in the man who failed to be king, Akbar's great-grandson, Dara Shikoh, who was a Sufi, spent long years in Kashmir translating the *Vedas* and *Upanishads* into Persian and preached that the only difference between the Hindu doctrine of Advaita and the Muslim-Sufi traditions was one of terminology. But 43-year-old Dara Shikoh lost the wars of succession to 39-year-old Aurangzeb, and history took a different turn. Yet it says something about the political policies of the Mughals that the grandmother and great-grandmother of the man who has come to symbolize Muslim bigotry, Aurangzeb, were Hindu Rajput princesses from Jaipur.

The traditions of harmony survived the inconstancy of a ruler or two, and, like the flame which was a favourite image of the poets of the time, Mughal Delhi was at its finest just before the Mughal was finally obliterated and Delhi became a provincial town of British India. This is the era known as the Residency period.

On 29 April 1639, at the precise moment decreed by the royal astrologers, the *subahdar* of Delhi ordered Shah Jahan's master architects, Ustad Ahmad and Ustad Hamid, to begin the excavation for the city of Shahjahanabad, which was to be the new capital of the Mughal Empire. On 19 April 1648, again after consulting the astrologers about the most auspicious moment, Shah Jahan entered the Daulat-Khanah-i-Khaas (Hall of Special Audience), sat on a special throne enclosed by a golden railing and inaugurated the capital with great gifts and festivities.

The astrologers had got it right. The city flourished. By the 1820s Thomas Fortescue could record the existence of 52 bazaars inside the walls and 36 *mandis* outside. A profusion of religious and cultural festivals were more often celebrated by both Hindus and Muslims: for instance, the fair at Hanuman Mandir at Jaisinghpura every Tuesday, or the fair at Kalkaji, next to the temple built by Akbar's minister, Kedarnath. Everyone went to see Ram Lila held at Shahji's Tank outside Ajmeri Gate and participated in the happy, riotous Holi and the sparkle of Diwali. The Id of Muslims was a traditional day for a display of inter-religious warmth, while in the pageantry of the Moharrum procession Hindus mingled with Muslims. Muslim saints were commonly revered, and the Urs at the *dargah* of Hazrat Nizamuddin Auliya was attended in vast numbers (as indeed it is to this date). The royal princes were always the chief guests at the celebrations of Basant Panchami, while the *Chharrion ka mela* was held each year on the estate of the Shia nawabs of Awadh, at Safdarjung's *madrasah* (college). Gulfaroshan, the festival of flower-sellers held each year in autumn on the estate of the Raja of Ballabgarh, was linked to both a Hindu temple and a Muslim *dargah*. By the 1820s more than 100,000 people were attending the festival. This was the period when the poetry of Ghalib, Zauq and Momin took the language of Urdu to unprecedented heights, and the miniatures of artists like Faiz Ali Khan, Jivan Ram, Mazhar Ali Khan, Ghulam Ali Khan and Ghulam Murtaza Khan were in enormous demand. A portrait of Sir David Ochterlony by Jivan Ram hangs today in the Victoria Memorial, Calcutta. One of the most colourful personalities of Company Raj, Sir David, a Scot, was twice Resident of Delhi, and liked wearing Indian dress, smoking a hookah, watching nautch-girls and taking the air every evening on his elephant accompanied by a large retinue of Indian wives, servants and their families.

It was this 'composite' Mughal culture (as the serviceable but rather ungainly phrase goes) which was the inheritance of families like the Nehrus, shaping their habits and their outlook: at one level, creating the preference for the *churidar* and *sherwani* over the dhoti, and at another making secularism a part of their natural instincts. To be communal was bad manners, and what could be a greater sin than that? And yet in that environment also lay the seed of a revivalist movement which was to have such enormous consequences that it would lead eventually to the division of the subcontinent – and, implicitly, to the greatest defeat of Mohandas Gandhi and Jawaharlal Nehru, a failure from which neither they nor the subcontinent quite recovered.

All the flowers of the Gulfaroshan, or the durbars for important guests, with processions, elephants, trumpeters, horsemen, foot soldiers and drummers could not hide the fact that the Emperor wore borrowed robes. The insolent young Company officers laughed openly at the cheap and gaudy finery that had now replaced the brocaded velvet from Turkey and the silk from China that in Shah Jahan's age roofed the Hall of Ordinary Audience (Daulat-Khanah-i-Khas-o-Am), more than seventy feet above the ground, raised on four silver pillars. Now, as Bishop Reginald Heber wrote with some sadness, the Diwan-i-Am was 'full of lumber of all descriptions, broken palanquins and empty boxes and the throne so covered with pigeons' dung that its ornaments were hardly discernible'. The Bishop recalled lines from Saadi:

The spider hath woven his web in the royal palace of the Caesars,
The owl standeth sentinel in the watchtowers of Afrasiab.

In 1817 Akbar Shah II sat on the Mughal throne, a pitiful bearer of a great name. The old empire was dead, and the new one, adolescent and cheeky, was growing. Akbar Shah was a puppet confined to the Red Fort, commanded by captains of the Company army and surrounded by high-born relatives who would often gather on the rooftops of the fort and scream at the citizens passing below, 'Ham bhookey marte hain!' ('We are dying of hunger!') Those in this penniless nobility who had some sense gave unto the Emperor that which was his due – loyalty – and unto the British that which they wanted – paid service.

Khwaja Farid was one such person. He worked for the British in Calcutta, Burma and Iran before taking on the impossible job of managing Akbar Shah's finances, a task which needed both dexterity and imagination. His daughter, Aziz al-Nisa, married a Sufi mystic, Mir Muttaqi, who became a recluse, and their son, Sayyid Ahmed Khan (1817–98), was brought up by the grandfather in the family *haveli*. The methods were traditional. The boy was banned from playing with children on the street to prevent any corruption of the chaste language he learned at home, and education was Urdu, Persian and mathematics after dinner. In addition, he acquired Arabic from an uncle and oriental medicine from a friend. Sayyid Ahmed did not try to learn English, although Delhi College was offering lessons by now; he shared the common Muslim prejudice against the West. His entertainment was true to his class; there were regular, if unpublished, visits to the *kothas* of Delhi for a spot of poetry, music and prostitution. But family circumstance soon ended the pleasures of youth. His brother, father and grandfather died in quick succession. To earn a livelihood, Sayyid Ahmed Khan joined the British judicial service as a reader (like Ganga Dhar Nehru) and later became a *munsif* or junior judge.

The man changed dramatically. Suddenly the plight of the Muslim élite began to dominate his thoughts; his own experience mirrored the downfall of the race. He took his first refuge in history, recreating the romance of the Mughal Empire in books which are also superb examples of Urdu prose. *Asar al-Sanadid*, a survey of Delhi's monuments, came out in 1842; his translation of Abul Fazl's *Ain-i-Akbari* in 1855. Along with this arose questions in his mind about the future of the community, and the quest for an answer. Inverting the logic, he came to a conclusion. Only the British had shown the ability to destroy Muslim power; therefore, if the Muslims wanted to recover their place in the sun, they had to learn the ways of the English. Upon receiving a copy of Sayyid Ahmed's translation the poet Ghalib had taunted him, 'Put away the *Ain-i-Akbari* and examine the Englishman.' Sayyid Ahmed took the advice with a dedication its giver had never intended. He became a fanatic devotee of the British.

At the time of the Indian Mutiny, Sayyid Ahmed was posted in Bijnor, given to the British by the rulers of Awadh in 1801. On 20 May 1857 Nawab Mahmud Khan, his sympathies with the Mutiny, seized control. Massacre was the most likely fate of the small British community there, headed by the collector, a man named Shakespeare. The Nawab immediately offered a place in his new administration to Sayyid Ahmed, but he not only saved the lives of all the Britishers but also turned the offer down with the words, 'By God, Nawab Sahib, I say that British sovereignty cannot be eliminated from India.' It was either treason or foresight or both. Anyway, Sayyid Ahmed's point was proved, and his faith in the supremacy of the English doubly reinforced. He did not hide this admiration; some of his unctuousness is embarrassing even at this distance. It was not as if he did not suffer during the Mutiny. When he returned to Delhi in September that year he found his house looted and his mother dying; she had been surviving on grain meant for horses and had not tasted a drop of water for three days. An old servant of the family died in front of him, and his mother survived only another month. But no matter. The British had found their 'foremost loyal Mohamedan'.

He now launched his movement to restore Muslim fortunes with British patronage. In 1860 appeared *The Loyal Mahomedans of India*. Sayyid Ahmed was even willing to use God in this crusade; he published a commentary stressing the similarities between Christianity and Islam. He did not mince words. He wrote: 'Without flattering the English, I can truly say that the natives of India, high and low, merchants and petty shopkeepers, educated and illiterate, when contrasted with the English in education, manners and uprightness, are as like them as a dirty animal is to an able and handsome man.' And so the Muslim salvation, he believed, lay in an English education. From this conviction came his greatest achievement, the foundation of the Mahomedan Anglo-Oriental College in Aligarh in 1875 (the same year incidentally when Swami Dayanand began the Arya Samaj in Bombay). The foundation-stone of the college was laid by the Viceroy himself.

This disciple of the British became hero to the élite of a community which had lost its pride and confidence after a century of stagnation;

whose leaders had degenerated from emperors to caricatures; whose poetry had collapsed from philosophy to self-deprecation or lament; whose vision was so debilitated that when asked to surrender self-respect in return for bread it happily did so. For a pat on the back and a knighthood, Sayyid Ahmed Khan happily denounced the bravery of those numerous Muslims who fought the British in the wars of 1857. Inevitably he could not resist becoming a bit of a caricature himself, wearing English clothes after his knighthood in 1888 and acquiring a knife and fork for his table. (But he still did his writing sitting on the floor.)

Sir Sayyid's most important influence on the future lay in the fact that he gave respectability to the idea of Muslim–British co-operation and interdependence – an idea which was anathema before 1857. It was a policy which his descendants would carry to far greater and more insidious lengths. A necessary element of this equation was that it had to operate, to a lesser or greater degree, at the expense of the Hindus. It was a policy which limited itself to sectional advantage. At one point Sir Sayyid even opposed the induction of Indians into the Civil Service because it would only bring 'Bengali babus' to the top and not Muslims. It was not as if Sir Sayyid was vigorously anti-Hindu; he was simply indifferent to their interests. His vision was controlled and conditioned by the religious divide, the only relieving feature being that he was utterly sincere and dedicated to the Muslim cause. Consciously or unconsciously, he created the groundwork for community-based politics, with all its attendant consequences. It is no surprise that his college at Aligarh became the intellectual cauldron for the ideas which later created Pakistan. He himself articulated the arguments which became constants in discussions about Muslims till 1947.

It is important to remember that Sir Sayyid was concerned only about the Muslim élite; and so he was largely their hero. He was firmly anti-democratic. Why? First: 'Men of good family would never like to trust their lives and prosperity to people of low rank, with whose humble origins they are well acquainted.' Second, under universal franchise the Muslim would be outvoted – for the Hindus, of course, would vote only for Hindus, and the Muslims only for Muslims. Since the population of Hindus was four times as much as the population of Muslims, the latter would be destroyed. 'It would be like a game of dice, in which one man had four dice and the other one.' It was such thinking which, with the ready help of the British, directly led to the demand for separate electorates and eventually to a separate country. The British needed Sir Sayyid, and he frequently had to visit the capital of his province, Allahabad. He bought a house there, from the government, for Rs 20,000. Sir William Moore, who attended the house-warming party, hoped in his speech that this large, palatial house in the Civil Lines of Allahabad, in the neighbourhood of the bungalows and administrative offices of governors and civil servants, would become the cement holding together the British Empire in India. Strangely, quite a different fate awaited this home. Sir Sayyid's son found the bungalow to be a bit of a white elephant and sold it off to Raja Ram Kumar Parmanand of Moradabad. In 1900 a brilliant new luminary from the legal world was looking for a residence to match his rising status and wealth. Price was no object. His eye fell on this sprawling bungalow, now run down, with even a raja unable to maintain it. Although not a very religious man, the lawyer did find some comfort in the fact that the address, 1 Church Road, was situated near the Bhardwaj Ashram, next to the confluence of the Ganga and Yamuna, a spot associated with episodes in the epic *Ramayana*. He bought the house for Rs 19,000 and named it – upon the advice of his friend, the poet Akbar Allahabadi – Anand Bhavan, the House of Joy.

The name of the lawyer was Motilal Nehru. And the house which was once conceived as a cementing institution of the British Empire became, as much as any house could claim such distinction, a cradle of the Indian revolution which removed the British from the subcontinent.

3 The Lawyers

There were not too many places to go for the upwardly mobile Indian in the second half of the nineteenth century. The administrative services had barely opened up; and, in any case, the Indian would have to be both far more civil and far more of a servant if he was to be allowed into the covenanted élite. Indian industry did not exist, and survival off the land required either birth or abject sycophancy to the English revenue collector, or, most often, both. Wealth and recognition could come only through the professions.

The generation that would mould twentieth-century India was born in the middle of the nineteenth. The oldest was Bal Gangadhar Tilak, born in Ratnagiri in Maharashtra on 23 July 1856, ten months before the Mutiny. Motilal Nehru and Rabindranath Tagore arrived within a day of each other in May 1861. Madan Mohan Malaviya was born in Allahabad on Christmas Day, six months later. Gopal Krishna Gokhale, the great moderate who persuaded Gandhi to return to India, was born on 9 May 1866 at Katluk in Ratnagiri in a poor family, unlike his famous near-contemporary Tilak. Baba Kharak Singh, the man who pioneered the Akali Dal, was born in Sialkot in 1867. Mohandas Karamchand Gandhi became on 2 October 1869 the youngest of three brothers and a sister in a family in Porbandar. Kasturba was born the same year in the same city. (Up north in Delhi the famous Urdu poet Ghalib passed away that year.) The great Bengali leader C. R. Das was born on 5 November 1870, and Sri Aurobindo, the revolutionary from Bengal, in Calcutta on 15 August 1872. In another corner of the world, Newcastle upon Tyne, the pacifist Reverend Charles Freer Andrews was born on 12 February 1871. In Nadiad, Gujarat, 31 October 1875 saw the birth of Vallabhbhai Jhaverbhai Patel. Muhammad Ali Jinnah, who created Pakistan, was born on Christmas Day 1876 in Karachi. The fiery philosopher-poet who inspired the idea, Sir Muhammad Iqbal, was born in Sialkot on 9 November, eleven months later. In 1879, on 13 February in Hyderabad, was born the poetess/freedom fighter Sarojini Naidu; and, a little to the south-east, in the district of Salem the same year came C. Rajagopalachari. The philosopher-guide from the south, Dr Sarvapalli Radhakrishnan, was born on 5 September 1888; while in the east the communist M. N. Roy was born on 21 March 1887. Dr Rajendra Prasad, the first President of India, was born in the un-known village of Ziradei in the barely known district of Siwan on 3 December 1884. Firoz Bakht, also known as Muhiyuddin Ahmed but to become famous as Maulana Abul Kalam Azad, was born in 1888. The next year, on 14 November, came his friend and the future Prime Minister, Jawaharlal Nehru. In 1890 was born the Frontier Gandhi, Khan Abdul Ghaffar Khan, in the north-west of undivided India; while in 1891 came the man who is called the father of India's Constitution, the 'untouchable' Bhimrao Ramji Ambedkar. And in the same year that Nehru was born, on 1 April in Nagpur, was born the man who created the organization which is the fountainhead of Hindu reactionary forces, Dr Baliram Keshavrao Hedgewar, the youngest of six children.

Most of them began as lawyers. Of all the professions, nothing was more appealing than the law. It was, in a sense, a profession fashioned by the historical moment; a way out for those whose self-respect did not allow them to work for the British against their countrymen, but who could simultaneously exploit the system to build their position in society and approach the British as equals. Understandably, then, the profession of law was a crowded one. The champagne-quaffing barrister sat over his pot of gold at one end of the rainbow, but at the other stood the *paisa*-less 'briefless barrister', with a frayed tie, a tatty collar, a loud mouth and nothing but time on his hands. Failure was easy.

The most dismal professional start was certainly that of Mohandas Karamchand Gandhi. In theory he had fulfilled every criterion for success. He was called to the Bar in England; the Inner Temple certified that Mohandas Karamchand Gandhi of 20 Baron's Court Road, West Kensington, was 'generally admitted of the Honourable Society of the Inner Temple on the sixth day of November, one thousand eight hundred and eighty-eight, and was called to the Bar by the same society on the tenth day of June, 1891'. He applied for permission as an advocate to the Bombay High Court in 1891; he was a callow twenty-two, and the Bombay Bar was dominated by the likes of Sir Badruddin Tyabji and Sir Pherozeshah Mehta. It took months of waiting for Gandhi to get his first brief: a case in the Small

Causes Court for a man called Manibhai, on a fee of Rs 30 a day. (The case was not likely to last longer than one day.) Gandhi stood up to cross-examine the plaintiff's witnesses, 'but my heart sank into my boots. My head was reeling and I felt as though the whole court was doing likewise. I could think of no question to ask. The judge must have laughed, and the *vakils* no doubt enjoyed the spectacle.' As he mentions in his autobiography, Gandhi sat down, returned the case and did not enter court again till he reached South Africa.

Far more successful a début was that of Muhammad Ali Jinnah. He began his career as a temporary third presidency magistrate (Bombay then had four such magistracies) and did very well in his six months there, dealing with cases ranging from ticketless travel to opium smuggling from Iraq. Sir Charles Ollivant, the judicial member of the Bombay government, offered him in 1901 a permanent place at the quite substantial salary of Rs 1,500 a month. Jinnah turned the offer down, saying, 'I will soon be able to earn that much in a single day.' He did. Stanley Wolpert quotes (in *Jinnah of Pakistan*, 1984) a contemporary on Jinnah: 'He was what God made him, a *great* pleader. He had a sixth sense: he could see around corners . . . When he stood up in Court, slowly looking towards the judge, placing his monocle in his eye – with the sense of timing you would expect from an actor – he became omnipotent. Yes, that is the word – omnipotent.'

For most of the men now honoured in law's hall of fame, struggle preceded success. C. R. Das spent fifteen years in poverty before his advocacy in the trial of Sri Aurobindo turned him into a star. Dr John Mathai received a bunch of bananas as payment for his first case. Motilal Nehru earned 5 rupees for his first case, but quickly built up a practice of over Rs 2,000 a month, a fair sum in those days.

Allahabad was an inevitable melting-pot of the professional classes. Probasi Bengali, the Muslim élite, the Kayasthas and the *émigré* Brahmins were the intelligentsia which filled the jobs in revenue, justice and police. The Allahabad Bar was, initially, dominated by British barristers, but by 1877 a second tier, the pleaders (whose examination Motilal had topped), had organized a Vakils' Association. The volume of litigation was rising, thanks to new British legislation, particularly on property. By the 1880s British primacy was under attack by Indian luminaries like Sir Sundarlal Dave (a Gujarati Brahmin), Bengalis like P. C. and L. M. Banerjee,

Kayasthas like Jwala Prasad, Sachchidananda Sinha and Munshi Ram Prasad and Kashmiri Pandits like Tej Bahadur Sapru, Bishambar Nath and Motilal Nehru. In 1896 Motilal was one of the four *vakils* honoured by being made advocates (the others were Sir Sundarlal, Munshi Ram Prasad and Jogendranath Choudhuri) by Chief Justice Sir John Edge. The ingredients of Motilal's extraordinary success ranged from striking looks to incisive arguments to repartee and to some very old-fashioned hard work. He reached the apex of his legal career when in 1909 he received permission to appear before the judicial committee of the Privy Council in Great Britain. Chief Justice Sir Grimwood Mears described Motilal's advocacy:

> He had a profusion of gifts; knowledge came easily to him, and as an advocate he had the art of presenting his case in its most attractive form . . . He had an exquisite public speaking voice and a charm of manner which made it a pleasure to listen to him . . . With his wide range of reading, and the pleasure that he had taken in travel he was a very delightful companion, and wherever he sat at a table that was the head of the table and there was the centre of interest.

This was Sir Grimwood's tribute in the newspaper *The Leader* on 8 February 1931, after the end of one of the most famous cases fought by Motilal, over the inheritance of the Lakhna estate. The case began in 1894 and kept Motilal and his opposing counsel Sapru in funds for the rest of their lives.

Motilal could laugh at himself and his clients. When asked, once, about the famous Dumraon case, which stretched through decades, whether there were any claimants besides the two contesting parties, Motilal replied that if the case went on for another five years he and C. R. Das (the opposing counsel) would be the only beneficiaries left. 'His laugh became famous in Allahabad,' remembers Jawaharlal in his autobiography. And so did his temper:

> I admired Father tremendously. He seemed to me the embodiment of strength and courage and cleverness, far above all the other men I saw, and I treasured the hope that when I grew up I would be rather like him. But much as I admired him and loved him I feared him also. I had seen him losing his temper at servants and others and he seemed to me terrible then and I shivered with fright, mixed sometimes with resentment, at the treatment of a servant.

Jawaharlal recalls one thrashing which left a deep scar, literally and mentally, when he was 'about five or six'. Concluding, rather rationally actually, that his father could not possibly require both the fountain-pens on his office desk at the same time, Jawaharlal pocketed one. A mighty search was conducted for the pen; in sheer fright Jawaharlal kept quiet. The pen was eventually discovered and his guilt established: 'Father was very angry and he gave me a tremendous thrashing. Almost blind with pain and mortification at my disgrace I rushed to Mother, and for several days various creams and ointments were applied to my aching and quivering little body.' Motilal could be rude to people he did not care for. He was very much the aristocrat in his behaviour, both at home and in public. As he grew into a national figure, stories about him took on a life of their own. All his suits were tailored in Savile Row (not quite true; only those needed for special occasions); and his linen was sent to Paris for laundering (nonsense, of course).

Motilal's temperament encouraged such stories. He was unabashed in his enjoyment of all the luxuries. His ability to earn money was more than matched by his ability to spend it. He had never seen his father, and his early life was full of hardships. The first house he lived in was in the crowded Chowk Mirganj area of Allahabad, but with the first hint of success he moved into a spacious bungalow, 9 Elgin Road, in the Civil Lines, the exclusive residential area for the ruling white and Eurasian families. At one time, no Indians were allowed to live here, and there used to be a curfew against Indians between 9 p.m. and 6 a.m. But his ambitions were still higher, and he finally created his ideal home after he bought the house from Raja Parmanand of Moradabad at 1 Church Road.

Motilal wanted nothing but the best. Anand Bhavan was the first home in Allahabad to have its own swimming-pool, electricity and running water. Obviously the pool was a great attraction for friends, even for those who did not know swimming. There were 'bathing parties' at which the young Jawaharlal enjoyed himself by pushing nervous guests like Sir Tej Bahadur Sapru (then a junior at the Bar), who never allowed his foot to go deeper than fifteen inches of water, into the pool. Motilal would roar with laughter, though he himself was not a particularly good swimmer. 'He could,' his son recalls, 'just manage to go the length of the pool with set teeth and violent and exhausting effort.' No new invention was too expensive for

Motilal to order from Europe. The latest models of the growing novelty, the bicycle and tricycle, were ordered for Jawaharlal through Raja Ram Motilal Guzdar & Company (he was part owner of the firm). In 1904 he brought the first car to Allahabad; a famous picture shows Motilal at the wheel in coat and tweed cap, his young daughters wearing large bonnets. When he took his son to Europe to put him in Harrow in 1905 he bought another car. In 1909, again in Europe, he bought two more, a Lancia and a Fiat. He had a stable of fine Arabian horses, and the children learned to ride at a very early age. Jawaharlal on horseback would become a familiar sight to Indians – strapped in the saddle as a young child; or in boots, breeches and hat as a boy; in a dark *sherwani*, black cap and white *churidar* as the Congress president in 1929; and then in his familiar long coat, the rose in the second buttonhole, *churidar* and white *khadi* cap as a Prime Minister on holiday. One corner of the spreading grounds around Anand Bhavan was reserved for Motilal's favourite sport: wrestling. He would bring the finest wrestlers to his *akhara* (wrestling arena) and enjoy a drink of milk with them afterwards. He even took a wrestler once to Europe and arranged exhibition matches for him. For more sophisticated guests there were tennis and garden parties; an invitation became the symbol of acceptance to the highest of circles. It was during a tennis party that Jawaharlal was once discovered missing. He was seven, and had gone riding while his father and friends were playing tennis. He took a fall, and the horse, an Arab, returned home without him. An upset and worried Motilal formed a procession of his friends on whichever vehicle they could find, and search parties were sent out in every direction. Motilal met his son on the road, calmly walking back home, and his relief and joy were expressed in a tremendous fuss, which embarrassed the growing boy.

Every evening, at around seven, Motilal's friends would gather in the garden or the drawing-room, and the whisky and conversation would flow. Jawaharlal would often peep from behind a curtain, unable to restrain his curiosity about this adult world. Sometimes he would be caught peeping, and told to go to his father to apologize. A benevolent Motilal often sat the boy on his knee so that he could see for himself that there was nothing particularly conspiratorial about the adult laughter and drinking. Once Jawaharlal got a great fright while taking a peep; instead of whisky he saw his father drinking blood! He rushed to tell his mother this horrible story – and learned that Father was drinking nothing more dangerous than claret that evening.

Stories about Motilal's lavish household passed into lore. Motilal himself narrated to the historian B. N. Pande, who as a young Congress worker knew the Nehru family well in his native Allahabad, the story of the one man who had been able to snub him. A cook from Kathiawad in Gujarat came to Anand Bhavan and applied for a job in Motilal's kitchen. Motilal asked him to display his talents. The cook asked for a *seer* (a liquid measure) of ghee and some vegetables, and returned after a while with the cooked dish. Motilal's first remark was that the food looked terribly dry after the cook had taken a full *seer* of ghee. The cook immediately put the food in the cloth covering the dish, and he squeezed out a full *seer* of ghee from the food. Then, commenting that the stories he had heard of Motilal's greatness were obviously exaggerated, the cook walked off. Motilal was stunned into abashed silence.

If, therefore, the son learned to throw money about, the only complaint the father could legitimately have was that he was being profligate about something he had not yet earned. Despite an extremely generous allowance, the student in London was often in debt. Jawaharlal confessed in a letter to his father on 11 April 1912: 'If I had £5,000 a year I am sure I would spend it all with the greatest ease and then get into debt.' However, the lasting contribution of Motilal Nehru to the family that he created was the values he imparted, the philosophy and the approach to life that still permeate their thinking generations later. Of these, one of the most important was his attitude to religion.

There were few castes as rigid in their commitment to unthinking ritual as the Kashmiri Pandits at the turn of the last century. Motilal's eldest brother Bansi Dhar did not allow even his children to be present when he ate his meals. One of the first gestures of revolt which Motilal made was to start eating lunch at the High Court. It was a time when the sterility of priesthood and the vice-like grip of superstition had complete control, and the higher the caste the more vicious the hold. Reformers like Swami Vivekananda tried to arouse the community out of this mental swamp: 'I would rather see every one of you rank atheists,' he told Hindus, 'than superstitious fools, for the atheist is alive and you can make something of him.' It was this hidebound surrender to irrational ritual that Motilal opposed, preferring agnosticism to the rigid patterns of orthodoxy. One strong taboo, for instance, was against foreign travel. One of the first Kashmiri Pandits to go abroad was Mirza Mohan Jal Kashmerian, in the 1840s. He travelled through Central Asia before reaching Europe and meeting the young Queen Victoria. He, however, made his brethren's horror irrelevant by converting to Islam, marrying a lady from the Persian royal family and settling abroad. The first 'modern' Pandit of Allahabad to go abroad was Bishan Narayan Dhar, who went to be called to the Bar and was later to be an undistinguished president of the Congress; he had to perform a purification ceremony on his return.

Motilal refused to surrender before such humbug in 1899. He was nothing if not emphatic in his rebellion. Writing to his old mentor Pandit Prithinath, he said: 'I will not (come what may) indulge in the tomfoolery of *Proschit* [purification]. No, not even if I die for it . . . I know what your *biradiri* [caste] is and if necessary, in self-defence, I will ruthlessly and mercilessly lay bare the tattered fabric of its existence and tear it into the minutest possible shreds!' Motilal was excommunicated; he laughed in response. As he told a pious uncle who came to visit him, 'You may not dine with me without polluting yourself, but I suppose we could share whisky and soda?' His defiance helped destroy the taboo on foreign travel. And it also made him a target of the orthodox lobby. He did not much care. He quite consciously kept a personal servant called Hari, although Hari was an 'untouchable'. But Motilal did not impose his views on the household. His wife Swarup Rani, her widowed sister Rajvati and his sister-in-law Nandrani followed their own preferences. Swarup Rani fasted for her husband's welfare on Shiv Ratri and placed 100,000 *bel* leaves on Shiva's head. Rajvati had her separate kitchen and would entrance the boy Jawaharlal with stories from the Hindu epics as well as the hot *puris* she cooked.

However, there was a price to be paid in public life. Hindu Mahasabha leaders accused Motilal of apostasy and anti-Hinduism. At public meetings, questions about whether he ate beef would be planted to arouse mass anger against him. (Exactly the same charge would be made later against Jawaharlal; to this would be attached the accusation that it was the Nehru softness towards Muslims which made them 'hand over' Pakistan to Jinnah.) In the 1924 elections the three-man nexus of Lala Lajpat Rai (who had joined the Hindu Mahasabha by then), Madan Mohan Malaviya and Swami Shraddhanand made 'anti-Hinduism' a key charge against Motilal and his Swaraj Party. The president of the All-India Hindu Mahasabha in 1950, N. B. Khare, was only repeating an old story when he called Jawaharlal Nehru 'English by education, Muslim by culture and Hindu by an accident'. One reason why Motilal and Jawaharlal commanded the trust of the minorities is because they ignored these accusations without worrying too much about electoral consequences. B. R. Nanda, in his excellent book on this unique father and son, *The Nehrus*, describes Motilal's ethos thus:

> He was too absorbed by the daily struggle here and now to bother about the hereafter. He was a product of that late-Victorian 'free-thinking' rationalism, which was learning to dispense with divine explanations of the working of the universe and to pin its faith on the human intellect and on science to lead mankind along endless vistas of progress. This rationalism prevented Motilal from being swept off his feet by the tides of Hindu revivalism, which rose high at the turn of the century.

The words fit Jawaharlal easily. Secularism, reason, free-thinking, science and progress were the Pancha Sheela (Five Principles) on which the first Prime Minister of India founded his political life.

A second element of the Motilal philosophy was an admiration for the British, which, without any contradiction, happily coexisted with anger against British rule. Macaulay had wanted to produce 'Indians in blood and colour but European in opinion, in morals and intellect'. He got them in the Nehrus. What Macaulay did not bargain for was that this combination of modern opinion, morals and intellect would alchemize into a deep, powerful and unremitting nationalism. Motilal Nehru once, in the 1890s, even banned the use of any language other than English in the house. The result was dead silence; the women did not know English. But the occasional excess only underscored an admiration for the English temperament and a faith in Western education and ideas. Motilal could hardly not wonder at the qualities which enabled a handful of men from a small island thousands of miles away to control an empire as vast as India. But unlike Sir Sayyid, who was content with a master–servant relationship with the British on the grounds that the servants were at least certain to improve their standard of life, Motilal and his peers wanted to emulate the English the more easily to defeat them. A personal perspective – become better lawyers, evolve from *vakil* to barrister, to end the English domination of the Allahabad Bar, for example – slowly evolved into a conscious nationalism. If the English domination of the Allahabad Bar could be destroyed by the talents of Motilal Nehru and Munshi Ram Prasad, then British power in India could also be destroyed by the talents of this emerging professional class. But the evolution was slow, and Motilal was never given to overdue optimism. He preferred moderation to extremism all his life, even if his son swayed from one side to the other.

Motilal was impressed enough by Britishers to imitate them from his college days. He was a bit of a rowdy in college, and perhaps the adoption of Western clothes was also a part of the teenage rebellion syndrome. It must have been logical for Allahabad's rebel without a cause to wear shirts and trousers when only Indians in the fashionable Presidency cities attempted to dress like a sahib. From the moment he began to earn he consciously built an English life-style at home. The photograph portraits of the family say it all. The picture of Motilal as a boy shows him in *sherwani* and pyjama, but the young man has a striped tie and a high-buttoned coat. A picture of the couple is most interesting. Swarup Rani, in traditional sari and heavy jewellery, sits on a chair placed on a dais, while Motilal is seated casually on the dais itself, his right arm resting on the chair; he is dressed in boots, breeches and a thick-striped summer coat. Jawaharlal as a child is done up like an Indian prince for the camera, but the moment he reaches the age where he can sit on a tricycle he is given a Lord Fauntleroy dress. Certainly the fact that he was a home-bred *vakil* rather than an England-returned barrister must have jarred on this proud man; and Motilal took his revenge by not only being more-English-than-thou and more-successful-than-thou, but also making his own home the centre of social life where Englishmen would call on him rather than the other way round. Among his English friends he could count both Sir Harcourt Butler, who became governor of the province, and Sir John Edge, chief justice of the Allahabad High Court. Sir John, in fact, was very keen to make Motilal a member of the till then exclusively European Allahabad Club, but Motilal refused the dubious honour of all-white company.

Yet Jawaharlal's childhood had an equal, if less flamboyant, aspect; if the dominant father was Western, the other half was Indian. There is also a picture of Jawaharlal in 1902 after his thread ceremony, head shaved, an ascetic's stick in his hand, bare-bodied except for a dark dhoti, the thread which was the mark of a high-caste Brahmin hung diagonally across his body, from left shoulder to the right of the waist. This was the ritual of the Brahmin's second birth, the thread ceremony. This was the mother's world of belief and *puja* and faith. Jawaharlal preferred his father's intellect over his mother's tradition, but he was never contemptuous of religion. He understood its power, its hold over the popular imagination. The very emotional attachment which Jawaharlal developed with the river Ganga, for instance, could only have its roots in the world of his mother and grandmother and grand-aunts. No agnostic ever got so lyrical about a holy river; but this duality was an important element in the making of Nehru. He took his anger out, and very frequently, on 'organized religion', on orthodoxy, on communalism, but however much he may have privately disapproved of the appellation 'Panditji' (a caste term, after all) he never publicly renounced it.

As a young boy Jawaharlal, in his own words, 'had very hazy notions [of religion]. It seemed to be a woman's affair.' But he enjoyed the excitement of religious festivals, and in cosmopolitan Allahabad both Hindu and Muslim festivals. The colours and laughter of Holi had their obvious temptations, as did the dancing lamps of Diwali and the morality plays of Dussehra and Rama Lila. On Id, Jawaharlal would spend the morning with their estate manager, Munshi Mubarak Ali, for whom Motilal had a house built on the premises, and enjoy the rich *sewai* and embrace his friends in that Islamic gesture of unity and solidarity. There were some uniquely Kashmiri festivals, like Navroz, or New Year. The family never forgot its Kashmiri identity, although it was nearly 200 years since they left Kashmir – in fact, Jawaharlal's sisters were the first Nehrus to marry outside the community. It was the sisters, and then Jawaharlal's heirs, who turned the family into not only a national but an international conglomeration. There was no question of inter-caste marriage before that. It was not a matter of religion, but the more powerful instinct of race. The group identity, the fair skin, the sharp nose and the Aryan features had to be preserved; it was a small and proud community in a vast Indian sea. Motilal regularly took his holidays in Kashmir, enjoying the view, the weather, the house-boats on the Dal Lake, the hunting and riding, and the company of successful, well-dressed friends. He would often send scenic postcards to Jawaharlal in Harrow: a scene from Allahabad, with Motilal's scrawl at the top asking, 'What part of the city is this?' or a picture of Allahabad High Court with a caption, 'The scene of my labours'. The picture postcard sent on 15 December 1905 was a view of the river Jhelum in Kashmir, with Motilal's signed message: 'The motherland sends you greetings.' They might live in Allahabad, but there was no doubt about the motherland. Motherland was Kashmir.

4 The Options

There used to be a satirical slogan to describe the Mahomedan Anglo-Oriental College at Aligarh established by Sir Sayyid Ahmed Khan: 'Quam Khuda ka, college Sir Sayyid ka, hukm Beck Bahadur ka'; or: 'The people of God, the college of Sir Sayyid, and the orders of Beck Bahadur'. Beck referred to the principal of the college, Theodore Beck, who was virtually the government agent in Sir Sayyid's domain. Sir Sayyid attempted to buy a community's welfare in exchange for political subservience, thereby becoming the father of both Muslim progress and Muslim political self-destruction. This bargain was not the only contradiction in the ideas that shaped the thinking of the nineteenth century and flowered into the ruinous problems of the twentieth. There were, to use a methodology whose prime virtue is convenience, at least three other positions in the crucial Hindu–Muslim debate, which in turn was to become the insuperable hurdle in the path of Indian nationalism, unity and freedom. It would be stating the obvious to say there was much overlapping and that men often shifted, in the course of the long struggle, from one stream to the other; and that those in the 'secular' club were not always secular, just as those in the 'communal' ethos were not always communal. But very often it is essential to state the obvious; after all, we do forget it so often.

The first and crucial phase of British expansion came at the expense of Muslim power. It was perfectly logical, consequently, that the British first sought to destroy the Muslim nobility both politically and economically. In 1765 Robert Clive secured the revenue licence for Bengal from a weakened Shah Alam II; he collected a fixed sum from the zemindars, who in turn taxed the peasantry to the extent they could – the difference was their income. Under Lord Cornwallis the power of these zemindars was gradually whittled away; he disbanded their police forces and eventually set up a district-based administration under two white men, one the collector (literally) and the second the magistrate. But it was the Permanent Settlement of 1793 which was to alter fundamentally the nature of power in Bengal and have a far-reaching impact on Hindu–Muslim relations. Under the settlement, the British acquired the right to seize a zemindar's land and hand it to the next bidder for non-payment of dues. The catch lay in the character of the Muslim landed élite of Bengal. The Muslim gentry had become so thoroughly extravagant and irresponsible that in no time at all their lands had been taken over by Hindu money-lenders, speculators and the growing class of professionals who lived in Calcutta. As W. W. Hunter put it in *The Indian Mussalmans* (London: 1870. Reissued by Trubner and Company in 1971): 'Hundreds of ancient families were ruined, and the educational system of the Mussalmans, which was almost entirely maintained by rent-free grants, received its death blow.' Then came the second blow. In 1837 the British abolished the use of Persian and Urdu in Bengal and decided that the work of administration would be done either in English or in the local vernacular. The consequences were inevitable. To take one example, till 1851 there were more Muslim lawyers on the rolls of the Calcutta court than Hindus and Christians combined, but between 1852 and 1868 only one Muslim lawyer entered the rolls. Their share of government jobs had never been particularly high, but it sank to as low as 11.7 per cent in 1867 and less than 7 per cent by 1887. The Permanent Settlement, the Resumption Proceedings and the Education Circulars effectively destroyed Bengal's Muslim aristocracy. And the fate of the Muslims of north India was settled after the failure of the Mutiny. It is hardly an accident that Hindus were allowed to re-enter the deserted city of Delhi in October 1857, and Muslims only in August 1859, by which time the best properties had been resettled. (Delhi returned to some normalcy only around 1875 when its population reached 160,553, or approximately what it had been in 1847. But it could never recover its educational status; Delhi College lost out, and the Government College, Lahore, became the premier educational institution of north India. On 1 April 1877 the Punjab government finally closed down Delhi College. St Stephens was born as a palliative in 1881.)

To quote the civil servant W. W. Hunter, writing in 1868, again:

After the Mutiny, the British turned upon the Mussalmans as their real enemies so that failure of the revolt was much more disastrous to them than the Hindus ... In every district the descendant of some line of Muslim prince is sullenly eating his heart out in a roofless palace and weed-choked tanks. The Mussalmans are excluded from the army and the law. The judiciary was either Anglicized or Hinduized; while Permanent Settlement led to wholesale eviction of Muslim landlords.

King Bahadur Shah, as was his wont, expressed his anguish in verse:

Kahin aisa bhi hai sitam suna,
Ke di phaansi laakhon ko begunah;
Wale kalma-goyon ki taraf se
Abhi dil mein unke ghubar hai.

('Have you ever heard of such anger, that they hanged *lakhs*? They are still revengeful against those who say the Kalimah.')

Within months after the Mutiny, the Company appointed a commission to find what had gone wrong, and how British power could be best preserved in the future. The ageing and experienced Lord Elphinstone (he had been in the Company's service since 1796), then governor of Bombay, sent a minute to the commission which was unambiguous: '*Divide et impera* was the old Roman motto, and it should be ours. I might perhaps hesitate to express my conviction so decidedly if I were not able to show that my views upon this subject are entirely in accordance with those of the Duke of Wellington.' The playing-fields of Eton not only defeated Napoleon; they also preserved the Indian empire. (Harrow, however, got its revenge; its playing-fields produced Jawaharlal.) Lord Elphinstone was not alone. In a letter to Lord Elgin dated 3 March 1862, Sir Charles Wood, Secretary of State from 1858 to 1866, says: 'We have maintained our power by playing off one part against the other, and we must continue to do so . . . Do what you can, therefore, to prevent all having a common feeling.' And on 10 May, Wood wrote: 'We cannot afford in India to neglect any means of strengthening our position. Depend upon it, the natural antagonism of races is no inconsiderable element of our strength. If all India was to unite against us, how long could we maintain ourselves?' How long, indeed? Consequently, from the late 1860s British policy became less anti-Muslim and more even-handed as the British sought to create a 'Muslim card' as a balance against Hindus. The need was sharpened by the first stirrings of 'Hindu' protest: the anger against white indigo planters; the demand for the right to try white suspects in courts (as early as 1827 Raja Rammahun Roy organized a protest petition against the Jury Act which denied Hindus and Muslims the right to try Christians, including native converts); the insurrections of the Pune Brahmins; the trouble with the Sikh Kukas who rose to protect the cow; and the growing influence of reform movements among the Hindus with their strong underplay of patriotism.

One of the problems which Muslim theologians faced was that while the Quran and the Hadith had been so explicit on so many worldly issues, one subject on which they did not provide much guidance was how a Muslim should deal with the problem of being in a minority. There was enough to indicate how Muslims should deal with minorities when they were in power, but not the other way round. As Muslim thinkers tried to analyse what had gone wrong, and seek a course for the future, they inevitably went back to Islam's first principles. The Wahabis were the extremists of this revivalism. Others, like the followers of Shah Waliullah (1702–63), were more realistic in their analysis; while they agreed that Muslim decadence and the abandonment of Quranic simplicity and commitment were primary causes of Muslim decline, they realized that a new future could not be built without friendship and co-operation with Hindus. But common to both schools was an anti-British passion. When Delhi fell to the British in 1803, Shah Abdul Aziz (1746–1831), son of Shah Waliullah, issued a *fatwa* (decree) declaring India to be Dar-ul-Harb – the land where Islam was no longer safe. In other words, Muslims were commanded either to fight the British till martyrdom or victory, or to leave to go and live in a Muslim country. (Some *maulvis* in fact did run off to the Andaman Islands; while others went to Afghanistan.) Many *maulvi* sects fought bravely in the Mutiny of 1857. Abdul Qadir, one of the leading ulema of Lucknow, led his men to Delhi in Bahadur Shah's defence and, after defeat, escaped to the jungles of Patiala till an amnesty enabled his group to return to their homes. But their anger against the British remained undimmed, and when Sir Sayyid advised Muslims to boycott the Congress and support the British, Shah Muhammad, the son of Abdul Qadir, issued a *fatwa* along with 1,000 other *maulvis*, condemning Sir Sayyid. It was titled 'Nusral al-Ahrar' ('Victory of the Good') and became one of the pamphlets distributed at the Allahabad Congress in 1888. This group became famous as the Ahrars and played an extremely significant part in the freedom movement.

The followers of Shah Waliullah founded a monastic school at

Deoband in United Provinces in 1867 with five objectives: to teach
the word of Allah; to organize Muslims; to preach the message of
Shah Waliullah; to fight the British; and to challenge all aristocracy
and despotism and seek democratic and republican forms of self-
government. One of the finest products of this tradition was
Ubaydullah Sindhi (1872–1944), a Sikh who ran away from home,
became a Muslim in the deserts of Sind, wandered as a fakir for
twenty-five years across Afghanistan, Russia, Turkey and Hijaz and
came at the age of forty-five to Deoband. The message that he
preached could have gone into a Congress manifesto. India, he said,
is the home of many peoples and races; all must live peacefully. It has
a compact geography and an essentially common culture; it is, therefore, one nation. But each community has the right to develop its
own variation of language and culture, and therefore the new India
must be based on these principles: adult franchise, democracy, indigenous industry, workers' welfare, support for the peasant and
equality of all religions. This philosophy of unity, equality and individual rights and responsibilities is a logical extension of the Sufi
tradition in Indian Islam.

The Muslim clergy was split into two broad groups: one, whose
interest was Islam, and which spread the message of Islamic brotherhood and equality; and the other, whose primary interest was
Muslim power, Muslim welfare and the Muslim sword. While the
theocrats, therefore, were constantly exhorting a jihad, the Sufi-
influenced *maulvis* promoted the concept of the Umma-i-Wahid, a
concept of the Prophet Muhammad which became a symbol of a
composite Indian nation. It was based on the defence treaty which
the Prophet negotiated with the non-Muslims of Medina for the
protection of their common city against a common foe. In the fourteenth year of his prophethood Muhammad's pact with the Jews of
Medina specified that both parties would be free to follow their own
religions, but in all other ways Muslims and Jews would be considered one. The Sufis also preached Wahdat-al-Wujud, or the unity
of existence; many Sufis in India even argued that, since the concept
of Brahman was monotheistic, Hinduism should be included in the
religions of Adam. Certainly the Hindu tradition of creation is not
too different from the Quranic and biblical; the original human was
half man, half woman, which parallels Adam, who himself was half
Eve until God delivered Eve from his rib. The nationalist group of

the clergy banded together under the Jamat-e-Ulema, while the theocrats eventually created their separate Jamat-e-Islami, in the shadow of the Pakistan movement.

One of the questions which Pakistan was forced to answer, after even single-religion nationhood had not solved the problem of civil strife, was: who is a Muslim? The famous Munir Commission of the 1950s offered this reply:

> We cannot refrain from saying here that it was a matter of infinite regret to us that the ulema, whose first duty should be to have settled views, were hopelessly disagreed among themselves ... Keeping in view the several definitions given by the ulema, need we make any comment except that no two learned divines are agreed on this fundamental? ... And if we adopt the definition given by any one of the ulema, we remain Muslims according to the view of the *alim* but *kafirs* [unbelievers] according to the definition of everyone else ... The net result of all this is that neither Shias nor Sunnis nor Deobandis nor Akl-i-Hadith nor Barelvis [the anti-Deoband group] are Muslims.

It was a tough thing to discover *after* Pakistan was created.

Hinduism was no less in ferment at this time, for reasons both similar and different. If some Muslims were bemoaning the arrival of 'Christian imperialism', then some Hindus were flabbergasted at their inability after 800 years of Muslim kings in Delhi to replace them with one of their own. The answer once again ran from reform and regeneration to simple hatred of the outsider – the problem was that even the Muslim was condemned as an outsider by the extremists. Hinduism became the bedrock of this version of nationalism, leading, but naturally, to great resentment among Muslims. The last thing the Muslims wanted was to live under a permanent fog of suspicion about their 'true' loyalties. Islam, in any case, demands a transnational identity which is bound to arouse suspicions in a subnational faith whose religio-geographical anchors are the Ganga and the Himalayas and which not a hundred years ago considered overseas travel taboo.

There was, however, consciousness that Hinduism had largely itself to blame. The very pro-Hindu historian R. C. Majumdar admits (in *The History and Culture of the Indian People*, Vol. IX, 1965): 'There was undoubtedly a general deterioration in Hindu society [due to] blind faith impervious to reason.' The women were the worst victims. Even when suttee was finally abolished in Bengal,

1,146 signatories, including 120 Pandits, protested. An upper caste like the *kulin* Brahmins had converted marriage into a lucrative racket; since these twice-born commanded a great dowry, many of them married fifty times or more. Children were thrown into the Ganga in the name of religion. And in the grander families of Calcutta the festivities at Durga Puja became an excuse for expensive nautch and prostitution. Reginald Heber, Lord Bishop of Calcutta, could sniff from his pedestal: 'The term of Bengalee used to express anything which is roguish and cowardly; such as they are, however, I am far from disliking them.' The Marquess of Hastings told his diary on 2 October at Diamond Harbour:

> The Hindoo appears a being nearly limited to mere animal functions, and even in them indifferent. Their proficiency and skill in the several lines of occupation to which they are restricted are little more than the dexterity which any animal with similar conformation, but with no higher intellect than a dog, and an elephant, or a monkey, might be supposed capable of attaining.

Insult was not the only contribution from the West. It was the Western scholar who helped revive, through his research, memories of a golden past. The Bengalis who were to lead the renaissance grasped at this past as the idyllic world which could be recreated by modern will. Muslims became fashionable whipping-boys, as the evil which had interfered with the evolution of the golden Hindu age. The Hindu press of Calcutta did not mince its words; it referred to Muslims as *yavana jati* or barbarians. Even Dwarkanath Tagore, a liberal, had this to say in *The Englishman* of 6 December 1838:

> The present characteristic failings of natives are a want of truth, a want of integrity, a want of independence. These were not the characteristics of former days, before the religion was corrupted and education had disappeared. It is to the Mahomedan conquest that these evils are owing, and they are the inevitable results of the loss of liberty and national degradation. The Mahomedans introduced in this country all the vices of an ignorant, intolerant and licentious soldiery. The utter destruction of learning and science was an invariable part of their system, and the conquered, no longer able to protect their lives by arms and independence, fell into opposite extremes of abject submission, deceit and fraud. Such has been the condition of the Natives of Hindustan for centuries.

Bankim Chandra Chatterjee carried such views into literature, leaving through his novel *Ananda Math* and its song 'Bande Mataram' yet another controversy for the politicians of the twentieth century to ruin a subcontinent over.

From this rose the revivalist political position, articulated frankly enough by R. C. Majumdar: 'The basis of national unity in India is Hindu religion. Hindu nationality embraces all the Hindus of India irrespective of their locality or language. The Hindus are destined to be a religious nation.' Organizations like the Theosophical Society encouraged this revivalism, as its European intellectuals romanticized the 'golden age of Hinduism'.

Elsewhere, preachers like Swami Dayanand, founder of the Arya Samaj, railed against the evils within Hinduism like idol worship and caste. Dayanand promoted achievement-based élitism and abused 'mobocracy' as 'a mere collection of thousands of irresponsible, uneducated and ignorant masses (who exploit their birth in earning their bread) [which] cannot be called a meeting'. But his greatest anger was reserved for other religions. His views on Muslims are best summed up in the first comment on the subject in his book *The Light of Truth*: 'The Moslems say that the Quran is God's word. But ... its author is someone else.' Which rather ends the argument, at least as far as the Muslims are concerned. But this Gujarati preacher had wide influence, particularly among Punjabi Hindus, and some of the heroes of the Congress from that state, like Lala Lajpat Rai, were Dayanand's followers, while Bengali revolutionaries like Aurobindo Ghosh were deeply influenced by him.

Dayanand made Delhi into a centre of Hindu revivalism. The touchy business of cow slaughter had spurred a series of riots in the 1880s, aided by the accident of the calendar which put Moharrum and Dassehra within a few days of each other between 1884 and 1887. Religious organizations like the Ram Sabha sprouted up; and the first of these came up in our familiar Bazar Sitaram in 1884. In 1890 Delhi became the headquarters of the first all-India Hindu organization, the Bharat Dharm Mahamandal, founded in 1887 at Hardwar. By 1896–7 communal riots had become endemic, and only ceased with the arrival of an even greater disease, the plague. The Arya Samaj spurred the simmering tension with its reconversion programme; and by 1908–9 the Maulvi of Delhi, Abdul Haq, was telling Muslims in his sermons that Muslims would have to unite with Christians to protect themselves from the common enemy, the proselytizing Hindu. Sir Sayyid's ideas were finding a growing audience, in other words, wherever rising tensions and violence created the climate of fear.

The political fall-out of this thinking was evident in the rise of what are known as the Extremists in the Indian National Congress. Religion – Hinduism – was fused into their politics, as they sought not only to liberate the country from the British but also to rid its culture of both the influence of Islam and the new, but no less pervasive, influence of the West. They sought to build a Vedic Indian character as much as a Hindu-political India; and though they were defeated eventully by the Moderates (or, to put it more accurately, subsumed by Gandhi, who in effect made both varieties of Congress irrelevant), their impact is still apparent. Fortunately, any form of extremism does not really work in India. The balance of the Indian ethos tends to find a way out much in the manner of the turning, curving Ganga: the tendency to slide across or beside a problem, changing everything in one view and changing nothing in another. And so sops may be offered to the extreme, while the broad middle continues its languorous course.

The three main schools of politics influenced by revivalism were the Maharashtrians of Bal Gangadhar Tilak; the Punjab version led by Lala Lajpat Rai; and the Bengal chapter, headed by Bipin Chandra Pal and Aurobindo Ghosh. Tilak became a hard-liner even on social reform, challenging the Age of Consent Bill of 1891. In a deliberate attempt to Hinduize the Marathas, he began the practice of public celebrations of the festival of Lord Ganesh in 1893, and followed this up by formal glorification of the 'anti-Muslim nationalist hero' Shivaji; the first Shivaji festival was held on 15 April 1895. The Extremists, however, had one great advantage in terms of popular appeal over the Moderates in the Congress – they were far more anti-British, while the Moderates rarely hesitated to pledge their loyalty to the rulers. It was natural, consequently, that young men like the teenager Jawaharlal never quite appreciated why their fathers had opted for the Moderate camp.

5 Growing Up

The first two sentences of Jawaharlal Nehru's autobiography are a slightly abashed admission: 'An only son of prosperous parents is apt to be spoilt, especially so in India. And when that son happens to have been an only child for the first eleven years of his existence there is little hope for him to escape this spoiling.'

Jawaharlal was the third son born to Motilal, but the first to survive. Birth in those days was good news, but not good enough. Infant mortality was high. Jawaharlal's two sisters, however, were healthy babies. The lady the world came to know as Vijaylakshmi Pandit was born on 18 August 1900 and named Sarup Kumari; she was the first girl born into the Nehru family after nine boys. Since she was the little one of the family, her brother being already eleven years old, she was nicknamed 'Nanni', an affectionate Hindustani term for 'little one'. The English-speakers soon converted this to Nan (Miss 'Toopie' Hooper, the English governess, would have none of Nanni). Her upbringing included riding, English governesses and dancing classes – but no formal education. On 14 November 1905 (which, incidentally, was Jawaharlal's birthday too) a fourth son was born to Motilal but could not survive; the infant died within a month. On 2 November 1907 came Krishna, nicknamed 'Beti' ('daughter' in Hindi), and once again re-nicknamed by an English governess as Betty.

Swarup Rani suffered from poor health. She was semi-invalid for long spells and could barely look after her own children. Her great passion was her only surviving son, and the fuss she used to make over him, and the lengths to which she would go to protect Jawaharlal from *nazar* (the evil eye) became a bit of a joke in the crowded joint family. (There were about 40 family members living at Anand Bhavan, not to mention about 100 servants and the traditional ghost; legend had it that a previous owner had killed his wife and she haunted Anand Bhavan.) Swarup Rani would give her son a quiet snack before meals so that he did not eat too much in front of others at the table; the doting mother did not want anyone to comment on the appetite of a growing child and thereby cast 'the evil eye'. The superstition is very strong in India, and mothers are convinced that their children will suffer from a jealous and malicious comment. Remedies extend from prevention (a black dot on the forehead, for example, which repels *nazar*) to cure (circling the head with red chillies and then throwing the chillies into a fire while chanting a mantra). The normal quota of tensions apart, it was a happy joint family, with Motilal, affectionately known as Bhaiji (even his nephews, after all, were only a couple of years younger than him), as the presiding godfather.

Anand Bhavan was a happy instance of coexistence between the English and Indian styles of living: Motilal enjoying the former, his wife the latter, and the children enjoying both. There were two kitchens – the Western, staffed by Muslims and Goan-Christian cooks, supervised by the butler Asghar Ali, very impressive in his dark red coat and golden turban, and Bhola, Motilal's personal valet, who was a favourite of the children. There was a separate Muslim chef for Muslim food, while Hindu cooks and servants concentrated on the women's side. The manager of this substantial household was the dignified scion of a Muslim feudal family from Badayun which had been destroyed by the British after the Mutiny, Munshi Mubarak Ali, who had been given a separate cottage on the spreading lawns of the estate. There was a strong bond of love between the Munshi and Jawaharlal. As the latter recalls: 'With his fine grey beard he seemed to my young eyes very ancient and full of old-time lore, and I used to snuggle up to him and listen, wide-eyed, by the hour to his innumerable stories – old tales from the *Arabian Nights* or other sources, or accounts of the happenings in 1857 and 1858.' These stories were early fertilizer on budding nationalism. 'I mused,' remembers Jawaharlal, 'of Indian freedom and Asiatic freedom from the thraldom of Europe. I dreamt of brave deeds, of how, sword in hand, I would fight for India and help in freeing her.'

Motilal was prone to quicksilver shifts of mood. His violent temper could make the house tremble just as much as his laughter could make it quiver with joy. Once he caught a servant wiping a plate with his sleeve just as his guests were sitting to dinner and lost his temper to such a degree, and thrashed his servant so violently, that his embarrassed guests left the house. Only Munshi Mubarak Ali had the authority to tell Motilal that enough was enough. But when a dinner party went well it could be splendid. Motilal had one of the finest cellars; his kitchen was superb, his heart generous. We have one description by a Britain-and-USA-returned Indian journalist, St Nihal Singh, who spent twenty days at Anand Bhavan in 1910: 'The meals were good enough to be placed before royalty. Wine flowed liberally – wines of many kinds. With the dessert were brought boxes of cigars and cigarettes and liqueurs. A fair-sized bar could have been opened with the decanters placed in front of us.' The lavishness was not restricted to just the godfather or the godson. A story symbolizes the spirit of Anand Bhavan in those prosperous days. A cousin of Jawaharlal, Maharaj Kishan, liked to eat his chapatis very hot; and rather than keep them all on a single plate, he wanted them one by one, straight from the oven. He hit upon the ingenious practice of tying a rope around a boy servant's waist and yanking it whenever he needed a fresh chapati. One day he kept yanking the rope to no effect. When he finally went to find out he discovered that the boy had tied the rope to a tree and was happily flying kites.

For the privileged heir, it was idyllic: long hours of swimming in the summer, and riding in the winter. Birthdays were celebrated with royal munificence. Jawaharlal would first be weighed against bags of wheat and other gifts for the poor; then he would be weighed against new clothes which went to his wardrobe, and there would be a great party for the hero in the afternoon. No wonder he wanted birthdays to come a bit more often than once a year. There were holidays in Kashmir. His mother took him to shrines and family weddings, where the teenager would experience the first thrills of meeting the opposite sex: through a glance or a touch. Education was at home. Jawaharlal had started with two governesses, and then spent a few months in the local St Mary's Convent School, along with his cousin Shridhar. Motilal found the convent inadequate, and began Jawaharlal's tuition at home. Naturally, nothing less than the best would do. Sanskrit was taught by the great scholar Pandit Ganganath Jha. On the recommendation of the half-Irish, half-English and fully Indian nationalist Annie Besant, an Irish-French theosophist called Ferdinand T. Brooks became Jawaharlal's tutor when he was around eleven, and stayed for three years. Motilal, however, was determined that his son become a 'well-rounded' personality rather than just a bookworm, but Jawaharlal's inclinations were towards the non-academic library:

Lewis Carroll and Kipling (*Jungle Book* and *Kim*) to *Don Quixote* (with Gustave Doré's illustrations), adventures by Fridtjof Nansen (*Farthest North*), Scott, Dickens, Thackeray, H. G. Wells, Mark Twain and staple classics like *The Prisoner of Zenda* and *Three Men in a Boat*. He was fascinated by science, though, and spent long hours in his homespun laboratory over elementary experiments in physics and chemistry (he would later take a Natural Sciences tripos at Cambridge).

The most interesting early influence was not of literature or science but of Theosophy. The young Jawaharlal went to the weekly meetings in Brooks's rooms, where the talk swivelled from Dhammapada to Pythagoras to reincarnation to astral bodies. This was clearly the life! Annie Besant, a leader of the movement as well, came to Allahabad to give a few lectures, and fascination turned into conviction. Jawaharlal asked his father for permission to become a theosophist. A former victim himself, Motilal smiled and said yes. Annie Besant herself performed the initiation ceremony. A 'thrilled' Jawaharlal attended the theosophical convention at Benaras, and acquired a constant smug look of excessive piety. Motilal did not like this obsession and quietly eased Brooks out.

With Brooks, away also went Theosophy. Jawaharlal's interest, in any case, had less to do with religion and more to do with another fascination. As he recalls in his autobiography:

> I dreamt of astral bodies and imagined myself flying vast distances. This dream of flying high up in the air (without any appliance) has indeed been a frequent one throughout my life; and sometimes it has been vivid and realistic and the countryside seemed to lie underneath me in a vast panorama. I do not know how the modern interpreters of dreams, Freud and others, would interpret this dream.

This love of flying strengthened during his Harrow days. He was thrilled by 'the early growth of aviation. Those were the days of the Wright brothers and Santos Dumont (to be followed soon by Farman, Latham and Blériot), and I wrote to Father from Harrow, in my enthusiasm, that soon I might be able to pay him a weekend visit in India by air.' Father and son went to Berlin in 1909 to see Count Zeppelin arrive in his airship from Friedrichshafen and be welcomed by the Kaiser. (Jawaharlal kept the picture of Count

Zeppelin he got from his hotel, the Adlon, as a memento.) Two months later they were in Paris to see the first aeroplane fly over the city and circle the Eiffel Tower; and eighteen years later Jawaharlal (now with Indira on his shoulders) was again in Paris when Charles Lindbergh brought his plane across the Atlantic. This love of flying has travelled down the generations. Grandson Rajiv made flying a profession, his younger brother Sanjay a tragic obsession. (Sanjay died when the single-engine Pitts two-seater he was flying crashed over Delhi city on 23 June 1980.)

As Jawaharlal entered his teens, Motilal's reputation soared to new heights, and inevitably there were pressures to devote more of his time to politics. He concentrated, however, on becoming the best, and most expensive, barrister. His son made a perceptive observation when explaining why Motilal avoided politics in this phase of his life: 'He had no wish to join any movement or organization where he would have to play second fiddle. The aggressive spirit of his childhood and early youth had been outwardly curbed, but it had taken a new form, a new will to power.' The will to power would be another characteristic which would travel down the generations. But events, of course, would not wait. Along with Jawaharlal Nehru the Indian National Congress also entered its teens; after all, it was only four years older than Jawaharlal.

Who first conceived the idea of a Congress? Dr Pattabhi Sitaramayya offers three options: at discussions during the Great Durbar of 1877; during the international exhibition in Calcutta (in 1884), where again the élite of India gathered; or at a private meeting of seventeen men after the Theosophical convention in Madras in December 1884. All three, most likely: it was an idea waiting to be born. And perhaps Gopal Krishna Gokhale was right when he said that no Indian could have started it.

A Britisher did: Allan Octavian Hume, son of the Radical MP Joseph Hume, who had retired from the service in 1882 to devote the rest of his life to the science of ornithology, Theosophy and Indian causes. The last was no sudden development. He had been humiliated and denied promotion to the Viceroy's Council for being too pro-native. Hume, as secretary of the department of revenue, agriculture and commerce between 1871 and 1879, had repeatedly drawn his government's attention to the horrifying poverty of India's villages and the British indifference to it. His interest in Theosophy brought

Hume in touch with the professionals and intellectuals who were searching for ways to express the Indian interest in politics and government. On 1 March 1883 Hume sent a memorable circular to the graduates of Calcutta University, urging them to band together politically for the regeneration of the people of India. By May 1885 he was ready, and he informed the Viceroy, Lord Dufferin, about his intentions. The new party was almost christened the Indian National Liberal Union, but eventually the first session of the Congress Party of India was summoned in the historic city of Poona in Maharashtra. An outbreak of cholera transferred the honour to Bombay. Seventy-two delegates (including 39 lawyers, 14 journalists and one doctor) from 27 out of India's 250 districts, in formal top hats or silk turbans, gathered on the morning of 28 December 1885 at the Goculdas Tejpal Sanscrit College. It was (surely out of instinctive generosity rather than special political insight) a message from Florence Nightingale, sitting far away in the mother country, which hinted at the destiny of this fledgling: 'We are watching the birth of a new nationality in the oldest civilization in the world.'

The first objective of the Congress was a better deal for Indians within the empire – the creation of an Indian ruling class (administrative) in the governance of the Empire, and not independence. Hume first asked Lord Reay, the Bombay governor, to preside. But Dufferin advised Hume against too close a linkage with the Raj; Hume's job was to create a loyal opposition, because the British were getting apprehensive about newly evident 'dangerous' sentiments, particularly among the Hindus, and wanted safety-valves which they could regulate. Very few strategies of the British have collapsed as quickly as this one. As early as 1886 Hume himself was writing and publishing pamphlets, attacking the government and demanding representation, whose popularity in the north alarmed the British. Very innovatively they were printed in Indian languages as well as in English. On 8 October 1888 the lieutenant-governor of the North-Western Provinces, Sir Auckland Colvin, wrote bluntly to Hume that he was unleashing forces he would not be able to control. And just before he left at the end of his term, Lord Dufferin made the official position towards the Congress unambiguous at his St Andrew's Dinner speech at Calcutta on 30 November 1888: Hume and the Congress were seditious. The decision had been reached, and all those opposed to the Congress now knew they would get official patronage. Colvin also formally introduced the argument which would culminate in a separate country sixty years later: that the Congress was not a fully representative organization, and that the aims and aspirations of the Muslims of India were different from those of the Congress.

From the very first Congress the Muslim bogy was raised, among others by the correspondent of *The Times*, London: 'Only one great race was conspicuous by its absence; the Mahomedans of India were not there, they remained steadfast in their habitual separation.' But there were two leading Muslims present, R. N. Sayani and A. N. Dharamsi; and work, not intention, kept Badruddin and Kamruddin Tyabji away. Congress leaders challenged this conspiracy which sought to divide even before an all-India organization had been barely launched. Hume described it as a 'shameful libel' and in *The Indian National Congress: Its Origins, Aims and Objects* (Calcutta, 1888) bitterly denounced the British for encouraging the 'devil's . . . dismal doctrine of discord and disunion'. At the second Congress, under W. C. Bonnerjee's presidentship, there were fifty-five Muslim delegates. The next year Hume, who worked hard to encourage Muslims to join the Congress, persuaded Badruddin Tyabji to preside over the third session, at Madras. In response, the British signalled to their man, Sir Sayyid, and he readily obliged. On 28 December 1887, when the first Muslim president of the Congress was preaching Hindu–Muslim unity at Madras, Sir Sayyid in Lucknow gave a speech that for the first time outlined the 'two-nation' thesis. The Congress, he said, could never do any good to anybody, with its anti-British policies, except a few Bengalis 'who at the sight of a table-knife crawl under their chair'. Remain loyal to Queen Victoria, he warned both Hindu and Muslim. But for Muslims he offered a more substantive rationale for loyalty.

First, Sayyid argued, Hindus and Muslims are 'two different nations'. If the British left, what would happen? 'Is it possible that under these circumstances the two nations – the Muhammadans and the Hindus – could sit on the same throne and remain equal in power? Most certainly not. It is necessary that one of them will conquer the other and thrust it down.' Second, democracy would be a subterfuge for Hindu rule, since the Hindus outnumbered Muslims four to one. 'It would be like a game of dice, in which one man had four dice and the other one.' Third, only the Christian British were worthy of friendship because the Quran said so: 'our nation cannot expect friendship and affection from any other people'. Sir Sayyid's rhetorical flourishes were his own. But the substance of his arguments had been published in *The Pioneer*, the establishment newspaper, about a month before. The author was a Cambridge graduate who had just been appointed principal of the Mahomedan Anglo-Oriental College, Theodore Beck.

In 1888 the Congress met at Allahabad. Among the 1,400 delegates was 'Pandit Motilal, Hindu, Brahmin, Vakil of High Court, NWP'. His rising fame won him a place on the subjects committee in 1888. In 1892 when the Congress met again in Allahabad he was secretary of the reception committee. But for about a decade after that he kept away, preferring to concentrate on his work and on his family. In 1899 he went on a trip to Europe; it was probably during this visit that he decided that his son should study in the best school that the British Empire had to offer. On 13 May 1905 the fifteen-year-old Jawaharlal sailed for England on the SS *Macedonia*, along with his parents and his four-year-old baby sister, Nan. They reached Dover on 31 May. On the train to London, Jawaharlal read in the newspapers of the great Japanese naval victory over Russia at Tsushima. The news delighted him; an Asian nation had, at long last, inflicted a mighty defeat on a European power.

Their first full day in London was spent at the races, but the holiday mood was disturbed by failing health. Swarup Rani was perpetually ill, and Motilal himself was suffering from 'nervous prostration, the natural consequence of five years of hard, incessant work without rest'. Harrow was closed till September, but the headmaster, Dr Joseph Wood, advised that the young man should get some Latin in the meanwhile. And so Jawaharlal went to A. J. Atkins Esq. of 154 Dalston Lane, London E, to bone up. The family went off to Germany, first to Cologne and then to take the mineral waters of Bad Homburg, and to Bad Ems. The spendthrift in Motilal was alive; on his daughter's fifth birthday, at Bad Ems, he invited 400 schoolchildren, in two batches, from the neighbouring schools. But all the excitement could not hide the fact that Motilal was missing his beloved son deeply. This was the first time Jawaharlal had been separated from the family, and a stream of letters from the Continent kept up an incessant flow of advice: guard yourself against the cold, *et al*. The family returned to London to catch the boat home, and the time came to say goodbye. The S S *Macedonia* sailed on 20 October. Motilal's last letter before sailing was a touching and beautiful description of how much the son meant to the father:

> In you we are leaving the dearest treasure we have in this world, and perhaps in other worlds to come. We are suffering the pangs of separation from you simply for your own good. It is not a question of providing for you, as I can do that perhaps in one single year's income. It is a question of making a real man of you, which you are bound to be. It would be extremely selfish – I should say sinful – to keep you with us and leave you a fortune in gold with little or no education . . . I think I can without vanity say that I am the founder of the fortunes of the Nehru family. I look upon you, my dear son, as the man who will build upon the foundations I have laid and have the satisfaction of seeing a noble structure of renown rearing up its head to the skies.

It was a dream which Jawaharlal Nehru would fulfil.

On his return to India, Motilal fought the pain of separation with a well-tried weapon: work. He took on cases with a compulsive vengeance. 'To my mind it is simple enough. I want money, I work for it and I get it. There are many people who want it perhaps more than I do, but they do not work and naturally enough do not get it.' One other reason why he was pushing himself so hard was to earn enough, and quickly, so that he could afford another trip to Europe the following summer, to see his son.

6 Harrow

The SS *Macedonia* sailed from Marseilles at ten on the morning of 20 October. As they had promised each other, father and son began writing letters at once, Motilal a little after midnight, the son the moment he awoke that morning, 'as I was very anxious that something should reach you at Port Said'. As it so happened, the first bit of news he provided was of trouble; he had missed a lecture on Trafalgar and was warned of 'unpleasant results' the next day. Father wanted not only constant communication ('the greatest comfort we can look for – a letter in your own handwriting') to ease the 'shock of parting' but regular photographs as well ('Please have yourself photographed at once in your school clothes and send us ½ dozen at least of the photographs'). Jawaharlal shaved to look his best for the camera, and got this rather acerbic comment in response: 'I must say that I did not like your shaved face. All the natural brightness and intelligence which meets the eye in the other photo (that taken by Vandyke in South Kensington) has disappeared with your moustache. In other words you look like a fool.' To a biographer the difference in the before and after photographs is less dramatic, but who can compete with a father's eye? Motilal's emotions took a long while to calm. From the Red Sea he wrote: 'Thirteen days have passed since we parted with you! And yet it was but yesterday that you were hurrying up at Bailey's Hotel to catch your train at the Gloucester Road Station!' There were the most meticulous instructions: how to wear clothes, how to make friends, to cut away the collars of flannel shirts and so on.

Jawaharlal was dutiful, even restoring the thin, light adolescent excess on the upper lip which passed for a moustache. But what his father also wanted to know was: 'Give me a complete account of your first fagging day. I am so anxious to know what menial services are exacted at Harrow from the only and dearly beloved son of a man who employs more than 50 servants in India.' Jawaharlal told him what services were exacted: 'Besides lighting fires and carrying messages I had to turn on toshes [school slang for bath or footpan] for sixth formers after footer.' In reply Motilal commented: 'I wonder if you had ever lighted a fire in India with your own hands.' There were other details as the young student got used to the ways of Harrow:

> I have joined the Chess Club here . . . It is getting late now and I have my work for tomorrow morning to do. I was almost forgetting to write that we had singing again yesterday. It was much the same as it was the first time. I was fortunate enough to get nothing to sing though I nearly got one. Goodbye now till next week.

Motilal soon got into the public-school mood, and wanted his son to get involved as much as possible in all the extra-curricular activities including a 'real fight', though a little cautiously, particularly in areas like 'footer'. 'I say this simply because I have read of a case of broken bones in the book *The Brothers* recommended by you.' He was happily surprised that his son had started shooting, 'one of the most necessary qualifications of a well-educated man', and delighted in Jawaharlal's enthusiasm as 'sergeant' in the Officer Training Corps. Jawaharlal soon got a nickname – the sign of acceptance – from his schoolmates: the predictable 'Joe'.

There was some exciting news from Allahabad soon, when Jawaharlal learned of the birth of a brother, sixteen years his junior to the precise day. He had heard that the name Hiralal was being thought of and was sharp in his opinion: 'I don't like this at all and I hope you don't either.' The opinion was soon irrelevant; the child (eventually named Ratan Lal) died on 2 December. On the 4th Motilal wrote to his son about his dead brother: 'He brought us almost unbounded happiness and joy but this world of ours was not good enough for him . . . It seems now that our happiness was too great to last long. Unmixed and uninterrupted happiness is not given to the spirit which inhabits mortal clay and the true lesson of life lies in making proper use of one's misfortunes.' Motilal was back at the High Court by the 6th 'but did not argue any case' on that particular day.

For the seven years that Jawaharlal was abroad, returning to India for just two brief holidays, once in the summer of 1906 and the second time in the summer of 1908, father and son kept up a virtually uninterrupted exchange of letters. Motilal's great love for his son soon converted those letters into a unique literature of a human relationship. The correspondence is a catalogue of a father's ambitions, apprehensions, dreams – as steady and confident when the child was fifteen as they assuredly were when he was born and as they would be twenty-five years later. And Jawaharlal's replies become the history of a response to a powerful love and a great vision, a study in an individual's development and change, as slowly, intricately, the backdrop of great events envelops both lives, and their personalities merge into events. One listens in their written chatter first for an intelligent observer's sharp perception and slowly watches them become participants, till their views and actions are not only commenting on events but influencing them. Father and son could hardly have been as honest with each other if they had conversed face to face rather than through letters. But the still centre of this correspondence remains the vision that Motilal had of his son's future. In fact, it is expressed in one of the earliest postcards he sent, one of a series of pictures of Congress leaders, in July 1905. Under the picture of Romesh Chunder Dutt, president of the Congress in 1899, Motilal had inked in the caption: 'Future Jawaharlal Nehru'. Dutt was the child of a family with considerable achievements in academic, literary and bureaucratic life. In 1869, at the age of just twenty-one, he qualified for the Indian Civil Service, and was also called to the Bar before he returned to India to begin an outstanding career in the ICS which won high praise from both lieutenant-governors and governors-general. By the time he retired in 1897, to concentrate on his love for history, he had also acquired a reputation for being a brilliant orator who was unafraid to tell the British they were wrong. He taught history at the University of London; and his finest intellectual achievements were a three-volume *History of Civilization in Ancient India* (published in 1899), *Famines in India under Early British Rule* (1901) and the *Economic History of India in the Victorian Age* (1902). All this was in addition to translations of the great Sanskrit classics into English and Bengali. It was an intimidating role model. Motilal was very keen that his son enter the Indian Civil Service. Commenting on the first term report at Harrow, he would write: 'Nothing will please me more than to have in you the first Senior Wrangler of your year. The ICS will then be child's play for you.' And later, on 11 January 1906: 'Cricket is after all only a game but shooting is an art which stands a man in good stead in emergencies. You will require some of it when you are a District

Officer in India.' That fate, mercifully, was to elude Jawaharlal, but he would become one of the finest prose writers of his time. And if the economic welfare of India was the passion of the administrator of the British Raj, then planning and a new world would be the central achievement of the first Prime Minister of free India. But let us follow the story for a while through the letters.

Jawaharlal did all the things required of a public schoolboy: football, cricket, cross-country steeplechase, a mile and a half-mile on Field Day, skating, gymnasium work-outs, cheering loyally at 'cockhouse' matches ('It is such a pity we have not been cockhouse [winners] for over a dozen years'). By the end of the term he was also able to send the good news to his proud father that

> I was of course top of my form and I am told that a prize will be given to me. I had never thought of this happening and am rather nervous about it . . . I wasn't quite sure whether I would get it to the very end and when Dr Wood called out my name I felt very confused. He gave me the book with the usual formula of congratulation. The prize is Lamb's *Essays of Elia* very nicely bound together.

He could never, however, do well in Scripture. But this was Jawaharlal's best academic phase, as well as his most responsible financially. He protested at the fees that his father was being made to pay to the school doctor, for instance: 'In the bill the one thing which struck me most was the doctor's charge. He only saw my leg once and then twice asked me how it was getting along.' (Doctors Bindloss and Lambert, the official physicians, had charged 17 shillings for the Christmas term of 1905.) Motilal, on his side, provided a running commentary on life in Allahabad: from the million-strong crowds at the Kumbha *mela* ('The Kumbh fair is in full swing. The Kashmiri Swamiji [guru of the Maharaja of Kashmir] is still my guest and being thoroughly comfortable has no present intention of going elsewhere') to details about Nanni and her governess ('Miss Hooper is thriving . . . she is getting fat'). Jawaharlal would respond: 'Nanni in spectacles! It is unthinkable . . . I do not like at all women, and especially girls, to wear spectacles.'

In the summer of 1906 Jawaharlal came to see his parents in India, spending a few weeks in Mussoorie with them. His headmaster Dr Joseph Wood was happy enough about his ward's progress, writing on 19 May 1906: 'You have every reason to be proud of your son, who is doing excellently and making his mark in the school ... He is a thoroughly good fellow and ought to have a very bright future before him.' But there were enough indications that Jawaharlal had already got bored by Harrow, with both the level of education and the level of intelligence he encountered. On 4 March 1906 he wrote to his father:

> I must confess I cannot mix properly with English boys. My tastes and inclinations are quite different. Here boys, older than me and in higher forms than me, take great interest in things which appear to me childish ... I almost wish sometimes that I had not come to Harrow, but gone straight to the 'Varsity. I have no doubt that public schools are excellent things and their training essential to every boy, but I have come here very late to really enjoy the life.

Nor were his Indian contemporaries – princes like Paramjit Singh, son of the Maharaja of Kapurthala, who caused a great to-do when his gold-mounted cane was stolen, only to be returned *after* the Eton–Harrow match at Lord's – much better. If anything he despised them even more. The prevalent anti-Semitic prejudice also got to Jawaharlal, though he hurriedly confesses that 'in later years, I had many good friends among the Jews'. But his real problem was that he was far more interested in politics than his schoolmates, and 'there was not a soul in Harrow to whom I could talk about it'. For the prize that really influenced Jawaharlal's heart and mind was not *Essays of Elia*, which he got 'for good work at school', but G. M. Trevelyan's Garibaldi books. 'Visions of similar deeds in India came before me, of a gallant fight for freedom, and in my mind India and Italy got strangely mixed together. Harrow seemed a rather small and restricted place for these ideas and I wanted to go to the wider sphere of the University.' And yet 'when the time came to part I felt unhappy and tears came to my eyes. I had grown rather fond of the place and my departure for good put an end to one period in my life.'

Later Jawaharlal was to romanticize that fondness. When he was in prison in the 1930s he stuck pictures of Harrow in his diaries, and made lists of great men who had been there. A Harrow and Trinity combination like Byron was especially welcome. And the school songs were recalled with greater gusto than that with which they may have been originally sung. But of course those songs were infused with the Harrow ethos: 'Come, fill your glasses, one and all, and join the toast with me: / Prosperity to Harrow! all upstanding, three times three!'

'Tis not alone in Classic lore her manly sons excel;
The Cricket and the Rifle grounds their tale of triumph tell:
The Church, the Senate, camp and Bar with varied voice attest
That, wheresoe'er bright Honour calls, her sons are with the best.

Or 'Forty Years On', which was sung when Jawaharlal revisited his old school on 2 May 1960:

Forty years on, when afar and asunder
Parted are those who are singing today,
When you look back, and forgetfully wonder
What you were like in your work and your play,
Then, it may be there will often come o'er you,
Glimpses of notes like the catch of a song –
Visions of boyhood shall float them before you,
Echoes of dreamland shall bear them along.
Follow up! Follow up! Follow up! Follow up! Follow up!
    Follow up!
Till the field ring again and again
With the tramp of the twenty-two men.

Harrow had at least one unexpected benefit. The bureaucrats of the Raj tended to be kinder in their treatment, particularly in gaol, towards a product of a legendary public school. As *The Harrovian* of 12 May 1960 takes care to point out while reporting the Indian Prime Minister's visit to his old school: 'On the whole, however, he [Nehru] did not find himself harshly treated, and sometimes was embarrassed at the "man-to-man" treatment he received from British officials who knew he had been to a Public School.' The report also noted the irony that successive secretaries of state, Lord Templewood and Lord Zetland, who were to find Nehru 'least co-operative' before the war were also Old Harrovians. In his autobiography Jawaharlal feels obliged to criticize the élitism: 'The Public School type has had its day even in England ... In India it is still more out of place, and it can never fit in or co-operate with our aggressive nationalism.' But it was obviously a faked criticism, to support the radical image he had consciously acquired. Jawaharlal never allowed such sentiments to come in the way of placing his grandsons Rajiv and Sanjay in the Indian equivalent of Harrow, Doon School. This ambivalence infected the visit to the old school in 1960. Jawaharlal was cheered by the boys and praised by the masters, but the enthusiasm was equivocal. The sharp but anonymous reporter of *The Harrovian* wondered why:

> To be honest, there was, throughout the afternoon, a strange sense of bewilderment. The School sang very badly. Why? The day was cold and grey, it was in the middle of the afternoon, and right at the beginning of the term, with little time to practise; the Shakespeare curtains helped to deaden the sound. But above all one felt that Songs, for once, were out of place before this great philosopher-ruler; agnostic, socialist, democrat, nationalist; at once the Rousseau, the Robespierre and Napoleon of the new India; and that he, in his turn, could not feel sure how much was left, behind the façade, of the Harrow that had created them.

The short explanation is that Harrow was used to producing men who built empires, not ones who destroyed them. Even when Jawaharlal was at Harrow, his politics were firmly nationalist. In fact, he had his first major difference with his father at this time, for he thought Motilal too pro-British. Jawaharlal even became insolent, and invited a sharp rebuke from the normally indulgent Motilal. But those were stirring times in India, enough to turn a young man's head.

7 The Rise of Hindu Nationalism

Swaraj, swadharma, dharmatattwa. National rule, national religion, national identity. This version of patriotism found its first powerful proponents in the group which came to be known as the Extremist wing in the Congress. The northern line of the Extremist triangle was held by the Arya Samaji Lala Lajpat Rai in Punjab and Madan Mohan Malviya in United Provinces; the western by Bal Gangadhar Tilak in Poona; and in the heart of British India, Bengal, it was led by the revivalist combination of Aurobindo Ghosh and Bipin Behari Pal. Aurobindo Ghosh was the most articulate of the leaders and, as he put it in his famous Uttarpara speech (30 May, 1909): 'I say it is the Sanatan Dharma [Hinduism] which for us is nationalism. The Hindu nation was born with the Sanatan Dharma; with it it moves, and with it it grows.' Their religion was their politics. Hinduism was patriotism. Freedom could be achieved, they believed, only through the reawakening of a national identity; this could, in turn, be built only on the mother religion of India, Hinduism. India could be reawakened and purged of foreign imperialists only through the concept popularized in the writing of Bankim Chandra Chatterjee: *dharmatattwa*, or a return to the fundamentals of Hinduism, and to the past when Hindu kings presided over a golden age. If the Extremists hated the British, then they were utterly contemptuous of the Christian, English-educated or -influenced Indians who saw the progress of the West as the answer to Indian poverty and secular liberalism as the antidote to social tensions. These liberals were quislings of foreign rule. But the more serious impediment to their dream of a Hindu India came from a quarter of the Indian population: the Muslims. Hatred and distrust defined their attitude to Muslims, and their secret societies were always occupied on two fronts, the British on one side, and the Muslims on the other.

The much-abused decision of Lord Curzon to divide Bengal essentially on Hindu–Muslim lines was a godsend to the Extremists, who were quick to denounce this as a conspiracy of two 'foreigners' to divide Mother Bengal. Cartoons in newspapers and magazines left nothing to the imagination. The July edition of *Hindu Punch* (literally, Indian Punch) shows a grim Curzon holding an axe while a sari-clad Mother Bengal lies prostrate before him, severed above the knees and ankles to represent the carving out of East Bengal and Assam. Muslim reaction to the Extremists was predictable; and even those who did not respond with parallel extremism kept aloof from the Congress under its Tilak spell. Muhammad Ali's article in *The Comrade*, in 1912, summed up the Muslim sentiment adequately:

> Whatever may be the inspiration of Hinduism as a religious creed, the educated Hindus made it a rallying symbol for political unity ... Past history was ransacked for new political formulas; and by a natural and inevitable process 'nationality' and 'patriotism' began to be associated with Hinduism ... But the Muslims weigh on his consciousness, all the same, as a troublesome irrelevance; and he would thank his stars if some great exodus or even a geological cataclysm could give him riddance ... The 'communal patriots' amongst the Hindus treated him as a prisoner in the dock, and loudly complained of him as an impossible factor in the scheme of India's future.

The liberals, clubbed under the term Moderates, were fortunately in no mood to surrender the Congress to the Extremists. It was a very difficult time for them, for the British had handed the Extremists a tremendous propaganda coup with the division of Bengal, and public sentiment was running strongly in favour of the Extremists. Both groups understood the value of the Congress as a vehicle, and so the tussle for the driver's seat was bitter. The most important leader of the Moderates was the wise genius Gopal Krishna Gokhale, the man who later gave the freedom movement a unique gift called Mohandas Karamchand Gandhi. With Gokhale were the great lights of India at the time – Dadabhai Naoroji, Pherozeshah Mehta and Surendranath Bannerjea. Twice, in the post-Bengal-partition tension of the 1905 Congress at Benaras and the even more tense Calcutta session next year, Gokhale's diplomacy kept the Moderates in charge of the party, with their nominees being elected president, to the great frustration of the Extremists. Gokhale was gentle in public but devastating in private about the Extremist leaders. In a personal letter to a friend, Natesan, on 2 October 1906, this is how he described the current hero of Bengal, Bipin Pal:

Mr Pal has never worked for the Congress in the past. He is a very unscrupulous man and inordinately ambitious . . . He uses brave words, but behind these words there is neither courage nor character and, of course, there is no judgement, and I have little doubt that in a year or two we shall see this man's collapse, whatever noise he may succeed in making temporarily.

As for Tilak: 'Mr Tilak has a matchless capacity for intrigue and he is not burdened with an exacting conscience.'

Gokhale, not Tilak, was Motilal's hero. Motilal did not support the division of Bengal but he was repelled by the Hindu revivalism of the Extremists and the religious cant of the boycott movement launched from Calcutta, calling it 'the most stupid and, I may add, the most dishonest thing I have ever seen'. He could not resist, however, admiring the manner in which they had captured the popular imagination. In a letter to his son on 16 November 1905, he wrote:

The Swadeshi movement is the wonder of the age. The Bengali Babus have after all justified themselves. Poor Curzon goes away from India 'unwept, unhonoured and unsung' . . . In Bengal one shout of Bande Mataram brings thousands of Bengalis to the spot and paralyses the executive power. If this movement only continues you will on your return find an India quite different to the India you left.

Such was the optimism generated that Extremist leaders like G. S. Khaparde (1854–1938) were predicting a date for freedom – it would come after war and insurrection, by 1913. The young Jawaharlal preferred the romance of a war of freedom to his father's moderation. He followed Indian politics closely through newspapers. From Harrow he asked his father to send him an Indian newspaper – and specified that he did not want *The Pioneer*, which was owned and edited by Britishers from Allahabad. He got the official line from the London press. But even *The Times* had admitted that the Swadeshi movement had spread to Kashmir, and he wrote to his father, tongue in cheek: 'The movement must be strong indeed if it has reached even the Kashmiris. I would never have thought of it.' Motilal sent his son the *Indian People* and clippings from other publications to provide a more comprehensive account of what was happening. And relatives like Rameshwari Nehru, the wife of Jawaharlal's cousin Brijlal, kept him well informed of the mood at home through letters. The school principal in fact once complained to Motilal that such rebellious letters were not conducive to a proper upbringing.

Jawaharlal's interest in politics was not restricted to India. He followed the 1906 general election in Britain keenly, and he was the only boy in his class to remember the names of the full Campbell-Bannerman Cabinet when a teacher took an impromptu test. A 'mock parliament' in school at that time was one of the highlights of his early Harrow life. (The Conservatives won.)

Motilal was more an observer of politics than a participant in those years. He went to the Calcutta Congress in 1906, but only to keep the party safe from the wiles of the 'oily babus'. Motilal had even less admiration for the Extremist heroes than Gokhale, describing Bipin Pal, for instance, as 'the great bathroom hero of Barisal'. But his son was equally certain that his father was wrong. 'I do not see why you dislike the "oily" babus. Their erratic methods have made me respect them far more than I ever did . . . It is practically owing to them that the people here have begun to take some interest in India. It is not very much, I know, but still it is better than nothing.' He was delighted, however, that this dislike had finally pushed Motilal into active politics. Although Motilal had 'grave doubts' about this, 'entirely a new line for me', his son had none and was easy with brash advice: 'Your address is certain to be a very brilliant one in every respect, only I hope it will not be too moderate. Indians are as a rule too much so and require a little stirring up.' When he read the text of his father's presidential address to the provincial Congress in March, Jawaharlal shot off his congratulations: 'My expectations have been fully realized. I specially like the manner you have handled the Hindu–Mohamedan problem. You are still very moderate but I hardly expected you to become an extremist.' If there was a touch of patronizing there, Motilal ignored it. 1907 was a year of much stir in India, which Sir Denzil Ibbetson, the lieutenant-governor of Punjab, described thus in order to justify a policy of strong action: 'Everywhere people are sensible of a change, of a new air, a *nai hawa*, which is blowing through men's minds.' Far away in Harrow, it was also blowing through Jawaharlal's, and only increased in intensity when he moved on to Trinity, Cambridge, on 31 July. In September, Jawaharlal went to Dublin on a holiday, which, much to his excitement, coincided with disturbances against British rule. He wrote to his father on 12 September from Dublin: 'you asked me not to go near Belfast on account of the riots, but I would have dearly liked to have been there for them'. And then: 'Have you heard of the Sinn Fein in Ireland? . . . Their policy is not to beg for favours but to wrest them. They do not want to fight England by arms, but "to ignore her, boycott her, and quietly assume the administration of Irish affairs".'

Politics, serious (the arrest of Lala Lajpat Rai) or trivial (a pun in Hindi on the name of the Secretary of State for India, John Morley, nicknamed 'Jan Marli'), filled the letters between father and son. But while Motilal kept getting more Moderate, Jawaharlal travelled in the other direction. Jawaharlal was furious with Pal's betrayal when he appealed to the court for mitigation of his sentence; Pal should never have begged. He now even began criticizing Motilal directly, calling him 'immoderately moderate' after reading an article by Motilal in the British-owned *Pioneer*. Motilal reacted with some irritation, but the son became only more acerbic: 'The government must be feeling very pleased with you at your attitude. I wonder if the insulting offer of a Rai Bahadurship, or something equivalent to it, would make you less of a moderate than you are.'

This was too much for the proud Motilal to take. He lost his famous temper and even threatened to recall his insolent son. He did not say as much in his letter to Jawaharlal, but the family grape-vine carried the message. Jawaharlal apologized:

> I have been told that you did not like something I wrote to you a few weeks ago. I was rather surprised to know this as what I wrote to you was written purely in fun and it never dawned on me that it could offend you . . . I am sure you will pardon me for an offence I did not intend to commit.

That was sufficient to melt the heart of an indulgent father, who replied: 'I do not of course approve of your politics . . . This is, however, neither here nor there. My love for you knows no bounds, and unless there is some very remarkable change in me, I do not see how it can be affected.'

Jawaharlal was soon to appreciate that his father's views were based on a larger philosophy. On the last Sunday of November 1908,

Bipin Pal came to address the Indian Majlis at Cambridge. What he heard opened Jawaharlal's eyes. His comment is revealing:

> He [Pal] is not accustomed to addressing small gatherings and the way he thundered nearly made me deaf. Sometimes he grew very eloquent. But I objected greatly to his not taking the Mohammadans into consideration. Once or twice he did refer to them but then he was not very complimentary. Another thing which annoyed me was his repeated references to the spiritual mission of India. India, he said, was 'God's chosen country' and the Indians the 'chosen race' – a phrase which reminded me of Israel.

More than two decades later, writing in his autobiography, Jawaharlal would recall, while examining Motilal's position: 'The background of these movements was a religious nationalism which was alien to his nature. He did not look back to a revival in India of ancient times. He looked to the West and felt greatly attracted by Western progress . . . Socially speaking, the revival of Indian nationalism in 1907 was definitely reactionary.'

The first clash on politics with his father was also Jawaharlal's first major lesson in the secular legacy of Motilal Nehru. And he ruefully noted later of those days: 'Many a Congressman was a communalist under his nationalist cloak.' He must 'learn to beware of Congressmen in sheep's clothing'.

8 A British Response –
in League with the Muslims

Aurobindo Ghosh, unable to bend the Congress to his will, decided to split it. At his instance, on 27 December 1907, at the twenty-third session at Surat, a Maharashtrian delegate threw a shoe at the dais which set off an unholy fracas and broke India's premier political organization for the first time in its history. Nearly 1,600 delegates and 800 visitors had gathered on the banks of the Tapti river for the twenty-third Congress at Surat, under the presidentship of the Honourable Doctor Rash Behari Ghose, CIE. He began his address with an extravagant simile: 'In standing before you today I feel as if I was summoned to drive the Chariot of the Sun; and if I am spared the fate of Phaeton, I shall owe my good fortune only to your for-bearance and indulgent kindness on which I am confident I can safely rely.' The confidence was misplaced. The Extremists, led by Tilak and Ghosh, furious at having been robbed once again of the presidentship, set off a pandemonium which ended in chairs being hurled, sticks being brandished, heads being bruised and turbans rolling on the floor. Pretty high drama by the standards of 1907. The ultimate indignity was the arrival of the police to clear the place. The Congress would not fully recover from this split for almost a decade.

Lord Minto could gloat to the new secretary of state who had taken office after the Liberal victory of 1906, John Morley: 'Congress collapse [is] a great triumph for us.' The British, however, worried by the impact of rising Hindu nationalism, had already taken out a key insurance policy.

Sir Sayyid died an unhappy man. His son, Mahmud, suffered a nervous breakdown and quarrelled with him; a Hindu accountant of his college forged cheques and cheated the institution of a hundred thousand rupees; and even the British let him down when the government of the United Provinces finally sanctioned the use of Hindi in the courts in 1900. (Sir Sayyid obviously was an Urdu and Persian protagonist.) But he remained loyal to the British.

In August 1888 Sir Sayyid formed the United Indian Patriotic Association with an appeal to both Hindus and Muslims to help him counteract the 'false impression' in England that all Indians were behind the Congress. (Membership was pretty high at five rupees a month, but the members were the *rais*, the rich; so they could afford it.) This became defunct soon. On 30 December 1894 there was a meeting at Sir Sayyid's house in Aligarh. Theodore Beck argued that the time had come for Muslims and the English to become 'united in firm alliance' since both were minorities in India, and their common interests were under threat from Hindus. How? Witness the anti-cow-slaughter agitation whose object was to prevent Englishmen and Muslims 'from killing cows for good'. From here Sir Sayyid launched the Muhammadan Anglo-Oriental Defence Association of Upper India. Its aims were to protect the political interests of Muslims, to 'discourage popular agitation among Muhammadans' and to 'lend support to measures calculated to increase the stability of the British government and the security of the Empire'. The membership fee had been made more reasonable – three rupees annually – but this association could not get off the ground either. In contrast, the Congress intensified its efforts to become the platform of all communities, united under the single banner of the interests of India. As Surendranath Bannerjea put it at the eleventh Congress in Poona in 1895, it was 'the Congress of United India, of Hindus and Mahomedans, of Christians, of Parsees and of Sikhs'. Hume railed at Beck, saying he was acting like a Guy Fawkes to promote 'the sectional Muhammadan cabal', and personally wooed Muslims into the party he had founded. Perhaps no sentence described the Congress spirit better than one delivered at the 22nd session of the party, in Calcutta in 1906: 'The foundation upon which the Indian National Congress is based is that we [Hindus and Muslims] are all equal, that there should be no reservation for any class or community.' It was uttered by a young man just making his political reputation: Muhammad Ali Jinnah. Coincidentally, at precisely the same time that Jinnah was saying this, a new party was being formed in Dhaka, called the All-India Muslim League.

Sir Sayyid passed away on 27 March 1898. (We know the year of his birth and the date of his death; that presumably is what fame is all about.) By 1900 the Defence Association had withered away, and the secretary of an offshoot, the Literary Society, was merrily auctioning and selling the books and documents gifted by the government for its library. The political heirs of Sir Sayyid, the landed gentry of

United Provinces, like Nawab Viqar-ul-Mulk, were in confusion. In July 1903 they finally mustered together a Muslim Political Association at a public meeting in Saharanpur. It was stillborn.

George Nathaniel Curzon, first Baron Curzon of Kedleston, later first Marquess Curzon of Kedleston, reached India on 6 January 1899. It was a Friday, the day of prayer considered auspicious by Muslims. The *Moslem Chronicle* and the Defence Association immediately appealed to the new Viceroy for special attention towards the Muslims, and Lord Curzon promised that 'my heart would be dull, did it not respond'. Lord Curzon knew his India; he had been Under-Secretary of State for India in 1891–2 and Under-Secretary for Foreign Affairs from 1895 to 1898. He also knew what he wanted: to crush the Bengali 'babus' and destroy the Congress in its stronghold, Bengal. Calcutta, after all, was still the capital of British India, and hence the centre of the confrontation. Curzon's policies, in particular the partition of Bengal and the passions it evoked, began a chain of events which set the politics of India on a road leading, in violent fits and starts over forty years, towards the partition of the country. It is important to understand the genesis.

The Bengal Presidency then covered 189,900 square miles, including the whole of Bihar and Orissa, containing more than a quarter of the population of the country (78.5 million at the turn of the century). The capital, Calcutta, was the heart of the jewel in the crown, while the jurisdiction of Calcutta University and Calcutta High Court extended beyond the Presidency. If the British could not administer Bengal effectively, if they could not control the politics of the most powerful province of the Raj, their power would be weakened everywhere; this much was obvious. Curzon tried to destroy the potential ability of Bengal to challenge the Raj by dividing it. This would serve two purposes. It would not only split the state's interlinked economy, but also split the Bengalis along communal lines; Hindus were preponderant in the western half, Muslims in the east. Curzon's excuse, on paper, was that the province was simply too large to administer effectively, and it is true that this complaint had been voiced as early as in the time of Lord Dalhousie in 1853, and proposals of division had been often made. But it was finally Curzon who authorized the publication, on 3 December 1903, of the formal scheme for partition, called the Risley Paper (after Sir Herbert Risley, Home Secretary, Government of India).

There was – predictably – an uproar; less predictably, it was not restricted to the Hindus. Even the *Moslem Chronicle*, which had championed Sir Sayyid, thought this a bit much. Curzon answered this 'hysteria' with a campaign which was nothing if not insidious. He went on a tour of East Bengal (today's Bangladesh) and tempted Muslims with an apple of discord – the thought that this new overwhelmingly Muslim province would 'invest the Mahomedans in Eastern Bengal with unity which they have not enjoyed since the days of the old Musalman viceroys and kings'. On 6 July 1905 the Government of India announced from its summer capital in Simla its formal decision to divide Bengal. On 10 October, London published the partition papers but requested a postponement of three weeks. Curzon refused. On 16 October, Bengal was partitioned. (Curzon's hurry was owed partly to the fact that he was being forced to quit the viceroyalty following defeat in his power struggle with Lord Kitchener, then commander-in-chief.) The new province of Eastern Bengal and Assam was now 106,540 square miles with 18 million Muslims and 12 million Hindus in a total population of 31 million.

Curzon explained his reasons unambiguously to John Brodrick, Secretary of State for India:

Calcutta is the centre from which the Congress party is manipulated throughout the whole of Bengal, and indeed the whole of India. Its best wirepullers and its most frothy orators all reside here. The perfection of their machinery and the tyranny which it enables them to exercise are truly remarkable ... They dominate public opinion in Calcutta; they affect the High Court; they frighten the local Government of India. The whole of their activity is directed to creating an agency so powerful that they may one day be able to force a weak government to give them what they desire.

Curzon was also convinced that he would get away with his scheme, for Bengalis 'howl until a thing is settled and then they accept it'. But this time the howling would not stop. When Lord Hardinge announced the annulment of partition in 1911, he admitted as much. He said on 13 July 1911: 'the political power of the Bengali has not been broken'.

The problem was not the decibel level but the content of the howl. Motilal, and the Moderates in the Congress, saw through the 'religious nationalism' of Bengalis like Bipin Pal and Aurobindo and rejected it. But the Hindu nationalism of the Swadeshi leaders provided some Muslims with the opportunity to attempt a consolidation of Muslim interests. On 16 October 1905 the Muhammadan Union was formed with the patronage of Nawab Salimullah Bahadur of Dhaka. The objective was to challenge the Hindus with British help. When Lord Curzon's successor, the fourth Earl of Minto (also nicknamed 'Mr Rolly'), finally removed the notoriously anti-Hindu governor of Eastern Bengal, Bampfylde Fuller, there were cries of betrayal by 'loyalist' Muslims. Lord Minto quickly indicated to the Muslims that Fuller's departure was only retribution for excess, not a change of policy towards the community.

In 1906 a special committee was convened with a special mission: to present an 'address' during a formal call on the Viceroy, Lord Minto, on behalf of India's Muslims. The nudge had come from the British through W. A. J. Archbold, successor of Theodore Beck as principal of the Mahomedan Anglo-Oriental College, Aligarh. On 9 August 1906 Archbold wrote to J. Dunlop Smith, private secretary to Lord Minto (both were in Simla): 'If the Muhammadans were informed (privately) that a deputation would be received and a statement made, what would happen would be that representatives of Muhammadans from various parts of India would come to Simla and present a carefully drawn-up petition.' Indeed, very carefully drawn up. On 13 September the nod came, formally. Dunlop Smith wrote to Mohsinul Mulk (Nawab Mehdi Ali) informing him that 'His Excellency will have much pleasure in receiving the Deputation'. The leader of this move was the spiritual head of the Ismaili sect, His Highness Sultan Mahomed Shah Aga Khan, GCIE. Lord Minto did not have too high an opinion of this gentleman, describing the Aga Khan privately as a man 'who knew more about the second-class music halls of Europe than of Indian affairs', but of course this was precisely the kind of expert that the British were looking for. The text of the address was prepared by Nawab Mohsinul Mulk, S. H. Bilgrami and W. A. J. Archbold. But the strings were firmly in the hands of J. Dunlop Smith, the Viceroy's private secretary, as the Aga Khan confirmed in a note to Smith: 'I have also asked him [Mohsinul Mulk] not to move in any matter before first finding out if the step to be taken has the full approval of the government privately.'

The text was finalized on 16 September, cleared by the 18th and presented to Minto at the Viceregal Lodge in Simla on 1 October. Thirty-five nobles, *jaghirdars*, *talukdars*, lawyers, zemindars and merchants, self-appointed representatives of 62 million Muslims (by the 1901 census), entered the regal ballroom of the Simla palace. The list makes most interesting reading: the Aga Khan, of course; Prince Bakhtiar Shah of Mysore; Malik Omar Hayatt Khan of Tiwana; Khan Bahadur Mian Mohomed Shah Din of Lahore; Maulvi Sharfuddin of Patna; Khan Bahadur Syed Nawab Ali Chowdhury of Mymensingh; Nawab Bahadur Syed Amir Husain Khan of Calcutta; Naseer Husain Khan Khyyal of Calcutta; Khan Bahadur Mirza Shujaat Ali Beg; Syed Ali Imam and Nawab Sarfraz Husain Khan of Patna; Khan Bahadur Ahmad Mohiuddin Khan of the Carnatic family of Madras; Maulvi Rafiuddin Ahmed and Ebrahimbhoy Adamji Peerbhoy of Bombay; Abdur Rahim of Calcutta; Syed Allahdad Shah of Sind; Maulana H. M. Malak of Nagpur; Khalifa Syed Muhammad Hussain and Col. Abdul Majid Khan, both members of the Patiala government; Khwaja Yusuf Shah, Mian Muhammad Shafi and Shaikh Ghulam Sadik of Punjab; Hakim Ajmal Khan of Delhi; Munshi Ihtishan Ali, Syed Nabiullah, Maulvi Syed Karamat Husain, Syed Abdulraoof, Munshi Abdur Salam Khan, Khan Bahadur Muhammad Muzammil Ullah Khan, Muhammad Ismail Khan, Sahabzada Aftab Ahmed Khan, Maulvi Mushtaq Hussain, Maulvi Habibul Rahaman Khan and Maulvi Syed Mahdee Ally Khan of the United Provinces; and Nawab Syed Sirdar Ali Khan of Hyderabad. Also present was the Persian consul-general based at Murshidabad.

At 11 a.m. sharp Lord Minto entered the hall, and the address, printed on vellum, was read aloud.

After a dutiful appreciation of 'the incalculable benefits conferred by British rule', the address set out these substantive demands: that Muslims be elected only through Muslim electorates, and in a proportion that reflected their 'political importance' and 'the value of the contribution which they make to the defence of the Empire'; that there should be a guaranteed percentage of jobs in the services for them and promotion without competitive examinations; and that the principle be extended to local self-government bodies. There was great worry expressed about what democracy would mean for Muslims; it was likely, 'among other evils, to place our national

interests at the mercy of an unsympathetic majority'. Muslims, therefore, 'should never be an ineffective minority'. Such guarantees would
strengthen 'the basis of their [that is, Muslim] unswerving loyalty to
the Throne'.

Lord Minto, in reply, welcomed them 'heartily to Simla'. 'Your
presence here today,' he began, 'is very full of meaning.' He was
grateful, he said, 'for the opportunity you are affording me of express-
ing my appreciation of the just aims of the followers of Islam and
their determination to share in the political history of our empire'.
He praised them as 'descendants of a conquering and ruling race', a
devious touch designed to excite Muslim feudal vanity as much as
Hindu anger. Lord Minto traced British efforts to help Muslims from
the time when Warren Hastings established the Calcutta Madrasah
in 1782 to July 1875 when Lord Lytton laid the foundation-stone
at Aligarh. He then pointed out that the new province of Eastern
Bengal was yet another reward for Muslim loyalty. He recognized
the unrest prevalent in India: 'the political atmosphere is full of
change. We all feel it. Hopes and ambitions new to India are
making themselves felt.' But this discontent was only the work of
an educated élite – the 'babus' (Minto, however, did not use the
term), who were the weeds in the harvest of English education.
However, the Muslims should not worry about the imminent arrival of British-style democracy. 'I am entirely in accord with you',
said Lord Minto, that Muslim representation should be decided
separately. And he specifically promised: 'the Mohamedan community may rest assured that their political rights and interests as
a community will be safeguarded in any administrative reorganization with which I am concerned'.

It was Mary, Countess of Minto, who let the cat out of the bag for
future historians when she recorded in her diary, soon after the visit
of the 36-member delegation (six, including Nawab Khwaja Salimullah of Dhaka, could not come due to illness), that Dunlop Smith
had sent her a note saying: 'I must send Your Excellency a line to say
that a very, very big thing has happened today. A work of states-
manship that will affect India and Indian history for many a long
year. It is nothing less than the pulling back of sixty-two millions of
people from joining the ranks of the seditious opposition.'

Within three days of the deputation, these nobles and great landowners took another major decision. They agreed to create a

national political party, but one restricted purely to Muslims, based
on the Nawab of Dhaka's scheme for an All-Indian Muhammadan
Confederacy. On 30 December 1906 the president of the first session
of the new party, Nawab Viqar-ul-Mulk Mushtaq Hussain (1841–
1917), argued that 'defence, not defiance' was their motto. The
resolution was 'that a Political Association styled the All-India
Muslim League be formed', with the objectives to promote 'feelings
of loyalty [to the British]' and to 'protect and advance the political rights and interests of the Musalmans of India'. It was moved
by the Nawab of Dhaka and seconded by Hakim Ajmal Khan, a
famous doctor of Delhi who would later become president of the
Congress and die a Congressman. And so was born in Eastern Bengal
the All-India Muslim League which would travel through various
stages of inactivity and despair before it came under the control, in
the 1930s, of the man who would deliver a country in its name:
Jinnah.

The wonderful irony is, as the first honorary president of the
League, the Aga Khan, noted in another letter to a correspondent he
kept well informed, Dunlop Smith, the 'doughtiest opponent' of the
League in 1906 was Jinnah, who 'came out in bitter hostility toward
all that I and my friends had done and were trying to do. He was the
only well-known Muslim to take this attitude . . . He said our principle of separate electorates was dividing the nation against itself.'
Jinnah, at the very moment when the Muslim League was being born
in Dhaka, was attending the troubled Calcutta session of the Congress. One of a 45-member Muslim delegation, Jinnah was with the
Moderates; he had helped draft the presidential address of the great
but now ageing Dadabhai Naoroji. (Dadabhai was too weak to
deliver it himself, and Gokhale read it out for him.) It was at this
Calcutta Congress that the thirty-year-old Jinnah met the charismatic
poetess Sarojini Naidu, who dubbed him India's true 'ambassador of
Hindu–Muslim unity'. She immediately became fascinated by this
'rising lawyer and a coming politician' inspired by a 'virile patriotism', Jinnah, in Sarojini Naidu's words, was even in those young
days

> a little aloof and imperious of manner . . . the calm hauteur of his accus-
> tomed reserve but masks, for those who know him, a naïve and eager
> humanity, an intuition quick and tender as a woman's, a humour gay
> and winning as a child's – pre-eminently rational and practical, discreet

and dispassionate in his estimate and acceptance of life, the obvious sanity and serenity of his worldly wisdom effectively disguise a shy and splendid idealism which is the very essence of the man.

Lord Minto delivered on his promise. For nearly a quarter of a century the British had ignored or dismissed every Congress demand. But it took them just three years to institutionalize the guarantee to the Muslims through the principle of separate electorates in the famous Minto–Morley reforms of 1909. The Muslims had been given critical advantages over Hindus. Apart from separate electorates and weightage, voting was made easier for them. A Muslim could become a voter if he paid tax on an income of only Rs 3,000 per year while a Hindu had to have an income of Rs 3 lakhs (Rs 300,000). Similarly, in the graduate category, a Muslim needed to be a graduate of only three years' standing, while a Hindu required thirty.

It is interesting, in retrospect, that in 1906 the thirty-year-old Jinnah should have been a Moderate, and seventeen-year-old Nehru a fan of the Extremists. But politics was of only sideline interest to the schoolboy in England; even his father was as yet extremely uncertain about whether it was worth getting deeper into what he perceived as a rather big mess. And so while Jinnah, inspired by the experience of his first Congress session, was preaching the merits of Hindu–Muslim unity, Jawaharlal was enjoying his Christmas 'vac' (as the school slang for vacations went) in Paris.

9 Europe, 1907–12: Taking It Easy

It wasn't just Jawaharlal – a whole collection of cousins studying in London (at Motilal's expense) were off to Europe that winter. 'Birju Bhaiya' (Brijlal) was supposed to go to Rouen, but he was reluctant since it was too far away from the comforts of Paris; Shridhar was headed for Dieppe; while their friend Jivan Lal Katju had not made up his mind, wavering between Grantham and Paris. Jawaharlal knew what he wanted: Paris. Though he was normally quite communicative in his letters to his father, there is a discreet silence about how he blew his money in France. He did mention a visit to the theatre to see a French translation of *Julius Caesar* which 'was more amusing than anything else. I don't think the actors were quite sure whether it was a pantomime or a tragedy.' And he sought a bit of parental pity for wandering around Paris without cash. In reply he got a snub, mildly tempered by the advice that 'You must always keep some extra money with you'. But at least some of the money was going on good theatre. On his return to London he saw *Macbeth* at the Garrick, but he was not impressed by *Antony and Cleopatra* at His Majesty's.

It was not theatre, however, which filled Jawaharlal's mind but visions of university. A year at Harrow had convinced him he was learning nothing, and he had written to Sir Walter Fletcher, senior tutor and lecturer in Natural Sciences at Trinity College, Cambridge University, for permission to appear in the entrance examinations. Motilal would have preferred that his son wait but accepted the latter's decision: 'I will tell him [Wood] that you have no more time to spend at Harrow.' A surprised Wood gave Jawaharlal the necessary character certificate though he had not quite known him for the required two years; Jawaharlal, possibly in the belief that the English were absolute sticklers for detail, did point this out, but Wood waived the detail away. Actually by now Jawaharlal had simply lost interest in formal education, and he was never going to recover that interest. In November 1906 he wrote to his father from Harrow: 'And even if I came out on top [of my form], it would not do me much good.

I would get a prize and that would be the end of it.' When he was meant to be preparing for the entrance examinations, his priorities were elsewhere: 'it is doubtful if I can manage to drag myself from a good cricket match to work'. Perhaps the most valuable asset he acquired from Harrow was the stamp; it was a good club to belong to – all the viceroys in Jawaharlal's lifetime were products of Harrow or Eton barring Chelmsford and Wavell (both Winchester) and Mountbatten (Osborne). Yet Cambridge was even worse, in terms of intellectual growth. He had been elated with the 'adult freedom' of university, and properly self-conscious when he first wandered through the big courts and narrow streets of Cambridge: 'I had got out of the shackles of boyhood and felt at last that I could claim to be a grown-up.' But his obituary of university life was less than exciting. 'Three quiet years with little of disturbance in them, moving slowly on, like the sluggish Cam.'

In 1546 King Henry VIII amalgamated King's Hall and Michael-house, gave them a trifle from the wealth he had seized from the monasteries and founded Trinity College. By the Year of our Lord 1986, the post-office-cum-store opposite the Great Gate was owned by a former clerk of the Ministry of Information and Broadcasting of the Government of the Union of India, a man from a small town in Punjab, Ferozepur, who managed to migrate to England in November 1963. Bachan Singh Bhalla was now a respectable councillor of the Borough of Sandwell and a proud owner of two homes; he bought the lease on the shop when he discovered that it was on sale during a tourist's visit to the college of Jawaharlal Nehru. Elsewhere in the vicinity the Sultan Bar and Disco and the Mumtaz restaurant spoke of Britain's changing face, but in 1907 Jawaharlal had to be content with indifferent lodgings at 40 Green Street and then 'probably the rottenest rooms in the whole college': Number 6 in Whewell Court. The system of allotting rooms was more patriarchal then, with tra-ditional Cambridge families reserving the better ones for their kin. (It is all frightfully democratic now, involving ballots, seniority and a compensatory weightage which takes into account whether the ballot has given you a good room earlier or not. The best thing, conse-quently, is to be consistently middle class so that you are always assured of middling-decent rooms.)

As at Harrow, Jawaharlal entered his name for all the activities: riding, tennis, the Trinity Boat Club (at 8 stone 4 pounds, he coxed well) and debating at the Magpie and Stump (emblem: a stuffed bird in a glass case on a tree stump), to which his name was proposed by St John Philby and Charles Darwin, grandson of the great scientist. Surprisingly, the future orator was least active in the last. In three years he spoke just once, for 2 minutes 30 seconds, on the motion 'This house approves of the present public school system'. He paid fines rather than speak. Neither was he very vocal at the gatherings of the Majlis, the society of Indian students; only one mention, of a speech at an Id (a Muslim festival) dinner, is available. Jawaharlal did take an interest in British political events, at least enough for him to remember that he could get 5 to 1 in favour of the Liberals. He liked gambling: 'I was always, like my father, a bit of a gambler, at first with money and then for highest stakes, with the bigger issues of life.' He became a bit of a dilettante, perfecting the art of 'semi-highbrow talk' with the aid of only a few books and a lot of name-dropping: Nietzsche (who was the rage in Cambridge then) and Shaw (prefaces, of course; the plays were meant for the masses) and Havelock Ellis and Krafft-Ebing and Otto Weininger and naturally Walter Pater and Oscar Wilde. His formal subjects were chemistry, geology and physics, but he gave up the last for botany. He encountered Shaw for the first time at a lecture on Socialism and the University Man. Later, when his own fame began to match that of the playwright, the two got along well whenever they communicated. But it is stretching the point to say that Jawaharlal became a socialist or Fabian at this stage. By his own description: 'My general attitude to life at the time was a vague kind of Cyrenaicism . . . It is easy and gratifying to give a long Greek name to the desire for a soft life and pleasant experiences.' The wit in the sentence is a reflection of the confidence of a national hero writing his autobiography in a British gaol, and not the undergraduate. The undergraduate was a prig, with not a great deal to commend him. Contemporaries like Saifuddin Kitchlew, Syed Mahmud, J. M. Sengupta and Tasadduk Ahmad Sherwani gave better reason to suppose that a major political career lay ahead of them. Jawaharlal would resent anti-Indian discrimination when he saw or heard of it, as for instance in June 1911, when he went to see Cambridge University play the visiting Indian cricket side (Cambridge won by an innings and 71 runs) and heard the story of how the Chancellor had refused to get up when giving degrees at a convocation to the Maharaja of Bikaner and the Aga

Khan (the same Aga who loyally inspired the birth of the Muslim League). But this was about as far as his pro-India sentiments took him.

Motilal, never one to underestimate his beloved son's talents, kept prodding him to be some kind of Olympian who would dazzle society with his popularity and enter the record books with his academic brilliance. Such glories were beyond Jawaharlal's current ambitions, to the severe disappointment of his father, who applied what balm he could to his own feelings with occasional bouts of sarcasm. Jawaharlal had few illusions about his capabilities, however, writing to his father: 'You distress me greatly by confidently expecting me to get a First.' Jawaharlal's self-assessment about his academic abilities was, to put it mildly, gloomy. Eventually when he passed in the second half of the second class, Motilal was relieved enough to celebrate lavishly, with that typically unique mix of European taste and Indian generosity. The family was on holiday in Mussoorie in June 1910 when Motilal got the wire about his son's success; a lavish feast was organized, the champagne flowed freely, and all the servants were given gifts and increments – including those few fortunate enough to have been hired that very day. Jawaharlal also got a very generous gift of a hundred pounds for a holiday in France ('and pick up', said Daddy, 'the language while you are enjoying yourself'). Motilal was acutely terrified that his son might actually fail, so even such moderate results were cause for celebrations. He could not bear the thought of his son's failure. But now the sharp father began to suspect that his son might have pulled a fast one by deliberately painting such a despondent picture of his academic abilities so that an average result might come as good news. As Motilal put it in a letter to Jawaharlal: 'What a fraud you are.'

This gift almost cost Jawaharlal his life. He decided to spend it on a tour of Europe. He was trekking through Norway's mountains with a friend, and they stopped at a small place called Visnes. Tired, they asked the proprietor of the hotel they checked into where they could have a bath. Obviously, there were not too many requests for a bath in small hotels in Norway, and the best that the puzzled proprietor could do was direct them to a nearby stream emerging from a glacier. The cold water numbed them; Jawaharlal slipped and was swept away. His friend managed to get out and ran along the bank till he succeeded in catching Jawaharlal's leg and dragging him out.

Just two or three hundred yards away was a precipice over which the stream tumbled to form a 400-foot waterfall, the beauty spot of the area. Jawaharlal seemed exhilarated rather than subdued by this adventure, although he noted: 'I am sure I could not have stopped myself before I reached the bottom of the fall.' He wrote to his parents that they need not worry, since 'I am one of the most violently healthy persons I have come across.' The sentiment was not reciprocated by the anxious parents.

If Jawaharlal was indifferent to his studies, it was hardly because he was extra-attentive to women. He was pretty frank about sex in his autobiography: 'We considered ourselves very sophisticated and talked of sex and morality in a superior way . . . As a matter of fact, in spite of our brave talk, most of us were rather timid where sex was concerned. At any rate I was so, and my knowledge for many years, till after I had left Cambridge, remained confined to theory.' It wasn't morality which kept Jawaharlal pious, but shyness. Father, who had been married in his early teens, was wary about his son falling into the conventional trap of wanting to marry the first girl he met. There was sufficient opportunity, particularly since Jawaharlal enjoyed dancing. The manner in which Jawaharlal spent his first Christmas– New Year week at Cambridge (he had gone in 1906 to be with Birju during the holidays) must have set the old man thinking. There was dancing every night, including a fancy-dress ball with a generous quota of Cinderellas. There was even a staff ball at the 'hydro' where he was staying, where the visitors, for a change, waited on the servants. The prettiest girl of the lot sat at the table Jawaharlal was serving, and he was very keen to dance with her, or any of the other waitresses, to find out (he explained later) what it was like to socialize with the lower classes. There was a long queue even for the lower classes if you were pretty. He couldn't manage to get a dance, though his cousin Birju was luckier.

Jawaharlal's mother became exceedingly distressed when she heard all this. She was convinced that her beloved son was going to dances with white memsahibs every day, that he had given up the idea of studies altogether. He had to assure her that her fears were exaggerated. Still, the parents were in no mood to take any chances. Motilal started leading his son towards the idea of marriage. In a letter in January 1907 he promised Jawaharlal a 'real gem' of a girl from 'a large field of selection'. Jawaharlal replied a bit pompously:

'As for looks, who can help feeling keen enjoyment at the sight of a beautiful creature? . . . And yet sometimes this is not the case. Beauty is after all skin-deep and without certain other qualities would be more harmful than beneficial.' Two years later they were still discussing the subject. Jawaharlal, impressed by new ideas, wrote from Trinity College that 'everyone in India should marry outside his or her community' and, therefore, he did not necessarily want to marry a Kashmiri girl. The alarm bells began jangling nervously in Allahabad, and the autocrat in Motilal rose to meet this piece of impertinence. Within a week the son had apologized ('I am so sorry for all the trouble I am giving you') and surrendered 'in favour of your latest choice'. A bit of college humour clothed the surrender: 'Of marriage, in the abstract, I have a very high opinion; so much so that the practice of it is sure to disappoint me. This sounds like the saying of the Irishman who declared that he had such a great regard for truth that he refused to drag it into his own petty affairs, but really there is some sense in it.'

Sense or not, the decision was made *in absentia*. In December 1911 Motilal had decided who would be his daughter-in-law. Jawaharlal pleaded that a final decision be put off till he could see this girl, if possible. If not, he would abide by his father's decision. He sent a separate appeal to his mother: 'Would you like me to marry a girl who I may not like for the rest of my life or who may not like me?'

Jawaharlal was wasting his time, and his father's money, during these years. He was badly in debt, and his expenditure seemed to rise in direct proportion to his idleness. As he himself put it, he was trying to 'ape the prosperous and somewhat empty-headed Englishman who is called a man about town'. He had rooms in fashionable Holland Park, played tennis at the Queen's Club, gambled and went fashionably attired to the theatre: a life-style supported by incessant wires home asking for funds. He was once even forced to pawn his watch and chain. Often his cables to Motilal said nothing more – or less – meaningful than the single word 'Money'. His expenditure in 1911 was £800, enough to pay for three years of an ordinary student's existence. The sole redeeming element in his extravagance was buying books: in one spree (March 1911) he purchased a twenty-volume edition of Thackeray and a forty-volume edition of Dickens, and he wanted to order Oscar Wilde. He suggested that his father open an account for him at The Times Book

Club, and got a sharp reply saying he could not get '*carte blanche* to buy up the Times Book Library'. Jawaharlal sulked. He revived his old trick, which worked well enough at Trinity, of giving the impression that he might fail to become a barrister. Even as generous a father as Motilal got fed up. He wrote on 30 May 1912: 'I do not think there are many fathers in the world who are more indulgent than I am, but however indulgent I may be, I am not the man to stand nonsense.' Jawaharlal replied with that tone of injured innocence which can come only from too much pampering; he said he would return to Allahabad immediately. This time Motilal capitulated: 'You know as well as anyone else does that, whatever my shortcomings may be, and I know there are many, I cannot be guilty of either love of money or want of love for you.' Who can prevent the fatted calf from being killed for the prodigal son? However, on 19 June 1912 Jawaharlal was admitted to the Bar by the Inner Temple. The proud Motilal personally prepared an album of his son's photographs which he titled 'From the Cradle to the Bar'.

Jawaharlal took up studies at the Honourable Society of the Inner Temple on 11 January 1909, but only after some debate. Motilal had set his heart on sending his son to the Indian Civil Service, that pinnacle of success for the Victorian Indian. He had wanted Jawaharlal to be the 'first Senior Wrangler of your year' at Harrow so that 'the ICS will then be child's play for you'. He called the ICS the 'greatest of services in the world'. He was anxious about quick admission to Trinity so that future ICS regulations about age could be met. But the weak Second at the end of Cambridge persuaded Motilal that his son was unlikely to get through the tough ICS examinations. Moreover, the doting parents wanted their son to live with them in Allahabad rather than spend the rest of his life posted to districts. The Bar was a natural alternative – and, 'as for success at the Bar, leave it to me'. Motilal's confidence in himself was clearly far higher than his confidence in his son.

Jawaharlal was never hostile to joining the ICS, as long as it seemed practicable. It was certainly considered an enormous achievement for an Indian in those days. Opened to competitive examinations in 1858, it was a full ten years before the service allowed in its first Indian, Satyendranath Tagore. In 1869 four more Indians went through the gates of Heaven: B. L. Gupta, S. B. Thakur, R. C. Dutt and S. N. Bannerjea (the first two are forgotten; the second two have a niche of honour in Indian history). One of the great ifs is, what would have happened if men like Aurobindo Ghosh, Muhammad Ali, Jawaharlal and Subhas Bose had become district collectors and magistrates defending British rule rather than fighting it? They all wanted to join the I C S at some point or other. (Doubtless, the freedom movement would have thrown up other leaders, but at least this book might easily have been someone else's biography.) Jawaharlal would later express enormous relief at not having been sucked into the class which 'is most singularly dull and narrow-minded'.

After Cambridge, Jawaharlal wanted to go to Oxford (Cambridge was, he said, 'too full of Indians'), rather than be a 'mere lawyer' – a phrase singularly inappropriate in a letter to a man who had created a whole new world for his family through his legal skills and had one of the best law libraries in the country. Inevitably, Father's will prevailed. As a vague compromise Jawaharlal also wanted to enrol at the London School of Economics. Even so, his time was spent not in libraries but on ice-rinks, at Lord's, on the golf course at Crowborough and at music concerts, rather than in the lecture halls. He rationalized his habits by converting his spendthrift ways into an intellectual conceit ('I am afraid I have no money sense') and the convenient argument that examinations did not add up to an education.

After seven years in Britain, Jawaharlal may have had poor results, but he did acquire an extremely good library and a much broader mind. He also became a confirmed schizophrenic about Britain. Even ten years after his return, in May 1922, he would tell a British judge at his trial that 'I returned to India as much prejudiced in favour of England and the English as it was possible for an Indian to be.' He admired in particular the British commitment to freedom and patriotism. He wanted the same liberties as an Indian, in India, and grew to hate British rule with a passion he could not find for anything else.

The only time Jawaharlal became genuinely angry with his father was when he heard a rumour that Motilal was going to be knighted by George V during the latter's visit to India in 1911. It was Motilal's turn to clarify the impression hurriedly: not so, and he was not the kind of man who would curry favour with British officials to get this kind of appendage to the name. Yet however defensive Motilal Nehru may have been there was no doubt that he was excited and honoured by 'the command of His Gracious Majesty King-Emperor George V to be in attendance at Delhi' for the Great Durbar on 12 December 1911. The British had been wooing Motilal. There was much socializing with the lieutenant-governor, Leslie Porter; and when the time came to travel to Delhi for the Great Durbar, Motilal, Swarup Rani and their two daughters Sarup and Krishna travelled in the special train of the governor. The invitation had come months before – time enough to order the compulsory court dress, including sword, from Poole's in Britain, shoes from Knighton's, gloves from Travellette's, lounge suits fit for a king's audience and hats made to order. Swarup Rani, more sensibly, kept to the Kashmiri sari and classic Indian jewellery. Motilal looks a bit of a caricature in the formal photograph taken of him wearing this ceremonial dress. (Motilal was, though, sensible enough to re-check that he had been invited to the investiture before ordering these expensive clothes.) The invitation was a signal of status, sweet recognition that the boy who started as a penniless Mutiny refugee had finally arrived. His tent was placed in the United Provinces lieutenant-governor's special camp; and Swarup Rani was one of only two Indian ladies invited from the United Provinces. They were present at all the functions, and had a prominent place in the line. The King showed extra attention towards Motilal, while the Queen smiled at and 'almost spoke' to eleven-year-old Nan. The Nehrus were also invited to be in Calcutta during the Christmas week which the royal couple would spend in the original capital of the Raj, but Motilal decided that he had had enough of courtesy to the Emperor: 'We have come back from Delhi fed up with royalty.'

Jawaharlal's own tryst with royalty was a little different (though he did want to see his father's photograph in 'your court dress'). The coronation had taken place in June, and he wrote to his father: 'I have been foolish enough to waste some time over the various processions . . . We did not intend seeing the processions this morning, it was more or less forced on us. We were wandering about the neighbourhood when the procession started and so we stopped to see it.' But the mood was different at Allahabad. Motilal was flourishing, and the life-style at Anand Bhavan would have given royalty some competition. To take just one instance: since the normal dining-room could not hold forty, the number of guests at a party for the Gaekwars in January 1911, the inner courtyard was converted into a palm garden and covered with an awning to serve as a dining-place for one evening. Motilal was prosperous enough to refuse a client (a relative of the ex-Nawab of Awadh) offering £1,000 a week, simply because he did not feel up to it. He did not have to woo anyone any more. Telegrams pleading with him to appear on behalf of clients kept pouring in from wherever there was a high court. He could command his price. And did.

Motilal's one great disappointment was his son. He confessed that 'my fondest hope of seeing the Nehru name universally loved and respected' could now be honoured only by his brother Bansi Dhar's son, the 'scholar and scientist' Shridhar, who was not only a BA, a BSc (Allahabad), double MA (Cantab) and PhD (Heidelberg) but also now (after failing once) an ICS. To Jawaharlal he gave some sane advice on the eve of starting his career as a lawyer:

> This is not perhaps so bright a picture as the one I painted the other day when I talked of your having MA and LLD (Cantab) after your name but it means future success in life when academical honours will be forgotten and every man will stand or fall by that which is in him and not what follows his name on paper ... I do not believe in diverting genius from one course to another more than I believe in creating genius where none exists. All I wish you to bear in mind is that you have now decided to enter a profession which is no respecter of names and titles but insists on your ability to do the work and do it well.

Inevitably, after seven years Jawaharlal had mixed feelings about returning to 'this land of regrets' (Motilal's sarcastic phrase). But Father, as usual, gave the orders. Jawaharlal tried, at the last minute, to wangle a short stretch in Oxford. No. All he would be allowed was a three-month holiday to recoup his health. He was told to obtain all that was necesssary: character certificates, enrolment in the High Court of England ('It costs only a crown or so'), wig and gown *et al*. Money was wired for passage, and Brajlal was sent to Bombay to meet Jawaharlal's boat, while an excited family (along with about fifty servants) shifted to a huge mansion in the hills of Mussoorie to await the return of the beloved son; his ailing mother's health improved at just the thought of seeing him again.

All the children were given their best dresses to wear, and servants put on formal wear, as the huge household bustled in happy expectation. Motilal rode up to the Dehra Dun station to welcome his son. A clatter of hoofs on the courtyard signalled the return of the son and heir after seven long years. The women came out of the house, and Jawaharlal swung out of the saddle, handed the reins to a groom and ran towards his mother, lifting her off her feet in a joyous hug. In a minute all the women had engulfed him, welcoming him back Kashmiri style. A little later, over their heads, he spotted a little girl in a fine silk dress, standing hesitantly beside a pillar. He came up, picked up the little girl and said, 'You must be Choti Beti [Younger Daughter]', and kissed her. Jawaharlal had never seen his five-year-old sister, Krishna, before.

The first fee that he got as a new lawyer was a very substantial one of Rs 500. And this while he was still holidaying in Mussoorie after his return: it was an advance from a client called Rao Maharaj Singh. It was a tribute to the father's fame, not the son's ability. The man wanted merely to curry favour with Motilal. Jawaharlal worked hard on such briefs as came his way, but he always seemed to lose his assurance when he stood up to speak in open court. Perhaps Jawaharlal was just too indifferent to be a success in the courts. Life was easy; the world was dull, the routine 'pointless and futile'. Nor could he quite adjust to the company of the Indians in the Bar library or the club. He recalled E. M. Forster: 'And why can't the races meet? Simply because the Indians *bore* the English.' Jawaharlal had a bigger problem; both the English and the Indians bored him. There was little excitement in politics either. He went to the Bankipore session of the Congress in 1912 and tried to enter into the swing of the agitation against the indenture system for Indian workers in Fiji or on the South African situation, but the fizzle went out pretty quickly. He was attracted towards Gokhale's Servants of India Society, but not sufficiently to join.

Nevertheless a character, an inner philosophy, was evolving: that unique mix of humanity, emotion, passion and sheer love which would make Jawaharlal such a courageous hero of peace, particularly in the midst of death and killing. An incident describes the man waiting to flower. He once went on a shikar during a holiday in Kashmir. He hit an antelope once. 'This harmless little animal fell down at my feet, wounded to death, and looked up at me with great big eyes full of tears. Those eyes have often haunted me since.'

These inner, more real emotions were kept tightly wrapped under a very worldly wise sophistication, inevitable perhaps in an intelligent young man who went to Trinity when Oscar Wilde and Shaw were dominant influences. The affectations, though, were clearly more Shavian than Wildean. It was fashionable to carry a mild hint of jaundice in the eye, and naturally nothing was quite sacred. Jawaharlal was always careful to be respectful to his father, but it is impossible to read his letters and not detect a constant and very carefully modulated tone of irony. To take a random example, on 1 April 1910 he wrote to Motilal: 'I am extremely glad to hear that you and the cough have parted company at last. I did not have a very high opinion of homoeopathy till now, but henceforth I shall treat it with greater respect.' And this to an ill father who, having tried allopathic treatment for his recurrent asthma and piles and failed, had become something of a self-taught expert on homoeopathy. (Motilal's tragedy was that he managed to cure everyone else with his homoeopathic skills, but never himself.) When the subject was less sensitive, the young man let his irony have full play. On the death of Edward VII, for instance:

> The King's death upset functions; the Tripos unhappily remains unaffected . . . One of the saddest consequences of the death of Edward the VII of Blessed and Glorious memory has been, from my point of view, the loss of several days' work . . . It was such an inconvenient time for him to die, just when my Trip [colloquial for Tripos] was going to come off, and, as the New York papers said, just when Mr Roosevelt [Theodore] was going to visit England! However, if even Mr Roosevelt's forthcoming visit was not sufficient to put off the sad event, I have little cause to complain about Trip.

His comment on the formal passing out: 'The ceremony itself was a commendably short one. Each person knelt before the Vice-Chancellor with his hands joined together in front, in the Indian fashion. The V C muttered something about the grace of God in Latin and lo and behold! he was a graduate of Cambridge University.'

This was 'Joe' Nehru of Harrow and Trinity talking. With this, so to say, fashionable tinge of jaundice in one eye and a figurative monocle in the other, he slipped into the Indo-Anglian groove of Allahabad: the courts in the day, a drink in the evening, bridge, social calls, occasional late-night parties, revels and of course holidays in the Motherland, Kashmir. Pictures of him (the 'I was twenty-six . . .' variety) show him nattily dressed, seated on a well-designed chair, the three-quarters profile highlighting his handsome features – but quite unable to disguise a growing weakness, which would descend two generations to his grandsons: balding. The doting eye of Motilal had detected the problem, as usual, long before. As early as 8 March 1906, he had written to his son in Harrow: 'What about the little patch of baldness on your head? I have thought of it off and on but always forgot to write and ask. I hope it has disappeared. If not you must do something for it. If the barber's prescriptions do not do any good consult a doctor.' Jawaharlal liked the Congress handspun cap for more reasons than one.

This liability was however of little consequence in the crucial business of marriage. Motilal had searched far and wide, even among Kashmiris settled in Madras, for his perfect combination of brains and beauty. His efforts culminated in the choice of Kamala Kaul, the daughter of a business man of Bazar Sitaram, Pandit Jawaharmlal Kaul. Born on 1 August 1899, Kamala was only thirteen when the decision was made. Her father was the owner of a flour-mill, and she had been educated at home and knew only Urdu and Hindi. Having chosen the girl from good traditional stock, Motilal now began the process of training his future daughter-in-law for his son. Since Bazar Sitaram was hardly London, Kamala was sent off to the European governesses who had looked after Jawaharlal's sisters to try to become as much of a memsahib as possible and learn the graces necessary for acceptance in the anglicized Nehru family.

Vasant is a season India waits for: spring, the month in which Kamadeva, the god of love (a handsome youth riding on a parrot, his bow made of sugar-cane, his bowstring a line of bees, his arrows tipped with flowers), is worshipped. Vasant starts in the month of Magha, which comes during January–February, and its other deity is Saraswati, goddess of learning, wisdom and fine arts, the benign aspect of Shakti (female energy). Saraswati's favourite day is on the first full moon of Magha, the day venerated as Vasant Panchami. It was on this auspicious day, which fell on 8 February in 1916, that Kamala and Jawaharlal were wed in Delhi. The style, of course, was grand; this was 55-year-old Motilal's proudest moment. A special train was hired to take the Nehru 'clan and friendship society' from Allahabad to Delhi, where a Nehru wedding camp was pitched and became the arena of week-long celebrations. The formal card sent from Anand Bhavan itself extended the invitation to three days: 'Mr and Mrs Motilal Nehru request the pleasure of your company on the occasion of the marriage of their son Jawaharlal Nehru with Kamala Kaul, daughter of Pandit Jawaharmal Kaul, at Delhi, on the 7th February 1916, and afterwards on February 8th and 9th, 1916. An answer will oblige.' That was only the beginning of the festivities. When they came back to Allahabad with the bride, the badminton, tennis, tea- and dinner-parties went on for weeks, interspersed with *mushairas, kavi sammelans* (poetry recitals) and music concerts.

Summer in such an eventful year could only mean another trip to the motherland, Kashmir. Jawaharlal left his young wife behind and, with a cousin and friend, went off for a trek-cum-shooting-stint high up in the mountains to the Zojila pass. It was here that Jawaharlal shot a bear and the antelope which so affected him. And it was here that, within less than six years, he almost died a second time. Jawaharlal describes the experience with an unrepressed thrill in the autobiography he would write nearly two decades later:

> We had left our camp at four in the morning and after twelve hours' almost continuous climbing we were rewarded by the sight of a huge ice-field. This was a magnificent sight surrounded as it was by snow-peaks, like a diadem or an amphitheatre of the gods ... We had now to cross this ice-field, a distance probably of half a mile ... It was a tricky business as there were many crevasses and the fresh snow often covered a dangerous spot. It was this fresh snow that almost proved my undoing, for I stepped upon it and it gave way and down I went into a huge and yawning crevasse. It was a tremendous fissure and anything that went right down it could be assured of safekeeping and preservation for some geological ages. But the rope held and I clutched to the side of the crevasse and was pulled out.

The memory of this, his second escape from death, stirred the lonely author in a cell of a British gaol. He thought of the promise he had made to himself so many times, to return to the strange and exciting and energizing desolation of these Himalayas and to the wonder-lake of Tibet, Mansarovar, next to the holy mountain of Kailas:

> Instead of going up mountains or crossing the seas, I have to satisfy my wanderlust by coming to prison. But still I plan, for that is a joy that no one can deny even in prison, and besides, what else can one do in

prison? And I dream of the day when I reach that lake and mountain of my desire. But meanwhile the sands of life run on and youth passes into middle age and that will give place to something worse, and sometimes I think I may grow too old to reach Kailas and Mansarovar.

Those lonely thoughts belonged to a still unimagined future. The family returned from Kashmir. Motilal's health had now begun to ebb, even as his list of clients kept flowing. Jawaharlal returned to his junior's desk in Anand Bhavan, and to the familiar round of socializing and reading *Punch* and the weekly magazines from London on Sundays. Fortunately, Jawaharlal was intelligent enough to get thoroughly bored with such an existence.

10 Three Muslims, Three Paths to 1947

No man had a lovelier excuse for failing the most crucial test of his young life: 'thanks to an English spring, and a young man's more or less foolish fancy'. Muhammad Ali had failed his examinations for the Indian Civil Service but lost not a whit of his impish confidence. His mother, a tough and noble widow called Bi Amman who had pawned her jewellery to provide her two sons with an English education, sought to soften his 'grief' at failure by recalling her son from England to marry a long-betrothed cousin. Muhammad returned, married and then went back to the land of his 'foolish fancy', England. But he did pick up from Oxford a BA in modern history before he returned to India to settle down. Otherwise generous about personal details in the snatches which add up to a partial autobiography (*My Life: A Fragment*, written, as was normal then, in gaol), Muhammad Ali has cheated us out of this fancy's name. Yet by the time this tempestuous life had played out its historic role in 1931, the English would have regretted the fact that the ICS had not had the good sense to absorb Muhammad Ali. For if Sir Sayyid dragged the Muslims towards the British in the last quarter of the nineteenth century, then it was Muhammad Ali (later to acquire the appellation of Maulana) who drove them with passionate enthusiasm back into the heart of the nationalist movement in the first quarter of the twentieth. Sir Sayyid Ahmed Khan, Maulana Muhammad Ali, Muhammad Ali Jinnah and Maulana Abul Kalam Azad: these were the four pivotal figures in the transition of the Indian Muslims from the day their empire died in 1857 to the blood-stained freedom of 1947.

Born within a dozen years of one another, the lives of Ali (1878–1931), Jinnah (1876–1948) and Azad (1888–1958) became representative of the options which the Muslims played with during their search for a place in the Indian mix. Obviously their paths crossed, but that is less interesting than the manner in which their political orbits probed different and often self-contradictory directions in search of an answer. Jinnah began as the secular constitutionalist, the brilliant lawyer who was convinced of his own eminence, and with good reason – the man who saw himself as the natural leader of India on a platform of Hindu–Muslim unity created through pacts debated and decided in drawing-rooms. It was his personal disgust at the mass-based, religion-coated politics of Gandhi and Muhammad Ali which made him angrily leave, in 1920, the Congress Party whose highest platforms he had graced when the others were clad in different masks. When Jinnah was helping write Dadabhai Naoroji's presidential address to the Congress in 1906, Ali was an official in Sayaji Rao Gaekwar's court at Baroda and trying to edge on to the Muslim League platform. Azad was in Calcutta, on the fringes of both the revolutionary cells led by Aurobindo Ghosh and the League convention summoned by Nawab Salimullah in Dhaka. Mohandas Karamchand Gandhi was in the process of renouncing sex, prior to the launch of yet another struggle in South Africa. Motilal Nehru was busy with his practice and indifferent to, when not caustic about, the shenanigans of the Congress Party, while Jawaharlal Nehru was still struggling with Latin and fagging in Harrow. And so in 1920 the most famous Muslim politician of the first twenty years of this century left centre stage to concentrate on an established practice and a temperamental wife. He would re-emerge only when the Gandhi–Ali movement had lost momentum and, in the late 1920s, when pact politics had once again replaced mass politics.

Of the three, only Azad remained constant to the beliefs with which he began his life: uncompromising faith in Allah, and total commitment to the principle of Indian unity. The same vision inspired him through the long rising curves of fame and glory, the sudden plunge towards despair and defeat in 1947 and the soggy ease of a Cabinet position that allowed him to die blandly in free India. The course of the other two lives illustrates the pressures that changed the most liberated and brilliant minds that modern Indian Islam has produced. From an Oxford training for the ICS to the life of a sparkling courtier in Baroda to the passionate espousal of the cause of Turkey in the First World War; from silk shirts and nautch-girls to the baggy, handspun trousers of the Maulana; from the man who called the Muslim League delegation to the Viceroy in 1906 a 'command performance' to squalid participation in the first Round-Table Conference, which the Congress had boycotted; and finally to a premature, tired death and burial in Jerusalem, Muhammad Ali epitomized the failure of a Muslim to come to terms even with a Gandhi. And the upright Jinnah, so disdainful once of religion that he could not swallow Gandhi's *bhajan*-singing and souped-up morality, became so obsessed and paranoid about Hindus that he consciously led the Muslims to a theocratic state which eventually divided and destroyed the *qaum* in South Asia – exactly as Azad had warned it would. Ali died, a broken man, before he was fifty-two. Jinnah died, of wasting tuberculosis, a tragic and bewildered hero, drowned in the tears of hundreds of thousands of widows and orphans. Azad died fatigued, almost willingly, his spirit unable to recover from the partition he had been unable to prevent. These three men made history, for better, and then for worse. Without understanding their politics, it is impossible to understand why Jawaharlal became the first Prime Minister of a divided rather than a united India.

Muhammad Ali was born in the princely state of Rampur, the fifth son of Abdul Ali, a favourite courtier of Nawab Yusuf Ali Khan. Abdul Ali was a well-meaning wastrel: when he died of cholera at the age of thirty, the two sons who would become famous, Shaukat and Muhammad, were eight and two. His tough widow, Bi Amman, inherited a debt of Rs 30,000 rather than any legacy with which to nurture her children. But her determination was extraordinary. She pawned her jewellery to send her sons to an English school in Bareilly when her conservative brothers-in-law refused to finance an 'infidel' education. The boys went on, with the help of scholarships, to the Mahomedan Anglo-Oriental College in Aligarh. Muhammad was both brilliant and mischievous: considered bright enough to be allowed to attend Nomani Shibli's lectures on the Quran at the college although still technically in school, but prankish enough to spend his time writing verses during these theology classes. His love of mischief did not prevent him from coming first in the final B A results of the Allahabad University (to which the Aligarh college was then affiliated). Shaukat, who had by then joined the provincial Civil Service of United Provinces, agreed to finance his younger brother's studies at Oxford to prepare him for the I C S. Muhammad was more keen on living a good life at Lincoln College and failed to enter the I C S. He gave the British yet another chance to tame him upon his return to India, but the English principal of the Aligarh M A O College refused his application for a job as a lecturer. He turned to his Oxford pal, the Crown Prince of Baroda, Fateh Singh; and the friendship paid off. He joined the state Civil Service, where he quickly acquired a reputation for wit, command of the English language and a passion for matching ties and handkerchiefs. He was not famous for politics yet, though he did get leave to attend the inaugural session of the Muslim League in Dhaka in 1906. At this stage he was clear in his mind that the League could be relevant only if it worked for Indian unity and made 'an effort at integration'. His writing indicated that he understood the true nature of the Hindu–Muslim problem. As he would articulate later in *My Life: A Fragment*: 'ultimately all communal interests had to be adjusted in order to harmonize with the paramount interests of India'. He recognized the culprits shrewdly: 'The greater portion of bigotry agitates not the bosoms of the ignorant and the illiterate but excites to fury and to madness the little-learned of the land.' When some Muslims protested against the reunification of Bengal, he advised them in 1912 to accept it in the larger interests of the country. He appreciated too the dangers of separate electorates, though he was not willing to challenge the popular mood by arguing publicly against them. He accepted separate electorates as 'a hateful necessity – like divorce which was accepted by Islam as a hateful necessity'.

Life as a civil servant in a princely state soon began to pall, and Muhammad Ali came down to the capital of British India, Calcutta, to start his own newspaper, named *The Comrade*. It had a rather valiant motto:

> Stand upright, speak thy thought, declare
> The truth thou hast that all may share.
> Be bold, proclaim it everywhere;
> They only live who dare.

The motto was the man. His editorial policy was enunciated in the first issue: 'if the Muslims or the Hindus attempt to achieve success in opposition to or even without the co-operation of one another, they will not only fail, but fail ignominiously'.

Use of the power of the pen was not limited to Muhammad Ali alone. Someone ten years younger than him not only had the same idea and a similar philosophy but also used journalism far more effectively: Maulana Abul Kalam Azad. His family had come to India from Herat in Babar's reign. One forefather, Maulana Jamaluddin, was a religious divine in the great Emperor Akbar's time; another, Muhammad Hadi, a governor of the most important Mughal fort at Agra in Shah Jahan's days; a third, Maulana Munawaruddin, the culture-educational czar in the dusk of a wilting empire. His father, the scholar Maulana Khairuddin, emigrated to the holy city of Mecca, where his ten-volume work in Arabic (published in Egypt) earned him lasting fame. Sultan Abdul Majid of the Islamic empire of Turkey, the Khalifa (Caliph) of Islam, however, was to give him the Majidi Medal, First Class, for a different achievement – solving the perennial water problem of the holy city by raising Rs 20 lakhs for the repair of the Nahr Zubeida, first constructed by the wife of the legendary Khalifa Haroun-al-Rashid. (The repair meant reconstructing the canal in such a way as to protect it from the marauding Bedouin.)

Firoz Bakht, Maulana Khairuddin's son, was born in Mecca in 1888. He was only two when his father decided to return to India; and then because he wanted competent medical attention for a broken shinbone he decided to come to Calcutta. His admirers never let him leave the city. Firoz received a traditional education, in Persian, Arabic and Islamic theology, from the most eminent scholars Calcutta had. His talents were obvious soon enough. By the time he was sixteen he had completed a course normally finished by students in their twenties. His father had, incidentally, added Mohiuddin Ahmed to his name by now.

The teenager was already straining hard at the leash of conventions. Firoz's mother had died when he was three, after which life became a sequence of strict discipline and learning. Firoz's first act of rebellion was learning the English language. Influenced by Sir Sayyid's views on education, he went at the age of sixteen to Maulvi Yusuf Jafri, then chief examiner of Oriental studies, to learn the Roman alphabet – with the help of Peary Chund Sarkar's *First Book*. Once he had grasped the basics, he taught himself English through one of the finest methods possible: by reading the King James Bible, with Persian and Urdu translations alongside. This mood of rebellion inevitably included a less learned element. He had been married at the age of thirteen, to Zuleikha; now he 'fell in love', as he himself later politely described it, with another woman. The most momentous night of this rebel phase was when he decided to stop a practice which had been synonymous with his upbringing, the saying of prayers five times a day. It was at this time also that he rejected the name given by his father, Firoz Bakht Mohiuddin Ahmed, and took on the name by which the world would get to know him: Abul Kalam Azad. *Azad* means 'free'. The Maulana was a title in honour of his religious learning.

Politics was an early attraction. A sister, Fatima, recalled how he loved, even as a child, playing the orator and then demanding applause from the circle of admiring sisters. When the Swadeshi movement shook Bengal, Azad was drawn into it. Through a person called Shyam Sunder Chakravarty he came into contact with Aurobindo Ghosh; the revolutionaries were greatly surprised at the sight of a 'Muslim patriot', but accepted him. This, however, did not prevent the eighteen-year-old Azad from also attending the inaugural session of the Muslim League in 1906, but his verdict came in quickly: they were collaborators with the British. And that was a sin he would not forgive, all his life.

We have noted the strong anti-British tradition in a section of the Muslim clergy, caused primarily by the decay of the Mughal Empire. Azad was heir to this tradition, but did not, as some others did, later convert this sentiment into the demand for another Muslim empire (in the shape of Pakistan). He believed without compromise in two things: Islam and freedom. And he would accept dilution in neither case. He was twenty (and had just suffered the death of his only son, Haseen, at the age of four) when he went on a tour of Iraq, Syria, Egypt and Turkey; it was a journey which reinforced both his identification with the Muslim world and his anger against the rule of the British. On his return he became convinced that the greatest immediate necessity was the creation of public opinion, and so he started *Al Hilal*, a weekly Urdu journal. It was, in Azad's words,

a turning-point in the history of Urdu journalism . . . The leadership of Muslim politics at this time was in the hands of the Aligarh Party. Its members regarded themselves as the trustees of Sir Syed Ahmed's policies. Their basic tenet was that Musalmans must be loyal to the British Crown and remain aloof from the freedom movement. When *Al Hilal* raised a different slogan and its popularity and circulation increased fast, they felt that their leadership was threatened. They therefore began to oppose *Al Hilal* and even went to the extent of threatening to kill its editor. The more the old leadership opposed, the more popular *Al Hilal* became with the community. Within two years, *Al Hilal* reached a circulation of 26,000 copies per week, a figure which was till then unheard of in Urdu journalism.

This is an important fact, particularly in the context of pre-independence Muslim politics. The experience of *Al Hilal* helped Azad understand the great dichotomy in the Muslim situation: that the aims and politics of its leadership had little correlation to the needs of the masses. Time after time the Congress leaders would make this point, deriding the League bosses who spoke in their name, but both the League and the British dismissed this as only a self-serving claim. The British reaction to *Al Hilal* and its young editor was simple: they harassed it, fined it and by 1915 confiscated it. Azad started a new paper, *Al Balagh*, within five months. This time the British used both the Press Act and the Defence of India Rules. Azad was externed from Calcutta and refused entry by the governments of United Provinces, Punjab, Delhi and Bombay. He went to Ranchi. By the end of 1916 he was interned and remained in confinement till 31 December 1919, being released by the King's decree the next day. In other words, Azad was the first leader of the Nehru generation to go to gaol.

Today's world is divided by a plethora of passports. In the imperialist-feudal order that existed before the First World War, there were fewer boundaries and far greater common cross-currents which influenced different countries within an empire. There was at least one unifying point among subject nations: the overthrow of a common colonizing enemy, in the case of that part of the world painted red, the British. Anything which weakened the British in any part of their Empire would be of obvious benefit to anyone fighting the common yoke. It was, logically, a far more international world under imperialism. Muslims, part of a pan-Islamic reality, found it easy to merge their nationalism with pan-Islamism, particularly since Turkey, the inheritor of the caliphate, had adopted an anti-British policy. The rumble of war began to be heard over Europe by 1911, and Indian Muslims quickly took positions. The followers of Sir Sayyid supported the British. The nationalist Muslims, happy to find God and Caesar on the same side for a change, passionately endorsed

Turkey. For a dozen years, from 1911 to 1923–4, Turkey became one of the critical factors in the shaping of the Indian struggle against the British. The great irony, of course, was that the caliphate was no longer a cause which deserved to be defended, but the reasons which provoked Indian Muslims had more to do with their own welfare than with the welfare of the caliphs. Even by 1911 Turkey had become a caricature of its former glory; as one contemporary observer put it, its army wore Russian uniforms, carried Belgian rifles, used a Hungarian saddle, wielded an English sword and practised French drill. Only the hat, the fez, was Turkish. No matter: it was also anti-British.

In 1911 Italy suddenly attacked Tripoli, then under Turkish control, and the British in Egypt refused to allow Turkish reinforcements through. Libya fell. In central Europe, the Balkan War broke out with the revolt of the Christian provinces against the Ottoman Empire. The Bulgars, Serbs and Greeks freed themselves from Turkey's control. Indian Muslims were convinced that this was all part of the British plan to destroy Muslim power in the world and gobble up the Turkish Empire (not, incidentally, too far-fetched an assessment), and a wave of anti-British sentiment swept the Muslims of India. One person who seemed to take the Turkish situation a bit too personally was Muhammad Ali. On the day he read the Reuters report that the Bulgarians (Bulgarians!) were only twenty-five miles from the city which for 500 years had been the symbol of Muslim might, Constantinople, Muhammad Ali became so depressed that he seriously began to contemplate suicide. Luckily, just at that point, an Oxonian friend turned up and insisted on dragging Muhammad Ali to a private nautch-party, which was scheduled to be topped by an even more private orgy, and Muhammad Ali was saved for greater deeds. (The story is from Ali's autobiography: proof enough of his impish humour, as also of his refusal to turn himself into a holy cow.) Shaukat, his elder brother, angrily resigned his British Civil Service job, grew a shaggy beard and changed from silk shirts to the Bombay-style crumpled loose green coat, as a gesture of re-identification with prevalent Muslim dress patterns. Later the brothers would acquire wool caps with the Islamic moon emblazoned on them, and since their remaining pictures are of this period this is the dominant visual image we have been left with. The brothers set about organizing aid for Turkey. Women impulsively gave their

ornaments for the Turkish interest, and a medical mission was organized which was received by the Sultan of Turkey with 'tears in his
eyes'. The mission did not do all that much for the wounded, but its
impact lay in defiance of the British. It also converted an interna-
tionally respected surgeon, who had a ward named after him in
London's Charing Cross Hospital for his services, Dr Mukhtar
Ahmed Ansari (1880–1936), into a national hero of the Muslims. He
was the leader of the mission. One of the members was a young
Aligarh student called Chaudhry Khaliquzzaman.

The Muslim leaders who were to dominate the country's politics
for the next twenty years were created by this pro-Turkey stir, which
became famous as the Khilafat movement and merged into the larger
Congress struggle under Gandhi. But that was still years away. In
1913 Muslim sentiments were further provoked by what has come to
be known as the Kanpur Mosque incident. An administrative plan
for road realignment in the industrialized city of Kanpur in the
United Provinces demanded that a part of a mosque be pulled down.
It was. Angry Muslims tried to rebuild this portion; the police opened
fire, and several Muslims died on the spot. Eventually the Viceroy,
Lord Hardinge, managed to persuade the UP governor, Sir James
Meston, to restore this portion, but not before an unprecedented
uproar in the community. Ali took a delegation to London to protest.
And it was in London that Ali and another member of the delegation,
Syed Wazir Hussain (1874–1947), met Jinnah and persuaded him
that he should begin to take a larger interest in Muslim League
affairs too on his return. (Jinnah had gone on a long eight-month
trip that year with Gokhale: a sojourn indicative of the close relationship between the two at the time. Surely they must have discussed
India and its future a great deal, but unfortunately we know next to
nothing because neither left a record of what transpired.)

Jinnah had attended a council meeting of the League in Bankipur
in December 1912, and a few months later sat with Mrs Sarojini
Naidu on a League platform in Lucknow convened to adopt a more
liberal party constitution. As a Congressman he had not as yet
formally joined the League; when he did, he had one condition, that
his 'loyalty to the Muslim League and the Muslim interest would in
no way and at no time imply even the shadow of disloyalty to the
larger national cause to which his life was dedicated' (Sarojini Naidu,
ed., *Mohammad Ali Jinnah: His Speeches and Writings, 1912–1917*,

1918). No one can accuse Jinnah of not being aware of the implications of joining the Muslim League. Suffice it to say that Jinnah felt no compulsion to clarify his patriotic ideals before any Congress session – for the very good reason that even the suspicion never arose. But now in 1913, for the first time, Jinnah would attend both Congress and League sessions, despite the fact that he had to travel some distance to do so. Two days after his birthday, on 27 December, he was in Karachi for the 1913 Congress and delighted in the opportunity of meeting boyhood friends whom he had not seen for over seventeen years. From Karachi he left for what was then the middle of India, Agra, for the League session. But Jinnah was, in fact, planning something very dramatic, even sensational, with his new resolve to keep a foot in either camp. He wanted to become the bridge, the ambassador of Hindu–Muslim unity, as his great friend and admirer Sarojini Naidu put it. It was a unique moment for Jinnah. Both his feet were on the ground, if straddled a bit; his head was high, and he had the ear of the English. And by 1916 Jinnah achieved his ambition – four years before Gandhi came and changed all the rules of the game by simply ignoring drawing-room pact politics and going straight to the people.

Jinnah was helped not a little by another turn of history. With the outbreak of the First World War, all the pro-Khilafat leaders, including the Ali brothers and Azad, were under arrest, and Jinnah was left without either peer or foe. Jinnah of course did not go to gaol. He had the longest career of all the leaders of the freedom movement, being there virtually from the start and certainly there at the finish. But not once in those more than five decades of active politics did the British feel the necessity of putting him behind bars.

At Agra in 1913 Jinnah appealed to the League to postpone a decision on separate electorates in the interests of a joint Congress–League solution to the Hindu–Muslim problem which he was trying to bring about. The League was not impressed, and rejected his appeal. Jinnah did not give up. In April 1914 he went to London with a delegation to urge reform. The mission failed. War broke out, with the British (Lord Kitchener apart) leaders generally confident of quick victory. But as it dragged on with a terrible fury, India's support in men, food, ores and supplies became a critical element of the war effort. Need bred new interest, and India once again returned to the centre of Whitehall's calculations. As a matter of record, the Muslim regiments fought loyally enough on the battlefields of Mesopotamia, Egypt and Europe (only a few units in Singapore had to be disarmed), but civilian Muslims were in ferment. The Muslim League leadership, once again performing to command, cancelled its 1914 session rather than risk the expression of any anti-British sentiment from its platforms. The next year began with an event of far-reaching significance, though of course no one would measure it that way then.

The historic *satyagraha* (non-co-operation or civil disobedience) struggle which Mohandas Karamchand Gandhi had launched with his vows of total personal renunciation in September 1906 finally came to an end on 21 January 1914 with the Gandhi–Smuts agreement. On 26 June 1914 the Indians' Relief Bill was passed by 60 votes to 24, and all the Indian demands were granted: the £3 tax was abolished, marriages deemed legal in India became legal in South Africa, and the domicile certificate became sufficient right to enter the Union. Gandhi was now finished with South Africa and was anxious to return to India. But a message came from a man lying ill in London, Gopal Krishna Gokhale: return to India via London. On July 18 the Mayor of Durban presided over a formal tribute to this unique hero, the climax of fortnight-long farewell ceremonies. There were messages of congratulation for what he had achieved from the Bishop of Natal and from General Smuts. (While in gaol Gandhi had made a pair of sandals for his adversary, Smuts, which he presented to him when he was freed. Smuts, touched, wore them for years.) That day, accompanied by his devoted wife Kasturba and his devoted disciple Hermann Kallenbach, Gandhi left by boat for England. The three travelled third class. At Madeira, they learned that war was imminent. On 4 August, two days before Gandhi touched Britain, the First World War began. Gandhi was warmly received in London; among those present at a reception at Cecil Hotel on 8 August was Jinnah, who paid fulsome tribute to the victor of the South African struggle. Gandhi joined the war effort and organized an ambulance corps, and only a fit of pleurisy prevented him from going to France's battlefields. Then Gokhale stepped in: Gandhi's real work lay ahead in India. On 19 December, Kasturba and Gandhi boarded a P&O steamer for Bombay. Kallenbach could not come because he was a German and could not obtain a passport. The couple travelled second class – there was no third-class passage available on the P&O line. They landed at Apollo Bunder at Bombay on 9 January 1915. The first thing Gandhi did when he landed was change to Indian clothes: dhoti, Kathiawadi cloak and turban. All were made from textiles manufactured in India. Then he went into the background.

Jinnah, in contrast, was a senior leader of the Congress. He, Tilak (just allowed back after six years of exile in Mandalay) and Annie Besant first unified the party and then intensified efforts to reach an understanding with the League. The 1915 sessions of the two parties were deliberately held in the same city, Bombay – for the first time ever. The Congress, under the presidentship of Satyendra Prasanna Sinha (later to become Baron Sinha of Raipur and to pilot the Act of 1919 through the House of Lords), had little problem endorsing Jinnah's effort. The trouble arose in the League, meeting under the presidentship of a barrister, Mazharul Haq (1866–1921). Haq himself urged *rapprochement* with the Congress: 'When unity is evolved out of diversity, then there is real and abiding national progress.' But the Urdu-speaking lobby in particular was determined to sabotage any such 'national progress'. Jinnah was booed; and a number of volatile Pathans rushed at him. Discretion proving the better part of valour, Jinnah left the venue. Outside he found an amused commissioner of police, S. M. Edwardes, who refused to interfere with the commotion inside. The session was reconvened on New Year's Day in the less egalitarian Taj Mahal Hotel, with attendance limited to those who had come to praise Jinnah and not to bury him. Jinnah's resolution demanding a 'scheme of reforms . . . in the name of United India' was passed.

The man appointed by the Congress to help draft this scheme in co-operation with Jinnah was Motilal Nehru. Motilal had gradually been drawn into the centre of Congress politics; his eminence ensured that much, if nothing else. Motilal remained a champion of the Moderate cause, much to the continued dismay of his son, whose interest in politics at this stage was strictly of the armchair variety. Father and son had long arguments, but politics was only an intellectual or weekend passion; real life was about briefs and law courts. In his more worrisome moments Motilal wondered whether this disease called patriotism would turn his son into some kind of revolutionary and lead him to the gallows, but there was little fear of that. Terrorism was very much in the air, but far from 'heading straight for the violent courses adopted by some of the young men of

Bengal', Jawaharlal had not even conquered his stage fright: 'I can imagine nothing more terrifying than having to speak in public.' He concentrated on reading: politics (Addington Symond's *Renaissance in Italy*), history (John Morley's *Notes on History and Politics*), biography (John Drinkwater's *Swinburne*). The do-gooder side of him found expression in Red Cross work, and he became, for a while, joint secretary of the Allahabad branch of the St John Ambulance Brigade. The nearest he came to direct politics was raising funds, as for instance for Gandhi's struggle in South Africa. Jawaharlal did use the opportunity provided by the environment of Anand Bhavan to meet and have long talks with a succession of great leaders. Dr Tej Bahadur Sapru and Pandit Madan Mohan Malaviya find special mention in this context in Jawaharlal's autobiography. As for his father, in his autobiography Jawaharlal recalls: 'from 1915 to 1917 he was still unsure of what to do, and the doubts in him, added to his worries about me, did not make him a peaceful talker on the public issues of the day. Often enough our talks ended abruptly by his losing his temper with us.'

If anyone in the Congress was suited to sit with Jinnah it was Motilal. Contemptuous of the thinly disguised 'Hindu nationalism' of the Extremists, he was outraged when the Moderates compromised at the 1910 Allahabad session (Sir W. Wedderburn was president) and sponsored the birth of the All-India Hindu Mahasabha. Motilal wrote that this would 'sap the foundation of the Congress itself. I opposed the formation of this Sabha, brought round Surendranath Bannerjea and Bhupendra Basu, but the great majority of the so-called leaders of upper India, specially those of the Punjab, had worked themselves to a high pitch and could not be made to listen to reason' (*Selected Works of Motilal Nehru*, Vol. 1). If taking such a stance meant being abused by the Hindu press, so be it. In the provincial Assembly in 1916, for instance, when he took a pro-Muslim line on the Jehangirabad amendment to the Municipal Bill, he was pilloried by them. There were some wise comments in that speech by Motilal opposing the motion (for instance: 'No feeling that is stirred by racial or religious animosity is ever unreal, however ill advised it may be') which indicate that Motilal had a down-to-earth grasp of the communal problem, an understanding that extended beyond the theories of what was 'right' for a community to what was practicable at any given moment.

In the heat of April 1916 Jinnah and Motilal sat down in Anand
Bhavan to draft the 'Freedom Pact': a singularly appropriate name,
since both leaders knew that if they could crack the Hindu–Muslim
code for peace, no power could prevent India's freedom. The key to
that code was identity. The Muslims had been warned by Sir Sayyid
that they would be submerged in a united India awash with a three-
fourths Hindu population. Motilal Nehru and Jinnah thought they
had found the answer – in clause 4 of the first part of the 'Congress
and Moslem League Scheme of Reforms'. It needs to be quoted in
full:

Adequate provision should be made for the representation of important
minorities by election, and the Mahomedans should be represented
through special electorates on the Provincial Legislative Councils in the
following proportions: Punjab – one-half of the elected Indian members;
United Provinces – 30 per cent; Central Provinces – 15 per cent; Madras –
15 per cent; Bombay – one-third. Provided that no Mahomedan shall
participate in any of the elections to the Imperial or Provincial Legislative
Councils, save and except those by electorates representing special interests. Provided further that no bill, nor any clause thereof, nor a resolution introduced by a non-official member affecting one or the other
community, which question is to be determined by the members of that
community in the Legislative Council concerned, shall be proceeded
with, if three-fourths of the members of that community in the particular
Council, Imperial or Provincial, oppose the bill or any clause thereof or
the resolution.

Long after the Lucknow Pact was forgotten, the principle established
here was still operative – essentially, that legislation affecting the
vital interests of a particular community would not be passed without
the overwhelming support (three-quarters) of the representatives of
the community. This was the guarantee against laws passed in the
name of 'progress' and 'logic' which might militate against the beliefs
of a particular faith. The Muslims in particular were afraid that their
religious laws would become vulnerable to a common 'Hindu-
inspired' civil code. The shadows of this contract have extended long
beyond, and even into the India of forty years after freedom.

After the labours of April, Jinnah went for a two-month holiday
to his friend Sir Dinshaw Manockjee Petit's (Petit from the French
petit; the original Sir Dinshaw was known as 'Le Petit Parsi' by

friendly French business merchants) bungalow in Darjeeling and fell madly in love with his friend's sixteen-year-old 'fairy princess' daughter, Ruttie. Her father was furious, but she ran away to marry the handsome and brilliant Jinnah on the day she turned eighteen. Love seemed to chase success; at forty Jinnah seemed destined for the highest pinnacles. Indians hoped that their co-operation in the war effort would be rewarded with dominion status as soon as the war was over. And who was more likely to don the mantle of executive authority over this vast nation than young, brilliant Jinnah, lean, superbly styled, a hero of women and the youth? The Lucknow sessions of the Congress and the League in 1916 were a personal triumph for him; he was declared president of the League for the first time and from that platform made the most inspiring speech of his life. 'The whole country,' he told the 'gentlemen' of the All-India Muslim League, 'is awakening to the call of its destiny and is scanning the new horizons with eager hope. A new spirit of earnestness, confidence and resolution is abroad in the land. In all directions are visible the stirrings of a new life.' He challenged the 'shallow, bastard and desperate political maxims' which the British used to stop the march of 'Indian patriots'. At the Congress session in Kaiser Bagh (Royal Garden), Lucknow, the president Ambikacharan Muzumdar intoned piously: 'Blessed are the peacemakers.'

Yet there was still a long way to go before they inherited the earth. In the session was a forty-six-year-old man who watched it all quietly. On 3 June 1915, about six months after he returned to India, he was awarded the Kaiser-i-Hind medal for public services (the other Indian honoured was Rabindranath Tagore, with a knighthood). Gandhi was famous, but not yet for anything done in India. He was still sizing up the country and its leaders. On 4 February 1916 he was invited to a grand occasion: the laying of the foundation-stone of the Benaras Hindu University. Even the Viceroy, Lord Hardinge, had come; a glittering galaxy of princes were in attendance, as were the country's most famous political leaders. Invited by Pandit Madan Mohan Malaviya, Gandhi came dressed in his coarse *khadi* dhoti, Kathiawadi cloak and turban. As this select audience listened to him that day, they began to sense that here was a different voice. He said many things in that speech 'of a man who allows himself to think audibly'. But the core of the message was:

The Congress has passed a resolution about self-government, and I have no doubt that the All-India Congress Committee and the Muslim League will do their duty and come forward with some tangible suggestions. But I, for one, must frankly confess that I am not so much interested in what they will be able to produce as I am interested in anything that the student world is going to produce or the masses are going to produce. No paper contribution will ever give us self-government.

It was a most dramatically unusual speech. Gandhi attacked the princes, sitting there laden with jewels, the administrators and the establishment for their total neglect of the people. The future, he said, lay not with the English-speaking élite, but with the illiterate masses. The impact was immediate. Gandhi's speech was disturbed, most notably by an angry Annie Besant. He would have been stopped had not the audience prevented it with cries of 'Go on!' The speech however did end abruptly, when the man in the chair, the Maharaja of Darbhanga, simply got up and left, unable to take any more. Gandhi impishly remarked: 'I have seen audiences going away from boredom; I have seen speakers made to sit down; but I have never seen the president himself abandon the meeting.'

That evening the police wrote out an order for the externment of Gandhi from Benaras, but Malaviya persuaded them not to serve it. Gandhi left the next day voluntarily. After that Gandhi made a string of speeches: at Poona, on Gokhale's first death anniversary, at Hardwar and Karachi and Madras, before the Missionary Conference on 14 February. 'Princes and potentates, whether they are Indian-born or foreigners, have hardly touched the vast masses except for collecting revenue,' he declared. The answer was Swadeshi and harmony between Hindu and Muslim; India had to first liberate itself from its weaknesses before it could take on the might of the British Empire. 'India', he said, 'cannot live for Lancashire or any other country before she lives for herself.' A new politics was being launched which would soon make the politics of the past irrelevant.

No one knew this in 1916. The man of the hour was Jinnah, not Gandhi. The 'united India demand', the liberal president of the Muslim League thundered, 'must eventually prove irresistible'. With the restoration of peace 'India will have to be granted her birthright as a free, responsible and equal member of the British Empire.' The Muslim League was later to find the sentiments of Hindu–Muslim unity so embarrassing that it censored portions of Jinnah's speech from official documents reproduced by the enthusiasts of the Pakistan Movement. It is a tremendous irony that both the first speeches of Jinnah, his first as League president and his first address to the Pakistan Assembly as the nominated Governor-General of a new country, have proved embarrassing to those who inherited his legacy.

In 1916, at the age of twenty-seven, Jawaharlal was itching for heroics but unable to find them. He became joint secretary of the provincial Home Rule League started by Tilak and Annie Besant, the Extremist leaders, and always seemed (much to his father's concern, as we have noted) on the verge of doing something dramatic, but his revolution never went beyond the armchair variety. Roger Casement's speech at the Easter Rising trial inspired him, and vague ideas of Utopian socialism filled his head; his reading dipped in favour of Bertrand Russell, and his letters to the editor of *The Leader* railed against the moribund politics of resolution-passers, but Jawaharlal was far from ready for real battle. Moreover, he had not found his leader. Gandhi was 'very distant and different and unpolitical to many of us young men'.

Bibliographies which publish a chronology of Jawaharlal's life leave a neat blank between his marriage and his eventual entry into what Gandhi would call professional politics in 1920. Jawaharlal's state of mind is best described by a story in Gopal's biography about the time when a heckler interrupted a Motilal Nehru speech in August 1917. Motilal lost his temper and dared the heckler to identify himself. The heckler never did. But Sachidananda Sinha, who was present, has left for posterity the identity of the heckler: Jawaharlal himself. He might think freedom, and ache for it, but he was not yet prepared to do anything other than heckle for it.

Bernard Shaw has said that those who can, do, while those who can't, teach. Well, they also sometimes take jobs on newspapers. Journalism was the way Jawaharlal discovered to salve his conscience without surrendering his barrister's robes. It does not seem a coincidence, in the light of his lifelong commitment to a free press, that the first public speech he made, on 20 June 1916 at Hardinge Theatre, was in protest against the Press Act. (Echoing Jefferson, Jawaharlal would say after becoming Prime Minister: 'I would rather have a completely free press with all the dangers involved in the wrong use of that freedom than a suppressed or regulated press.') The Indian

Press Act of 1910 allowed the government to demand security of up to Rs 2,000 from a new press or newspaper, and Rs 5,000 from an established one. In 1916 the government used it against Mrs Annie Besant (1847–1933), and protests broke out all over an agitated India. Jawaharlal had very vague memories about what he said in that speech, but he vividly recalled his terror at the thought of speaking in public, and then speaking in Hindi. He was embarrassed when Sir Tej Bahadur emotionally embraced him after the speech. *The Leader* of 23 June 1916 reported Jawaharlal as having said that 'The poisonous Press Act was growing in strength and that was the time when everyone felt that he should demand its repeal. There was no hope in this world for Indians who thought otherwise . . . The speaker hoped with Carlyle that there could be no compromise with the devil.' It was clearly not oratory which had provoked *The Leader* into reporting this speech at reasonable length, nor the fame of the speaker. Just the simple fact that Jawaharlal was son of the boss.

The Nehrus were very conscious of the role of print media and, more important, of the slant that the British-owned and British-controlled newspapers gave to information. As Jawaharlal wrote:

> A reader of the newspapers would hardly imagine that a vast peasantry and millions of workers existed in India or had any importance. The British-owned Anglo-Indian newspapers were full of the doings of high officials; English social life in the big cities and in the hill stations was described at great length with its parties, fancy-dress balls and amateur theatricals. Indian politics, from the Indian point of view, were almost completely ignored by them, even the Congress sessions being disposed of in a few lines on a back page.

It was to remedy this that Motilal and a group of conscientious friends sought to challenge the dominance of the English-owned *Pioneer*. The indigenous efforts so far – weekly papers like *Indian Opinion* in Allahabad and *Advocate* in Lucknow – had proved less than successful, though the *Opinion* had been of some comfort to Jawaharlal at Harrow. Motilal was elected the first chairman of the board of directors of Newspapers Ltd, and in October 1909 *The Leader* appeared. Thus began a relationship between the family and newspapers which would take some fascinating turns. The first editor was Pandit Madan Mohan Malaviya. Motilal soon got his first lesson

in the whims and egos of journalists when one of his assistant
editors, Nagendra Nath Gupta, resigned in a huff when the other,
C. Y. Chintamani, got a Rs 50 rise as a reward for his hard work.
(Mr Gupta lived by the clock. Chintamani became a famous name in
Indian journalism.) Motilal was determined to make the paper a
powerful weapon. As he told the visiting journalist Nihal Singh, 'So
long as a single brick is left on top of another in my house, I will
defend the right of *The Leader* to fight in the cause of freedom'–
but, of course, fight according to his ideas. By the summer of 1917 dif-
ferences arose with Chintamani, who had become the editor.
Chintamani preferred a constitutional approach to the struggle, while
Motilal and Jawaharlal (incensed by Annie Besant's imprisonment in
June) called for confrontation.

Jawaharlal wrote angry pieces in *The Leader*; his letter of 21 June
1917 condemning the arrest of Mrs Besant began: 'Quos Deus vult
perdere, prius dementat' (Those whom God would destroy, He first
makes mad). The influence of Harrow was still there, but the young
man was gradually taking wing. 'Ours,' he railed in the letter, 'have
been the politics of cowards and opium-eaters long enough and it is
time we thought and acted like live men and women who place the
honour and interests of their country above the frowns and smiles of
every Tom, Dick and Harry who has ICS attached to his name.' He
also had a practical if radical solution to offer: every Indian with an
honorary position in the government should resign. 'If Sir Sankaran
Nair [1857–1934; then judge of Madras High Court, and later to
resign from the Viceroy's Council over the Jallianwala Bagh incident]
and Mr Rajagopalacharya [1862–1927; then member of Madras
executive council] are not merely hirelings ... they must sever all
connection with the Government.' As a personal protest Jawaharlal
withdrew his application for special military training under the Defence of India Force Act.

It was Chintamani who won the boardroom battle for control of
the newspaper. Motilal resigned but would not accept defeat. He
launched a new company, Nationalist Journals, and a new paper,
The Independent, appeared on 5 February 1919. The new name was
chosen with care. Jawaharlal, Syed Hyder Mehdi, Syed Nabi Ullah
and Janki Nath Chak were the other directors. Motilal's chief adviser
was the famous editor of the *Bombay Chronicle*, B. G. Horniman,
who sent one of his best assistant editors, Syud Hossain, to edit the

new paper. The paper was hurt by poor management from the very start. Then for personal reasons the editor left, and Jawaharlal for a brief while tried the job himself. He learned quickly enough that it is far easier to turn out a bright leader than to run a full-scale newspaper. Here is a typical catalogue of troubles, narrated in just one letter from Jawaharlal to his father (on 19 August 1919). A much-expected nominee for assistant editor, Upendranath Neogee, had not turned up for his interview. Assistant manager Hridaynath Sapru wanted to leave soon, at latest by the end of the month. Gopi Iyer wanted a managerial job but neither could be trusted nor knew Urdu. The journalist Motilal wanted to hire, Kali Nath Ray, was too staunch a Moderate in Jawaharlal's view; moreover he had ridiculed *The Independent* when it had come out. There was no competent mechanic for the machines.

By February 1920 Motilal was also seriously worried by the great drain on his bank balance, particularly now that it was no longer being amply nourished by legal fees (the Nehrus had joined Gandhi's non-co-operation movement). Motilal was keen to close down the paper; Jawaharlal wanted one last effort made. Motilal went to Calcutta to persuade a few financiers to invest in exchange for shares. No luck. What he did manage to get was a famous editor, the revolutionary of the Swadeshi days, Bipin Chandra Pal. This did not prove to be a terribly inspired decision either. Pal began as a regular writer (four articles a week for 60 rupees, and payment punctually every Saturday please), and went on to become editor (on a salary of Rs 500 a month). No sooner had he done so than he hired one son as sub-editor (at Rs 100 per month) and another as foreign correspondent in London (for £6 a week). As if nepotism was not bad enough, Pal promptly began to bite the hand which fed him. Instead of attacking the British, he began to abuse the Congress and Gandhi. One attack on Gandhi was beyond Motilal's tolerance levels, and Pal was told to go. By October, Motilal had lost Rs 80,000 of his own money, and was forced to appeal to friends for help. But there was compensation on two counts. First, the paper gave Jawaharlal a vehicle to develop his superb skills as an essayist in the English language even as it honed his political mind. Second, there was the pride of promoting the nationalist cause. As Motilal happily pointed out to Gandhi in a letter written on 17 September 1920: '[*The Independent*] is the only English daily in India to support the full programme of non-co-operation.' By 1919 and 1920 the freedom struggle needed a voice like *The Independent*, and Motilal was the proud owner of that voice. If the period between 1916 and 1919 was the time of the phoney war in the struggle against the British, then it was perhaps just as well that the Nehrus were spending their time in journalism rather than in the Sabarmati ashram with Gandhi. The time to fall in step with Gandhi would come.

For eight years, between 1912 and 1920, Jawaharlal practised at the Bar; it was not inspired advocacy, but his work was never slipshod nor his research less than meticulous. Very methodical in his habit of preserving his papers, Jawaharlal has left behind notes about his preparations of cases. The famous lawyer and jurist M. C. Chagla has described these notes: 'The cases by themselves are not important, but they disclose the extraordinary industry and love of research of the young lawyer.' At the same time, Jawaharlal's ear was close to the music of politics and ideas. One of the most interesting articles he wrote is an incomplete review of Bertrand Russell's book, *Roads to Freedom* (Grant Allen, 1918). Jawaharlal had problems with both unfettered capitalism and fettered socialism:

> Present-day democracy manipulated by the unholy alliance of capital, property, militarism and an overgrown bureaucracy, and assisted by a capitalist press, has proved a delusion and a snare . . . But this is not the fault of democracy. Rather it is due to the many-sided influences which capitalists, aided and abetted by a host of others who fatten under the present regime, have exercised over the governments of the West.

Socialism was not the automatic answer:

> Orthodox Socialism does not give us much hope. The war has shown that an all-powerful state is no lover of individual liberty. It is the breeding ground for the bureaucrat, who, in the West as in the East, is most intolerant of criticism and is seldom enamoured of progress. Life under Socialism would be a joyless and soulless thing, regulated to the minutest detail by rules and orders framed by the all-powerful official Cortes.

The review was written in the middle of 1919, a little before Jawaharlal's thirtieth birthday; it is tempting to think that he left it incomplete because he still had not made up his mind as to what the course between these two options should be like.

By the middle of 1919 India was in the middle of a great storm, the first organized by the man who would now never leave the headlines until he died in 1948. One of those who came to attend the historic Congress session at Lucknow in 1916 was a peasant from the district of Champaran in the north-west corner of Bihar, just below the Himalayas. His name was Rajkumar Shukla, and he was anxiously trying to get the attention of the high-and-mighty leaders gathered there to help solve a problem which was breaking the back of the people of Champaran: the oppression suffered by the indigo cultivators. Only one man found time to listen to him: Gandhi. Gandhi had already taken up his first battle in India, against indentured labour. This was a thinly disguised form of slavery. Able-bodied men were picked up from destitute villages and taken under 'contract' to distant colonies like Fiji or the West Indies to work the plantations in total bondage to their employers. Gandhi had been attacking this practice for decades; his first protest petition on the subject was drafted in 1894.

Gandhi was considered a strange piece of work by the politicians of the day, 'rather an eccentric specimen of an England-returned-educated Indian' (in J. B. Kripalani's words) who lived in voluntary poverty, travelled the length of India in third-class compartments pursuing his social crusades against child marriage, untouchability and spinning, while simultaneously being more loyal than the King in defence of the British Empire's war against Germany. His crusades were not confined only to social ills. When all his polite appeals to Lord Chelmsford to stop indentured labour had failed, Gandhi went on the move in February 1917, travelling throughout the country to raise consciousness against this political evil. The response at every railway station from Karachi to Calcutta was extraordinary and kept growing. It was in this phase that a term began increasingly to be used to describe this man with a smile and a loincloth: Mahatma. Even the rich got into the swing; a women's deputation including Lady Tata and Mrs Dinshaw Petit (Jinnah's mother-in-law) called on the Viceroy to voice their anger. (This may have proved the last straw; if high society ladies of Bombay could be so inspired, anything might happen!) On 12 April 1917 a very reluctant Lord Chelmsford was forced to stop the indenture policy for the duration of the war (this was later ratified by the formal abolition of the system on 1 January 1920).

His first victory on the horizon, Gandhi immediately launched into his second battle. He reached Patna *en route* to Champaran on 10 April. Shukla met him at the station and took him to rest at the house of a lawyer with a growing reputation, Babu Rajendra Prasad, who would become the first President of free India. Prasad was not at home, and his servant first snubbed this visitor in a loincloth, who looked too impoverished to be a social equal of his master. They then went to a friend of Gandhi's from his London days, and president of the Muslim League in 1915, Mazharul Haque. That evening, having rested, Gandhi left for Muzaffarpur, the largest city of north Bihar. His host here was a professor in the government college, a young man called J. B. Kripalani, who would become one of the stalwarts of the freedom struggle and president of the Congress in the last days of British rule. Gandhi stayed in Kripalani's hostel that night. The next day an embarrassed Rajendra Prasad turned up. Lawyers and prominent citizens called on Gandhi, and discussions began on what should be done. Gandhi had only strategy: if the peasants wanted to defeat the nexus of planters and the British government they had to first destroy one thing – their fear. He saw at once it would not be easy: 'I had thought that I should be able to leave from here in two days, but now I realize that the work might take even two years.' He told those who met him that they must be ready for sacrifice, even if it meant prison; in fact, they should go to prison, and not plead in self-defence. (The lawyers were a bit taken aback at such a client.)

The administration at Champaran, which had been hearing rumours of Gandhi's arrival since March 1916, was perturbed. When the police asked for directions on how to handle Gandhi, the special assistant to the deputy inspector-general, Bihar, Special Branch, replied: 'We quite agree with you that his mere presence is undesirable . . . [But] he has a biggish following and one needs to be very careful in dealing with men of his notoriety.' On 11 April, Gandhi, as was his wont, told the secretary of the planters' association, Mr Wilson, his intentions; Mr Wilson replied curtly that he had no business being there. On 12 April, Gandhi requested an interview with the commissioner of the district, L. F. Morshead, and met him the next day. He told Morshead, 'My mission is that of making peace with honour.' But then Gandhi's honour was hard to satisfy in a struggle. The same evening Gandhi asked the local Congressmen to invite him formally, through a letter, to hold an inquiry into the situation of the peasants in Champaran so that the world might know the truth. On 14 April, Morshead asked the district magistrate, W. B. Heycock, to issue an order telling Gandhi to stay out of Champaran district.

Gandhi, of course, was ready for it, and he knew precisely what he was going to do in response: disobey and seek arrest. Fear was the key. It was this fear of the British Raj which had to be driven out of the peasant's heart. The only question was where he should be arrested, Motihari or Bettiah. He organized what should be done after his arrest, and on 15 April left Muzaffarpur by the midday train, reaching Motihari by three o'clock, where a large crowd was already waiting for him at the station. He was not apprehended, so he went to spend the night at the home of Gorakh Prasad. The next morning Gandhi got on to an elephant for the journey to the villages, reaching Chandrahia, about nine miles away, by midday. It was here, in one of the 2,841 villages of Champaran, that he was served the order and taken to Motihari. Gandhi responded to the district magistrate that 'I feel it to be my duty to say that I am unable to leave the district but, if it so pleases the authorities, I shall submit to the order by suffering the penalty of disobedience. My desire is purely and simply for a genuine search for knowledge.' In just four days the whole of India had become seized by excitement at the sight of one man in a loincloth challenging the might of the British Empire. The leaders who did not have much time for Gandhi at the Congress sessions suddenly began sending telegrams volunteering support and participation. On 17 April the police mounted a round-the-clock watch on Gandhi and took down the names of all his visitors. Gandhi simply ignored the police. India waited with a tense thrill as, at a quarter past twelve, Gandhi left for his trial in a carriage, accompanied by two interpreters (Gandhi could not understand the local dialect, Bhojpuri). In the carriage his companions told him that if he went to gaol they would follow. A delighted Gandhi said, 'Now I know we shall succeed.' Thousands waited outside the court room. Armed police were needed to control the agitated peasants. Inside, the government lawyer was armed with a barrage of law books.

Gandhi confounded the world with a simple statement. 'In obedience to the higher law of our being, the voice of conscience,' he pleaded guilty to breaking the lesser law of the British Raj.

The trial was over in half an hour. A thoroughly perplexed magistrate postponed judgement. Gandhi returned to his residence and immediately wired the full details to the Viceroy, to Congress leaders and to friends. He returned at three o'clock to the court to hear the magistrate's orders. It was the judge who was now pleading for time. He said he would pass orders on 21 April and released Gandhi on bail of Rs 100 in the meantime. Gandhi saw another chance and drove his point in again; he had no money for bail, he said, nor anyone to bail him out. The district magistrate told him to go away anyway. The Bihar government, in the meanwhile, was furious with Morshead. The chief secretary wrote to the commissioner on 20 April: 'Mr Gandhi is doubtless eager to adopt the role of the martyr which as you know he has already played in South Africa, and nothing perhaps would suit him better than to undergo a term of imprisonment at the hands of an "unjust" magistracy.' The same day the lieutenant-governor ordered by wire that the case be withdrawn.

In one stroke Gandhi was a national hero. He had humbled the Empire. The *Amrita Bazar Patrika* of Calcutta put the nationalist point of view pithily: 'God bless Gandhi and his work. How we wish we had only half a dozen Gandhis in India to teach our people self-abnegation and selfless patriotism.' As it so happened, one Gandhi would be sufficient. For the labourer in the field earning a wage of 10 pice a day, the woman earning 6 and the child 3 (the average daily wage for agricultural labour of the time) Gandhi became both a mahatma and a *bapu* (father) who would deliver them from their bondage. W. H. Lewis, the subdivisional officer for Bettiah, wrote to his district magistrate Heycock: 'We may look on Mr Gandhi as an idealist, a fanatic or a revolutionary according to our particular opinions. But to the *raiyats* he is their liberator, and they credit him with extraordinary powers.' Lewis had seen this when Gandhi's train reached Bettiah on 22 April on his way back from Motihari. The train had to be stopped long before it reached the platform; the crowds had simply spilled over beyond and on to the tracks. The people of India, Hindu and Muslim, were rallying behind their Mahatma.

If the Mahatma had entered the villages, the traditional politicians stirred the cities. Annie Besant and Lokmanya Tilak were in the van of the movement for Home Rule. On 16 June, Lord Pentland, the governor of Madras, ordered the arrest of Annie Besant, thus giving the movement an extra injection of momentum. Reflecting the new harmony, a special joint meeting of the All-India Congress Committee and the Council of the Muslim League, convened on 28 July, demanded the release of Mrs Besant as also of detainees like the Ali brothers and Maulana Azad. Tilak suggested that extra pressure be put on the government by electing Mrs Besant president of the next Congress. On 17 September she was released and immediately plunged right back into agitation. Jawaharlal was among those waiting on the platform when she arrived in Allahabad on 5 October; in the fashion of the day, her carriage was unhorsed, and volunteers pulled it through the streets decorated with bunting and ringing with cries of 'Besant mata ki jai!' Motilal gave a formal speech of welcome. The tenor of her reply was even sharper than before, for in these intervening months India had sacrificed thousands of its sons on the fields of Gallipoli, Flanders, Mesopotamia and Egypt in defence of the Empire. There was complete agreement among all shades of leadership that the Empire had to be defended, but the feeling had also grown that the reward of dominion status was a legitimate post-war aspiration – 'under a free crown in a free commonwealth of nations', in Annie Besant's words.

Lord Montagu, who had replaced Austen Chamberlain as Secretary of State for India after the mismanagement of the Indian war effort, responded to the new mood soon after taking office with a statement in the Commons on 20 August 1917, accepting the need for the 'increasing association of Indians in every branch of administration, and the gradual development of self-governing institutions with a view to the progressive realization of responsible government in India as an integral part of the British Empire'. Montagu was buying Indian support for the war and making no bones about it. He quickly embarked on a historic visit to India, the first by a Secretary for India, landing in Bombay in early November. There were other worries too: about the spreading impact of the Russian Revolution, for instance. Experienced ICS hands like Sir James Meston warned that not only was nationalist feeling greater than ever, but that Hindus and Muslims were united. On 26 November, Montagu met a delegation which included Gandhi and Jinnah; the next day he held discussions with Tilak and Motilal, among others. Montagu confessed his intentions to his diary: 'He [Tilak] is at the moment probably the most powerful in India, and he has in his power, if he chooses, to help materially in war effort' (*An Indian Diary*, 1930).

That year, the sessions of the Congress and the League were again held in the same city, Calcutta. Rabindranath Tagore opened the Congress session by reciting 'India's prayer'. The Congress expressed its 'deep loyalty and profound attachment to the throne' but now inserted a time limit in its self-government resolution. Gandhi made his views clear in a letter to Lord Chelmsford on 30 April 1918:

> I recognize that in the hour of its danger we must give, as we have decided to give, ungrudging and unequivocal support to the empire of which we aspire in the near future to be partners in the same sense as the dominions overseas. But it is the simple truth that our response is due to the expectation that our goal will be reached all the more speedily.

When the 'reward' came it was discovered to be, not to put too fine a sentiment on it, 'entirely unacceptable', to use Tilak's phrase. A special session of the Congress met under Syed Hasan Imam in Bombay on 29 August 1918 and found London's proposals for reform 'disappointing and unsatisfactory'. The British reactivated the Moderates, who gathered under the banner of the All-India Conference of the Moderate Party (soon to become the National Liberal Federation of India before becoming completely irrelevant) under the leadership of Surendranath (once nicknamed 'Surrender Not' but now, alas, full of surrender) Bannerjea. This time Motilal, much to the delight of Jawaharlal, was firmly on the other side. Speaking in the United Provinces legislature Motilal challenged the timidity of the Moderates who had been advocating the government line that Indians must learn to stand before they could walk. 'We cannot learn to walk,' he said, 'unless you give us the opportunity to exercise the function. If we keep lying all the time, then goodbye to all benefits of the exercise.'

Motilal and Jawaharlal attended the special Congress session in Bombay, and Motilal spoke on the main resolution at the plenary session. The normal session of the Congress that year was a damp squib. Tilak had been elected president but went off to England to fight a libel case against Sir Valentine Chirol, and Pandit Madan Mohan Malaviya took the chair instead. Gandhi was too ill to attend. Yet the Delhi Congress did sound the alarm on an issue which would soon rally India as nothing had done before, lead to Jallianwala Bagh, bring Gandhi to the forefront and change the course of history.

In the same week that the Montagu–Chelmsford reforms were announced appeared a less heralded but potentially far more volatile paper called the Sedition Committee Report. On 10 December 1917 Lord Chelmsford had appointed a committee to tell the government how to deal with 'criminal conspiracies connected with the revolutionary movement in India' through legislation. It was headed by Justice Rowlatt, judge of the King's Bench division of His Majesty's High Court of Justice, and had as its other members Sir Basil Scott, chief justice of the Bombay High Court, Sir Verney Lovett, member of the Board of Revenue, United Provinces, C. V. Kumaraswami Sastri, judge of the Madras High Court, and Probhash Chandra Mitter, *vakil* of the Calcutta High Court. It was formally known as the Sedition Committee, and sat in camera. It submitted its report in April 1918. Among its recommendations: special legislation, both preventive and punitive, suspending the ordinary law safeguarding the rights and liberties of the individual and leaving him at the mercy of the administration or the police. Many of these provisions existed in the wartime Defence of India Rules; now they were sought to be extended into peacetime. On the basis of the report the government framed two Bills. One was a temporary measure, designed to deal with the void arising out of the expiry of the Defence of India Rules. The second, the substantive legislation, was eventually passed: the Anarchical and Revolutionary Crimes Act, 1919. It allowed a special court, of three judges, for quick trials; no appeals were allowed from this court, which could meet in camera and consider evidence not admissible under the Indian Evidence Act. Any suspect's freedom of movement could be curtailed, arrests and searches could take place without a warrant, and anyone could be gaoled on mere suspicion. While a person dealt with by this Act could appear, in camera, before an investigation committee of three persons, the suspect had no right to engage a lawyer. The Bill was introduced in the Imperial Legislative Council on 6 February, passed on 18 March and placed on the statute books on 21 March 1919. Instead of being given a reward for its help in the war, India had been slapped. It stung.

Gandhi was severely ill at that time, in fact at death's door – thanks to his loyalty to the British war effort. His tour of Gujarat to mobilize recruits to fight Britain's war had led to an acute attack of dysentery, and he seemed to be weakening. He was only fifty years old, but it had been a very hectic life. Gandhi was recuperating in Ahmedabad when he read, in February, that the government had introduced the legislation. The first person he discussed his worry with was a lieutenant who, though young, had already become close to him, Vallabhbhai Patel. What should they do? Gandhi had an answer: 'If even a handful of men can be found to sign the pledge of resistance, and the proposed measure is passed into law in defiance of it, we ought to offer *satyagraha*.' On 24 February a small group signed a *satyagraha* pledge drafted by Gandhi at the Sabarmati Ashram: Patel, Sarojini Naidu, Horniman, Umar Sobani, Shankarlal Banker and Indulal Yagnik. Gandhi described the pledge as 'probably the most momentous in the history of India'. It may have seemed exaggeration then, but he knew what he was talking about.

All the Indians in the Council protested. Jinnah could not conceive how the government could any longer claim to be civilized, and Srinivasa Sastri declared in the House, 'If our appeals fall flat, if the Act goes through, I do not believe there is anyone here who would be doing his duty if he did not join the agitation.' Gandhi went to hear the debate: the only time in his life he heard the proceedings of the central legislature. He wrote protesting to the Viceroy. No purchase. He was a careful planner and now set about building his support in the south. He had received an invitation from a lawyer who had left his home town Salem to practise in Madras; Gandhi went to stay with him. The host was Chakravarti Rajagopalachari, whose daughter would marry Gandhi's son and who would replace Mountbatten as the first Governor-General of a free country. Gandhi was in Madras when the Rowlatt Act was passed; he was ill, and his heart was giving him trouble. Discussions about how to conduct *satyagraha* seemed to come to no specific end, when Gandhi had a dream. As he told Rajagopalachari the next morning, 'The idea came to me last night in a dream, that we should call upon the country to observe a general hartal' (a complete cessation of work). The dream seems a convenient mechanism, a bit like Gandhi's conscience. No matter – it was an inspired idea, and it had never been done before. The day was fixed: 6 April.

The people distilled the essence of imperialism into a superbly simple sentence: 'Na vakil, na appeal, na dalil' ('No lawyer, no appeal, no argument'). All over the country chapters of the Satyagraha Sabha started by Gandhi in Sabarmati sprouted without any prodding. When Gandhi had landed in Bombay in 1915 he thought that it would take about five years before he could hope to launch *satyagraha* in India. Events had forced the pace, just a little. The country was excited, awake, eager to try out this new strategy if a little unsure about the details. Gandhi started a pamphlet, *Satyagraha*, priced at one pice to chart the movement. The mood was expectant. The senior politicians could not quite stomach the thought of such 'extra-constitutional' and 'lawless' methods, and some of the most respected heavyweights signed a manifesto in protest against *satyagraha*. But the people, whose anger had already been inflamed by the suffering caused by an influenza epidemic which had taken 6 million lives since 1918, were ready to march against British rule.

In Allahabad, Jawaharlal Nehru announced that he was joining the Satyagraha Sabha. Motilal Nehru was shocked. It was not as if Motilal supported the Rowlatt Act, but his position was akin to Jinnah's; as a committed laywer, a believer in the law, he was perturbed by the concept of making lawlessness into a creed. Gandhi could always argue his way out by reference to a higher 'call', the 'voice of conscience' (as indeed he did, à la Champaran, in his Madras speech on 30 March), but Motilal's conscience was still in harmony with the law. He might not agree with a particular law, but as long as it existed he could not break it without becoming a criminal. Jawaharlal appreciated his father's logic too, but his mind was slowly getting ready for a different destiny. *The Leader* of 3 April reported that Jawaharlal had become a signatory to the *satyagraha* pledge to disobey the Rowlatt Act and a member of the committee formed to propagate the idea in other districts. Motilal condemned the thought of going to prison as 'preposterous', and father and son had long arguments about how far to go along Gandhi's way. Motilal's appeals to his son ranged from the intellectual to the emotional. Jawaharlal tried to ease the pain of a dispute which was extracting a terrible price in the close father–son relationship, but his mind was made up; he had to follow Gandhi. Motilal sensed the determination and, as Jawaharlal discovered much later, secretly began practising sleeping on the floor to get a taste of what life in prison might be like. Motilal's love for his son was so powerful that he was ready to give up a lifetime's convictions and follow his son to an inconceivable prison rather than risk a break between the two.

There was only one man who could resolve this conflict, and Motilal turned to him. He invited Gandhi to Allahabad, and Gandhi came to Anand Bhavan in the second week of March. The two elders had long private conversations (Jawaharlal was not included). Before he left, Gandhi told Jawaharlal that his relationship with his father was more important at the moment than participation in *satyagraha*. Jawaharlal was terribly unhappy at being balked by the man he had chosen to follow, but Gandhi refused to take him along to the Sabarmati Ashram. In hindsight it seems clear that Gandhi wanted both father and son, and he was prepared to wait till wisdom followed youth. As he must have anticipated, he did not have to wait long. In the bargain he had won Motilal's undying gratitude. In fact, when the next opportunity arose, Motilal would be ahead of his son when the call came. Within a month of Gandhi's visit to Anand Bhavan an event took place on the other side of the land that roused the nation to fury and in the heat of that fury melted all differences of strategy and united Indians as never before.

Three Sundays that summer shook India. On 30 March, Delhi and Amritsar observed *satyagraha* and showed how the might of British bullets and bayonets could be met with non-violence. On 6 April the hartal was a complete success in Bombay. The next day, the first issue of the consciously unregistered weekly one-page pamphlet, *Satyagraha*, was on sale for one pice, scheduled to appear every Monday at 10 a.m., carrying specific instructions from Gandhi on how exactly to break the law non-violently and invite arrest. On 8 April, Gandhi set out for Delhi but was taken off the train at Palwal, near the border, the next day and sent back via a goods train and a passenger train to Bombay. News of this arrest angered the people, but the anger was reserved for the British. On the streets, Hindus, Muslims and Sikhs made deliberate displays of unity, raising common slogans. Violence could not always be prevented; in Pydhuni in Bombay and Ahmedabad, Gandhi had to intervene personally to calm the popular mood.

Ramnavami (the celebration of the birth of Rama) was on 9 April that year. In Amritsar it passed off amid great scenes of communal harmony, but on 10 April the British arrested two local leaders, Dr Saifuddin Kitchlew and Dr Satyapal, under the Defence of India Rules. As news spread, a procession formed, demanding their release.

The police stopped the crowd at a railway crossing and opened fire. Many died. In anger, the mob retaliated; half a dozen Englishmen sitting in their offices were seized and killed. On 11 April, Brigadier-General R. E. H. Dyer arrived to take charge. On 12 April, the *satyagrahis* announced that they would hold a meeting the next day at 4.30 in the afternoon a few hundred yards away from the Golden Temple in a park called Jallianwala Bagh. That Sunday was also the day of Baisakhi, a joyous spring celebration that is accompanied by a colourful *mela*. The Jallianwala Bagh was crowded with more than *satyagrahis*; there were at least 10,000 people in that walled space with but a single narrow lane to serve as an outlet. General Dyer decided to teach the natives a lesson in the might of British power. With no provocation whatsoever, his troops fired a non-stop fusillade of 1,650 rounds within ten impossible minutes that afternoon, killing, by the official count, 379 people and leaving 200 gasping for life on the ground. That evening the provincial government requested the Viceroy to establish martial law in Punjab; the request was granted on 15 April. Censorship cloaked all news of the Jallianwala tragedy from India.

The Empire was already terrified by the sudden political earthquake. The Viceroy had sent the Governor of Burma a message on 12 April that he might deport Gandhi along with five others (including Sarojini Naidu) to Burma. Some prominent Indians, quite unused to upheaval, began to worry that things might have gone too far; as early as 12 April, Sir Rabindranath Tagore wrote to Gandhi urging restraint. 'Power', the poet said,

> in all its forms is irrational – it is like the horse that drags the carriage blindfold. The moral element in it is only represented in the man who drives the horse. Passive resistance is a force which is not necessarily moral in itself; it can be used against truth as well as for it. The danger inherent in all force grows stronger when it is likely to gain success, for then it becomes temptation.

In other words, stop. On 18 April, Gandhi called a temporary suspension of the movement. By now, however, word was trickling out about Jallianwala. Gandhi wired the Viceroy requesting permission to visit Punjab; it was refused. But such horror can hardly be kept hidden. India soon knew. On 30 May, Tagore wrote to Lord

Chelmsford renouncing the knighthood he had received in 1915 in protest against Jallianwala. On 8 June, the All-India Congress Committee met at Allahabad and announced that it would conduct an inquiry into the atrocities in Punjab. A committee to collect funds for the work was formed; its members were Motilal Nehru, Swami Shraddhanand and Madan Mohan Malaviya. With the partial lifting of martial law on 11 June (it went totally on 25 August) it was possible to travel without restraint, and Motilal went on his own initiative to defend those being hounded by the authorities. Swami Shraddhanand and Malaviya took charge of the relief work, and Motilal concentrated on the inquiry committee appointed by the Congress on 8 October, consisting of Gandhi, Motilal, C. R. Das, Abbas Tyabji and Fazlul Haq. (M. R. Jayakar replaced Motilal after the latter was named president of the 1919 Amritsar Congress as a gesture of appreciation for the work he had done in Punjab.) The secretary of the committee was K. Santanam. For more than a month before that Jawaharlal had already been at work, searching to piece together the truth about Jallianwala on behalf of his father.

Jawaharlal reached Amritsar in August and stayed till 7 September, when he left for Simla. The detailed notes in his diary would do credit to the most meticulous investigative reporter. Specimen:

> Walked round and saw numerous bullet marks – Counted 67 on one part of one wall ... One bullet mark on a balcony just outside the Bagh facing lane over canal – Most peculiar ... Visited the lane [Durga Koti Lane] where people were made to crawl on their bellies. Told that one respectable woman raped in a neighbouring house. General misbehaviour of tommies.

He also had a reporter's eye for the human interest story. He described an incident on 10 April after the firing on the procession. His informant was a person called Maqbul Mohammad (a pleader in the High Court and a resident of Amritsar):

> Mr G. S. Salaria, Dr Dhanpat Rai and I first came to dress a stout young lad of about 18 who lay badly wounded with his intestines and abdominal viscera turned out and lying in the dusty road. He made signs for water. I brought it in my cap and poured some of it into his mouth. He revived a

little and could then blurt out a few words. Dr Dhanpat Rai then came to attend on him. The young man with faltering accents said: 'Meri koi ummeed naheen; mere naal ke bhai ka intezam karo' ['There is no hope for me; try to save the brother who is lying near by']. He stopped, then gasped brokenly: 'Hindu Musulman ki jai' ['Victory to Hindu and Muslims'] and expired.

From the Punjab experiences of Jawaharlal emerges a story which is so fascinating that it appears in just about anything written on him, so it must find its place in a biography. The best thing to do is let Jawaharlal tell it:

> Towards the end of that year [1919] I travelled from Amritsar to Delhi by the night train. The compartment I entered was almost full and all the berths, except one upper one, were occupied by sleeping passengers. I took the vacant upper berth. In the morning I discovered that all my fellow-passengers were military officers. They conversed with each other in loud voices which I could not help overhearing. One of them was holding forth in an aggressive and triumphant tone and soon I discovered that he was Dyer, the hero of Jallianwala Bagh, and he was describing his Amritsar experiences. He pointed out how he had the whole town at his mercy and he had felt like reducing the rebellious city to a heap of ashes, but he took pity on it and refrained. He was evidently coming back from Lahore after giving his evidence before the Hunter Committee of Inquiry. I was greatly shocked to hear his conversation and to observe his callous manner. He descended at Delhi station in pyjamas with bright pink stripes, and a dressing gown.

It was an experience which starkly illuminated the arrogance and cold brutality of British power.

Gandhi's slogan, first heard in Amritsar, 'Hindu–Musulman ki jai', became the theme of his politics for the next thirty years. And that was the bedrock of Jawaharlal's social philosophy. His interest in the law dwindled, and it was obvious that it was only a question of time before the freedom movement became his sole occupation. The bonds between Motilal and Gandhi had strengthened during the committee work on Jallianwala. By the time of the Amritsar Congress, Motilal had fallen, as much as his son, under the Mahatma's spell. Motilal was the president, but Gandhi was the hero of the Amritsar Congress, notwithstanding the fact that sharing the stage with him were such luminaries as Tilak, Jinnah, Annie Besant, C. R.

Das and Malaviya. As Jawaharlal later put it: 'The Amritsar Congress was the first Gandhi Congress.' He noted in his autobiography: 'Of the other prominent Congress leaders only one, Motilal Nehru, supported Gandhi in the early stages. But there was no doubting the temper of the average Congressman or the man in the street, or the masses. Gandhi carried them off their feet, almost hypnotized them.'

The Amritsar Congress was sweetened by the passage of the Montagu–Chelmsford reforms, which became the Government of India Act on 23 December, bringing in its wake a little extra self-government; and sugared by a royal amnesty for all political prisoners from King-Emperor George V on the same day. But nothing could quite take away the bitter taste of Jallianwalla and British repression. In his three-hour speech Motilal revealed that, since the agitations had started against the Rowlatt Bills in Punjab, 108 persons had been condemned to death and the combined total of imprisonments was 7,371 years. 'The figures for whipping, forfeiture, fines and impositions on villages and towns are not available,' he added.

The irony is that during the three years of its life the Rowlatt Act was never once used by the British. It is quite astonishing how much governments are prepared to lose in the defence of the indefensible.

12 Stumbling towards Destiny

'Greatness', Jawaharlal wrote to his father on 14 May 1920 from the elegant Savoy Hotel in that exquisite hill station, Mussoorie, 'is being thrust on me.' It was the opening line of a strange story which played a significant part in completing the transition from lawyer to politician.

For eight years Jawaharlal had combined an industrious if uninspiring commitment to the court room with an irresistible flirtation with politics. The spirit of the non-co-operation movement proved a pervasive influence. The life-style at Anand Bhavan had, among other things, begun to irritate him, and he began to ask his father some embarrassing questions – as for instance whether any of the English civil servants who so happily lapped up the lavish hospitality of Motilal ever thought of asking him back to their homes. Not many of the memsahibs wanted to entertain a 'black' or a marginally paler Indian version. C. F. Andrews, who came to know Motilal intimately during the Congress inquiry committee work, has written (quoted in *The Great Nehrus*: J. S. Bright [Delhi: Tagore Memorial Publications, 1961]):

> More and more he [Motilal] had adopted, after each visit to Europe, the expensive standard of living common to the West. Exceedingly foolish stories about his Western habits were spread widely over the north of India, which were ridiculous to those who knew him in his own house. . . . He was far too deeply wedded to his own country and its traditions to make him ever forget his birthright.

Father and son were on the same wavelength only on those occasions when Motilal lost his temper at some unbearable perfidy, as for instance when the official report of Lord Hunter's committee on the happenings in Punjab appeared in March 1920. (The Indians on the committee had refused to endorse the European version, which was accepted as the formal findings.) 'My blood is boiling,' Motilal wrote to his favourite correspondent, his son, although the latter's blood had been at that temperature for some time.

Motilal's ardour was, however, cooled by the munificent fees he was commanding from his practice. The most famous of his law-court exploits, the Dumraon case, in which he battled with his great friend C. R. Das, has entered legend. At one point during the hearings Motilal was truly foxed by his adversary in the court room: 'I cannot for the life of me understand the tactics he employed today. He has tendered *our* documents as *his* evidence.' Fumed Motilal to his son, 'You would simply be shocked at the practices to which the big guns of the Calcutta Bar lend themselves.' But such anxieties found more than adequate compensation; in eight months Motilal received a fee of Rs 200,000 for this case alone. Das and Motilal added an extra dimension to the popular stories by their out-of-court behaviour. After arguing vehemently through the day they would sit down together in the evenings for a friendly drink and discussions on poetry, thus generating an endless round of romantic stories of how great lawyers behaved, to the unbounded titillation of an emerging middle class. These tales of wealth (true) and life-style (exaggerated) only serve to stress the distance the Nehrus were to travel in terms of self-denial and sacrifice when they became non-co-operators in October 1920.

One story, strenuously denied by Jawaharlal in his autobiography (cynics suspect for political reasons), nicely bridges the two worlds. The story was also told by Arthur Moore, a former editor of *The Statesman*, who was a friend of both the men involved, in a brief memoir called 'My Friend's Son', which was part of *A Study of Nehru* edited by Dr Rafiq Zakaria and published by *The Times of India* in November 1959. Arthur Moore insisted, however, that the story was true despite Jawaharlal's denials, which he attributed to the fact that the father did not tell his son everything; his source, claimed Moore, was Motilal himself. Motilal and the governor of United Provinces at that time, Sir Harcourt Butler, were very good friends. 'Motilal', writes Moore,

was dining with Sir Harcourt and, no doubt feeling his political views changing under his son's influence, and possibly shades of the prison house beginning to close around him, said laughingly to Sir Harcourt over their champagne (Motilal liked good wine) that one day soon he might be in prison. To which Sir Harcourt replied, 'Well, if that happens, I'll see that you get champagne.' It passed as a jest, but this, Motilal told me, is what happened. His first morning in prison an ADC from Government House arrived at lunchtime with a half-bottle of champagne wrapped in a napkin, and every single day of his imprisonment this was repeated.

Whether the champagne came or not, it is perfectly true that Sir Harcourt allowed his old friend to eat food brought from home rather than prison fare. In any case, the story got around, and Aldous Huxley brought it up when he met Motilal during a dinner-party in Delhi on an Indian visit, says B. R. Nanda in *The Nehrus*. (By that time, maple furniture had also been placed in Motilal's cell in the stories.) Motilal laughed in response and said, 'No, it is not true. But in the good old days, rivers of champagne must have flowed between us.' Which is as happy an ending to the anecdote as one might wish for.

It was Sir Harcourt Butler who decided to thrust greatness upon Jawaharlal in May. An Afghan delegation had booked into the Savoy at the same time and, as Jawaharlal complained, taken all the best rooms which he normally hired for himself. Sir Harcourt, quite out of the blue, sent Jawaharlal a letter demanding a positive undertaking that he would not visit or have 'any communication' with this delegation. Jawaharlal barely knew of this delegation's existence and had no desire whatsoever to have anything to do with it. But the thought of the British ordering him to do anything incensed him. He would not take orders from the British. It was a question of principle.

It was, however, not surprising that Sir Harcourt should worry more about the son than the father. Jawaharlal had become a virtual disciple of Gandhi already, and the old Mahatma had reciprocated with a fatherly affection. In February 1920 Jawaharlal had participated in a district conference of the Congress and by July become vice-president of the Allahabad unit. It was not as if Motilal was averse to his son's entering politics; in fact, he had an eye on a constituency from which Jawaharlal could enter the provincial council. What he objected to was Gandhian politics, with its demand of total non-co-operation, including a boycott of the courts. Only Motilal's beady eye kept Jawaharlal from formally declaring his commitment to Gandhi. Jawaharlal had, in his new enthusiasm, become quite careless even about his wife and child. Kamala was never very well, and her health had begun to break after the strain of bearing a child. Even so, Jawaharlal, his mind full of politics, was too 'busy' even to decipher a homoeopathic physician's prescription for his wife. His father retorted with a classic Motilal rebuke: 'There is nothing very complicated about Dr Ray's letter if you will only read it carefully after divesting your mind of the Khilafat and Satyagraha.'

The holiday in Mussoorie was scheduled to be a long one. Both Swarup Rani and Kamala had fallen ill. The doctors, as was the general practice then, at once ordered a stay in the hills. Jawaharlal even put his sister Betty into a local school: Hampton Court School, 'situated a little under Fitche's shop'. The Afghan delegation, on the other hand, had very different motives for coming to Mussoorie; it had come to negotiate the terms of peace after minor hostilities with the British in 1919, when King Amanullah took the throne. It was a season of rumour and apprehension. Congress–Khilafat co-operation was the talk of the country, and the British were very worried about any 'secret' negotiations between Congress leaders and Muslims outside India. This fear brought a superintendent of police with that fateful letter from the United Provinces government to Jawaharlal. Rather than accept the British condition, Jawaharlal returned to Allahabad. Motilal wrote to his friend Sir Harcourt asking what could have prompted such an order. The governor knew in his bones what was coming and while defending the government decision added that he hoped that in private life 'nothing will interfere with the friendly relations that have existed between us for thirty years'. Motilal told Sir Harcourt that, in case the health of the ladies worsened, he and his son would go to Mussoorie, order or no order. As it so happened, the order was withdrawn within a fortnight, but by then, quite accidentally, Jawaharlal had been drawn into a powerful peasant agitation that was then raging through his province. The peasants took him to the poverty of their villages, which the Harrow and Cambridge lawyer was to see for the first time. The experience changed his life. All doubts, all arguments about the choices before him, dissolved. As he put it in his autobiography: 'I have sometimes wondered what would have happened if I had not been externed and had not been in Allahabad just then with no engagements.'

13 Politics among the Peasants

Like just about any other problem, this one too had a part of its origins in the fear that had enveloped the British after the Mutiny. The Company had annexed its most prized possession, Awadh, from Nawab Wajid Ali Shah on 13 February 1856. Seeking, and without delay, to maximize their chief source of income – land revenue – the Company's immediate impulse was to prop up village-level landowners against the corrupt and despotic but extremely powerful *taluqdars*. Awadh was a delicious prize; its twelve districts were known as the garden of India. But within fifteen months of the annexation the Mutiny broke out, and the British found these *taluqdars* rallying against them, from the safety of their fortresses, while the villagers were either indifferent or also hostile. As Lord Canning, the Governor-General, commented: 'Not an individual dared to be loyal to the government.' He now needed little persuasion from James Outram, the chief commissioner of Lucknow, to revert to the rule; loyalty to the Raj would be the price for new membership of the old class. On 15 March 1858 the British confiscated all the land of Awadh and redistributed it to the corrupt *taluqdars* who promised loyalty in return. The only ones left undisturbed were the six landowners who had stayed with the Company during the Mutiny. The Talookdaree Settlement came into force on 1 May 1858, and Major L. Barrow, the special commissioner of revenue in Awadh, tossed about 'estates as large as shires and whole kingdoms with the wave of his hand, just as Napoleon used to fling away empires or a juggler knocks balls about', in the words of one eyewitness, William Howard Russell (*My Indian Mutiny Diary*, 1957), quoted by Kapil Kumar in *Peasants in Revolt* (1984). By March 1861, with the help of an agent from Bengal, Duckinah Runjun Mookerjee, the pro-British *taluqdars* formed the British Indian Association of Awadh, for which Mr Mookerjee was rewarded with part of the confiscated estate of the patriotic Rana Beni Madho of Shankarpur. (Others who shared the estates were Sikhs who had fought on the side of the British, the Raja of Khajurgarh and English officers.) Complete loyalty to the British was the *sine qua non* of those allowed to hold *jaghirs*. In exchange, the largely Thakur *taluqdars* were allowed to indulge in brutal and whimsical exploitation of the peasantry, and nowhere was the cruelty worse than in the districts of Pratapgarh, Sultanpur, Rae Bareli and Amethi.

In 1864, in a small village in the Mahratta state of Gwalior, a Brahmin boy called Shridhar Balwant Jodhpurkar was born. The misery of poverty was compounded by the cruelty of a stepmother, and he ran away from home. He worked where he could: as a coolie, or vendor, or labourer in the fields. In 1905 he became one of thousands sent to Fiji as indentured labour. In order to conceal his Maharashtrian Brahmin identity in Fiji, Jodhpurkar changed his name to Ram Chandra Rao, and he began organizing these men substituting for slaves. By the time he returned to India in 1916 he had already acquired a reputation as an 'agitator'. He began touring the villages of the United Provinces to preach his new gospel of a peasant awakening, colouring his message in religious imagery and symbolism, claiming divine visions, stressing *Ram-bhakti* (worship of Rama) and repeating verses from the Ramayana to inspire the people against the *taluqdar*–British nexus. It was a clever use of religion in politics.

The peasants were ready for an insurrection. The nature of the oppression was vicious. From the lower castes like Chamar, Kurmi, Koiri or Lodh, a man could be turned into bonded labour for as little as a loan of Rs 40; and with sharks keeping the 'accounts', the bondage was almost always transferred to the next generation. Rents would be enhanced illegally; the practice was called *beshi*. Then there was the system of *nazrana* or the 'gift': in reality, an arbitrary tax. If in Lucknow a peasant had to pay Rs 10 per bigha of land as *nazrana*, including a rupee each to the *patwari* (the village official) and the *zilledar* (landlord's agent), the rate could climb to an astronomical Rs 125 in the worst-affected Pratapgarh. Tenants were often forced to sell their daughters to pay for this evil. A report of the district deputy commissioner of Pratapgarh, V. N. Mehta, in November 1920 records a number of such tragedies: a five-year-old girl sold to a forty-year-old man for Rs 300 by her brother; fathers selling daughters to middle-aged or dying men for two or three hundred rupees. The practice was so prevalent it acquired a formal name: *kanya vikray* (sale of the daughter). A tenant had no hereditary rights. *Murdafaroshi* (literally, sale of corpses) was the norm; a tenant's holding was sold to the highest bidder as soon as he died. A special kind of priest became popular who would be paid to pray for an epidemic so that peasants might die and the landlord might raise more funds through *murdafaroshi*. On top of all this, the tenants had to finance every new expense, every sudden whim of the *taluqdar*. One woman *taluqdarni* of Pratapgarh, for instance, spent Rs 15,000 on mendicants to appease the gods so that her septic boil might heal and recovered the money from her tenants, calling this tax Pakawan (the Septic Tax). If a *taluqdar* wanted to buy a horse, the Ghorawan (Horse Tax) would be imposed. When a horse became old and useless, a forced lottery was conducted to dispose of the animal to the 'lucky' winner. The *hathiavan* (*hathi* means elephant) was followed by the *motrawan* (motors, in the age of cars), as the *taluqdar*'s preferred means of transport changed from the horse and the elephant to motor cars. Any charity – as for instance the Rs 50,000 given by the Sessendi estate to Lucknow University – came through the same 'gift' by the people. Virtually every item of household use, and any service, had to be provided by the tenants.

The anger burst through in April 1920 with one of the most militant of the backward castes, the Kurmis, in the van. It was led by Baba Ram Chandra, now a familiar mystic-hero of the peasantry. April was the month when the landlords would begin their punitive evictions, with the harvest in and past dues taken. The Baba began addressing large rallies exhorting the tenants to pay just their legal rents but not a paisa more to the *taluqdars*. As the momentum built up, and the *taluqdars* responded with redoubled oppression, the peasants felt the need for help. Who else to turn to but Gandhi? After Champaran his name had travelled to the remotest village. By June, Baba Rama Chandra had set up an organizational network, with about fifty branches, called the Kisan Sabha. On the auspicious occasion of the Saptami bathing day in early June, he set out at the head of a group of 500 peasants on a seventy-kilometre trek from Patti to Allahabad, in the belief that Gandhi would stop there on his way back from a Congress meeting in Benaras. And if Gandhi was in Allahabad, where else would he stay but at Anand Bhavan?

Gandhi, however, was still in Benaras. Motilal was in Arrah, arguing a case. Jawaharlal should have been in Mussoorie enjoying his holiday; instead he was alone at home with nothing to do, thanks to the externment order. Even then it took three days for the peasants to persuade the Allahabad politicians that their case was serious enough for the attention of the Nehrus. On the evening of 7 June, at the Balua river bank, Baba Ram Chandra met Jawaharlal and some of his friends, like Purushottam Das Tandon and Gauri Shankar Misra, to plead for a Champaran-style inquiry into their situation. Jawaharlal was not particularly enthused by the idea of visiting villages situated in one of the hottest regions of the country in the hottest month of the year. But, as he recalled in his autobiography: 'They would accept no denial and literally clung to us. At last I promised to visit them two days or so later.'

The first and fortuitous visit to 'real India' changed Jawaharlal dramatically. This sight of poverty was a revelation which left an imperishable impact on his psyche. Nineteen twenty was a crossroads year for him in any case, caught as he was between the Gandhian call of voluntary poverty and total involvement with the freedom struggle, and the more conventional tug of his father, urging freedom too but through less drastic methods. The enthusiasm of the peasants, the sheer enormity of their suffering and the soaring arc of their hopes moved him immensely. He was touched when he learned that hundreds of ill-clad villagers had built roads for him overnight so that his car could take him to the innermost recesses of rural India; or saw the eagerness with which they physically lifted his car when it got stuck in the soft mud. After all, he was still an Indian sahib in a hat and silk underwear. Jawaharlal reported that introduction to India in some vivid prose: 'The sun scorched and blinded. I was quite unused to going out in the sun and ever since my return from England I had gone to the hills for part of every summer. And now I was wandering about all day in the open sun with not even a sun-hat.' The excitement of discovery made the weather irrelevant:

We found the whole countryside afire with enthusiasm and full of a strange excitement. Enormous gatherings would take place at the briefest notice by word of mouth. One village would communicate with another, and the second with the third, and so on, and presently whole villages would empty out, and all over the fields there would be men and women and children on the march to the meeting place. Or, more swiftly still, the cry of *Sita Ram* – *Sita Ra-a-a-m* – would fill the air, travel far in all directions and be echoed back from other villages, and then people would come streaming out or even running as fast as they could. They were in miserable rags, men and women, but their faces were full of excitement and their eyes glistened and seemed to expect strange happenings which would, as if by a miracle, put an end to their long misery. They showered their affection on us and looked on us with loving and hopeful eyes as if we were the bearers of good tidings, the guides who were to lead them to the promised land. Looking at them and their misery and overflowing gratitude, I was filled with shame and sorrow, shame at my own easygoing and comfortable life and our petty politics of the city which ignored this vast multitude of semi-naked sons and daughters of India, sorrow at the degradation and overwhelming poverty of India.

Revelation. Promised land. There is little doubt that this is the nearest that the young agnostic came to a spiritual experience. This was the emotion which would henceforth sustain his political heart. His socialism was constructed more around a deep desire to end this wretched poverty than around the works of Karl Marx or any other ideologue. Even in that emotional wrench of the first experience, he was irritated by the anarchic-religious sentiments of Baba Rama Chandra, and never encouraged any movement beyond the acceptable limits prescribed by society. However, three decades later when he was Prime Minister, among his very first initiatives was to abolish the *taluqdari* system.

What is significant in the history of this peasant revolt is how both Gandhi from his pedestal and Jawaharlal from much lower down helped keep the sentiment within check, or at least prevented it from taking a Bolshevik dimension. Both were conscious of the storm of change just north of Kashmir, and they were as keen as the British government to ensure that it remained on the other side of the mountains. The sap, however, was just beginning to rise in June 1920, and the peasant movement would see much drama and violence before it burnt itself out. Jawaharlal became a great champion of the peasants, publicizing their cause in uninhibited prose in *The Independent* and touring the province at length. The government tried to stop both his journalism and the speeches, and failed. Ingenious solutions were often used to circumvent government efforts. When once he was banned from addressing a meeting at a place called Bhiti, Jawaharlal simply marched with the whole crowd for four and a half miles till they reached the next district, where there was no ban, and delivered his speech there. The government's CID agents of course followed him everywhere; occasionally there was the honour of a deputy collector himself trailing the blossoming orator. Jawaharlal recalls, in his autobiography, one particular specimen: 'The deputy collector was a somewhat effeminate youth from Lucknow and he turned up in patent leather pumps! He begged us sometimes to restrain our ardour and I think he ultimately dropped out, being unable to keep up with us.'

Jawaharlal was anxious to channel this exhilarating peasant power into the national movement rather than let it remain concentrated against the *taluqdars*. He brought Gandhi to Pratapgarh in November 1920. The British intelligence report of the United Provinces government felt that Gandhi came less to enthuse the peasants and more to frighten the landlords into supporting the Congress. Yet the anger of the peasants kept rising, and the CID thought that the 'Bolshevik idea is also rapidly spreading'. The government got a fright when *The Pioneer* reported that 'soviets' had been set up by the peasants; but it was only an instance of bad reporting. The journalist had confused a 'Kisan Sabha' with a 'soviet'. Gandhi's call at the Nagpur session for *swaraj* (self-government) within a year only excited passions further. Nobody quite knew what *swaraj* meant, so everyone interpreted it according to his needs. The peasant saw it as good cloth at four annas a yard. On 5 January 1921 about forty people led by Ram Gulam Pasi even went up to a *bania* shopkeeper, Badaria, in Tiloi and demanded cloth at that price. He refused, of course, and they looted the shop. That same week, other mobs had burnt the crops belonging to prominent *taluqdars* in separate incidents. South Awadh was in violent ferment. (In the process, a few peasants even tried to reform the mores of some *taluqdars*. One protest took place against Tribhuwan Bahadur Singh's kept prostitute Achhijan; the peasants wanted his rightful wife restored.) By the 6th, police were opening fire at many places. The first incident was at Fursatganj. The crowd, consisting of both Hindus and Muslims, raised slogans in praise of Gandhi, Ram Chandra and the Ali brothers.

There was firing too at Munshiganj. Jawaharlal reached the scene while it was going on. Once again he had been reluctant to come; he was tired after the just-concluded Nagpur Congress session but finally succumbed to the pressure of a telegram from Rae Bareli. When he reached the town he heard that the peasants had been stopped across a nearby river. He hurried there. The district magistrate sent him a note asking him to go back; he ignored it. When he reached the bridge he could see and hear the firing on the peasants. He was stopped here by the army, and before he knew it a crowd of peasants who had been hiding on this side of the river collected around him, frightened, but drawing strength from his presence. He reassured and comforted them, before the magistrate led him away. Jawaharlal wrote in *The Independent* of 22 January that for one moment his blood was up, before the discipline of non-violence calmed him again. Motilal joined his son the next day, but he seemed to have an eye on the main chance; he thought this area would become a safe seat for his son in the elections to the provincial council, 'in spite of the Raja Bahadur of Pratapgarh'. History has its own unique way of both fulfilling dreams and lacing them with irony. Decades later, three generations of Nehrus would be elected and re-elected from the constituencies of Rae Bareli and the adjoining Amethi, in some part at least because of the links forged by Jawaharlal in this agitation. But the Pratapgarh seat would remain outside the family ken – largely because the Raja Bahadur of Pratapgarh's descendants had become respectable Congressmen and were Congress candidates themselves.

Gandhi had, even in 1920, no desire to alienate the *taluqdars* completely from the Congress or encourage a peasant movement to the point where it took on the dimensions of an armed revolution. He was as clear then about communism as he would be a few months before his death in 1948, when he told a group of communists who had come to call on him: 'What to me is even more pathetic is that you regard Russia as your spiritual home. Despising Indian culture, you dream of planting the Russian system here.' Gandhi had deliberately refused to include the non-payment of rent in the non-co-operation programme finalized at Nagpur in 1920. And when the All-India Congress Committee passed a resolution on the subject in November 1921 it asked *satyagrahis* not to pay taxes to the government, but rent was still to be given to the *taluqdars*. Gandhi wanted both the landlord and the peasant on his side, just as he wanted both the capitalist and the worker. A place had to be found for all in the freedom movement; and, inevitably, a place had to be found for both sides of the economic divide in free India, leading in turn to the interesting animal called a mixed economy. The

November 1921 resolution bore the stamp of Gandhi's will. By then Gandhi had already become dictator of the Congress after an extraordinary coup in September 1920. One of the commanders of the pro-Gandhi coup was Motilal Nehru, to the unconcealed delight of Jawaharlal.

14 Conversion of the Nehrus: 'What a Fall, My Countrymen!'

Gandhi took his historic vow on 24 February 1919:

> Being conscientiously of opinion that the Bills known as the Indian Criminal Law (Amendment) Bill No. 1 of 1919 and the Criminal (Emergency Powers) Bill No. 2 of 1919 are unjust, subversive of the principles of liberty and justice, and destructive of the elementary rights of individuals on which the safety of the community as a whole and the state itself is based, we solemnly affirm that in the event of these Bills becoming law, and until they are withdrawn, we shall refuse civilly to obey these laws and such other laws as a committee, to be hereafter appointed, may think fit, and we further affirm that in this struggle we will faithfully follow truth and refrain from violence to life, person or property.

What history would be created by this pledge!

The moment was right for Gandhi to march. The Muslims were in ferment with the Khilafat struggle; anger against the Rowlatt Act and later Jallianwala gave everyone a reason for revolt. Gandhi channelled this anger into an unprecedented challenge to British authority; and for a while he buried the greatest obstacle to freedom, Hindu–Muslim tensions, in an avalanche of emotion created by a common ambition.

Gandhi had met Maulana Muhammad Ali in 1915. 'It was a question of love at first sight between us,' he would say later. The love did not wane despite differing views on the Great War. The Ali brothers went to gaol for four years for supporting Turkey, while Gandhi raised volunteers for the British Army. Gandhi wrote to the Viceroy in 1918 arguing that the brothers be released. The brothers told visitors like Chaudhury Khaliquzzaman in Lansdowne gaol that 'he alone [Gandhi] can be our man'. In a letter to Lord Chelmsford from gaol the Ali brothers called Gandhi 'our guide, philosopher and friend'. By the time Muhammad Ali was released in December 1919, India was already in ferment.

Muslim anger against the British only became worse in 1920. With the defeat of Turkey, the Holy Lands had passed, for the first time in the history of Islam, into non-Muslim control. Indian Muslims wanted Britain to let the Khalifa of Turkey keep custody over Islam's holiest places of pilgrimage, and were worried that the British would rule through an agent like the Bedouin chief propped up by T. E. Lawrence, Emir Feisal. Muhammad Ali led a four-member delegation to London to plead Turkey's cause in early 1920, when the terms of the peace were being settled in London. They met the British Prime Minister on 19 March, but Lloyd George had nothing to offer. On 22 March 1920 *The Times* of London reported Lloyd George as saying:

> I do not want any Muslim in India to imagine that we are applying one principle to Christian countries and another to a Muslim country. But neither do I want any Muslim in India to imagine that we are going to abandon, when we come to Turkey, the principles which we have ruthlessly applied to Christian countries like Germany and Austria.

This was British fair play; the victors would be equally ruthless with everyone. 'Why should Turkey escape?' asked Lloyd George. The terms for Turkey announced in May confirmed that it would not. Turkey lost every colony. Hejaz (now Saudi Arabia) went to Feisal; France got its chance to 'advise and assist' Syria; and Britain took over Palestine, and thereby direct control of the Al Aqsa mosque, and Iraq, which had Karbala – both places of reverence for Muslims.

In May 1920 appeared the Hunter Committee Report on Jallianwala, a laboured whitewash of Dyer's brutality. The House of Lords added insult by condoning Dyer's actions, while a chauvinist lobby in Britain presented him with a sword and purse of £20,000 for saving the Empire. An angry Muhammad Ali demanded that Sir Sayyid's Mahomedan Anglo-Oriental College at Aligarh cut its links with the Raj in protest. When the college refused, pro-Khilafat students walked out in droves, leading eventually to the founding of the nationalist alternative, the Jamia Millia Islamia, near Delhi. Gandhi appealed to the poet Iqbal to be the first rector of the Jamia, but the latter refused, and Ali himself filled that chair. Muslim sentiment turned against the League because of its British links, and leaders like Hakim Ajmal Khan, who had appeared on both Congress and League platforms till now, abandoned the League. What Gandhi was doing was exposing the contradictions and the evasiveness which lay behind so many public masks, the men who spoke for India in the day and supped with the Raj at night. He demanded that everyone stand up and be counted. Those who still insisted on hide-and-seek either became irrelevant or went in one logical direction and served the British from then on. V. S. Srinivasa Sastri, to take one example, became a delegate to the Imperial Conference in London in 1921 and then a member of the Privy Council, finding his ultimate reward in 1928 with the award of the British Order of Companion of Honour.

On 1 August 1920 Gandhi launched non-co-operation, in support of the Khilafat movement, by returning his Kaiser-i-Hind gold medal, his Zulu War medal and his Boer War medal to Lord Chelmsford, though 'not without a pang', as he wrote in his letter to the Viceroy. The return of honours symbolized the beginning of his anti-British phase. The decision had enormous impact upon Muslims. Some Congressmen like Pandit Madan Mohan Malaviya protested that Gandhi was becoming too pro-Muslim; there were even appeals that the movement be suspended. But Gandhi had launched non-co-operation on his own, without reference to the Congress. He would not withdraw: 'For me to suspend non-co-operation would be to prove untrue to the Musalman brethren.' The 1st of August 1920 can be called the day when the old politics was destroyed and the Gandhian era in the history of India began. The death of the revered Bal Gangadhar Tilak, in Bombay, on that very day seems a symbolic coincidence, because he was the only one who could have come in the way of Gandhi's pre-eminence on the Indian political scene. A special session of the Congress was summoned to consider whether the Congress should support or oppose Gandhi's call for non-co-operation; the venue was Calcutta, between 4 and 9 September.

Most historians stress that the coup by which Gandhi captured the Congress that year was not easy, and quote Gandhi's own comment that his plight was 'pitiable'. But the point lies elsewhere. This was also the first manifestation of Gandhi's power in India; the Congress needed him more than he needed the Congress. The people were with Gandhi; that was his strength. He was quite blunt about it. He said: 'When one has an unshakable faith in a particular policy or action, it would be folly to wait for the Congress pronouncement. On the contrary, one must act and demonstrate its efficacy so as to command acceptance by the nation.' The vow he took in his ashram in Ahmedabad on 24 February 1919 was not by permission of the Congress president of the day. He spoke directly to the people – as Congress leaders of both the pre-1920 vintage and the post-1920 generations were to learn, very often painfully. In 1919 and 1920 it was his slogan which echoed in every heart: 'Hindu–Mussalman ki jai' ('Victory to Hindu and Muslim'). He explained to the people, writes Tendulkar, that 'There should be only three cries recognized, "Allah-o-Akbar", to be joyously sung out by Hindus and Muslims showing that God alone was great and no other. The second should be "Bande Mataram" or "Bharat Mata-ki-jai". The third should be "Hindu–Mussalman ki jai".' His message was: 'I never realize any distinction between a Hindu and a Muslim. Both are sons of Mother India . . . When the Hindus and the Muslims act towards each other like blood brothers, then alone can there be true unity, then alone can the dawn of freedom break for India.' This was the base, non-violence the path. Non-violence did not mean passive resistance but was a powerful and positive force, not only an answer to the British but also an antidote to the destructive acid of religious violence which was by far the most dangerous element in India's complex inheritance. Non-violence was not just the chariot on which the freedom movement would ride; it was the only vehicle which could take a united nation towards progress. Order, peace, sacrifice, fearlessness and unflinching determination: those were the values which could liberate the motherland. (Incidentally, Gandhi had one very interesting solution for 'mobocracy': music. He wanted to make the singing of national songs compulsory. 'Music', he said, 'means rhythm, order. Unfortunately in India, music has been the prerogative of the few. It has never become nationalized.')

The old guard of the Congress was determined to stop Gandhi at the special session in Calcutta. They were all there, ready for battle: Annie Besant, Jinnah, Malaviya, C. R. Das, Bipin Pal and Lala Lajpat Rai, just returned from America, who was named president of the session. The drama at Calcutta deserves narration. The Tilak group led by G. S. Khaparde joined forces with the Bengal group (B. C. Pal, Motilal Ghose, editor of the *Amrita Bazar Patrika*, and B. Chakravarti) and on 1 September they met and decided to oppose Gandhi. Then there was the Constitutionalist group, whose anger was not against Gandhi's secularism but against his defiance of the law, which they were convinced would lead to anarchy. On 3 September, Motilal Nehru, a leader of this lobby, went to Howrah railway station to meet and brief his ally, Jinnah, who had come by train. The two agreed to join forces with C. R. Das, Annie Besant and Malaviya against Gandhi. They met and decided that very day that, while they would accept non-co-operation in principle, they would not agree to Gandhi's programme.

Gandhi reached Calcutta in the company of his Khilafat comrades. At the 'request' of Shaukat Ali (Gandhi always preferred a 'request') he drafted his famous non-co-operation resolution on the train itself. He asked for a seven-point programme: surrender of honours and nominated posts; boycott of official and semi-official functions; gradual withdrawal of children from schools and colleges; withdrawal from the courts (a measure aimed at the lawyers who packed the Congress leadership); no recruitment for army service in Mesopotamia; withdrawal by candidates from elections to reformed councils and boycott by voters; and boycott of foreign goods. Lala Lajpat Rai opened the Congress on Saturday 4 September but did not exercise his option of a presidential address. He himself was with the anti-Gandhi phalanx but felt it was his duty to become an 'impartial ringmaster' during the bitter battle ahead. The war began, with all the ferocity Indian politics is capable of, on 5 September, with the arguments in the subjects committee. Gandhi went into battle with a determination which shook everyone. Khaparde noted in his diary that Gandhi was trying to dominate the discussions; it was not a situation the old guard could quite swallow. Gandhi made excellent use of his favourite ace: that tiny voice called conscience which at the end of the day would be his final arbiter. If the majority voted against him, well, he said, he would then be guided by his conscience. The Congress leaders would have to keep Gandhi with them on his terms or watch him depart. C. R. Das led the opposition to Gandhi in the subjects committee, but when the vote was taken on 7 September, Gandhi barely scraped through, by just twelve votes: 144 against 132. All the Muslims in the committee, barring Jinnah, voted for Gandhi, but this by itself would not have been enough. Gandhi's victory came thanks to a critical last-minute defection, which occurred on the morning of the vote and took the old guard completely by surprise. The man who had switched and given Gandhi this historic victory was Motilal Nehru. With him had come enough minor defections to tilt the vote in Gandhi's favour.

Outside, in the open session, Gandhi did not need any help. There were 20,000 delegates under the *shamiana*, the largest gathering in Congress history, as also the largest Muslim contingent ever. They were massively for Gandhi. During the speeches, even Annie Besant was shouted down. The voting here was an elaborate affair which took six hours, but Gandhi won handsomely on 9 September: by 1,855 votes to 873. His comment at the session was, in fact, the obituary of an era of Congress politics: 'I do not rely merely upon the lawyer class or highly educated men to carry out all the stages of non-co-operation. My hope is more with the masses.' A dejected Jinnah told the special session of the Muslim League held concurrently in Calcutta as per the 1916 practice: 'There is no other course open to the people except to inaugurate the policy of non-co-operation, though not necessarily the programme of Mr Gandhi.'

At the regular Congress session at Nagpur in December, Jinnah tried hard to reverse the Gandhi tide. On the eve of the Nagpur session he wrote in reply to a conciliatory letter from Gandhi:

Our extreme programme has for the moment struck the imagination mostly of the inexperienced youth and the ignorant and the illiterate. All this means complete disorganization and chaos. What the consequences of this may be, I shudder to contemplate . . . I have no voice or power to remove the cause; but at the same time I do not wish my countrymen to be dragged to the brink of a precipice in order to be shattered.

Perhaps it was this reference to the ignorant and the illiterate which made Jawaharlal write a decade later in his autobiography: 'The enthusiasm of the people struck him [Jinnah] as mob hysteria. There was as much difference between him and the Indian masses as between Savile Row and Bond Street and the Indian village with its mud-huts. He suggested once privately that only matriculates should be taken into the Congress.' The contempt Jawaharlal developed for the Jinnah kind of politician is obvious.

Overwhelming popular support had its impact, and the pro-Gandhi mood had become a storm by the time the regular year-end Congress session at Nagpur came around. This session had the highest percentage of Muslims ever: 1,050 out of 13,532 delegates. Anti-

Gandhi Congress leaders were booed off the rostrum at Nagpur. No one felt this humiliation more keenly than Jinnah. While Gandhi, now firmly a Mahatma, could barely be heard for the cheers, Jinnah was not allowed to speak. He was 'howled down' with boos and cries of 'Shame, shame!' He was literally driven off the platform, while Gandhi watched. The moment of Gandhi's triumph was thus also that of Jinnah's defeat. Twenty-seven years later the world would see precisely the opposite happen: Jinnah's greatest triumph coincide with Gandhi's greatest defeat. Jinnah was so disgusted at Nagpur that he took the next available train to Delhi along with Ruttie. He would never return to this Congress Party which had branded him a coward. As far as the Muslim League session, still taking place in the vicinity, was concerned, Jinnah did not even go there. No one of any consequence was with the League. Nothing was happening there.

September in Calcutta and December in Nagpur signalled a liberation for Jawaharlal, and in more senses than the purely political. When, on 7 September, Motilal switched to the side of Gandhi, he joined not only a new politics but a totally new life. No one is sure why Motilal changed, but it is clear from reading his letters that he had realized that if he did not stand by Gandhi at this vital juncture he would lose his son. To the marginal extent that coincidences have their impact on the course of history, Jawaharlal's commitment to Gandhi, more than anything else, led Motilal to the Gandhi camp; the disciple had, in other words, helped the master at the very outset. Personally, Motilal could not quite swallow Gandhi. The epicure was on the eve of his sixtieth birthday, too late to develop suddenly a taste for the ascetic. Motilal had struggled and worked enormously hard to achieve the opulence of his life-style and had little desire for sacrifice. Jawaharlal was born into luxury; for him it was the ascetic who held the romance of challenge. But Motilal was nothing if not a man of commitment. Once he had decided, he became a Gandhian with a vengeance, at least for a while.

The change was as quick as it was dramatic. Motilal's youngest child, Krishna (later Krishna Hutheesingh), was withdrawn from school, the legal practice was wound down, and he resigned his seat on the provincial council. This, in effect, met the terms of the non-co-operation resolution. Motilal was determined to go the extra mile, however. Anand Bhavan underwent a radical change. The wine cellar disappeared, along with all the paraphernalia of luxury: crystal, china, horses, carriages and the wardrobe. From now on, there would be no competition with the Jinnahs in Savile Row suits; homespun, turned into *kurta*, pyjama and dhoti, would serve. The cuisine became simple and vegetarian. Motilal mused on the change, not without a trace of wonder. He wrote to Gandhi from a health resort during a holiday in the summer of 1921:

> The brass cooker . . . has taken the place of two kitchens . . . one square meal of rice, dal, vegetable, sometimes *khir* [a milk and rice savoury] in the middle of the day, that of breakfast, lunch and dinner 'à l'Anglaise' . . . The *shikar* [hunt] has given place to long walks, and rifles and guns to books, magazines and newspapers (the favourite book being Edwin Arnold's *Song Celestial* which is undergoing its third reading). 'What a fall, my countrymen!' But, really, I have never enjoyed life better.

Motilal might have added that the Gandhi cap had replaced the London hats. Still, at least the Nehrus had not thrown away their Shakespeare along with their English baggage.

The women of the house, of course, loved this transformation. This was the Indian life-style which appealed to their instincts. For Jawaharlal the conversion was the triumph of right over doubt. Gandhi, on his part, never forgot the role Motilal had played in the Calcutta Congress. The Mahatma's revolution would undoubtedly have continued without Motilal's vote in the subjects committee: but his conquest of the Congress might well have been delayed. Gandhi would return the favour in precisely nine years' time.

Jawaharlal, his mind tuned by a secular Western education, his nature more comfortable in the company of Bertrand Russell than the Scriptures, was always uneasy about the use of religion by Gandhi in the Khilafat movement. He looked askance at the large number of religious leaders. 'I used to be troubled sometimes', he writes in his autobiography,

> at the growth of this religious element in our politics, both on the Hindu and Muslim side. I did not like it at all. Much that Moulvies and Maulanas and Swamis and the like said in their public addresses seemed to me most unfortunate. Their history and sociology and economics appeared to me all wrong, and the religious twist that was given to everything prevented all clear thinking. Even some of Gandhiji's phrases sometimes

jarred upon me – thus his frequent reference to *Ram Raj* as a golden age which was to return.

It was an image which the Muslim League would later adroitly exploit to charge Gandhi with really wanting to create a 'Hindu Raj' under the label of 'Ram Raj'. Gandhi was guilty of many things in his life, and indeed no one could have been as merciless about his mistakes as he was with himself, but to accuse him of wanting a Hindu India is about as slanderous as it is possible to get. That Gandhi was handing his present and future opponent, Jinnah, a weapon, however, was something that Gandhi's heir sensed early. He also realized he could do nothing about it and opted to busy himself in the roaring excitement of a tremendous popular upsurge. He simply ignored his own doubts about Gandhi. He wrote: 'Having put our faith in him we gave him an almost blank cheque, for the time being at least. Often we discussed his fads and peculiarities among ourselves and said, half-humorously, that when Swaraj came these fads must not be encouraged.' Some doubts were not merely about fads. Jawaharlal could not, for instance, accept the doctrine of non-violence in its absolute form. He recognized that a state had to have the means of protecting its integrity, and often through the use of violence. These compromises over Gandhi's philosophy were justified by the logic of means and ends, but the Nehru of 1950 is also visible in the Nehru of 1920.

Gandhi was always more than the sum of the parts. He transcended Hindu nationalism and Muslim revivalism and sought, out of the confusion of half-awake desires, to light the fuse of long-submerged Indian nationalism.

15 Prison: At Last

The history of the pre-independence Congress can be divided into two parts. The first, extending from 1885 to 1920, can be called the struggle for self-respect; the second, from September 1920 to August 1947, the struggle for self-rule. Allan Hume was a reformer. From the moment he joined the Bengal Civil Service in 1849, in his first posting, at Etawah, where he stayed for eighteen long years, he built a reputation as a friend of Indians. His scheme for elementary education won wide praise. He financed the teaching of over 500 children through 'voluntary taxes' from the *taluqdars*. The Hindi paper he began in 1859 was aptly named *Lokmitra*, or *People's Friend*. Even his private passion, ornithology, in a sense helped India; *The Game Birds of India* was a brilliant study which he published at his own expense (over £4,000). Hume was the father of the first Congress philosophy, whose ultimate ambition was an India ruled by an Indian élite within the British Empire. Gandhi, the father of the second stage of Congress, wanted to make it the instrument which would bring total freedom from the British. (Both fathers were vegetarian. Hume became convinced that eating flesh led to an 'intricate network of evils (bodily, mental and oral)', a sentiment Gandhi would have heartily endorsed.)

In 1920 Gandhi promised *swaraj* within one year, but refused to become specific about what it meant. As Jawaharlal recalls, he was 'delightfully vague'. Gandhi did not want to get entangled in debates over a clause here and a law there. He knew it was going to be a long battle, and that there was only one way to win it – through the support of the people. They would have to be educated first in strategy, in non-violence (otherwise British 'aeroplanes will then bomb the people, their Dyers will shoot into them, and their Smiths will uncover the veils of our women'). The very first thing Gandhi did with the Congress was to draft a new constitution, to make the structure more rational and democratic. As he explained in a letter to N. C. Kelkar on 2 July 1920: 'I have attempted to give the Congress a representative character such as would make its demands irresistible.'

He wanted to build both a new popular base and a new leadership which would replace the ageing lawyers – young men who would get out of the drawing-rooms and work among the masses. Jinnah was one person who understood that the Congress and its goals had changed. He asked at the Nagpur session in 1920, while challenging Gandhi's call for 'unadulterated' *swaraj*: 'Is it possible for us to stand on the same platform after this creed is passed, one saying that he wants to keep the British connection and another that he does not want it?'

Nineteen twenty-one was the year of khaddar (homespun), of the *charkha* (the spinning-wheel), of the Gandhi topi, of mass upheaval and of direct confrontation with the British. Jawaharlal Nehru was in the forefront. In fact, his political career coincides almost exactly with Gandhi's revolution. Both, in totally different and contrasting environments, searched for a path between 1915 and 1919 and then found their course – one as master, the other as disciple. Gandhi was the perfect navigator for Jawaharlal's nationalism. And it was a relationship which was strengthened by a unique dimension: love, the love of a father towards a son.

Jawaharlal rode the slogan of the year: 'Go to the villages!' He concentrated on the progress of the non-co-operation movement in his province, particularly in the villages. The peasant unrest had given him access. Khaddar, the cloth woven on the spinning-wheel (which Jawaharlal later described as the livery of freedom), was the uniform; *swaraj* and Khilafat were the battle-cries. Many villages could not quite understand what Khilafat meant – Turkey was obviously too distant a concept – but it was enough for them that the word sounded analogous to the Urdu word for 'opposition'. They wanted to oppose, and get their *swaraj*. The infection touched everyone. A station-master once found Jawaharlal stranded on the platform, having missed his train. Using rare abilities of improvisation, he put the young leader on a trolley which could roll along the tracks and which did in fact take Jawaharlal nearly thirty miles to his next meeting. (The unfortunate station-master lost his job later.) Spinning-wheels were distributed, shops selling foreign cloth picketed; bonfires of foreign cloth were common; and tailors were asked not to sew anything but *khadi*. This deep commitment around the concept of self-reliance later helped Jawaharlal to build an economy around the idea.

The Nehrus, already famous during their opulent years, had become heroes in their abstinence. India loves no one more than the man with nothing. (It will accept, follow, even occasionally admire the man who has everything; but what it will almost never do is tolerate any hypocrite in between.) In the summer of 1921 Motilal went to Almora to recover from a severe attack of asthma. It was a small town in the Himalayas, with the added advantage of having a nephew as the Indian civil servant in charge of the district – Shridhar Nehru, the young man whose brilliant academic career and success in the ICS had sent a paternal twinge of regret through Motilal's heart a decade before, when he compared them with his own son's indifferent academic abilities. The same Shridhar now seemed uncomfortable about hosting his mentor and winced each time a crowd gathered to glimpse Motilal and rent the air with a 'Jai!' ('Victory!').

Spirits in the nationalist camp were very high, and the government had begun to display nerves. The British were both puzzled and apprehensive. Fed on tales of the mysterious East, as labyrinthine in its lanes as in its minds, they refused to trust the apparent. A movement led by an unclad man spinning out cloth and political parables could not be what it seemed; this strange business of non-violence must be the camouflage behind which a great armed upheaval was being planned. Such fears led to a most amusing incident. Motilal, after duly consulting the stars, had fixed 10 May as the day for the marriage of his elder daughter Sarup (who later took the name Vijaylakshmi) to a barrister from Rajkot, Ranjit Pandit. Naturally, there was a large congregation of Congressmen from all over the country. This set off an absurd fear psychosis. A rumour spread through the town that these Congressmen had gathered in Allahabad for a sinister reason; 10 May would mark another armed uprising. Wasn't 10 May the anniversary of the Indian Mutiny of 1857? Even Englishmen who had so often enjoyed Motilal's champagne began carrying revolvers on their person, and there was talk of shifting the community to the fort for their protection.

Jawaharlal used the wedding guests for far less sinister purposes. He organized a district conference, presided over by Muhammad Ali and with Gandhi present. In September 1921 the Ali brothers were arrested once again, this time for trying to subvert the Indian Army. Both Motilal and Jawaharlal signed a manifesto (prepared by

Gandhi) pronouncing that the Ali brothers had done no wrong. The Viceroy, Lord Reading, wanted to split the movement along the familiar Hindu–Muslim lines, so Hindus were carefully left free.

The impending visit of the Prince of Wales finally forced Lord Reading to forget about such dubious distinctions. No one would be allowed to disturb the peace, not even Hindu Congressmen.

In a most interesting coincidence, another career was also just beginning. In the Prince's party on the 246-day tour was a 21-year-old cousin, Louis Francis Albert Victor Nicholas Mountbatten. (Albert and Victor were included at Queen Victoria's insistence; it was a pyrrhic victory, for he was never called by any of these names and became known as Dicky.) It would be a very happy sojourn for Dicky on his first visit to India. A year before, at a ball given by Mrs Cornelius Vanderbilt, he had met the spirited Edwina Ashley, great-grandchild of the Earl of Shaftesbury on one side and grandchild of the Jewish banker Sir Ernest Cassel on the other; in other words, she inherited noble blood from one side and money from the other – a perfect combination. Mountbatten could really boast only of his descent. The richness of royal blood in his veins was tempered by an absence of liquidity in the cash flow. She had more than 2 million pounds in inheritance, and he an annual income of £610, but true love conquered all. Edwina joined the Viceroy's house party in Delhi to be near her Dicky. The Prince of Wales approved of the match, though Lady Reading sniffed. As she wrote to Edwina's aunt: 'I hoped she [Edwina] would have cared for someone older, with more of a career before him.' In any case, it was an astrologer at the court of the Maharaja of Mysore, Professor Coomaraswamy, who had the last word. He made two predictions, that Dicky would marry soon, and excel in polo. Professor Coomaraswamy was right. Dicky did both. On 14 February 1922, at the Viceroy's Palace in Delhi, Dicky proposed and Edwina accepted. A large silver cup was filled with champagne; seventeen élite guests sipped half of it, and Dicky drained the other half (next morning he promised never to do anything so silly again).

Not all that far from Delhi, at that moment Jawaharlal was nursing his father in a British gaol. He and Mountbatten did not know one another then, but their lives would become deeply intertwined in a personal and political relationship which would have the most significant implications for the destiny of India.

Jawaharlal was so eager to be arrested that even the Viceroy could not have prevented it any more. Lord Reading had stopped the United Provinces government once, in June, from prosecuting Jawaharlal for seditious articles in *The Independent*. But, by November, Jawaharlal's volunteer squads were successfully closing down town after town with one hartal after another. The visit of the Prince of Wales only spurred Jawaharlal to greater anti-government activity. This was clearly unacceptable. Thanks to Jawaharlal, the movement was most successful at Allahabad. The 'volunteer boards' were declared illegal on 22 November, and on 6 December 1921 father and son were arrested for the first time in their lives. The once-reluctant Motilal now felt as exhilarated as his son. As early as 24 June of that year Motilal had written to Tej Bahadur Sapru saying: 'Jawaharlal and I both know what is coming and are prepared for it.' On the morning of the 6th George Joseph, then editor of *The Independent*, Purshottam Das Tandon, Syed Kamaluddin Jafri and Gauri Shankar Misra were picked up. Motilal was in his office at Anand Bhavan that afternoon examining papers put up to him by M. S. Godbole, the office secretary of the All-India Congress Committee, when a servant announced that the police were at the door. It was the police officer who was a bit nervous, but he did not forget to be polite. 'Adab arz,' he said, using the Urdu form of greeting, and then showed Motilal a search warrant. Motilal replied that he would be happy to open his house for a search, but if they really wanted to do justice to the idea a thorough search would take at least six months in Anand Bhavan. The officer did not know how to react to this witty sarcasm but finally managed to convey that he had arrest warrants for father and son too.

Having got up very early that day, at four, Jawaharlal had spent the morning writing the accounts of Swaraj Sabha and working on his Jallianwala research. After a short while in the office he went to the district court to attend the trial of Kapil Dev Malviya and was pleased at the high spirits of the Congressmen. 'The poor judge in a bad way,' he recorded in his diary. 'He appeared to be the convict and the prisoners the judges.' On his return to his office he got the first intimations of trouble; the police had searched the Congress office in his absence. He continued working, writing letters, arrest still far from his mind. He had just completed a note to his friend Khaliquzzaman saying that he was coming to Lucknow on the 8th, when excited messengers brought news that Anand Bhavan was being searched. Bechu, a family servant, came soon after; Motilal had sent for his son. He reached Anand Bhavan at about 6.30 p.m. Motilal was eating his now sparse evening meal, of bread and milk, and giving last-minute instructions. Everyone seemed excited rather than depressed. Kamala was very composed and 'behaved admirably'. Only two people were visibly upset: Swarup Rani, whose face had lost colour, and little Indira, who irritably refused her food. Father and son were given a warm and emotional farewell as they went off in a car. Motilal left a message for his countrymen: 'Having served you to the best of my ability, it is now my high privilege to serve the motherland by going to gaol with my only son.' Swarup Rani held back her tears; this was not a moment for the display of any weakness. A journalist interviewed her as her husband and son were being taken away. Yes, she said, she felt the 'wrench of separation'. Then she added, 'Mahatma Gandhi told me once that others in the world have also their only sons.'

The government had prepared its case very badly against Motilal in the improvised court room of K. N. Knox, I C S. (Jawaharlal was tried in Lucknow, where he was taken on the night of the arrest.) The government advocate, Banerjee, was visibly edgy. His main witness, an illiterate called Kirpa Ram Bahadur, held the document upside down as he formally 'verified' Motilal's handwriting. Motilal could have torn apart the case but he cheerfully refused to defend himself except to note that the whole show was a farce. He was sentenced to six months' imprisonment and a fine of Rs 500. Since, as a non-co-operator, he would not pay the fine, the authorities in a display of petty vindictiveness seized carpets and furniture worth many times more the next day from Anand Bhavan. Motilal requested, and received, only one concession through the brief trial: he kept his four-year-old granddaughter, Indira, in his arms while the farce was conducted. She was the only one to protest angrily when the police vandalized their home.

Gandhi, on hearing what had happened, invited the Nehru women to come over to Ahmedabad, where the Congress session of 1921 was being held. That was the first time in their lives that the ladies travelled by third class in a train.

The Nehrus were now heroes, and the youth, in particular, had found their idol: Jawaharlal. It was his first journey to a prison, but there would be many more trips before freedom came a quarter of a century later. Between December 1921 and August 1942 Jawaharlal was sentenced nine times. He spent 3,262 days of his life in the gaols of Lucknow, Naini (Allahabad), Bareilly, Dehra Dun, Almora and Gorakhpur in the United Provinces, Ahmednagar Fort in Bombay state and, worst of all, in the princely state of Nabha. The first term lasted 87 days: from 6 December 1921 to 2 March 1922; the second extended between 11 May 1922 and 31 January 1923; the third, in Nabha, was a short spell of 12 days between 22 September and 4 October 1923; the fourth went on for six months from 14 April to 11 October 1930; the fifth followed quickly after, between 19 October 1930 and 26 January 1931; the sixth was a long spell, from 26 December 1931 to 30 August 1933; the seventh was more than a year and a half, from 12 February 1934 to 4 September 1935; the eighth came after the beginning of the Second World War, from 31 October 1940 to 3 December 1941; and the last internment was by far the longest, a full 1,040 days after the Congress had told the British to quit India – from 9 August 1942 to 15 June 1945. Nine of the prime years of his life were spent in British prisons, but not once did he flinch from the sacrifice, even through moments of deep depression and loneliness. Jawaharlal's war for freedom went on for more than twenty-five years, and the price was heavy. There were desertions along the way, and long moments when nothing seemed possible but failure and more failure. In the end, however, it was the British who collapsed, exhausted.

The official reason for Jawaharlal's first arrest was that he was distributing a pamphlet in Lucknow urging a boycott of the visit of the Prince of Wales, scheduled to be in Lucknow on 9 December. The handbill, titled 'Mahatma Gandhi's Order', demanded that it was 'our national and religious duty to observe hartal in the city with peace and perseverance'; and 'those who will not do so will be considered guilty in the eyes of God and the country'. As the police sub-inspector Hari Singh testified before Mohammad Shafi, the Lucknow city magistrate, when the trial began on 15 December, he had seen 'Pandit Nehru, the accused, distributing notices with others near the Congress office in Holaganj on 3 December 1921'. The others were Khaliquzzaman, Syed Mohammad Nawab and Dr Shivaraj Narain Saxena of Wazirganj. They had also been seen travelling up and down the city in a car distributing those handbills. A charge was brought under Section 17(2) of Act XIV of 1908, which prohibited participation in an 'unlawful association'.

'Are you a member of the Central Volunteer Board, appointed on 24 or 25 November 1921, to organize Volunteer Corps in the United Provinces?' the government asked the defendant.

'I do not recognize the British government in India, and I do not regard this as a court. I regard these proceedings as farce or show. This court carries out what has only been decided,' replied Jawaharlal.

'Did you attend a meeting of the Congress Committee on 3 December 1921 in Lucknow?' the accused was asked.

'I do not wish to give a reply to this question, or to any question,' answered Jawaharlal.

And that of course should have been that. But it was not quite. By the time he delivered the judgement on 17 December, the magistrate realized that he had been prosecuting Jawaharlal under the wrong clause; the relevant provision, considering the evidence produced, was Section 17(1) and not Section 17(2). The difference was not ornamental. The maximum imprisonment for the first was six months, while for the second it was three years. The mistake did not bother the judge. He had tried Jawaharlal under one clause but convicted him under the other. Jawaharlal was sentenced to six months' imprisonment and a fine of Rs 100, with another month in gaol for default.

On 3 March, Jawaharlal was released after a revising authority admitted that he had been wrongly sentenced. The release, however, brought little joy. For during these eighty-seven days of prison Mahatma Gandhi had done the unthinkable; he had called off the non-co-operation movement. The Mahatma's reason? Indians were not yet ready for *swaraj*. His evidence? A small village called Chauri Chaura.

16 Chauri Chaura: Withdrawal Symptoms

The incident took place on the night of 5 February 1922. The village of Chauri Chaura, which has become an indelible part of the history of the nation, was then an unknown and remote hamlet in the backward district of Gorakhpur in United Provinces, and it took time for word to filter through. The world learned of it only on the morning of the 8th. Gandhi did not wait. He had started his movement on 1 August 1919 without asking the permission of the Congress. Gandhi ended it without asking anyone either. Congressmen were furious at his arbitrary behaviour, but no one dared challenge him. On 11 February, the Congress working committee quietly substituted the revolutionary call of mass civil disobedience with a 'constructive programme' of spinning, temperance, education and reform. They hated the thought, but no one could conceive of breaking with the pious dictator. As usual, Gandhi produced a rationale no one could argue with. To do anything else, he said, would be to succumb to the voice of Satan.

All his exhortations notwithstanding, violence had erupted in the course of this eighteen-month movement: at Ahmedabad, Viramgam, Kheda, Amritsar . . . The worst incidents took place in Bombay on 17 November, when the Prince of Wales arrived; fifty-eight were killed. 'This *swaraj* stinks in my nostrils,' was Gandhi's instinctive reaction to the Bombay violence. The incident at Chauri Chaura became the cut-off point. A procession had been taken out in the village in support of civil disobedience. As it passed the police station, an altercation arose between the constables on duty and stragglers at the tail-end. Words were exchanged which soon became taunts, and these led to scuffles. The stragglers called out to the other processionists for help, and they returned. The constables took fright and opened fire into the crowd to disperse it. But they were not prepared for such a confrontation, and their ammunition soon ran out, at which point they ran and took shelter in the police station. The enraged crowd set the station on fire. Twenty-two constables perished, either burnt alive inside or hacked to pieces when they tried to escape the burning trap.

Gandhi decided that he had no choice left now. He blamed himself for having condoned the violence of the past and went on a self-purification fast for five days. 'I must undergo personal cleansing. I must become a fitter instrument able to register the slightest variation in the moral atmosphere about me,' he wrote in *Young India* of 16 February. It was not only the pressure of morality, he continued: 'The tragedy of Chauri Chaura is really the index-finger. It shows the way India may easily go, if drastic precautions be not taken.' Others, particularly new converts like Motilal, were not easily going to understand or accept a decision like this without protest. Motilal's logical mind simply could not fathom why a whole nation's effort should be penalized for the errors of a single village in Gorakhpur. Jawaharlal could conceal neither his amazement nor his anger. He, unlike Gandhi, did not consider non-violence more than a strategy, a policy. He could not find a rational answer from Gandhi to his bitter questions. If one Chauri Chaura was sufficient to stop this massive, nation-wide struggle for freedom, then the British could always employ *agents provocateurs* to sabotage the freedom movement.

Gandhi was convinced about what he was doing. His humiliation, in any case, was greater than anyone else's. Annie Besant had taunted him at the Ahmedabad Congress barely six weeks before, saying, '*Swaraj* was to arrive on 30 September or 1 October; on 31 October; on 31 December, at the Congress; it is as far off as ever.' After the session the anti-Gandhi group within the Congress actually sought the help of Jinnah, whose bona fides with the government were naturally excellent, to mediate a settlement with the British, and Jinnah and Malaviya convened an all-party conference on 14 January in Bombay. They wanted to buy peace with the British by ditching the Ali brothers, who were still in gaol; but Gandhi insisted that their release had to be one of the main conditions for any settlement. Side-stepping the January deadlock, Gandhi now went ahead with his plans for a different and complementary struggle: the Bardoli civil disobedience campaign. His task was still the same – to drive the fear of 100,000 Englishmen on Indian soil from the hearts of 320 million Indians. On 1 February 1921 Gandhi sent an ultimatum to the Viceroy that the Bardoli campaign would begin, unless the government conceded his demands. By 6 February the government had rejected every demand. Gandhi reached Bardoli on the 7th and sent his final letter to the Viceroy. The nation was again on edge, waiting for the climactic confrontation between the fakir and the Lat Sahab. Then suddenly, because of Chauri Chaura, Gandhi withdrew all his disobedience campaigns on 8 February. If ever there was an anti-climax, this was it. What is interesting is that Gandhi wrote to pacify Jawaharlal in gaol on 19 February, but not to Motilal.

The British of course celebrated this victory which had come from an 'own goal'. Lord Reading was now convinced that Gandhi had run out of steam, and he would have found enough buyers for his proposition in the gloom of withdrawal. Lord Birkenhead and Edwin Montagu taunted India that Great Britain had the 'vigour' and 'hard fibre' to show Gandhi his place. Gaol, which was to come on 10 March, was something of a relief to Gandhi. He would not be able to launch another national movement like this for another decade – and, when he did so again, he assured Jawaharlal that no Chauri Chaura would come in the way this time. However, in 1922 Gandhi still had to deal with the frustrations of one group who had idolized him, trusted him completely and believed he could, and would, deliver: the Muslims.

The Congress–Khilafat movement had been a unique achievement in the long and tortured history of Hindu–Muslim relationships. The gestures which the two sides made to each other were extravagant, and both leaders and ordinary people went out of their way to demonstrate their unity. Brahmins asked Muslims over to their homes for meals. Swami Shraddhanand was invited to address a congregation at the Jama Masjid. The Ali brothers travelled, like Gandhi, to every corner of the country. Muhammad Ali had made a typically flamboyant promise at the Amritsar Congress in 1919 after his release. 'I have come from prison,' he said, 'with a return ticket.' He now declared: 'After the Prophet, on whom be peace, I consider it my duty to carry out the commands of Gandhiji' (Afzal Iqbal, *Life and Times of Mahomed Ali*, 1978). As a gesture to Gandhi, Muslims were urged to stop eating beef. Many Muslim leaders, like M. A. Ansari (president of the League in 1920), deserted the League completely, and Hakim Ajmal Khan, who was a member of the 1906 delegation to the Viceroy, became Congress president in 1921. More important, the generation which was to take over in 1947 – Jawaharlal, Azad, Rajagopalachari, Patel, Rajendra Prasad – was blooded in this movement. Azad's oratory was different from Ali's but no less moving. Always handy with labels, the Muslims named him Amir-ul-Hind (Leader of India). Azad used parallels from the Prophet's life extremely effectively to promote the new spirit. He spoke of how the Prophet had prepared a covenant with the Jews of Medina after his migration from Mecca, in pursuit of the concept of *ummah vahidah* ('one nation'). 'Thus, if I say that the Muslims of India cannot perform their duty unless they are united with the Hindus, it is in accordance with the tradition of the Prophet, who himself wanted to make a nation of Muslims and non-Muslims,' declaimed Azad.

There was one significant difference between the philosophy of Muslims and that of Gandhi: the former did not see non-violence as more than useful policy. For Gandhi non-violence might have been a religion, but Islam had no argument with violence in the cause of justice. Gandhi's decision to call off the movement after Chauri Chaura was, consequently, even more bitterly inexplicable to the Muslims than it was to Nehru. Gandhi's lieutenants were confident that dominion status for India was within reach if the mass campaign pushed the British hard enough. Britain finally surrendered after the Second World War, but it was exhausted after the first Great War too. The British themselves acknowledged privately how close Gandhi had come to success. The governor of Bombay, Lord Lloyd, put it all together in these words: 'He gave us a scare. Gandhi's colossal experiment came within an inch of succeeding' (quoted in Michael Brecher's biography, *Nehru*, 1959). And if Gandhi had travelled another inch? India would have begun to come into its own simultaneously with Lenin's Soviet Union and Mustafa Kamal Pasha's Turkey (who embarrassed the Khilafat activists by going one step ahead of the British and destroying the sultanate itself). Self-government in 1922 would have meant a united India forged by a movement created by Gandhi and Motilal and Muhammad Ali, with a great generation of successors, not one marked at birth by religious violence, with Jinnah and Jawaharlal stumbling through blood. In his solitary cell in Bijapur, Muhammad Ali, who had been rearrested on a charge of sedition on 14 September 1921 at Waltair, could not understand the 'surrender'. In fact, Gandhi had been with Ali when the police came to arrest him; they were on their way to Malabar. Gandhi commented on that moment, writes Iqbal: 'With a smile on his lips he waved goodbye. I understood the meaning. I was to keep the flag flying.' The two were going to Malabar at a very difficult time. In August the Muslims of Malabar had revolted, first against the government and then, as the passion of violence released other long-suppressed frustrations, turning against Hindu landlords amidst chants of an independent Muslim state. In a long frenzy as many as 2,339 were killed by the official count alone. Yet such was the mood of India then that this barely disturbed the Hindu–Muslim unity in the north of the country where communal passions were traditionally more volatile. The Bardoli mass civil disobedience programme was partly Gandhi's response to the arrest of the brothers. Now suddenly the flag had been lowered. The Khilafat conference was defeated.

The government of Lord Reading had wanted to arrest Gandhi as early as 12 February in response to pressure from Montagu, who in turn was reflecting the anger in England. Orders, the Viceroy reported to the Secretary, had in fact been sent to the Bombay government for Gandhi's arrest on the 14th, but the Indian members in the Viceroy's Council protested, and the decision was postponed. Such an environment was extremely conducive to rumours. On 9 March in an article for circulation Gandhi asked the people to turn the day of his imminent arrest into a day of rejoicing rather than anger. The next day the police turned up at Sabarmati. Gandhi had a word each with all the inmates, asked everyone to join in a hymn written by Narsinh Mehta, gave a special hug to Hasrat Mohani, the Khilafat leader who was visiting Sabarmati, and got into the car with Kasturbai, who was allowed to accompany him till the prison gates. Gandhi took with him one extra loincloth, two blankets and five books: the *Gita*, the *Ramayana*, the Quran, Sabarmati's hymn book and a copy of the Sermon on the Mount. In the court records he described himself as a farmer and a weaver, and the famous trial began on Saturday 18 March before C. N. Broomfield, ICS, ending with the judgement that is a tribute to British honour. Judge Broomfield's remarks have become legendary:

> The law is no respecter of persons. Nevertheless it will be impossible to ignore the fact that you are in a different category from any person I have ever tried or am likely to have to try ... There are probably few people in India who do not sincerely regret that you should have made it impossible for any government to leave you at liberty.

But the law was served along with honour, and Gandhi was given a

six-year sentence. The poet Sarojini Naidu was in the court room
when her 'beloved master' was sentenced. Tendulkar (*Mahatma*,
1969) quotes her description:

> The most epic event of modern times ended quickly. The pent-up
> emotion of the people burst in a storm of sorrow as a long, slow
> procession moved towards him in a mournful pilgrimage of farewell,
> clinging to the hands that had toiled so incessantly, bowing over the
> feet that had journeyed so continuously in the service of his country. In
> the midst of all this poignant scene of many-voiced and myriad-hearted
> grief he stood, untroubled, in all his transcendent simplicity, the
> embodied symbol of the Indian nation – its living sacrifice and sacrament
> in one.

Gandhi was released prematurely, on medical grounds, on 5
February 1924, after an operation for acute appendicitis, but by
then the world was a different place. Muhammad Ali was Congress
president for the 1923 session at Coconada, and Gandhi himself
the next year, at Belgaum in 1924, for the only time in his life. For
all the words of mutual praise, however, the relationship was quali-
tatively different; it was now marked with unease at best, suspicion
and anger at worst. As usual, Gandhi himself was most frank. From
his hospital bed he wrote to Ali in his first letter after his release:
'This unity, which I fondly believed in 1922 had been nearly
achieved, has so far as the Hindus and Musalmans are concerned,
I observe, suffered a severe check. Mutual trust has given place to
distrust.' It was all going to be downhill from now. A series of
riots in early 1924 reflected the new but growing bitterness, and
the Hindu–Muslim violence in Kohat in the North-West Frontier
Province was so bad that Gandhi went on a 21-day purification
fast 'as prayer to Hindus and Muslims not to commit suicide'.
Always in the quest for symbols, he chose Muhammad Ali's house
in Delhi, quite deliberately, as the venue of his fast. His host was
furious, afraid that if Gandhi did not survive the Hindus would
explode and revenge themselves on him and on Muslims. But
Gandhi always moved men with his sheer sincerity; as soon as he
came to stay, the whole Ali household became vegetarian, and on
the last day of the fast, as a special gesture, Muhammad Ali bought
a cow from a butcher and sent it to survive at a cow-home. Even

so, the Kohat riots finally separated Gandhi and Ali. They came to different conclusions on who was guilty. Two years before, this would have been unthinkable.

Just after his release in February, Gandhi went to recuperate at the Bombay beach-house of one of the most important Indian industrialists, Ghanshyam Das Birla. Like so many other national leaders, the Nehrus too came to visit Gandhi here. One day, recalled Birla in a short memoir written for a volume of birthday tributes to Nehru, published in 1949, Gandhi turned to him and said, 'Do you know Jawaharlal?' Jawaharlal was sitting in a corner of the veranda, reading a copy of the *Bhagavad Gita*.

'I have only seen him from a distance, never met him,' replied Birla.

'Then,' ordered Gandhi, 'meet him and try to become friendly to him.'

Gandhi was, of course, thinking ahead, building the bridges which would help a young man he loved walk into a difficult future. It was the young man who could not always understand. He was eager to follow, but found the master disappointingly hesitant to lead. In his autobiography, Jawaharlal describes this period with some irritation: 'Gandhiji did not resolve a single one of my doubts. As is usual with him, he refused to look into the future, or lay down any long-distance programme. We were to carry on patiently "serving" the people.' The ironic punctuation marks around 'serving' point to Jawaharlal's state of mind. The young man in his thirties had been 'serving' for three years without getting anywhere. It was, moreover, a time of doubt on every front. Stalwarts like Sir Tej Bahadur Sapru and Srinivasa Sastri were busy praising the Empire in return for rewards. Sapru told the Imperial Conference in London in 1923 that 'I can say with pride that it is my country that makes the Empire imperial.' Pride? During Gandhi's years in gaol the Congress had fallen into the old morass. 'In the place of ideals there were intrigues,' writes Jawaharlal, 'and various cliques were trying to capture the Congress machinery by the usual methods which have made politics a hateful word to those who are at all sensitive.' Gandhi's own role was under question. The British thought they had ended this particular menace. In a telegram to Whitehall, Lord Reading described the Congress mood: 'disintegration and disorganization set in; enthusiasm evaporated; disillusionment and discouragement prevailed in the ranks.' The masses were still with Gandhi, but how was anyone to know that?

The old dispute over whether to contest the elections and enter the councils or not revived. Those opposed to Gandhi in September 1920 demanded their price; now that non-co-operation had failed, they wanted another round of co-operation. The issue was resolved by the formation of the Swaraj Party, essentially a party of Congressmen co-operating with the government to the extent of contesting elections. Motilal and C. R. Das were the chief Swarajists. Jinnah might have been with them, but he had already drifted too far away from the Congress and would sit in the Council as an independent, though often working in co-operation with the Swarajists.

Jawaharlal was adrift and literally sought the bleak comfort of the Empire's prison as some anchorage. 'One feels almost lonely outside the gaol, and selfishness prompts a quick return,' he said during his statement at his second trial. Well, the Raj was happy enough to oblige.

After his release on 3 March 1922, Jawaharlal concentrated on that part of the movement which had not been withdrawn, the boycott of foreign cloth. This was one of the shrewdest decisions of Gandhi, because while it attacked economic exploitation, it simultaneously brought the peasant and the weaver into the forefront of the anti-British struggle. Jawaharlal saw the whole point and later explained it extremely well to his daughter in a letter written from prison on 1 December 1932 (collected in *Glimpses of World History*, Kitabistan 1934–5, under the title 'The Indian Artisan Goes to the Wall'). The impact of Romesh Chundra Dutt's work on the history of the Indian economy was very visible on Jawaharlal. In the eighteenth century India was a great manufacturing and agricultural country; its handlooms spun the finest cloth for Asia and Europe. 'Weaving', said Dutt, 'was the national industry of the people and spinning was the pursuit of millions of women.' This India was converted by the Raj, wrote Jawaharlal, into

> just a consumer of British goods. The machine did not come to India, as it might have done in the ordinary course; but machine-made goods came from outside. The current which was flowing from India, bearing Indian goods to foreign countries, and bringing back gold and silver, was reversed . . . The textile industry of India was the first to collapse before this onslaught.

This in turn led to de-urbanization; the deprived artisan had to return to the village, increasing the pressure on land. Agriculture had always been buffeted by the vagaries of weather, and poverty was the normal condition. Now poverty deteriorated into famine. As has been well documented by others, the British Raj in India began and ended with the most colossal famines known on the subcontinent. Not all of them can be attributed to the infidelities of the white man, but there is sufficient evidence for an extremely good case against him.

On 23 June 1757 Robert Clive defeated Siraj-ud-Daula at Plassey and extracted a fortune in gold and 882 square miles of land, the twenty-four *parganas*, from the puppet successor Mir Jafar. The first chronicler of British oppression was Macaulay himself. As Annie Besant pointed out in her introduction to *How India Wrought Her Freedom* (1915), the Report of the Famine Commission of 1880 had recorded eighteen major calamities, and there were four more by the turn of the century. More than 10 million died in Bengal in 1770. Madras was hit in 1783, Oudh in 1784, Bombay and Madras in 1792, Bombay again in 1803, north India in 1804 and Madras in 1807. In 1813 it was Bombay's turn again, and Madras felt the lash in 1823 and 1833. (The latter year was particularly gruesome; half the population of Guntur district was wiped out, and the dead lay unburied and uncremated on the streets of Madras.) A million people at the least died in the north in 1837. It was back to Madras in 1854, and in 1866 one-third of Orissa died, along with half a million in Madras, making a toll of one and a half million. More than a million died in the north in 1869; a million went in Bengal in 1874; and it was much worse in Madras in 1877. In 1889 Madras and Orissa suffered; in 1892 Madras, Bengal and Rajputana. In 1896-7 almost the whole of British India was hit. And in 1899 north India, Central Provinces and Bombay reeled with hunger.

Instead of only making fiery speeches, like Annie Besant, Gandhi tapped this terrible anger and powered the national movement with it. What galled the patriotic intelligentsia further was the conclusion, in the words of Asoka Mehta and Achyut Patwardhan (*The Communal Triangle in India*, 1942), that 'twice in less than a century, India was conquered by the British with *Indian money*'. First India paid for the Company armies which campaign by campaign reached Delhi, and then the country was burdened with the cost of suppressing the Mutiny. (The latter was estimated at Rs 40 crores.) There was also the constant drain of India's wealth towards London; the Company was earning £30,000,000 per year by the 1850s and remitting 11⅔ per cent back to England. Under the rule of the Crown it was worse. By 1876–7 £13,500,000 was going to London out of annual revenues of £56,000,000, or 24 per cent. The impoverishment in the villages took on an extraordinary magnitude by the turn of this century. Even the government figures for the landless labourers showed the number rising from 18.69 millions in 1901 to 46.50 millions by the time Gandhi launched his movement twenty years later. To turn foreign cloth into the symbol, and consequently the target, of non-co-operation was as brilliant a device to give a real meaning to freedom as it was possible to conceive. Gandhi understood the people of India, and their hunger for both God and Mammon, perfectly. His politics were constructed around this perception.

In August 1921, under the pressure of Jawaharlal's volunteers, the cloth dealers of Allahabad had taken a pledge not to purchase foreign cloth till the end of 1922. A *vyapar mandal* (business association) was set up to ensure compliance of the oath through fines or, when this failed, picketing. As soon as non-co-operation was withdrawn and Gandhi arrested, the merchants reverted to the old ways. In March 1922 some of the dealers bought foreign cloth. On 25 April the recently released Jawaharlal announced in a speech at the Swaraj Sabha grounds that picketing would begin the next day. On 2 May the police seized a pamphlet signed by him and two others, Bishambar Nath Bajpai and Raghunath Prasad Kapoor, asking, 'Ap kidher hain?' ('On which side are you?'). On 11 May, Jawaharlal went to Lucknow to visit his father, who was still serving his sentence. During the visit the gaol superintendent asked him to step out. At the gate of the gaol the police were waiting. Jawaharlal was charged under Sections 116, 117, 385 and 506 of the Indian Penal Code – for abetting an offence, extortion, threatening citizens and criminal intimidation. The now familiar K. N. Knox, who had sent Motilal to gaol, was in the magistrate's seat. The charge-sheet was read, and the accused was asked, 'Do you plead guilty?'

Jawaharlal replied, 'I refuse to plead.' All he asked for, on 17 May, was an opportunity to make a statement but 'not in order to defend myself . . . I do not recognize this court as a court where justice is administered.'

On the occasion of his first arrest Jawaharlal had sent messages to his province and to his city; but this statement was addressed to India, the first such message in a life which would be overcrowded with them. British censorship could not dilute the impact. He began by saying that when he had come to India from Harrow and Cambridge less than ten years before he was 'as much prejudiced in favour of England and the English as it was possible to be' and 'perhaps more an Englishman than an Indian'. The speech became a powerful description of the distance Jawaharlal had travelled since then. He was now a Gandhian and a nationalist:

Loyalty is a fine thing. But in India some words have lost their meaning and loyalty has come to be almost a synonym for treason to the Motherland, and a loyalist is he who is not loyal to his God or his country but merely hangs on to the coat-tails of his alien master. Today, however, we have rescued the word from the depths, and in almost every jail in India will be found true loyalists who have put their cause and their faith and their country above everything else . . . England is a mighty country with her armies and her navies, but today she is confronted with something that is mightier . . . We are fighting for our freedom, for the freedom of our country and faith . . . India will be free; of that there is no doubt, but if England seeks the friendship of a free India she must repent and purge herself of her many sins, so that she may be worthy of a place in the coming order of things. I shall go to jail again most willingly and joyfully. Jail has indeed become a heaven for us, a holy place of pilgrimage since our saintly and beloved leader was sentenced . . . I marvel at my good fortune. To serve India in the battle of freedom is honour enough. To serve her under a leader like Mahatma Gandhi is doubly fortunate.

K. N. Knox delivered his judgement at 9.30 in the morning of 19 May: eighteen months' rigorous imprisonment and a fine of Rs 100 or three further months. The others, sentenced to lesser terms on the same charges, were Keshav Dev Malaviya, Khudayar Khan, Bhairon Prasad, Munni Lal, Ananadi Prasad, Chhote Lal, Amar Nath and V. S. Venkat Rama Iyer. Jawaharlal had got the long sentence he wanted – and become a hero of the country. Motilal discovered his son's new eminence when he went on a nation-wide tour later that year. For the first time in his life he was cheered, in Delhi, because he was Jawaharlal's father. The young man who had been so diffident about speaking in public in 1916 had come a very long way; on

Wednesday 17 May 1922 the nation heard an orator created not by tricks or techniques but by the love of his country. There was, in fact, more wrong than right in the technique. His voice was feeble and often could not be heard. But the force of his sincerity, the strength of his patriotism and that glorious turn of phrase lent a unique dimension to his speeches. Motilal, who was once so disappointed that his son could not make it into the Indian Civil Service, could now say, 'On reading your statement I felt I was the proudest father in the world.'

17 Among the Heavyweights

Jawaharlal's second spell in prison ended prematurely too. On 31 January 1923, after serving just half his term, Prisoner Number 4,126 was released, thanks to a general amnesty announced by the United Provinces government for 107 political prisoners. Gaol had been bad for his physical but good for his intellectual health. Jawaharlal used the time to indulge a very catholic taste in books. He kept a diary which provides a detailed account of his life in the district gaol of Allahabad (till 20 May) and Lucknow. To cure his body he took homoeopathic treatment (mainly arsenic and sulphur, 'according to Father's written directions', as the entry for 16 July 1922 puts it) and stuck to very simple fare. There was spinning and physical exercise in the mornings – running and walking. He fasted often, including joining Muslims during a Ramzan fast. Most of the time went on newspapers, journals (*New Statesman*, *The Nation*, *Modern Review*) and a colossal range of books: history (Havell's *Aryan Rule in India*, Bryce's *Holy Roman Empire*, *Babarnama*), classics, poetry (the Romantics in particular), politics and religion (the Bible, the Quran and the *Gita*). There was a profusion of arbitrary reading too. The isolation of gaol always brought out the poet in Jawaharlal, though his favoured form of expression was prose. In the evenings he gazed at the stars or dreamt about the holidays he would enjoy when free; he even drew up a long itinerary for a visit to the motherland, Kashmir.

The authorities made sure that all this idyllic life was restricted purely to the imagination. It was a difficult existence. First there was the utter lack of privacy in a barrack. Then, later, as one of the seven most difficult 'trouble-makers' he was transferred to separate confinement. 'The food', he remembered, 'was quite amazingly bad.' His mother was of course very upset but advised him to celebrate his birthday with penance, so he kept aside five rupees for charity. But his colleagues in gaol made a grand day of it, even preparing a special meal and putting up illuminations. It was now that he wrote his first letters to his daughter, Indira. For instance: 'To dear Indu, love from her Papu ... Have you plied the new spinning-wheel which Dadu [grandfather] has brought for you? Send me some of your yarn. Do you join mother in prayers every day?' It was this practice which would flower into two of the greatest classics of Indian writing: first, *Glimpses of World History*, in the 1930s, and then *The Discovery of India* in the 1940s. Jawaharlal exercised his mind with notes on the wide range of books he went through. Occasionally there was the sad experience of cruelty. A minor breach of discipline by a teenager who had styled himself Azad ('free') was punished by fifteen lashes inside prison. 'He was stripped and tied to the whipping triangle, and as each stripe fell on him and cut into his flesh, he shouted "Mahatma Gandhi ki jai." Every stripe brought forth the slogan till the boy fainted.' This lad would enter the pages of India's history as the *brahmachari* revolutionary Chandrashekar Azad (1906–31), who along with Bhagat Singh and Ramprasad Bismil made the Hindustan Socialist Republican army a terror for the British. When Azad was betrayed and surrounded by the police in Alfred Park on 27 February 1931, he shot himself rather than surrender.

The first letter that Jawaharlal chanced to see at home upon his release from gaol was from Sir Grimwood Mears, by now the chief justice of Allahabad High Court, inviting Jawaharlal to drop by and see him as frequently as was possible. A story was then current in English circles that the real reason why the champagne-drinking Motilal had become a nationalist was because he had been refused membership of the European Allahabad Club. This was patently absurd. The incident went back to the 1890s when Sir John Edge, then chief justice, had tried to persuade Motilal to become the first to break the barrier, but Motilal had declined, saying he did not want to join a club where his application might be blackballed by any subaltern. There had been a quarter-century of wining and dining with Englishmen after that, so the club affair could hardly have been responsible for a sudden attack of nationalism. Still, the English clearly did not want to take any chances with the son. Sir Grimwood hinted at a straight deal: would Jawaharlal give up the Congress and like to become education minister in the provincial government? The British had been successful with others; even old lions like S. N. Bannerjea had left the Congress to become ministers, as he was in Bengal between 1921 and 1923. As for the liberals, they were very liberally helping the Empire. But Jawaharlal's nationalism was too secure, although he did yearn for the chance to do something constructive rather than spend his whole youth in challenge. 'Destruction and agitation and non-co-operation are hardly normal activities for human beings,' he wrote in his autobiography. Yet he was reconciled to the idea that his own life might be spent on the shifting sands of struggle, and the building might have to be left to be 'done by our children or our children's children'.

In the meantime, the Congress was split. Jawaharlal, along with Maulana Azad, sought to maintain an 'atmosphere of charity and goodwill' between the two groups, but both commodities were in very short supply, particularly since men like C. R. Das were convinced that Gandhi's unorthodox methods would hurt rather than help progress towards *swaraj*. It was not Motilal but C. R. Das who tried hard to persuade Jawaharlal to join the new party; perhaps the father knew the strength of his son's loyalty to Gandhi. The son was, in fact, depressed and confused, and he tried to camouflage his frustration. He became general secretary of the All-India Congress Committee in May 1923 and launched into his job with excessive zeal.

One of the things Jawaharlal tried to do as general secretary was abolish the use of 'Mahatma' before Gandhi's name. It was not just the 'Mahatma' he was after, though, but the whole lock, stock and barrel of titles acquired by virtue of either caste or religion or wealth. And so, no 'Maulana' for his president, and no 'Pandit' for himself, no 'Sheikh' or 'Syed' or 'Munshi' or 'Moulvi' or even the newly popular 'Sriyut' and 'Shri', not to speak of 'Mr' and 'Esquire', said the circular he sent. This was the agnostic egalitarian at work, determined to root out artificial distinctions from the Congress. Wiser counsel prevailed, and did so by order. Muhammad Ali directed him by telegram to stop such changes at once and never, but never, to address Gandhi as anything but Mahatma. Jawaharlal learned this lesson quickly, and henceforth the 'Pandit' in front of his own name was left undisturbed.

One thing about which Jawaharlal had no doubt was that he would not break with Gandhi. Gandhi had won against his father before 1920 and was doing so again. The tension between father and son flared up once more, forcing Gandhi again to intervene. As late as 2 September 1924 Gandhi wrote to Motilal:

This letter like the former is meant to be a plea for Jawaharlal. He is one of the loneliest young men of my acquaintance in India. The idea of your mental desertion of him hurts me. Physical desertion I hold to be impossible. Needless to say Manzar Ali [Sokhta, a friend of Jawaharlal] and I often talked of the Nehrus when we were in Yeravda. He said once that if there was one thing for which you lived more than any other, it was for Jawahar. His remark seemed to be so true. I don't want to be the cause direct or indirect of the slightest breach in that wonderful affection.

Nevertheless he was. Jawaharlal would have loved nothing more than agreement between Gandhi and his father, whose stand had been in many ways vindicated by the handsome victories won by the Swarajists in the November 1923 elections, but Gandhi refused to compromise then. Jawaharlal had, in addition, to face the ridicule of those, like Sardar Patel, who were unencumbered by Swarajist fathers. No wonder, as S. Gopal mentions, Jawaharlal remarked to his friend Sri Prakasa, 'I wish we would not hurt each other's hearts so easily and constantly.' With the self-deprecation of an Englishman, Jawaharlal wrote to another friend, A. M. Khwaja, on 6 June 1923:

> I am developing into a kind of 'Pooh-Bah' [a character in Gilbert and Sullivan's *Mikado* who had more jobs than he knew what to do with]. They forced me to take up the working secretaryship of the AICC at Bombay. When I say I am going to resign from the Municipal Chairmanship, there is a howl and I am told that it might almost result in a petty riot. Meanwhile I must carry on the Provincial Congress work and of course I cannot desert the Allahabad Town Congress Committee of which I am president! A pleasant outlook! I am thoroughly distressed and troubled.

In August he would repeat the sentiment in a letter of condolence to Mahadev Desai on the death of the latter's father: 'I am weary and sick at heart.' Fortunately, chance threw in Jawaharlal's way that year work which could utilize his distracted energies. He became chairman of Allahabad's municipality. It was his first spell in public office – and he proved good at it.

Following the Swarajists, the Congress in United Provinces decided to contest the local bodies and municipal elections. Needless to add, they won. The man first selected by the party as its candidate for municipal chairman, Purshottam Das Tandon, was opposed by the Muslims. For the first time but certainly not the last, a consensus was eventually possible only on a Nehru. Less than an hour before he became chairman Jawaharlal was not even aware that he was in the running. That was the year when Congressmen captured the cities: C. R. Das became mayor of Calcutta; Vithalbhai Patel president of Bombay Corporation; Vallabhbhai Patel mayor of Ahmedabad. Complaining initially that this job would divert his energies from the national struggle, Jawaharlal slowly began to enjoy the pleasures of constructive work. Typically, among the very first things he did was publicly rebuke his colleagues for idleness. (Though they forced him to recant, he had made his point.) He laid down his policy: no patronage, no favours and no hypocrisy. One vice-chairman, Zahur Ahmed, learned to his cost that bluff would not work with this man; when, in a huff, he offered his resignation, Jawaharlal accepted it, and Ahmed had to plead to be retained. On 24 April 1923 Jawaharlal noted:

> I have been pestered with applications for appointments ... Chits and recommendations have been brought to me from friends and attempts have been made to influence me in favour of various applicants ... Personally I have an almost unconquerable aversion to the 'chit' system. Nearly everybody in India gives a testimonial and nearly everyone flaunts these 'chits' in the face of a long-suffering people. I would suggest that such 'chits' or testimonials should be made taboo.

When the municipal employees wanted a holiday to mourn Jallianwala Bagh's anniversary, he said a flat no: they were interested only in a holiday, not in mourning. Any sign of excessive Congressism (like proposing to sit on the floor rather than on chairs) was rejected; but khaddar of course was encouraged. The bureaucrats found him a surprisingly good boss – as they would later too – though he was severe on incompetence. Two employees of the dispatch department were suspended for delaying a letter. 'No kind of effective work is possible', Jawaharlal said in an official note, 'unless our office is run on business lines.' And it was in this job that he first displayed another trait; while he was willing to protect officers from trivial harassment he could as easily become the champion of the people against negligent administration, playing both administrator and agitator in a double role.

One of the most endearing campaigns Jawaharlal undertook as chairman was on behalf of the city's prostitutes, who were being subjected to one of those periodic fits of morality that mark a hypocritical establishment. Since you could not realistically abolish the practice, Jawaharlal maintained, the proper thing was to treat the problem sensibly. Start clinics for venereal disease, he suggested, prevent prostitutes from going near schools and colleges, try to check soliciting. He would allow no injustice to prostitutes. There was an effort to prevent one, Akhtari Bai, from purchasing a house in Mohalla Chowk. Jawaharlal brought out the book and pointed out that the law of sales and purchase did not discriminate against a prostitute buying a house anywhere, and it was a perfectly legal transaction. He lashed out against the double standards which men adopted: 'Prostitutes do not carry on their ancient trade by themselves. They are only one party to the transaction. I seldom hear anything against the other party, the man who exploits the poor woman and casts all the blame on her.' In this note in a file dated 10 June 1923 he added: 'I do not believe in issuing a fiat that prostitutes must not live in any part of the city of Allahabad except a remote corner. If this is done I would think it equally reasonable to reserve another part of Allahabad for the men who exploit women and because of whom prostitution flourishes.'

Jawaharlal introduced national songs and symbols into the city life. Iqbal's 'Sare Jehan se acha Hindustan hamara' ('Our Hindustan is the most beautiful place in the world') became a part of the school curriculum. The 1st of August (Tilak's death anniversary) and 18 March (the day Gandhi was sentenced) were declared public holidays. He snubbed the British by organizing civic addresses for Congress leaders, and pointedly ignored a visit by the Viceroy Lord Reading to the city. He sent a note to the Board on 25 October 1923 which ended: 'I am weak and powerless but I too have a little pride – the pride of the weak perhaps it may be. And I would sooner be trampled by Lord Reading's soldiery and ground to dust, rather than bow down to welcome a person who was responsible for so much sorrow to my country and countrymen.' Spinning and weaving became a part of school education; everyone was slowly infected by the 'new spirit'. Water, roads, finances, redressing the grievances of horse-carriage drivers, preparing the bathing-ghat for the Kumbha *mela*: the chairman was everywhere. He eventually relinquished office in January 1925 to concentrate on national politics, but the memory of this experience lured him to try again for the job in 1928. When he had not wanted it in 1923 he was forcefully elected. When he wanted it in 1928 he was defeated – by one vote.

Within all this 'Pooh-Bah' activity, Jawaharlal still had found time for yet another trip to gaol. A special session of the Congress was held in Delhi in September under the presidentship of the 35-year-old Maulana Azad: the youngest president in its history, but one who proved adept at organizing the compromises which had eluded Jawaharlal. The highlight of Jawaharlal's trip north for this session was a 'strange and unexpected adventure' in the small princely state of Nabha in the Punjab. The British agent in charge was a man called J. Wilson Johnston (1876–1933). Johnston, ICS, was the power behind the throne in Nabha. It was a petty throne, but that made him admirably suited to the job, for he was a petty man.

The princely order of British India did not quite cover itself with glory. By the twentieth century many of its scions were either perverts or caricatures, and very often both. Waste and the most puerile form of sexual excitement seemed their dominant passions, and their only apparent interests were the quality of their horses, the number of their women and the potency of their aphrodisiacs. The British were most content with this state of affairs. Perhaps most notorious of all was Patiala; it was also one of the most favoured families. Later, its ruling prince, Maharaja Bhupinder Singh, would become the chancellor of the Chamber of Princes during the partition discussions. One of the more dramatic things the ruling prince of this clan apparently did was appear naked once a year in front of the people to display the size of his penis, suitably reinforced for the occasion with doses of *shilajat*, an aphrodisiac made from herbs grown in the remote Himalayas. But the British needed men like him and were happy to oblige when he wanted a sworn enemy of his, Maharaja Ripudaman Singh of Nabha, deposed. The British placed a minor on the throne and sent Johnston as administrator to run the state.

The Sikhs of Punjab had in 1920 started a major agitation against the control of their *gurdwaras* by Hindu *mahants*. They had good reason, for the *mahants* had far more time for extortion and lechery than for the Sikh faith. The British supported the *mahants*, and a confrontation developed. The Sikhs conquered the imagination of the nation by the manner in which they won their battle – through an extraordinary display of non-violence. Groups (up to a maximum of 100), called *jathas*, would take a vow of non-violence in a *gurdwara* in the morning and then set out for an appointed spot to offer arrest there. The police might try to drive them away with cudgels and lathis and even open fire, but they would hold their ground. It was this show of courage and discipline that Jawaharlal wanted to see. For a change, he was not seeking gaol; he was more a political tourist.

The special Congress over, Jawaharlal left on 19 September for Nabha along with two friends, K. Santhanam and A. T. Gidwani (1891–1935, for many years principal of Gujarat Vidyapith). They reached Muktsar by train, where they addressed a Sikh meeting on the 20th. The next day, travelling by horse and bullock cart, they proceeded towards Jaito where *jathas* from many places were scheduled to congregate. About three miles from Jaito they came across one such *jatha* and decided to walk with it the rest of the way. When the police stopped this *jatha*, Jawaharlal and his friends stepped aside and sat under a tree to see what would happen next. The police asked them what they wanted. Nothing, they replied; just looking. At that moment the superintendent of police came up and ordered them to leave Nabha immediately. Actually, they had no plan to stay – their train tickets for a return journey to Delhi had been booked for that very evening; but on hearing an 'order' Jawaharlal's blood rose. He said he did not intend to leave Jaito right then and would wait till the time came to catch the train. All three were arrested under Section 188. When Jawaharlal's two friends protested that there was no written order for their arrest, the district magistrate pronounced, very promptly, an *oral* order under Section 144 for breach of peace. The reason for arrest given was that they were Congressmen and, consequently, bound to make trouble. Johnston's worry was not the law but this now famous nationalist leader. He was Dyer's child and relished the opportunity to flaunt Britain's power. The three were handcuffed, Santhanam's left wrist tied to Jawaharlal's right, and a policeman led them through the streets by a chain and put them on the evening train from Jaito to the main city, Nabha. It was, as Jawaharlal recalled, like 'a dog being led by chain'.

Jawaharlal had done at least one sensible thing already. From the police station at Jaito he had sent off two letters, one to his wife Kamala, and the other to his father. The theme was the same: 'Please don't worry.' But that was clearly asking too much of the proudest father in the world. Motilal had seen the vagaries of the legal system all his life, and he knew how vicious it could get in vindictive hands in a princely state. He was not wrong. The handcuffs were taken off only after twenty hours. Jawaharlal's cell was 'small and damp, with a low ceiling which we could almost touch. At night we slept on the floor, and I would wake up with a start, full of horror, to find that a rat or mouse had just passed over my face' (from *An Autobiography*). The trial was 'most extraordinary and Gilbertian', except that this was very black comedy. The judge was illiterate and terrified of the English administrator; he would do nothing, howsoever minor, without checking. (In any case, the normal practice in Nabha was summary arrest and detention without trial, which was the general fate of the supporters of the deposed maharaja.) Motilal sent off two telegrams before he boarded the Punjab Mail for Nabha on 23 September. One was to his old friend from the Jallianwala inquiry days, Harkishenlal, who had become a provincial minister. The other was to the highest authority of them all, the Viceroy. 'Expect there will be no interference or molestation by subordinate officials in exercise of my natural right,' the second cable said. The expectations were belied. On the 24th Motilal received a message from Johnston at his camp in the railway station waiting-room that he would be allowed to see his son only if he left Nabha state immediately afterwards. Motilal shifted to Ambala, from where he sent another telegram to the Viceroy accusing the authorities of conducting a mock trial. That, in fact, was putting it mildly. Late in the evening of the 24th, to take one instance, the charge against Jawaharlal was suddenly replaced by one under Section 145 of the Indian Penal Code; the authorities had discovered that the first charge was untenable even in Gilbertian Nabha. It finally needed the Viceroy's intervention to enable father and son to meet at Nabha gaol.

Motilal was stunned to discover that Jawaharlal was irritated about all that his father had done to get him out of gaol. The temptation to be a hero was overwhelming, causing a petulant Jawaharlal to become rude and insensitive to his father. He had prepared a very heroic draft statement to read in court – sample statement: 'I rejoice that I am being tried for a cause which the Sikhs have made their own.' Only Motilal's enormous love for his son could have persuaded him to swallow his substantial pride. He kept his temper in check, cut out the frippery from the statement and reshaped it into a cooler, more legally sound document. But he left Nabha deeply hurt and sent his son a letter dripping with some choice irony:

> My dear J., I was pained to find that, instead of affording you any relief, my visit of yesterday only had the effect of disturbing the even tenor of your happy gaol life. After much anxious thinking, I have come to the conclusion that I can do no good either to you or to myself by repeating my visits . . . Please do not bother about me at all. I am as happy outside the gaol as you are in it.

Jawaharlal was quickly contrite.

Meanwhile, Delhi instructed Johnston on the 24th to tell the judge to let Jawaharlal off with a mild sentence, nothing more than an expulsion order. Johnston was furious. He wanted Jawaharlal to serve a 2½-year sentence in that damp, rat-infested cell. But petty officials cannot argue beyond a certain point with a Viceroy, and Jawaharlal and his two friends eventually left by the night train on 4 October. As Jawaharlal noted in his autobiography: 'discretion was preferred to valour'. On both sides, it needs to be stressed. But the Nabha experience gave him an indelible insight into three realities: the raw edge of British rule; the tragic farce that existed in so much of 'Indian' India; and the quality of the Akali movement which emerged in this struggle. While the first may only have deepened his anger against British rule, the second and third played a significant part in shaping his mind for the struggle ahead. The goodwill that he built up with the Sikhs would be particularly useful in both pre-partition and independent India. The All-India Congress Committee now put him in charge of Punjab affairs. The Viceroy, for his part, was convinced that he had 'substantially defeated . . . Nehru and his son' by his generosity.

Whatever marginal chance there might have been of making *The Independent* work had been killed by the demands that politics made on father and son. Their frequent absence from Allahabad compounded the 'amazing degree of incompetence' in the management of the paper, and what ensued was a nightmare of squabbles. *The Independent* died in early 1923. Jawaharlal, who was a director, was profoundly relieved. It gave him much more time to concentrate on his work as general secretary of the party. Among other things, he immediately introduced a strange new element to the job: accountability for expenses from all the leaders. He even stopped a leader like Muhammad Ali's bills and answered protests by formally requesting him, through a letter on 7 March 1925, to lay down the norms – the class of ticket, the permissible reasons for travel (only to attend meetings, or also for doing other work, such as going to resolve Hindu–Muslim disputes) and whether the expenses of an accompanying servant were to be paid by Congress or not. As he wrote to Gauri Shankar Misra on 3 April 1925: 'You might be interested to know that among others I am troubling Muhammad Ali, Santanam, Mrs Naidu [Sarojini] and George Joseph for detailed accounts.'

Jawaharlal had good reason for caution. The Khilafat movement at that time had become embroiled in a scandal whose stink would become a permanent whiff in its history. The charge was that about Rs 16 lakhs of Khilafat funds had been embezzled. The Ali brothers were indiscriminate both in taking money and in spending it (which was why Jawaharlal was particularly chary). There was never enough, and becoming Congress president did not improve matters. Muhammad Ali wanted to revive *The Comrade* in August 1924 and could not; eventually the generosity of Haji Abdullah Haroon (who would become later one of the architects of Pakistan) and a donation of Rs 10,000 enabled *The Comrade* to appear in November. But the Ali brothers were also getting money at this moment from sources which were less than healthy. According to British government reports, the brothers were now supporting Ibn Saud in return for ready cash – much to the distress of colleagues like Hasrat Mohani, who had always opposed Saud as a British agent against Turkey. By May 1925, however, *The Comrade* was a shambles, and not much support was coming from the Muslim masses either, who suspected their money was being misused. On the day of Id in Delhi, in April 1925, Muhammad Ali could collect only 153 rupees. The deposed Maharaja of Nabha temporarily rescued Ali with a grant of Rs 6,000 in the hope that the brothers would do propaganda for his restoration. By January 1926 *The Comrade* had shut down. Muhammad Ali, though only forty-seven, was already a mental and physical wreck, his politics destroyed by confusion and betrayal, his health by diabetes. To compound his sorrow, his beloved daughter Amnae died on 11 March 1924. Events had overtaken the glorious phase of unity; the slogans of love had been replaced by the screams of hate.

One of the most perceptive modern political thinkers of India, the Communist leader Hiren Mukherjee, has noted in a monograph (*Was India's Partition Unavoidable?*, Calcutta: Manisha, 1987) that in the last two hundred years India has not produced a single outstanding atheist: the point being that religion was too ingrained in the Indian psyche to allow an ideology to develop totally outside its framework. Those who used the religio-political identity constructively built harmony, and from there created prosperity. Those who aroused the destructive dimensions of religion inevitably wounded the people. Gandhi put his finger on the former pulse. The 'mad wanderer' (as the Bengali poet Nazrul Islam described Gandhi) managed such a brilliant fusion of religion and politics in 1919, 1920 and 1921 that it lit hearts and created a national movement unknown in Indian history. By abruptly calling it off, however, he also signalled that neither he nor the country was yet ready for success. He had the moral strength to understand this. Others did not.

Maulana Azad, blunt and unsparing, said Gandhi had ruptured the Hindu–Muslim unity he himself had built. Yet Azad was one of those who remained by Gandhi's side all his life. Others fell prey to suspicion; suspicion slowly festered into anger; anger burst out in spasmodic violence. The communalists among both Hindus and Muslims, who had been driven into sullen silence by Gandhi, now re-emerged, particularly when Gandhi was in gaol. Those who had cloaked latent motives in Gandhi's shadow now reasserted their other selves. The Arya Samaji, Swami Shraddhanand, who had once preached unity from the ramparts of the Jama Masjid in Delhi, now returned to the original missionary purpose of this organization created by Dayanand Saraswati and relaunched the *shuddhi* and *sangathan* movements for purity and reconversion to Hinduism. Muslims, including a few who had been flag-bearers of communal unity, like Saifuddin Kitchlew of Amritsar, replied with the *tanzeem* and *tabligh* movements. (A contemporary and friend of Jawaharlal at Cambridge, Kitchlew joined the national movement as early as in 1912. His career took many turns before he died in 1963. Among his achievements was the Lenin Peace Prize in 1952.)

The elections of 1923, consequently, were fought amid mounting

Hindu–Muslim tension. The Swarajists under Motilal and C. R. Das won a handsome forty-two seats. Jinnah, a shoo-in from Bombay, formed a separate seventeen-member independent group in the Council. It is an interesting fact that Motilal had more Muslims with him than Jinnah: eight against three (out of which one soon died; so Jinnah really had only one other Muslim). Among Motilal's legislators was Nawab Ismail Khan of Meerut, who would play a critical role during the Jinnah–Jawaharlal confrontation over ministry-making in the United Provinces after the 1937 elections. The decline of Gandhi saw the resurrection of Jinnah, and for a year and a half there followed what can best be described as the phase of the 'co-operation movement'. Motilal and Jinnah joined forces in the National Assembly, which met for the first time in New Delhi on 31 January 1924; together, they could take on the thirty-six official appointees any time they wanted. By February 1924 they had forced Lord Reading to appoint a Reforms Inquiry Committee, headed by the home member Sir Alexander Muddiman, to 'take steps to have the Government of India Act revised with a view to establish full responsible Government in India'.

Jinnah rarely let an opportunity pass to express his now quite intense dislike of Gandhi. He even forced the Muslim League to abandon the practice of holding its session in the same city as the Congress when he learned that Gandhi would be president at Belgaum in December 1924. Motilal entreated, but Jinnah took the specious plea that it was too late to shift the venue back again. From this moment, relations between Jinnah and Motilal began to deteriorate. Motilal could not forgive this deliberate affront to Gandhi. But Jinnah was on the top of his little world. His prestige was high. Lord Reading had offered him a knighthood which he easily turned down (his response, 'I prefer to be plain Mr Jinnah', became famous); more to the point, he was confident that the Muddiman Committee would vindicate his view that *swaraj* and 'responsible government' would be achieved only through co-operation with the British and not through non-co-operation by half-naked rabble-rousers. The informal Jinnah–Motilal alliance withered. The reality of British will was brought home to its greatest co-operator when on 7 July 1925 the Tory Secretary of State for India, Lord Birkenhead, made it very clear in the House of Lords that there would be no immediate reform. David Page (*Prelude to Partition*, 1982) quotes Jinnah's speech on 8 September 1925 in the Council, his anger breaking through his normal icy calm:

> I ask Lord Birkenhead, I ask Lord Reading, what is your answer to those men who have co-operated with you? None. Your answer to me as one who has not non-co-operated with you is this: will you bring a section of the politically minded people, who happen to be the largest political party, will you bring them down to their knees? Will you bring Pandit Motilal Nehru to bow before the throne at Viceregal Lodge and say: 'Sir, I am humble, I crawl before you, and will you now graciously be pleased to give me a Royal Commission?' Is that what you want? What has Pandit Motilal Nehru been doing in this Assembly? Has he not been co-operating with you? . . . Have you no eyes, have you no ears, have you no brains?

The 'co-operation movement' was soon buried by the obstinacy of the imperialists. Gandhi, however, had little time for satisfaction. Other problems, simmering in the background, had worked their way to the fore. It was when he was presiding over the Congress at Belgaum that the Hindu Mahasabha emerged as a powerful force in the country's politics.

In 1905 Lord Curzon partitioned Bengal. In 1906 the British set up the Muslim League. In response, 1907 saw the formation of the United Bengal Hindu Movement and the Punjab Hindu Sabha (logical; Bengal and Punjab were the two great Muslim-majority provinces). The leaders of these groups were also Congressmen, and influential ones too. At the 1909 session in Lahore the president, Pandit Madan Mohan Malaviya, recognized the Sabha as a Congress forum. In December 1913, on the initiative of the Punjab Hindu Sabha, a historic meeting took place at Allahabad (what a city!) to launch an All-India Hindu Mahasabha. It had its first session next year in Hardwar, the holy pilgrimage centre where the Ganga emerges from the Himalayas. Sessions of the Sabha were held alongside the Congress after that; and Malaviya and Lala Lajpat Rai emerged as its principal leaders, products of the 'Lal–Bal–Pal' school of Extremist politics in the pre-Gandhi Congress. In 1923 the Sabha took its annual show elsewhere – for Muhammad Ali was to preside at the Kakinada Congress. It met instead at Benaras, with Malaviya as president and the Maharaja of

Benaras as the host. Among the important leaders in attendance were Dr Bhagwan Das, father of Jawaharlal's friend Sri Prakasa, Dr B. S. Moonje, the Arya Samaj leader Bhai Parmanand and, very interestingly, Dr Rajendra Prasad. (Much later, as the first President of India, Dr Prasad would object vehemently when Prime Minister Jawaharlal Nehru legislated reforms in the civil laws of the Hindu community.)

It was at Benaras that the Hindu Mahasabha formally adopted the programme which was to spark off riots all over India: *shuddhi*. The 1911 Punjab Census Report defined it thus: '*Shuddhi* is a Sanskrit word which means purification. In religious terminology it is now applied to (1) conversion to Hinduism of persons belonging to foreign religions, (2) reconversion of those who have recently, or at some remote period, adopted one of the foreign religions and (3) reclamation, i.e. raising the status of the depressed classes.' The most important activist was Swami Shraddhanand, born in 1856 as Munshi Ram. Within less than two months, by the last week of February, the proselytizers began work on a group called the Malkana Rajputs in north India: Muslims of Rajput stock who, socially and culturally, retained many Hindu practices – not the least of them being casteism, a practice forbidden in Islam. The elimination of untouchability was also one of the formal aims of the movement, but as Lala Lajpat Rai himself recorded, they were half-hearted about this. What they were full-hearted about was Muslims. At Belgaum they made it clear to Gandhi that they would not allow any more unity at the cost of 'Hindu' interests. Lala Lajpat Rai had published thirteen articles in *The Tribune* between 26 November and 17 December 1924 defining Hindu aims. A committee was set up. Its members included Lajpat Rai, C. Y. Chintamani, B. S. Moonje, N. C. Kelkar, Jairamdas Daulatram, M. S. Aney, T. Prakasam and Rajendra Prasad. Among the first things it did was sabotage an all-party conference called in Delhi on 23 January 1925 to iron out Hindu–Muslim differences. Chintamani went as far as to say that every future decision of the Congress would have to be ratified by the Sabha. Leaders like Malaviya began campaigning against the 'rights' that Muslims had acquired – for instance, that no music would be played outside a mosque during prayers, a perennial if thoroughly artificial cause of friction. At the Calcutta session in 1925, president Lala Lajpat Rai announced the full programme of the Sabha: to set up chapters all over the country; to organize relief for Hindu victims of riots; reconversion of those 'forcibly converted' to Islam (which in their interpretation meant virtually everyone); to start gymnasiums (on the health-is-strength principle); and to popularize Hindi. This became the manifesto of Hindu communalism. Long after the Sabha declined and was replaced in importance by organizations like the Rashtriya Swayamsevak Sangh, this was still the *de facto* programme of Hindu communalism. The Mahasabha was always quite explicit about Muslims. As Craig Baxter mentions in *The Jana Sangh* (1971), its president at the Ajmer session in 1933, Bhai Parmanand (1874–1948), explained: 'Hindustan is the land of the Hindus alone, and Musalmans and Christians and other nations living in India are only our guests. They can live here as long as they wish to remain as guests.' As for the language preferred by north Indian Muslims, the Mahasabha resolved: 'Urdu is a foreign language which is a living monument to our slavery. It must be eradicated from the page of existence. Urdu is the language of the Malechas which has done great harm to our national ends by attaining popularity in India.'

One of the most influential thinkers of the Mahasabha was Vinayak Damodar Savarkar (1883–1966), a Chitpawan Brahmin, son of a Sanskrit scholar, virulently anti-Muslim in his politics and a protégé of Tilak. Exiled in 1911 by the British to the Andaman Islands for his militant revolutionary activities, he returned to the mainland in 1924. He was barred from politics, however, and only in 1937 could he formally take over as president of the Hindu Mahasabha – the first of seven terms, until he retired in guilt after the assassination of Mahatma Gandhi in 1948. His major work, *Hindutva*, was published on his return in 1924 and became a guiding thesis to a generation of Hindu chauvinists.

As history is witness, these Hindu communal organizations never achieved the mass support among the Hindus of which they dreamed, which could carry them to power. Despite the heavyweights who were their leaders, from Malaviya to Savarkar to Shyamaprasad Mukherjee to N.C. Chatterjee to Guru Golwalkar, they, or their surrogates, were humiliated in election after election. At best their activists or sympathizers (like Rajendra Prasad) became influential within the Congress. They were never more than a fringe force. But what enormous damage they did from that fringe! The Muslim League exploited their propaganda to justify its secession; the poisonous propaganda of Hindu communalists was the nectar which would revive a dormant and disused League, before the British picked their creation up one last time and used it for a neatly executed endgame.

'Please do not Pandit me too much,' Jawaharlal wrote to his Oxbridge and Congress colleague K. M. Panikkar (later to serve as India's ambassador to China, France and Egypt) on 20 May 1924. The caste nomenclature was becoming popular in a country with deep reservoirs of reverence for the Brahmin, but at least privately Jawaharlal fought shy of the implicit bow to caste prejudice. He did not like his given name either. When he learned that his very dear friend Syed Mahmud wanted to name his son after him he wrote in a letter dated 3 June 1925: 'For heaven's sake don't call your son Jawaharlal. Jawahar by itself might pass, but the addition of "lal" makes it odious.' Depressed by the wave of Hindu–Muslim riots, he was bitter against the play of religion in the country's politics. In the same letter he told Mahmud: 'I have no idea who will preside at the Cawnpore Congress, nor am I very much interested.' The indifference was a comment on the acrid politics of those years.

Jawaharlal received a hero's welcome when he reached home after the Nabha experience. As he wrote to Sri Prakasa on 7 October 1923: 'I have returned to Allahabad twice before after serving much longer periods in gaol but nobody took much notice of my return. Yesterday, however, there was quite a seething mass of humanity at the station to welcome and embarrass me!' The elation was quickly dampened by surrounding realities. His presidential address to the United Provinces Congress in Varanasi on 13 October (which was read out; he was too ill with fever to attend) reflected his depression: 'In 1920 and 1921 we were full of faith and confidence. We did not sit down to debate and argue. We knew we were right and we marched on from victory to victory ... [But now] Senseless and criminal bigotry struts about in the name of religion and instils hatred and violence into the people.' It was not just Hindu–Muslim problems that had arisen; in Punjab tension was mounting between Hindus and Akalis, who were leading the reform movement among the Sikhs. Lala Lajpat Rai had begun urging the Congress to stop any help to the Akalis. On 27 March 1924 Jawaharlal wrote to Panikkar: 'You have already noticed the unfriendly feeling between Hindus and Sikhs. If possible you should try to induce the various Hindu and Sikh newspapers to refrain from hurting each other.' The newspapers did not stop. Fifty years later they would be largely if not chiefly responsible for the rise of the 'Khalistani' challenge to Indian unity. But as early as 2 April 1924 Jawaharlal had analysed the complex Punjab conundrum brilliantly. Punjab was a historical curiosity, and all its three communities suffered in some way from a minority complex. The Muslims, a majority in Punjab, were a minority nationally. The Hindus had the reverse syndrome. And the Sikhs were a minority in the grip of a dream – a land where they could rule as a majority. Jawaharlal's insight into this triangle was clean, free from bias or humbug. He wrote to Panikkar:

> I am inclined to think that you are right in saying that the Hindus in Amritsar are narrow-minded and are taking up an undesirable attitude. Still I think this is not the sole cause of the bad relations between the two communities. The Sikhs have been largely to blame. There have been times when a generous word or gesture from them would have brought over the Hindus to them. But they did not care to make it. Their movement is largely a separatist movement so far as religion is concerned and this has naturally reacted in the social and political sphere. The almost general belief amongst the Hindus that the Akalis are arrogant and in their pride do not care for the feelings and sentiments of the Hindus is not without foundation. Sikhs have not been keen enough to win the Hindus in spite of their professions. The bitterness of the Hindu against the Sikh and the Muslim is chiefly due to the realization of his utter weakness and humiliation, and being narrow-minded and bigoted this bitterness instead of urging him to better himself or make himself stronger turns to hatred and curses.

Decades later, this whirlpool is still spinning as viciously, at that same point in Punjab's psyche. Jawaharlal's analysis remains equally valid.

Jawaharlal's letters of this period often become an intimate form of reportage: narrative leavened with insight and opinion, an occasional smile or, more often, despair. On 12 September 1924 he tells 'Respected Bapuji' (he had begun calling Gandhi 'Bapu' or 'Father' by now) that he has refused to mediate in a Hindu–Muslim riot in Amethi, about fifty kilometres from Lucknow (and a constituency which both his grandsons, Sanjay and Rajiv, would represent in Parliament): 'Whom would I represent? The Hindus are not going to accept me, and why should the Muslims do so?' The frustration resulted from his experiences when he went to Moradabad and Sambhal on 8, 9 and 10 September to inquire about the Moharrum riots there. 'Prima facie the Hindus are the aggrieved party,' he accepted, but concluded that 'there was a considerable amount of lying on both sides'.

The story is ageless. The causes are almost always the same: music played before a mosque; or a stone thrown on a Hindu procession; desecration of a temple or a graveyard; or simply the right of way. But these incidents are only the visible rash on the body. The disease lies in the mind, and minds are influenced by the past and the future even more than by the present. As if these complications are not enough, sub-plots have their own ramifications. Take the following instance of the riot in Sambhal, whose story Jawaharlal went to find out and noted for an AICC file.

Sambhal is one of the very few surviving ancient towns, being mentioned as early as in the Puranas. Prithvi Raj built a fine temple there, which the Muslims subsequently converted into an equally fine mosque. Being ancient, it was full of pilgrimage places and sacred wells, and the Hindus believe that the next *avatar* will come from here. Shiva, with Ganesha on either side, is worshipped at the main temple; near by was a temple to Hanuman, who burnt Lanka in aid of Lord Rama. Right next to that temple was a graveyard. A little before the riots, a Hindu Sabha had turned some local Hindus into great supporters of the *shuddhi* movement. Encouraged, the Sabha started litigation to recover property which it claimed had been illegally appropriated by the Muslims. The tension was building. Bakr-Id, when Muslims sacrifice an animal to Allah after the fashion of Abraham, and Moharrum, when pageantry commemorates the battle of Kerbala, are the two occasions when the knives come out. During Moharrum the tension finally burst. Everyone knew it was coming: the constable, the subdivisional officer, the *pujari* at the temple, the drumbeaters in the Moharrum procession. At nine that night, the Muslims attacked the temple, threw one Hindu into a well (he was later saved), wounded seventeen, stripped the little a sadhu was wearing and stole Rs 1,305 in cash from him, chipped the image of Shiva and broke one of Ganesh, and then went off, their thirst satisfied. It was all over in about half an hour. In a typically Indian twist to this story, the subdivisional officer was asleep at home while all this was happening.

Of such trivia was hatred built. The consequences, however, were far from trivial. Jawaharlal was even more upset by riots in his own Allahabad which began virtually as soon as he returned from gaol, on 7 October, which was also the day of Dussehra that year. The 'peace' promised by leaders at the Delhi Unity Conference had had no effect on the masses. 'The contributory causes here', he said in his report, dated 19 October, to Gandhi on the Allahabad disturbance, 'have been the same as elsewhere – Sangathan and Aligol, separate *akharas* [gymnasiums] – and the deliberate preaching of distrust and fear.' The Hindu strategy, recognizing that the upper castes were not too eager to engage in battle, had changed: 'the Hindu Sabha might have expected that the lower classes – *chamars*, *pasis*, etc. – would be useful in a conflict with the Muslims. These classes, for the last few years, have been asked to take part in the Ram Lila processions.' It is only logical that this experience with the bitter side of religion drove Jawaharlal back to atheists like his favourite Bertrand Russell. As he wrote to Syed Mahmud from Geneva on 12 September 1926: 'I think what is required in India most is a course of study of Bertrand Russell's books . . . Religion as practised in India has become the old man of the sea for us and it has not only broken our backs but stifled and almost killed all originality of thought and mind.' He was now convinced that 'religion in India will kill that country and its peoples if it is not subdued'.

The situation in 1926 was as bad as, if not worse than, in 1925. Calcutta, always a volatile city, went through a severe bout. Muhammad Ali warned the Hindu Mahasabha that the Calcutta riots would be the precursor of a much bloodier war and asked the Muslims to prepare for such a war. Congress Muslims like Dr M. A. Ansari who refused to provoke such passions were dejected and silent; but Muhammad Ali had no such inhibitions. The Khilafat conference, at a special session in Delhi in May 1926, made an emotional call for 'self-defence' even as it passionately denounced Hindu Mahasabha and Arya Samaj leaders for having let loose this demon once again. The fact that this was an election year only made matters worse, since there were rewards to be reaped from communalism in a voting system based on separate electorates, and with the franchise limited to the upper and at best educated middle classes.

Punjab, with its triangular balance (or imbalance), became the deadliest vortex of religious passions. A pamphlet called *Rangeela Rasul* appeared which inflamed Muslims because of its utterly malicious and false attacks on the Prophet. The Raj watched with happy unconcern. When Motilal and the Swarajists in the Central Legislative Assembly proposed legislation to curb communalism, the home member actually turned down the idea on the grounds that it would be violative of civil liberty! Such worry about human rights had never disturbed the Raj before. Writers like the incomparable Prem Chand were hounded by the government, and he was eventually dismissed from the education department for his left-secular nationalism. But, then, the British understood too well the power of literature. It is not widely known, for instance, how they influenced one of the most controversial books of recent times, Bankim Chandra Chatterjee's *Ananda Math*. Chatterjee is a great hero of Bengali letters, but the *Ananda Math* is heavily biased against Muslims. The first version of the novel, published in *Bangadarshana*, however, exhibited nearly as much hostility to the British as to the Muslims. Chatterjee was a deputy collector in the Raj bureaucracy at that time and was told at once that such creativity would come in the way of promotions. Chatterjee deleted many of the anti-British references, and what finally emerged was largely an anti-Muslim work.

A high point of danger was reached when a Muslim fanatic, Abdul Rashid, killed the Arya Damaj leader Swami Shraddhanand at four o'clock on the afternoon of 23 December 1926 and then boasted that he was happy to have done so and looked forward to heaven as his reward. Gandhi immediately gave Lajpat Rai the responsibility of preventing Hindu revenge assaults in Punjab, and Rai did so successfully. Despite this, there were angry hartals in Karachi, Bombay, Kanpur, Varanasi, Patna, Roorkee and Jawaharlal's Allahabad. Jawaharlal captures the ruptured spirit of those times beautifully in his autobiography by describing the change that had come in the celebration of a festival which till then had been the common property of both Hindu and Muslim, Ram Lila:

How well I remember my visits to it, when I was a child! How excited we used to get! And the vast crowds that came to see it from all over the district and even from other towns. It was a Hindu festival, but it was an open-air affair, and Muslims also swelled the crowds, and there was joy and light-heartedness everywhere . . . And now . . . the children of Alla-habad, not to mention the grown-ups, have had no chance of seeing this show and having a bright day of joyful excitement in the dull routine of their lives. And all because of trivial disputes and conflicts! Surely religion and the spirit of religion have much to answer for. What kill-joys they have been!

It was inevitable that, at such a time, the thinly cloaked Hindu chauvinists would once again try to take over the Congress. Gandhi was dormant, the Swarajists had got nowhere in particular, and the flames were spreading outside. Jawaharlal thus describes the situation: 'The Congress was in a quandary. Sensitive to and representative of national feeling as it was, these communal passions were bound to affect it. Many a Congressman was a communalist under his national cloak.'

Motilal was dispirited too, but he had not lost his zest and was determined to challenge the Hindu Mahasabha Congressmen who had contested the 1926 elections under the label of the Nationalist Party. Motilal described the campaign in a letter to Jawaharlal written on 2 December 1926 (printed in *A Bunch of Old Letters*, 1958): 'It was simply beyond me to meet the kind of propaganda started against me under the auspices of the [Madan Mohan] Malaviya–Lala [Lajpat Rai] gang. Publicly I was denounced as an anti-Hindu and pro-Mohammedan but privately almost every individual voter was told that I was a beef-eater in league with the Mohammedans to legalize cow slaughter in public places at all times.' He went on to explain the larger ambitions of this group:

> The Malaviya–Lala gang aided by Birla's money are making frantic efforts to capture the Congress [at the forthcoming Guwahati session]. They will probably succeed as no counter-effort is possible from our side. I shall probably make a public declaration after the Congress and with it resign my seat . . . My National Union for Hindu–Muslim Unity is of course there but in the present state of communal tension my voice will be a cry in the wilderness. I shall consult Gandhiji but as you know his hobbies do not interest me beyond a certain point. You can hardly advise from the distance which separates us but I shall be glad to have your views.

As it so happened, Motilal's pessimism was unjustified. Although

Swami Shraddhanand's assassination had provoked intense communal bitterness (Motilal feared the greatest danger from 'the Bengal revolutionaries who have unfortunately been tainted with communalism to a very considerable extent'), the liberal Congressmen managed to stave off the Malaviya–Lala–Birla combination. As Motilal happily reported in another letter to his son on 30 December 1926: 'the Gauhati Congress has been a greater success than was expected. We have stood firm against all reactionaries and carried everything we wanted by overwhelming majorities.' Jawaharlal was not at Gauhati; he was taking a much-earned, though accidental, rest.

We must, in retrospect, be thankful for the physical distance which separated father and son then. For if Jawaharlal had been at Anand Bhavan these extremely revealing letters would not have been written. Fortunately for the endless stream of wordsmiths who would make use of some part of this letter to prove one point or the other, Jawaharlal, in December 1926, was in Geneva. The deteriorating tuberculosis of his wife, Kamala, had enforced this sojourn.

19 Europe: Pass Marx

'I wish you could give yourself and Kamala a holiday,' Gandhi wrote to 'my dear Jawahar' on 30 September 1925. (The Mahatma was then involved in yet another of his minor passions: writing with his left hand, so the letter was pretty much of a scrawl.) Jawaharlal was in a bad way, suffering from repeated bouts of fever. His wife Kamala was in even worse shape; her body was being eaten away by consumption. In November 1924 she had borne a son, but the baby died within a week. (The telegram of condolence from Gandhi read: 'Sorry about baby's death. God's will be done.') In the autumn and winter of 1925 she was forced to spend months in a Lucknow hospital. Finally they decided to take her to a sanatorium in Switzerland. Gandhi wanted Jawaharlal to take a break too. 'I expect great results from this trip,' he wrote to Motilal, 'not only for Kamala but also for Jawaharlal.' The results were such that Jawaharlal almost broke with Gandhi on his return – the only time in his life that this happened.

The Jawaharlal who sailed on 1 March 1926 from Bombay for Venice, *en route* to the mountain sanatorium of Montana and Geneva, was politically a complete Gandhian: his sympathy and concern for the poor born out of the morality of renunciation, his ideology conditioned by his visual rather than intellectual experience, his commitment to nationalism and economic change an extension of his liberal spirit. The year and three-quarters in Europe, to which he was returning after thirteen years, would give him the opportunity to rediscover what the rest of the world was thinking, as much as the time to find an individual mould for his own thinking. Apart from that burst of rebelliousness that provoked him to ignore Gandhi in the first flush of his return in December 1927, and which resulted in a severe rebuke from the Mahatma, Jawaharlal never stepped out of the Gandhi line again, but it was equally true that there was a distinctive Nehruvian thrust to the policies he now espoused. There was, of course, no need to disagree with Gandhi on the critical issues of the freedom movement:

the Hindu–Muslim question, or the strategy against the British. But there was disagreement over economic policy and the course to be followed as a free power. On foreign policy, Gandhi generally let Jawaharlal have his head.

Obtaining a passport was no problem. The British were still keen to keep Motilal in good humour. Jawaharlal was a little nervous about the Europe he would find after thirteen years, altered so dramatically by a great war and a great revolution; a continent now in the ferment of change, trembling between the pressures of new ideas and the obduracy of old institutions. He also wondered, in a letter of 29 January 1926 to his beloved friend Padmaja ('Bebee'), daughter of the great poet-nationalist Sarojini, how much he would miss his country: 'India is so like a woman – she attracts and repels.' For the moment he was content to ignore the attraction. He set up an inexpensive house in Geneva, took his daughter Indira, who had hardly seen him after about four, to school and back each day, nursed Kamala, wrote lots of letters, attended political lectures and courses, learned French and of course dipped heavily into his favourite authors. New prescriptions opened up for old ills. In the letter to Syed Mahmud of 12 September 1926 he said he had had enough of 'generosity of heart'; now he wanted it leavened by 'coldly reasoned tolerance'. Bread and education were the answers to the stranglehold of religion. 'Most of us', he wrote again to Syed Mahmud on 12 January 1927,

> acquire a smattering of the three R's and a little else during our years at school and college and consider that our education is complete and we are learned. In India especially the standard is extraordinarily low and I think most of our difficulties are due to this want of knowledge. Take Lajpat Rai's case as an example. He considers himself, I presume, a highly educated person and a keen political thinker and many others perhaps think likewise. My own opinion about him is that he has not sufficient intellectual or cultural background and is really a very badly educated person. Hence his peculiar behaviour in public life.

Jawaharlal also clearly defined his differences with Gandhi in that letter: 'I have become an even greater believer in khaddar than I was, but khaddar as an economic doctrine and not as an offshoot of religion. I have no patience left with the legitimate and illegitimate offspring of religion.'

A public airing of such views about the sacred cows of the Indian freedom movement would have been nothing short of blasphemy, but then Jawaharlal was not any kinder to the real sacred cows themselves. On 1 December 1926 he wrote from Montana to Devdas Gandhi:

> I wish the Cow Conference or the Cow Sabha or whatever it is called would send a deputation of the elect to have a look at the cow in this part of the world. It would do them good. And they might get some brighter ideas than keeping enormous *pinjrapoles* [a sort of old cows' home] for the halt and the lame!

This particular 'cow conference' had been presided over by none other than the Mahatma himself, at a special Congress week in Belgaum.

It was this distance from orthodox, caste-based Hinduism which made the Nehrus a particular target of the conservative Hindu lobby. The accusation of being 'beef-eating', 'un-Indian', 'pro-Muslim' and 'insensitive' to majority sentiment began with Motilal and has travelled down to every succeeding generation. The story of one such confrontation sums it up. On 20 May 1928 Jawaharlal had made yet another of his attacks on obscurantism, this time at a students' gathering at Bombay. Among the things he said were:

> I always feel irritated when anybody talks of our immortal past ... Much is said about the superiority of our religion, art, music and philosophy. But what are they today? Your religion has become a thing of the kitchen, as to what you can eat, and what you cannot eat, as to whom you can touch, and whom you cannot touch, whom you could see and whom not.

There was an uproar. One United Provinces Brahmin Congress leader, Gauri Shankar Misra, launched a campaign against Jawaharlal for abusing the 'superior glory of the Vedic religion' and Indian literature, rounding his accusations off by describing Jawaharlal as anti-Indian. In a devastating letter to *Abhyudaya* (published on 30 June, in Hindi) Jawaharlal first demolished Misra, before caustically signing off with this: 'I wish to state that Gauri Shankar Misra is mistaken in the idea that I was born in England. I have been told by persons, who should be considered reliable in this matter, that it was in the holy city of Prayag that I first beheld this world.'

Gandhi left Jawaharlal alone in these matters. It was clear that he was building Jawaharlal up; he gave his protégé a great deal of rope as he launched into his intense affair with socialism.

The means were unclear and being debated, but the idea of equality, of redistribution of wealth, was part of the intellectual vision that was emerging in India at the turn of the century. Giants like Rabindranath Tagore recognized its appeal. In the ferment of the nationalist struggle of 1905 there was also heard a call for a 'toilers' republic'. In 1907 the twelfth International Socialist Congress was held at Stuttgart with all the familiar faces present: Rosa Luxemburg from the host country, Jean Jaurès from France and Vladimir Ilyich Lenin with the Russian delegation. The unfamiliar participant was India; a Parsi lady who lived in Paris, Madame Bhikaji Rustom Cama, and Sardar Singh Rana constituted the formal delegation, while a brother of Sarojini Naidu, Virendranath Chattopadhyay, better known as 'Chatto', attended as an observer. The last day of the three-day session, 22 August, was devoted exclusively to India, and Madame Cama made a tremendous impression with her fiery oratory. The man who led the opposition to a resolution on Indian nationalism, and in fact sabotaged a vote on the motion, was Ramsay MacDonald. (No wonder Gandhi would warn Jawaharlal after his return from Europe not to put too much faith in British socialists: all their class rivalries disappeared when it came to imperial exploitation of India. It would be MacDonald, after all, who would fertilize the seeds of separation with the Communal Award.)

Lenin kept in touch with Indian nationalists of all hues: socialists like Chattopadhyay, pan-Islamists and revolutionaries like Maulana Barkatullah and Raja Mohendra Pratap. (Books gifted by Pratap to Lenin can still be seen in the latter's personal library preserved at the Kremlin.) The success of the Bolsheviks naturally had a tremendous impact on Asia. Moscow began to see a red glow in the East; and in October 1920 a combination of socialists and Muslim Muhajirs formed the Communist Party of India in Tashkent. The growing influence of the Soviet Revolution was best summed up in a short story written by the brilliant Bengali poet Kazi Nazrul Islam, who was serving in the wartime army and was stationed in Karachi in 1918; 'Byathar Dan' ('The Gift of Pain') is the story of an Indian who crosses the mountains across Central Asia and joins the Red Army. Brilliant young men like M. N. Roy (1887–1954) and Sripat Dange turned to the cause. The Chief of Intelligence, Government of India, Cecil Kaye, reported to his government: 'In UP and Bengal, the Kisan Sabha and Ryot Sabha are frankly pro-Bolshevik ... The Bolshevik method on the question of distribution of land has greatly attracted the Indian masses.' Then Kaye added most perceptively: 'Lenin certainly desires revolution in India but I think that Lenin is quite content to allow the Indian revolution to proceed along its own peculiar course.' *The Times*, London, was less perceptive; it saw a foreign hand in the non-co-operation movement started by Gandhi, calling it on 20 March 1919 part of the 'Bolshevik plans to raise revolution in India'. On 16 December the same year the paper was alleging that 'Secret leaders were in touch with the Russian Bolshevik movement.' More likely, *The Times* correspondent was secretly in touch with Cecil Kaye, for Gandhi made his antagonism to a red revolution clear from the very beginning.

Jawaharlal's mind dragged him leftwards. His instinct, experience and dogged faith in Gandhi's leadership stopped him a long way short of Marxism. In fertile company, however, he could be more socialist than thou. His first big opportunity came in February 1927, at Brussels, during the International Congress against Colonial Oppression and Imperialism, which he attended as the representative of the Indian National Congress. The Soviet Union did not send a delegation to this theoretically non-partisan gathering, but there was no shortage of Soviet fellow-travellers. (Among those present was Willi Muenzenberg, who invented the term.) Brussels that month was teeming with single, double and even triple agents of the great powers. The conference was the brain-child of a pro-Bolshevik group in Berlin and always at the mercy of a nod from Moscow. The idea was to provide a forum for anyone in the world pitted against imperialism, especially of the British variety, but not underestimating the 'threat of the rising imperialism of the United States' to Latin American nations too. The three 'chief planks', however, were to be China, India, and Mexico to 'take the lead in the consolidation of

Latin America against the United States'. (The quotations are from Jawaharlal's formal report on the conference to the Indian National Congress.) Funds also came from the enthusiastic Chinese and Mexicans, but typically the problem was not so much the money as the ideological hair-splitting. The Second International (founded in Paris in 1889 and commanding the allegiance of the socialist and social democratic parties of Europe) wanted to boycott Brussels because of its allegiance to the Third International (or Comintern, founded by Lenin in Moscow in 1919 and dissolved by Stalin in 1943). The charge was a familiar one: that the strings were held by Moscow. The dispute was resolved when the Russians kept away. Delegations came from 'Egypt, Persia, Syria, Dutch East Indies, Annam, Korea, Morocco, French North Africa (both Arab and Negro), South Africa (both Negro and White Labour), United States (Negroes and White representatives of the minority movements), Mexico, and States of Central and South America'. There were famous leaders of Britain's Left: ex-Labour minister George Lansbury (1859–1940), Fenner Brockway, Ellen Wilkinson, who became a close friend of Jawaharlal's, and Harry Pollitt (1890–1960), leader of the British Communist Party. Authors like Henri Barbusse and Ernst Toller (1893–1939) were present. Messages came from Mahatma Gandhi, Romain Rolland and Albert Einstein.

Jawaharlal was very excited by this first international conference he was attending. He found the Chinese, contrary to image, 'very young and full of energy and enthusiasm'. The Indonesian Muslims 'bore a striking resemblance to the higher-caste Hindus'. The Negroes, 'from the inkiest black to every shade of brown . . . full of eloquence and energy, but they all bore traces of the long martyrdom which their race had suffered'. The Arabs were 'typical fighting men, who understood independence and fighting for it and little else, and were wholly untainted with the slave mentality of more intellectual races'. Jawaharlal was made a member of the presiding committee, which set the agenda each morning. He arrived on the evening of 6 February and took part in all the preparatory meetings. He addressed the press on the 9th (there was heavy censorship of the reporting) and was one of those who delivered the opening addresses. The languages of the conference were French, English and German; one speaker attempted Hebrew and was told to stop because no one else understood it. He drafted the resolution on India; and the joint declaration with China was the first statement of a belief that would be shattered only at the very end of his life, thirty-five years later – that friendship between India and China had to be the core of pan-Asianism. The influence of this conference on Jawaharlal's thinking can hardly be overstated, but what was truly remarkable was the perception with which he viewed the future. An example: 'What is more likely is that England in order to save herself from extinction will become a satellite of the United States and incite the imperialism and capitalism of America to fight by her side.' Or:

[A Communist victory] does not mean that the Chinese Republic will be fashioned wholly on the lines laid down by Marx. Even Soviet Russia, owing to the pressure of the peasantry, has had to give up part of its communism, and in China where the small peasant is the deciding factor, the departure from pure communism will be all the greater.

Jawaharlal made a tremendous impression at this conference and was appointed a member of the executive committee and honorary president of the League against Imperialism and for National Independence which emerged out of the conference. It was a distinct honour. The other members were Einstein, Romain Rolland, George Lansbury and Soong Ching-ling (Madame Sun Yat-sen).

Jawaharlal had, however, no illusions about the value of this League. He was then, and continued to be, sceptical of British leftists and Labourites when it came to India. (In a speech in Lucknow on 29 August 1928 he would describe them as 'the sanctimonious and canting humbugs who lead the Labour Party in England'.) He had no illusions either about the Soviet Union. 'It is thus probable that the Russians will try to utilize the League to further their own ends,' he wrote in his secret report to his party's working committee. 'Personally I have the strongest objection to being led by the nose by the Russians or by anybody else.' If Jawaharlal was not born in England, he was not born in the Soviet Union either. This did not prevent the British from trying to persecute him as a communist upon his return, citing as evidence his association with the League and his continuing correspondence (a weekly affair, when the mail was allowed to pass by the censors) with 'Chatto', who was a communist. The British even tried to implicate Jawaharlal in the Meerut 'conspiracy case' by forging a letter purportedly from the communist leader Manabendra

Nath Roy. Roy, incidentally, was not his real name, which was Narendra Nath Bhattacharya. Roy changed his name after leaving India in 1915, at the age of twenty-two, during his travels in Mexico. He played a prominent part in the Comintern discussions on India in 1920, differing with Lenin's thesis that the Indian Communists should ally, in the first stage, with the national bourgeoisie. He returned to India in 1930, after differences with the Comintern in 1928, went to gaol for six years, joined the Congress, left it, formed a radical party and died in 1954.

In August 1928 the government released a letter, allegedly written by Roy, describing Jawaharlal as the 'liaison agent between Moscow and India'; it was Defence Exhibit 148(5) in the Meerut conspiracy case. Jawaharlal ridiculed the notion that he was anyone's agent. Writing to 'Chatto' on 4 April, he said: 'You will find that the League against Imperialism figures prominently as an organization "controlled by and subject to" the Communist International. It is unfortunate that the British Government is so extraordinarily stupid. I hate stupidity in my opponent.' This did not stop him from praising as often as he wanted the merits of communism. He told the All-Bengal Students' Conference on 22 September 1928:

> Socialism frightens some of our friends, but what of communism? Our elders sitting in their council chambers shake their grey heads and stroke their beards in alarm at the mere mention of the word ... I wish to tell you that though personally I do not agree with many of the methods of communists, and I am by no means sure to what extent communism can suit present conditions in India, I do believe in communism as an ideal of society. For essentially it is socialism, and socialism, I think, is the only way if the world is to escape disaster.

The Russians, and more so the Indian Communists, would have loved to see Jawaharlal turn Communist. 'Chatto', who had attended the third Congress of the Communist International in Moscow in 1921, kept urging him to revolt against Gandhi. In one of his letters in 1928 he said:

> According to my reading of the Indian situation the revolutionary ferment will come to a head just after the Simon Commission has reported to Parliament and the Government prepares a plan of reforms for the purchase of the owning class. If you are organizationally prepared by this

time, you will be able to strike a blow, just as Gandhi was able to do in 1921. But I hope that this time there will be no sentimental nonsense about the shedding of a few litres of blood, and that the revolutionary movement will be led on purely materialistic lines by trained Marxian revolutionaries.

Moscow had more than charity towards Indian nationalism in mind when wooing the Nehrus. The success of the Bolsheviks had altered the geopolitics of the north-west of India dramatically. The British began strengthening the defence of India. The Washington Naval Conferences of 1921–2 led to the construction from 1924 of the naval base in Singapore to facilitate quick transport of troops from Australia. (A new Labour government stopped work on it in 1924, but the Conservatives took Singapore up again on their return to power in 1926. It was completed in 1938.) The vital port of Trincomalee, on the eastern coast of Ceylon, in British hands since 1795 and strategically placed to monitor the Bay of Bengal, was also developed. Construction of the Khyber railway was sanctioned in September 1920; the work was completed by 2 November 1925. A sophisticated airbase was established at Karachi, with smaller bases in the North-West Frontier Province; and the area soon saw a concentration of tanks and planes. With the Central Asian republics still full of the 'bandits' fighting Moscow (they would not be subdued till the early 1930s), the Russians were extremely anxious about British rearmament in this region – a worry heightened by the break in diplomatic relations by Britain in 1927. Moscow feared a British invasion through Afghanistan; Britain feared precisely the opposite. Both powers, consequently, wooed King Amanullah of Afghanistan, who happily basked in the luxury of such unfamiliar courtship.

Moscow was, therefore, very keen to find friends in the Congress Party. What better gesture than to invite one of the five honorary presidents of the League against Imperialism to the tenth anniversary of the November Revolution? In the autumn of 1927 Motilal had joined his son, taking a holiday in Europe after nineteen long years. In Berlin both received an invitation, via the Soviet ambassador, to come to Moscow. That, incidentally, was also probably the last year an invitation could have been sent. In 1928 Moscow, at the sixth Congress of the Third International, abandoned the Lenin line, and Gandhi's Congress turned from bourgeois revolutionary to 'reformist and class-collaborationist'. That November was also the last opportunity to see Lenin's Soviet Union, for in December 1927 the Soviet Union under Stalin launched its offensive against the kulak, and nothing was ever the same again.

Most of the Nehru family were in Europe at that point. Nineteen-year-old Betty (Krishna) had broken tradition, ignored her mother's ardent pleas against going unchaperoned to licentious Europe and joined her brother in March 1926. The only promise she made was to her father. On the eve of her departure, just after a two-hour harangue from her mother, she was summoned by Motilal. What he told her says as much about Motilal as about the family. 'Now, darling,' he began,

> sit down and don't interrupt, I only want you to bear one thing in mind. You have the gambling spirit. You are going to be alone on a ship that takes seventeen days to reach Italy. Do not play cards aboard ship, because I am not going to pay your debts. And secondly, I want you to remember your duty to us, and I want you to be, as you always have been, frank and straightforward with me. Promise me that you won't do anything about which you cannot write me.

As Krishna Hutheesingh recalls in *We Nehrus* (1967): 'I don't think I ever broke my promise to him.'

Life with her Bhai (Brother) was austere: no taxis, and a small flat ('Bhai's little flat delighted me because I had never before lived in anything so small'). His warmth and his relaxed company more than compensated for the minor discomforts. There was skiing and skating. Jawaharlal was always trim and athletic, keeping fit with a daily session of yoga. There was also the inevitable compensation of travelling with him (as his secretary, after she had learned typing) and meeting a range of fascinating people. The Communist and pan-Islamist exiles, of course, were in touch. There were meetings with Raja Mahendra Pratap in Montreux (Jawaharlal remembers him in his autobiography as a 'delightful optimist, living completely in the air and refusing to have anything to do with realities'); with Madame Cama in Paris ('rather fierce and terrifying as she came up to you and peered into your face, and, pointing at you, asked abruptly who you were. The answer made no difference'); with Moulvi Obeidulla in Italy ('He had produced a scheme for the "United States" or "United Republics of India", which was quite an able attempt to solve the communal problem'); and of course with 'Chatto', who was always broke. Albert Einstein came to the flat one day, and there were calls on Romain Rolland, who had written Gandhi's biography even without meeting him. But the most important friend Jawaharlal made during this European sojourn was a dark man with burning eyes, a great hook-nose and an intense air: V. L. Krishna Menon.

Born on 3 May 1896 at Panniankara, Calicut, in Kerala, Menon had exchanged life in a prosperous Nair lawyer's family for a miserable existence in London, running the India League to publicize the freedom movement at a time when censorship and bias kept the British public ignorant or misinformed. He had come to London in 1924 to take a teacher's diploma, which he duly got in 1925, and then went on to teach history at St Christopher's School in Hertfordshire. He joined the London School of Economics and took his degree in 1927, obtaining an M A from University College in 1930 and an M Sc from LSE in 1934. He was called to the Bar from the Middle Temple the same year. A Labour activist, he became a borough councillor for St Pancras, but his important role was as *de facto* ambassador in London of the Congress Party. He and Jawaharlal became very good friends, and after freedom the Prime Minister of India honoured Menon's contribution by naming him High Commissioner in London. Menon bought a beautiful mansion at 9 Kensington Palace Gardens in 'Millionaires' Row' as the official residence of the High Commissioner, but preferred to live in a small room adjoining his office in India House. His only luxuries were endless cups of tea – and a prolific tongue, which would play its part in the international politics of the 1950s.

By the autumn of 1926 it was clear that Kamala's health was not improving. She had to leave the flat and go to a sanatorium high in the Alps, at Montana–Vermala, near Bex, where the nine-year-old Indira (nicknamed Indu) was at school. This left Jawaharlal more free to travel (with the British secret service generally on his trail). By the summer of 1927 Kamala was far better. Motilal, who could not come to Europe earlier because of work on the Lakhna inheritance case (perhaps his most famous; it began in 1894 and took more than three decades in the courts), finally reached Switzerland. The quality of life immediately became much better; with Motilal present, they lived and travelled *de luxe*.

When the invitation to visit the Soviet Union reached them, Motilal dismissed the idea as a waste of time. Jawaharlal, however, was very keen, and the son once again prevailed. All five – father, son, Kamala, Indu and Krishna – took the long and uncomfortable 28-hour train trip from Berlin through Poland. They reached the Russian border on the night of 7 November and Moscow the next afternoon, to find there was nothing grand left about Moscow's Grand Hotel. The Communists had covered the plush czarist furniture with coarse covers to make it more socialist. Neither would socialism allow hot water for a bath. Motilal made a great fuss. An unrepentant bourgeois, he refused to be impressed by the poorly stocked shops or the proletariat officialdom. He finally lost his famous temper when the Soviet foreign commissar, G. V. Chicherin, gave him an appointment for four in the morning. His temper did not fetch him hot water but it did help change the appointment to the marginally more reasonable hour of 1 p.m.

Between 700 and 800 guests had been invited from all over the world by the Society for Cultural Relations with Foreign Countries (among the other Indians was S. J. Saklatvala, a relation of the top Indian industrialist family of Tatas, who had become a communist in Britain). The Nehrus had, in fact, missed the real anniversary celebrations on the 7th, when Kalinin took the salute from a march-past, to the strains of the Internationale, of a million soldiers, workers and children – a day-long procession culminating in a break-neck charge across Red Square by the Cossack cavalry. There was nevertheless enough to see and banquets to be enjoyed during their four days. Jawaharlal noted, not without irony, that large crowds (chiefly women) were still going into the ancient chapel dedicated to the Virgin Mary right next to the Kremlin, ignoring Marx's famous message, inscribed in large letters on an adjoining wall: 'Religion is the opium of the people.' What Jawaharlal admired most was the visible egalitarianism: the demolition of class distinctions in both behaviour and dress; the sight of ordinary people at the magnificent State Opera House, with its seven golden tiers; the unique relationship between rulers and ruled. A revolutionary film, *The Last Days of Petrograd*, impressed him; the Museum of the Revolution did not. The Nehrus were certainly treated as a little more than five among 800. Their schedule included a call on Kalinin, the President of the Soviet Union, in his small, simply furnished flat in the Kremlin.

The Soviet visit provoked Jawaharlal to an intensive bout of reading on the subject. Always voracious, he now concentrated on learning about the revolution from books such as *The Russian Experiment 1917–1927* by Professor K. T. Shah, *Karl Marx's Capital* by A. D. Lindsay, *Karl Marx and Modern Socialism*, Bukharin's *Historic Materialism* and *Economic Theory of the Leisure Class*, Bogdonoff's *Short Course of Economic Science*, Lenin's *Imperialism – The Last Stage of Capitalism*, Karl Kautsky's *The Labour Revolution*, Trotsky's *In Defence of Terrorism* and *Where Is Britain Going?*, Norman Angell's *Must Britain Follow the Moscow Road?*, *The Bolshevik Theory* by R. W. Postgate, *My Reminiscences of the Russian Revolution* by M. Phillips Price, *Lenin and Gandhi* by René Fulop-Miller, Emil Ludwig's *Genius and Character* and of course John Reed's *Ten Days That Shook the World*. Always searching for parallels between the Russian experience and the Indian, Jawaharlal found himself in broad agreement with the way the revolutionaries had tackled the problem of religion. He could also – tongue only a little in cheek – see some similarities in Lenin asking his shocked comrades to join the tsarist Duma after the failure of the 1905 Revolution and his father entering the British Council after the failure of Gandhi's non-co-operation movement. He absorbed a great deal more than one might expect from a four-day visit. 'Russia apart,' he wrote in *Towards Freedom* (1941), 'the theory and philosophy of Marxism lightened up many a dark corner of my mind . . . I was filled with a new excitement.'

Jawaharlal returned deeply impressed by this near-decade of Bolshevik achievement. A series of articles, most of which appeared in *The Hindu*, Madras, were compiled and published by Lala Ram Mohan Lal of University Road, Allahabad, in December 1928; it was his first book. Later, the British used this book as 'evidence' against Jawaharlal in the Meerut conspiracy case. The controversy over why Jawaharlal was not eventually charged in the conspiracy case continues; the accusation has been made that Motilal's influence with the British got his son off the hook. Jawaharlal himself did not know what to expect. While he agreed with his father that there should be a perceptible distance between him and the Communist Party, he also gave up smoking in preparation for another spell in gaol. The Communists were not amused by Jawaharlal's ambivalence. Muzaffar Ahmed branded him a 'tepid reformist', while others less charitable called him a Britsh stooge. (This was how the Communists accused in the Meerut conspiracy case described the major Indian Congress leaders: Motilal was 'a dangerous patriot'; Subhas Bose a 'bourgeois and ludicrous careerist'; C. R. Das a 'poltroon'; Lala Lajpat Rai a 'scoundrel, and politically dangerous'. As for the arch-criminal Gandhi, he was not only religious-minded, an awful sin in itself, but also 'a grotesque reactionary'.)

Jawaharlal landed at Madras with his wife, daughter and sister after twenty months in Europe, just in time to join the forty-second session of the Indian National Congress held in the city. Motilal Nehru, who had attended the forty-first session in Guwahati, stayed back in Europe to enjoy a longer holiday. The next year they would be together again at a Congress session, in Calcutta – and, with the open help of Gandhi, make history. But before that the Moscow-returned 38-year-old almost stumbled out of Gandhi's embrace.

20 The Truant Child

The family generally celebrated Motilal's birthday with a high tea. It was not without a touch of fun. The invitation sent by the three children, for instance, for his sixty-fourth birthday in 1925 (celebrated on 20 April and not 6 May) asks the guest over for a 'Book Tea . . . You should represent a well-known book in English, Hindi or Urdu, or any other book of international reputation. You will be required to guess the names of the books represented by others. The highbrows who make the largest number of correct guesses will be installed in seats of honour and presented with souvenirs of the occasion.' But in 1927 the children were in Europe, and Motilal was in a low mood on his birthday. He wrote to Gandhi that day: 'Looking back through the vista of 66 long years it presents to myself an almost unbroken record of time wasted and opportunities missed.' There was just one thing he now wanted: 'the crown' for his son. 'The crown' was the leadership of the Congress – a term Gandhi had introduced.

When Gandhi became Congress president for the only time in his life in 1924, Jawaharlal described it as an anticlimax. For a super-president had descended to the status of just another president. Gandhi had been in self-imposed retirement since then, waiting for some answer to his prayer for guidance out of the political stalemate. Nevertheless, no important decision of the Congress could be taken without his nod. That summer, as usual each year, discussions began on who should be nominated Congress president for the next session. A lobby was pushing for Motilal in the conviction that only he could bring about the peace which eluded the country. Gandhi was reluctant; if the Muslims trusted Motilal, then Hindus like Lala Lajpat Rai and Malaviya detested him with equal passion. Motilal then hinted that 'the crown' might be offered to his son. Such was Jawaharlal's growing reputation that the idea was not dismissed outright as nepotism. Gandhi thought the idea had an 'irresistible appeal', but wondered if the time had fully come for Jawaharlal to be saddled with such a responsibility. He bounced the ball, through a letter to Switzerland, to Jawaharlal himself, mentioning that only Jawaharlal could now bring the masses back to the Congress. Jawaharlal, of course, declined – but then one could hardly expect him to grasp at a gift. Gandhi offered a kinder explanation to Motilal for rejecting his son: 'He is too high-souled to stand the anarchy and hooliganism that seem to be growing in the Congress.' The real problem, as Jawaharlal recognized when similar excuses blocked his nomination the next year too, was elsewhere. As he wrote to his friend and confidant Syed Mahmud on 30 June 1928: 'As for my presidentship of the Congress, don't worry. I had rather not preside. The real objection to me is not youth or jealousy but fear of my radical ideas. I do not propose to tone down my ideas for the presidentship.'

In retrospect the most 'radical' of these ideas does not seem all that radical. It was like the chalk line which cannot be crossed; once you have stepped over it you wonder what the fuss was all about. The most important of the differences between the not-so-young Jawaharlal and the senior leaders in December 1927 and 1928 – including and particularly Gandhi – was over a resolution to be passed by the Congress demanding freedom. Should it be 'full' freedom, or diluted by a connection to the Raj? Should it be complete independence or dominion status? Jawaharlal wanted full freedom. Gandhi told him not to be foolish.

Jawaharlal issued a statement to the press when his ship reached Colombo on 19 December, dealing largely with the attitude of London and Hindu–Muslim problems. There was at least one memorable remark about religion and politics: 'The less we talk of and worry about the next world, the more good we are likely to do to our fellow countrymen and country.' They reached Madras on the 22nd, and Kamala and Krishna (Betty) immediately stitched some *khadi* clothes for Jawaharlal to wear to the session. The subjects committee met on the 25th, and Jawaharlal submitted his controversial resolution for discussion:

This Congress declares the goal of the Indian people to be independence with full control over the defence forces of the country, the financial and economic policy and the relations with foreign countries. The Congress demands that this right of the people of India should be forthwith recognized and given effect to, in particular by the complete withdrawal of the alien army of occupation.

There was great consternation. An old co-operator like C. Vijia-raghavachariar dismissed the thought of such self-government as silly, and Dr Rajendra Prasad (who was in the anti-Nehru lobby) was convinced that such a resolution would make the Congress the laughing-stock of the world. Jawaharlal was furious; he considered it degrading even to think of self-rule within the British Empire and he directly attacked Rajendra Prasad, accusing him of being overly influenced by 'Anglo-Indian' journals. Mrs Annie Besant even questioned whether a demand for full independence was consonant with the creed. Eventually the elders whittled the resolution down to: 'This Congress declares the goal of the Indian people to be complete national independence.' No one had any wish to do anything to pursue such a goal; it was only accepted as a sop to Jawaharlal. But, sop or not, for the first time the concept of 'complete national independence' had become part of the Congress resolve.

Congress leaders were more concerned with their resolutions on the Simon Commission, the drafting of an Indian Constitution and communalism. M. A. Ansari had been made president, in the hope of promoting Hindu–Muslim unity, and the wide-ranging resolution on the subject attempted a solution to the problem: joint electorates, reservation of seats, reforms in North-West Frontier Province and Baluchistan and no decision on any communal issue without the support of three-fourths of members of the community affected. It was at Madras too that the Congress first demanded the restructuring of provinces on a linguistic basis and the immediate formation of Andhra, Karnataka, Orissa (Utkal) and Sind. Jawaharlal decided to start lobby-groups to push his message of independence, on the valid assumption that the Congress would not do so. He resigned as general secretary to concentrate on the Republican Congress, which had its first session on 28 December 1927 under the Congress *shamiana*, and later the Independence for India League, set up on the evening of 30 August 1928, with a provisional committee consisting of Jawaharlal and two rising young freedom fighters: Subhas Chandra Bose and Dr Zakir Husain (1897–1969). Ansari insisted on retaining him, however, and he continued as general secretary till his father became Congress president in December 1928.

The man Jawaharlal was most upset with was none other than his leader, the Mahatma himself. He was convinced that the Congress had lost momentum, was 'drifting to middle-class or babu politics', as he said in his address to the Republican Congress, and he was extremely angry with Gandhi for refusing to give any lead. Just after the Congress session he sent such a strong letter to Gandhi that the Mahatma preferred to destroy it. 'Your first letter I destroyed after reading and replying to it. The second I am keeping,' wrote Gandhi to his protégé on 17 January. Jawaharlal was livid at Gandhi's assertion in an article in *Young India* that his independence resolution was 'hastily conceived and thoughtlessly passed'. Jawaharlal had not much minded the criticism of the Mahasabha lobby or that of the Moderates; he did not expect anything else from them. As he wrote in his second letter to Gandhi on 11 January:

> I do not care what they say or do. But I do care very much for what you say and do . . . You know how intensely I have admired you and believed in you as a leader who can lead this country to victory and freedom . . . I have asked you many times what you expected to do in the future and your answers have been far from satisfying.

Now the young man began lecturing the old, not only for this 'extra-ordinary' criticism of what after all was a formal resolution of the Congress, but also for all his peculiar views on religion, the West *et al.* (Among other things that Jawaharlal found himself unable to accept was Gandhi's condemnation of the use of contraceptives.) He knew by the end of the letter that he had overreached himself: 'But I must stop. I have already exceeded all reasonable limits. My only excuse is my mental agitation.' He hoped Gandhi would forgive him – but he did not withhold the letter.

Gandhi was very ready to forgive, but he introduced a dangerous sting in the tail. He replied on 17 January:

> I see quite clearly that you must carry on open warfare against me and my views. For if I am wrong I am evidently doing irreparable harm to the country and it is your duty after having known it to rise in revolt against me . . . The differences between you and me appear to me to be so vast and radical that there seems to be no meeting ground between us. I can't conceal from you my grief that I should lose a comrade so valiant, so faithful, so able and honest as you have always been; but in serving a cause, comradeships have got to be sacrificed.

The sting: he offered to make the differences publicly known.

Such a break would have pleased a lot of people, none more than the communalists within the Congress who wanted to take over Gandhi and make him the Mahatma of Hindu India rather than India. This lobby was powerful and well financed by industrialists like the Birlas. Jugal Kishore and Ghanshyamdas Birla sat on the top committees of the Hindu Mahasabha. A history of the organization, published by the Akil Bhartiya Hindu Mahasabha in December 1938, includes a piece by Jugal Kishore Birla, and Ghanshyamdas was a member of the Shraddhanand Memorial Fund. The Birlas took the precaution of wooing Gandhi simultaneously; and the Mahatma in turn used them to keep the 'Hindu' lobby of the Congress in line. As far as preferences among industrialists were concerned, the Nehrus kept on the side of business men like the Tatas. (At one point, when Jawaharlal was into one of his moods again and embarrassed about still being dependent for money on his father, he nearly took a job with the Tatas.) The leftists wanted Jawaharlal not to resign from the Congress but to act as their agent. Chattopadhyay wrote to him on 29 August 1928:

> It would be a serious political blunder if you resign your position as general secretary of the Congress. The reactionaries, among whom must, of course, be included Subhas Bose, will take advantage of the situation created by your retirement in order to make the Congress revert to its old position, abandon the Independence Resolution and sever the connection of the Congress with the League [Against Imperialism].

News about the conflict between Jawaharlal and Gandhi was spread with much glee by both the pro-British press and the anti-Nehru Mahasabhaites. Hostile newspapers deliberately played up differences, real or imaginary. On 21 January, Jawaharlal was forced to complain to the editor of *The Leader*, protesting about the report of a speech he made in Benaras where the paper said he had called Gandhi 'effete and fossilized'. In this letter, published on 25 January, of 21 January 1928, Jawaharlal said that no one in his senses could call Gandhi 'old in spirit . . . We who talk of youth and the call of youth are pygmies before his giant and irrepressible youth.' Two days earlier he had sent a very contrite letter to 'My dear Bapuji' in which he explained the distortions which had made Gandhi think

that Jawaharlal was in revolt. Warning Gandhi not to believe everything he read in the papers, and promising to visit him as soon as
possible, Jawaharlal wrote: 'Am I not your child in politics, though
perhaps a truant and errant child?' The prodigal was forgiven.

Gandhi had travelled incessantly all through 1927, including a visit
to Ceylon, and now prepared to pause for a while in his ashram at
Sabarmati. One reason for his irritation with Jawaharlal's hurry in
pushing through an independence resolution was that he was not
clear about the follow-up. As he knew only too well, if the demand
for freedom was not backed by mass action it would indeed become
a laughing-stock of the world. Gandhi had a perceptive reason for
believing that the call was premature; it was still an élitist demand.
As he wrote in *Young India* on 12 January: 'We the English-
educated Indians often unconsciously make the terrible mistake of
thinking that the microscopic minority of the English-speaking
Indians is the whole of India.' He wanted freedom, but the kind
that had relevance to every Indian, and until that consciousness
was created he was not ready to give the call. There was another
typically Gandhian reason too. He had been sentenced to six years'
imprisonment in 1922 and released because of his illness in 1924,
but he felt morally bound to refrain from active politics till these
six years expired. That period would end only in March 1928.
Perhaps there *is* something called the historic moment defined by
destiny – because it was in February that the India which had
gone to sleep after the non-co-operation movement, a sleep punc-
tuated only by the nightmares of communal violence, was suddenly
ready to wake up to another dawn.

Motilal, abroad in the winter of 1927–8, had intended to enjoy a
longer holiday in Europe. Among other things, he had had a good
time at the Monte Carlo casino, winning, in three trips, about 2,000
francs. He returned to India when a medical check-up showed traces
of albumen and glaucoma, implying, as he wrote to his son on 4
January 1928, 'stone blindness sooner or later'. His diagnosis of
blindness proved to be an exaggeration; perhaps he was only feeling
lonely and homesick in Europe and wanted to return to 'the old
familiar surroundings'. Actually, they were not all that familiar or
old, for he had just constructed another house in addition to Anand
Bhavan on the estate. The original reason for the new house was
puritanical. Jawaharlal had been insisting that the old home was too

palatial. Motilal started out to build a spartan home, then got fed up with his son's sacrificing spirit and built himself an even grander home – not in size, but certainly in quality. He was his own architect; and the helpful Tatas sent him a specialist engineer. Motilal Nehru too was back home by February.

Sir John Simon landed at Bombay on 3 February 1928.

21 Leader of a New Mood

When Edward Frederick Lindley Wood, Baron Irwin, later Earl of Halifax, the high-Tory, good-Christian Viceroy of India from 1926 to 1931, sat down to write about his life, in *Fullness of Days*, he finally admitted that he had made a mistake in believing that the Hindus and Muslims would never co-operate in 1928. His advisers could, however, hardly be blamed for making such an assumption. The riots of the last five years had scarred hearts as nothing else in living memory, and hate-inspired proselytizers on both sides had filled the vacuum left by Gandhi's withdrawal from politics. Lord Irwin, however, chided himself for not seeing what he described as a 'new force' in India, inspiring every section of the people to revolt. The young in particular were restless and waiting for the signal. The growing Communist influence caused a spate of strikes – in Tata's steel mills at Jamshedpur, in the cotton mills at Sholapur, in the jute mills of Calcutta and the woollen mills at Kanpur: 31 million working days were lost in 1928. Jawaharlal was in greater harmony with this mood than the Congress.

The Montagu–Chelmsford Report of 1919 on Indian constitutional reforms had promised a review of the constitutional position in ten years. A Royal Commission was consequently due in 1929. But Frederick Edwin Smith (1872–1930), the first Earl of Birkenhead, Secretary of State for India between 1924, when the Tories replaced the Labour government, and 1928, preferred not to wait till 1929. The eagerness had nothing to do with love of India. An imperialist to the right of Churchill, Birkenhead was convinced that if Labour won the next election and got a chance to set up the commission it would sell out to the Congress. He was terrified of what Labourites like the first Viscount Stansgate, Colonel Wedgwood Benn (1877–1960), might concede. His apprehensions about a Tory defeat were justified, for the Colonel did become Secretary for India between 1929 and 1931; but he might have been reassured by Nehru's assessment that Labour was under the control of men like Ramsay MacDonald, 'who probably are a shade worse in regard to India than even Birkenhead'.

Taking no chances, Birkenhead had the relevant provision in the Act of 1919 amended and on 8 November 1927 announced the appointment of a seven-member commission, consisting of British MPs and headed by Sir John Simon (1873–1954).

India, with one voice, described this as an insult. It would not accept its fate once again being determined solely by the British; not a single Indian had been included in the commission. As in the case of the Rowlatt Bill, the commission's actual work became an irrelevant footnote to history, but while it was touring India it managed to do what even Gandhi had almost despaired of doing – it restored to India a single aim and a common voice. Birkenhead's response was contemptuous. Indians, he said, could never, would never, agree on a common Constitution. The Congress took up his challenge at its Madras session. On 15 January an all-party meeting presided over by Dr Ansari decided to observe a complete hartal on 3 February, the day Sir John was scheduled to land in Bombay. India would boycott the Simon Commission. The next task was to show Britain that Indians could write a Constitution for themselves. Between 12 and 22 February the All-Parties Conference worked out the details for the march towards 'full responsible government', and in May in Bombay a subcommittee was set up to write out the principles of an Indian Constitution. Its members were: Sir Ali Imam and Shuaib Qureshi to represent the Muslims; the Hindu Mahasabhaites M. S. Aney and M. R. Jayakar (1873–1959); Mangal Singh from the Sikh League; labour leaders N. M. Joshi and G. R. Pradhan; the old Allahabad liberal lawyer Sir Tej Bahadur Sapru; and, as president, Motilal Nehru. Jawaharlal was a secretary to the committee. The real problem, as everyone knew, hinged on a single question: the place of minorities in the power structure. By the end of June, as Ansari wrote to Gandhi, there was complete deadlock. The Sikhs wanted no reservation of seats at all; the Hindu Mahasabhaites accepted partial reservations; and the Muslims wanted just about everything reserved. When Sir Tej Bahadur saw Motilal's draft, however, on 21 July, he found it to be 'A-1'. By the end of August all the parties had been persuaded to accept the principles behind the recommendations, but had introduced so many mutually contradictory amendments that only chaos could result. In the meanwhile, Jinnah began creating a fuss, this time with help from the Ali brothers.

It was a bad time for Jinnah, both politically and personally. He had, of course, opposed the Simon Commission but saw with concern the resurgence of Congress in the forefront of a rising national storm. During the Budget session of the National Assembly in March he approached Lord Irwin and offered to sell out (the precise words Irwin used were 'take the brunt of the attack in India') if the Viceroy agreed to one of two things: put an Indian in Simon's commission, or establish, alongside, a separate Indian commission. But Birkenhead was in an aggressive mood. In a speech at Lancaster on 17 February 1928 he taunted the boycotters that they would be exposed as having no support. Rather carelessly, he spelled out (as *The Indian Annual Register* of 1928, edited by N. N. Mitra, Vol. 1, reports) the constituency of the Raj:

> I would add this, that those who are organizing boycott of this Commission will, in my judgement, discover month by month how little representative they are of that vast and heterogeneous community of which we are the responsible trustees. They will discover millions of Muslims, millions of the depressed classes, millions of the business and Anglo-Indian communities who intend to put their case [before the Simon Commission].

The British ignored Jinnah's advice – but the link was, as we shall see, maintained.

Jinnah returned from Delhi to his Bombay home, South Court, to find that Ruttie had left him and gone to live in a rented suite at the famous Taj Mahal Hotel in Bombay. She sailed for Europe with her mother on 10 April 1928; Jinnah followed a month later. In London he received an urgent message that Ruttie was ill and dying in Paris. He rushed there, checked into the George V and then set about saving his wife, changing doctors, hospitals *et al*. She recovered but did not return to him; they did not meet again. Motilal, unable to talk to Jinnah in these months, did the next best thing and discussed his report with Jinnah's favourite junior and secretary, the 27-year-old Mohammad Cureem Chagla. Motilal was inclined to accept the principle of separate electorates. It was Chagla who differed, pointing out very validly that they were drafting a Constitution not for the moment but also for the future – for a free India. The Nehru Committee recommended joint electorates. Jinnah was furious that Chagla had co-operated in reaching a compromise and upon his return from Europe started sabotaging Motilal's efforts. He labelled it a 'Hindu report'. Motilal (and who could have been less Hindu than him?) was shocked at this betrayal by a man he always considered a fellow liberal. Jinnah gave a 'call' to the Muslims to 'organize themselves, stand united and . . . press every reasonable point for the protection of their community', as if some great crisis had descended. Motilal, upon reading this, invited Jinnah, who was president of the Muslim League, to join his committee. Jinnah refused. By early November, Jinnah began talking about the 'parting of ways' with the Congress, but he was isolated. Almost all the senior League leaders – even the Raja of Mahmudabad, the previous year's president – wanted to accept the Nehru Report as a settlement of the Hindu–Muslim question. Yet Jinnah kept insisting it was a 'Hindu' document. Motilal, Dr Ansari and Maulana Azad pleaded with him to attend a special meeting in December. No, said Jinnah. The most loyal admirer he had, Chagla, just could not understand why this 'man of integrity' was so obviously playing an obstructionist game. Chagla argued so effectively for the report at the League meeting on 23 November that Jinnah postponed a vote, knowing that he would lose if a vote was taken that day. At the League session on 26 December, Jinnah advised a total rejection of the Nehru Report. On the one hand, he kept saying that he wanted Hindu–Muslim unity; but with equal ease he kept rejecting the report. Under pressure from his League colleagues, he joined the national convention called by the Congress on 28 December. Sir Tej Bahadur Sapru could not understand Jinnah's lonely obstinacy when every other League leader had been won over and described him as a 'spoilt child, a naughty child'. That day in Calcutta, Jinnah was more than just spoilt. Alone, and without a single Muslim leader by his side, he told the others at the convention, 'Let us part as friends.' Lord Birkenhead did not have the support of the 'millions of Muslims' that year; but he had the vital, if still formally disguised, connivance of a very determined leader of 'Muslim India' – a term used by Jinnah in that speech which his biographer Stanley Wolpert describes as Jinnah's 'swan-song to Indian nationalism'.

Why had Jinnah sung that song so early? Nothing had happened till 1928. None of the 'reasons' that so many theorists would use to justify Jinnah's push for Pakistan – the failure of a possible Congress–League coalition after the 1937 elections, for instance, or the Cabinet

Mission plan, or the great riots of 1946, or anything else – had happened in 1928, and yet Jinnah had trilled his 'swan-song to Indian nationalism'. Why? What made Jinnah spurn nationalism in 1928, sabotage the Nehru Report and destroy yet another historic chance of unity? Every rational Muslim leader was with Motilal, including all those who would later become Pakistanis. Only a pro-British, obscurantist rump of the League, headed by the Aga Khan, was against the Nehru Report. Why did the great self-proclaimed nationalist, Jinnah, join them? It is a question his apologists ignore, because the answer would greatly reduce the heroic image of Jinnah they construct. The truth is that the Jinnah of 1928 was not so much a Muslim nationalist as a collaborationist. He left the main League session at Calcutta that year and went straight to Delhi where the small pro-British rump of the Muslim League was holding its separate session.

The Aga Khan, that same expert of second-class music-halls who had led the 1906 delegation to the Viceroy at the beckoning of Dunlop-Smith, now welcomed Jinnah gloatingly on New Year's Day in Delhi in 1929. Jinnah's defection to this camp meant a quantum leap towards respectability.

Motilal Nehru had been defeated in the drawing-room politics of 1928, but his son had won a major victory on the streets. Jawaharlal's enthusiasm for the boycott campaign bubbled through the text of his first circular to all provincial Congress committees on 7 January 1928. A diligent stream of messages ensued. The British had claimed that the Muslims would support the Simon Commission, and Jawaharlal was worried that they might not join the hartal in Allahabad. Although a section of the Muslims did succumb to British pressure, the Allahabad hartal was an 'amazing success'. But Jawaharlal was not content and wrote to Syed Mahmud on 4 February: 'I am not going to leave them [the bigoted and reactionary Muslims] in peace ... And so I, a Hindu, though a nominal one, have to face the Maulanas and the like!' The martial spirit had seized him, and he was impatient with any sign of romanticism, even in a friend. There was an absolute nugget in the same letter to Mahmud:

> Your letters are thoroughly dismal reading. Why should you put on a woebegone expression and be always dissatisfied with yourself and the world? I think it is the effect of Urdu poetry. People brought up on such

sickly and sentimental and soppy stuff are bound to become a decadent people. Get rid of this outlook. Become a little more aggressive and you will see that the world does offer something to live and fight for!

That was certainly his theme of the year: a battle-inspired optimism marred only by the relapse suffered by Kamala in summer.

The Simon Commission ended its first tour of India in the spring. When it returned in the autumn, the demonstrations asking it to 'Go back!' resumed with even greater vigour. On 30 October the 'seven uninvited gentlemen' reached Lahore in the afternoon by the government's special train. The citizens had prepared a very special kind of reception. At 1 p.m. several thousand people of all three communities started from Mochi Gate towards the railway station carrying black flags with a now famous message: 'Simon go back.' At the head were Lala Lajpat Rai, Pandit Malaviya, Sardar Mangal Singh, Abdul Qadir Kasuri, Dr Alam, Sardul Singh Cavesheer and others. Crossing Brandeth Road, Landa Bazar, it reached the point on Mulchand Temple Road, about 200 yards from the railway station, where it was stopped by barbed wire and wooden barricades. Lala Lajpat Rai had arrived from Etawa just that morning and had initially been disinclined to join the procession; but once there, he was in the front. Suddenly, the superintendent of police, a man named Scott, along with a few constables, began raining blows on the front row of boycotters. Using his knobbed hunter, Scott hit two direct blows at Lala, one of them at his heart. A constable added two blows of his own. Others near by suffered severe injuries too: Raizada Hansraj, Dr Alam, Dr Gopichand, Dr Satyapal. In a remarkable display of non-violent discipline, the leaders kept calm as they were being hit, and the young men behind them simply sat down, ready to take their share of the police attack. The ageing Lion of Punjab could not survive the injuries he suffered that day; on 17 November, Lala Lajpat Rai died. If the anger sweeping India needed any further provocation, this was it.

The only Indians who refused to be angry were the collaborators. It is very interesting to read the names of those Indians who co-operated with the Simon Commission at Lahore. Almost every one of them would play, at some point, a dubious role in the tragedies which would unfold over the next fifteen years: Captain Sikandar Hayat Khan and Chaudhury Chotu Ram, knights at the head of the

Unionist government in Punjab; Raja Narindernath, a communal Hindu Mahasabha activist; Dr Gokulchand Narang; Sir Muhammad Shafi, of the Aga Khan rump of the Muslim League; Sir Mahomed Iqbal, general secretary of the Punjab Muslim League and poet-philosopher of Pakistan; Sir Sundar Singh Majithia from the Sikhs; Sir Fazle Hussain, another Leaguer. Among the incidentally interesting co-operators, in Karachi, were Zulfiqar Ali Bhutto's father, Shah Nawaz Bhutto, and Girija Shankar Bajpai, one of the more famous bureaucrats to serve under Nehru. Perhaps the most interesting coincidence was the presence of a major-turned-MP on the commission. His name: Clement Attlee.

India officially mourned the Lala on 29 November; it was declared the Lala Lajpat Rai day. That was also the day the Simon Seven arrived on Jawaharlal Nehru's turf, the United Provinces. They left Delhi on the 28th, paused at Agra to see the Taj Mahal the next day and reached Lucknow on the morning of the 29th. Jawaharlal was not content with just another show of strength that day. He wanted protest on an unprecedented scale.

He had been building the tempo. There were Congress meetings on the 23rd and 24th; on the 25th Jawaharlal himself reached Lucknow and warned the city that he would boycott the boycott if they did not put up a truly massive demonstration. A vast procession was taken out on the 26th, a sort of dress rehearsal which infuriated the local police. In revenge, they lathi-charged the next procession, on the 28th. Jawaharlal had left Lucknow but returned on the 29th. He was walking with a group of a dozen volunteers (including a colleague who would become the first Congress chief minister of United Provinces, Govind Ballabh Pant) towards a meeting when he heard a clatter of hoofs behind him; mounted policemen were bearing down on them. The first temptation was to run, but then 'some other instinct held me to my place'. The first charge of the horsemen scattered the others, and suddenly, in a few seconds, Jawaharlal found himself alone in the middle of the road. 'The line,' he recalled in his autobiography, 'between cowardice and courage was a thin one and I might as well have been on the other side.' But courage was the finest quality of that generation. A mounted policeman came brandishing a long, new baton and cracked two blows on his back. Jawaharlal was stunned and shaken, but he did not fall. An angry crowd quickly collected, and now the police opted for discretion.

Rather than risk more trouble, the police now escorted the group to their destination.

News of the attack on Jawaharlal spread instantly. Motilal, Swarup Rani and Krishna were enjoying a quiet day in Allahabad; a telephone call from his son brought word, and Motilal was frantic with worry. The last train had gone, and he decided to drive the 146 miles to Lucknow. But the chauffeur had gone for the night. Krishna stepped in, offering to drive their shiny new Delage limousine. Motilal was very dubious about Krishna's abilities; in the end, love for the son outweighed fear of the daughter's skills, and they set out. They reached Lucknow just as the injured Jawaharlal was setting off for the railway station to participate in yet another boycott demonstration. Motilal wanted to join in, but his son, aware of the dangerous mood of the police, would not hear of this. It was just as well. A confrontation occurred with the authorities over how near the procession could get to the members of the commission, and once again the mounted policemen came. The cavalry charged straight and venomously into a non-violent crowd, but the volunteers held their ground, and hundreds were injured in the 'tremendous hammering'. Jawaharlal was 'half-blinded with the blows' on his back, legs and shoulders. The police, led by the deputy commissioner, Gwynne, whom Jawaharlal described as the *deus ex machina*, clearly had a special fate in store for him, but the bravery of some young men, to whom Jawaharlal was a great hero, saved him. Students of the Lucknow University simply covered Jawaharlal (as well as Pant and Suniti Devi Mitra, a woman volunteer near him) with their bodies and took the baton blows on themselves. Jawaharlal tried to play down the incident, but that only made him a bigger hero all over the country. He kept his wit, as much as his wits, about him. On 3 December he telegraphed friends in London to calm their anxiety: 'Thanks. Injuries severe but not serious. Hope survive the British Empire.' Which, of course, he did – in style.

Gandhi sent a fond letter of congratulations from Wardha on 3 December: 'My dear Jawahar, My love to you. It was all done bravely. You have braver things to do. May God spare you for many a long year to come and make you His chosen instrument for freeing India from the yoke.' There was no mistaking the import of this message. But the problem in 1928 at least was that Gandhi was still clinging to the yoke, as was Motilal. Jawaharlal just could not understand why the Nehru Report should demand nothing more than dominion status, on a par with Canada, Australia, New Zealand, South Africa and the Irish Free State, to be known as 'the Commonwealth of India'. Father and son had disagreed before, but never so much. As Motilal told his nephew Braj Kumar Nehru, 'Father and son are atilt. But Jawahar would not be my son if he did not stick to his guns.'

Reflecting the mood of the younger generation, Jawaharlal refused to support the Nehru Report when it came up for ratification at the All-Parties Conference in August 1928, and then again at the Calcutta Congress, to the great irritation of Gandhi. Eventually Gandhi negotiated a typical compromise to maintain unity: if the government did not accept the demands of the Nehru Report within one year, the Congress would then seek full independence. It merely meant that the inevitable had only been postponed by a year, since there was no chance whatsoever of Lord Irwin, or the new Labour government in Britain of Ramsay MacDonald, accepting dominion status. In fact, as Jawaharlal had often expressed, the MacDonald–Wedgwood Benn combination proved even worse than the Tory government on the India question. The Calcutta Congress of 1928 (hosted with much martial pomp and ceremony by Subhas Bose), consequently, became the last session dominated by the elders whose dreams had never really stretched beyond home rule. Motilal was, symbolically, the perfect president. As perfect, indeed, as Jawaharlal would be the next year, 1929, when he became the first president to release India's heart and mind from the yoke, even if the body was still chained. Gandhi was the bridge, and he prepared for 1929 by asking Jawaharlal to tour every province that year and reawaken the masses. Jawaharlal kept pushing his audiences (in particular youth) to strive for complete independence, even if the wiser Motilal impressed upon them the necessity of a transition period as a tactical step. 'Pure idealism,' as he put it, 'divorced from realities has no place in politics.' Gandhi, in fact, was not at all sure whether the Congress of 1929 would be the appropriate moment. In fact in January he was contemplating a foreign tour from April to October which would take him through Russia, Austria, Germany, Poland, France, England, the United States, Italy, Turkey and Egypt to deliver his message to the world; but the journey never came off.

Too much was happening in India, yet it was action without

direction. Gandhi was arrested in March 1929 in Calcutta, although it proved a damp squib when someone paid the one rupee fine without his knowledge. On 8 April two young men, Bhagat Singh and B. K. Dutt, wrote their names into national lore by throwing bombs into the Legislative Assembly, 'not to kill but to make the deaf hear'. In the absence of an organized movement, terrorist violence erupted in spasms. In March, thirty-one Communists were arrested, marking the beginning of the 3½-year-long Meerut conspiracy case. The Raj sprinkled oil on troubled flames by making it clear that even dominion status was an unacceptable ambition. Irwin did use the phrase in his 31 October declaration announcing the first Round-Table Conference, saying that 'the natural issue of India's constitutional progress . . . is the attainment of Dominion Status'. The British Parliament threw a fit, however, and the strong reaction in England destroyed any positive impact this declaration might have made in India.

The schism within the Congress was soon being mirrored in the country. The young were drifting away from the inactive Gandhi, towards Subhas and Jawaharlal. The latter's nation-wide tours for two years had built a hidden wave, waiting to burst. Jawaharlal's oratory voiced the emotions and ideas of the young as no one else's had done. Take one instance: his address to the Punjab provincial conference at Amritsar on 11 April 1928. 'The gods of yesterday,' he said, 'are neglected and lie almost forgotten, and new ideas and new myths convulse the people.' He aroused the pride of his audience: 'What is the British Empire today . . .? If we leave out India and the dependencies, it is like the famous Cheshire cat in *Alice in Wonderland* whose body has entirely disappeared and only the grin has remained.' His ideal of free India was an 'independent democratic state, and I would add a socialistic state'. This could not be achieved through terrorism. 'Violence . . . is today in India the very reverse of revolution.' What was the major obstacle to freedom?

The real problem before you is how to exorcise communalism . . . It may be a giant today, but it has feet of clay. It is the outcome largely of anger and passion, and when we regain our tempers it will fade into nothingness. It is a myth with no connection with reality and it cannot endure. It is really the creation of our educated classes in search of office and employment . . . If this question of culture is settled satisfactorily, and sufficient safeguards are provided for the interests of minorities and groups which may be in danger of suppression, what remains of communalism?

Was it just a loving father's partisan interest which made Motilal write to Gandhi on 13 July 1929 when once again the summer air was full of talk of the next Congress president? Motilal first paid due homage: Gandhi would be the ideal choice for the Lahore session, since 'You are the real power.' Then he came to the point; Gandhi must accept that

> The revolt of youth has become an accomplished fact ... It would be sheer flattery to say that you [Gandhi] have today the same influence as you had on the youth of the country some years ago, and most of them make no secret of the fact. All this would indicate that the need of the hour is the head of Gandhi and the voice of Jawahar ... There are strong reasons for either you or Jawahar to wear the 'crown', and if you and Jawahar stand together, as to which there is no doubt in my mind, it does not really matter who it is that stands in front and who behind.

The anti-Nehru lobby in the Congress tried to sabotage this move by putting up their own candidate to challenge Jawaharlal; and in fact there was more support for Sardar Vallabhbhai Patel than for Jawaharlal among the provincial Congress committees. But the key lay with Gandhi; 'the crown' would go in the direction of his nod. Jawaharlal was edgy. On 9 July 1929 he wrote to Gandhi: 'I am very nervous about the matter and do not like the idea at all.' He put forward a number of excuses, including a couple of silly ones – like wanting to retire for a while to a village instead of becoming Congress president, as if there had been no opportunity to do so before and none would come again.

Gandhi, who had in 1928 prayed that God make Jawaharlal his chosen instrument, now decided that the time had come to play God. In August he suggested publicly that Jawaharlal be given the honour. On 21 August, from Calcutta, Jawaharlal sent him a telegram: 'Beg of you not to press my name for Presidentship.' Gandhi summoned him to Sabarmati Ashram; at the end of the discussions, options were still open, at least theoretically. But Gandhi was not someone who would venture on such a course without having thought it out quite completely; he was consciously, deliberately nominating

Jawaharlal as the leader of a session that would launch the decisive phase of the freedom movement with its call for *purna swaraj*, or full independence. On 28 September at Lucknow he told the All-India Congress Committee to elect Jawaharlal Nehru. They did so, unanimously on paper, although with resentment barely disguised in some quarters.

There were no such reservations among the people. The congratulations poured in from all over the world. Sarojini Naidu indulged her imagery in her letter to Jawaharlal the next day:

I lay awake until late into the night thinking of the significance of the words I had used so often in reference to you, that you were predestined to a splendid martyrdom. As I watched your face while you were being given the rousing ovation on your election, I felt I was envisaging both the Coronation and the Crucifixion ... they are synonyms today especially for you, because you are so sensitive and so fastidious in your spiritual response and reaction and you will suffer a hundredfold more poignantly than men and women of less fine fibre and less vivid perception and apprehension, in dealing with the ugliness of weakness, falsehood, backsliding, betrayal.

'I wonder,' ended Sarojini, 'if in the whole of India there was yesterday a prouder heart than your father's or a heavier heart than yours.'

In 1928 Motilal had written to B. K. Nehru: 'If Jawahar lives for ten years he will change the face of India', and then added sadly, 'Such men do not usually live long; they are consumed by the fire within them.' Jawaharlal Nehru would live much longer. The fire would one day consume him, but not before he had shown destiny that its demands were not outside the capabilities of a man's will, courage and dreams.

22 India Claims Freedom

The story is told by D. G. Tendulkar that Mohandas Karamchand Gandhi was once informed that Lord Irwin, who took his Christianity very seriously, never did anything without praying to God. It was hardly an unfamiliar dialogue, at least as far as Gandhi was concerned; his own relationship with the Almighty was advertised often enough. Gandhi knew the uses of God as an alibi. Hence his comment, 'What a pity God gives him such bad advice.'

On the eve of the Lahore Congress, in December 1929, Lord Irwin tried his best to sabotage the independence resolution which Jawaharlal was itching to push through. Using his allies – Jinnah from the League and the Liberals Sir Tej Bahadur Sapru and V. J. Patel – he built up pressure for a meeting to defuse the coming confrontation. The Congress was committed to a non-co-operation movement if the British did not accept dominion status; but that was a demand which had been dismissed as subversive by Lord Reading, scorned by Lloyd George, abused by Birkenhead and called insulting by Sir John Simon. Jawaharlal described this last-minute call for talks by Irwin as 'mere eyewash' (in a letter to Frances J. Spratt on 20 November), but Gandhi, accompanied by Motilal, went on 23 December to the new and gleaming Viceroy's House at New Delhi. As coincidence would have it, that was Gandhi's day of silence, so the talks could not start before 4.15 p.m. when he broke his silence. It did save him the bother of discussing the proposed talks during the day with Patel, Sapru and Jinnah. The agenda was limited to political prisoners, the date of the first Round-Table Conference (1930 or 1931) and who should participate in it. It was as unreal an agenda as possible. The anger outside was searching for something far greater. On that very day a terrorist bomb had exploded near Delhi under the carriage of the Viceroy's train. Non-violent Gandhi expressed his horror at the incident; but there was no more conciliation. Gandhi and Motilal pointed out that dominion status was not an idea which had just been introduced to English ears; for more than a decade India had been agitating for it. What was wrong with dominion status now? Lord Irwin thought this argument unreasonable. And Jinnah, Patel and Sapru thought what Irwin thought. The moment had come for the nationalists and the pro-British elements within the freedom movement to go their different ways. It is interesting that, during the fifteen-minute journey from V. J. Patel's home to the Viceroy's Lodge, Jinnah, Sapru and Patel travelled in one car, and Motilal and Gandhi in another. Their ways had parted already.

On Christmas Day the forty-year-old Congress president-elect paraded through Lahore on a white charger. The packed crowds on either side of the narrow streets cheered, and women showered flower petals from the balconies. Exactly ten years before, in nearby Amritsar, Motilal had become president of the Congress for the first time; but he knew that this was something very different from 1919. He described the difference in a Persian phrase: 'Herche ke pidar natawanad, pesar tamam kunad' ('What the father cannot achieve, the son does').

Father and mother watched their son's coronation procession from the balcony of the Bhalla Shoe Company in the famous market, Anarkali. The photographs of the session show father and son in long, black *sherwanis* and black Gandhi caps; one can sense the tingle of excitement even in the few and indistinct pictures. On the night of 29 December, for the first time, Jawaharlal unfurled the flag of free India. Freedom had become the Congress resolve, and the mind was unchained. They danced around the flag at midnight on the banks of the Ravi, Jawaharlal himself leading this emotional outpouring of joy. Calling this the 'most momentous session' of the Congress, Jawaharlal declared:

> The flag under which you stand today and which you have just now saluted does not belong to any community . . . All those who stand today under this flag are Indians, not Hindus, not Muslims, but Indians . . . Remember once again, now that this flag is unfurled, it must not be lowered so long as a single Indian, man, woman or child, lives in India.

That flag would never come down. Nowhere did it fly more proudly after the Lahore session than at Anand Bhavan. On 9 April 1930 Motilal dedicated Anand Bhavan to the nation, and it was renamed Swaraj Bhavan, or Freedom House.

Sir Tej Bahadur Sapru thought the Congress had gone mad, and all the pro-British or communal politicians, from Jinnah to Malaviya, nodded their wise heads in solemn agreement. They even tried, on 26 February 1930, to formulate a separate solution. No one bothered. The country was in a different thrall.

The first call for full independence from a Congress platform had been given by the emotional Hasrat Mohani at the Ahmedabad Congress in 1921. Motilal demanded dominion status in the manifesto of the Swaraj Party in 1923 and placed it formally in the Assembly in February 1924. Jawaharlal took up his cry of full freedom at the Brussels Conference in February 1927. Gandhi objected to Jawaharlal's haste at Madras in 1928, uncertain about whether the 300 millions of Indians understood what it meant. But now he had endorsed the resolve, the first thing he set out to do was to give this freedom a real meaning to the 300 millions. On 2 January 1930 the new Congress working committee sanctioned Gandhi's plan. He wanted every village and town in India to celebrate this demand for independence with a pledge. The chosen day: Sunday 26 January. When India became free, it would adopt its Constitution and declare the nation a republic precisely twenty years later on this day.

This Independence Day pledge had a four-part message. Exploitation had reduced the Indian to an average income of seven pice a day: end it. Politically, India had been degraded: restore liberty. Culturally, India had been made to love the very chains which enslaved it: break the chains. Finally, the British had made the country impotent by the theory that its defence was safe only as part of the Empire: change that thinking. 'We hold it to be a crime against man and God to submit any longer to [this] rule,' said the pledge. The people responded with unprecedented enthusiasm. Gandhi was relieved, as Tendulkar writes; 'Thank God,' he said, 'they have unity in their starvation.'

Gandhi now expanded the four points to eleven. The Congress would call off civil disobedience if the British accepted these demands: total prohibition; restoration of the exchange rate to 1s 4d; 50 per cent reduction in land revenue; abolition of salt tax; military expenditure reduced to half; Civil Service salaries reduced to half; tariff against foreign cloth; a coastal reservation Bill; discharge of all political prisoners except those convicted of murder; abolition of CID; and the issuing of licences for firearms for self-defence. (Those who misunderstand the relationship between non-violence and the needs of security might consider that last point.) The British would never accept, of course. (The Raj might collapse, but it is doubtful if the salaries of the Civil Service would ever be cut!) Gandhi cheerfully admitted inconsistencies and explained: 'Mere withdrawal of the English is not independence. By mentioning the eleven points I have given a body in part to the illusive word "independence".' The stage was being further set. When the time came, Gandhi picked up the most elemental of these demands and converted it, with a magic only a Mahatma could conjure, into the mantra of the freedom movement. He picked up a handful of salt.

The original Mughal firman which allowed the East India Company a toehold in India in 1619 had specifically restricted the company only to overseas trade. When the Mughal weakened in Delhi, the *Angrez* grew bolder in Calcutta. The Court of Directors' General Letter of 26 April 1765 accepted that what it was now doing was illegal, but it was nevertheless delighted to rake in profits from the Company's newly flourishing inland trade in three commodities: betel nuts, tobacco and salt. That same year Robert Clive legalized the illegality. Shah Alam II was, after all, a pawn vulnerable to every knight on the Indian chessboard. The Fort William Council immediately vested the trade in these three items in a monopoly, and imposed a 35 per cent duty on 18 September 1765. While betel nuts and tobacco were, comparatively, luxuries, salt was not; and the growth of the British Empire was matched by a continuing rise in the salt tax. When Gandhi used the same symbol he knew that the people would at once understand, in a real way, what they were fighting and what they were fighting for. Liberty had to mean salt, or it would be nothing more than an upper-class slogan. Gandhi wrote to Lord Irwin on 2 March 1930: 'The [salt] tax shows itself more burdensome on the poor man, when it is remembered that salt is the one thing he must eat more than the rich.'

This time the excitement was building across the world, and not just in India, as the day of Gandhi's 'final conflict' approached. Journalists sent word of this unique story to every corner, and messages of support came from men of politics, men of religion and ordinary men who had no greater desire than to see fellow human beings freed from imperial chains. The crowds each day on the banks of the Sabarmati that March were unprecedented. Through prayer, sermon and example Gandhi gave them simple lessons which they would never forget. And each day was filled with rumours, as speculation raged on whether the government would allow the Mahatma to begin his Salt March to Dandi or not.

The very Christian Lord Irwin did not communicate only with the biblical Almighty, apparently; he also kept in touch with Hindu gods. The story may seem unbelievable, but there it is. In his note to Wedgwood Benn dated 7 April 1930, Lord Irwin said he wanted neither to make Gandhi an unnecessary martyr, nor to give the impression that anyone was 'unarrestable'. He faced the true dilemma of a man of power who recognized that at the core of his apparent strength was a weakness and vulnerability which this fakir had exposed. A frustrated Irwin told Benn that the best thing that could happen to the British was the death of Gandhi. Irwin said he was convinced that Gandhi would die that year, and therefore he should be allowed whatever took his fancy in his last days. How could Irwin be sure? The astrologers had predicted it. If this proves nothing else, it proves that astrologers were making fools of Delhi's rulers long before they started wearing khaddar. The stars had, as it transpired, planned the death of the Empire before the death of the Mahatma: not by much, but still before.

There were no women among the band of seventy-nine *satyagrahis* who set off at 6.30 on the morning of 12 March for a village which had once boasted a lighthouse but was now a deserted spot on the Gujarat sea-coast 241 miles from Sabarmati Ashram. Gandhi's reason for the absence of women: 'A delicate sense of chivalry.' He may also have been prompted by his English disciple Mirabehn's desire to join the march; as he had once done with Charlie Andrews, Gandhi kept the Britisher, however well meaning and genuine, out of a gesture which had to be seen by India's masses as a totally Indian effort. He wanted India to be independent of both enemy and friend, to fight alone. At sixty-one, he was the oldest on the march; the youngest was sixteen, numerically opposite. The *satyagrahis* came from Punjab, Gujarat, Maharashtra, United Provinces, Kutch, Sind, Kerala, Rajputana, Andhra, Karnataka, Bombay, Tamil Nadu, Bihar, Bengal, Orissa, Nepal and Fiji. The whole of India was with Gandhi: Hindus, Muslims, untouchables, Christians. His goal: to reach Dandi on 5 April, so that he could break the law by preparing salt on 6 April. It was a date which married different strands of history. Eleven years before, Gandhi had called a hartal in protest against the Rowlatt

Act. The 6th of April was the anniversary of Jallianwala Bagh, and every year 6 to 13 April was observed as National Week.

The 24-day Dandi march was an unparalleled triumph played out in front of the world's cameras and print media. At 8.30 on the morning of 6 April, soon after his prayers, Gandhi walked into the sea and picked up a lump of natural salt. The signal that India was waiting for had been given. Gandhi declared open 'this war against the salt tax'. He told the country through *Young India*: 'Let me distinguish between the call of 1920 and the present call. The call of 1920 was a call for preparation, today it is a call for engaging in a final conflict.'

The man who welcomed this difference most eagerly was waiting in Allahabad. He had been very busy organizing the party and motivating the people; there were circulars and letters and statements to the press. 'How I wish', Jawaharlal wrote to 'Bapuji' on 7 March, 'I could join your gallant band or at least could see it start off bravely on the morning of the 12th.' But all Congress leaders were meant to be in their provinces, to lead civil disobedience in their areas. On the 12th Jawaharlal sent a detailed circular to the provinces outlining the plan of action (beginning 'Dear Comrade'); on the 13th he described what needed to be done if the Mahatma were arrested. On 24 March there was a passionate article for *Young India* which summed up his emotions: '*Inquilab zindabad! Inquilab zindabad!* Loud the shouts rang out in conference and meeting hall, and the echo answered, *Inquilab zindabad* . . . India was going to be free. The youths had decided it.' And he asked those youths who wanted to remain on-lookers: 'What shall it profit you to get your empty degrees and your mess of pottage if the millions starve and your motherland continues in bondage? Who lives if India dies? Who dies if India lives?'

On the evening of 10 April, Jawaharlal led the first batch of Allahabad *satyagrahis*; anxious, eager to be arrested. It was a superb turn-out. His wife Kamala and his sister Krishna were with him. The city erupted. Muslims vied with Hindus to garland the *satyagrahis*; once again the amity of a Gandhian movement had destroyed the machinations of the communalists. Jawaharlal wrote to Sitla Sahai: 'I have never seen Allahabad quite so excited.' He was eager to be arrested, but the Viceroy would not oblige. Congressmen were being picked up: Krishna Datt Paliwal in Agra, Hariharnath Shastri in Kanpur, Mata Prasad Misra in Rae Bareli. Jawaharlal knew his turn was only a matter of time. He nominated Gandhi as the party president of Congress in case of his absence. Gandhi declined, and Motilal took the job back. The 'great day!' (as Jawaharlal noted in his pocket diary) came on 14 April, just after the end of National Week.

He was on his way to Raipur in Central Provinces to preside over the third session of the Hindi provincial conference. With him was a man whose eight-volume biography of Gandhi was to become a classic, the Cambridge-educated D. G. Tendulkar (1909–71). The first leg was a shuttle to Cheoki, to join the Bombay Mail which would take him to Raipur. At 7.35 in the morning the police picked him up at Cheoki and took him to Naini by car, choosing this isolated station to avoid any popular demonstrations against the arrest. The trial in front of the magistrate, J. S. Grose, took place the same day. It lasted two hours. The accused happily admitted his 'guilt' under Section 9(c) of the Indian Salt Act XII of 1882. According to Shiv Dayal, the salt inspector, the accused had filtered a mixture of saline earth and water through a tin and, when the salt was finally ready, put it in a piece of paper. Naim-ul-Haq, the sub-inspector of police, corroborated the evidence. Six months. Off to Naini Central Prison.

On 17 April, Jawaharlal recorded in his diary that he had been arrested and convicted on an auspicious day: Vaisakh 1987, or the New Year's Day of the Samvat calendar. That day, however, marked the beginning of more than half a decade of loneliness, tragedy and, inevitably, bouts of severe depression. Though he played his part in sabotaging a conciliation effort between the Viceroy and Gandhi in July 1930, Jawaharlal was effectively marginalized from Congress politics till Gandhi brought him back to centre stage in 1936 – once again on the eve of a historic moment: the first elections in which the Congress participated. But till then Jawaharlal would spend most of his days in gaol. It was a time of personal tragedy too; his beloved father and his extraordinary wife passed away, one of age, the other of illness. Whether he realized it when they were alive or not, both were enormous reservoirs of strength on whom he depended. His father was the great patriarch-friend who guided his son's destiny with both a seen and an unseen hand as and when he was able to – or was allowed to. As for Kamala, Jawaharlal took her for granted until the intimations of her departure magnified the consciousness of the loss. The sole consolation of these five years of wilderness, of life without parents, without the warmth of a wife or a beautiful growing daughter, was that it gave Jawaharlal time to indulge his passion for reading and writing. It is to British gaols that we owe some fine writing: essays in history, culture, politics, religion, a diary which measures the heartbeat of this sentimental hero and an autobiography which is an important contribution to history.

On 14 April 1930 Jawaharlal could hardly have been blamed for being in very high spirits. This was the revolution he had been dreaming about all his life. The news from outside the 'circular wall' of the prison was exhilarating: the movement had got a fillip with his arrest. Police opened fire on protesting crowds in Calcutta, Madras and Karachi, three far-flung corners of the subcontinent. Bombay displayed its anger with distinct panache: six donkeys were decked in foreign clothes – hats included – and paraded on all the main streets. In Peshawar the movement took a tragic turn when the Khudai Khidmatgar (the non-violent Servants of God) challenged armoured cars to protest the arrest of their leader Khan Abdul Ghaffar Khan; there were hundreds of deaths and casualties. One particular incident sparkled with the new spirit of India; the Hindu troops of two platoons of the Second Battalion of the 18th Royal Garhwal Rifles refused to fire on Muslim demonstrators, and in fact handed over their arms. For a while, the people took control of Peshawar; it needed reinforcements and air support to bring the city back under British control by 4 May. That was also the day Gandhi was finally arrested: forty-five minutes after midnight the district magistrate of Surat, two police officers and thirty policemen, all armed, surrounded his camp at Karadi, three miles from Dandi. The Mahatma asked gently, 'You want me?' He wanted a little time to get himself ready and then requested a fellow *satyagrahi* to recite his favourite hymn, 'Vaishnavajan'. He heard it standing, his head bent, his eyes closed. At ten past one, a constable picked up his two *khadi* satchels; and they put him in a lorry and took him away to Yeravda Central Gaol.

The year ended on a high note for the interned Jawaharlal. Released on 11 October, it took him just eight days to return to prison. On 19 October he was charged under Section 124(A) of the Indian Penal Code – a law intended for anyone who excited feelings of disaffection against the government. It was added to the Penal Code in 1870 but first used against Tilak in 1897. Punishment could range up to transportation for life. On 12 October, Jawaharlal had addressed a meeting which gave the authorities sufficient cause to prosecute, but they waited till he had gone and seen his ill father in Mussoorie. On 18 October the police came while he was addressing a peasants' conference at Allahabad at 7.30 in the morning. He declined to accept the initial order. At 8.30 that night his car was stopped as he was returning from a public meeting and he was back in Naini Central Prison. Naim-ul-Haq was back in the witness-box. The sentence this time was eighteen months plus a fine of Rs 500, or a further three months in gaol.

Jawaharlal's forty-first birthday was celebrated all over the country, on the orders of Motilal, the nominated president of the Congress, as Jawahar Day. As he noted exultantly in his prison diary when news reached him in prison about the events of 14 November: 'Jawahar Day! Arrests – convictions – lathi charges all over the country!' About twenty people died in police firing; 1,500 were wounded, 1,679 arrested. Excerpts were publicly read out from his pamphlet, *The Eight Days Interlude*, describing his eight days out of gaol. It was also a day on which Motilal could feel legitimate pride in this son who had, against all expectations, fulfilled a father's greatest dreams. Jawahar Day over, Motilal's weakening body collapsed.

Only one man in India could have asked Mahatma Gandhi for a drink. And because he could, he did. The man was Motilal Nehru. It was not a drink that he really wanted so much as to tease the prohibitionist Mahatma. Gandhi touched his elder friend's arm and said, 'Motilal, you should not think of earthly things like drinks. You should recite the *Gita* and try to think of unworldly, spiritual things.' Gandhi's mind was on the next life; but Motilal replied with a flash of his devastating repartee: 'I leave unworldly things to you and my wife. While I'm on earth I will be earthy.'

There was not much time left on earth. Motilal was on his deathbed.

The exhaustion of the last great campaign against the British had finally proved too much for this seventy-year-old lion. His mind still roared, but his body was wasting under the attack of piles and the chronic asthma that had troubled him for decades and had now caused fibrosis of the lungs and a tumour in the right side of the chest. On 17 November 1930 he left for Calcutta to be examined by three of the most famous doctors of the day, the three friends, as he put it, to whom he had handed over his body for safekeeping: Jivraj Mehta, Nilratan Sarkar and B. C. Roy – who was allowed out of Alipore Central Gaol for a few hours to take a look at Motilal. He moved to a garden house in Calcutta to rest. On 1 January, Kamala, who had become a heroine in her own right with her work, particularly among the women, during this civil disobedience campaign (from gaol Jawaharlal called it, in a letter to Indira, 'a pleasant New Year gift to me'), was arrested and sent to Lucknow Central Gaol. Motilal rushed back to Allahabad. When he went to see Jawaharlal on 12 January for the permitted fortnightly visit, his son got a shock. He recalled in his autobiography: 'his face was even more swollen. He had some difficulty in speaking, and his mind was not always quite clear. But his old will remained, and this held on and kept the body and mind functioning.' Not for long. By the time the Congress leaders were released on 26 January, Motilal was clearly dying. Jawaharlal was in fact released a few hours earlier to be with his father. Gandhi left Bombay within a day for Allahabad. Motilal's last wish was to participate in a Congress working committee meeting in his old home, now called Swaraj Bhavan. Gandhi reached there late at night, but Motilal was awake, waiting for him.

Gandhi comforted him: 'We shall surely win *swaraj* if you survive this crisis.'

Motilal was a realist: 'I am going soon, Mahatmaji, and I shall not be here to see *swaraj*. But I know that you have won it and will soon have it.'

He could still be mischievous, as his daughter Krishna (who also left behind the story about the drink) recalls in *We Nehrus*. At one point, when he seemed to be in a coma, he suddenly opened his eyes and told Gandhi who was sitting beside him:

Bapu, if you and I happened to die at the same time, you, being a saintly man, would presumably go to heaven right off. But, with due deference, I think this is what would happen: you would come to our River of Death; you would stand on the bank and then, most probably, you would walk across it, perhaps alone or maybe holding on to the tail of a cow. I would arrive much later. I'd get into a fast new motor boat, shoot past you, and get there ahead of you. Of course, being very worldly, I might not be allowed into heaven – if there is one.

On 4 February, Motilal's doctors made one last effort to save him, taking him to Lucknow, where he stayed at the palace of one of those rare *taluqdars* who were sympathetic to the freedom movement, Raja Awadhesh Singh. He insisted he wanted to die in Anand Bhavan, but his doctors would not listen. Jawaharlal remembers: 'Early next morning, February 6th, I was watching by his bedside. He had had a troublesome and restless night; suddenly I noticed that his face grew calm and the sense of struggle vanished from it.'

Gandhi said in a statement: 'What I have lost through the death of Motilalji is a loss for ever: "Rock of ages, cleft for me, let me hide myself in thee".' On 7 March at a public meeting in Delhi he revealed: 'I may tell you that when on the last day of his presence on earth he referred to the Garhwalis, only I was by his side ... I consider that as his last will and testament to me.' The Garhwalis were the Hindu troops who had refused to fire at the red-shirt *satyagrahis* in Peshawar the year before. And that surely was Motilal's greatest testament: his unwavering commitment to Hindu–Muslim unity. When in June 1912 Jawaharlal returned from Cambridge, neither son nor father ever imagined the historic part they would play in the nation's life, but even in 1912 Motilal was warning his colleagues in the Congress about the dangers of flirting with the Hindu Mahasabha. As his participation in political life increased, so did his commitment against Hindu chauvinism. In the 1920s, when Gandhi left a vacuum with his withdrawal from active politics, Motilal stepped in; it was a vital contribution, for in his absence the legislatures might have gone totally into the hands of Hindu or Muslim communalists. Muhammad Ali acknowledged this when he said in 1925 that the only Hindus whom the Muslims trusted were Gandhi and the two Nehrus. It was this trust which, in turn, confirmed every dark suspicion of the bigoted Hindu, who found both the Mughal–Muslim and the British–Christian influences in Motilal and his son abhorrent.

Motilal was an irreligious realist. He was never hypocritical. He had the confidence of a man who knew his mind and was never afraid of his convictions. When the tides seemed to turn against him, as in late 1926, he might get depressed, but he refused to get defeated – not by the Lajpat Rais, not by the Malaviyas, not by the Birlas. His secularism was not garbed in religiosity, as it was with Gandhi. It was a product of the Mughal court culture, of an education that included Sanskrit and Persian and of a liberal outlook which was rooted in generosity towards one's fellow man. There was no shortage of patriots in that era, but there was some need for patriots who were not overt or covert bigots. Motilal's legacy also shaped the thinking of India's first Prime Minister. The liberal temperament bred a scientific approach; and both father and son exulted in the blessings of technological advance. If Gandhi was Jawaharlal's spiritual parent, then Motilal was the true father of a modern prime minister. No commitment in Motilal's life was greater than his love for his son. The faith in Jawaharlal's greatness was almost fanatical. Gandhi, who understood both well enough to know what he was talking about, was once asked what was Motilal's most striking quality. Love for his son, replied Gandhi. Not love for his country? came a follow-up question. 'No,' said Gandhi. 'Motilal's love for India was derived from his love for Jawaharlal.'

Jawaharlal missed his father immensely and could not reconcile himself to the patriarch's absence. On a holiday in Ceylon in the summer of 1931, he almost wired his father to join them. He was puzzled by a letter which reached him in May 1931, bearing innumerable stamps of post offices around the world. His name on the envelope was in his father's handwriting. Amazed, he opened it to discover that the letter had been sent more than five years before, on 28 February 1926, and was meant to reach him in Bombay, care of the Italian Lloyd steamer on which he was travelling to Europe. It was a letter of farewell.

It was but natural that Motilal would dominate him in death in a way he never could in life. This post-mortem hero-worship reached a point where Jawaharlal told Gandhi after the Karachi Congress ratified the Gandhi–Irwin pact that, if his father had been alive, the Congress might have achieved more. The remark hurt Gandhi bitterly.

The only Indians at the first Round-Table Conference were members of the Raj lobby: leaders of communal organizations, princes, landowners, industrialists. Some of the worthies were Jinnah, Muhammad Ali, the Aga Khan, Raja Narendra Nath and Moonje (the Hindu Mahasabhaites), the princes of Bhopal, Patiala, Baroda, Alwar *et al.* At noon on 12 November 1930 King-Emperor George V inaugurated the first Round-Table Conference; his speech was

broadcast to the world on the radio. After ten weeks of tepid disagreement the conference limped to a dismal end. India, in any case,
was with the man in gaol, Gandhi, and not with these men sitting in
the Royal Palace at St James's. The flamboyant Muhammad Ali
reminded King George V that if he did not watch out he would lose
India just as his ancestor had lost America. Ali was ill. Perhaps it was
a premonition of death which had made him borrow money to take
his wife along on this last journey. On the eve of his death he once
again became an advocate of Hindu–Muslim harmony, dictating a
letter to Ramsay MacDonald on this subject on 3 January. That
evening he suffered a stroke; the next morning he was dead. He was
buried in Jerusalem near the Dome of the Rock, marked by the
inscription: 'Here lies al-Sayyid Muhammad Ali al-Hindi.'

There were far more Muslims with Gandhi then than with the
Aga Khan or with Jinnah (in fact, Abbas Tyabji had been nominated
to lead the Dandi march in case of Gandhi's arrest). An appropriately
named Congress Muslim Party was far more active than the League.
The pitiful condition of the League was reflected in the very thin
attendance at its session in December at Allahabad presided over by
the famous poet-philosopher Muhammad Iqbal (1877–1938). Jinnah
had handed over the presidentship because he was fed up. Jinnah
went off to London, along with his daughter Dina and sister Fatima,
took a passport which described England as his place of residence,
set up a practice, in which he was eminently successful, and lobbied
hard to become a member of the House of Commons, with no
success. Wolpert quotes a Labour leader on Jinnah: 'We don't want
a toff like that!' The toff turned to the Tories, hoping that such
qualities would find more appeal here. The Tories had a different
problem with him: he was not the right colour. It was a time of great
frustration for Jinnah.

The British realized at the end of the first Round-Table Conference
that they would have to deal with Gandhi. Release, on 26 January
(now celebrated as Independence Day by the Congress) 1931, was
the first step. Then Sapru, Jayakar and Srinivasa Sastri were sent
with a message to Gandhi that Irwin wanted a dialogue. Gandhi
agreed, and thus began one of the duels that lend romance to the
dusty story of politics. Lord Montagu had wondered in 1919 at this
man 'dressed like a coolie . . . who lives practically on air'. Now
Lord Irwin learned that Gandhi actually lived on dates and goat's

milk though, of course, he still dressed like a coolie. At half-past two on the afternoon of 17 February the Gandhi–Irwin talks began at the Viceroy's Palace in Delhi and on the first day continued till six. Gandhi stayed at Dr Ansari's house and would often walk the five miles from the palace alone.

In London, Churchill thundered at the coolie:

> It is alarming and also nauseating to see Mr Gandhi, a seditious Middle Temple lawyer, now posing as a fakir of a type well known in the East, striding half-naked up the steps of the Viceregal palace while he is still organizing and conducting a defiant campaign of civil disobedience, to parley on equal terms with the representative of the King-Emperor.

Churchill was right about the terms being equal; if anything, Gandhi was the superior. That in itself had never happened before: an Indian in a dhoti getting more attention from India and the world than the Viceroy! The psychological impact on an enslaved nation was extraordinary. They now came in hundreds of thousands to his prayer-meetings in Delhi; even the Muslim League tottered, and Sir Muhammad Shafi requested Gandhi (who, in official League parlance, was only the leader of 21 crore Hindus) to address its council. The speech made there on 22 February is as definitive a statement of Gandhi's position on the Hindu–Muslim question as one can come across:

> Brethren, I am a *bania*, and there is no limit to my greed. It had always been my dream and heart's desire to speak not only for 21 crores but for the 30 crores [300 million] of Indians. Today you may not accept that position of mine. But I may assure you that my early upbringing and training in my childhood and youth have been to strive for Hindu–Muslim unity, and none today may dismiss it merely as a craze of my old age. My heart is, however, confident that God will grant me that position when I may speak for the whole of India, and if I may have to die striving for that ideal, I shall achieve the peace of my heart.

Gandhi and Irwin grew fond of each other. On 1 March the Mahatma even had his dinner of dates and a pint of goat's milk in the company of the Viceroy. The talks, however, were going badly at that point. It was personal chemistry, as much as political judgement, which finally enabled Irwin to concede enough to Gandhi; a settlement was reached at half-past one on the night of 4–5 March.

(London was irritated by this personal chemistry. Irwin's successor was Lord Willingdon, who was rude enough to put any Indian off. Willingdon had even insulted Jinnah's wife Ruttie at a dinner-party when he was governor of Bombay – a discourtesy Jinnah never forgave.) At twelve on 5 March, after eight meetings totalling twenty-four hours, Irwin and Gandhi signed their famous pact and toasted their success with a cup of tea. Gandhi, ever prepared with symbols, took out a paper bag from his shawl. 'Thank you,' he told the Viceroy. 'I will put some of this salt into my tea to remind us of the famous Boston Tea-Party.' They both laughed, but who could miss that Gandhi had made both his immediate and future point? He had used illegal salt at the Viceroy's Palace and hinted broadly what the next step would be – the tea-party was the prelude to freedom from Britain. When he left the Viceroy that day, Gandhi forgot his shawl. Lord Irwin saw it, picked it up and gave it back with a gentle smile, saying, 'Gandhi, you haven't so much on, you know, that you can afford to leave this behind.'

Civil disobedience was 'discontinued'. The boycott was withdrawn as a political weapon, and picketing was curbed. In return the Raj accepted the concept of 'Indian responsibility' and invited the Congress to the second Round-Table talks. Jawaharlal, however, wept when he heard the terms of the Gandhi–Irwin pact. As far as he was concerned, it was a sell-out. His *purna swaraj* had not been achieved. Once again Gandhi had to bring him into line. Totally against his will, but bowing to party discipline, he moved the re-solution ratifying the Gandhi–Irwin settlement at the Karachi Congress at the end of March. As he remembers in his autobiography, he kept his unhappiness to himself: 'I lay and pondered on that March night, and in my heart there was a great emptiness as of something precious gone, almost beyond recall. *"This is the way the world ends. Not with a bang, but a whimper."*'

There were other reasons for distress that March night. Lord Irwin had ignored one plea made by Gandhi, a plea which voiced the feelings of the whole country, and gone ahead with the hanging of Bhagat Singh, Sukhdev and Rajguru. On the night of 23 March the three revolutionaries had died on the gallows. 'The corpse of Bhagat Singh,' declared Jawaharlal, 'shall stand between us and England.' The wave of anger which swept the country would have washed away the Gandhi–Irwin pact, but the Mahatma virtually ordered the

Congress to stand by the commitment he had made to Irwin, and no one dared defy him. The young demonstrated in Karachi, shouting, 'Gandhi's truce has sent Bhagat Singh to the gallows!' Using all the tact and steel at his command, Gandhi steered this Congress session, whose president was Sardar Patel, in the direction he wanted. Slowly, India fell silent.

Silent, that is, except for the sound of a familiar frenzy: communal riots broke out in Kanpur, Agra, Benaras, Mirzapur and other cities. Jawaharlal's health broke down, and he went with Kamala on a much-needed holiday to Ceylon. On his return in June, he returned to his old fight, of the peasants against the *taluqdars*. Suspicious – and rightly too – of Gandhi's ambivalence on this issue, he launched an independent movement to stop payment of rents. After long months of public meetings and fruitless discussions with government officials, the district Congress committees of Rae Bareli, Etawah, Kanpur, Unnao and Allahabad were given the signal, on 6 December, to begin a no-rent campaign. On 14 December, at the request of the United Provinces government, Delhi promulgated the United Provinces Instigation and Emergency Powers Ordinance. On 21 December, Nehru was served an order under Section 5 not to leave Allahabad and not to speak at public meetings or publish anything. He refused. On 26 December he was arrested. On 4 January he was produced before a magistrate, for the first time an Indian, Sohan Lal Srivastava. The judgement: two years' rigorous imprisonment and a fine of Rs 500 or a further six months in gaol. Naturally he did not pay the fine, and the government seized a car registered in the name of Indira. (It was bought later at an auction by a certain Mrs L. Singh, for Rs 1,150, who requested the government to keep her name strictly confidential.) Apart from two brief spells outside, he would be in gaol till September 1935 – by which time his wife Kamala would be on her death-bed.

Gandhi was on his way back from the second Round-Table Conference when Jawaharlal was arrested. The omens had been all wrong. Gandhi should have read the true intentions of the British when they refused to allow him to keep Dr M. A. Ansari in his delegation. When Gandhi sailed on the *Rajputana* on 29 August 1931, with him were Malaviya, Sarojini Naidu, Prabhashankar Pattani, Mahadev Desai, Pyarelal, his son Devadas and Mirabehn. G. D. Birla was also on the same boat and headed for the same conference but representing the Federation of Indian Chambers of Commerce. To put it bluntly, there were no Muslims with Gandhi. The British would not allow Gandhi the right to represent Muslims; that right would belong only to the Raj-approved Muslim leaders. Gandhi admitted in London that leaving Ansari behind had been a fatal blunder, and he had no one else to blame but himself. Congress Muslims swallowed their bitterness and stayed with Gandhi. Ghaffar Khan, in fact, merged his Khudai Khidmatgars into the Congress only that year.

The Muslim League had just adumbrated, in the meanwhile, the ghost of another idea. Speaking to his motley gathering in Allahabad at the League session of 1930, the Persian and Urdu poet who had degrees from Heidelberg, Munich and Trinity, Cambridge, in addition to being a barrister from Lincoln's Inn, Muhammad Iqbal, asked for a 'Muslim India'. And he defined this Muslim India: 'I would like to see the Punjab, the North-West Frontier Province, Sind and Baluchistan amalgamated into a single state.' That is exactly what the 'final destiny' of Pakistan has been, after a country twice that size was created in 1947 and then broken apart by a civil war in 1971.

23 The Most Exclusive School in the World

'CHEERIO GET WELL SOON AND BRING THE HOWLING INFANT HERE FOR DISPLAY AND CRITICISM LOVE JAWAHAR.' The new head of the Nehru family was obviously in a Wodehousean mood when he sent that telegram from Almora prison in February 1935 to his 'Beti', the younger sister, who had just given birth to the first boy in the family to survive in forty-five years – that is, since the birth of Jawaharlal himself. (Male Nehrus had been born, including to Jawaharlal, but had not survived.) Krishna took her son, Harsha, to her Bhai, and recalls in *We Nehrus*: 'So he had his first glimpse of a prison at the age of six weeks, which is rather early even for a Nehru.' Point. Every Nehru went to gaol, including Motilal's wife Swarup Rani; this brave lady even had to suffer the brutality of a lathi charge during the National Week (6 to 13 April, now commemorating Jallianwala, Rowlatt movement and Dandi march) of 1932. A procession she was leading in Allahabad was halted by the police. Unconcerned and determined, she sat down in the middle of the road; the only concession she allowed herself was the comfort of a chair. The police charged to clear the road of the *satyagrahis*. She was hit repeatedly on the head and fell unconscious with blood flowing from her wounds. A rumour ran through the city that night that she had died, and angry Allahabadis attacked the police. But she survived, and wrote on 16 April 1932 to her son in Bareilly gaol (where his barracks were 6 feet below ground level, the walls consequently over 21 feet high, prompting Jawaharlal to label them the Great Wall of China): 'The mother of a brave son is also somewhat like him. It was only a lathi – had it been a gun I would have bared my chest.'

A conscious insult by the gaoler sent Jawaharlal into a fury. Seething at the manner in which his daughter Indira had been treated when she came to visit him, he set a self-imposed ban on their visits, which he broke only after eight months on Gandhi's intervention. He deeply missed his wife, whose love he had rediscovered on their holiday in Ceylon the previous year, and his growing daughter, now in her teens. In June 1932 he was shifted from Bareilly to the cooler prison in the hill resort of Dehra Dun. To his relief, the super-intendent here, a Captain Falvey, had once been a disciple of Eamon de Valera and quietly sympathized with another nationalist strug-gling against British rule. Subhas Bose had once sneered at Jawa-harlal's 'sentimental politics'; the accusation had some truth, be-cause his heart was always an enormous influence on his head. Prison life could rouse him as easily to poetry as to tears. 'One misses many things in prison,' he wrote in his autobiography, 'but perhaps most of all one misses the sound of women's voices and children's laugh-ter.' He found great comfort in nature:

> Upon that little tent of blue
> Which prisoners call the sky,
> And at every drifting cloud that went
> With sails of silver by.

One of the worst days he spent in prison was the Christmas Eve of 1932 in Dehra Dun. A thunderstorm had turned the Himalayan winter into a special torture. But suddenly the sky cleared in the evening, and all misery vanished as he saw his beloved mountains again, now gently covered by a mantle of snow. He enjoyed the miracle of changing seasons, saw with surprise four giant *peepul* trees quickly drop all their leaves and watched with joy a million little bits of green suddenly turned into spring leaves.

It was a little tough, but Jawaharlal did manage to establish peace-ful relations with the small animals and insects living in his cell or in the yard outside. However, there could be no truce with bedbugs, mosquitoes and flies, though wasps and hornets he tolerated. They tolerated him too – as he put it: 'We respected each other.' Of bats he had a horror; silently, soundlessly, they seemed to pass within an inch of his face, and he was terrified that they would hit him. But he welcomed the occasional presence of a snake; well, if not quite the snake, then at least the diversion caused by the ensuing commotion. He was not particularly frightened of snakes. Centipedes alarmed him much more, and there was a nightmarish memory of one crawling over him at night in Calcutta's Alipore gaol. He was fas-cinated by scorpions, frequent visitors after rains. He once kept a brutish specimen in a bottle for a while, feeding it with flies until it escaped. In Lucknow he made friends with a squirrel, which often scurried up his stationary leg as he sat under a tree, reading. What he was most grateful for, however, was the company of dogs; they were intelligent friends, and he had always been fond of them. Anand Bhavan was once full of them.

Still, nothing could compensate for the frustration of inactivity, even as great events took place outside the prison walls. The news of Gandhi's fast against the decision of Ramsay MacDonald to award separate electorates to untouchables irritated him. This was another British attempt at divide in order to rule, another communal card with which to trump the freedom movement: divide untouchables from Hindus, play off the two and turn the hero of the untouchables, Dr B. R. Ambedkar, into an equivalent of Jinnah. Dr Ambedkar had in fact begun to encourage untouchables to convert to Buddhism, so we might well have had a Buddhist League, if Gandhi had not personally taken up the challenge. A compromise was reached: no separate electorates for the untouchables but reserved seats – a practice prevalent in India till the moment of writing. Gandhi broke his fast on 26 September 1932. But in prison Nehru thought Gandhi was risking his life unnecessarily and was irritated at 'his religious and sentimental approach to a political question . . . And his frequent references to God – God has made him do this, God even indicated the date of the fast, etc. – were most irritating.' He was relieved to hear of the settlement.

Jawaharlal was fretting at his inactivity. As he wrote to Indira on 3 October (she had been with Gandhi during this fast and met Rabindranath Tagore as well, so she had her share of excitement too): 'Well, the excitement is over now and Bapu leaves his mango tree and goes back to his cell, and you go back to your school routine, and I, well, I remain where I was! And I read and write and spin and stand on my head.' He had become an expert at yoga. Often he succumbed to depression:

The years I have spent in prison! Sitting alone, wrapped in my thoughts, how many seasons I have seen go by, following each other into oblivion! How many moons I have watched wax and wane, and the pageant of the stars moving along inexorably and majestically! How many yesterdays of my youth lie buried here; and sometimes I see the ghosts of these dead yesterdays rise up, bringing poignant memories, and whispering to me: 'Was it worthwhile?'

Outside prison, it always seemed worth the while; inside, matters often looked different.

His diary entry for Sunday 4 September said: 'We did get through August at last! But it took some doing.' Then he quoted two rather ordinary lines of Urdu poetry: 'Subah hoti hai, shaam hoti hai / Umar yun hi tamam hoti hai' ('The day passes, the evening passes / This is how life passes'). It was the same man who wrote just five years before to his dear friend Syed Mahmud, wondering why the latter indulged in the sentimental nonsense of Urdu poetry. There was only one escape route: 'Heigh-ho! What a life! The same round, day after day, and nothing to distinguish one day from another . . . And books, books – what would one do without them to escape from ennui and depression?' Posterity should, however, thank fortune for those enforced spells of ennui. Jawaharlal's appetite for books was always legendary. One particular order has been widely quoted; there is no reason why it should not be repeated here. On 14 February 1929 he sent an order to The Times Book Club in London for forty-nine books on science, technology, politics, socialism, history (biographies of Tamerlane, Genghis Khan, Lenin), exploitation (from Upton Sinclair's *The Profits of Religion* to Sidney and Beatrice Webb's *The Decay of Capitalist Civilization*), the Soviet Union (John Reed, Bukharin), China, British colonial policy, Africa, classics like Samuel Butler's *Erewhon* and new works like Isadora Duncan's *My Life*. Now he took up Arnold Toynbee, Harold Laski, Julian Huxley, Tagore and a dozen others in addition to Indian epics like the *Bhagavad Gita*, *Ramayana* and *Mahabharata*. His favourite British papers included the *New Statesman* and *The Spectator*.

Prison became a kind of enforced sabbatical. No wonder, while comforting his sister Krishna once on her way towards gaol, Nehru described prison as the most exclusive school in the world. He did both reading and writing at this school. We owe three classics to his prison days: *Glimpses of World History* (1934–5), *An Autobiography* and *The Discovery of India* (1946). *Glimpses* was the best gift an itinerant father could ever give his child. As he wrote to Indira on her thirteenth birthday: 'My presents cannot be very material or solid. They can only be of the air and of the mind and spirit, such as a good fairy might have bestowed on you – things that even the high walls of prison cannot stop.' These letters, begun tentatively and then continued because Indira loved them, developed into an amazing (given that Jawaharlal was writing without references) and fascinating history of civilization, dipping into near and remote corners of human experience and turning events and impressions into a collage that could capture a growing child's insatiable mind. The letters were also an intellectual release from incarceration. On 19 May 1932 he wrote, to give just one example of dozens:

> I feel often enough that I am not at all a good guide for you through the maze of past history. I get lost myself. How, then, can I guide you aright? But again I think that perhaps I might be of a little help to you, and so I continue these letters. To me certainly they are of great help. As I write them and think of you, my dear, I forget that the temperature in the shade and where I sit is 112 degrees and the hot *looh* is blowing. And I forget even sometimes that I am in the District Gaol of Bareilly. My last letter carried you right up to the end of the fourteenth century in Malaysia. And yet in northern India we have not gone beyond King Harsha's time.

If he erred it was only on the side of Indian nationalism and an anti-colonial bias – no bad thing for a daughter who would one day become Prime Minister in her own right.

In June 1934, 'in a mood of self-questioning', Jawaharlal began the story of his own life, first titled 'In and Out of Prison' but published simply as *An Autobiography*. (Was he, at the age of forty-five, influenced by the fact that Gandhi had also written his autobiography a few years earlier?) His attempt, he said, would trace his mental development, not history. When it was published in the spring of 1936 it was at once acclaimed as a valuable insight into one of the great contemporary minds. It became a best-seller and went into many editions. Its appeal lay both in its content and in its style; even Nehru's targets applauded an enemy they could respect. The only ones who found nothing illuminating were the anti-Nehru politicians of India who predictably commented that Jawaharlal did not understand the 'soul of India'. Their anger was against not the book but the author. They could not take a man who had written pamphlets for Congressmen like this one on unemployment in India in April 1929: 'It is said that there are 52 lakh sadhus and beggars in India. Possibly some of them are honest. But there is no doubt that most of them are completely useless people, who wish to dupe others and live on their earnings without working themselves ... Our country is overburdened by these lakhs of worthless people and idlers.' The Hindu Mahasabhaites could hardly take kindly to a man who attacked the *pandas* at places of pilgrimage as quacks. *The Discovery of India*, a mix of reminiscence and essays, was the result of his last term in prison, written in five months between April and September 1944 and dedicated 'To my colleagues and co-prisoners in the Ahmadnagar Fort Prison Camp from 9 August 1942 to 28 March 1945'. *An Autobiography* had a dedication of six bare words: 'To Kamala who is no more'.

Kamala died at five in the morning on Friday 28 February 1936 at Lausanne in Switzerland where she had gone to a sanatorium for her last battle against death, in severe pain but conscious to the end, her body eaten away by tuberculosis. She was thirty-seven.

   Kamala had been born in a large house in that fortress of Delhi's Kashmiri Pandits, Bazar Sitaram, the first child of Rajpati and Jawaharmal Kaul. As was the custom of the times, education was the prerogative of men; Kamala had to be content with Hindu and Sanskrit scriptures at home, a fact she bitterly regretted. In her last years, women's education became a favourite cause of hers. She was just thirteen when Motilal, having heard of her beauty, came to see if she could be a fit bride for the son on whom he doted. The decision made, Motilal brought her to Anand Bhavan to educate her in the Western manners that a Harrow and Cambridge man would expect from a wife. Motilal had demanded four qualities in a future daughter-in-law: beauty, intelligence, temperament and health. Perhaps the abundance of the first three had to be compensated by the absence of the last. Tuberculosis was detected in 1919, and the disease destroyed her body. Kamala was pregnant thrice, but only Indira survived. A premature son died after only two days in 1925, and in 1928 she had a miscarriage. Between her illness and Jawaharlal's total commitment to politics, she virtually lost her husband for a decade. Finally, since she could not defeat politics in the competition for her husband's affections, she decided to join it. To Jawaharlal's great joy, she soon proved that she deserved a place of her own in the history of the freedom movement. Her struggle really began the day her husband inspired the nation with his call for *purna swaraj* (complete independence) on 29 December 1929. When Jawaharlal went to prison on 14 April 1930, Kamala fulfilled a promise she had made to herself as early as in 1926, when she wrote to Syed Mahmud from Geneva that she would get together with his wife and the two of them should 'urge them [Indian women] to place their trust in God and fight for their own freedom'. Her participation in the civil disobedience movement was a unique tonic – for a change she was healthy. She would join the Congress volunteers' drill in the morning and face the police during the day.

One day Kamala went to the local government college to persuade the students to join the boycott. One of the students was watching her exertions with some amusement when, because of the heat and strain, she fainted. He rushed to get water and a fan to revive her. Soon he too joined the Congress, and he grew very close to her. His name was Feroze Gandhi.

On 1 January 1931 Kamala was at a public demonstration defiantly reading the speech for which her husband had yet again been sent to gaol, when the police came. A journalist asked for a message as they took her away. She said, 'I am happy beyond measure and proud to follow in the footsteps of my husband. I hope the people will keep the flag flying.' Jawaharlal was thrilled beyond measure when he heard that she too had gone to gaol – he called it a wonderful New Year gift. That was in many ways the happiest year of their lives, particularly when just Jawaharlal, Kamala and Indira spent a seven-week holiday together in Ceylon, flying to the island by a small chartered plane. Jawaharlal recalled this period in his autobiography: 'We seemed to have discovered each other anew. All the past years that we had passed together had been but a preparation for this new and more intimate relationship.' He was delighted when Kamala addressed a group of women assembled at Sarojini Naidu's house in Hyderabad, where they had halted on their way to Ceylon. Her call for emancipation had at least one convert. A few weeks later Jawaharlal got an angry letter from a distracted husband saying that his *purdah-nashin* (veiled) wife had begun acting 'strangely' – she no longer took orders from him.

After the high point of that summer, once again that shadow of disease came between a man who could pause only in gaol and a woman who simply could not keep pace. Kamala busied herself, when health permitted, in social work, most notably in a hospital established next to Swaraj Bhavan. As her mother-in-law aged, she gradually took on more of the household responsibilities; after Motilal's death, it was her husband who was the head of the family after all. When Krishna married Gonottam (Raja) Hutheesingh on 20 October 1933 (by civil registration, for her husband was a Jain), it was Kamala who organized the trousseau, and she was very upset that the family no longer had the money to marry a daughter in the old style. With Motilal had also gone the finances to organize a 'Nehru wedding camp'. All they could now afford was a little jewellery and lunch for the family, the only outsiders on the guest-list being the Hutheesinghs. (However, the Nehru clan added up to something like 150.) Even Nan had a trousseau of 101 saris, diamonds, pearls, matched necklaces and much else; but, of course, it was Motilal who was in charge then. Jawaharlal felt the difference. When he went to bring the bride down, he could not help remarking that Krishna did not look much like a bride. Then, on an impulse, he picked a rose from a vase, put it in her hair and said, 'Well, now you look better.' It was all he could afford.

Jawaharlal and Kamala spent all their time together during that brief sojourn out of gaol between August 1933 and 12 February 1934. In January they went to Calcutta and Santiniketan to meet Tagore and arrange to put Indira in Tagore's ashram school. Mother and daughter were extremely close. One of the thoughts most unbearable to Kamala was the worry that Indira might inherit or catch her contagious disease. In July 1934 Kamala suffered a severe relapse. The attack of pleurisy was accompanied by high temperature, and she was declared to be in danger. Jawaharlal was allowed out of prison to be near her. As he noted in his prison diary on 24 August 1934 after going back to gaol: 'In and Out – Out & In! After eleven days of freedom back I come to Naini Prison. Eleven days of meeting crowds of friends, discussions and of course Kamala's illness. Eleven days of comfortable living. And now I am back to the loneliness of solitary jail life.' There were suggestions from the British that he could obtain his freedom in return for a guarantee that he would not indulge in politics. The idea of such a compromise, of course, went against the grain. Kamala would not consider it either. She had now to move to sanatoriums, first at Bhowali in the Himalayas and then in Europe. Bedridden, haunted by early death, she sought refuge in spirituality. It was at this time that Feroze Gandhi became attached to her – first spending time with her at Bhowali and then following her to Europe after Kamala and Indira had gone abroad. Jawaharlal had been shifted to Almora gaol and saw her, under prison escort, about once a month. In May 1935, accompanied by Indira and a cousin, Dr Madan Atal, Kamala left by sea for the Badenweiler sanatorium in the Black Forest. Indira consequently had to leave Santiniketan after only a few months. Tagore wrote to Jawaharlal on 20 April 1935: 'It is with a heavy heart we bade farewell to Indira, for she was such an asset in our place. I have watched her very closely and have felt admiration for the way you have brought her up.'

For Kamala it was now just a question of living out the days. On 2 September a telegram came from her doctors saying she was critical. Jawaharlal's sentence was suspended: released on 4 September, he flew to Germany to be at Kamala's side. By the middle of December she had to be shifted to the Clinique Sylvana in Lausanne; Indira was placed in a school in Bex. It was here that Jawaharlal learned that Gandhi had made him president of the Congress for a second time: for the next session at Lucknow in April. The terms of his release had indicated that he would be rearrested if he returned to India before his gaol term ended in February. Politics called. According to a letter sent to Swami Abhayananda of Belur Math, Calcutta, he planned to leave Switzerland by air on 29 February, leaving Kamala behind. On 28 February, Kamala died, with her rediscovered husband at her side. 'And all our bright dreams were also dead and turned to ashes. She is no more, Kamala is no more, my mind kept on repeating,' wrote Jawaharlal. He cremated his wife in Switzerland and brought the ashes back with him when he reached Karachi by air on 10 March. For the rest of his life he kept a part of her ashes always with him, in his bedroom or gaol cell; these were to be mingled with his own after he died. A man of his qualities, of his temperament, intellect and power, was bound to attract women, and Jawaharlal certainly did not always spurn those who sought a relationship. But Kamala would be the only woman he truly loved. Jawaharlal Nehru often acknowledged the debt he owed to his father, Motilal, and his Bapu, Gandhi; it was after Kamala's death that he fully realized the debt he owed this girl who came into his life when she was seventeen and saw him, in twenty years, evolve from a bored lawyer to one of the great men of the twentieth century. When Jawaharlal Nehru's first grandchild was born on 20 August 1944, the name he chose for his grandson was Rajiv. Rajiv means lotus; so does Kamala.

Later, the royalties would supplement it, but in 1935 Jawaharlal had a total income of only Rs 750 a month with which to keep the large establishment at Anand Bhavan going. He even had difficulty finding money for Kamala's treatment abroad, and a friend, Jal Naoroji (Dadabhai's son), quietly found her a better cabin in the ship. 'I do not know about the rights and wrongs of using capitalistic influence to secure better cabins for the wives of super-kisans, but at any rate you are not fit enough to be subjected to the outcome of theories of this character at present,' Jal told Kamala. The financial situation of the Nehrus was hardly a secret. The Birlas sent quiet word to Jawaharlal that they could pay a substantial monthly sum to help out. He was livid. This socialist would not become another investment of a capitalist, even an Indian one.

Gandhi has been sneered at as a *bania* (trader) by those opposed to him, both the Muslim Leaguers and the Communists. As a literal statement it was accurate enough; he belonged to the trading community which has acquired a reputation for deviousness. The charge was that his politics were built on similar characteristics; that his very obvious saintliness was a camouflage for a mind which was manipulative, and an intention which was dishonest. The Muslim League leaders needed to create this image of a Hindu Gandhi dreaming of a Hindu kingdom (*Ram rajya*) in order to justify their own existence; for in the 1930s the only other justification for their existence was the unabashed support from the British for the most sensational demands, including some which emerged only from the fertile brains of Whitehall.

Gandhi's problem was not that his intentions were complex, but that India was complex – and that this intrinsic complexity was constantly used and manipulated by the British to rationalize their existence as the one authority which could create some sense out of this confusion. It was necessary to create a white man's burden, through literature and history and journalism, in order to justify colonialism. Indian pawns, Hindu, Muslim or Sikh, were well rewarded with wealth, titles and social status. Gandhi's total commitment to freedom was built on the foundations of Indian unity and self-respect: and of the masses more so than the leaders. He was willing to let every other problem wait for the day when Indians controlled their own destiny. A man who had spent his whole life matching his talents against a mighty empire, he never underestimated its strength, or its ability to destroy the morale of a people, or its mastery of the critical weapons of suspicion and doubt. Gandhi's genius prevented an enormous catastrophe in the 1930s; and because it was prevented it has not perhaps been as widely recognized as it should have been.

The British were determined to create another communal party among the untouchables, by distancing them from the caste Hindus and turning Dr Babasaheb Ambedkar into an untouchables' Jinnah. They gave the untouchables a place at the Round-Table Conferences, thereby politicizing yet another social problem in India. Gandhi's miracle of 1932 tempts one to believe that, if he had been working in India in the first decade of the century rather than in South Africa, the Muslim League would never have been born, or at least would have been aborted very soon. No one could accuse the British, of course, of creating the problem; no social sin of India has been more horrendous than untouchability. But a lesser man than Gandhi could not perhaps have prevented the creation of a 'Buddhistan'. Yet while Gandhi concentrated on stopping the conversion of harijans (the children of God) to Buddhism, by opening temple after restricted temple to them, and living with them, the Congress got snared by the problems that inevitably consume an organization when its vision has been clouded. The repression of 1932 and 1933 by Lord Willingdon had dampened the civil disobedience movement, and Ramsay MacDonald's Communal Award, presented to the British Parliament in August 1932, let loose the wasps of communalism into the debate within India.

Gandhi lamented in 1931 at a meeting in Delhi, 'What after all are the things you are quarrelling for? Not, indeed, for air and water. It is for seats in the legislatures and local bodies . . . I am sick of these squabbles for the seats, this scramble for the shadow of power.' Nevertheless the shadow of power, to the undisguised glee of the British, was enough to create the mad scramble. The Congress was hardly immune from the influence of the environment. A distinct Right and Left had emerged in the last five years. While such definitions can only be very general, and there are enough exceptions on both sides to qualify any label one might use, one could describe the

Right as nearer capitalism in its economic philosophy and closer to the Hindu Mahasabha in its social outlook. The Left was as leftist as it could become in the Congress fold, but it was as secular as anyone could have wished in its commitment to peace between the various religions of India. The pillars of the Right were men like Sardar Patel, Rajendra Prasad and C. Rajagopalachari (whose daughter Laxmi married Gandhi's son Devadas in June 1933). The Left consisted of the younger lot: Nehru, Jayaprakash Narayan, Achyut Patwardhan, Rammanohar Lohia and Acharya Narendra Dev. Gandhi often supported the Right, because he in turn needed their support. He knew that though they might not have the mass appeal of the Left, they had vital influence on Indian industry, on a growing middle class and on the religious fringe. Gandhi made it very clear that the Congress would have to find a place for both a Jawaharlal and a Patel, as much as for a Vinoba Bhave and a Birla. But the fascinating reality is that when he had a choice, he always ensured that the primacy of power remained in the hands of the leftists, of a Jawaharlal rather than a Patel. Gandhi made Jawaharlal president in 1929, the year of the *purna swaraj* resolution; then, in 1936 and 1937, leader of the Congress in its first elections; and then of course, in 1946, leader of the first Congress government. Despite his seniority Sardar Patel always took second place. Gandhi was conscious that the Prime Minister of India always had to have the trust of the minorities, even if the deputy did not, but he also stressed the need for compromise, to work together along an acceptable median. This conundrum obviously created its dilemmas; as long as Gandhi was alive he could rap whichever knuckle, he wanted, as harshly as he desired. In 1936, having given the leadership to Jawaharlal, he also gave him a lesson on precisely how far a leader could travel in any direction, and taught him that a leader became a lost individual without a team.

'I must frankly confess,' Jawaharlal Nehru had told the first Congress session he addressed as president in 1929, 'that I am a socialist and a republican and am no believer in kings and princes, or in the order which produces the modern kings of industry, who have greater power over the lives and fortunes of men than even kings of old, and whose methods are as predatory as those of the old feudal aristocracy.' It was little wonder that the Communists valued him as India's Kerensky. But the shift in Moscow's policy made them drop him in 1931; he was expelled from the League against Imperialism – he had now become a 'traitor to the cause'. Jawaharlal, however, kept his intellectual links with the faith. The books read in gaol, and friends like Krishna Menon, ensured that he would serve the Left, but never at the expense of Gandhi. In 1934, in protest against Congress resolutions on private property and the treatment of the working class, a group of young men led by Rafi Ahmed Kidwai and Bose formed the Congress Socialist Party as a pressure group and appealed to Jawaharlal to take the lead against 'reactionaries'. One target of the more volatile element among the Socialists was no less than Gandhi. It was a revolt which Gandhi quickly snuffed in his own way. In a statement on 17 September 1934 he said: 'The rumour that I had contemplated severing all physical connection with the Congress was true.' He said later: 'I have welcomed the formation of the socialist group. Many of them are respected and self-sacrificing co-workers. With all this, I have fundamental differences with them on the programme published in their authorized pamphlets ... If they gain ascendancy in the Congress, as they well may, I cannot remain in the Congress.' That threat was sufficient. The interesting thing is that a right-winger like Patel agreed that it was time for Gandhi 'to retire from the Congress'; perhaps he was provoking an open split on the issue, knowing full well that in a confrontation it would be the Socialists who would be driven out, and never Gandhi. In any case, Nehru made it absolutely clear that there was no question of staying in a Congress without Gandhi. Jawaharlal may have been intellectually a socialist, but politically he was a Gandhian.

During the visit to Europe for Kamala's treatment, Jawaharlal's friendship with Krishna Menon had strengthened. What he saw in Europe only confirmed his view that fascism was as great a threat as colonialism. As a personal gesture, he shopped only at Jewish stores; in contrast, Subhas Bose was drifting in the other direction. When the Communists learned of his nomination as the next Congress president they got in touch. R. Palme Dutt, leader of the Communist Party of Great Britain, extracted a promise from him that he would help the Indian comrades. The Communists were to be disappointed, but only because their expectations were too high. Nehru's analysis in his presidential address at Lucknow was beyond Communist reproach:

Fascism and imperialism thus stood out as the two faces of the now decaying capitalism . . . Thus we see the world divided up into two vast groups today – the imperialist and fascist on one side, the socialist and nationalist on the other . . . Where do we stand, then, we who labour for a free India? Inevitably we take our stand with progressive forces of the world which are ranged against fascism and imperialism.

He committed himself specifically, demanding an end, for instance, to private property 'except in a restricted sense'. There was, however, a caveat: 'Much as I wish for the advancement of socialism in this country, I have no desire to force the issue in the Congress and thereby create difficulties in the way of our struggle for independence.' Gandhi punctured any hopes of a formal resolution of the Congress reflecting such sentiments. G. D. Birla, who had been worried about what Jawaharlal might do, could boast in a letter to Purushottamdas Thakurdas on 20 April 1936: 'Mahatmaji kept his promise and without his uttering a word, he saw that no new commitments were made. Jawaharlalji's speech in a way was thrown into the waste paper basket because all the resolutions that were passed were against the spirit of his speech.'

Neither did Gandhi allow Jawaharlal to pack his working committee with comrades. Only Acharya Narendra Dave, Jayaprakash Narayan, Achyut Patwardhan and Bose could be counted as socialists out of fourteen members, and Bose was in prison. Worse, Jawaharlal was totally outmanoeuvred on the question of whether the Congress should participate in the coming elections and accept office if it won. Expectedly, the radical Nehru wanted neither until his 'complete independence'. The Congress right wing pushed through the decision to participate in the elections at Lucknow and would manoeuvre the acceptance of office when the time came in 1937. What Jawaharlal had with him in 1936 was crowds. The masses were with him; his popularity was second only to Gandhi's. Jawaharlal continued his private battle with Indian capitalists in his speeches, accusing them of being neo-fascists and allies of British imperialism. In his opening campaign speech in Bombay he called for socialism without violence – and warned that change and progress were the only guarantee against a popular upheaval. A group of twenty-one Indian business men issued a manifesto against Jawaharlal; his reply, as quoted in *The Tribune* of 9 June 1936, was spirited: the situation in a poverty-stricken country whose economy was in the grip of a small handful 'is not a pleasant picture. I do not like it, and as I see it, sometimes my blood freezes and sometimes it boils with indignation that such things should be.'

Jawaharlal never allowed even the suspicion of a challenge to Gandhi to arise, no matter how much of a rebuke he might have to suffer. Gandhi, for instance, pulled Jawaharlal up severely at the Wardha working committee meeting in the first week of July 1936 after Rajendra Prasad complained about his leadership. Gandhi accused him bluntly of not understanding the nature of office, of arrogance, intolerance and a lack of a sense of humour. On 15 July 1936 Gandhi wrote to Jawaharlal from Seagon, Wardha, rebuking him for displaying to his colleagues his

> magisterial manner and above all your arrogation of what has appeared to them your infallibility and superior knowledge ... You are in office by their unanimous choice but you are not in power yet. To put you in office was an attempt to find you in power quicker than you would otherwise have been. Anyway that was at the back of my mind when I suggested your name for the crown of thorns. Keep it on, though the head be bruised.

Although Gandhi softened the blow by keeping the letter secret, Jawaharlal was left with no illusions about how far tolerance of his weaknesses would go. His working committee colleagues soon found him delightful.

Nehru never wavered on two things: Gandhi would always be his leader and the Congress would always be his party. Freedom was the first priority; socialism could come later. If this meant the ridicule of his foes and the deep disappointment of his friends, so be it. When the time came to draft the manifesto for the first elections which the Congress Party would contest, the economic programme did not go beyond the resolutions passed at the Karachi session in 1931. There was no mention of socialism.

As Gandhi had so correctly predicted to Narendra Dave as early as 2 August 1934, Jawaharlal Nehru had once again 'hastened slowly'. But on the sidelines another problem was brewing whose consequences would be immensely more dramatic for Nehru, Gandhi and India than the prospects or otherwise of socialism. This was that familiar horror, communalism. Its teething problems were over. Now it began to display its fangs.

24 The Stir of the Monster

Bazar Sitaram, once again. This time: 1884. The first organization created specifically to protect Hindus and Hinduism was formed in this crowded *mohalla* in Delhi in the wake of a series of riots over cow slaughter. Its name: Ram Sabha. The reform movement of Dayanand Saraswati, with its aggressive anti-minority overtones, was institutionalized in the Arya Samaj on 1 November 1878; and Hindu–Muslim tensions were being sharpened by Arya priests 'reconverting' Muslims and mullahs protecting their flock. In 1887 the first all-India Hindu organization, the Bharat Dharm Mahamandal, was formed in Hardwar. A long decade of intermittent violence was doused only by the greater misery of a plague that swept through Delhi in 1898. The Muslim League came in 1906, and by the end of the decade the Hindu Mahasabha, growing alongside the Congress till by 1925 it was in a position to flex its muscles. In 1925 another Hindu organization was born, with aims similar to the Mahasabha, but outside the Congress embrace. For it believed that the freedom of India could be achieved only by Hindus, and that minorities like the Muslims were foreigners whose loyalty to India would always be suspect; Hinduism was nationalism.

Like Nehru, Keshav Baliram Hedgewar was born in 1889: in Nagpur, the city which is still the headquarters of the organization he founded. He began to participate in politics while taking a medical degree in Calcutta, and his inclinations drew him towards the Hindu Mahasabha. But on Vijaydashami in 1925 (the festival which marks the triumph of Rama over Ravana) Hedgewar, with four associates, M. N. Ghatate, Appaji Joshi, Bala Sahib Apte and Dada Parmarth, started the Rashtriya Swayamsevak Sangh (RSS) in Nagpur. Till 1932 the founder concentrated on building a core group of dedicated disciples, and only one branch was permitted, in the holy city of Varanasi, under the charge of a bright young man, Madhavrao Sadashiv Golwalkar. It was Golwalkar who would be handed the succession by the founder on his death-bed and lead the RSS in its most influential phase. Golwalkar's thinking was best summed up in these words from *We, or Our Nationhood Defined* (1947), his principal ideological work, written in 1939:

> The non-Hindu peoples in Hindustan must either adopt the Hindu culture and language, must learn to respect and hold in reverence Hindu religion, must entertain no ideas but those of glorification of the Hindu race and culture . . . in a word they must cease to be foreigners, or may stay in this country, wholly subordinated to the Hindu nation, claiming nothing, deserving no privileges, far less any preferential treatment – not even citizen's rights.

It served as excellent propaganda for the Muslim communalists, who constantly described such ambitions as the true will of Hindu-majority India, a will which would become a reality the moment the British left and the Hindu majority won unbridled control over this country.

In the 1930s it was the Hindu Mahasabha which was the premier voice of majority communalism. It had a range of exceptional leaders, apart from holding a number of senior Congressmen in its spell: B. S. Moonje, Bhai Parmanand, M. R. Jayakar, N. C. Kelkar, Vinayak Damodar Savarkar and men like Shyama Prasad Mookerjee and Nirmal Chandra Chatterjee from Bengal – the first an educationist, the second a lawyer-judge. The Mahasabha made no secret of its intentions. At its Ajmer session in 1933 it said, for instance, what it thought of the preferred language of north India's Muslims, which later became the national language of Pakistan: 'Urdu is a foreign language which is a living monument to our slavery. It must be eradicated from the page of existence. Urdu is the language of the Malechhas which has done great harm to our national ends by attaining popularity in India.'

A language cooked in the melting-pots of medieval India was called 'foreign' only because the Muslims used it, though hardly exclusively. But since Muslims had to be condemned as foreigners, their language had to be similarly characterized. Nor were Muslim communalists alone in describing Muslims as a separate nation rather than only as a separate religion. The president of the Ajmer session of the Mahasabha, Bhai Parmanand, told his audience: 'Hindustan is the land of Hindus alone, and Musalmans and Christians and other nations living in India are only our guests. They can live here as long as they wish to remain as guests' (see *The Jana Sangh* by Craig

Baxter, 1971). This bondage to charity was, obviously, not terribly popular with Indian Muslims. The Mahasabha was to play its part in the 1937 elections and then, through its successor party, the Jana Sangh, to lead the first Prime Minister of free India into a terrible morass in Kashmir. The Mahasabha collapsed after the assassination of Mahatma Gandhi, when its leader, Savarkar, accepted his moral guilt and retired from politics. But the RSS was there to continue the mission.

In 1932 the founder of the RSS, Dr Hedgewar, decided that the time had come to set up more branches, first in other parts of Maharashtra and then eastwards from Nagpur into the Central Provinces (now Madhya Pradesh), and he set off on a tour to organize the expansion. One of his aides on this tour was a man called Nathuram Godse.

In the meanwhile, some Muslims were not only happy to be called foreigners but had begun to talk of a separate land in the name of this separate identity. This rather exposed the contradictions in the position taken by the Hindu communalists. On the one hand, they condemned Muslims as foreigners; then when some Muslims went and behaved like foreigners, the Hindu communalists condemned them as traitors. Pakistan was the product of communalism, both Hindu and Muslim. Both papered over the cracks in their logic with the strident bugle-notes of a bogus super-patriotism.

Nineteen thirty-two was a year during which the British set many policies in motion. In August 1932 Ramsay MacDonald's government announced the Communal Award, guaranteeing Muslim control over Bengal and Punjab. By the end of the third Round-Table Conference, on 24 December, Sir Samuel Hoare had granted every outstanding Muslim demand. In the same year an obscure student of Cambridge University, Chaudhry Rahmat Ali (1897–1951), with the help of three even more obscure associates, published a pamphlet called *Now or Never* with the subtitle 'Are we to live or perish for ever?' Ali described himself as the founder of PAKSTAN (this was how he wrote the acronym) on the basis of that pamphlet. In this scheme, the land area of Punjab, Afghan province (North-West Frontier Province), Kashmir, Sind and Baluchistan would be consolidated into a Muslim nation, and that would, for ever and ever, solve the Hindu–Muslim problem in India. Iqbal in 1930 had spoken of a Muslim India within the framework of a federal unity. Messrs Rahmat Ali and the other 'students', Mohammad Aslam Khan, Sheikh Mohammad Sadiq and Inayat Ullah Khan, pronounced: 'There can be no peace and tranquillity in the land if we, the Muslims, are duped into a Hindu-dominated Federation where we cannot be the masters of our own destiny and captains of our own souls.' The interesting thing is the unanimity with which this idea was rejected as foolish. The inconsistencies were glaring. To begin with, the proposed PAKSTAN contained only a fraction of the Muslims living in the subcontinent, so how could it possibly be a solution for the problems of India's Muslims, spread as they were in virtually every village and town of this sprawling land? Jinnah, who was in London, dismissed the idea as nonsense and refused to meet these students. The only people who took the scheme seriously were the members of the India lobby in Britain. What makes the suspicion of British involvement into a reasonable surmise is the enthusiasm with which the stalwarts of colonialism promoted the idea. Stanley Wolpert himself provides two instances in his sympathetic biography of Jinnah: that of Sir Michael O'Dwyer (1864–1940), governor of Punjab at the time of Jallianwala Bagh, and Sir Reginald Craddock (1868–1937), a former home member of the Government of India and at the time a Conservative MP.

Long after Chaudhry Rahmat Ali made his scheme public, not many people were even aware of it, for no Indian took it seriously. The British were not so dismissive. In March 1933 (the details are from Reginald Coupland's *The Constitutional Problem in India*, 1944), Whitehall published a White Paper, and in April a joint committee from both Houses was set up under Lord Linlithgow to 'consider the future government of India'. The committee was alive for eighteen months and examined 120 witnesses over 159 meetings, including twenty-eight Indians. The Indians, however, were strictly of the pro-British or at least non-Congress variety, like the Aga Khan, M. R. Jayakar, B. R. Ambedkar, Sir Akbar Hydari, Sir Mirza Ismail and Sir Tej Bahadur Sapru. Virtually every aspect of India and Indian policy was examined intensely. On 12 December 1934 a motion that a Bill be submitted to Parliament on the lines of the Linlithgow Committee Report was passed; on 19 December the Bill was introduced; and, after a forty-three-day debate in which Winston Churchill fought determinedly to prevent what he thought was surrender to Indians, the Bill was passed. On 4 August 1935 it received royal assent and it eventually became the Government of India Act of 1935. On 1 April 1937 it came into effect as the new Constitution.

At the committee hearings, Sir Michael O'Dwyer argued against the idea of an all-India federation and suggested that, if the Hindu majority tried to 'force its will' on Muslim-majority provinces, 'What is to prevent a breakaway of the Punjab, Sind, Baluchistan and NWF as already foreshadowed and their possibly forming a Muslim Federation of their own?' Foreshadowed by whom, by what? Even Iqbal, when he spoke of his land for Muslim India, had retained it within a composite Indian federation. No leader of the Muslim League had so far voiced such an idea. No one had even hinted such a possibility in any resolution. In fact, all the bitter squabbling about reservation of seats in the legislatures, and the urge to protect a Muslim dominance in Bengal and Punjab, were attempts to guarantee Muslim rights in a united India. There would be no sense in one-third representation for Muslims in a Pakistan, would there? Who had heard of Rahmat Ali? No one. Abdullah Zafrulla Khan (1893–1981), president of the Muslim League in 1932, had no inkling of even the term 'Pakistan'. And Abdullah Yusuf Ali, appearing before the Linlithgow Committee as a representative of the Frontier Province, wondered aloud why he was being questioned about this idea by Sir Reginald Craddock. 'As far as I know, it is only a student's scheme,' he said; 'no responsible people have put it forward.' Then he dismissed the notion as 'chimerical and impracticable'. Craddock persisted that he had received 'communications about the proposal of forming a Federation of certain Muslim States under the name of Pakistan'. From whom? Muslims of the non-Congress ilk were sitting in front of him, and not one was aware of any such proposals; but Sir Reginald Craddock was in the know of this scheme. Sir Reginald's remark at this point of the evidence was absolutely fascinating: 'you advance very quickly in India, and it may be, when those students grow up, it will be put forward; that scheme must be in the minds of the people anyhow'.

Which people? Not the Congressmen. Not yet the Muslim League. Not the princes. Not anyone in India. But yes: definitely in the minds of a few people in Britain – some in power, and determined never to relinquish India to Indians in their lifetimes; and some their student-stooges. As Sir Reginald so confidently asserted: 'you advance very quickly in India'. Particularly when someone is prodding you from behind.

Jawaharlal Nehru's solution to this bubbling communal crisis was outlined in a statement to the press issued, from Allahabad, on 5 January 1934, in reaction to the White Paper, which he called a 'travesty of a Constitution'. He argued for a Constituent Assembly elected on the widest franchise, which would then write the Constitution (rather than electing an Assembly after this Constitution was passed). He accepted the temporary need for separate electorates 'in order to remove all suspicion from the minds of a minority'. He added that

> if the Muslim-elected representatives for this Constituent Assembly adhere to certain communal demands I shall press for their acceptance. Much as I dislike communalism I realize that it does not disappear by suppression but by a removal of the feeling of fear . . . We should therefore remove this fear complex and make the Muslim masses realize that they can have any protection that they really desire.

He was convinced that communalism was an upper-class disease: 'Communalism is essentially a hunt for favours from a third party – the ruling power.' Nehru said: 'Communalism thus becomes another name for political and social reaction, and the British government, being the citadel of this reaction in India, naturally throws its sheltering wings over a useful ally.' He had no illusions either about some of his *khadi*-clad brethren: 'It is time that Congressmen and others who have flirted with Hindu or Muslim or Sikh or any other communalism should understand this position and make their choice. No one can have it both ways, and the choice lies between political and social progress and stark reaction.'

Jawaharlal Nehru may not always have been able to defeat the entrenched communalism within his own party, but once he took wing among the masses he was supreme. Few products of the upper classes, all through history, have had the kind of support and adulation which Jawaharlal Nehru enjoyed among the people. Even his opponents accepted his unique mass appeal and readily allowed him to lead when elections came around – no matter how much they tried to trip him up in between. In 1936 and 1937 Gandhi and Nehru led the Congress to a spectacular victory over communal forces; then one went back to his ashram and the other to his loneliness, while others dipped their fingers in the tasty nectar of power for the first time in their lives.

25 'Rituraj'

The golden jubilee session of the Congress at Faizpur in December
1936 was the first to be held in a village. Gandhi's decision, of
course. He was very excited about this culture-shock he was going to
impose on his urban, if not necessarily urbane, Congress leadership,
and he warned the organizers that they were not to turn Faizpur into
a city; no city amenities, they must make do with only what the
village had to offer. He summoned the famous painter Nandalal
Bose and pleaded with him to design the venue: 'This Congress will
be for villagers and not for townsfolk. Its setting should be made by
village artisans out of materials commonly obtainable in the village.'
One newspaper inevitably labelled Bose's creation the Bamboo City.
Gandhi personally supervised the construction of the venue and its
facilities – a massive job, with some 100,000 delegates scheduled to
attend this session, the biggest ever. They came from Cape Comorin
and from the Frontier; from Bombay and from Bengal: Hindus,
Muslims, Christians, Parsis, all united by a single zeal. Jawaharlal
was the president of this session too and was not terribly enthusiastic
about a village session. But Gandhi even made the presidential procession rural; instead of riding a magnificent horse, the Congress
president came on a 'beautifully designed and decorated chariot
drawn by six pairs of bullocks'.

Gandhi had more than one reason to celebrate the fiftieth session
of the Congress in a village. While the thought of making the city-
dulled Congressmen wash and scavenge for themselves and grind
their own flour doubtless pleased him beyond measure, he was also
sending out a vital political signal, that Congress was now an organization of the villagers, the masses. The Faizpur session closed with
these words from Gandhi: 'We want this contact with villagers to
grow. It will be like Kumbha Mela when lakhs of pilgrims gather.
But this *mela* will welcome Muslims, Sikhs, Parsis and others, and all
will join together to pray for *swaraj* . . . Your Constituent Assembly
can meet anywhere you like, but the real Constituent Assembly will
be in the villages like Faizpur.' Equally to the point was the fact

that within days would come the most important elections in the history of India, with a franchise widened to include, for the first time, a part of the peasantry. It was an appropriate moment to signal an affinity with rural India.

The Government of India Act of 1935 (which also separated Burma from India, ending at least one threat to Congressmen, that of deportation to Burma) continued the process of communalizing the politics of India. The 1909 Morley–Minto reforms had divided the electorate into four parts, the Montagu–Chelmsford reforms into ten. The combined genius of Ramsay MacDonald, Sir Samuel Hoare, Lord Willingdon and Lord Linlithgow turned the number of special electorates into seventeen. The scheduled castes, Indian Christians and even categories of women were given separate electorates. The Muslims so far could vote in both general constituencies and separate electorates; they were now stopped from the latter; the separation of interests was total. At the core of this pernicious philosophy was the wretched belief that one community would never – could never – be concerned about the interests of another. Since the British found it convenient to insist, to use the words of the historian of imperialism, Reginald Coupland, that the Congress was 'dominantly Hindu in fact, though non-communal in principle', they had to extend that principle and say that only Muslims could truly represent Muslims.

The 1935 Act also obeyed the famous dictum of Lord Minto: 'The position of a community should be estimated not on its numerical strength but in respect of its political position and the services it has rendered to the Empire.' And so the obedient princely states, occupying 23 per cent of India, had 33 per cent of the voting power in the Lower House and 40 per cent in the Upper House. In order to buy the Muslims out of the Gandhian nationalist movement, they were given a larger share of seats in Bengal and Punjab than their population allowed. According to the 1931 census, Muslims formed 54.8 per cent of Bengal's population and Hindus 44.8. The former got 119 seats instead of 109, and Hindus 80 seats instead of 90. (The greatest bias was reserved naturally for the Europeans. Despite being only 0.01 per cent of the population, they had 25 seats in Bengal. It was their Raj, after all.) Sir Samuel Hoare had granted the two most important Muslim demands on 24 December 1932 by separating Sind from Bombay, thereby creating another Muslim-majority province, and promising that Muslims would get one-third of the seats in the central legislature (the League, as a matter of fact, had demanded a little less, only 32 per cent). To sum up, everything possible had been arranged to ensure that the Muslim vote would go not to the Congress but to the pro-British groups, either the League or the traditional parties like the feudal Agriculturist Party. With so many seats guaranteed to anti-Congress blocs, like the Europeans, a Congress majority was always going to be a difficult task, unless it got an exceptional popular endorsement. Everything was stacked against a Congress victory. The franchise was limited. Total adult franchise, which Gandhi wanted, would have made Congress victory easier, for the poor were with Gandhi. A limited franchise was automatically weighted in favour of the affluent and better suited an élitist party like the Muslim League, which could never dream of mass action, or indeed of holding a session in a village. Last, but hardly least, the power of government, and of its supporters like the *taluqdars*, was used heavily against the Congress. The influence which local land-lords still have in Indian elections in the 1980s should be an indication of the power of their bullying and terror then. And yet the results were a stunning defeat for the British and their fraternal party, the Muslim League. That was the finest hour of the young Congress president, Jawaharlal Nehru.

On 8 March 1936 the poet Rabindranath Tagore told the inmates of his ashram in a talk in memory of Kamala Nehru:

> Today is the day of our Holi festival, the festival of spring. In the midst of the fallen and sere leaves, Nature is making preparations to mark the death-triumphing entry of a new life, to which the newly sprouted leaves bring their offerings of joy. On this occasion it will be meet to associate the stirring of new life in the nation with that of the springtime. And Jawaharlal is the *Rituraj*, representing the season of youth and triumphant joy, of an invincible spirit of fight and uncompromising loyalty to the cause of freedom.

The poet had summed up what Jawaharlal symbolized beautifully: India looked up to him, and he led his party from the front, to a famous victory. However, before Jawaharlal could take on his adversaries in the Muslim League he first had to confront a few opponents nearer home – in the Congress itself.

The death of Kamala, the strain of prison, the doubts generated by the passive leadership of Gandhi in 1934 and 1935 had all begun to affect his fragile temperament. He was always a very emotional man and never quite able to disguise it. His temperament was always on public display. He could weep like a child when in the company of Gandhi (as he did when accusing the Mahatma, after the pact with Irwin, of betraying the nation); or his anger would bubble up in public if he felt the sting of injustice or heard the voice of prejudice. In particular, he never had any patience with communalists, of either the Hindu or Muslim variety. One incident at the 1936 Lucknow session was typical.

Gandhi's Congress was not, of course, a party in the denominational sense; people of every conviction, from Arya Samajis to Communists, could be and were members of the All-India Congress Committee. At the Lucknow session some Sanatanists from the sacred city of Benaras began heckling Jawaharlal. He ignored it for a while, then suddenly lost his famous temper, jumped from the rostrum and charged straight into the saffron hecklers. A friend, Sri Prakasa, who quite accidentally also happened to be from Benaras, tried to restrain Jawaharlal. Brusquely, he pushed Sri Prakasa aside, saying, 'Go to hell, you Benaras people!' When Sri Prakasa complained later, Jawaharlal apologized in a letter sent on 3 May 1936 but also explained:

> Like you, many things and persons and groups in India at present oppress me. But my reaction to them is somewhat different from yours. It is an aggressive reaction and often an impertinent and undignified one. The mere fact that conditions become adverse and individuals lukewarm makes me feel more combative. I have not undertaken this job to please others or because of others but because I have felt a strong urge to do so. All my intellect pushed me in the direction, so also my emotions and pride . . . Then there is today, I feel, a severe tug-of-war in India between rival ideologies. This is partly apparent and partly hidden but is important. I find myself very much on the side of one ideology and I am distressed at some of my colleagues going the other way.

Those colleagues were equally distressed with the reasonably socialist and aggressively secular Jawaharlal. With his magnificent effort on the campaign trail from April to December, Jawaharlal was infusing every corner of the country with his ideology, and his views became synonymous among the masses with those of the Congress.

His influence on the election manifesto adopted at the AICC meeting on 22 August 1936 indicated his rising power within the party; both the 'Fundamental Rights Resolution' of the 1931 Karachi Congress and the Agrarian Programme of the 1936 Lucknow Congress were incorporated. These commitments in the manifesto in turn forced the Congress governments, after they took office in 1937, to initiate reform; for instance, through their efforts to reduce the burden of agricultural debt. Peasant agitations got a renewed lease of energy at the sight of Congress premiers. In Bihar the peasants stormed the Assembly House, persuading a petrified capitalist like Birla to threaten the Congress that he would lead a flight of capital away from provinces like Bombay and United Provinces to the safer havens of princely India where the 'indiscipline' of socialism could still be trammelled by rulers who preferred the virtues of a Birla to the passions of a Nehru. Even Gandhi was frightened by the 'turbulent wind', a phrase he used in a letter to Patel on 9 October 1937. However, the Congress government of 1937 might never have sat in office if Nehru had had his way. All through the election campaign of 1936 and early 1937 he maintained that the Congress was contesting these elections not to strengthen the 'steel frame' of the Raj but to break it: not to give legitimacy to the British-created Constitution of 1935 but to destroy it and replace it with one written by an Indian Constituent Assembly. As he told the Allahabad district Congress committee on 19 February 1937: 'The main question before us is how to wreck the Constitution.'

None of this was very comforting for the Congress right wing. When Gandhi indicated that Jawaharlal should be renominated president for another term at the Faizpur Congress in December 1936, the right wing again chose Sardar Vallabhbhai Patel as the leader of its challenge to Nehru. Jawaharlal was willing to accept victory or defeat in this internal battle with equal equanimity; all he wanted, he said, was that he be judged on the issues. Gandhi carefully avoided taking sides on issues such as socialism and land reform. His own interpretations were, to put it mildly, rather unique. At the exhibition grounds of the Faizpur Congress, on 27 December, for instance, he explained how he understood socialism:

> Real socialism has been handed down to us by our ancestors who taught:
> 'All land belongs to Gopal, where then is the boundary line?

Man is the maker of that line and he can, therefore, unmake it' . . . In modern language it [Gopal] means the state, that is, the people. That the land today does not belong to the people is too true. But the fault is not in the teaching. It is in us who have not lived up to it.

Frustration is the mildest reaction possible to such an interpretation. But it was Gandhi who alone had the power to keep the Congress crown on the more rational socialist's head. Patel eventually withdrew his challenge to Nehru, although not before issuing a stern statement in which he made no secret of the fact that he did not endorse many of the party president's views. 'Indeed,' he said, 'the Congressmen know that on some vital matters my views are in conflict with those held by Jawaharlal.' He specifically mentioned socialism and office acceptance; Patel was averse to the former and keen on the latter. Patel also warned the president of his party that he had 'no dictatorial powers . . . The Congress does not part with its powers by electing any individual, no matter who he is.' Patel, who would make a fetish of the same principle of 'equality' as Nehru's deputy in free India's first government, need not have worried about any potential Nehruvian dictatorship or even pomposity.

Jawaharlal's strength came from the people. No one, not even the Patels, could ignore the response he received from every part of the country. In a note he prepared at the end of the polls, Jawaharlal recounted (*Eighteen Months in India*, 1938) that he had covered nearly 50,000 miles in 130 days of mainly rural campaigning:

about 26,000 miles by railway, 22,500 by road (chiefly by car) and 1,600 by air. The means of transport varied greatly. They included aeroplanes, railway (usually third-class travelling, sometimes second-class, and on two occasions special trains for short distances); motor cars (from a Rolls-Royce to a fifteen-year-old Ford); motor lorry; horse carriage, tonga, *ekka*, bullock cart, bicycle, elephant, camel, horse, steamer, paddle boat, canoe and on foot.

He addressed more than 10 million people and met millions more in brief roadside stopovers. Once, on 16 September 1936, he was motoring along the Rohtak–Delhi road, anxious to catch his train at Delhi, when suddenly his car was brought to a halt by 'a crowd of men and women, some with torches in their hands'. They had been checking every car since the afternoon to see if Jawaharlal was in it; now they had found him. He began an instant dialogue with them about the meaning of the slogan these Jat villagers were raising: 'Qaumi nara ... Bande Mataram ... Bharat Mata ki jai' ('Our national slogan ... *Bande Mataram* ... Victory to Mother India'). Jawaharlal's message was: 'Remember that Bharat Mata is you and it is your own *jai*.' He still reached Delhi in time for his train: 'And so on into the darkness to Delhi city and the train, and then a long sleep.' It was the kind of tiredness he adored.

Jawaharlal savoured each experience, even a fall while cycling, on 14 September, towards a remote interior village in the Etawah district of United Provinces. His excited happiness during this period is reflected in a letter he wrote to his friend Norah, the nickname of Purnima Banerjee, a comrade in the freedom struggle and sister of Aruna Asaf Ali, who was to enter legend by raising the flag of freedom after Gandhi's call to the British to quit India in 1942. 'My dear Norah,' wrote Jawaharlal,

> Your letter. I have survived the cycle accident as I propose to survive other accidents ... I have read a good part of Aldous Huxley's book [*Eyeless in Gaza*]. I have been carrying it about with me during my tour but have had no time to finish it yet. As for the answers to the problems of life, do you know what Marx said about it? The only way history answers questions is by putting further questions.

As he raced through Bombay, Punjab, Sind, Delhi, UP, Andhra, Tamil Nadu, Nagpur, Mahakosal, Maharashtra, Bengal and Kerala, he felt moved by 'those millions of eyes out of which India looked at us'.

There were always practical problems for the president of the party to settle. The Urdu press had turned hostile towards Gandhi over the Hindu–Urdu controversy, and someone had to counter the false Muslim League propaganda. On 5 October 1936 he wrote to Syed Mahmud:

> Is it our fate that always the reactionary Muslims should take the lead in everything and the nationalists should follow in their wake like dumb-driven cattle? That has been the case often enough in the past. Is it going to continue? I hope not ... This talk of separate Muslim parties also

must not be encouraged. I write in haste in the moving train. At every station there are vast crowds. Love.

That talk of separate Muslim parties would soon haunt Jawaharlal, but in 1936 the League was still in slumber. In 1927 the League's membership was only 1,330, and its activities till 1933 were so few that its annual expenditure did not exceed Rs 3,000. No one really bothered, either inside it or about it. Just ten members of its council of 310 were considered sufficient for a quorum, since it was often difficult to get more members interested. Since Muslim interests were its rallying cry, the generous Communal Award had left the League with little else to demand. Other neo-Muslim parties, like the Ahrars, with a more radical economic programme, had far more influence in the north, particularly in Bihar. By 1933 the League had split a second time. The fractious leaders discovered there was only one thing on which they could agree: that the only chance the party had of survival lay in bringing Jinnah back from Hampstead and handing the party over to him. On 1 and 2 April 1934 some forty-odd members of the League Council enthusiastically welcomed the idea and asked Jinnah to set the date, place and agenda of that year's session. Jinnah returned to London on 23 April, where his legal practice was earning him more than £2,000 a year. He came back to Bombay in December, but it was only in October 1935 that he took up the reorganization of the League. In April 1936 the League finally sat in session in Bombay. Jinnah was named the permanent president.

Muhammad Ali Jinnah became the party. It was reborn with him and it died with him, despite an inheritance as enormous as Pakistan. The decisions of the League now reflected Jinnah's evolving ambitions. The logic, will and determination for which Jinnah was justly famous were not the only determinants of his politics; there was also a cold but quietly violent anger against Gandhi and his lieutenants like Nehru and Azad for continuously denying him his 'position as a tribune of the people', to use Chagla's phrase. But this Jinnah was no longer the kind of tribune Chagla wanted. Jinnah picked up new young disciples: Hussain Shaheed Suhrawardy (1893–1962) of Bengal, Liaquat Ali Khan (1895–1951) of the United Provinces, Ismail J. Chundrigar (1897–1968) of Bombay, the industrialist Mirza Abol Hassain Ispahani of Calcutta and Amir Ahmad Khan, the new Raja of Mahmudabad, whose estate provided an annual income of two million rupees – men of wealth and property. Little wonder that the League was always and very loudly opposed to any movement that aimed at the expropriation of private property. But the party was still a scattered crowd.

Jinnah stepped up the ante. Even though he avoided any direct reference to the scheme being promoted through hysterical pamphlets from 16 Montague Road, Cambridge, by Rahmat Ali, now self-labelled founder of the Pakistan National Movement, he launched the cry that was to echo with increasing ferocity for the next decade: 'Islam is in danger!' Free India would mean Hindu Raj. The transition was subtly done. Jinnah frightened the upper classes by warning them that Nehru's 'red pen' would take Congress towards 'socialistic and communistic ideas', while the middle class was showered with propaganda that its religion as well as its language would be buried by the Hindu-Congress avalanche. (Jinnah did not have to worry about the truly poor; they still had not got the franchise.) Jawaharlal was damned if he was going to let this pass unchallenged.

On 3 January 1937 Jinnah claimed at a public meeting in Calcutta that he represented the third party in the country, the Muslims (the British and the Congress were the other two). Nehru replied to this proprietorial claim over India's Muslims from Purnea, on the eastern fringe of Bihar, on 10 January. He called Jinnah's views 'communalism raised to the nth power' and 'medieval and out of date'. As for the League:

> It represents a group of Muslims, no doubt highly estimable persons, but functioning in the higher regions of the upper middle classes and having no contacts with the Muslim masses and few even with the Muslim lower middle class. May I suggest to Mr Jinnah that I come into greater touch with the Muslim masses than most of the members of the Muslim League?

He described his own faith:

> I represent the hunger and poverty of the masses, Muslim as well as Hindu; the demand for bread and land and work and relief from innumerable burdens which crush them; the urge to freedom from an intolerable oppression. I represent all this because the Congress represents

it, and I have been charged by the Congress to hold aloft its principles and the torch that it has lighted to bring hope and strength and brightness to the dark corners of our land and to the suffering hearts of our people.

He dug his knife in: 'I am sorry to see the way Mr Jinnah's mind works.'

At a speech in Ambala on 16 January 1937 Jawaharlal said:

All those people who talk in terms of Hindu rights and Muslim interests are job-hunters, pure and simple, and fight for the loaves and fishes of office. How long are you going to tolerate this nonsense, this absurdity? . . . There are only two forces in the country, the Congress and the government. Those who are standing midway shall have to choose between the two.

On 19 January, Jinnah replied: 'The League does not believe in assuming a non-communal label, with a few adventurers or credulous persons belonging to other communities thrown in and who have no backing of the people.' 'Adventurers' had a specific connotation: these Muslims were men who would sell their services for reward.

This was enough to send Jawaharlal's short temper flaring. He thundered in Bombay on 9 February: 'There are Muslims in the Congress who can provide inspiration to a thousand Jinnahs. Let not Mr Jinnah pour ridicule on the Muslims in the Congress. What does he know of their steadfastness, their patriotism, their struggle, their heroism and their sacrifices?' At the end of that speech Nehru regretted a bad mistake which had already been made: 'I am sorry that the Congress did not set up more Muslim candidates . . . The voters of the UP, whether they were Hindus or Muslims, were all anxious to vote for the Congress.' He also dismissed speculation of a secret deal between the two parties, calling it 'false and malicious'. He added: 'How on earth can I sign a pact with the Jinnah who I have seen only once during the last five years and that too for five minutes at a students' meeting in Allahabad?'

When Nehru sneered at the League as a 'drawing-room party' which did not even have the courage to challenge British imperialism he had the weight of evidence on his side. Not only did the League manifesto avoid any demand for independence (the Ahrars, in fact, broke with the League over this), but its president at Bombay at the twenty-fourth session in April 1936, Syed Wazir Hasan, told the 200-odd delegates that Muslims should be thankful for the 'fortunate connection between India and the British Crown'.

Jawaharlal made two telling points in his Purnea statement. First, he remarked on the similarity between Jinnah's positions and those adopted by the leader of the Hindu Mahasabha, Bhai Parmanand. The two communal parties were of course one in their perception that there should be a Hindu party and a Muslim party rather than any common party. Equally interesting was their agreement on economic policies, for in this lay evidence of the class character of the communal politics of British India. As Bipan Chandra notes in *Communalism in Modern India* (1984), the two opposed anti-landlord measures, while the Mahasabha went the extra mile by bitterly fighting any anti-money-lender legislation to give relief to peasants. The League opposed the Tenancy Bill brought by the Congress in United Provinces in 1938 and the agrarian programme of Fazlul Haq in Bengal – later demanding as the price of its alliance with Haq the suppression of the progressives in the Haq fold. The Mahasabha's antipathy to the 'demon of communism' was no less virulent than Jinnah's. What both were unable to do in 1937 was co-opt their communalism to the rising radicalism of the peasantry. The second insight lay in Nehru's assessment of the fate that lay in store for communal parties: 'Because no common principle or policy binds them, at the touch of any real problem they break apart.' Witness what happened to the Muslim League after Jinnah created Pakistan.

Jinnah replied with salt and pepper. The salt lay in the adjectives he used for Nehru ('busybody', 'sole custodian of the masses', *et al.*), and the pepper was used in speeches to rouse Muslims in the name of Islam. Jawaharlal responded by damning the League and the Hindu Mahasabha as fascists in the same breath. Talking to the press at Lahore on 17 October 1937, to give one instance, he said:

It is interesting to note that Bhai Parmanand has fully appreciated the Muslim League policy [of organizing Muslims in the name of Islam]. The next step should obviously be for the Muslim League and Hindu Mahasabha, in the sacred name of religion, to join together to protect their respective vested interests against the incursion of the common people of India. This is a fascist development. Behind the veil of religion and culture, there is this attempt to consolidate vested interests and groups of privileged people.

No one could accuse Nehru of not making his mind clear. In the same interview he added: 'The League and its supporters stand clearly and definitely today for the division of India, even on a political and economic plane, into religious groups.'

Jawaharlal's confidence in his political line was reinforced by the dramatic results of the elections in January and February 1937. In 1920, 7 million Indians had been eligible for the vote; this time the electorate was 36 million spread over 1,585 seats in the eleven provincial legislatures of British India in a total population of some 300 million. Of them 808 were general seats, and 777 were 'tied' or reserved for special representation – for Muslims, of course, but also for landlords, Europeans, business men, etc. Despite the odds, the Congress won 456 of the 808 general seats, securing absolute majorities in the United Provinces, Madras, Central Provinces, Bihar and Orissa and emerging as the single largest party in Bombay, Bengal, Assam and the North-West Frontier Province. As Jawaharlal exulted to Sir Stafford Cripps, who had just formed a Socialist League under his leadership along with Keir Hardie's Independent Labour Party and the Communists, on 22 February 1937: 'We had the government apparatus and all other vested interests against us and all means, fair and otherwise, were employed to defeat us. But the enthusiasm for the Congress was so tremendous that it swept everything before it.' *The Indian Annual Register* for 1937 (edited by Nripendra Nath Mitra) quoted a review article by H. N. Brailsford in the *New Statesman and Nation*: 'The solid interior of the Peninsula belongs to it [the Congress] in an unbroken block from the Himalayas to the Cape Comorin ... The result of this plebiscite is unambiguous.'

The breakdown for the Congress was: 65 per cent of the votes and 159 seats out of 215 in Madras; 75 per cent of the vote and 98 out of 152 seats in Bihar; 61 per cent of the vote and 70 out of 112 seats in Central Provinces and Berar; 56 per cent of the vote and 86 of 175 seats in Bombay; 65 per cent of the vote and 134 out of 228 seats in United Provinces; and 60 per cent of the vote and 36 out of 60 seats in Orissa. The party also did well in NWFP, with 38 per cent of the vote and 19 out of 50 seats, and was easily able to form a government when the signal from the working committee came. It had fared at best reasonably in Bengal (25 per cent of the vote and 56 seats out of 250 – Bengal was the largest province) and Assam, with 33 seats out of 108. But the party was routed in Sind (7 seats out of 60) and Punjab (18 seats out of 175) where the landlords and smaller land-owners effectively reduced the Congress to an urban Hindu party, and neither the Sikh nor the Muslim peasantry were willing to vote Congress in preference to the Unionists, whose policy centred around an agile ability to negotiate with everyone and anyone as long as their special interest was preserved.

Jawaharlal was particularly elated that the Congress had overcome the challenge posed by both Hindu and Muslim communalism, as well as reactionaries like the landlord-dominated National Agri-culturist Party of Agra and Awadh upon whom the British had been banking heavily; the NAP got only 13 seats in Agra and 12 in Awadh. He had every right to gloat at the discomfiture of the League. The party created in the name of 'Muslim India' found surprisingly few Muslims in its ranks, though its leader was prominent enough: of the total Muslim votes cast (7,319,445) the League got only 321,772 or an abysmal 4.4 per cent. It must be stressed once again that the elec-torates were communal, so Muslims only had the choice of a selection of Muslims in their constituencies – despite which they rejected the League quite decisively. In Madras the League got 10 of the 28 Muslim seats; in Bombay 20 out of 29; in Assam 9 out of 34; in Bengal 39 out of 117; in UP 27 out of 64; and in Punjab just 2 out of 84. In the Frontier they did not win a single seat out of 36, and none also of the 39 seats in Bihar, 14 seats in Central Provinces and 4 seats in Orissa.

The League was badly defeated in all the provinces where the Muslims were in a minority. It did comparatively better only in areas where not only were Muslims in a majority but the 'ruling ethos' of the past, as well as the influence of the left-overs of Muslim feudalism, was stronger. The striking difference in the results of UP and Bihar is especially remarkable. The poorer Bihari Muslims were more in-fluenced by the radical programme of pro-Kisan parties like the Ahrars and were totally unwilling to buy the League's hate-Hindu philosophy. It was this recognition that made Jawaharlal despair of the serious error which the Congress parliamentary board (headed by Sardar Patel) had made in not putting up enough Muslim candidates in its name. Jawaharlal admitted to Cripps in his letter of 22 February 1937 that the Congress has 'not succeeded in regard to Muslim candidates. Partly this was due to our own timidity as we ran few Muslim candidates.' His experience at mass meetings had convinced him that Muslim Congressmen would indeed have been a match for a thousand Jinnahs. But he was not going to take solace only in excuses. In the letter, he accepted that there was a problem:

> But it is true that the Muslim masses are more apathetic. They have been too long doped with communal cries. They have no leaders of their own and they are a little hesitant in casting their lot completely with the others. Still it is obvious that even these Muslim masses are getting out of the rut of communalism and are thinking along economic lines. Equally significant is the change that is coming over the younger generation of Muslims ... The Hindu communalists have been largely swept away by the Congress and they count for little. The Muslim communal leaders still function but their position weakens for they have no reply to the questions about poverty and hunger and unemployment and independence that their own people put to them. They can think only in terms of jobs for the upper classes.

The Hindu Mahasabha, incidentally, had won only two seats in Bengal, one in CP (considered to be its fortress) and four in Sind. Its ally, the Congress Nationalist Party, won just one seat in Punjab and one in Bombay.

The paradox of the Muslim League's lopsided election results is not as paradoxical as it might seem at first glance. For the fact was that, despite all of Jinnah's rhetoric about one Muslim *quam* in India, there was nothing called a common political identity among Indian Muslims. Naturally there was a Muslim identity, just as there was a Hindu identity and indeed a Christian one; but there was little reflection of it in politics. The politics of the Muslims in a particular province were far more reflective of their regional environment than of any national perceptions. Punjab's Muslims, for instance, had quite different interests from those of United Provinces, which is why they voted differently.

According to the 1931 census, the 77,677,545 Muslims of the subcontinent formed 22.16 per cent of the population overall, but the average was a most unreliable indicator of their strength. Looking at India from east to west, Muslims formed over 25 per cent of the population of Assam, over 50 per cent of Bengal and about 20 per cent of UP and Bihar. They were less than 10 per cent in CP, Madras, Maharashtra, Gujarat, Mysore and Kerala, but the percentage grew in Muslim-ruled Hyderabad. In Sind they were in a majority; they dominated West Punjab and formed over 90 per cent of the population in the Frontier and Baluchistan. The Muslims were broadly divided into three groups: those living in Muslim feudal states where their minority status was more than adequately compensated by their possession of power; those in the Muslim-majority provinces like Punjab, Bengal and Sind, where their ambitions were tailored to the institutionalization of Muslim control over political power; and in the provinces where the Muslims were in a minority and where the struggle for loaves and fishes acquired the most virulent dimensions.

The subahdars of the Muslim-majority provinces like Punjab fought bitterly to achieve a Muslim advantage in the legislatures, which in turn confirmed their grip on power; once they had got as much under the Communal Award of 16 August 1932 and the Government of India Act of 1935, they were not the least bit interested in Jinnah's struggle to 'liberate' Muslim India. The Act gave residency powers to the provinces (through the creation of federal, provincial and concurrent lists), confirmed separate electorates and even gave more seats to Muslims than their population percentage warranted. Muslims had 82 of the 250 seats in the federal assembly, and the Muslim-majority provinces were guaranteed preferential treatment. Their only subsequent aim was to ensure, in any new Constitution, that the centre remained weak, a puppet of strong provinces, so that this situation could not be reversed in a changed dispensation.

The Unionist Party in Punjab had been in power since 1920 thanks to its policy of communal unity based on the common interests of the peasantry, and it wanted very little to do with either the urban-*bania*-influenced Congress or the shrieking savants of the League. It was this confidence which made the Punjab Unionist Party leader Fazl-i-Husain snub Jinnah when he was requested to join the Muslim League parliamentary board in 1936. Husain told Jinnah to keep 'his finger out of the Punjab pie' (quoted by Z. H. Zaidi in his introduction to *The Jinnah–Ispahani Correspondence* (Karachi: 1976)) and told him that all he was doing was encouraging 'vociferous tendencies among Muslims'. There were eleven members from Punjab on Jinnah's 34-member central parliamentary board; only *two* were willing to represent Jinnah in the 1937 elections, and one of them quickly became a Unionist. Jinnah left Punjab swearing, 'I shall never come to the Punjab again; it is such a hopeless place', as Azim Husain mentions in his biography of Fazl-i-Husain.

The ground was both a little more and a little less fertile for the League in Bengal. The Bengali Muslim peasant, weighed down by the most abject poverty and exploitation (from his non-resident zemindar to the village money-lender, who charged unbelievably exorbitant multiple interest), and bearing the social stigma of 'inferiority' to the Bengali *bhadralok*, did not have the confidence of his landowning, milk-fed Punjabi counterpart. So while the potential of broad Muslim unity did exist against 'Hindu' tyranny, it had to be based on a radical economic platform. You needed a Muslim Nehru in Bengal, but all you had on offer was a Muslim Jinnah. The League was a party of *taluqdars* and rajas and Bombay and Calcutta business men; it was hardly going to challenge private property. Moreover, the ties of culture, language and emotional outlook created an interweave in Bengal which could not be unravelled easily. A leader like A. K. Fazlul Haq (1873–1962), who was not famous for his scruples, was yet perceptive enough to understand that he could not win votes on the pro-rich League ticket. While Jinnah packed the League with landlords, the manifesto of Haq's Krishak Praja (Farmer and Tenant) Party demanded the abolition of zemindari without compensation. Haq refused a pact with Jinnah, and the election results proved his point. He won 31.78 per cent of the rural votes against the League's 26.5 per cent, and the margins would have been far bigger in Haq's favour if the franchise had been wider. The League predictably outperformed him in the urban areas, winning 61.4 per cent of the votes against 26.5 per cent for Haq; but the urban Muslim vote was a natural prize for a right-wing, communal-interest party, given the nature of the franchise and the concessions to Muslims in the qualifications required to become voters. (Jawaharlal, reacting to a similar phenomenon in UP, dismissed the League as a *qasba* party, unrepresentative of the India where the masses lived, the villages.) Haq, whose political acumen was infinitely more reliable than his morality, had no hesitation in joining the League after the elections in order to become premier of Bengal. He had come to an informal alliance with the Congress before the elections, though Nehru had no illusions about his morals. In a speech in Calcutta on 3 May 1937 in support of the strike of over 200,000 jute workers, Nehru revealed: 'Six months ago, I visited Calcutta when Mr A. K. Fazlul Haq, at present premier of Bengal, saw me and declared himself as a *khadem* [servant] of the Congress and even wanted money from the Congress to help him in his election expenses.' Anderson, the governor of Bengal, wrote to Linlithgow on 3 December 1936 that irrespective of his current stance Haq would make a deal with anyone after the elections by 'selling himself . . . to the highest bidder'. Haq, he said, was 'devoid of principle and trusted by nobody'. The coalition which Haq patched together (two minister-ships to his own party, four to the League, three to caste Hindus, two to scheduled castes) sank all the noble promises about abolition of zemindari. As many as twenty-eight of the Praja legislators deserted Haq in anger at the sell-out, but he kept his majority at the cost of his programme.

The Muslims of the United Provinces were unable to find a suitable equation. Heavily influenced by the Doomsday preaching of Sir Sayyid, they were consumed by uncertainty about the future even as they licked the shards of a destroyed glory. And there were no heroes left. Jinnah filled the vacuum, promising to 'save' the Muslims from the Congress. Jinnah was not personally a communal man and never would be; he was too sophisticated for that. But he was now the leader of a communal idea, and he was resolved to turn that idea into a determinant for future generations, to become one of the architects of history rather than yet another forgotten footnote.

His own life had been headed towards a whimper in London. All he had was a quiet existence in Hampstead, his faithful sister Fatima seated at the other end of an often empty table. His thirteen-year-old daughter, Dina, with her mother's smile and beauty, was home only during brief holidays from her boarding-school but pampered as only a lonely, doting father can spoil his one daughter. A black Dobermann and a white West Highland terrier provided what joy pets can offer. Breakfast was punctually at nine, after which his chauffeur Bradbury drove him in a Bentley to his City chambers. (Though his practice took him before the Privy Council, he was never given an honour he wanted, of being made a judge.) He would dine with visiting friends like Durga Das at Simpson's or some other expensive restaurant; the theatre was a favourite form of relaxation. Yet this surface comfort was a pale substitute for what he truly loved: involvement in the great affairs of state. Jinnah, the brilliant 'Round-Tabler', was not even invited to the third and concluding Round-Table, though he lived at the time in London itself. If Jinnah's career had ended in this twilight, at best he might have had a street named after him in Bombay. His singular will, instead, was going to make him into the father of a new nation. An artificial nation perhaps, but still a nation. There are not many men in history who can claim such an achievement.

Jinnah shrewdly realized on his return to India that his main battle would be fought not in Punjab and not in Bengal, where his country would be created, but in United Provinces and Bihar. The logic of his arguments all pertained to the real or imagined insecurities in those provinces where Muslims were in a minority, and where pleas for special protection or economic preference found a ready audience. But it was Iqbal's Muslim India which was eventually born, with Bengal tagged on to it, an extra hump which had to be operated out of the strangely constructed camel. The Muslims who made Jinnah relevant once again in the 1930s became refugees in their own promised land; and their descendants are, many decades later, in the midst of another violent battle over that eternal question of the subcontinent: who and what is a nation?

In 1937 Jinnah set out to answer this question; it was the last campaign of a long career. The tuberculosis in his lungs had now secretly begun to eat away his body. The world was told that his cough was only a 'smoker's cough', for the truth might shatter the dream. But the idea of Pakistan was always as vulnerable as one individual's life. In the race between tuberculosis and Pakistan, Pakistan just nipped ahead.

Three points are generally advertised as the landmarks on the road to Pakistan. The first is the collapse of the negotiations to settle the Hindu–Muslim question through the Nehru Report in 1928. The second is Jawaharlal Nehru's 'sabotage', through his influence as Congress president, of the proposed Congress–League coalition ministry in the United Provinces after the 1937 elections. And the third is Jawaharlal Nehru's rejection of the Cabinet Mission plan for a federal India in 1946. The first we have encountered, and the third will come up later. The second arises at this point of our journey through the life of Jawaharlal. The central pro-Pakistan argument in all three, however, is the same: a conciliatory Jinnah offered his hand; a devious/callous/overconfident/irrational Nehru/Congress refused the offer, confirmed Jinnah's view that it was impossible to co-operate honourably with the Hindus and forced him to break the country. It is the kind of argument which avoids every relevant question, including the most basic one of them all: how did partition solve the problem of Hindu–Muslim relations on the subcontinent? Those Muslims with a sense of insecurity remained precisely where they were; those who had nothing to fear from Hindus formed a separate country in the name of fear. It is the Hindus who had the sense of insecurity in Punjab or East Bengal, so according to the logic of 'protection' and 'security' in a 'motherland' perhaps Pakistan should have been scattered in bits and pieces within the Gangetic plain and 'Hindustan' scattered through the Indus and Padma plains. However, even such simplistic arguments as those employed by the defenders of the League do not survive the scrutiny of evidence.

26 Hero on a Roller-Coaster

Nineteen thirty-seven was Jawaharlal's year. Gandhi had laid the moral-political line at the meeting of 'the real constituent assembly' in the last week of 1936 at Faizpur. He had brought 100,000 Congress workers to this village in Maharashtra, given them unpolished rice, hand-ground flour and jaggery to eat and turned the Brahmins into scavengers by making them responsible for the sanitation (Appa Patwardhan was in charge). He comforted the impatient ('though progress may seem slow, it will prove quickest in the long run'); warned the Hindus that, until they removed untouchability and communalism, *swaraj* would elude them; and lifted the spirits of both the workers and the president of the party with extravagant praise in the speech with which he closed the Faizpur Congress. Then the Mahatma went off to the princely state of Travancore to celebrate the opening of temples to harijans and devoted himself to social reform and religion. His lieutenants went off on their election campaigns across India.

The crowds that came to Jawaharlal's meetings were unprecedented. Even in a cold wave at Gaya in Bihar they waited till three in the morning for their hero to arrive. The man's style was infectious, his politics passionately pro-poor, and he seemed to have a fatal attraction for the women in particular. History of a kind was made at Ranchi on 9 January 1937 when women mobbed him. It was perhaps inevitable that a whiff of scandal would trail a man so attractive to women, particularly to the younger firebrands in the Congress who doted on him as a political-personal idol. The older puritan leaders had been sniffing angrily at this new culture being introduced by these young men and women, particularly of the Congress Socialist Party, with the active encouragement of Jawaharlal. Sardar Patel cried out in horror, 'Stinking atmosphere is prevailing in the country. Reading of socialist and sex literature is the order of the day.' One of the targets, the beautiful Kamaladevi Chattopadhyaya, refused to be intimidated by the age or power of even a Vallabhbhai Patel and took him on in the party pamphlet *Congress Socialist* (vol. 1, no. 13). She wrote:

> The young generation is in revolt against the old order . . . That is what old Sardar is railing against. It is an order in which his power is threatened, his creed mocked. He is of the band of conservatives . . . who would turn their back upon the rising golden light and try to envelop themselves in the vague security of medieval twilight.

Jawaharlal gave further provocation by his open friendship with women, a public familiarity which was Western. Tongues would wag when he shared, for instance, a train compartment with a woman friend on the campaign trail, refusing to be intimidated by the rising fingers of the middle class. He liked the company of intelligent women; they adored him; and he obviously trusted them too. He sent Kamaladevi to Bombay straight after the Faizpur Congress to find out from J. R. D. Tata, the industrialist who pioneered air travel in India, if it was possible to hire one of his planes. It was. By the middle of January, Jawaharlal had set yet another precedent in the nation's democratic annals: campaign by air. The *Amrita Bazar Patrika* printed pictures on 22 January 1937 of the Congress president with his special plane in Punjab and noted with wonder that Nehru had done 900 miles by air in ten flying hours and over 500 miles by car in one swing. The crowds once again had been tumultuous. In Amritsar, said the paper, the landing of the plane had been delayed by half an hour because of the rush of people on the ground. (When the Punjab results came out, however, the Congress discovered that it had won barely two seats, starting yet another tradition in Indian politics: the jibe that the crowds had come to see the plane rather than the politician.)

There was much turbulence for the Western-modern Jawaharlal. His opponents (and there were many more of them in the Congress than in the opposition) spread the story that he was about to marry a socialist graduate girl, and, as if such licentiousness was not bad enough, he was going to do so not by the normal Hindu rites but by civil ceremony. The whispers said that the recently widowed Jawaharlal was having an affair with a beautiful colleague; 'socialist' and 'graduate' were identification marks within Congress circles. Jawaharlal was sufficiently worried to issue a denial. A story was planted on the Allahabad correspondent of the *Amrita Bazar Patrika*, then the most powerful pro-Congress paper in the country, and appeared in the edition of 6 January 1937. It began with a two-deck headline and said:

A BASELESS REPORT

Pt Jawaharlal has no intention of marrying
From Our Own Correspondent

Allahabad, 5 January: There is absolutely no foundation for the report published in a local Hindi paper, which has been reproduced by several English papers, to the effect that Pandit Jawaharlal Nehru shortly proposes marrying a socialist graduate girl under the Civil Marriage Act.

On inquiries being made by me today at Anand Bhavan regarding this report, Pandit Nehru's closest relations characterized this 'news' as entirely baseless. Great indignation was expressed that such irresponsible reports should be published in respectable papers.

It was further pointed out that those responsible for this baseless news should have remembered that Pandit Nehru was greatly attached to his deceased wife and that any talk of marriage so soon after death (sic) was nonsense.

As it happened, any talk of marriage for the rest of his life was nonsense; but allegations of affairs with attractive women never stopped. Far from sinking his reputation, these stories only added to Jawaharlal's glamour, particularly among the poor who had little use for either the middle class or its morality. Certainly the results of the first elections Jawaharlal fought proved this much, as did the results of every subsequent one. He never lost an election conducted under his leadership.

A look at copies of the *Amrita Bazar Patrika* in the first week of 1937 provides a flavour of that unique year. The advertisements were on page one, of course; and the last page was given over entirely to picture journalism. The new year opened with exciting news of a special plane being arranged for the Congress president, a dramatic adaptation of Rabindranath's *Gora* playing to full houses in Calcutta, Haile Selassie's silver being auctioned at Puttick & Simpson's, Clement Attlee suing successfully for being called a Jew and Don Bradman's Australia getting ready to take on Gubby Allen's England in the Third Test of the Ashes.

On 2 January came reports that Krishna Menon in London had chaired a special meeting of Indians and Ceylonese, prompted by Jawaharlal Nehru, in support of democracy in Spain; the elections to the Darjeeling seat had had to be postponed because of the death of Sardar Bahadur Laden La, and Subhas Bose was in the Calcutta Medical College, where an X-ray had been taken of him, and the results were awaited.

On 3 January the paper reported the first Congress victory; polling and results were staggered, but this result from the Frontier was in early because Dr Khan Sahib had been elected unopposed. Larwood was in Bombay *en route* to London after being sent back from the Australian tour. The Tata firm TISCO, in another first, had announced a gratuity of half a year's salary to its retiring workers. The features section of the paper had articles on 'The Leopard: Can It Be Tamed and Milked Like a Cow?' and 'The Censorship of Sex in Films' (some things are ageless in journalism).

On 4 January, the paper reported Jinnah's controversial speech at the Muhammad Ali Park in Calcutta where the Muslim League leader warned Nehru to leave the Muslims alone in response to Nehru's assertion that only two real parties existed in the country, the Congress and the government. (Jinnah's speech had to be translated by an interpreter into Urdu, since the leader's Urdu was inadequate.) The paper's London correspondent thought readers might like to know that he had bumped into Dr B. R. Ambedkar at HMSO in the Aldwych and found him ordering a copy of the Communal Award.

Next day India learned of another first in Congress history: disciplinary action against a Congressman for violating party orders and contesting against the official candidate. (The erring Congressman was Guru Raghubar Dayal of Kanpur; the official candidate was called Dr Jawaharlal, and presumably the name had nothing to do with the party president's decision. The 75-year-old Pandit Malaviya had also set up rebel candidates on the Hindu Nationalist Party ticket, but no action was taken against him in deference to his age.) An ailing Mrs Rudyard Kipling entered Middlesex Hospital, and Gandhi celebrated the temple entry of harijans in Travancore.

The next day it was Sardar Patel's turn to go to hospital, for dysentery, while Bradman took up most of the sports section with a superb 248 not out which settled the fate of the Test. (Australia eventually won by 365 runs.)

Readers learned on the 7th that Tagore had decided not to campaign for anyone and that the US State Department had finally allowed an arms dealer the licence to sell $400,000 worth of weapons to the Madrid government, while on the last page Shirley Temple, dolled up as The Spirit of 1937, pushed Old Man 1936 out of the way. (Her film *Dimples* had just been released in Calcutta.) As reports of Nehru's swing through Bihar brought news of milling crowds, it was becoming evident that the Congress was heading for a historic victory.

As in any other campaign, however, there was no end of controversy and internal bickering – over money, over policy, over ego, over just about anything Indians could devise. A joke made the rounds which later was to be reincarnated in many variations: 'One Indian, a philosopher; two Indians, a squabble; three Indians, foreign rule.' There were controversies about whether industrialists like the Birlas and the Tatas had contributed funds to Congress. Nehru, in *The Discovery of India*, conceded that some funds did indeed come but they never went to the Congress worker, whose expenses came out of membership fees (a full-time worker received about Rs 75, then the equivalent of $25, a month). The Muslim League, intent on creating the image of the Congress as nothing but a Hindu-*bania*-controlled organization, played up the Birla link. Nehru repeatedly clarified that while such industrialists might finance Gandhi's social reform activities, they had no influence over the political decisions of the Congress. Gandhi himself never had any hesitation about accepting money from the rich; one of his Indian financers during the South Africa days was in fact Sir Ratan Tata. But Gandhi could never be accused of misusing this money for personal benefit. The problem before a Congress president was another matter.

On 4 January, as we have noted, Jinnah warned Nehru to leave Muslims alone and accept them and the League as the third party in India. The election results exposed the League's claims. In the United Provinces the Muslims were at a loss. The traditional saviours, the landlords, nesting in the Agriculturist Party, had suffered stunning defeats after having lived in the legislatures for more than a decade. And the *qasba*-elected Muslim League just did not have enough seats to make a rational bid for a place in power. The Congress reacted to its great victory with a fierce internal debate on whether to accept office. Thus far, the Congress had avoided a formal answer to the question as to why it was contesting the elections, for the good reason that the two camps were bitterly divided over the answer. Nehru treated the polls as the opportunity to wreck the Constitution written by the British from within, while the Congress Right, led by the Patel–Rajagopalachari axis, was equally determined to sit in office, even though the 1935 Act had not even conceded dominion status.

Nehru had support from all the Socialists – including one very interesting comrade from Britain. On 3 March 1937 Stafford Cripps wrote to Jawaharlal hoping the Congress would refuse 'to partake of the empty fruits of office which can do nothing but poison the pure and free spirit of the Congress'. The first signs were propitious. At its Wardha meeting on 27–28 February and 1 March the Congress working committee had said very categorically:

> The Congress has entered the legislatures not to co-operate with the new Constitution or the government but to combat the Act and the policy underlying it, as this Act and policy are intended to tighten the hold of British imperialism on India and to continue the exploitation of the Indian people. The immediate objective is to resist the introduction and working of the federal part of the Act, and to lay stress on the nation's demand for a Constituent Assembly.

On 7 March the UPPCC, at Lucknow, rejected office acceptance by a comfortable majority of thirty votes, and Jawaharlal was heartened enough to warn against 'loose talk' about ministries, by Congressmen and newspapers. In the middle of the month Nehru went to Delhi (he stayed with Dr Ansari) for the All-India Congress Committee on 17–18 March and then the All-India Convention of Congress Legislators on 19 March. This was when the cookie crumbled. Under severe pressure from Patel and Rajagopalachari, Gandhi first patted Nehru on the back and then quietly tripped him up. The working committee endorsed the party president's view that the results had proved very convincingly that the people wanted the Congress to wreck the Constitution – and then authorized qualified acceptance of office. A short paragraph at the end dictated by (who else?) Gandhi opened a path for Congress governments, although there was still some way to go. It read:

In pursuance of the policy summed up in the foregoing paragraphs, the All-India Congress Committee authorizes and permits the acceptance of offices in Provinces where the Congress commands a majority in the legislature, provided the ministerships shall not be accepted unless the leader of the Congress Party in the legislature is satisfied and is able to state publicly that the Governor will not use his special powers of interference or set aside the office of ministers in regard to their constitutional activities.

Gandhi had bridged the compromise with the proviso that the governors would have to give the assurance that they would not use their arbitrary powers of dismissal, but Jawaharlal recognized defeat when he saw it. M. N. Roy recalls that one afternoon Jawaharlal walked into his house in Delhi, threw himself on a bed and, on the point of tears, talked of resignation after the way Gandhiji had sabotaged his resolution. After he reached Allahabad, Nehru wrote to Menon, on 28 March: 'I feel tired and rather empty . . . What I want badly is rest to refresh a jaded mind.'

The British, however, were in no mood to provide the Congress even with this fig-leaf. Why should they, when thirsty leaders like Rajagopalachari were already conspiring with them? As Lord Erskine, the governor of Madras, noted in a telegram to the Viceroy on 11 June, Rajagopalachari had told him that if the British facilitated the induction of Congress governments, it would end the civil disobedience mentality of the Congress for good. Needless to say, this was precisely Jawaharlal's worry; he wanted a 'revolutionary' seizure of power, not this petty hunger for British-manipulated ministries. By April the non-Congress provinces had elected their premiers: A. K. Fazlul Haq in Bengal, Sir Sikander Hayat Khan in Punjab, Sir Syed Muhammad Saadulla in Assam, Sir G. H. Hidayatullah in Sind. Elsewhere, the British nominated premiers from their quota of the faithful: the Nawab of Chattari in United Provinces, Sir K. V. Reddi in Madras, Sir D. B. Cooper in Bombay, Mr Yunus in Bihar, Dr Rao in Central Provinces, Sir A. Quaiyum Khan in the Frontier and the Maharaja of Parlakimedi in Orissa. On 22 June, after long negotiations during which the Congress president was conspicuous by his absence (he was on a tour of Burma and Malaya, both to restore his jaded nerves and to avoid getting on anyone else's), Lord Linlithgow issued a statement which dwelt at great length on power and responsibility and practice growing out of experience rather than rigid convention but did not surrender on Gandhi's last paragraph. Even this was sufficient for Messrs Patel and Rajagopalachari. On 7 July the Congress working committee resolved 'that Congressmen be permitted to accept office where they may be invited thereto'. The eager C. Rajagopalachari became premier in Madras, B. G. Kher in Bombay, Pandit G. B. Pant in UP, Srikrishna Sinha in Bihar, Dr N. B. Khare in CP, Dr Khan Sahib in NWFP and Biswanath Das in Orissa. A little later, Bordoloi replaced Saadullah in Assam.

That settled one problem – and started another.

The Congress had put up just nine candidates for the sixty-four Muslim seats of United Provinces, even leading to speculation that there was some secret alliance with the League. (Nehru did admit to supporting some League candidates, if they met two conditions: if there was no Congress candidate in the constituency, and the Leaguer was 'progressive'.) It lost all. (Its one seat came later.) Nehru took the defeat in Muslim seats personally and used every opportunity to urge colleagues and workers to rise to the challenge and intensify work among the Muslim masses. He thought it might be difficult to change the Muslim mood in the small towns in the short run but was quite confident of sweeping the rural vote on an economic platform the next time around. The British, naturally, did what they could to sabotage any Muslim support the Congress might have. The case of Maulvi Abul Qasim of Shahjahanpur was typical; the British arrested him for a speech made at an informal Muslim conference organized in the Congress interest. We know of this incident because of a letter Nehru wrote to Kailas Nath Katju on 10 July 1937 requesting Katju to appear in the Maulvi's defence. Nehru noted: 'There is a set attempt being made on the part of the government to control and suppress Muslim workers on behalf of the Congress and it is up to us to give such persons as much help as we can.' (Later, Maulvi Abul Qasim became a communist and migrated to Pakistan, where he was gaoled for four years for his alleged role in a conspiracy case. The Maulvi returned to Nehru's India and died in 1973 – after having lived to see the sundering of Pakistan in 1971.)

Nehru announced a 'mass contact' programme aimed at wooing Muslims. On 31 March he sent a circular to all the provincial Congress committees with a self-explanatory heading: 'The need for greater contacts with Muslims'. He set up a separate department in the party and made preparations for the launch of an Urdu weekly, *Hindusthan*, in July from 6 Neill Road, Lucknow. Orders were issued that all party pamphlets and notices be prepared in both the Devanagari and Urdu scripts. The mass contact programme made the Muslim League leaders, already smarting under the rejection of the electorate, absolutely furious. Maulana Shaukat Ali, always ready to threaten doom where a mere objection might serve, lashed out in a statement to the press on 21 April:

> All that is being talked and written in the press about Muslim mass contact and the Muslim League would have been very amusing if it was not so tragic and full of danger. Howsoever Pandit Jawaharlal may be encouraged by what paid or unpaid Muslims may say to him, he will fail unless he meets real Muslims. Efforts like this will only widen the gulf and lead to a fearful catastrophe.

The statement is particularly interesting because it establishes the themes of the Muslim League propaganda in that dangerous decade between 1937 and 1947: first, that the only 'real' Muslims were those who were in the Muslim League; second, that any Muslim who opted for Gandhi and the secularism of the Congress was nothing more than a paid agent of Hindus and therefore despicable; third, that the Congress had no right to seek the support of any Muslims, who were the preserve of either the Muslim League or those leaders and parties who had been certified by the League. Finally, there was, as always, the threat that there would be some cataclysmic catastrophe if the Muslim League's due demands were not conceded – including, and in particular, the League's right to represent all Muslims. There was nothing new in the central charge; when Khan Abdul Ghaffar Khan merged his Khudai Khidmatgars (Servants of God) into the Congress he had to face the same propaganda. As Mushirul Hasan notes in 'Congress Muslims' (*Struggling and Ruling: The Indian National Congress 1885–1985*), Ghaffar Khan defended himself in November 1931:

> People complain against me for having joined the Congress by selling my nation. The Congress is a national and not a Hindu body. It is a *jirga* composed of Hindus, Jews, Sikhs, Parsis and Muslims. The Congress as

a body is working against the British. The British nation is the enemy of the Congress and of the Pathans. I have therefore joined it and made common cause with the Congress to get rid of the British.

Even while the Maulana Shaukat Alis huffed and puffed in public, a silent deal with the Congress was being forged by common friends. The most important of these was Nehru's old friend Chaudhry Khaliquzzaman, scion of a *taluqdar* family who traced his ancestry to no less than the first Caliph of Islam, Abu Bakar Siddiq. He was almost an exact contemporary of Jawaharlal, born about six weeks later, on Christmas Day of 1889. Nehru was in England getting his degree when Khaliq took a break from Aligarh Muslim University in 1912 to join the famous medical mission to Turkey under Dr M. A. Ansari, which gave him an entrée into politics. Whenever he came to Allahabad for political meetings, Anand Bhavan was his abode, and a warm friendship developed with Jawaharlal. But though he was party president, in addition to being a friend, it was not through Jawaharlal that the first approach to the Congress was made. It was a former secretary of Motilal Nehru, Abdul Walli (1885–1941), who had worked for Motilal in the Swarajist Party days of 1923–6 and now published an Urdu monthly, *Maloomat*, who first gave Jawaharlal an idea of what was going on. In a letter sent on 28 March 1937 Walli told the Congress president that Khaliq was hatching a scheme for a Congress–League coalition in United Provinces. Walli put his finger on the nub of the issue when he wrote in his letter: 'Once the Congress enters into a pact with the Muslim League it loses the right to ask the Muslims to join it.' This old Congressman had struck a deep and fundamental note, for at stake lay the very ideology of the Congress. Was every Indian equal in its ranks or not? If yes, then how could the Congress ever hand over the Muslims of the country as the sole property of the League?

Nehru saw the point at once; it was in his mind already. After a sad reference to Khaliq –

I have myself been much put out at the way he has been drifting away from the Congress. For so many years past I have had a warm corner in my heart for him and I believe that my affection for him is reciprocated ... For nearly a year I have neither seen him nor corresponded with him. I would be happy indeed if he broke loose from the reactionaries who surround him ...

– Nehru mentioned, in his reply, that he was surprised to hear of a 'scheme being hatched . . . I have not heard anything about it. I am entirely opposed to this as I am opposed to all pacts and coalitions with small groups at the top.' He added that Maulana Azad was also definitely opposed to the idea. The story soon broke, a debate started, and Jinnah, already thoroughly irritated by Nehru, chose to spar with the younger man on this issue. When *Jayabharat*, a Bombay daily, editorially suggested in April that Congress should accept Jinnah's offer of co-operation, Nehru avoided a direct answer and sent a wire saying that Congress was still bound by its resolution to reject the new Constitution.

Jinnah immediately took umbrage and replied: 'It appears to me that he has taken the position of a dictator. It comes to this, "Accept what I have already decided and then I shall talk to you." This is not the way to arrive at a settlement.'

Nehru's rejoinder, in a statement to the press from Allahabad on 25 April, was sharp and spicy: 'I am sorry that anything that I have said or done should lead Mr Jinnah to think that I want to function as a dictator. Far from dictating to others, I cannot even dictate to myself . . . Personally I find it difficult to think of any question on communal lines. I think on political and economic lines.' Adding that Congress attached the greatest importance to the removal of suspicions between various religious groups, he nevertheless insisted: 'It cannot be a unity of subjection.' The same day Nehru released a long statement on Congress and Muslims where he admitted that his party had neglected the Muslim masses, but he asserted that the whole League position was bogus because 'Only a lunatic can think that the Muslims can be dominated and coerced by any religious majority in India.' In any case, the Congress had declared categorically over and over again 'that the fundamental and basic rights of all Indians contain provisions for the free exercise of religion, for freedom of conscience, for the protection of the culture, language and script of minorities'. This was the manifesto of unity. Against this, 'to think in terms of communal groups functioning politically is to think in terms of medievalism. And that is the reason why communal groups in India fail so dismally in the political field.'

Jinnah was furious. On 29 April he responded: 'It is quite clear that he [Nehru] is talking as if he were a sovereign authority.'

It is hard to conceive, in the light of the bitter personal and ideological differences between the two party leaders, how this alliance was ever going to come about, but Khaliq's desire to become one of the two Muslim League ministers in the alliance government gave the idea enough momentum to keep it going. Nehru catalogued the reasons why the idea could never work in another statement on 2 May, from Allahabad. The most important of them remained the same that prevented the Congress from allying with the Hindu Mahasabha: that these were communal parties. In any case, the one condition that Jinnah insisted on, that the Congress stop working among Muslims, made the very idea a non-starter: 'The objection is not political, it is communal . . .'

The bitterness was reinforced by the events of the Bundelkhand by-election in July, and if Nehru had even the smallest hope of the League becoming less reactionary it disappeared after the experience of the campaign. He explained his position in a long letter to Khaliquzzaman on 1 July, in which he tried to bring his friend back to the Congress and the 'progressive side':

> The Bundelkhand election has a certain temporary value but, after all, it is a small affair and will pass. The Muslim League has a perfect right to put up a candidate to represent its policy. It is not that I object to it but the astounding notices that are coming show the depths to which the League has fallen. Even Jinnah has no other argument left in a political contest but to appeal in the name of Allah and the Holy Koran . . . Fortunately there are many Muslims who do not adopt these tactics and they will serve their community as well as the larger cause far better.

He then entered his ideological objections:

> Is the League a democratic organization or is it just a close preserve of certain individuals? Why should I accept it as the representatives of the Muslims of India when I know it represents the handful of Muslims at the top who deliberately seek refuge in the name of religion to avoid discussing mass problems? . . . Do you not see that this communal policy which the Muslim League here has fathered is a policy more injurious to the Muslims of India than anything that a majority could do would be?

One can only comment by quoting Khaliquzzaman himself. Just

before he died he gave an interview to the well-known Pakistani journalist M.B. Naqvi in which he accepted that Pakistan had been a mistake – that it had hurt Muslims, not helped them.

Jawaharlal had also been provoked to write this letter by a statement signed by Khaliquzzaman, among others, which said: 'Mussalmans ... have been ordered ... by God and His Prophet to support the Muslim League candidate [in Bundelkhand] to give a crushing reply to the non-Muslim organization so that in future it will not dare to interfere in the affairs of Mussalmans.' The League had decided that its most reliable campaigner was going to be Allah. Jinnah added to this by reasserting in a statement on 1 July that only he could be the spokesman of Indian Muslims:

> In my opinion this policy of mass contacts with Mussalmans by Congress is fraught with very serious consequences. There is plenty of scope for Pandit Jawaharlal Nehru to improve his own people, the Hindus, as there is a lot of undesirable element among them. Similarly the Muslim League should do the same thing, as there is plenty of undesirable element among the Mussalmans.

Nehru replied in a statement from Wardha on 3 July: 'I am advised by Mr Jinnah to improve my own people, the Hindus. Not being religiously or communally inclined, I venture to think of my people as the Indian people as a whole ...'

As it happened, it was not Islam but a hangover of an undesirable element of Hinduism which helped the League candidate Rafiuddin Ahmed defeat Congressman Nisar Ahmad Shervani by a margin of 727 votes (4,557 votes were cast out of an electorate of 7,500). Rafiuddin Ahmed had been converted from the Hindu caste of Malkhan Rajputs, and caste affinity had survived conversion to the casteless brotherhood of Islam. A caste panchayat (council) had ordered every member of this community, which was a quarter of the electorate, to vote for Rafiuddin on pain of penalties. Not only was Islam in danger for the League candidate, but caste was also apparently in danger.

The tensions generated by this election were substantial. A group of League hoodlums even stoned Jawaharlal's car and smashed a window pane in yet another first incident of its kind. Luckily, no one was hurt. However, negotiations for a coalition were not allowed to melt in the heat of election rhetoric. The League wanted two seats in the ministry, one for Khaliq and the other for Nawab Ismail Khan, the president of the UP League board. Maulana Azad handled the negotiations on behalf of the Congress and was tempted by the offer; he felt that this coalition would lead to the absorption of the League into the Congress. Nehru was reluctant and worried about the impact this might have on Muslims loyal to the Congress. But Pant, Azad, Acharya Kripalani and Narendra Dev prevailed over his objections, and the Congress offered its conditions for the alliance. First, the Congress working committee resolution in March on Congress policy on the legislatures had to be accepted fully by the League to prevent any misapprehensions. Second, the Muslim League group would be wound up, including the UP parliamentary board. Third, all League MLAs would become full members of the Congress (though they were exempted adherence to the Congress pledge). Fourth, all would be subjected to Congress discipline. Fifth, there would be no separate candidates in by-elections. Khaliq replied that they could not accept two of the conditions. Nehru was relieved at the temporary impasse, repelled as he was by the whole deal, particularly with Bundelkhand's propaganda ringing in his ears and the anger of Muslim Congressmen rising as they heard whispers about those not terribly secret negotiations. Maulana Azad had his own reservations too; he did not want Nawab Ismail Khan because of his feudal background and suggested a young man, Hafiz Ibrahim, as the League minister in the coalition instead.

The Assembly session was due to start on 27 July; formal discussions between the parties began on 12 July. A second round of talks took place on 15 July. On 24 July, Maulana Azad gave a final draft to Khaliquzzaman. The next day the Maulana got a telephone call from Khaliq: instead of the expected agreement, the Congress leaders heard of a totally new demand. In Khaliquzzaman's own words in his autobiography, *Pathway to Pakistan* (1961), the new proviso was: 'Provided that the Muslim League Party members in the UP Assembly will be free to vote in accordance with their conscience, on communal matters.' Azad was shocked and upset at this. Both he and Pant knew that there was no need to even refer this new condition to Nehru. The League had sabotaged the idea by its final communal demand, for the League had arrogated to itself exclusive rights on Muslim questions, as if Congressmen could not be trusted on the matter. It was obviously impossible for any Congressman to accept this condition. Simply wishing a contradiction as fundamental as this away does not make it disappear. Nehru's objections to the deal were ideological, but he had allowed Azad and Pant the opportunity to try to see if a bridge could be built out of such flimsy material. And, as Khaliquzzaman's account in any case proves, it was the League which scuttled the deal with this last-minute condition. Azad would later give currency to the allegation that Nehru had become the unwitting sponsor of the League by rejecting the agreement, but as Jawaharlal pointed out at a meeting of Muslims in Ahmedabad on 17 September 1937: 'The Congress is a political body whose doors are open to all. [The League's] policy and programme differ from those of the Congress. How can there be unity between the two bodies unless the Congress gives up its ideals?' He insisted that it was the duty of the Congress to rout both the Hindu Mahasabha (which it had done) and the Muslim League.

After the last-minute condition had sabotaged the chance of an agreement, Jinnah exploited Jawaharlal's ideological reservations against the coalition extremely brilliantly. Jinnah's propaganda converted this failure into the evidence that was necessary to prove that the 'Hindu' Congress would never co-operate with 'Muslims'. (In Jinnah's view, of course, 'true' Muslims did not exist outside the League.) It is evident that the sharp taste of defeat in the January and February elections had convinced Jinnah that the only hope lay in shedding the last vestiges of moderation and plunging into extremism – hardly an unusual phenomenon in politics. By the time of the next test for the Muslim vote, in the by-election of Bijnor, the League's communal propaganda, not to mention its use of violence, had become even more extreme. Nehru was upset at N. A. K. Sherwani's defeat in Bundelkhand, but he had taken comfort in the comparatively reasonable margin, and in the fact that the rural Muslim vote had gone almost entirely for the Congress. At Bijnor much more was at stake than at Bundelkhand, for it was a revenge election. Muslim landlords had begun to shift towards the League from 1936, a process spurred by the rout of their Agriculturist Party in the elections. Although Nawab Liaquat Ali Khan takes credit for being among those who persuaded Jinnah to return from London to take over the defunct League, he himself was not one of the 39 League candidates (27 rural and 12 urban) in 1937. Men like Raja Shaban Ali Khan of

Salempur, however, had come over to the League in October 1936, and their arrival made the party only more reactionary, to the dismay of some of the younger men. When the Raja of Salempur became the state president, the tensions led to a number of resignations. Among those who left was a man who had been a UP council member of Motilal's Swaraj Party between 1923 and 1926, Hafiz Muhammad Ibrahim (1889–1964), who formally joined the Congress. Since he had won the 1937 election on the League ticket, he honourably resigned his seat and sought re-election from his constituency, Bijnor, on a Congress ticket.

The manifesto issued by the joint secretary of the UP Muslim League parliamentary board for the Bijnor election said that the Congress wanted to suppress, dominate and cripple Indian Muslims so that they might never rise again. How? What the Congress wanted to do, it explained, was to make the Muslims prostrate before Gandhi and Jawaharlal rather than before Allah. In their speeches the League orators claimed that the Congress wanted to eliminate Urdu, ban cow slaughter and force people to wear the 'Hindu' dhoti instead of the 'Muslim' pyjama. The propaganda was as crude as this. In an effort to win the support of the Shias, who had at the All-India Shia Conference on 11–12 October at Lucknow resolved to support the Congress, the League also alleged that the Congress government would ban the *tazia* pageant during Moharrum. The only Muslims with the Congress, the League leaders said, were the ulema who had been bribed. A personal letter from Jawaharlal to Rafi Ahmed Kidwai in which he had discussed election travel expenditure had found its way to Rafiuddin Ahmed, the League candidate at Bundelkhand, by mistake; this was touted by no less a person than Jinnah as evidence of 'bribery' of the ulemas by the Congress. The implication was that Muslim stooges were being financed to fight their selfless, honest brethren in the League. Lies were freely used. Nehru was accused of having snatched and torn every flag bearing the Islamic slogan 'Allah-o-Akbar' ('God is Great') at Najibabad. It was an utter canard, of course, but truth was at a premium. Maulana Shaukat Ali was evocative in his vilification. Congress leaders like Dr K. M. Ashraf were accused of having said that, like Stalin, Mussolini and Hitler, the Congress too would destroy religion. Violence was freely used; thugs entered Indian electioneering for the first time. Even an institution like Aligarh University, from where restraint if not ideological sobriety might have been expected, became the scene of communal violence. The League's slogans were unabashed incitement to anti-Hindu violence: 'Congress murdabad, Gandhi murdabad; Hindu kafir hain, unko maarne se ham bahisht jaenge' ('Death to Congress, death to Gandhi; Hindus are infidels, we shall reach heaven by killing them'). Nehru was horrified at this political depravity and wrote to Krishna Menon on 11 November 1937: 'Everything up to murder on religious grounds is preached and the worst type of fanaticism aroused.' Nehru tried every appeal for calm and sense, but no one was listening.

The Congress position on minorities had been restated at the All-India Congress Committee meeting in Calcutta between 26 October and 1 November through a comprehensive resolution promising to protect the various rights of minorities and stressing that 'The objective of the Congress is an independent and united India where no class or group or majority or minority may exploit another to its own advantage . . .' It is interesting, in passing, that gradually the adjective 'united' began to be stressed, as the shadow of another possibility began to disturb Congress minds. Nehru appealed to people he knew on the social level, but who were now in the League, to bring some restraint into their campaigning. In a letter to Nawab Ismail Khan (1886–1958) on 10 November he refuted each one of the allegations made by the League in specific detail, exposed the absurdity of each League claim, and then asked on a personal note:

> Can we have any public life, or any life, if this is the background in which we function? With what self-respect can we look into each other's eyes, or into the eyes of the foreigner, if we forget the elemental courtesies and decencies of life? You and I and many of us have been entangled in public affairs for a long stretch of years and we have seen many ups and downs. We have, I hope, a measure of respect for each other. We came to politics not to find a profession, for we could have done well otherwise also. We came because we wanted to work for an objective we had at heart. We tried to live up to certain ideals and even when sorrow and difficulty encompassed us the thought of that objective and those ideals kept us going. It has not been a politician's game of electioneering that has kept us up to the mark. Elections come and go; we win or lose. But there are other things in life which have attracted us and given us strength even when disaster seemed to threaten us. But if those things go, life itself would lose its flavour, and public affairs would become a curse and an abomination.

These were not the words of a manipulator, the image of Jawaharlal Nehru that Jinnah was trying to create. These were the words of an idealist and a humanist staring at reality and fighting off the disillusionment that could so easily break the will where abuse and vilification would not.

Hafiz Ibrahim won comfortably in Bijnor, by 5,000 votes, defeating this awesome barrage of propaganda (he would remain in India after partition and serve as minister in every Congress government till he passed away in 1964, as governor of Punjab), but the result only inspired the League to greater levels of communalism. The Bijnor campaign by the Muslim League provoked tension all over the province, and the usual rash of disputes over familiar issues like cow slaughter threatened to make it a bloodstained winter. As president, Nehru's instruction to his party men was unambiguous. He wrote to Mela Ram on 31 December 1937: 'It is better to err on the side of generosity.' But it was a time when the limits of generosity were being severely taxed. A lead had been given, and now opportunist leaders like Fazlul Haq dipped into this bubbling well of communalism to water a fresh crop. At a meeting of the All-India Muslim Students' Federation at Calcutta on 28 December 1937, the premier of Bengal made an explicit call for violence: 'We are surrounded by enemies on all sides and we must therefore be ready for the fight.' Between the December of 1936 and the December of 1937 much had changed. And one of the most significant events on this very dramatic and crowded calendar was the Muslim League session at Lucknow between 15 and 18 October.

In 1937 Jinnah was at the very apex of his professional life, earning a standard fee of Rs 1,500 a day, one of the highest in the country, his income supplemented by the rent from seven flats in London's Mayfair and a bulging portfolio of stocks which brought at least Rs 40,000 annually. He belonged to the very small club in the country required to pay 'super tax' – though it is another matter that he never paid his taxes on time. He had changed his Bombay residence from the house on Little Gibbs Road to a virtual palace on Malabar Hill, 15,000 square yards of wooded land on Mount Pleasant Road. Plus there was a bungalow in Delhi at 10 Aurangzeb Road (now the Dutch embassy). At the age of sixty Jinnah had only two serious problems: a disease in his lungs and a political career that still seemed stuck on a low base. He could not do anything about the first except hide it. But he could show the world that there was still a great deal he could do about the second. Jinnah knew he had tuberculosis but guarded the information as closely as a state secret – which, come to think of it, it certainly was. Nothing would have sabotaged his plans more effectively than news that his life was nearing its end.

When Jinnah reached Lucknow from Bombay on the evening of 13 October 1937 he had achieved at least one of his objectives: he was the supreme authority in his party. The 1937 elections had, however, rather exposed the pretensions; it was not a party worth being supreme authority of. As Iqbal, the poet-philosopher who led the Punjab League, said in his letter to Jinnah on 28 May 1937, the League needed a new political *raison d'être* for sheer survival. Its commitment to upper-class Muslim interests (an analysis which coincided with Nehru's view of the League) was responsible for its current hopeless state, Iqbal wrote, and the League had to address itself to the vital question of Muslim poverty. But Jinnah, with his own ideas on class and property being what they were, was in no mood to offer any radical economic programme, either on socialist lines or even on the precepts of equality and justice offered by the Quran, as Iqbal advised. The economic philosophy of the League was based on the premiss that Muslim prosperity was linked to the power and influence of Muslim zemindars and business men. Hence the League's attack on the Congress schemes for the abolition of zemindari at the Lucknow session, and on Nehru's socialism.

The fertile mind of Iqbal offered another idea, a step forward from his famous speech at the League session in Allahabad on 29 December 1930 when he had demanded a Muslim state in the north-west. (The League was so moribund then that the meeting did not even have its quorum of seventy-five members.) On 21 June 1937 Iqbal wrote to Jinnah: 'Why should not the Muslims of North-West India and Bengal be considered as nations entitled to self-determination just as other nations in India are? Personally I think that the Muslims of North-West India and Bengal ought at present [to] ignore Muslim minority provinces.' It was a most interesting thought. Jinnah, however, immensely more practical and political than Iqbal, saw no reason why he should ignore the Muslim-minority provinces, when the far more sensible thing to do would be to feed their frustrations, build their anger and then exploit their strength for a dream in which eventually they would have no place. It was no accident that after Lucknow the next session of the League was held in Patna. The League's effective propaganda machine found an ideal target: the Congress Hindu premiers in United Provinces and Bihar who had taken office in late 1937. Everything the Congress did became an attack on Muslim culture. While objections to Vande Mataram had some partial merit (the Congress, in response, amended the version it used), to call the hoisting of the Congress tricolour an insult to Muslims was more consistent with the level of League propaganda. All this was flavoured with Jinnah's constant charge that the Congress had only one aim in mind: to annihilate the Muslim wherever it was in power.

By October 1937 Jinnah knew that the League would not survive unless he could make it something more than a shadow of his own personal stature. The crowds that welcomed him at Lucknow station, brought by Khaliq and the Raja of Mahmudabad, were large and emotional, yet Jinnah knew he needed a new political charter in order to expand his strength. His strategy was to concentrate on the centre, to leave the provinces to the local satraps in return for their endorsement of him as the sole voice of Muslims at the national level. It was a claim which would have no meaning without the support of Punjab and Bengal. He was willing to pay any price for this, and so simply liquidated the League in these two provinces in exchange for the support of the two premiers. Simultaneously wanting to keep a useful line open to the British, he was hesitant about the now obligatory resolution demanding full independence at this session of the League, until Khaliquzzaman convinced him that any milder option at this stage would destroy whatever credibility the League had among the people.

The 14th of October was a historic day, for Jinnah got what he wanted from the premiers of Punjab and Bengal. Sir Sikandar Hayat Khan, looking no further than the preservation of his Unionist government, thought he had extracted a very heavy price from the League in exchange for the pact with Jinnah. He had, on the one hand, ensured the obliteration of the League in Punjab, which would go down well with his partners in the coalition like Sir Chotu Ram, while his own loyalty to the League was left as even less than nominal. Bengal was much easier for Jinnah, for all he had to do was ensure that Fazlul Haq retained his chair, which Jinnah did by ditching

Haq's bitter foe and his own loyalist, Khwaja Nazimuddin. Haq predictably became more loyal than the king, promising revenge against Hindus in Bengal if any Muslim was touched under any Congress Raj. In his speech on 17 October at the League session he orated: 'If the Hindu Congress ministries continue their policy of oppression of the Muslim minorities in their provinces, I declare it from this platform that I shall retaliate in Bengal even if it costs my life ... hypocrisy, untruth and deceit are the basis of Congress policies and the Congress is trying to establish a Hindu raj in India.' As the British governor of Bengal had noted in another context, these adjectives were more applicable to Haq than to anyone else. Some of the League leaders were embarrassed by the passion of this new convert; and Nehru was disgusted. He wrote to Subhas Bose on 20 October: 'The recent meeting of the Muslim League and the fulminations of Fazlul Haq there have shown the recrudescence of an intensive and low type of communalism.' Jinnah kept his counsel. He had found the allies he would need. As his biographer Stanley Wolpert puts it in *Jinnah of Pakistan*:

> The Punjab was Pakistan's first and most important capital letter; and by luring Sir Sikandar into his party's tent, Jinnah raised the green flag with its giant 'P' over the League's Kaisar Bagh ('Royal Garden') outside Mahmudabad House, signalling the birth of an inchoate nation that was to remain in the womb of British India for precisely one decade. Fazlul Haq closed ranks as well that fateful day in 1937, adding a remote Eastern wing to the nation of South Asian Muslims now in the making. By sundown Jinnah knew that this second Lucknow Pact he had negotiated would tear asunder the subcontinent.

When Jinnah reached Lucknow for that session he was still in the clothes he had worn all his life: British suits and a sola topi. Clothes make the man. The man had changed; so would the clothes. As he prepared himself for the opening day of the Lucknow session he put on, for the first time in his life, a long, black *sherwani* – the formal dress of the Muslim élite of United Provinces. As he reached the door through which he would walk towards the *shamiana* he found Nawab Ismail Khan standing there, wearing a woollen cap. On an impulse, Jinnah plucked it from his colleague's head, put it on, studied himself in a mirror, was pleased with what he saw and walked towards the 5,000 delegates assembled on the lawns of the palace of the Raja of Mahmudabad. Thus was born the Jinnah cap, which at once became the Muslim League's answer to the Gandhi cap of the Congressmen. And nothing symbolizes the difference between the two parties better. Gandhi created his cap out of hand-spun cotton and fashioned it on the headwear given to him in a South African prison. Jinnah's cap came from a nawab's head.

That day, on 15 October 1937, Jinnah gave the Muslim League session the outlines of a new future. He did not exaggerate when he described this session as the most critical in the history of the League. There was a 'magic power', he told the Muslims, in their hands with which they could, with unity and sacrifice, forge a new future; a decision they took now would be 'grave and momentous'. What was this future which Jinnah wanted the Muslims to equip themselves for?

> No individual or people can achieve anything without industry, suffering and sacrifice. There are forces which might bully you, tyrannize over you and intimidate you, and you may even have to suffer. But it is by going through this crucible of the fire of persecution which may be levelled against you, the tyranny that may be exercised, the threats and intimidations that may unnerve you – it is by resisting, by overcoming, by facing these disadvantages, hardships and suffering, and maintaining your true convictions and loyalty, that a nation will emerge, worthy of its past glory and history, and will live to make its future history greater and more glorious not only in India but the annals of the world.

In ten years this nation would emerge, less illustrious than promised, with a destiny more troubled than that pristine dream, and for reasons as much to do with British policy as Muslim will; but it would emerge, nevertheless, leaving a wound across South Asia which would never heal. Pakistan was not created because the president of the Congress for the year 1937 could not stomach the idea of handing the fate of India's Muslims to a self-avowed communal party. It was created because some ambitions would settle for nothing less.

27 Her Father's Daughter

He first proposed to Indira when she was sixteen, before she was sent to Shantiniketan to study at the school founded and presided over by the great poet and family friend Rabindranath Tagore. Indira turned Feroze Gandhi down and was very upset with him when he complained to her mother, Kamala, about her rejection. Feroze Gandhi (no relation of the Mahatma's) had entered the Nehru house after that chance encounter with Kamala described earlier. Krishna Hutheesingh, Jawaharlal's sister, remembers the Feroze of those days in her book *We Nehrus*:

> As a young man he had admired Kamala in a romantic, Dante-and-Beatrice way, content if he could just be near her. Because of her he had given up his college education to join the movement; but all he did was to follow her on her journeys to the villages carrying a little box with her tea or coffee and some sandwiches in it, because she was unwell and not allowed to eat everything. I can see him now, a stocky, fair young man, walking just behind her carrying the little box.

Indira's childhood had been unique. The emotional security of the great love of her parents was juxtaposed with the insecurity of their absence. Father was either in gaol or on the move; Mother was increasingly bedridden or trying to recover in a sanatorium. For long spells Indira lived in boarding-schools. Loneliness became a part of her life. There is a famous story about her. One day a visitor came to Anand Bhavan during the Salt Satyagraha movement. In a very grave and solemn tone, she told him, 'I'm sorry, but my grandfather, father and mummy are all in prison.' It was only too true. Her school life was constantly interrupted, if not by politics then by the need to go abroad with her mother, as in 1926–7, when she was just nine. After her return she went to a convent and hated it. Then Jawaharlal sent her for a while to one of the most liberal institutions of the time, the Pupil's Own School in Poona, which was co-educational as early as then. Her teens were spent watching both her parents on the political trail. She took her Senior Cambridge examinations before joining Shantiniketan. Then, when Kamala's health collapsed, she went with her mother to Switzerland.

Feroze Gandhi could not keep himself away. He persuaded a rich aunt to finance a trip to England, ostensibly to study journalism; but he was soon in Lausanne, beside Kamala's bedside. After her mother's death, Indira went to Badminton School in England to learn the classics. Feroze was there too, and here the friendship deepened to love. Indira went on to Oxford, where she took a course in Modern History. She had the option of studying in Paris, but Indira Gandhi recalls in the interview-based book *My Truth* (1981): 'One reason for choosing Oxford was that Feroze was in England. I considered him more as a friend; it was a link with the family and with India.' Indira returned to India in November 1938 for a few months in the company of her father, who finally managed to take an oft-yearned-for summer trip to Europe after leaving the Congress presidentship in 1938. She went back to London in April 1939, via Paris. 'I had gone first, and Feroze joined me there,' remembered Indira Gandhi. 'That's when I finally said yes, on the steps of Montmartre. But we didn't tell anyone.'

Father, in other words, did not know, which was perhaps just as well. He would be upset when he did. Nobody quite said it – everyone was too sophisticated for that – but one of the stumbling-blocks to this marriage was the fact that Feroze Gandhi was not a Hindu but a Parsi. The problem had arisen before in the Nehru family, with Vijaylakshmi Pandit, when she became friendly with a Muslim journalist working on *The Independent*, Syud Hossain, but Motilal had managed to nip the idea before it prospered. Jawaharlal was undergoing yet another spell in prison when he learned of Indira's desire to marry Feroze, and he began fretting. He tried the ploy that Indira had just come back from London and should get to know more men before she finally made up her mind. He told her to consult her aunts. Vijaylakshmi was adamant: no marriage. Krishna writes that she first offered the same answer: 'With a flash of Nehru temper and considerable logic Indu said, "Why? It took you only ten days to make up your mind to marry Raja Bhai; and I have known Feroze for years. So why should I have to wait, and why should I have to meet other young men?"'

There was obviously no answer to that. This was no longer the Indira of Shantiniketan. There is a very interesting picture of her with other students clustered around for a typical group photograph with Rabindranath. Everyone is looking at the camera, with differing degrees of self-confidence. The only one with her head tilted down and away from the camera is Indira. Now, however, she was a confident and beautiful woman, one who did not make up her mind in a hurry but, once she did, would rarely be swerved from her intention. Jawaharlal's reluctance was understandable. The mood of the times was hardly conducive to such liberal gestures in personal life. He was certain that the Hindu chauvinists would pounce upon this inter-religious marriage as a 'betrayal' of Hinduism. He might be an atheist in private, but he shied away, as a public figure and prospective Prime Minister of India, from alienating himself from Hindu sentiment so sharply. Yet his conscience would not allow him to forbid the marriage. The storm that arose when news spread told its own story. The relatives, of course, were furious; as if being a Parsi was not bad enough, Feroze had no money either, which compounded his crime at a time when a queue of the richest princes in the land were lining up for Indira's hand. Despite all this, in the end there was no way Jawaharlal was going to hurt the daughter he loved with as much intensity as his own father had loved him, the natural love of an emotional and generous nature heightened by its concentration on an only child.

The letters which Jawaharlal wrote to his daughter when she was in London only reiterate the great need he felt for her, a dependence which was eventually bound to cause a strain in her marriage. Jawaharlal needed his daughter as much as Motilal needed his son (he often called her 'Indu-boy'). She was his trusted confidante, a person he could unburden himself to in a way he could not with a sister or a friend, particularly when trapped by depression. When she left in April 1939 for Oxford, 'Papu' wrote to her, on 12 April:

Darling, So you have gone and I wonder when and where we shall meet again in this mad world. More and more I have been thinking that it was right for you to go to Europe. India is not a happy country at present at any rate for those who are sensitive ... I spent yesterday with Shah, Mahmud and company. Shah left in the evening and then I sat till late at night with Mahmud. Old ties hold when one is depressed ... I read those old letters which I had sent you again and I felt how terribly far away that time was, when I wrote them.

The next day he wrote again (Syed Mahmud had stayed on in Allahabad to keep his depressed friend company), quoting lines from Alfred de Musset:

> J'ai perdu ma force et ma vie,
> Et mes amis et ma gaieté;
> J'ai perdu jusqu'à la fierté,
> Qui faisait croire à mon génie.

('I have lost my strength and my life / And my friends and my cheerfulness; / I have lost even my pride / Which used to make me believe in my genius.')

Indira would respond like a friend. On 26 April her father wrote: 'You give me a lot of good advice, my dear, to keep smiling, etc. of course, but it is a little difficult. I suppose age is telling upon me and I am losing my resilience.' By 3 July little had happened to lift the father's spirits:

> It is long since I have written to you – two weeks or so . . . Often I think of writing to you, for you are always in my mind, but I hesitate and put it off. A vague feeling that too frequent letters might be a nuisance and a burden to you holds me back . . . I am withdrawing into myself more and more and my incursions into the outer world are being limited . . . Here in Allahabad the introvert prevails and I live in this big house in absolute silence with very few interruptions . . . I reach Anand Bhavan and come up to my room and pay a visit to yours and look round and see the familiar pictures and books and articles. Then back to my room where I live day and night except for brief visits down below for food or to see an occasional visitor. I do not encourage visitors and I am glad that they respect my wishes. I am beginning to think that there is something in the old Hindu idea of *sanyasa* after a certain age. There is no chance of my becoming a *sanyasi* but the idea is not without attraction.

When another milestone, the fiftieth birthday, did come around, Papu was in uneven spirits. The letters of this phase offer a very touching and a very endearingly witty glimpse into the deep and mature bonds that existed between father and daughter. On 16 November 1937, two days after his birthday, Nehru wrote:

Darling Indu, Your message was very welcome because of the news it gave about your progress to health. The reminder of the birthday is not a pleasant one after one approaches or passes a certain age. In China I believe the fiftieth birthday is a great event for age is honoured there and everyone is keen on appearing older than he is. My own enthusiasm for age is not so great and the figure fifty in connection with my age frightens me. Perhaps wisdom comes with the years, but wisdom by itself does not take one very far. There must be the urge and capacity to act up to that wisdom. *Si jeunesse savait, si vieillesse pouvait.* [If youth knew, if old age could.]

The letter quickly went on to news: how friends had forced a new *sherwani* on him on his birthday (when the tailors, Hope Brothers, came they reminded him that the last coat he had had made was exactly a decade before, for the Lahore Congress); that he had been given a mere Rs 2,500 or so as royalties from *Letters from a Father to His Daughter* (Kitabistan, 1938) against the publisher's profits of Rs 20,000 but had now given the rights to universities. And: 'The Calcutta *Statesman* offered me Rs 500/- a month for a column a week – 4 columns a month of comments on international affairs. I rejected it of course.' There would be no question of writing for pro-British papers. By 13 December, the mood had become far brighter. Cripps was staying with him at Anand Bhavan, and the excitement of politics was once again serving as adrenalin. He could look at his age in chattier perspective:

The fifty years do not bother me much, so do not worry. I have been told, on the unimpeachable authority of an astrologer (the man who has made most of the family horoscopes), that I have now entered some new phase which is under the influence of the moon, and this is supposed to be a very good one for me!

Then again someone told me he had discovered the secret of my activity. He was a believer in Cheiro and had closely studied his theory of numbers. It appears I am under the influence of No. 5 because I was born on the 14th of this month (4 + 1 = 5). No. 5 denotes activity. So now you know.

In the same letter he mentioned a young man who was to become a devoted family friend:

We have a young Pathan boy staying with us for the last six weeks. He is named Yunus. Abdul Ghaffar Khan sent him to me for some kind of training. He is a very charming boy. But what will interest you is that he has got 41 brothers and sisters – in all they are 42! One father but I think 7 or eight mothers. He is about 22, his eldest brother is 70. Bit of a record, I should think. Everyone who hears about it collapses.

The home that echoed with the roar of decades of history was, however, now silent. The old were dead, and the young had moved on to their own abodes of bliss. Swarup Rani, Jawaharlal's ageing mother, had passed away in January 1938, on a day on which the family was together, for a change. It was late evening, for they were waiting up with Vijaylakshmi, who was to take the night train to Lucknow. At around eleven Swarup Rani leaned forward to give a goodbye kiss to her elder daughter and collapsed. Jawaharlal caught her before she fell; she was already unconscious. That night she passed away in her sleep – it had been a massive stroke. In one of those utterly unbelievable coincidences, her faithful widowed sister Bibi Amma, who had so devotedly looked after Swarup Rani all her life, died within twenty-four hours, in her sleep too and at the same hour as Swarup Rani, five in the morning. Anand Bhavan's role in the freedom movement was really over. Vijaylakshmi, now a minister in the Congress government in United Provinces, lived in Lucknow; Krishna was in Bombay with Raja and her two sons; and Jawaharlal was always a wanderer. But Anand Bhavan would come to life one more time: on 26 March 1942, the day Indira wedded Feroze.

Nehru, with characteristic honesty, decided to confront the controversy about the marriage (the volume of hate-mail was heavy, but Indira was coolly unperturbed). He issued a formal statement to the press on 26 February 1942. Marriage was a personal affair, he said, and this statement was only a realistic concession to his place in public affairs. 'Feroze Gandhi', Jawaharlal said, 'is a young Parsi who has been a friend and colleague of ours for many years, and I expect him to serve our country and our cause efficiently and well. But on whomsoever my daughter's choice would have fallen, I would have accepted it or been false to the principles I have held.' Moreover, 'Mahatma Gandhi, whose opinion I value not only in public affairs but in private matters also, gave his blessing to the proposal.' Yet it was not as principled as all that. The ceremony was not under the civil act but through Vedic rites – for which purpose Feroze had to go through the process of becoming a Hindu. A concession was made to the hate-mail. All controversy seemed nevertheless to disappear as the bride waited for the 'auspicious' hour at Anand Bhavan. She wore a shell-pink sari made from *khadi* spun by Jawaharlal himself. The mantras were chanted on a marble platform with removable slabs at the centre for the holy fire. Jawaharlal escorted his daughter, looking lovelier than ever, to the fire to sit beside Feroze. Beside him, a place was kept empty; it was for the missing Kamala. After a short honeymoon, the new couple took a small house in Allahabad. Yet another child of Anand Bhavan had moved away.

That summer Indira went with her father for a holiday to Kulu. Feroze stayed behind in Allahabad on some work. He joined Indira after Jawaharlal had finished his holiday, and then the couple went to Kashmir where they were guests of a good friend of the family and a man whose destiny – as well as his family's – was going to be linked to the Nehrus for generations: Sheikh Muhammad Abdullah.

'One of the reasons I got married', recalled Indira Gandhi in *My Truth*, 'was that I was determined to have children, yet I went through a bad time because a doctor had said that I may not survive child-bearing.' The first child was, surprisingly therefore, a perfectly normal baby – not too many labour pains, mother healthy. He was born in Bombay on 20 August 1944. Jawaharlal, as usual, was in gaol and received the news by telegram. He was sent a list of about twenty options, from which he, as head of the family, might choose the name of his first grandson. Jawaharlal chose Rajiv, a Sanskrit word for 'lotus'. He had named his grandson after his wife, Kamala, which also means 'lotus'. Indira added another name: Ratna, meaning 'jewel' (a synonym for 'jewel' is Jawahar). The full name, then, was Rajiv Ratna Gandhi, although the sixth Prime Minister of free India is popularly known only as Rajiv Gandhi.

Jawaharlal saw his grandson for the first time in the darkness of the night outside Naini gaol in Allahabad, where he had been forced to halt on his way from Ahmednagar Fort; it was the last spell in a British gaol. Indira and Feroze had heard a rumour that he might be passing through Naini, and they took their son and waited, hoping for the chance to give Nehru a glimpse of his grandchild. Indira Gandhi remembered the incident in *My Truth*: 'We went to prison and waited outside. They arrived late at night, because the British always did things in the dark. I lifted the baby up under a very dim roadside light. My father peered at him.'

It was the darkness just before the dawn.

28 Mr Chanakya, and Other Masks

In its long and illustrious career the British Broadcasting Corporation has often influenced the lives of politicians, sometimes for the better; more often (news being essentially a dangerous commodity) for the worse. One wonders if the world's best-known news corporation is quite aware of what it did to the fair name of Jawaharlal. The 'ha-haing' of a BBC announcer irritated the future Prime Minister of India to such an extent that he even tried to change his name. On 25 March 1937 Jawaharlal Nehru wrote to his dear friend Krishna Menon:

> Allahabad
> March 25, 1937
>
> My dear Krishna,
> ... One small matter. I am getting rather fed up with my name. It is always being misspelt and mispronounced. The other day a BBC announcer got hopelessly muddled over it and went on ha-haing. Unfortunately I cannot change my name but I propose to make a slight change in the way it is written. Jawaharlal consists really of two Hindustani words: Jawahar and Lal. In India one usually combines the two, but this long word has a terrifying look about it and foreigners cannot get hold of it. So it would be better in future to separate the two. My name should therefore be given as: Jawahar Lal Nehru.

The Congress president may have been, like politicians before and after him, only making the media a convenient excuse for indulging a whim, but in March 1937 Jawahar Lal was ready to change the world according to his tastes, so changing his name was truly a small matter. Confident, and inspired by the crowds he inspired in turn, with a historic victory in the elections behind him, Nehru was on a peak in his forty-eighth year. By the end of 1937 he was back in the valley.

In February 1937 he wrote the foreword for a book of 101 cartoons by K. Shankar Pillai, who drew for the *Hindusthan Times* between 1932 and 1946 before starting his own *Shankar's Weekly*. It was a liberal's tribute to the relationship between a cartoonist with bite, but 'without the least bit of malice or ill will'. He ended with: 'I hope that he [Shankar] will long continue to enlighten us and amuse us and pull us down a peg or two.' By October 1937 Nehru had become his own Shankar. On 5 October he reached Anand Bhavan from Lucknow for a short, four-day break from his perpetual tours and penned, as an 'after-dinner exercise', a devastating self-portrait. Then, without getting it typed by a secretary or typing it himself, he posted it to his very dear friend Bebee (the nickname of Padmaja Naidu) suggesting that she pass it on to the *Modern Review*, edited by Ramananda Chatterjee from Calcutta, for publication. Anonymously. Nehru was quite pleased by the mischief. The editor published it in good faith as a severe lampoon of the high-striding Congress president, and Nehru was most amused by the various reactions the piece aroused. He recommended it to John Gunther, the American writer, six months later as an article where 'I considered judiciously my virtues and gave praise for them in full measure'. He admitted it was a bit of a trick, but the point was that, like all good lampoons, the mockery was truth thinly exaggerated in either direction. Nehru titled the piece 'The Rashtrapati' ('The President') and signed it 'Chanakya' (the fourth-century B C Indian political theorist). The piece does not really bear slicing and has to be read fully to be savoured, but the essential point he made was that, though he loved standing 'on the seat of the car, balancing himself rather well, straight and seemingly tall, like a god', he was no Caesar. 'Chanakya' wrote: 'Jawaharlal is certainly not a fascist, not only by conviction but by temperament. He is far too much of an aristocrat for the crudity and vulgarity of fascism.' And later:

> Jawaharlal cannot become a fascist. And yet he has all the makings of a dictator in him – vast popularity, a strong will directed to a well-defined purpose, energy, pride, organizational capacity, ability, hardness, and, with all his love of the crowd, an intolerance of others and a certain contempt of the weak and the inefficient. His flashes of temper are well known and even when they are controlled, the curling of the lips betrays him.

Was Nehru trying to achieve anything more than an after-dinner intellectual game? He was. There were suggestions that he should be kept president for a third term, and with the Congress in office against his wishes he had no desire for that. 'Jawaharlal is obviously tired and stale,' 'Chanakya' wrote. Jawaharlal was fed up and for the first time could not be persuaded to become general secretary after Subhas Bose became president at the Haripura Congress. He even wanted to resign from the working committee, but that would have been seen as a sign of open confrontation with Bose, so he let his name remain there. But he did not hide his lack of interest. And so the internationalist in him set off to explore those frontiers in Europe and Asia that his heart longed for, but which his national commitments had denied him.

The behaviour of the Congress ministries had proved his worst expectations. C. Rajagopalachari seemed to have forgotten that he was a Congressman. In a note to Sir Geoffrey Bracken dated 30 January 1939, Lord Erskine, the governor, described his Congress premier as 'too much of a Tory even for me'. In Bombay, home minister K. M. Munshi wanted the British governor to help him deal with the Communists and trade unionists: a prospect that was anathema to Nehru. As long as he was president of the party, however, he loyally defended his governments. With Subhas Bose taking over, the aggressive anti-fascist stance of the Congress was also in danger of being diluted. Nehru's conviction that the fascism of Hitler and Mussolini was a greater danger to the world than British imperialism was to remain steady throughout these very difficult years ahead, even when the evidence from the battlefield suggested that Indian nationalism might prosper from a different course. An imperialist like Winston Churchill made support for the Allies even more difficult. But Nehru did not waver. As we have seen, he tried to use only Jewish shops when in Europe. At one point he even proposed settling Jews seeking refuge from Germany in India, and Gandhi agreed whole-heartedly with him. On 31 August 1938 Gandhi wrote to Jawaharlal from Segaon, Wardha:

> Then about the Jews. I feel entirely like you. I boycott foreign goods not foreign ability. And I feel keenly for the persecuted Jews. As a concrete proposal I suggest your collecting the names of the most deserving ones and making it plain to them that they must be prepared to throw in their lot with us and accept our standard of living.

It was the Raj which threw cold water on the idea, by insisting that each refugee be guaranteed a job before being allowed in, and nothing came of it.

In the early part of 1938 there was a long exchange of letters with Jinnah on the interminable communal question, though by now the two were repeating themselves. Nehru's arguments however were beginning to have some effect at least. Even a man like S. Wazir Hasan, who had presided over the Bombay session of the Muslim League in 1936, had finally reacted against the communalism of Jinnah. He wrote to Nehru on 11 February 1938:

> This propaganda of misrepresentation, lies and religious and communal hatred, not only between Mussalmans and Hindus, but also between Mussalmans and Mussalmans, was initiated in the presidential address of the Muslim League session at Lucknow in October last. It is being carried on from day to day with ever increasing false statements of facts under the guise of the rights of minorities and religious hatred.

Wazir Hasan wanted Nehru and Azad to launch an immediate counter-offensive, but Nehru was too tired. The Haripura Congress over, he decided it was time to indulge in a little wanderlust, 'to get out of the old rut and cross mountains and seas and make acquaintance with new countries, new people'. He wrote a piece on 7 April 1936 (published in the *Modern Review* of May) about this desire to go somewhere which had possessed him: 'It was not physical tiredness, but a weariness of the mind which hungered for change and refreshment . . . Political life was an exhausting business and I had had enough for a while . . . my mind was elsewhere . . . It panted for escape from the troubles and problems that encompassed us, for peace and quiet and the gentle sigh of the wind.' He went to the Indian hills, to Almora, where 'Sometimes I would lie under the pine-trees and listen to the voice of the wandering wind, whispering many strange things into my ears, and lulling my senses, and cooling the fever in my brain.' After the Indian hills, his thoughts turned to Europe: 'Hitler was marching into Austria and I heard the tramp of barbarian feet over the pleasant gardens of Vienna. Was this the prelude to that world catastrophe which had hung over us for so long? Was this war?'

There was no relief from controversy, in matters major or minor. Foreign travel always excites an undercurrent of resentment in India, as if it is a vaguely anti-Indian thing to do. (Surely this latent irritation has at least something to do with the old Hindu prejudice against crossing the seas.) Gandhi had purified himself in 1890 after returning from abroad, and even in 1929 as famous a Congress socialist as Jayaprakash Narayan preferred to appease conservative Hindu sentiment by doing *prayaschit* after his return from overseas. (Motilal, if you recall, had sneered at the thought and shocked respectable India by doing so.) The criticism is never quite open, perhaps out of embarrassment; it finds expression in different forms. Nehru now found he had to defend his practice of wearing European clothes in Europe. On his return, he issued a statement from Anand Bhavan, on 2 December 1938: 'It seems to me as absurd for me to wear a dhoti and *kurta* in Paris or London as to wear European attire in the villages of India.' He had no desire to tempt a Swiss winter with *khadi*. 'This has nothing to do with Indian nationalism,' Nehru wrote crossly. Gandhi might go to see the King in a bare body in 1931, but Nehru neither was Gandhi nor wanted to be. Moreover, his tour of Europe was well photographed and reported. Nehru was news. So India got more than a glimpse of what he was doing abroad.

One posed portrait of Nehru during this foreign tour shows him in a well-cut, dark, three-piece suit, the tie wound in a single knot, white cuffs linked by studs, the left hand in his trouser pocket and a cigarette-holder between the index and middle fingers of his right hand (the ash still on the edge of the half-consumed cigarette). This was the legacy of Harrow. In Egypt, where he stopped on his way to Europe, he wore Western clothes: both when talking to Nahas Pasha and posing in front of the Sphinx. (He also tried to look inscrutable.) When he wanted to cover his near-bald head he put on a hat rather than the Gandhi cap. But when he addressed an anti-fascist rally at Trafalgar Square on 17 July 1938, under the auspices of the Aid to Spain Committee, he was very much the Indian leader, wearing a black *sherwani* (long coat ending at the knees) and black Congress cap.

Nehru first stopped off briefly in Egypt in July *en route* to Europe, then sped off via Italy to Spain as a guest of the Republican government. The romance of the Republican cause was heady stuff. He visited the front, met officers and comrade-soldiers at General Lister's headquarters and experienced air raids during his five days in

Barcelona. Predictably, he felt an urge to join the International Brigade. He was now convinced that the British government was tacitly supporting Franco. He preferred the Britain which suited his kind of leftism: a commitment to socialism, democracy and compromise in equal parts. The Socialist League, the Left Book Club and the *New Statesman* idolized him. He further comforted the British Left by giving Gandhi one hundred per cent on sainthood and nationalism but distancing himself from Gandhi's economic programmes, which he described as a romantic throw-back to a past which was best forgotten. Invitations to the country for weekends, however, cut across party lines. Lord Lothian, who had been in correspondence with him, had him over, and he suffered (silently) Nancy Astor's diatribes against socialism. A whole range of people called on Nehru, including Jewish leaders. Lord Linlithgow, who was then on home leave, invited him for a chat. In a note written years later, on 24 October 1955, Nehru recalled he told the Viceroy that 'I gave England at the outside ten years before India was independent. I was not so far out.' Zetland discussed Spain with Nehru; naturally the two disagreed. From London, Nehru went to Paris, Prague (where he supported the resistance to Hitler), Germany and Geneva before coming back to a London charged with war fever. He visited the House of Commons to hear Chamberlain announce that he was flying the next day to Munich for talks with Hitler and Mussolini (the 'peace in our time' pact); he was sarcastic about Chamberlain's peace offensive and tried out a gas mask. He wanted to return overland to India through Central Asia, an old dream of his, but could not get the visas.

Among those who wooed him during this trip were the Nazis. The fascist powers naturally had a serious interest in India, the jewel and the treasury of the British Empire. On his journey back to India after the second Round-Table Conference, Gandhi had stopped in Rome, wanting to meet two people, the Pope and the Duce. The Pope had no time for the fakir, but the Duce not only found the time but invited Gandhi to be a state guest. Gandhi, conscious that this might be construed as tolerance of fascism, refused the second offer. Mussolini, however, was keen to do Gandhi honour and made a rare gesture by walking down the famous huge hall in front of his office to greet Gandhi at the door. The Mahatma, however, quickly disillusioned the dictator, telling Mussolini bluntly that he was only building a house of cards. Gandhi summed up Mussolini in five short sharp words: 'His eyes are never still.' The fascists turned their restless eyes on the younger Indian leaders. In July 1933 when Subhas Bose reached Germany during a European tour, the German Foreign Office instructed the Indo-German Society to arrange meetings with National Socialist Party leaders and to help Bose in every way possible. A meeting with either Hitler or Goebbels, however, was not possible. Hitler did not think too highly of Indians as a race, as his assessment in *Mein Kampf* amply proves:

> England will lose India only if it allows its administrative machinery to be dominated by Indians or when it will be forced to give up India by a more powerful enemy of England. The Indian rebels will never be able to realize this . . . I, as a German, prefer to see India, in spite of everything, under British domination than under the domination of any other country.

Even when Hitler finally granted an interview to Bose on 29 May 1942, he crudely clarified that in his view India would not be able to rule itself for another 150 years. Bose wanted to use the Germans against the British, but Jawaharlal was always clear in his mind that no compromise was possible with the Nazis for whatever cause. During this trip he spent two days in Munich. The German consul in Bombay had sent word in May 1938 to Nehru asking whether he would accept a formal invitation to be a guest of the Nazi government; Nehru had turned down the suggestion. In Munich he stayed as a private tourist. (It is an interesting, though not commonly known, fact that Jinnah sent Khaliquzzaman and A. R. Siddiqi to Europe in 1939 to contact German and Italian governments and suggest that they court him too, and not just Nehru.)

It is no huge surprise, consequently, that the man who moved the first – and, as it turned out, definitive – Congress resolution on war policy was Jawaharlal Nehru. What might sound surprising is that he did this not in 1938 or 1939 but in the winter of 1927 – at the same Madras session where he tried to force a complete independence resolution and was sneered at by colleagues and rebuked by Gandhi for doing such a 'childish' thing. War-clouds were a permanent feature of the European sky between the two wars; Nehru saw them darken in 1927 because of the millions being spent on the construction of the Singapore naval base, the upgrading of the Trincomalee base in Ceylon, the construction of the Khyber railway and his belief that Britain was considering a pre-emptive strike through Central Asia towards Turkey and the Balkan countries, with the help of Afghanistan and Iraq. Nehru's speech proposing the resolution showed a fine understanding of the world's nerves:

> Today Europe is perhaps a greater powder magazine than it was in 1914 when the last Great War broke out. War has not broken out yet because all nations are exhausted. But all the seeds of war are present, and present in greater number than they were thirteen years ago. When you look at the Balkans, Poland, Italy, Czechoslovakia, Lithuania and Russia, everywhere there is preparation for war, and there is chance for war.

What then should be the Congress attitude to Britain in a European war? To prevent India from becoming 'again a tool in the hands of foreign imperialists'. How? 'It will be the duty of the people of India to refuse to take any part in such a war or to co-operate with them in any way whatsoever.'

The rise of German fascism in the 1930s did introduce a new element into the equation, for Nehru's abhorrence of fascism was as intense as his anger against imperialism. There was, unlike for Bose, never any question of ambivalence on this. Bose as president of the Congress met the German consul in Bombay in December 1938; Berlin must have been doubly pleased when he was re-elected at Tripuri, winning, unthinkably, against the wishes of Gandhi, who wanted Maulana Azad as the president that year. Bose was sabotaged by his working committee after this stunning victory, with Gandhi effectively using the old guard to trip a president he did not want. Jawaharlal was very unhappy at this rift, but though he stayed neutral in the working committee politics, he refused to break with Gandhi, as Bose was prepared to do. Bose taunted Nehru as an inveterate supporter of lost causes like Spain and China; his champions were Germany and Japan. Nehru wanted India with the Allies. His only, but fundamental, qualification was that this decision should be made by Indians and not be forced on the country by the Raj. He would not accept a decision if it were arbitrarily made on India's behalf by an imperial Britain, no matter how much he might agree with the decision; he would not accept the status of a slave.

Bose resigned and left the Congress to form his own party, Forward Bloc; with this ended any serious opposition to the Nehru line on war policy. Babu Rajendra Prasad replaced Bose for the remaining months of Bose's second term. At a meeting on 1 May 1939 the All-India Congress Committee strongly disapproved of the dispatch of Indian troops to the front lines of the British war effort, Egypt and Singapore, on the grounds that India was being involved without the formal consent of Indians. At Wardha between 9 and 12 August the working committee reasserted 'its determination to oppose all attempts to impose a war on India'.

On 24 August came the Ribbentrop–Molotov pact, leading eventually to another split in the ranks of the freedom movement; the Communists decided that their war policy would be tailored to Soviet needs rather than Indian perceptions. On 25 August the British Foreign Office announced the Anglo-Polish Pact, but Hitler was not impressed by a man who could be fooled by a piece of paper. Germany attacked Poland on 1 September, and the world got ready for the coming catastrophe. Two meatless days a week were decreed in Italy, and the value of government bonds in Bombay and Calcutta fell sharply even as prices of everything else jumped up in British India. On Sunday 3 September at nine o'clock in the morning Sir Nevile Henderson, His Majesty's ambassador in Berlin, informed the German government that unless its forces began to withdraw promptly from Poland, and promptly meant by 11 a.m., there would be war. Hitler ignored the deadline.

At 11.45 Chamberlain spoke over the air to the British people from the Cabinet Room at 10 Downing Street: 'I have to tell you now that no such undertaking has been received and in consequence this country is at war with Germany.' The Prime Minister informed the House of Commons: 'It is a sad day for all of us, but for none is it sadder than for me. Everything I have done, worked for, hoped for and believed in during my public life has crashed in ruins.'

That night His Majesty King-Emperor George VI told his Empire: 'In this grave hour, perhaps the most fateful hour in our history, I send every household of my peoples, both at home and overseas, this message spoken with the same depth of feeling for each one of you as if I were able to cross your threshold and speak to you myself.' When a King wants to drop in and see you, it generally means bad news; for good news he summons you to his palace. The reason why the King wanted all 'my peoples' to unite for the big fight was a curious one:

> We have been forced into a conflict, for we are called with our allies to meet a challenge of a principle which, if it were to prevail, would be fatal to any civilized order in the world. It is a principle which permits a state, in selfish pursuit of power, to disregard its treaties and solemn pledges, which sanctions the use of force or threat of force against the sovereignty and independence of other states.

Curious, because this was precisely the complaint which the colonies had against Britain.

In Delhi, His Excellency the Marquis of Linlithgow, Viceroy of India, did not even have the courtesy to wait for the King's broadcast, far from having the wisdom to consult Indian leaders, before he declared war on behalf of India. However, why did His Excellency feel so strongly that India must fight Germany? Because, 'Confronted with the demand that she should accept the dictation of a foreign power in relation to her own territory and her own subjects, Poland has elected to stand firm.' It is astonishing that the irony of their double standards was lost on these British rulers. 'Nowhere do these great principles mean more than in India,' His Excellency said in his message declaring war. The Congress decided to show him that he was absolutely right.

Gandhi had been invited to meet the Viceroy through a telegram which reached him at Wardha on Saturday 2 September. He left for Simla that night. Other Indian leaders, Jinnah, Bose *et al.*, were similarly summoned and informed rather than consulted. Gandhi told the Viceroy that he could not reach any understanding with the Viceroy because the Congress working committee had given him no such authority. As far as he was concerned, he viewed the war 'with an English heart', but if the Viceroy wanted to know the national mood he would have to check with the Congress, which might not necessarily be as generous as him. Nehru was in China, on a long-planned tour, enjoying the experience enormously as he indulged his two favourite pleasures: diplomacy and journalism. (He sent a regular diary to his paper, the *National Herald*, and many other newspapers happily helped themselves after its publication.) He flew into China via Vietnam. It took five hours from Saigon to Hanoi in the Air France plane *La Ville de Calcutta* – the name was written in Bengali on one side of the aircraft. He visited Kunming, Chungking and Chengtu and was due to go north-west to meet Mao Tse-tung when the outbreak of the much-expected war forced him to rush back.

Nehru's views on the war were well known. To his relief the Congress governments had opposed the Government of India Act Amending Bill which aimed at mobilizing Indian resources for war purposes, and he made his views known through speeches, articles and editorials. As he wrote to Krishna Menon on 26 April 1939: 'I have been writing in the *National Herald* on the subject also, though I have preferred doing so lately in the form of unsigned editorials.' When Bose was absent from the AICC session in Calcutta on 1 May 1939, Nehru moved the resolution on the war danger, which once again committed the Congress to opposing any attempt to drag India into the war without the consent of the Indian people. He saw no contradiction between this and his views on fascism; the contradiction lay not in his attitude, but in the circumstances. He was bitter about Chamberlain's appeasement of fascism, and repeatedly claimed that British imperialism was in fact a closer ally of fascism. In an article called 'The Hoax', written in England on 15 October 1938 and published in the *National Herald* on 25 October, he wrote:

While Europe shakes and trembles, the British Parliament is on holiday and the Prime Minister of Britain goes afishing. And *The Times*, that thunderer of old, has sunk to the level of Herr Hitler's own well-managed press and sings his praises from day to day. Even *Punch*, that very respectable organ of the British middle classes, has lost its temper with *The Times*, and in biting satire of a *Times* leader writes:

> 'Justice alone was yielded
> And everyone was right:
> The sword that Hitler wielded
> Was not a sword of might.
> The French and we were tender
> And took the kindliest course:
> The Czechs did not surrender

To fear nor yet to force.
Lord! I could write a column
Of tripe to this intent,
As smooth – as suave – as solemn –
If England gave up Kent.'

In an interview to the press in New Delhi on 21 March 1939, reported in the *Hindusthan Times* the next day, Nehru categorically stated his position:

India's sympathies are very strongly anti-fascist and therefore she will inevitably wish for the defeat of fascism and the triumph of democracy. The policy which Mr Chamberlain has pursued since the last crisis is highly repugnant to India, and she has dissociated herself from it in every way. [But] it must be emphasized that India will not submit to any form of exploitation to further Britain's war effort . . . how can India fight for democracy if she herself does not have it? India's participation in any war will have to be decided by herself.

War fever, however, had seized India too. Special editions in Calcutta were selling out as fast as in London. As sad queues of young couples formed outside the offices where special licences for marriage were issued in England, Germany and Austria, women registered themselves for war work in Calcutta, and Germans began to be picked up and detained. The Congress working committee gathered at Wardha for a crucial meeting. (Maulana Azad was summoned from Lucknow, where he had gone to settle a Shia–Sunni dispute.) Nehru's mind was very clear. On 8 September he gave an interview to Associated Press in Rangoon on his way back from China, where he said: 'This war is going to change the face of things. The old order is dead and cannot be revived. If we are making for a new order, let us do so consciously, defining it clearly and acting up to it from now onwards.' He would always side with democracy over fascism, he reiterated, but demanded that the decision be his, not the Viceroy's. On landing in India, he rushed to Wardha. He authored the draft for the Congress's statement on the war, issued on 14 September. As a first step, Congressmen were ordered to boycott the next session of the Central Legislative Assembly. The statement took a grave view of the manner in which India had been turned into a belligerent in the war. It condemned Nazism and Nazi aggression, but told the British that co-operation would never come through compulsion; only a free India would gladly associate itself in the war to protect freedom. It taunted the princes, who had quickly announced support to the British, and suggested the introduction of a bit of democracy in their states. The Congress motto was: A slave India cannot help Britain.

Gandhi endorsed this statement, which he described as a manifesto to all the exploited nations of the world, but added a chuckle to his endorsement. He wrote:

> The author of the statement is an artist. Though he cannot be surpassed in his implacable opposition to imperialism in any shape or form, he is a friend of the English people. Indeed he is more English than Indian in his thoughts and make-up. He is often more at home with Englishmen than with his own countrymen. And he is a humanitarian in the sense that he reacts to every wrong, no matter where perpetrated. Though, therefore, he is an ardent nationalist his nationalism is enriched by his fine internationalism.

Gandhi rubber-stamped Nehru's position: make India free, and you also make every Indian a British ally.

Nothing helped Jinnah's dream more than the Congress war policy. Where Nehru, on his point of principle, broke with the British, Jinnah offered to fill Britain's armies with the Muslims of India. Where Gandhi had evaded the Viceroy's questions with sweet talk, Jinnah in the first week of September did hard bargaining. Jawaharlal Nehru was among the first to recognize this implication; he saw two wars coming – a war across the world, and a civil war across India. Just before he left for China he wrote a moving letter to his friend Sri Prakasa where he opened his mind: 'As you know I am overwhelmed with this sense of impending catastrophe. I find that few persons even among our leading politicians have this sense of tension and this premonition of approaching disaster. I fear we are rapidly heading for what might be called civil war in the real sense of the word in India.' He understood how far British imperialism would go to keep Indian nationalism at bay, 'behind the scenes, exploiting all manner of other groups to this end'.

Jawaharlal Nehru wrote this letter on 15 August 1939. Exactly eight years later, to the day, that civil war would break India, with imperialists manipulating the strings till the very last minute.

29 Pakistan: Emerging from the Closet

It was a journalist who dreamed up the title: Quaid-e-Azam, the Great Leader. On 10 December 1938 Maulana Mazharuddin Ahmad proclaimed in his daily Urdu newspaper *Al-Aman* that Muhammad Ali Jinnah should be known as the Quaid in recognition of his services to Muslims. When Jinnah reached Patna a fortnight later for the League session, the crowds hailed him as a Quaid. Lucknow 1937. Patna 1938. Lahore 1940. The last would not have been possible without the two before. Jinnah was not particularly worried about who ruled Calcutta, Lahore or Karachi as long as Muslim India made him its voice in the dialogue with British India. His own party gave him anything he wanted, of course. Resolution 4 at Patna, for instance, handed him the power to resort to 'direct action', a weapon he kept in reserve for a critical moment. He was cheered as he lambasted Gandhi and the Congress at Patna:

> The Congress is nothing but a Hindu body ... The presence of a few Muslims, the few misled and misguided ones, and the few who are there with ulterior motives, does not, cannot, make it a national body ... Who is the genius behind it? Mr Gandhi ... He is the one man responsible for turning the Congress into an instrument for the revival of Hinduism. His ideal is to revive the Hindu religion and establish Hindu raj in this country.

It was, however, one thing claiming support, and quite another being recognized as having it.

Lord Brabourne, who deputed for Linlithgow in the latter's absence, was sympathetic to Jinnah. When the Viceroy was away in London, in August 1938, Jinnah approached Brabourne with a deal: he would guarantee Muslim support for the British at the Centre if the latter would protect the League in the provinces. The secret meeting took place at the Viceregal Lodge in Simla on Tuesday 16 August 1938 at 6.30 p.m. Brabourne was even a little startled by the temerity of the offer. My Lords Zetland, Linlithgow and Brabourne were a bit wary initially, but, as the summer brought the war on to the horizon they changed gear. With Nehru there, they would never get support in the war effort from the Congress. With their usual foresight, six months before the war broke out, the British added Section 126(A) to the 1935 Act, which enabled the Centre to acquire full executive powers in any province if it so deemed necessary during an emergency – as, for instance, war or threat of war.

Circumstances also gave Jinnah another formidable card in his hands: the Indian Army.

Before 1857 the Company army was divided into units determined by numbers, not caste or religion. Lord John Lawrence, who had to defeat parts of this very army in order to quell the Mutiny, decided, when he became Viceroy, that the Empire could not afford an army where intermingling dissolved racial and other prejudices and consequently fostered a non-regional identity. Tribe, sect and caste became the new definitions for battalions and regiments. In the first phase of the reorganization, the army was virtually closed to Muslims, but Sir Sayyid's loyalty presaged the new policy of using Muslims as a lever against the growing nationalism in the Hindu middle class. The creation of the Muslim League, courtesy Colonel Dunlop Smith and Lord Minto, and the Minto–Morley reforms were accompanied by a rise in Muslim recruitment, partly also as a counterpoise to the Civil Service, where the Indian element was overwhelmingly Hindu. By 1914 the Indian army had this communal composition: Sikhs 19.2 per cent, Punjab Muslims 11.1 per cent, Pathans 6.29 per cent, Gurkhas 13.1 per cent, Garhwalis 1.9 per cent, UP Rajputs 6.4 per cent, Hindustani Muslims 4.1 per cent, Brahmins 1.8 per cent, Marathas 4.9 per cent, Madras Muslims 3.5 per cent, Tamils 2.5 per cent. In other words, Muslims (including Pathans) formed 24.9 per cent of the army, of whom 17.3 per cent came from Punjab and the Frontier. By 1930 a more interesting phenomenon had taken place; the Hindustani and Madras Muslims had been eliminated, but this loss was more than compensated from the north-west of India. The Punjabi Muslims now numbered 22.6 per cent, more than double the number of sixteen years before. Another reason was a deliberate reduction in Sikh recruitment, which was down to 13.6 per cent. The Pathans remained steady at 6.35 per cent, but north-west Muslims made up a huge 29 per cent of the Indian army and an even larger percentage of the *Indians* in the army. Volume one of the report of the Simon

Commission has a map providing details of the combatant troops from the different parts of India in 1929: Punjab alone supplied more than half, 86,000 out of a total of 158,200; the Frontier provided 5,600, UP 16,500, Kashmir 6,500, Rajputana 7,000, Nepal 19,000, Bombay 7,000, Madras 4,000, CP 200; Bihar and Orissa 300, Burma 3,000, Hyderabad 700, Mysore 100; Bengal, with a population of 48 millions, gave not a single soldier. By 1939 more than Rs 100 million went from the military budget to Punjab alone in pay, pensions, stores, etc. It was Britain's Indian sword.

The British, in other words, could afford to sneer at Fazlul Haq but not at Sir Sikandar. With such a high proportion of Muslims, Sir Sikandar and Jinnah had to be kept pleased. Jinnah understood this power and discreetly underscored it during his speech in the Legislative Assembly on 23 August 1938: 'If I instigate the army today, it will be only disastrous to me and not to the opponent whom I want to hit.' His opponent was the Congress, not Britain, and he happily offered full support to Britain's war effort – at a price.

On 4 September 1939 Jinnah's opportunity came. He had waited for this chance and did not want any intrusions. He was furious when Sir Sikandar announced that the Muslims would be loyal to the British even before he had got his chance to bargain with Linlithgow. Gandhi had given the Viceroy nothing in two hours of conversation but sympathy; Jinnah offered men. In return he wanted 'something positive'. His price: the dismissal of the Congress governments. Glendoven in *Linlithgow* quotes Jinnah as telling the Viceroy: 'Yes! Turn them out at once. Nothing else will bring them to their senses ... They will never stand by you.' In the same conversation he revealed his mind: that the only solution 'lay in partition'. His mind was made up, as the record proves, long before either the Cripps or the Cabinet Mission came. All his excuses and accusations and actions had but this purpose. The much-trumpeted differences with Nehru that were supposed to have convinced him that there was no hope for Muslims in a united India were only another ploy. Anita Inder Singh has made the point well in her book (*The Origins of the Partition of India 1936–1947*, 1987) that the Lahore resolution was the culmination of a political curve, not the beginning of one. The British knew what Jinnah wanted; and they knew what their needs were. They let the idea fester in the expanding communal swamp.

Khaliquzzaman in his autobiography *Pathway to Pakistan* exposes the British–League collusion explicitly, although in a spirit of ex-ultation and achievement rather than embarrassment. On 14 March 1939 in London he was granted an interview by Colonel Muirhead, Under-Secretary of State for India. The colonel asked how the British could help Muslims. 'We have got great sympathy with you but we do not know how to help,' Khaliquzzaman recalls Muir-head telling him. He walked up to the map of India hanging in his room and simply pointed to the north-west and east of the sub-continent. The colonel smiled and said, 'Yes, that is an alternative. Have you talked about it to Lord Zetland?' No, replied Khaliquzza-man. Such was the colonel's keenness that he organized this meeting with the Secretary of State within a week, before the 21st, when Khaliquzzaman was scheduled to catch his boat home. They met on the afternoon of 20 March, and Zetland asked him about his plan to prevent the 'enslavement' of Muslims. Khaliquzzaman replied, 'You may partition the Muslim areas from the rest of India and proceed with your scheme of federation of the Indian provinces without including the Muslim areas, which should be independent from the rest.' Lord Zetland gave the League leader one and a half hours and, before the meeting was over, learned that the League was going to announce this demand for partition at its next session – still a full year away. Jinnah had discussed and confirmed this plan with his confidants already.

In view of all this evidence it is a total mystery how Nehru or the Congress leaders can be held responsible for Pakistan. These leaders of the Muslim League spent years preparing the ground for secession, exploiting every situation in order to make an impossible idea pos-sible. They had the support of the Raj; it was a collusion of interests which could not be made public for obvious reasons. Pakistan was, in other words, created by the will of the people who wanted it, not the mistakes of those who did not. It is pointless to *blame* the British – they were foreigners, not Indians; they had only their own interests to serve, not India's.

On his return to India, Khaliquzzaman told Jinnah, on 12 May 1939, that he was certain the British would 'ultimately concede par-tition'. Jinnah heard out his disciple very carefully.

Jinnah now did not agree with the Congress, because he would not agree with the Congress. That much became obvious in Sep-tember 1939, when Linlithgow attempted to create a defence liaison committee consisting of Congressmen, League politicians and princes. Still hopeful of weaning the more conciliatory Gandhi towards co-operation in the war, he invited Gandhi for talks, and the non-violent Mahatma (accompanied by Mahadev Desai and Rajkumari Amrit Kaur) set off again for Simla on 25 September, sending a note to Nehru that he hoped he would come too if invited: 'I am off to Simla again. I go only to act as intermediary. You will send me instructions if any. I do hope you will be ready to answer invitation, if it comes. Love. Bapu.'

Linlithgow wanted Gandhi and Jinnah together. Jinnah was suddenly too busy to come. Those League leaders not in the know about his plans for partition kept wondering why Jinnah did not go. Gandhi told the Viceroy he could not convince the Congress; the Viceroy informed him that he could no longer, in that case, disregard the 'legitimate claims' of the princes and the Muslim League in any future settlement. The threat was obvious. Their talks went on for three and a half hours. Gandhi begged the Viceroy to ignore the Muslim League, but the Viceroy was interested in protecting Britain's Empire, not in protecting India's unity. It was nearly six when Gandhi left the Viceroy's Lodge. He did not give more than a minute to the journalists clustered around his car – just a smile and 'How are you?' Reporters had to remain content that day with human-interest stories, like the one about Amrit Kaur's terrier getting into the Viceregal rickshaw and refusing to let Gandhi go alone for his meeting. There were suggestions that Gandhi stay on for talks, but he took the train for Wardha that very evening at seven. The very next day Zetland chided the Congress in the House of Lords. Gandhi's response was to restate the Congress position and repeat that the Congress represented everyone, including Muslims. 'I maintain', Gandhi said in a statement,

> that the Congress is an all-inclusive body. Without offence to anybody it can be said of it that it is the one body that has represented for over half a century, without a rival, the vast masses of India, irrespective of class or creed. It has not a single interest opposed to that of the Mussalmans or that of the people of the states.

Nehru, as head of the party's subcommittee on war policy (the other members were Azad and Patel), issued a statement on the same lines.

On Tuesday 3 October, Nehru and Prasad (who was Congress president then) left Birla House at ten thirty in the morning in the industrialist's cream Packard for the Viceroy's Palace for yet another round of talks; when they returned a little after one, nothing had changed. There was more excitement generated by speculation surrounding a dinner meeting between Nehru and Jinnah, at the house of a common friend, on the initiative of Sir Sikandar Hayat; talk of a new pact and Congress–League coalition governments in all provinces filled the air. This was consistent with the new Congress line. With war declared, the Congress had anxiously begun trying to build a joint front with the League against the British. Jinnah was even invited to participate in the crucial working committee meeting at Wardha, an unusual and generous signal of goodwill. Jinnah declined. Sir Sikandar, who often roamed through the growing distance between the Congress and the League, played the honest broker. A compromise was suggested even as late as the third week of October: the Congress would recognize the League as an *important* party of the Muslims, but not the sole party. The hard-liner, Nehru, was amenable; as long as the League was not given exclusive rights to the Muslim interest, it was fine with him. This compromise had the added merit of reflecting the truth. On 18 October, Nehru made another gesture. He wrote to Jinnah apologizing for not having contributed 'anything substantial' to the solution of the Hindu–Muslim question and appealing to both Jinnah and his vanity: 'With your goodwill and commanding position in the Muslim League that should not be so difficult as people imagine.' Nehru pleaded for co-operation against the British, who 'take us for granted as hangers-on of their system, to be ordered about when and where they will'. But Jinnah kept the Congress hanging on to this hope, while he secretly pursued a different line with the Viceroy. Sir Sikandar obviously knew about this duality and, even if he did not totally approve of what Jinnah was doing, he had no reason to ditch Jinnah for the Congress. Publicly, he denied reports of acting as the broker. In Delhi on 5 October, for instance, he anxiously disclaimed any connection with Congress leaders, telling the Associated Press that he had come to Delhi only to talk to Jinnah and disassociating himself from all this talk of a Congress–League settlement.

That same day, a Thursday, was Jinnah's turn to meet Linlithgow. Jinnah profusely thanked the Viceroy for protecting Muslim interests.

On 18 September the League had passed a resolution offering support to the British if the Viceroy treated it as 'the only organization that can speak on behalf of India's Muslims'. On 22 October the League would formally thank the Viceroy for having done so. Linlithgow had to meet this condition; the League was now the third party in the negotiations for the future and the princes were the fourth. While the princes acquired this status by treaty, the League had edged in by policy. On 5 October, however, Linlithgow also made it clear to Jinnah that it was a political deal and not a natural one. He had found no truth in Jinnah's charge that Congress ministries had been oppressing Muslims. But Jinnah was not disturbed by niceties. His plan was on course. Privately, Linlithgow was extremely relieved at having kept the League on his side. As he wrote to Zetland, had Jinnah and Gandhi 'confronted me with a joint demand, the strain upon me and His Majesty's Government would have been very great indeed'.

The Congress now took the next logical step. After a full day's deliberations in Wardha on 22 October, the working committee called upon all Congress governments to resign, since the Viceroy's final promise of dominion status was insufficient. By 30 October the resignations began to be handed in, starting with Madras and United Provinces. A last effort was initiated on 1 November by the Viceroy to see if some agreement could still be found. Gandhi, as the Mahatma, and Rajendra Prasad, as party president, gathered at Jinnah's house at 10 Aurangzeb Road and drove in Jinnah's Packard Eight to Linlithgow's palace. It was the first time after the three Round-Table Conferences that the British were talking to leaders of more than one party together; the League was now formally on par with the Congress. These last talks were so futile that they ended quickly. Gandhi had summed it all up even before the summit, on October 30: 'Janab Jinnah Saheb looks to the British power to safeguard the Muslim rights. Nothing that the Congress can do or concede will satisfy him.' The British, in turn, looked to Jinnah. Jinnah had got his veto.

Privately Linlithgow was both relieved and stunned at the extent of the sell-out by the League leaders. In his note to Zetland on 24 October 1939 (quoted by Anita Inder Singh) he could not quite believe his success and feared that Jinnah would not be able to sell this pro-British line to the rest of his party: 'Their platform is essentially anti-national and anti-democratic, and I feel sure their younger leaders will soon grow restive about a policy so utterly sterile. I therefore do not regard Moslem support as something upon which, by itself, we can safely afford to build any long-term policy.' Statements like this convince the present author that the greatest legacy of the British, greater even than their language, was their archives, their belief in preserving the record. Who would have accepted such an analysis if it had come only from Jawaharlal Nehru? On 28 November, Linlithgow happily told Zetland that the League's policy could be called 'the sole' or 'most important' obstacle to the achievement of Indian independence – so why should the Viceroy of India quarrel with it?

That year the festival of Id fell on 13 November. The British allowed Jinnah to broadcast a special Id message to the Muslims of India. It was the first time such a thing had happened. The Quaid-e-Azam was being publicly awarded the status of spokesman of Muslim India. What Jinnah had not been able to achieve through mass support in the elections he had done through strategy and manipulation. Never a victim of impulse, and never losing sight of his enemy, Gandhi's Congress, he had worked his way skilfully through the threat of a civil war in India and the existence of a world war to prepare the ground for the final thrust towards his dream.

Gandhi, with great sadness, saw it coming too. In *The Harijan* of 7 November 1939 he wrote: 'I hope that the League does not want to vivisect India.' Yet that was precisely what Jinnah wanted. On 2 December, Jinnah dramatically announced that the Muslims would celebrate Friday 22 December as a 'day of deliverance and thanksgiving' to proclaim their relief at the fall of Congress governments. Nehru was livid. He wrote to Mahadev Desai on 9 December: 'There is a limit even to political falsehood and indecency but all limits have been passed. I do not see how I can even meet Jinnah now.' Even an ardent Jinnah admirer like Ispahani was shocked; people like him had followed Jinnah but were still not ready to follow him into a civil war. He wrote to his leader on 12 December 1939: 'I did not expect such a command from you ... The progressive elements in the League who followed you blindly when you actively took up cudgels on behalf of the unfortunate downtrodden Muslims of India find, to their utmost regret and disappointment, that you are gradually drifting more and more into the arms of reactionaries and *jee huzoors* [yes-men].'

Men like Ispahani reflected the mood on the ground. Abdur Rahaman Siddiqui, an M L A from Bengal and member of the League working committee, was furious. In a statement issued on 8 December, quoted in the *Hindusthan Standard*, he said:

> The mountain in labour, in our case Malabar Hill, has produced the proverbial mole ... He [Jinnah] cannot be allowed to play havoc with the fundamental principles of the Muslim League or run riot with the cherished ambitions and ideals of the progressive section of his co-religionists ... The psychology of fear so sedulously preached among the Muslims in India, fear of the Hindu, fear of the Britisher, fear even of our own selves, must give place to a mentality of confidence in ourselves and absolute trust in the divine message entrusted to us. Slaves and cowards have never achieved anything.

Siddiqui charged – correctly – that Jinnah was intent upon destroying India's unity rather than winning India's freedom. On 9 December sixteen Muslim M L A s of Bengal agreed with him, saying in a statement:

> He [Jinnah] has tried to undermine the forces which make for Indian unity and freedom, and played into the hands, if one takes the most charitable view, of reactionary imperialism ... Mr Jinnah, who is never tired of waiting in the Viceregal anteroom, has always mounted the High Horse when it came to an interview with the representatives of the Congress to reach a settlement.

Other League leaders still hoped that there would be a League–Congress *rapprochement*, a round of Jinnah–Nehru talks was even proposed for December. Nehru kept asking the League leaders for specific charges of atrocities against Muslims by Congress governments. The notoriously voluble Haq challenged Nehru to sit with him in a joint inquiry. Nehru promptly accepted the challenge, and Haq then wriggled away saying that what he really wanted was a Royal Commission. Jinnah's once-devoted secretary, M. C. Chagla, protested from Bombay on 8 December against the call for the 'deliverance day':

> Every decent-minded Mussulman who loves his country will be shocked and horrified ... The creed of the League is still independence, not of

a community, but of the whole country ... How can they [League members] sit quiet and see the country, which they are pledged to liberate, torn into pieces by tactics which Mr Jinnah proposes in the statement, and why does Mr Jinnah drag God into every controversy?
(*Hindusthan Standard*, 9 December 1939)

Jinnah needed God as an alibi to change the party's creed from independence for the country to independence for a community. In the early hours of Saturday 23 March 1940 the subjects committee of the League met in Lahore to discuss the draft of the resolution which would tear India first into two and then, a quarter-century later, into three. The critical third paragraph of the first resolution on the second day of the session, moved by Fazlul Haq, with Jinnah in the chair, said that 'the areas in which the Muslims are numerically in a majority, as in the North-Western and Eastern zones of India, should be grouped to constitute independent states in which the constituent units shall be autonomous and sovereign'. This was the core of the Lahore Resolution. Fazlul Haq was quite pleased at the thought; he felt he was also asking for an independent Bengal. After all, Pakistan was nowhere specifically mentioned, and the phrasing was vague enough. But a journalist asked Jinnah to clarify the confusion, and the next day's newspapers were more accurate; they called it the Pakistan Resolution.

Nehru described it as fantastic, mad. In his speech at Allahabad on 13 April 1940 he explained that a Congress–League dialogue was no longer possible after this latest stand at Lahore:

Without mincing words, I want to say that we will have nothing to do with this mad scheme ... The League is not interested in the Indian nation but in something else, and hence there can be no common meeting ground between the Congress and the League. On the other hand, it has become the clear duty of the Congress to fight out the League and its scheme of denationalizing India ... Look at the picture presented by the League leadership today, with its contempt for the country and its hymn of hatred. It has at last unmasked itself and left no room for mis-understanding. We will, of course, oppose the partition scheme, but our goal is clear and we will march on our path. A struggle is inevitable now.

The Congress would not say yes to partition. And the British would not say no. Jinnah waited in the middle, biding his time, holding in his hand the tremendous weapon which the British had given him, the veto. It was not long before this weapon would be used, by both the British and Jinnah, to defeat Gandhi and Nehru.

30 Scrambled Eggs

The lean, ascetic and vegetarian leftist Richard Stafford Cripps (1889–1952) came three times to India before independence, though only two visits are famous, as the Cripps Mission and the Cabinet Mission. His first trip, in 1939, was on the face of it a personal visit to spend time with his friend Jawaharlal Nehru, but there was little doubt that he was sounding out Indian and in particular Congress opinion at the beginning of the war. Of exactly the same age, Cripps and Nehru discovered an affinity in politics in the 1930s. Both were left-of-centre ideologues committed to socialism and anti-imperialism. In 1936 Cripps, a lawyer on the left wing of the Labour Party, had created a United Front of the Socialist League (which he headed), the Independent Labour Party and the Communist Party to oppose the Conservatives. The idea received Nehru's warm approval. (Nehru to Cripps, 22 February 1937: 'This was pleasing news and I felt it was laying the foundation of bigger things to come.') Along with Aneurin Bevan, Cripps had founded *Tribune*, and Nehru was sent a complimentary copy of the paper (which he also wrote for). Acquaintance turned to friendship. When in 1937 Nehru's publisher John Lane went into liquidation, leading to a temporary cessation of royalties, Nehru asked Cripps for advice and accepted his friend's view that a legal contest was not worth the while.

The war situation made Cripps's political background a valuable asset to the British establishment. Churchill took the inspired decision to send him as ambassador to the Soviet Union in 1940, when Moscow was an ally of Nazi Germany. Cripps ended an extremely successful stint on a triumphant note by bringing off the Anglo-Soviet pact of July 1941. In recognition, he was given the high office of Lord Privy Seal and made a member of the War Cabinet on 19 February 1942. However, the first Cripps Mission was Chamberlain's idea, not Churchill's.

A KLM flight brought Cripps to Karachi airport on 7 December 1939 *en route* to Anand Bhavan. Dressed in a check coat and flannel trousers, Cripps chatted with the press, making no secret of his intentions for the eighteen days he provisionally wanted to spend in India. He would meet leaders of all parties and the Viceroy to see if he could take back any practical suggestions to London. 'It is wise on the part of Gandhiji not to have hurried things and kept open the doors,' he told the gathered journalists in Karachi, adding, 'There is a distinct change even on the part of Conservatives with regard to India, and nobody wants to alienate the sympathies of India. A movement is rapidly gaining ground in England in favour of India, and some are making careful investigations in this direction.'

That was artful thinking. No one was in any mood for compromises. Nehru had mounted an offensive against British imperialism and its 'retrograde' ally, the Muslim League, which was organizing its 'deliverance day' for 22 December. By the time Cripps flew off to Rangoon on 26 December on his way to China, where he would spend a month, nothing had emerged to change anything. London's concentration was on the collapsing war front, and the mood in India slowly hardened. In a typically poetic phrase, Nehru described the next phase as a time to travel through 'the valley of the shadow' (in a Christmas Day letter to Madame Chiang Kai-shek in 1939). Gandhi was not prepared for an immediate mass struggle, and Nehru retired to the loneliness of inactivity. He, along with Azad, wanted another popular movement against the British, but Gandhi would not go beyond passive non-co-operation. Nehru took up spinning seriously again after four years and hoped to count out the days with a visit to neutral Switzerland (where Indira was living) and the still neutral United States. At the working committee meeting on 1 March 1940 he and Azad urged Gandhi to start mass action, but even six months later, at the AICC of 15 September, Gandhi would go only as far as individual *satyagraha*. Acharya Vinoba Bhave was selected as the first *satyagrahi*, Nehru as the second. On 17 October, Bhave launched the Congress anti-war movement. Nehru's turn was scheduled for 6 November. He was ready for gaol. In a piece written in October, 'On the Verge' (included in *The Unity of India*, 1948) he says:

Now that Satyagraha seems at hand the whispering [about arrests] grows fiercer, and all manner of good advice is given to us by our well-wishers. Our letters are opened, our telephone conversations tapped, our bank accounts secretly examined by the emissaries of the Government. True. But why worry or get excited? . . . Why blame the Government? An alien imperialist Government must, so long as it exists, function in that way. It must have recourse to coercion, exploitation, methods of terror, corruption, secret police and the like . . . If we go to bed with a tiger, why wonder if it digs its claws into us and tries to make a meal of us?

On 30 October the police picked up Nehru at Cheoki railway station on his way back to Allahabad from Wardha, where he had been visiting Gandhi. Three days later he was produced before district magistrate E. de V. Moss in a small tent erected in the Gorakhpur gaol compound. Charge: spreading disaffection by speeches at Deoria, Maharajganj and Laldiggi; prosecution under Rules 34(6) and 38(1) of the Defence of India Rules. Police sub-inspector Dalsingar Singh deposed as witness. Nehru, as usual, refused to defend himself. On 4 November came the sentence: three consecutive terms of rigorous imprisonment of sixteen months each, adding up to four years.

Both Churchill and his new Secretary of State for India, Leopold S. Amery, were shocked at the severity of the Government of India's action. London directed Linlithgow on 14 November not to treat Nehru like a common criminal, but Linlithgow was determined to be vicious with Jawaharlal. This was Nehru's worst spell in prison since those mercifully few days at Nabha. The Viceroy took a personal interest in ensuring that the rigours of rigorous imprisonment were not lightened by sympathetic gaolers. For a while he was even placed in the 'gallow cell' of the Dehra Dun prison and not allowed a washerman or barber, while the petty insults were too numerous to bear mention. He could receive only one letter a week, as entitled to by regulations.

Nehru actually enjoyed being denied privileges and settled down to a disciplined routine. He took strength from reading the *Bhagavad Gita*, kept himself physically fit with yoga, became a diligent gardener and returned to serious writing. (His work here and during his next and last spell in gaol would flower into *The Discovery of India*.) By the end of 1941 the Viceroy's War Cabinet decided that the Congress challenge had been contained and its leaders could be safely released. Sir Maurice Hallett, the governor of UP, agreed – except for one man: Nehru. Hallett argued that the Muslim League would be demoralized by Nehru's reappearance in public. Churchill agreed with Hallett; in fact, Churchill refused to be selective and wanted all the Congressmen kept in. But the War Cabinet stuck to its decision despite Churchill's objections. ('When you lose India, don't blame me,' he said, according to Glendoven in *The Viceroy at Bay*, 1971.)

Jawaharlal Nehru was freed on 4 December 1941. Three days later the volatile world changed again. Japan attacked Pearl Harbor.

Singapore fell on 15 February, Rangoon on 7 March. But apart from the Far East, there was generally good news for the Allies. The United States had been forced into the war by Pearl Harbor; in Africa, Auchinleck had raised the siege of Tobruk and was advancing in the western desert; in Russia, the German offensive had been halted; and in the Atlantic British shipping was now suffering far less damage from U-boats. But the Pacific caved in to a conquering Japan, and a catastrophic defeat lay at India's doors. Churchill now anxiously needed the Congressmen he had wanted interned only weeks before. And while Roosevelt was an extremely welcome ally he also brought along an unwelcome suggestion: give India dominion status at once so that it could become a whole-hearted ally. Nehru, on his part, was more than ready to fight Japan. He publicly called for resistance, including violent resistance, if the Japanese entered India. The world's concern was reflected in the sudden visit to India by Marshal Chiang Kai-shek and his wife, who hoped to use their personal equation with Nehru to persuade him, and through him Gandhi, to support Britain unconditionally. The Mahatma, despite all his seeming flexibility, was now in no mood to listen to such advice. He had already reached a most perceptive analysis of the war. As D. G. Tendulkar notes in Volume 6 of his eight-volume biography, Gandhi was convinced about the outcome as early as February 1942:

> Personally I think the end of this giant war will be what happened in the fabled *Mahabharata* war. The *Mahabharata* has been aptly described by a Travancorean as the permanent history of man. What is described in that great epic is happening today before our very eyes. The warring nations are destroying themselves with such fury and ferocity that the end will be mutual exhaustion. The victor will share the same fate that awaited

the surviving Pandavas. The mighty warrior Arjuna was looted in broad daylight by a petty robber. And out of this holocaust must arise a new order for which the exploited millions of toilers have so long thirsted.

The Mahatma was prepared to sit in either his ashram or a gaol and wait. Churchill could not afford that luxury. By February, Churchill was worried that east India (including Calcutta), Ceylon and a part of Australia could soon be in Japanese hands. He was willing to consider India's complete freedom, within the British Commonwealth, after the war. In the interim there would be an Indian Council of Defence and an Indian on the Viceroy's Executive Council; and after the war could come a new Constitution of India as the last prelude to freedom.

The Viceroy sabotaged the idea, arguing that it would be insufficient to win over the Congress and sufficient to lose the Muslim League. A special committee was set up under Attlee, with Viscount Simon, Sir John Anderson, Sir James Grigg and Sir Stafford Cripps as members. It took care to retain a loophole clause to protect the Muslim League; its proposals included the 'option to any province not wishing to accede to the new Constitution to stand out'. The League's pound of flesh was once again spelt out specifically, the commitment restated that there would be a Pakistan after the war. Now Linlithgow decided to drive the point further in. He claimed that, while this idea satisfied Muslim aspirations in the majority provinces, there was nothing in the proposals equally to satisfy the Muslims in the minority provinces like UP, or to appease groups like the Sikhs and the scheduled castes. The Sikhs had a double problem, he noted; they would be a minority in either dispensation. With cables still being exchanged between London and Delhi on these interminable disputes, Churchill decided to announce a special mission by Cripps to India. On 11 March the House of Commons was duly informed.

The Congress chose guarded optimism as its initial response. The party president, Maulana Azad, would go no further than, 'I would welcome him [Cripps] as a friend.' The Mahatma kept his tongue close to his cheek, telling the press agency UPI after Churchill's announcement, 'Sir Stafford Cripps and I are both food faddists, and that is the similarity between us.' The party revolutionary was in Allahabad, busy in the arrangements for his daughter's wedding, and he too kept his reactions in check. 'The time for comment', said Nehru 'will come later.' (The quotations are from the *Hindusthan Standard*.) Jinnah also chose silence, though for completely different reasons. He was a little worried about the precise colour of the cat in the latest Cripps bag. The only ones who were unreservedly happy were the Americans: Senator Connally, chairman of the Senate Foreign Affairs Committee, praised 'Britain's enlightened policy towards her dominions'. The mood of India was best summed up by the *Hindusthan Standard* headline on Thursday 12 March: 'Statement on India at last'. There was genuine relief that the impasse was about to be broken, and that Cripps was coming by the 'fastest available plane'.

The plane bringing Cripps landed in Delhi on 22 March, and at once the familiar round of meetings with Indian leaders of every hue began: Azad and Nehru; Jinnah and Sir Sikandar; Fazlul Haq (who had by now launched the Azad Muslim Party after breaking with the League); Veer Savarkar of the Hindu Mahasabha; Ambedkar of the depressed classes; Sapru and M. R. Jayakar from the liberals; Jamsaheb of Nawanagar as chancellor of the Chamber of Princes; and Gandhi because he was Gandhi (he was not a member of the Congress that year). The brunt of the negotiations was of course with the Congress; that was the deal which had to be negotiated. Cripps leavened the atmosphere with witty press conferences, but no formal announcement of his proposals was made till Sunday 29 March. The drama eventually went on till 12 April, almost a week after Gandhi left Delhi for his ashram on 4 April, but the fact is that the Cripps Mission had died long before. The proposals failed to come anywhere near the Congress positions either on questions of principle or on problems of practice.

The Congress leaders were clearly misled by the statement made by Cripps in his opening conversation with Azad. They believed that India was being promised a national government similar to the British Cabinet, with the Viceroy becoming the equivalent of the King. If true, it meant a genuine sharing of power. The Congress had (despite Gandhi's reservations) adopted the Nehru line that co-operation in defence was not only possible but necessary because of the common commitment against fascism: the caveat being that it had to be the co-operation of equals. The paradox is that it was precisely on defence that Cripps displayed to Azad and Nehru exactly how unequal they still were. The Congress might have settled with Cripps if he had established his bona fides through agreement over the defence member's responsibilities. However, Cripps made it very clear that His Majesty's Government would not surrender control over the defence of India. While Cripps envisaged the appointment of 'some suitable Indian' as the defence member in the War Cabinet, he would not accept Nehru and Azad's view that this Indian must be the superior of the commander-in-chief. The Viceroy would not hear of any such thing, while the commander-in-chief, Wavell, curtly insulted Nehru and Azad when they met to discuss the issue, saying bluntly that if this was their position there was nothing to discuss. There was much pressure to settle from the Americans, through Colonel Louis Johnson, a personal envoy of President Roosevelt, and on 8 April a very specific formula was devised on the sharing of powers. But now London pulled up Cripps, saying he was going too far in his desire to reach a compromise. There would be no question of any dilution in the commander-in-chief's powers. Before he left on 12 April, Cripps tried to explain, in a broadcast over the radio, that reorganization of the defence secretariat would mean 'an unscrambling of eggs scrambled many years ago'. But that was, naturally, the point. Nehru and Azad had been fighting all their lives to unscramble the imperialist eggs. Churchill told the Commons much later, on 12 December 1946, that Cripps had far overstepped his brief in his effort to get a settlement. However, Linlithgow and Wavell were there in March and April 1942 to ensure that the enthusiasms of the moment did not prejudice the British interest, and they did this most effectively. It seems that the Cripps offer was only an illusion to satisfy the liberal in Roosevelt.

Non-violent Gandhi, thoroughly uninterested in a defence minister's powers, had warned Nehru against accepting Cripps's offer much before. At two in the morning he scribbled an undated personal note to Nehru written on the back of a dentist's bill (the bill was dated 27 March 1942) saying: 'It will ruin the country.' After the mission collapsed he explained his reasons (Tendulkar, Volume 6) for rejecting 'that ill-fated proposal'. Describing it as 'ridiculous', he asked, first, how could Congress accept dominion status? Second, accepting Cripps's proposals meant a virtual dismemberment of India. Gandhi commented: 'He [Cripps] knew too that the proposal contemplated the splitting up of India into three parts, each having different ideas of governance.' Finally, no Indian would ever get control of defence, so what value was there in Cripps's offer? The editors of the *Hindusthan Standard* had caught the Gandhi mood in their front page of 30 March revealing the Cripps proposals. The four-deck lead-story headlines ran like this:

Cripps Declaration has no pep
Dominion Status of new variety
Princes & Pakistanwallas given free hand
Prospect of too many Ulsters in post-war India

Jinnah was relieved. He had been very anxious that the pro-Nehru Cripps might scuttle all he had achieved through Brabourne and Linlithgow. He forgot what Gandhi remembered: that the Cripps with a mission was a representative of an imperial power, not the radical of Labour politics. Cripps's account of his interview with Jinnah on 25 March 1942 (Mansergh and Moon, eds., *The Transfer of Power*, 1981, Vol. 1, p. 480) notes how readily Jinnah accepted the proposals once he saw that the idea of Pakistan had been given its due place. In his eve-of-departure broadcast, Cripps made it a point to use the Muslims as a weapon against the Congress demand for self-rule:

It is easy to understand that the great minorities of India would never accept such a system. Nor could His Majesty's Government, who had given pledges to those minorities, consent to their being placed un-protected, while the existing constitution lasts, under a simple and possibly inimical majority rule. It would be a breach of all the pledges we have given.

This was the radical Cripps himself equating Congress rule with 'inimical majority rule' – after negotiating with a Congress president named Maulana Azad! Amery made the same point in the House of Commons on 28 April, saying there was never any question of con-ceding to a rule 'presumably of Congress or, at any rate, of Hindus'. And of course Cripps confirmed that pledges had been given.

C. Rajagopalachari, disappointed that the Cripps Mission had not led to a settlement which would restore him to office, got two resolutions passed by the Congress members of the Madras legislature on 23 April 1942. The Congress, said the first, should now accept the Muslim League's claim for partition. The second wanted a Congress government in Madras. On 29 April the Congress high command, meeting at Allahabad, rejected both ideas outright. Gandhi rebuked his in-law by marriage publicly: 'I see the same difference between him and me that there is between chalk and cheese. He yields the right of secession now to buy unity in the hope of keeping away the Japanese. I consider the vivisection of India to be a sin.' Nehru was livid with Rajagopalachari, accusing him of seeking to destroy the Congress. But these quarrels were to become irrelevant in the face of a new plan Gandhi had begun to promote.

Asked on 29 March what he thought of the Cripps Mission, Gandhi said, 'My advice will be, this is a post-dated cheque. Accept or leave it as you like.' Some imaginative person tagged on a phrase, and the sentence became famous as 'a post-dated cheque on a crashing bank'. Gandhi now decided that the time had finally come to check out the strength of the bank. In *The Harijan* of 26 April 1942 he made his plan public for the first time. Gandhi demanded the complete withdrawal of the British from India:

Whatever the consequences, therefore, to India, her real safety and of Britain's too lie in orderly and timely British withdrawal from India. All talk of treaties with the princes and obligations towards minorities are a British creation designed for the preservation of the British rule and British interests . . . The fiction of majority and minority will vanish like the mist before the morning sun of liberty.

The failure of the Cripps Mission had not changed Nehru's views on fascists. He assured the British and the Americans that he would participate in a guerrilla war if the Japanese broke through. At a press conference on 12 April he even said bluntly that he would oppose Japan's Indian ally Subhas Bose and his Indian National Army if ever the situation came to that. (On 28 March a report made the front pages of India's newspapers that Subhas Bose had died in an air crash. It was denied two days later, after many condolence messages, including from Gandhi and Nehru, had been published.) Gandhi was worried that the vacuum left behind by the failure of the Cripps Mission might throw the Congress leaders into contradictory directions. A focal point was needed to bring the freedom movement back on the rails. As he told Louis Fischer, 'The original idea of asking the British to go burst upon me suddenly. It was the Cripps fiasco which inspired the idea. Hardly had he gone, when it seized hold of me.' Gandhi took out the whip and brought Nehru back in line; Nehru retracted his promise to fight a guerrilla war, now saying he was committed to non-violence. In turn, Gandhi gave his commitment that a free India would sign a defence treaty with the Allies. The Mahatma had made up his mind, and when that happened little was allowed to stand in the way. He even wanted Azad removed from the Congress presidentship when he found out that Azad favoured yet another round of talks with the British, this time with Roosevelt as arbiter. The British, for their part, went back to being tough. Amery suggested to Churchill that Gandhi and the working committee be arrested the moment they passed any resolution demanding British withdrawal from India. Delhi preferred to wait till an AICC session had ratified such a resolution. The working committee met at Wardha on 6 July. Gandhi decided to become a Congressman once again and was 'requested' to resume the leadership.

On 14 July 1942 the most important resolution in the history of the Congress, exactly 1,700 words, was passed by the working committee, unanimously. The draft was not Mahatma Gandhi's but Jawaharlal Nehru's. It attacked Nazism, fascism, Japanese imperialism, the Indian reactionary classes, vested interests and communalists. There was enough socialism in it to satisfy Nehru and enough nationalism to satisfy everyone else. This resolution had one purpose: 'the withdrawal of British rule from India'. Gandhi, however, left no one in any doubt about who was the boss. He told a press conference after the working committee meeting on 14 July, 'Of course, if the resolution had not met with my approval, it would not have been passed.' His message to the British was clear: 'Leave India to God or anarchy.' His message to Indians was reported in the *Hindusthan Standard* the next day: 'There is no question of one more chance. After all, it is an open rebellion.'

India divided into those who supported Gandhi's open rebellion and those who did not. The latter included elements as disparate as the Communists, the Muslim League, the Hindu Mahasabha, scheduled caste leaders like Ambedkar and rebels like Rajagopalachari (who resigned from the Congress). P. C. Joshi, general secretary of the Communist Party of India, said: 'We Indian Communists are trying to convince our fellow patriots that the course of action suggested by Congress leadership does not lead to freedom, but cuts the nation away from freedom's battle and divides the progressive forces in Britain and India.' Rajagopalachari wrote to Gandhi warning that this move 'must involve the dissolution of the state and society itself'. Veer Savarkar of the Hindu Mahasabha ordered his followers, including Shyama Prosad Mookerjee, to ignore the Congress call. His recipe for freedom, given at Srinagar on 17 July, was: 'Hinduize all politics and militarize all Hindudom.' Jinnah, of course, accused Gandhi of having already achieved that. In a statement, he charged 'Mr Gandhi and his Hindu Congress of blackmailing the British and coercing them to concede a system of government which would establish a Hindu Raj immediately'. (What is fascinating is that this champion of militant Islam should soon ally himself with the champion of militant Hinduism in a coalition government in Bengal.) Everyone who supported the British had something to gain. On 23 July the ban on the Communists was removed (it was London's gesture; the ban on the Canadian Communists was removed the same day). But R. S. Nimbkar, the labour welfare officer of the Government of India, left the comrades with no illusions. As he put it, on behalf of the government: 'I am sure the Communists will help a good deal in checking to some extent this inopportune move of Mr Gandhi.'

The only political force which no longer wanted anything from the British was the Congress. On 17 July Nehru, accompanied by his colleague and good friend Mridula Sarabhai, told his party men at the town hall in Meerut: 'We have all to be prepared, as in these months and years the fate of the country is going to be decided.' Nehru, more concerned than others about world reaction, had decided to ignore the international outcry over Gandhi's call. The *New York Times*, for instance, had commented on 16 July that 'Mr Gandhi may do more dreadful harm to his people than Ghengis Khan'. Cripps, broadcasting to the USA on 27 July to whip up anti-Indian sentiment, once again flaunted the Muslim card and attacked Gandhi as a man who no longer understood reality, either in multi-religious India, or in a world at war. Nehru's attitude was summed up at a press conference in Delhi the same day: 'I am not interested at the present moment in what America is going to do after the war.' His leader was Gandhi, not Roosevelt. Gandhi's determination was unbending. Tendulkar quotes him as saying: 'All the manufactured criticism that I find being made today is sheer tomfoolery, meant to overawe me and to demoralize the Congress ranks. It is a foul game. They do not know the fire that is raging in my breast.'

That fire would soon spread from his breast and set a nation aflame.

31 In the Name of God, Go!

Neither Gandhi, who inspired the movement, nor Nehru, who drafted the resolution, actually used the slogan which would become imperishable in the memory of generations of Indians: Quit India. The term was in fact the shorthand that newspapers adopted to sum up the more cumbrous phrasing of the formal resolution. It became an instant hit. Gandhi told the country that 'Quit India' would be his last movement – the biggest – and it would either end British rule or end him. The excitement of the people was palpable as the day of the All-India Congress Committee meeting called in Bombay to ratify the working committee resolution, 7 August, neared. Statements and speeches by Congress leaders spurred this nervous excitement. On 1 August, Tilak day, Nehru cried out in Allahabad: 'Struggle, eternal struggle! That is my reply to Mr Amery and Sir Stafford Cripps!' He very neatly turned Amery's famous speech in the Commons demanding Chamberlain's resignation; now Nehru quoted Cromwell to demand the end of the Raj: 'You have sat too long here for any good you have been doing. Depart, I say, and let us have done with you. In the name of God, go!' At other times he could be cruder: 'Get out.'

On Monday 3 August, Gandhi reached Dadar Station along with his wife Kasturba and his secretaries Mahadev Desai and Pyarelal. There were huge crowds at the station; but, Monday being his day of silence, he had only his lovable toothless smile and a wave for them, before he drove off to Birla House in Bombay. Nehru and Acharya Kripalani arrived the same day, getting off at the city's other main station, the splendidly Victorian Victoria Terminus. Once again, large crowds cheered the arriving heroes. Gandhi broke his silence at four and immediately went into a huddle with Nehru, Patel and Kripalani. The party president Azad came by the Bombay Mail from Calcutta the next day, and full-scale working committee meetings began: Azad, Nehru, Patel, Kripalani, Pant, P. C. Ghosh, Asaf Ali, Sarojini Naidu, Pattabhi Sitaramayya, Syed Mahmud, Harekrushna Mahtab, plus of course the man above all mortal status symbols, the Mahatma himself.

The Bombay Pradesh Congress Committee, and the Congress mayor, Yusuf Meherally, were making hectic arrangements for what everyone recognized as a session for the history books. An area of 30,000 square feet was fenced at Gowalia Tank, in the heart of the city, and covered by 'double tarpaulin' as protection against the heavy monsoon rains that lash Bombay in August. Provisions were made to house 7,500 delegates; 250 fans were brought for the *shamiana*, and tables and chairs organized for full AICC members and more than 300 newsmen from India and all over the world who had gathered to cover the session. The British, in the meantime, were making plans of their own to try to defuse the building momentum. On 31 July, a rumour went around that they were planning to install a 'national government' headed by M. N. Roy and Jinnah, and Roy even issued a conciliatory statement in expectation! From Dehra Dun, he put out a written statement to the press: 'Immediate establishment of such a broad-based wartime government will isolate Congress and may, once for all, put an end to the bluff and bluster of a group of bankrupt politicians' (*Hindusthan Standard*, 1 August). In an effort to discredit the Congress, the government released forged documents purported to have been seized during raids on Congress offices in Allahabad. (The forgery was exposed within days.) A secret circular was distributed by Sir Frederick Puckle; pro-British politicians like Sapru proposed another Round-Table Conference, on 26 July; while others, like Ambedkar, called the Congress move both irresponsible and insane (27 July). Cripps, from London, continued to make threats while saying, 'We make no threats' (5 August). But the Congress leadership was now past caring.

Jawaharlal stayed in Bombay with the younger of his two sisters, Krishna, and his brother-in-law Raja Hutheesingh, in their large apartment at Sakina Mansions on Carmichael Road. The spacious, quiet, three-bedroom flat became crowded and chaotic the day the future Prime Minister turned up. With him came his 'Indu-boy', Indira, along with her husband, Feroze. With Nehru taking, as usual, the guest room, Krishna's sons Harsha and Ajit in their normal bedroom and Indira and Feroze in the third, Krishna and Raja ended up sharing the flat of their neighbour Chinni Sundaram. Krishna's flat became a Congress waiting-room, with a constant stream of leaders and workers from all over the country bustling about for their appointment with history.

At 2.45 on the afternoon of Friday 7 August the AICC session began its first sitting with about 200 members and 10,000 visitors who paid between Rs 10 and Rs 500 for tickets, which were sold out two days in advance. More than 3,000 volunteers helped inside, while more than 5,000 people thronged outside the *pandal* despite the rain. The proceedings began with women volunteers singing 'Vande Mataram'.

The minutes of the last session were read out. Then the president, Azad, stood up. Zero hour, he said in the course of a moving 100-minute speech, was approaching, and the confrontation had been thrust on India despite its willingness to fight alongside the allies. 'What this resolution says is this: Let us have a declaration of Indian independence forthwith and we, on our part, shall immediately enter into a treaty of alliance with the United Nations for the sole purpose of fighting and winning this war.'

The crowds had cheered each leader's arrival; but the Mahatma of course was supreme – the ovation was deafening as he came resting on his two young women aides. His smile broad, his mood happy, his spirit soaring, he explained once again his philosophy and his reasoning. 'Occasions like the present do not occur in everybody's and but rarely in anybody's life,' he said in a nine-minute speech. Only in 'a democracy established by non-violence, there will be equal freedom for all. Everybody will be his own master. It is to join a struggle for such democracy that I invite you today. Once you realize this you will forget the differences between the Hindus and Muslims and think of yourselves as Indians only, engaged in the common struggle for independence.' Fight, he said, but not with hatred – either between yourselves or against the British. Seek freedom, not power.

Now the moment came to move the historic resolution, and who else would do so but Mohandas Karamchand Gandhi's anointed heir, Jawaharlal Nehru? 'The immediate ending of British rule in India is an urgent necessity, both for the sake of India and for the success of the cause of the United Nations.' He was, not very surprisingly, emotional. 'I hate poverty,' he said. 'My grievance against the British is that they have made Indians miserable, poverty-stricken wrecks of humanity. We are now taking a step from which there will be no going back ... It is going to be a fight to the finish. The Congress has now burnt its boats and is about to embark upon a desperate campaign.' Sardar Patel seconded the resolution. Gandhi was good at defining hierarchy through such signals. As for his own role, he said mischievously, referring to the taunt often made against him by Muslim League leaders: 'I am a real *bania* [trader]. My business is to obtain *swaraj*.'

At about six o'clock the next evening the AICC passed the resolution Gandhi wanted – with only thirteen objections, from the Communists. He spoke for two hours after that, in both English and Hindustani. That speech was a distillation of twenty-two years of leadership, of his dreams, of the solutions he sought, a message of the heart and mind that was the essence of all that Gandhi would mean to the generations that lived with him and would come later, a speech that was a stream of Gandhian consciousness and inspiration. He knew, on 8 August, that he would not get an opportunity to talk to his people like this for a long while. As he always maintained, making the British leave was far easier than knowing what to do after they had left. The time had come for the message which would bind that future beyond tomorrow's gaol. And that future could be fully secured only by one idea: unity – unity between religions, between majority and minority, and unity between classes, between the prince and the worker too, so that through common effort and mutual understanding a median could be found, an axis on which this complex world of India could balance.

Gandhi started by congratulating the thirteen Communists who had voted against the Quit India resolution – congratulated them for their courage, and then reprimanded them for their error of judgement. That was his style. The substance followed. The first essential was to solve the Hindu–Muslim problem, to restore the magic of the Khilafat movement, 'when every Mussalman claimed the whole of India', when he and the Ali brothers had demanded freedom in one voice. He rejected the idea that only he could solve the Hindu–Muslim problem satisfactorily; the idea flattered him but did not appeal to his reason. He recalled his childhood and his early politics and the bridges he had consciously built ('I shocked Hindus by dining with Mussalmans'). This personal and political friendship was never at the cost of either his or the Muslim's faith. He worshipped the cow; the Muslim ate it. But 'The cow, like the Khilafat, stood on her own merits.' Why had he today become the target of Jinnah's venom? 'Because the canker of suspicion has entered his heart.' He said:

May God bless him [Jinnah] with long life, but when I am gone, he will realize and admit that I had no designs on Mussalmans and that I had never betrayed their interests ... My life is entirely at their disposal. They are free to put an end to it, whenever they wish to do so ... But if someone were to shoot me in the belief that he was getting rid of a rascal, he would kill not the real Gandhi, but the one that appeared to him a rascal.

Someone did shoot Gandhi in the end, for being a rascal who wanted to protect Muslims. The assassin was a Hindu fascist. Gandhi attacked this breed bitterly in this speech: 'Those Hindus who, like Dr Moonje and Shri Savarkar [leaders of the Hindu Mahasabha], believe in the doctrine of the sword may seek to keep the Mussalmans under the Hindu domination. I do not represent that section. I represent the Congress.' He explained the philosophy of the party he had nurtured: 'The Congress does not believe in the domination of any group or community. It believes in democracy which includes in its orbit Muslims, Hindus, Christians, Parsis, Jews – every one of the communities inhabiting this vast country ... The Congress does not belong to any one class or community; it belongs to the whole nation.' The moment had come for this whole nation to declare that it was free: 'The bond of the slave is snapped the moment he considers himself to be a free being.' There would now be no more talks with the Raj, no more pacts with viceroys. 'The mantra is: "Do or Die." We shall either free India or die in the attempt; we shall not live to see the perpetuation of our slavery ... This is an open rebellion. In this struggle, secrecy is a sin.' Everyone must join in, in their own way – students, journalists, soldiers (remain at your posts, but do not fire at your own people). 'I have given you my message,' he told the Congress, 'and through you I have delivered it to the whole of India.' He declared, 'I want freedom immediately, this very night, before dawn, if it can be had.'

Before dawn, however, came imprisonment. As usual Gandhi woke at four and began his day with prayers. The police commissioner reached Birla House just as the prayers were over, with warrants for Gandhi, his secretary Mahadev Desai and his favourite disciple Mirabehn. The Mahatma breakfasted on his normal goat's milk and fruit juice. His favourite hymn, 'Vaishnav Jayato', was then sung, and verses were read from the Quran. He picked up a copy of the

Bhagavad Gita, a Quran, the Sevagram hymn book and an Urdu primer, then gave his final instruction to the nation before the last journey to gaol: 'Let every non-violent soldier of freedom write out the slogan "Do or Die" on a piece of paper or cloth and stick it on his clothes, so that in case he died in the course of offering *satyagraha* he might be distinguished by that sign from other elements who do not subscribe to non-violence.'

If Gandhi had addressed the nation, Nehru spoke to the world on 8 August:

> This resolution is not a threat [to the Allies]. It is an invitation. It is an explanation. It is an offer of co-operation . . . On any other terms there will be no co-operation . . . All I can say to those Englishmen and Americans who consider that it is not right for the Indian people to decide for themselves is that they do not know what it is to be under subjection.

He was bitter against the British and the man he was convinced was their creation, Jinnah:

> We are told that we cannot send Muslims to represent the Congress. This is an insult to our great organization and revered president . . . Whenever we knocked at the doors [of the League] we found them bolted, and we knocked ourselves against a wall . . . Are we going to be kicked about by men who have made no sacrifice for the freedom of India and who can never think in terms of freedom at all?

The flat in Sakina Mahal was crowded that night. As Krishna Hutheesingh recalls in *We Nehrus*: 'They were half-elated, half-appalled by what they had done.' Nehru retired at midnight. The knock came at five in the morning. Indira woke him up at 5.45. 'The police have come,' she said and quietly packed his suitcase and his bedding. The courtyard was ablaze with lights, which seemed all the more startling because of the wartime blackouts. Policemen packed the apartment, and the inspector was nervous and impatient as he waited for his captive to get ready. Krishna silenced him, at least temporarily, with 'You'll have to wait until he is ready, and he's not going without having his breakfast, for I don't know what he'll get for the next few months.' It would, as a matter of fact, be the last good breakfast for years. Indira was calm and helped keep things as calm as she could. Nehru was in no mood for courtesy towards the police. When Krishna informed him that the inspector was urging him to hurry, he replied irritably, 'Tell him to go to hell!' She went out and told the inspector precisely that. But this version of that morning's events is Krishna Hutheesingh's account. In his prison diary Nehru does not mention the very English breakfast or the loss of temper.

The household staff were hardly unfamiliar with arrests. They quickly laid out a breakfast which Jawaharlal loved: a bowl of cornflakes, eggs, bacon, toast, coffee. The inspector saw the spread and said there was no time for breakfast. 'Shut up!' said Nehru. 'I intend having breakfast before I go.' The heir refused to start the morning on goat's milk and fruit juice, although he still reached Victoria Terminus, from where a special train would take them to gaol, before the Mahatma. But then there was no *bhajan* singing at Sakina Mahal. They were arrested under Section 26(i)(b) of the Defence of India Act, which allowed detention without trial. On the way to the station Nehru saw a young socialist comrade and waved to him; he waved back and disappeared into the underground movement from where he would elude the police till 20 May 1944. His name: Ram Manohar Lohia.

Krishna, Indira and Feroze followed Jawaharlal to the railway station in their friend Chinni Sundaram's (son of C. P. Ramaswamy Aiyar) car, then sped to Birla House, when they learned that Kasturba had not been arrested. Krishna Hutheesingh has an interesting story to narrate. A little after they reached Birla House, one of the younger Birlas (not Ghanshyam Das consequently) came and said, 'Please quit my house. I don't want it confiscated.' When the Nehrus protested, he explained, 'You don't understand. We are not in politics, we are business people. We don't want anything to do with any of you, so please leave immediately.' The visitors left, but was it fear such as this which persuaded Kasturba that her hosts had turned gutless, and her place was in gaol beside her husband? That evening she invited arrest by announcing that she would address a protest meeting. The British obliged. She would not leave that prison alive. Gandhi would lose the two people closest to him during this term in gaol: his secretary Mahadev Desai (who died within a week of arrest, on 15 August) and later his beloved Kasturba. (Gandhi nearly died himself during his 21-day fast from after breakfast on 9 February 1943. The Congress leader and physician Dr B. C. Roy commented after that fast, 'He was very near death. Mahatmaji fooled us all.')

Jawaharlal Nehru was straining at the leash that non-violence had imposed on him. One incident, more than his remarks at breakfast, indicates his feelings. Orders had been issued that the special train carrying the Congress leaders was not to stop till it reached its two destinations: a small station near Pune from where Gandhi would be driven to the Aga Khan's palace which was to be his prison; and then to Ahmednagar Fort where the members of the Congress working committee would be kept. But a red signal halted the train at Pune station, and when the crowd on the platform recognized Jawaharlal sitting inside they surged towards him. The police countered with a baton charge. Nehru was so furious at this that he jumped through the train's window and on to the platform towards the policemen to halt their batons. It needed half a dozen policemen to force him back into the train.

A new Indian heroine was born on the morning of 9 August: Aruna, wife of the sophisticated Congressman and friend of Nehru, Asaf Ali. (Asaf Ali died as India's ambassador in Switzerland in April 1953.) According to the original Congress programme, Jawaharlal had been scheduled to unfurl the tricolour that morning at Gowalia Tank. Aruna came to Victoria Terminus, watched the special train leave at seven, then went to Gowalia Tank and defiantly raised the tricolour; it was a gesture which became symbolic of India's thirst for freedom. She joined the underground movement which simply ignored Gandhi's commitment to non-violence, though it never ignored Gandhi. The Mahatma formally disapproved, of course, and even ordered her to surrender to the authorities – but he could not hide his sheer fondness for her and his admiration for her courage. Aruna was the symbol of young India: radical, secular (she had married a Muslim over her upper-caste Bengali Hindu father's objections), idealistic and courageous. The British could not nab her despite all their efforts. Finally, on 29 January 1946 they withdrew the warrant of arrest, and Gandhi sent her a telegram saying 'SO YOU HAD YOUR WAY. EXPECT LETTER. BAPU.'

The newspapers, severely hampered by authoritarian pressure, still managed to convey some of the anger of those weeks. Seven were killed (or at least that was the number the authorities were admitting to) in Bombay on 9 August itself; there was violence in Pune and Allahabad (Nehru's home town). By 11 August, the government was admitting 31 deaths in Bombay alone, 12 in Delhi, 2 in Calcutta, 4 in Madras, 3 in Allahabad, 5 in Dhaka. The number of wounded was at least ten times that. There was firing in Patna, Kanpur, Agra, Benaras, Bangalore, Gorakhpur, Katihar, Madurai and even Wardha, the town where Gandhi had created an ashram. The toll of dead and wounded kept rising till 19 August when the nationalist newspapers closed down in anger against throttling censorship. The government used the whip – literally; the Emergency Whipping Act was revived. In eastern United Provinces, in and around Ballia, the government had to kill mercilessly to control a serious revolt. Villagers attacked all government property – police stations, post offices, government godowns and small bridges – and hoisted national flags on government buildings. When Nehru learned that the people had not submitted tamely he was pleased.

This was to be Jawaharlal Nehru's last, longest (1,040 days, from 9 August 1942 to 15 June 1945) and loneliest spell in prison. He was lonely despite the fact that his comrades in the working committee were in the same gaol till May 1945, when each leader was sent to his province for a few weeks prior to release. (Nehru shifted to Naini first, then Bareilly, then to the hills of Almora.) He was dogged by a sense of isolation; for a long while there was not even the comfort of newspapers, nor the satisfaction of the 'interview' with his few loved ones: his sisters or the daughter he so doted on. (When, later, books were allowed, each page was checked for any message sent in invisible ink!) In any case, the privilege of family visits would have been pointless; for a while virtually the whole Nehru family was in gaol. On 13 August, Vijaylakshmi was taken to Naini prison. On the 20th she saw with surprise her eldest daughter, eighteen-year-old Chandralekha, walk in – she had joined a protest demonstration. On 11 September, Indira turned up; another gesture of defiance had led to her arrest. (Her sari was torn when the people reacted angrily to her arrest at a women's meeting.) That evening Feroze was picked up. His crime? Well, he had married a Nehru and therefore was subversive! He got a year's sentence. On 19 September, another Nehru family husband went in, the scholarly Ranjit Pandit, husband of Vijaylakshmi. (Raja Hutheesingh was already in a cell.) Ranjit

Pandit would not survive; his asthma and pleurisy worsened in prison conditions, and he was beyond recovery when he was released on health grounds in October 1943. He died on 14 January 1944. Indira fell prey again in prison to pleurisy. The disease had been diagnosed in November 1942, but she was released only in June 1943. Feroze was given his freedom a little later, and the couple moved to Lucknow where he became the manager to the successor of *The Independent*, the *National Herald*. (Nehru, always tempted by journalism, had started this paper in 1938.) Raja Hutheesingh was released in November 1943, because the harsh prison had broken his health. Few families can claim such a contribution to the freedom movement.

After Quit India, it became a story of the immovable object and the irresistible force: Churchill, who had warned Irwin against giving respectability to a half-naked fakir on one side, and the smiling but utterly determined fakir himself on the other. Gandhi wanted his freedom now. And Winston Churchill would not even consider the thought. In a speech at the Lord Mayor's banquet on 10 November 1942 he said: 'Let me, however, make this clear – let there be no mistake about it in any quarter. We mean to hold our own. I have not become the King's Minister in order to preside over the liquidation of the British Empire.'

32 Zero Hour

One of the many fascinating bits of Nehru *memorabilia* to have survived is his verbal doodling during the Congress working committee meeting on 5 August 1942, just before the Quit India resolution. These scrawled, disjointed sentences on notepaper are a revelation of a mind anchored in ideas and commitment, and an experience which had traversed the full range of possibilities. The sentences were partly reactions to the conversation taking place behind closed doors, partly ideas which had struck him then and partly the day-dream of a man yearning for freedom. A random selection of sentences and phrases will suggest the flavour:

> Emotional reactions – debasement of moral standards . . . Demoralization – falsehood . . . Danger of being swept away by passion. Go to the people – find out what they feel or say . . . Spending our lives in prison. Not the action of the moment but due to deep-seated conviction and urges before which all else is secondary and immaterial. Something more than politics . . . We do not wish to have dominion over others – but we cannot tolerate dominion over us . . . I do charge the British Government with bitter hostility to the people of India, with deliberate falsity and perversion, with every attempt to disrupt India – with enmity to the Congress. Sowing bitter seeds of hatred and now the harvest approaches. Every fibre of my body rebels against the British Government.

Two phrases in particular leap off the page. The first: 'Zero hour of the world.' The second: 'If – Out of chaos – dancing stars of freedom.' The two seem to sum up Nehru's own life between August 1942 and August 1947.

Zero hour began in Ahmednagar Fort. Jawaharlal Nehru had taken three books with him to gaol: Plato's *Republic*, Proust's *Remembrance of Things Past* and Lin Yutang's *With Love and Irony*. As the Congress leaders knew, it was going to be a long winter. He sent a list of about seventy-five books he wanted to the government. By the end of the first month, newspapers began trickling in: *The Times of India* and the *Bombay Chronicle*, then a letter or two. Life in the beginning had its moments, particularly as the leaders suddenly discovered that they had the opportunity to get to know one another as more than political colleagues. Nehru's friendship with Maulana Azad, for instance, deepened. In his first letter to Indira (on 18 September 1942) Nehru remarked: 'Maulana is an extraordinarily interesting companion. The more I know him, and I have known him now for over 21 years, the more I find in him. I wish I could profit more by this enforced companionship. Meanwhile, I am having a peep into Urdu poetry. He tells me, or rather writes for me, a verse or two daily.' Nehru understood Urdu; he had translated Azad's superb speech at the Ramgarh session in 1940 brilliantly, winning praise from Azad. But he had little taste for Urdu verse and no knowledge of the script. This peep was going to become a fad as the days passed, and Urdu verses are sprinkled liberally in the prison diary and the letters he sent. He was, naturally, familiar with ways of spending time in prison; there was, for example, always some new world to discover in a secret of nature – pebbles, and their amazing colours, to name one. Yet there was an unreality about this calm idleness in the middle of a world storm, which he could only resent. He reacted bitterly even to minor decisions. On 1 September 1942 the government introduced a new standard time to save an hour's daylight. Nehru commented: 'There is some new-fangled time abroad we are told, a trick to save daylight. We see no reason to abide by it and so we carry on with the old time.' One can hardly miss the bile.

The books – a quarter of them, that is – came by the middle of September. (Maulana, already an expert on Plato, Aristotle, Arab Spain, the Middle Ages and Muslims in India, ordered a large assortment of books on nineteenth-century India.) Gardening, badminton, classics, science, Sherlock Holmes, Lewis Carroll's diary or letters filled Nehru's time. They had a bit of a party on his first gaol birthday – his fifty-third in life. G. B. Pant organized eleven bouquets so that everyone could present flowers. Maulana added a garland, and Harekrushna Mahtab wrote an Oriya poem. Asaf Ali persuaded the gaoler to go and buy a cigarette holder from the bazaar and gave it to Nehru. Syed Mahmud wrote a long sentimental letter describing their friendship from the time they had first met in London in 1909. (Mahmud would soon be unable to take the psychological strain of prison.) One man for whom Nehru's admiration kept growing was the Maulana, particularly when in his thoughts he contrasted him with Jinnah: 'Compared to him ... Jinnah, who has made good in his own way, is just an uncultured, untaught politician, with a politician's flair and instinct, and nothing more' (diary entry, Christmas Day 1942).

Outside, everything seemed to be going Jinnah's way. Even Sir Sikandar, who now had become vocal against the Pakistan idea, describing it as a 'counsel of despair', passed away that winter, leaving Jinnah without powerful challenge in Punjab. In May, Allah Bux, the Sind leader who opposed Pakistan, was shot dead while travelling in a tonga. His assassin was never discovered. Jinnah had once, in a fit of rage, wondered if he would ever be rid of Allah Bux. Nehru commented in his diary: 'It must therefore be the culmination of the Muslim League's persecution of Allah Bux.' Some of Gandhi's moves were no help, such as his toying with the idea of negotiating a release. Nehru was relieved when on 31 March 1943 the British clarified that there was no 'change of heart in Mr Gandhi'.

By the summer of 1943 the strain had begun to show. Most of the Congress leaders were ill: Patel, Pattabhi Sitaramayya, Acharya Narendra Dev, Pant, Asaf Ali, Syed Mahmud, Kripalani. The enforced intimacy made the ageing men get on one another's nerves. Nehru's own temper was hardly under control, and poor best-friend Mahmud got the worst of it. Depression was the most common ailment. Nehru, with his new Urdu, quoted a verse from Ghalib, which reflected his feelings, in a letter to Indira on 14 May:

> Unke dekhe se jo aa jaati hai munh par raunak
> Woh samajhte hain ke beemar ka haal acha hai.

('My face lights up upon a glance from her, / And she thinks that this lovesick man is healthy!') After this he added: 'Last evening, a little after sunset, I saw a curious sight. The 8- or 9-day moon looked quite green. I had never seen it so. Fed up, I suppose, with the goings-on in this world.' But a sense of humour remained intact: 'I have exceeded all bounds in this letter – I fear it is much more than 500 words! So my apologies to the censors.' The days were bad enough; the nights were impossible. He used to get constant nightmares and moan a great deal in his sleep. His entry for 2 July says: 'The nightmare is not vivid and I forget it soon after waking. But just on waking I remember it. Usually it has to do with struggle and conflict and a certain inability on my part to reach the person or thing which is troubling me. I then shout out either for help or as a warning to someone.'

Soon the first anniversary of the prison term came around. Kripalani and P. C. Ghosh organized a special dinner, and the superintendent even sent around a birthday cake with '1' marked on it. Outside, bombs exploded in Bombay, Surat and Karachi. News of the great famines all over India, but most particularly in Bengal, began to come through. Nehru was bitterly angry. On 21 September he wrote: 'Some homilies in the English press about food scarcity and our failings. But they will know one day, the world will know. Meanwhile, we know.' And of course there was this threat of Pakistan to taunt him:

> The Pakistan business – often my thoughts have turned to it. How mad and foolish it is . . . mad and foolish and fantastic and criminal and all that, and yet a huge barrier to all progress. What a lot Jinnah and his Muslim League have to answer for! They have lowered the whole tone of our public life, embittered it, increased mutual dislike and hatreds, and made us contemptible before the outside world. I cannot help thinking that ultimately the Muslim in India will suffer most.

A perceptive assessment, and one which Azad would share and grieve about, being convinced that the Muslims of the minority provinces would become orphans in both India and Pakistan. Letters brought some news of life outside. Nehru worried about his daughter's pregnancy, recalling that Kamala had never really recovered after Indira's birth. On 13 April 1944 he began his last book, *The Discovery of India*: a loose collection of articles, impressions, experiences, autobiographical memories, viewpoints, essays and, from chapter four, a long tour of the history and culture of India, before it returned to the contemporary experiences of the author. It was a work spun out by a prison need rather than held together by the strength of Nehruvian passion. The prose is more flat than in *An Autobiography*, and the history less riveting than in *Glimpses*. He finished the 998 handwritten pages on 7 September 1944.

It was not a good moment for the dozen in Ahmednagar Fort. They were all upset by the news that Gandhi was meeting Jinnah for talks in Bombay on 9 September. The British had allowed Gandhi nearly to die during his fast in 1943. But on 6 May 1944 they suddenly released him unconditionally on health grounds. His departure was less elaborate than his arrival; the inspector-general of police came and drove him to freedom in his own car. Till 15 June, Gandhi kept quiet – literally – most of the time (an average of 20 hours a day when not 24). Then he began his politics. The government would not let him meet the Congress working committee; he experimented with the Rajagopalachari approach. A four-point formula was published by Rajagopalachari on 10 July: the League would endorse the Congress demand for independence; a post-war plebiscite would determine the fate of Muslim-majority areas; if they separated, defence, commerce and communications pacts would be signed; the terms would be binding only after the departure of the British. On 17 July, Gandhi sent 'Brother Jinnah' an invitation to talk (the letter was in Gujarati).

Brother Jinnah was elated. The Mahatma had come to the mountain – and had accepted partition in principle! It was as unbelievable to him as it was to the Congress working committee in gaol. At five minutes to four on 9 September, Gandhi, accompanied by Pyarelal, was met by Jinnah at the latter's palatial Bombay residence, and the two smiled broadly for the cameras before a private discussion that went on for three and a quarter hours. Jinnah treated both Gandhi and the Rajagopalachari formula with contempt; he had won his battle already. He had forced Gandhi to admit, by the very idea of talking to him, that he was the man to be dealt with, as far as the Muslim question was concerned. As for Rajagopalachari's formula: Jinnah wanted Pakistan from the British, not from the Congress; and before the British left, not after. Gandhi, says Tendulkar, was appalled by Jinnah's 'staggering contempt'. By 26 September the Gandhi–Rajagopalachari initiative had not only injured Congress policy, but had established Jinnah's eminence beyond any doubt. This Gandhian recognition of Jinnah was resented most of all by the Congress Muslims. At the end of the talks, Gandhi told the *News Chronicle* in Bombay, 'Mr Jinnah is sincere, but I think he is suffering from hallucination when he imagines that an unnatural division of India could bring either happiness or prosperity to the people concerned.' But after touting the Rajagopalachari formula it was a dud charge to make.

There was a new Viceroy in Delhi by then, Lord Wavell. And Wavell wrote a fine epitaph of what had happened in his journal on 30 September 1944: 'This surely must blast Gandhi's reputation as a leader. Jinnah had an easy task, he merely had to keep on telling Gandhi he was talking nonsense, which was true, and he did so rather rudely, without having to disclose any of the weaknesses of his own position, or define his Pakistan in any way.'

Morale in Ahmednagar Fort was further dampened by the defection of Syed Mahmud. Unable to take prison any longer, he wrote secretly on 19 August 1944 to the government supporting the war effort and was released. Nehru was furious, particularly since the allegation was bandied around that he (and the Maulana) had agreed with his friend's betrayal. Though Nehru and Mahmud shared a cell, the truth was that since April the two had fought so much that they were not on proper talking terms. Syed Mahmud later met Gandhi and apologized; Gandhi forgave him. But Nehru had little generosity to offer. 'What a bloody fool Mahmud has been!' he wrote on 22 October. 'If all this is not cowardly, sneaky and lying behaviour I do not know what it is.' Nehru was angry enough to reject a new privilege from the authorities, permission for 'interviews' with friends and relatives. He was lonely and yet wanted nothing remotely generous from the hated British government. On 3 October he wrote to Krishna Hutheesingh:

It struck me as an odd and arresting fact that for nearly 26 months – for 785 days to be exact – I had not seen a woman even from a distance. Previously it was not so, for even in prison we had interviews occasionally. And I began to wonder. What are women like? how do they work? how do they talk and sit and walk?

The touch of self-pity can surely be understood.

The first time that Nehru got a decent cook after his breakfast at Krishna's flat three years before was in June 1945, at Almora gaol, where a Congress prisoner, Mangal Singh, turned out to be a minor chef. 'Even knows how to deal with eggs,' Nehru wrote in his diary on Thursday 14 June 1945. That night at nine in the evening the gaoler came with some exciting news. He had just heard a broadcast on the radio by Lord Wavell and learned that the big leaders, Gandhi, Jinnah, et cetera, were being invited for a conference at Simla on 25 June.

The next day, Friday 15 June, at fifty minutes past seven in the morning, Jawaharlal Nehru and the now ten working committee colleagues were informed that they had been released unconditionally. Zero hour was over.

33 Other Men's Flowers

Some Britishers had the most curious notions of how Indians would manage in their absence. No less a person than Leopold Amery, Secretary of State, thought, in a note to Lord Linlithgow on 1 October 1943:

> If India is to be really capable of holding its own in the future without direct British control from outside, I am not sure that it will not need an increasing fusion of stronger Nordic blood, whether by settlement or intermarriage or otherwise. Possibly it has been a real mistake of ours in the past not to encourage Indian Princes to marry English wives for a succession of generations and so breed a more virile type of native ruler.

Extraordinary thought. Fortunately, the man Amery and Churchill chose to replace Linlithgow that very month got more sensible advice from his predecessor. 'The chief factors', Linlithgow told Wavell on 19 October 1943, 'of the problem of Indian political progress were the stupidity of the Indian and the dishonesty of the British' (Wavell, *Viceroy's Journal*, 1973).

Archibald Percival Wavell stepped on India's red carpet on the evening of Sunday 17 October 1943. He had not particularly wanted the job of Viceroy of India, but Churchill left him little choice; it was the very best upstairs Wavell could be kicked to after a succession of failures on the battlefield. It was Wavell's fate to be defeated before his successor became a victorious hero. It happened each time. Erwin Rommel broke him in the desert; when the time came for British victories, Montgomery was there to win the kudos. From commander-in-chief of the Middle East he became commander-in-chief of the Far East in 1941. Now the Japanese smashed his armies in the mountain jungles of Burma and India, and only the inadequacy of supply lines prevented the Japanese from pursuing their 'march to Delhi'. In the winter of 1942 Wavell sent the 14th Indian Division into Arakan to capture the Akyab port, and another division followed in support. His counter-offensive was battered out of shape. By May

1943 the British–Indian armies were lucky that they had returned to their starting-point. Winston Churchill was furious and publicly vented his anger on Wavell at the slightest opportunity. Churchill wanted a younger, more imaginative Supreme Commander for the East and pushed his candidate through the hostility of the senior officers and politicians (including Attlee) in Britain with the help of the Americans. (Roosevelt and Eisenhower were delighted.) Churchill's man was Mountbatten. On 24 August 1943 Churchill announced the appointment. Mountbatten was happily stunned at the honour and the responsibility. It was Mountbatten who took the surrender of the Japanese on 15 September 1945.

Wavell was not Churchill's first choice for Viceroy. For a while Churchill toyed with the idea of sending Anthony Eden, then his Foreign Minister, to India. Wavell himself wanted the Supreme Commander's job. (He was not alone.) Over dinner on 14 June 1943 Churchill told Wavell it was the viceroyalty. And it would be a war appointment; in other words, if the war ended in less than five years, Wavell would have to return.

One of the people who called on Wavell before he left England was an author and an economist, Edward Thompson. Thompson was a good friend of Nehru. About a year later, Thompson sent via Wavell two books for Nehru to read in prison. Thus on 10 November 1944 Nehru received, in his cell, a parcel, sealed, unopened, uncensored and personally delivered by the prison superintendent, Major M. Sendak. Nehru was surprised, and his surprise became laced with worry when he learned that the parcel had come from the Viceroy; after the Syed Mahmud incident, and the mischievous effort to link him and Azad with Mahmud's letter to the government, he was very apprehensive of warders bearing gifts. Two books were by and from Thompson; the third was an anthology of poetry put together by Wavell, *Other Men's Flowers*, published that very year. There was a personal letter from Wavell as well, a private one 'in view of our respective positions'. Nehru's immediate reaction (as his diary indicates) was very positive. 'Letters', he notes, 'are often self-revealing . . . Wavell's letter was a good one and indicated the decency of the man.' He was in a fix, though. If he told his colleagues about the letter, they would gossip; if he did not, it could become a scandal if word ever leaked out. He decided to confide in Azad and Sardar Patel about Wavell's gift. Well, diaries can be self-revealing too.

'Ultimately I changed my mind about Vallabhbhai and decided not to mention the matter to him. I spoke only to Maulana and Pantji,' Jawaharlal wrote. Nehru simply did not trust Patel enough; he was far closer to Pant and Azad.

Other Men's Flowers seems a most appropriate summation of Wavell's viceroyalty. On 14 June 1945 Lord Wavell broadcast his new scheme for settlement: an interim national government consisting of representatives of the main communities, with Muslims and 'caste Hindus' in equal numbers; the release of all Congress leaders; and a conference, from 25 June, at the summer capital, Simla. Twenty-one leaders were invited: the official party leaders in the Central Assembly and Council of State; past and present premiers of the provinces; a leader of the scheduled castes, Rao Bahadur N. Siva Raj; a leader of the Sikhs, Master Tara Singh; and the two 'superstars', Jinnah from the League and Gandhi from the Congress.

Gandhi's first reaction was to demur. He was no one in the Congress, he pointed out. True enough. It was Azad who was president. But it was obvious that Gandhi had seen through the trap. Jinnah was being invited to Simla on his terms – as the representative of *all* the Muslims of India, where he would deal as an equal of *the leader of the Hindus*, Gandhi. Azad was a Muslim. If both the Congress and the Muslim League were represented by Muslims, it would rather knock the self-acquired 'sole spokesman' status of Jinnah. Gandhi refused. Wavell gave in. On Monday 18 June, Azad was invited. Gandhi was also perturbed at this intrusion of something called 'caste Hindus' as the equal of Muslims; the British were dividing Hindus now, along caste and untouchable lines, in formal talks. When Gandhi finally accepted the offer to attend the conference after Wavell had also invited Azad, he made his intentions plain. His telegram to the Viceroy was quite specific: 'The Congress has never identified itself with Caste or Non-Caste Hindus and never can even to gain independence which will be one-sided, untrue and suicidal.' He bluntly told the Viceroy that it was the Hindu Mahasabha which 'is the body claiming to represent solely Hindu interests', not the Congress. The Hindu Mahasabha was not invited. Jinnah and Wavell wanted to treat Gandhi as the Indian Hindu leader, not Veer Savarkar.

Churchill's paranoid hatred for Congressmen was even greater than his hatred for Indians. Amery's diary entry for 9 September

1942 quotes Churchill telling his Secretary of State for India, 'I hate Indians. They are a beastly people with a beastly religion.' At a Cabinet meeting on 1 September, Churchill pointed out that the suppression of the Quit India movement had confirmed 'that Congress really represents hardly anybody except lawyers, money-lenders and the Hindu priesthood' (quoted in Wolpert's *Jinnah*). Churchill was proud of British rule in India and happy with the League's politics of co-operation; he feared that the Labour members in his War Cabinet would sell out to the Congress if allowed any sway. Cripps was distanced from Indian affairs and made minister of aircraft production on 22 September 1942. Within days of the arrest of the Congress leaders on 9 August, the British installed a League ministry in Assam; Mohammad Saadullah's majority was possible only because Congress MLAs were in gaol. In October in Sind the pro-Congress Allah Baksh was dismissed by Sir Hugh Dow, the governor, on Linlithgow's orders, for renouncing his official honours, and G. H. Hidayatullah became premier; he joined the League soon after. On 31 March 1943 Sir John Herbert dismissed Fazlul Haq in Bengal, and the League's Nizamuddin formed a government with the support of the twenty-five European legislators. The next month even the Congress stronghold of NWFP was taken. Although Aurangzeb Khan never had the support of more than 19 of the 43 members of the Assembly, his League–Akali coalition was put in power.

Wavell could not conceal his astonishment at the blatant discrimination, at least when writing his journal. His entries on two key issues of the time expose the extent of Churchill's perfidy. He asked Winston Churchill for food for the millions dying in Bengal, and this was the response (5 July 1944): 'Winston sent me a peevish telegram to ask why Gandhi hadn't died yet! He has never answered my telegram about food.' In March 1945, with the war unwinding, Wavell went to London. He met Churchill on 29 March to discuss what should now be done. This is what he says about the meeting in his journal: 'The PM then launched into a long jeremiad about India which lasted for about 40 minutes. He seems to favour partition into Pakistan, Hindustan, Princestan, etc.' This is as clear a description of British intent as is possible to find. The plan to divide India had festered in Churchill's mind for a long while, and he was determined to hand Pakistan over to Jinnah, and if possible break the

subcontinent into many parts. Wavell, moreover, already knew
something by then which was a secret to everyone in India but
Jinnah and his personal doctor. On 10 March, Wavell wrote: 'Jinnah
who was to have seen me on 7 March is sick, I am told he has a touch
of pleurisy and may be laid up for some time.' British intelligence
had done its work; none of India's politicians were aware of this
disease. The time had come for the next step.

Despite the advantage of participating in the provincial governments, the League was once again tottering. In Bengal the squabbling
between Haq, Nizamuddin and Shaheed Suhrawardy had taken its
toll. In Punjab the Unionists had broken the Sikhandar–Jinnah pact.
The Frontier was back with the Congress. In Sind the League was
split. On what basis, consequently, Lord Wavell awarded Jinnah the
right to represent India's Muslims at the Simla Conference is difficult
to understand, except in terms of a private deal. Even Wavell was
forced to concede during the talks that Jinnah could not possibly be
given the right to nominate *all* the five Muslims on the proposed
Executive Council; the Unionists had their claim, not to mention
Congress president Azad's right to nominate himself if he chose to.
The Congress naturally would not concede this communal right to
Jinnah. This very same principle had destroyed the coalition talks in
UP in 1937, and the Congress had not become a 'Hindu' party since
then. Jinnah, with nothing to lose, stuck to this demand. The Con-
gress was reasonable, as Wavell admitted; and Azad, in turn, found
Wavell frank and sincere rather than devious. At one point, on 30
June, Wavell even considered the possibility of going ahead without
Jinnah – but he was pulled up at once by London. As Penderel Moon
observes in his notes to *The Viceroy's Journal* (1973): 'Churchill,
who was still Prime Minister, and many of his Ministers had only
reluctantly consented to the Simla Conference being held at all. They
would have been outraged if its upshot had been a proposal to form
a Congress-dominated Council unbalanced by the League.'

Churchill's ally was Jinnah, and he would protect his man. And
why not? League leaders were quite ready to talk his language. Lord
Wavell's diary for 4 April 1945 reports the proceedings of a London
Cabinet meeting which Sir Firoz Khan Noon was asked to attend:
'Firoz Khan Noon said rather optimistically that everyone in India
was united in wishing to remain in the Empire.' Wavell tried to find
a way out of this extremely complicated thicket at the Simla talks.

On 29 June he told Jinnah, 'I am no dialectician and do not propose to argue. I have put you a simple proposal which everyone else seems to understand. Are you or are you not prepared to submit me a list of names?' Jinnah parried and stalled; on his request the conference was postponed by a fortnight. On 8 July, Jinnah met Wavell again, privately. He knew that his and the Muslim League's bluff was on the point of being called. This is how Wavell recalls the meeting in his journal entry for 9 July:

> I had 1½ hours with Jinnah yesterday evening which left us where we began. He spent practically the whole time trying to get me to agree that none except himself as head of the Muslim League could nominate the Muslims on the new Council. I refused to accept this, and he finally refused to give me his list of names, though he left a loophole in the end by asking me to write to him, which I have done this morning. He was obviously in a high state of nervous tension, and said to me more than once, 'I am at the end of my tether'; he also said, 'I ask you not to wreck the League.'

The entry needs little comment. It was an abject appeal for help. If the British recognized any other Muslim spokesman, it would have been, in Jinnah's own words, his 'death warrant'. But even Wavell, who was convinced that the League did not want a settlement at Simla, would not go ahead and settle with the Congress or Khizr Hayat's Unionists, ignoring the League, despite having enough reason to do so. Instead, he declared failure and closed the Simla Conference.

One of the finest assessments of the Muslim situation in India at that time, just two years before partition, was made by Andrew Clow, governor of Assam. On 22 August 1945 (I owe this to Ayesha Jalal's *The Sole Spokesman*, 1985) Clow admitted that it was the British who had 'contributed to make Pakistan a live issue'. Punjab and Bengal, he added, would never vote to partition their provinces, and Jinnah's ideas were preposterous – his strength lay in vagueness, for the details would expose him in front of the Muslim masses: 'Muslims would realize fairly quickly that Pakistan was not worthwhile and would be more ready to compromise on concessions at the Centre. As it is, a good many more of them have this in view than dare to avow it openly.' Jinnah, after having been saved by Wavell at Simla, now resurrected his chant that only he and Pakistan now stood between Muslims and slavery in the 'Hindu Raj' of Congress-ruled India. Anyone who offered a less extremist view was branded a 'traitor' or 'Congress showboy'. Simultaneously the League had also begun preparations for violence. Wavell noticed this. On 10 June 1944 he wrote in his diary: 'Although Jinnah is a most un-orthodox Moslem (to say the least of it) he seems to be able to wave the banner of religion and frighten them all to heel with it. We shall have more trouble with J. and his private army, the Moslem National Guards.' Those guards, urged by no less hysterical leaders, now whipped up another slogan: 'Lar ke lenge Pakistan' ('We will fight to get our Pakistan'). An ill wind was beginning to rise in the land.

By the summer of 1945 Churchill had won the war and lost his government. In May, Germany surrendered; on 23 May a caretaker government filled in time pending post-war elections; in July, Clement Attlee became Prime Minister with a 'monstrous' majority, and Nehru's socialist friends were finally in power untrammelled by Conservatives. Wavell worried that the Attlee government might produce a pro-Congress solution to India.

In June 1938 Nehru (along with Indira and Krishna Menon) had spent his first weekend in England at Filkins, Stafford Cripps's country house. The other guests included Attlee, Aneurin Bevan, Harold Laski and members of the Labour shadow Cabinet; Nehru was confident after the Filkins discussions that a future Labour government would support the idea of India as an independent ally of Britain in the coming war. Now Nehru felt cheated by Cripps; he was so bitter that he did not even reply to a friendly telegram from Cripps after his release. Wavell's worries abated in direct proportion to Nehru's rising disappointment. The Viceroy wryly noted, on 24 December 1946: 'Bevan like everyone else hates the idea of our leaving India, but like everyone else has no alternative to suggest . . . Both he and [A. V.] Alexander are in reality imperialists and dislike any idea of leaving India.' It still took some convincing. The imperialists finally gave up when that most formidable of institutions, the Indian Army, started showing signs of strain.

Spurned by Adolf Hitler, Subhas Bose took a German U-Boat to Tokyo. On 8 February 1943, at dawn, Bose and a comrade, Abid Hassan, boarded a Type IX at Kiel commanded by Werner Mus-enberg. On 28 April they transferred by a rubber boat to a Japanese submarine in the Indian Ocean, 400 nautical miles south-south-west of Madagascar. The next day the Japanese crew celebrated the Emperor's birthday – and the Indians, sheer survival; it had been a tough journey. They reached Sabang on 6 May, where a plane picked up Bose and Hassan; they reached Tokyo on 16 May. In the first week of June, Bose met Prime (and War) Minister Tojo. The war was no longer going well for the Axis powers: the Germans had withdrawn from Stalingrad; the African front had collapsed; and the Americans were making gains in the Pacific. But there was good news still from the Far East, and Burma. On 16 June, Tojo declared in the Japanese Diet:

> We are indignant about the fact that India is still under ruthless suppression of Britain and are in full sympathy with her desperate struggle for independence. We are determined to extend every possible assistance to the cause of India's independence. It is our belief that the day is not far off when India will enjoy freedom and prosperity after winning independence.

This was the signal for an offensive against India. Japan would replace Britain as the imperial power, and Bose head the pro-Axis Indian government. On 19 June, Bose announced, at a press conference, his resolve to fight: 'The enemy that has drawn the sword must be fought with the sword.' On 23 June, Bose left for Singapore, landing on 27 June. On 5 July he took command of the Indian National Army. On 15 February 1942 Colonel Hunt, the British commander, had surrendered to the Japanese with over 40,000 Indian soldiers and officers after the fall of Singapore. The Japanese declared that the Indians would be treated differently, as their war was with the British, not Indians. About 13,000 officers and men had by now banded together into the INA. 'Delhi chalo!' ('Towards Delhi!') Bose called out to the troops lined up in the city square of Singapore under a scorching sun. 'How many of us will individually survive this war of freedom', Bose declared, 'I do not know. But I do know this, that we shall ultimately win, and our task will not end until our surviving heroes hold the victory parade on another graveyard of the British Empire: the Lal Qila [Red Fort] of ancient Delhi.'

Well, the INA did touch Indian soil on 6 April 1944, but just barely: no further than Kohima. On 4 April, Bose appointed Lieutenant-Colonel A. C. Chatterjee as governor of the 'liberated' territories, but when the INA did reach the Red Fort it was only as prisoners – those, that is, who did not re-defect when the British drove them back from Imphal. Nehru had no sympathy with Bose's collaboration. He made it very clear – and did so in Bose's city, Calcutta – that he would even oppose Bose at the head of his army. But when the British committed their last great folly, his blood rose. The Raj announced that it would put several hundred of the 20,000 INA prisoners on trial from 5 November 1945. The only concession, made at Azad's request, was to hold the trial in public.

On Saturday 3 November, Nehru lashed out at the government at a mass rally in Delhi, demanding both the freedom of the INA prisoners and the freedom of the country. He helped organize the defence committee of lawyers, and when the trial of Captain Shah Nawaz, Captain P. K. Sehgal and Lieutenant Gurbaksh Singh Dhillon opened on Monday, Nehru himself was in the lawyer's robes he had discarded twenty-five years before. By a remarkable coincidence, one of the three accused was a Muslim, one a Hindu and one a Sikh; the national movement could not have found better symbols. India was outraged. In city after city police had to open fire. As students and young men died, the anger became an avalanche. Nehru, characteristically, both rode and fuelled the anger. On 3 November 1945 Jawaharlal launched the Congress campaign for the next elections in Delhi, and his meetings had a volcanic force in that charged atmosphere. 'We don't want to fight our countrymen,' he said in Delhi, 'we want to fight for the freedom of our country.' In Jinnah's home town, Bombay, he lambasted the British and the Muslim League, which he called imperialist agents. Freedom, he told a meeting in Bombay on Sunday 11 November, 'will be neither Hindu Raj nor Muslim Raj but Hindustan Raj', of equality and socialism. The next day he gave a call to Indians: 'It is the duty of every Indian, who is a slave, to revolt and carry on the revolt till he is a free man. Every country which is dominated by another nation must revolt against that authority. I am using the word "revolt" after great consideration and thought.' The government was worried, and there was talk once again of arrest. William Cove, a sympathetic Labour MP, told UPI in London on 12 November: 'I can only hope and pray that no one will be so rash and foolish as to arrest Pandit Jawaharlal Nehru, the very embodiment of India's struggle for freedom.' The Nehru passion rang out, undeterred. On 20 November he told a rally in Lahore: 'We are now terribly sick of this British government. We may go to hell but this government must get out of our country. There is a fire raging in our hearts. We must be free soon.' There was genuine fear of an open rebellion breaking out that winter.

This time the army and the police did not seem wholly eager to protect the British. In his autobiography *While Memory Serves* (1950), General Francis Tuker notes that anger over the INA trials was threatening to destroy the whole edifice of the Indian Army. And Azad, in his memoirs *India Wins Freedom* (1959), recalls:

> Wherever I went during this period, the young men of the Defence Forces came out to welcome me and express their sympathy and admiration without any regard for the reaction of their European officers. When I went to Karachi a group of naval officers came to see me . . . If there was a conflict between Congress and the Government they would side with the Congress.

In Lahore, Gurkha soldiers lined up in hundreds for a *darshan* (view) of Azad. In Calcutta, when Azad's car was caught in a traffic jam, constables from the nearby police headquarters, Lalbazar, mobbed him, saluting him and touching his feet. Even at Government House, where Azad went for a formal interview with the Bengal governor, the constables on duty shouted pro-Congress slogans when they saw him. The price of staying on was made irrevocably clear to the British by mutinies in the air force and the navy. If the first was muted, the second reached the world's headlines. On 19 February 1946 nearly 3,000 ratings of the Royal Indian Navy ripped up the Union Jack, raised the Indian tricolour and marched through Bombay's streets in open revolt. British troops fired on them. Workers struck in sympathy, shops closed down, and suddenly a conflagration lit the commercial heart of India. The Communists and radical Congress leaders like Aruna Asaf Ali wanted to extend the revolt, but Nehru, instead of fanning the flames of revolt, chose to quieten them – Gandhi had opposed the mutiny. Patel pacified the mutineers and negotiated a peace with the commander-in-chief, General Claude Auchinleck: no action would be taken against the mutineers, and their grievances would be examined and removed.

It was the first time since 1857 that the military had revolted, and the British caved in. The Empire was over. The British had seen it coming. On New Year's Day of 1946 Lord Pethick-Lawrence assured India in a broadcast from London that it would be free and there was no longer any need for 'organized pressure to secure this end'. On 19 February, exactly on the day that the mutiny had broken out, Clement Attlee announced in the House of Commons: 'Three British Cabinet Ministers are going to India to discuss with leaders of Indian opinion the framing of an Indian Constitution. They are Lord Pethick-Lawrence, Secretary of State for India, Sir Stafford Cripps, President of the Board of Trade, and Mr A. V. Alexander, First Lord of the Admiralty.' This was the Cabinet Mission. All the British wanted now was to get out with their skins intact. They would leave untouched, but Indian blood would flow bitterly over their legacy.

Jawaharlal Nehru was both a nationalist and an internationalist. He wanted freedom for the whole of the colonized world, and in particular for the Asian nations struggling to free themselves from the yoke of the war's victors: France in Indo-China, a British–Dutch combination in Indonesia, Britain in Malaya and Indonesia. He wanted to visit these countries for a first-hand report to the Congress. Permission to visit Indonesia and Burma was refused bluntly. He could come to Malaya, but his movements would be severely restricted – if, that is, he could find a car to travel in, in the first place. Suddenly there was a message from Singapore, assuring every facility. It had come from the Supreme Allied Commander, Lord Mountbatten.

When Nehru landed at Singapore he was quite startled by the reception; it was fit for a prime-minister-in-waiting. At the canteen, no less a person than the wife of the Supreme Commander waited to greet him. As they entered the inside room together, a wild rush of Indian soldiers ran into them. They had been waiting for Nehru and could not control their enthusiasm. He lost his hostess in the rush and was forced to get up on a chair to look for her; he soon discovered her crawling out of the crowd. As Nehru wryly reminisced to Dorothy Norman on 12 October 1963, when his life was near its end: 'That was an unusual introduction for us.' And the beginning of a famous friendship.

34 The Sole Problem Again: Who Shall Be the Spokesman?

There was never any question, naturally, of who led the Congress; it was a role which the Mahatma adopted or shed according to his inclinations. But there was always a question of who would be his successor. In the aftermath of the resignation of the Congress ministries, and the confusion created by the different interpretations of the Congress war policy, Chakravarti Rajagopalachari made his bid to settle with the Muslim League and the British, offering Pakistan to the former and co-operation to the latter, in return for a free and Congress-controlled India. It was, inevitably, also a bid for leadership of the Congress. His personal standing in the country was high enough; and he was also close to Gandhi – his daughter was married to Gandhi's son. There was a growing view that Rajagopalachari had replaced Jawaharlal in the Mahatma's affections, a change with obvious political connotations if true. Gandhi deliberately scotched any such impression. On 15 January 1942 Gandhi told the All-India Congress Committee at Wardha:

> Somebody suggested that Pandit Jawaharlal and I were estranged. It will require much more than differences of opinion to estrange us. We have had differences from the moment we became co-workers, and yet I have said for some years and say now that not Rajaji but Jawaharlal will be my successor. He says that he does not understand my language, and that he speaks a language foreign to me. This may or may not be true. But language is no bar to a union of hearts. And I know this, that when I am gone he will speak my language.

Little could have been more emphatic. Nor was it a sudden or recent decision; 'some years' is Gandhi's own phrase. Gandhi had been nurturing this disciple for the leadership of free India, and the very differences between them (on the attitude to science, or industry, or planning, for example) might have persuaded the Mahatma that Nehru would be a better Prime Minister for a modern nation than a more loyal Gandhian. Each time Gandhi made his disciple party president it was a historically significant year. It was forty-year-old Jawaharlal who first announced the Congress pledge of *purna swaraj*, or total freedom, on the banks of the Ravi in 1929. It was Jawaharlal whom Gandhi selected to lead the party during the crucial elections of 1937, keeping his protégé on for a second consecutive term in order to ensure that he remained president after the polling too. In 1942 Azad was the president, but Jawaharlal was given the honour of raising the flag of free India at Gowalia Tank on 9 August. (Aruna Asaf Ali did so after Nehru's arrest.) Now in the summer of 1946, when it was evident that the freedom movement had entered the home stretch, Gandhi made Jawaharlal Nehru president of the Congress once again. He forced the decision, in Simla, when the Congress leaders were busy planning out an interim Indian government in Delhi with the Viceroy of India, the Cabinet Mission from London and the Muslim League.

On 26 April 1946 Azad, who had been president for an unprece- dented six years, announced that he was leaving office and named Nehru as his nominee for successor. It was clear that it was not a unilateral choice; he had spent an hour with Gandhi before he made the announcement. The logic of the timing was evident from another story in the next day's *Hindusthan Standard*: there was a strong feeling that an interim government might be formed as early as in the first week of May, when the tripartite talks were scheduled to begin in Simla. The Congress president would naturally claim to head such an interim government, whenever it was formed. It needs to be mentioned that a 'voluntary' resignation was unprecedented; a new president took over only at a full Congress session, and the Meerut session of 1946 would begin only on 21 November. (When Prasad replaced Bose it was only because Bose left the Congress.) In his autobiography Azad can barely hide his disappointment at being denied the chance to head the Interim Government, but at least he was on the same wavelength as Nehru. There were other claimants who were not. (One nomination was also received for Subhas Bose; his ardent supporters were convinced that he had not died in an air crash but was alive and in hiding.) Once again, Nehru was chal- lenged. Both Sardar Vallabhbhai Patel and Acharya Kripalani had put up their names. The voting was scheduled to begin on 16 May. There was only one man who could ensure a unanimous decision in favour of Nehru, and Gandhi did so. On 9 May, Kripalani issued a communiqué in his capacity as general secretary of the party, saying that, the two other candidates having withdrawn, Nehru was declared automatically elected. That same day Nehru met Jinnah for talks on the future. It was the first time, reported the *Hindusthan Standard*, that they were meeting in seven years.

The Three Magi of the Cabinet Mission arrived on 24 March, but Wavell had his doubts about the quality of the gifts they were bearing. Wavell's notes about discussions at his Executive Council meeting the next day, 25 March, provide a most interesting look at the cross-section of views and expectations at this stage of the unwinding of Empire. B. R. Ambedkar supported the Pakistan idea but added that in ten years the Muslims would be sick of what they had created and rejoin India. N. B. Khare, the Hindu Mahasabha leader, who had joined the government, began dreaming of a Mahratta province as the base for modern Hindu power. The British position was put across by Sir Edward Benthall and Sir Archibald Rowlands: the army and police could no longer be trusted, civil war seemed possible, and the British must now concede Pakistan. This was yet more proof, if any more seems necessary, of the British desire to pay their debts to Jinnah. British officials, the true imperialists, had conceded Pakistan to Jinnah long before all the thrashing around by the politicians and the nit-picking over solutions. Wavell made it clear that he would play an active role in the coming negotiations, which would begin on 1 April; the Cabinet Mission would return only on 29 June. It was Sir Akbar Hydari who raised, however, the most relevant question. He himself would never accept Pakistan on principle, he said, but he would like to ask Mr Jinnah a question: could he define his Pakistan? On 4 April the Cabinet Mission also realized that even the father had no real clue about the contours of his proposed nation.

Wavell disliked Gandhi intensely, describing him as a 'malevolent old politician', and was appalled when Cripps personally stood up to receive the Mahatma as a mark of respect during their meeting on 3 April. Yet even Wavell found the man he preferred, Jinnah, thoroughly confusing the next day. Jinnah, writes Wavell, spent an hour on a 'largely fanciful' history of India and on differences between Hindus and Muslims. Then an hour and a half stonewalling all specific questions. And when in the last half-hour the Mission asked for his ideas about the boundaries of Pakistan, 'we got nothing much out of J.'. The other stars of the Muslim League were little better than their leader. On 8 April came Hussain Shaheed Suhrawardy. Comments Wavell: 'I have always regarded him as one of the most inefficient, conceited and crooked politicians in India, which is saying a good deal. He made a very bad impression on the delegation.' The only thing the League leaders were articulate about was in their 'hymn of hate against Hindus'. Four more leaders of the League came that day, from the Muslim-minority provinces of Bombay (Chundrigar), UP (Khaliquzzaman), CP (Syed Abdur Rauf Shah) and Madras (Md Ismail). They were even less impressive. 'They claimed that Pakistan would help the Muslim minorities in Hindu Provinces, but after an immense amount of verbiage – mainly from Bombay (Chundrigar) with UP (Chaudhry Khaliquzzaman) a close runner-up – could adduce no real argument, except vague phrases such as balance of power, prestige, psychological effect, but a good deal of hate against Hindus.'

This, do note, is essentially a friend of the Pakistan idea writing. Pakistan was a chimera created by an artificially induced hatred. The arguments which its most important theorists placed in front of the Cabinet Mission, where the destiny of the subcontinent was being decided, were appalling. Even from this brief glance it is obvious that the League leaders did not know what they wanted, except for hyped-up revenge against Hindus. One of the most remarkable aspects about Wavell's journal is that, while he finds enough scope to comment on the anti-Hindu sentiments of the League, he never heard any Congress leader speak the language of hate against Muslims. That was the difference between Jinnah's party and Gandhi's.

The Muslim-minority province leaders in particular had no clue about what they were demanding in a Pakistan, or how a nation formed in the north-west and north-east of India could protect Muslims in Bombay, Madras, United Provinces or Central Provinces. It was not surprising therefore that Jinnah was never publicly specific about the boundaries of his proposed nation. He had sold a lie to the Muslims of the Hindu-majority provinces in order to win their support, which he got in much greater measure in the 1945–6 elections than in 1937. The Muslim peasantry of Bengal also responded to the idea because it had much to gain out of separation from the Hindu landlord, but the League's support was tepid in Sind, Frontier and even Punjab. H. V. Hodson, the Reforms Commissioner, reported to

Linlithgow in 1941 that virtually every Muslim Leaguer saw Pakistan as something within a united Indian federation but ensuring an equal status between Muslims and Hindus in free India. This really was the concept that most Muslims who opted for the League banner believed in. The Ulster comparison was a well-used one after the Lahore Resolution, and I. I. Chundrigar often reassured his Bombay supporters that the proposed 'two nations' would be welded into a united India. The number of 'Pakistan' schemes that did the rounds further added to the confusion but simultaneously reinforced the view that it would all eventually remain a part of one India. Dr Rajendra Prasad in *India Divided* (reprinted 1986) mentions some of the schemes floating about both before and after the Lahore Resolution:

(1) A confederacy of India. This would consist of the Indus Regions' Federation (UP, CP, Bihar, parts of Bengal, Assam, Orissa, Madras, Bombay and some princely states); the Rajasthan Federation; the Deccan Federation (Hyderabad, Mysore, Bastar); and the Bengal Federation (East Bengal, Tripura, Muslim Assam).

(2) The Aligarh professors' scheme. This would divide the subcontinent into seven independent and sovereign countries: Pakistan; Bengal (the Muslim areas); Hyderabad (with Berar and Karnataka); Delhi; Malabar; and Hindustan (the rest).

(3) Rahmat Ali's scheme. The originator of the Pakistan idea in 1933 wanted by 1942 Muslim Islamic raj over the whole of South Asia, including Ceylon.

(4) Dr S. A. Latif's scheme. Highly decentralized cultural zones within an all-India federation. The Muslim zones would be: North-West Block; North-East Block; Delhi–Lucknow Block; Deccan Block. The Hindu Zones would be: Bengal (half of it); Orissa, West Bihar and UP; Rajput States; Gujarat; Mahratta; Dravidian Group; Hindu–Sikh Block.

(5) Sir Abdullah Haroon Committee's scheme. This was the committee of the Muslim League which began work in February 1940 and drew up a plan for partition. The Pakistan in the north-west and north-east of course are known. But it went further and demanded that all princely states ruled by Muslims, like Hyderabad, should become separate and sovereign feudalisms. After a long journey through complicated demographic mathematics

which had very little to do with reality, the committee discovered it had protected, at least on paper, 74.07 per cent of united India's Muslims.

(6) Sir Sikandar Hayat Khan's scheme. Seven zones in a united India: Assam and Bengal, with Sikkim; Bihar and Orissa; UP and UP states; Madras, Travancore, Coorg; Bombay, Hyderabad, Mysore and all the states here; Rajputana, Gwalior and central India, Bihar, Orissa, CP and Berar states; and Punjab, Sind, Frontier, Kashmir, Baluchistan, Bikaner, Jaisalmer and Punjab states in the last zone.

When Sir Sikandar finally realized that Jinnah would settle for nothing less than a sovereign Pakistan, he broke with the League and made his oft-quoted statement in the Punjab Legislature on 4 March 1941: 'We do not ask for freedom that there may be Muslim Raj here and Hindu Raj elsewhere. If that is what Pakistan means I will have nothing to do with it.' Sir Sikandar was the man who had drafted the 1940 resolution; but he passed away, and others continued to fudge and promote Jinnah's crusade for partition. Their confusion before the Cabinet Mission was nothing but a reflection of the contradictions that surrounded the Pakistan idea, the most critical one being that Jinnah's boundaries could never in fact serve the declared purpose for the creation of Pakistan: the protection of Muslims in Hindu-majority provinces. No wonder A. V. Alexander commented in his diary for 16 April 1946, referring to Jinnah: 'I have never seen a man with such a mind twisting and turning to avoid as far as possible direct answers.'

The story of the Cabinet Mission discussions could fill a book by itself, such are the twists and devious turns, so complicated are the squabbles and interpretations of every word. To make the story a trifle simpler: the Mission came with the purpose of setting up an Interim Government till full freedom and deciding the procedure for the preparation of the new Constitution for a free India. No Britisher, except for the Viceroy, would be a member of the Interim Government. The Congress wanted united India, the League a Pakistan. After two weeks of running around the familiar bushes, Jinnah was told that Pakistan would mean at best divided Punjab and Bengal, and no Assam. Instead he was offered Wavell's 'Three-Tier Constitution': a union government confined to control of defence, external affairs and communications; provinces; and groups or sub-federations of provinces. These provincial governments would be virtually autonomous – and a provision was suggested, to satisfy Jinnah, that a province could secede after five years if it wanted. The right to secession being present, Jinnah agreed to consider this as a basis for a settlement. On 15 April, Azad issued a statement explaining why Congress had accepted the idea. (Patel had reservations about whether the Centre could be effective enough with only three subjects, but Gandhi overruled him.) To begin with, Azad said, Pakistan as an idea was a double-edged disaster in his eyes; as an Indian he found it bad enough, but as a Muslim he found it worse. 'As a Muslim, I for one am not prepared for a moment to give up my right to treat the whole of India as my domain and to share in the shaping of its political and economic life.' Indian Muslims would, if they accepted partition, 'awaken overnight and discover that they have become aliens and foreigners'. However, the League propaganda and the 'attitude of certain communal extremists among the Hindus' had created a sense of fear among many Muslims. How could this fear be removed? First, by granting the necessary autonomy to the Muslim-majority provinces to assure them that they could develop as they willed, and yet influence the Centre on key issues. As Gladstone had said: 'the best cure for a man's fear of the water is to throw him into it . . . when India attains her destiny, she will forget the present chapter of communal suspicion and conflict and face the problems of modern life from a modern point of view. Differences will no doubt persist, but they will be economic, not political.'

This, of course, was precisely what Nehru had been saying. In a confidential note on the talks on 15 March, before leaving for Malaya on 17 March, he had said that the British should abdicate, leaving the final authority to a Constituent Assembly, and then questions such as Pakistan would be settled by mutual consent or by a plebiscite on the basis of adult suffrage in any province. (The hangover of this was visible later in his Kashmir policy.) Behind this lay the conviction that the British would take away with them the passing phase of communalism, particularly when the real problems of poverty and development seized the nation's attention.

Despite all the optimism, the second round of talks in May got off to an ominous start. The League and Congress delegations met at the sixty-year-old Viceregal Lodge at 10 a.m. on Sunday 5 May (also, incidentally, Wavell's sixty-third birthday). Jinnah refused to shake either Azad's or Khan Abdul Ghaffar Khan's hand. He shook hands only with Nehru and Patel. The old veto had reappeared; he would not recognize the legitimacy of any Muslim Congressman. He was the sole spokesman. The Mission published its 'Three-Tier' plan on 16 May. A short statement on 25 May clarified some points. On 6 June the League decided to accept the plan. On 16 June the Viceroy announced he had invited fourteen persons to serve on the Interim Government: Sardar Baldev Singh, Sir N. P. Engineer (the attorney-general), Jagjivan Ram, Nehru, Jinnah, Liaquat Ali Khan, H. K. Mahtab, Dr John Mathai, Md Ismail Khan, Khwaja Sir Nizamuddin, Sardar Abdur Rab Nishtar, S. Rajagopalachari, Dr Rajendra Prasad and Sardar Vallabhbhai Patel.

The announcement came as a surprise to the Congress, which had not yet, as a matter of fact, officially accepted the Cabinet Mission plan. Monday 17 June was Gandhi's weekly day of silence. On Tuesday he made his first objections public. Sarat Bose, Subhas Bose's brother, had not been included. Sir N. P. Engineer was a government servant; how was he there? And Nishtar had been defeated in the last elections. But these were not real hurdles. The real problem was that Wavell had arbitrarily conceded Jinnah's demand that only he could speak for Muslims. There was no nation-alist Muslim, no Muslim Congressman, on that list. All the five Muslims were leaders of the Muslim League. It was not a question of Azad or Ghaffar Khan being made a minister. For Gandhi and Nehru and Azad this was a question of life-and-death principle; they could not surrender the very ideological basis of the Congress. The British had already conceded League–Congress parity by keeping the talks tripartite; now, by choosing only Jinnah's Muslims, they were turning Congress into the Hindu party Jinnah had always declared it to be. On 24 June the Congress made it clear that while it accepted the plan in principle it could not accept an Interim Government where the only Muslims were members of the Muslim League. On 29 June the Mission left for London. A caretaker council was set up pending further negotiations. There was only one Indian in the eight-member government: Sir Akbar Hydari.

Jawaharlal took over as president at the All-India Congress Committee in Bombay in the first week of July. When he announced his working committee, some famous names had been dropped –

including that of one man who had challenged him for the presidentship, Acharya Kripalani, and the venerable Sarojini Naidu. He tried to soften the blow by making a special mention of their contribution to the party. Among the surprise newcomers were two good younger friends: Kamaladevi Chattopadhyay and Mridula Sarabhai. Appreciating the ripples this might cause, Nehru assured the world that Mahatma Gandhi had approved the names of such young blood for the working committee.

Nehru now returned to his favourite theme at the AICC on 7 July. The true sovereign body at which every problem would be finally settled, Nehru said, would be a Constituent Assembly; that is where the details of 'grouping', for instance, could be determined once the various provincial leaders made their viewpoints known. There was nothing illogical about this. A Constituent Assembly, by implication, was meant for this purpose. Nor would he, for purposes of agreement, concede any harmony between the ideology of the Congress and the League. Upon reaching Bombay he had said: 'The Congress idea of independence is certainly different from that of what the Muslim League and the Viceroy think.' But it was his comment at the 75-minute press conference at the Congress House on 10 July which set off an uproar. 'We agreed to go into the Constituent Assembly,' he said. 'We agreed to nothing else. True, we agreed to certain procedures for going into it. But we are absolutely free to act.'

Both Patel and Azad were livid. Patel wrote to D. P. Mishra on 29 July 1946 that Nehru's 'emotional insanity' had wrecked everything, and Azad, who had developed a sort of proprietorial right over the Cabinet Mission plan he negotiated, was upset that his work had been undone. In effect, they were reacting really to Jinnah's reaction. Azad admits that these remarks might have been forgotten if Jinnah had ignored them. But Jinnah exploited them to claim that this was the kind of betrayal that minorities would have to face under the Congress, that the whole deal was now off. The point needs to be repeated and stressed that Gandhi and the Congress had already rejected the Viceroy's list for an Interim Government, and had done so three weeks before, on the grounds that it implicitly accepted Jinnah's right to be the sole arbiter of Muslims. It was not Nehru's press conference on 10 July which changed anything, at least substantively. Yet Jinnah decided to use this one statement as 'evidence' of Congress–Hindu–Nehru anti-Muslim politics. On 27 July, Jinnah told the Muslim League Council that now Pakistan was the only option. The new Congress working committee met under Nehru on 8 August to pass a special resolution insisting that the party stood by its 7 July resolution endorsing the Cabinet Mission plan, but Jinnah had got his chance. It is obvious that Jinnah was looking for some way to break the commitment to the Mission plan. If not this press conference, then something else would have cropped up; there were enough differences and suspicions between the Congress and the League to provide many an opportunity. And, as we shall see when the League eventually entered the Interim Government, this co-operation was always hostage to the creation of a Pakistan, simultaneous with British withdrawal. Pakistan was created by Jinnah's will and Britain's willingness, not by Nehru's mistakes.

The game was rather given away by one of Jinnah's most faithful disciples, M. A. H. Ispahani, who has written in his book *Qaid-e-Azam Jinnah As I Knew Him* (1967) that Jinnah began regretting having accepted the Cabinet Mission plan within hours of doing so – long, long, that is, before Nehru's press conference. Jinnah actually sold his acceptance of the plan to his party by saying that it would put the League in a better position to obtain Pakistan. The Mission plan was not a solution for India's unity, but only another step towards partition, at least in Jinnah's eyes. Even when the League eventually joined the Interim Government led by Nehru, it stayed inside only to wreck the experiment and prove that there could never be co-operation between the League and Congress in any Cabinet, hence there was no practical option but separation. Jinnah's speech in Bombay on 27 July 1946 expressed what was in his heart: 'So long as the Congress and Mr Gandhi maintain that they represent the whole of India . . . so long as they deny true facts and the absolute truth that the Muslim League is the only authoritative organization of the Muslims, and so long as they continue in this vicious circle, there can and will be no compromise or freedom.'

Jinnah had by now decided to put into play more dangerous plans to wreck India. He announced that the League would organize a Direct Action Day on 16 August. A correspondent asked him whether it would be violent or non-violent. 'I am not prepared to discuss ethics,' replied the Father of Pakistan curtly.

The world would find out in Calcutta on Friday 16 August.

When millions were dying on the streets of Calcutta and the villages of Bengal from the genocide of Churchill's imposed famine in 1942 and 1943, Hussain Shaheed Suhrawardy was making millions of rupees by selling grain meant for the famished on the black market. 'Crooked', 'conceited', 'dishonest', 'self-seeking', 'careerist', 'unprincipled', 'shifty' and 'unattractive' were some of the adjectives Wavell used to describe him in his diaries. A weakness for silk suits, night-clubs and champagne did not prevent Suhrawardy from being the Muslim League premier of Bengal in 1946.

The Muslim League had never been coy about violence. They were constantly either giving their own, or taking Hindu blood, in their speeches – even the most moderate of them. Nehru was utterly depressed when, on 14 May 1943, he read in his cell that his old friend Khaliquzzaman had said at the League's Delhi session: 'Muslims believe in violence, and League ministries in five provinces will see to it that Pakistan is established in effect.' When the elected legislators of the League met in Delhi early April 1946, Jinnah made each one sign a solemn pledge in the name of Allah that he would do anything necessary to achieve Pakistan. Suhrawardy, always anxious to be extra loyal, asked while moving the pledge resolution: 'What next?' He answered his own question: 'I have long pondered whether the Muslims are prepared to fight. Let me honestly declare that every Muslim of Bengal is ready and prepared to lay down his life' (quoted by Pirzada in *Foundations of Pakistan*, 1969). The cue came on 29 July, with Jinnah's call for Direct Action.

Suhrawardy at once declared 16 August a holiday in Bengal. The other League coalition ministry, in Sind, left it as a normal working day; there was no trouble in Sind on 16 August. One day before 16 August, Nehru made a last bid to settle with Jinnah. On 6 August, Wavell had asked him to submit proposals for an Interim Government; and after accepting the responsibility, Nehru wrote to Jinnah on 13 August from Wardha pleading for co-operation. (Nehru was visiting Gandhi's ashram; at the public meeting to mark Quit India

Day he had predicted: 'We will be free in another year's time.') They met at 6 p.m. at Jinnah's Malabar Hill house. Nehru was willing even to concede the five positions the League had on the first list out of fourteen; all he wanted was that Congress should be allowed to name a Muslim if it so desired in its quota of five. Jinnah simply turned down the idea. Once again, he would not allow Congress to represent any Muslims. Nehru left Jinnah's house in despair. Jinnah had sabotaged the Cabinet Mission plan yet again. Exactly one year later would come partition. And the blood would begin to flow in twelve hours, on the other side of India.

When dawn came on 16 August, Calcutta had frozen into a shell of fear. With first light came processions carrying Muslim League banners, ostensibly for a public meeting to be addressed by Suhrawardy that afternoon beneath the Ochterlony Monument on the spacious park on the banks of the Hooghly river, stretching from Fort William to the palace of governor Sir Frederick Burrows. By seven, these wandering mobs began killing and looting at Maniktolla in the north-east of the city. There were no policemen to be seen, not even traffic policemen. The British brigadier in charge of Calcutta, J. P. C. Mackinlay, had ordered his troops confined to barracks for the day. All government servants had been given an unusual three-day weekend. Calcutta was left naked, for the mobs. In his speech that afternoon, the obese, silk-suited premier urged the looters on, rather than restrain them. Direct Action Day in Bengal, he said, would prove to be the first step towards Muslim emancipation. The killing and rioting were the worst between three in the afternoon and seven, when a sharp shower drove the rioters temporarily off the streets and dampened a few literal fires (as, for instance, at the *Hindusthan Standard*, whose offices at Burman Street had been torched at dusk). Curfew was finally declared only at nine that night. But the riots continued for three days, leaving in their wake a hate so powerful that it was now virtually impossible to control communal violence elsewhere in India. Lieutenant-General Sir Francis Tuker, GOC, Eastern Command, remembers in his autobiography: 'It was unbridled savagery with homicidal maniacs let loose to kill and kill and maim and burn. The underworld of Calcutta was taking charge of the city . . . The police were not controlling it.' When Wavell visited Calcutta on 25 and 26 August, General Sir Roy Bucher, acting army commander (who became C-in-C, Indian Army, 1948–9),

R. L. Walker, the chief secretary of Bengal, and O. M. Martin, his deputy (both from the ICS), all had the same story to tell: that Suhrawardy had been totally partisan in the riots. Bucher had driven with Suhrawardy on 18 August through the city and was shocked by the latter's attitude. Burrows, the governor, even suggested to Wavell that, since Suhrawardy had lost everyone's confidence after these riots, a new coalition ministry should be formed under Azizul Haque. This could be done easily since Suhrawardy's majority depended on the European votes in the Assembly. But Suhrawardy remained in power. The European vote stayed on his side.

By 19 August the army needed masks to ward off the stench of corpses; the government offered five rupees for every corpse collected from the gutters and bylanes of this congested city. Only Englishmen could be seen on the streets, wandering through piles of bodies dumped on handcarts, lying in clusters in lanes or forming an ugly flotilla on the river Hooghly. Thousands of ordinary people, always the victims of extraordinary ambitions, streamed out of this city of death, the first of the waves of human exodus that would leave indelible patterns of sorrow across the land. On 21 August, Wavell informed London that at least 3,000 had died in Calcutta and 17,000 were injured. The official figure was later raised to 5,000 dead and 15,000 wounded; unofficially, the figure was nearer 16,000 murdered, from both communities. (The proportions had evened out by the second and third day.)

The cancer spread quickly. On 23 August, 4 died and 43 were injured in communal clashes in Allahabad. On the 31st the League asked Muslims to observe a Black Day on 2 September to protest the installation of the Interim Government, and on the 1st serious riots broke out in Bombay. Hundreds died. Calcutta began to fester again after Black Day. By 9 September, Hindus had been attacked in East Bengal; and on 10 September, Jinnah complacently said in Bombay that India was on the edge of civil war. By the 14th there were riots again in Bombay, and Dhaka too succumbed to communal violence. The next day, Ahmedabad: two killed, three injured. By the 23rd both Dhaka and Calcutta were in flames again. And so on and on it went. On 10 October came Noakhali – more than 5,000 were to die in a matter of a week in Noakhali and Tippererah. Poor Azad: he had tried frantically to save Calcutta on 16 August, a day he described in his memoirs as the greatest tragedy in Indian history. Now, on 19

October, he pleaded: 'I would make a special appeal to Muslim brethren in East Bengal. Islam enjoins that the protection of one's neighbour is one's religious duty.' But who in the ranks of the Muslim League knew that Islam means 'peace'? Blood was the call of the hour. The riots intensified, now erupting without a pause. On 27 October the Hindus of Bihar began their organized revenge, massacring Muslims indiscriminately in Chapra and neighbouring villages, and by early November the violence had spread to Patna district. On 14 November, Jinnah repeated in a formal statement what he had said so often before: give me Pakistan, or the riots will not stop.

There was little trace of sympathy for the dead, the wounded, the orphaned, the desolate. Stanley Wolpert quotes what Jinnah told a foreign news agency after the Great Calcutta Killing: 'If Congress regimes are going to suppress and persecute the Mussalmans, it will be very difficult to control disturbances.' Where was the question of Congress venality then? Bengal had a League government, not a Congress one. What was Jinnah's solution? 'In my opinion, there is no alternative except the outright establishment of Pakistan.' Contrast this with the reactions of Nehru and Gandhi. On the 26th, to take just one instance from the period's newspapers, Nehru said: 'This new development of violence has ceased to be communal or political. It has become a challenge to every decent instinct of humanity and it should be treated as such.' Gandhi called the violence a 'hymn of obscenity'. Contrast also how the League tackled the riots in Bengal and the Congress in Bihar. Sir Roy Bucher wrote to Nehru on 13 November 1954 in a letter of reminiscence (part now of the Nehru Papers): 'Neither then [in August 1946], nor afterwards, did one member of that [League] Government give me any real assistance in bringing order out of disorder.' And this is how another Englishman recalls the Bihar riots: on 10 November 1946 Wavell noted that Nehru was so overwrought by the attitude of some of his own party men in Bihar, and had had such a rough time with Congressmen who thought the Interim Government under him should be a Hindu raj, that he was 'not far from a nervous breakdown'. (Nehru offered his resignation three times in five minutes before Wavell calmed him down a little. The combination of violence in the country and working with his intractable League ministers in the coalition was to prove too much for Nehru.) As for Gandhi, what he achieved in Bihar, the peace he brought with his personal tours, is something which still seems unbelievable. But the League-inspired riots had a specific political motive: the breakdown of hope in unity, and the alienation of Muslim from Hindu. The very eminent Indian journalist Nikhil Chakravartty, who was an eyewitness to the Great Calcutta Killing, made a most perceptive comment in an article for *The Telegraph* forty years later: 'The Calcutta killing of August 16, 1946, was the harbinger of a new type of organized communal clashes. In the politics of independent India this has persisted, as could be seen in Phizo's attempt at secession at one time and Laldenga's for some time, and more grotesquely in the current bloody clamour for Khalistan.' In other words, this was violence not out of emotion, not even for purely religious reasons, but violence as blackmail, to frighten a nation into accepting a demand for separation. Peace was the hostage, a new nation the ransom.

On 22 August 1946 Nehru wrote a private letter to Wavell, saying:

> Calcutta has been a terrible shock to you and to all of us . . . Our friends and relatives are involved in these bloody murders, and our children and dear ones may have to face the assassin's knife at any time. It is this grim reality that we face. We shall face it of course without shouting, but we are not going to shake hands with murder or allow it to determine the country's policy.

Yet murder would determine policy, as he would find out when he became a vice-president of the Executive Council on 2 September.

On 6 August, Wavell wrote to Nehru inviting proposals for an interim government; Nehru replied affirmatively on 10 August. Two days later the formal announcement was made. Now Nehru, as we have noted, implicitly accepting criticism of his press conference, went the extra mile to persuade the League to join his government. On 13 August he wrote to Jinnah seeking the latter's co-operation. Jinnah rebuffed him. Jinnah in fact had another idea for an interim government, but one which he dared not express publicly for fear of popular wrath. He had however outlined this clearly in a confidential meeting with Major Woodrow Wyatt, an assistant to the Cabinet Mission who had close links with the League (he was a good friend of the pretty granddaughter of Sir Muhammad Shafi, Mumtaz 'Tazi' Shah Nawaz), on Friday 24 May 1946. Jinnah's secret plan was, first, a 'surgical operation' to create Pakistan and India, one ruled by the League, the other by the Congress, with the British controlling the union government for another fifteen years and in charge of defence and external affairs. It was this perhaps which encouraged Wavell to think that the British could remain in India for fifteen to twenty years more, though, in his military view, they would need an additional three to four *British* divisions to do so. As we shall see, the Jinnah–Wyatt plan is not the only surprise to emerge from the twelve volumes of Nicholas Mansergh and Penderel Moon (eds.), *The Transfer of Power* (1981).

On the evening of 20 August, just before dinner, Wavell received Nehru's first list of ministers for the Interim Government. Six Congress nominees were unobjectionable: Nehru himself as Vice-President, Patel, Rajendra Prasad, Rajagopalachari, Sarat Bose and Jagjivan Ram, the Congress answer to Ambedkar. There was no problem over Asaf Ali either, who came in as the ranking Congress Muslim leader after Azad chose to keep out of the ministry. Nehru then made a laborious and not very edifying attempt to fill his Cabinet on the representation principle: Syed Ali Zaheer, president of the India Shia Conference (which had supported the Congress against the League), entered to satisfy his Shia brethren; Dr John Mathai was a Christian; Cooverji Hormusji Bhabha popped in from comparative obscurity on the Parsi ticket; and Frank Anthony came in as president of the Anglo-Indian Association. With Sardar Baldev Singh, nominee of the Panthic Prathinidhi Board, Sikhs were sought to be appeased. One post, for a Muslim, was left blank. The real surprise on the list was not the presence of Sir Shafaat Ahmad Khan, a landowner who had resigned from the League just a month before, but Fazlul Haq, the former Bengal premier. Nehru wanted a list of fifteen, rather than the original fourteen, to include an Anglo-Indian, but Wavell would not agree, so Anthony was dropped. On the morning of 22 August, Wavell strongly advised against including a man like Fazlul Haq. Nehru was clearly trying to side-track the League through ex-Leaguers, not a particularly intelligent thing to do at that point. He dropped Haq's name after the discussion with Wavell, and on 24 August the names of the ministers of the first Interim Government were announced.

Ambedkar displayed his ire by saying on 25 August that the scheduled castes would not obey or respect the Nehru government.

And the Muslim League made its response dangerously clear: Sir Shafaat was stabbed seven times by two League workers in Simla the day the announcement was made. He survived to become health minister but could not join the swearing-in on 2 September.

The 2nd of September was a Monday, Gandhi's day of silence. So he wrote out a message for the man he would describe in his evening prayer at Birla House that evening as the people's 'uncrowned king, Jawaharlal'. The Mahatma wrote to his heir: 'You have been in my thoughts since prayer. Abolish the salt tax. Remember the Dandi march. Unite Hindus and Muslims. Remove untouchability. Take to *khadi*.' Remove poverty. Achieve communal unity. Lift up the harijans. It was the very quintessence of the Mahatma's life in politics. He was living, on that visit to Delhi, in a colony of untouchables. All the ministers came to his hut in the Bhangi Colony that morning, to be garlanded with hand-spun yarn and receive a pat on the back. It was a day on which, Gandhi said, the 'door to *purna swaraj* has at last been opened'.

Jinnah now began to worry that, if the Congress succeeded in making this government work, the doors to his Pakistan might shut. Suddenly the man who had built his reputation around obstinacy became the epitome of conciliation. Wavell, unable to trust a government without his men inside, was as anxious to get the League inside the tent. It was now Gandhi's and Nehru's turn to signal no compromise. Wavell lobbied even the ageing Sarojini Naidu, inviting her for dinner on 10 September and asking her to intervene. On 16 September, Wavell met Nehru and Patel in the morning and Jinnah later. By 25 September, Jinnah had only two demands: make him and Nehru alternate vice-presidents rather than keep it only with Nehru, and settle without loss of prestige. Jinnah was even willing to surrender the sole-spokesman right, pleading only that the League be credited with representing the overwhelming majority of Muslims. Nehru was now openly suspicious of Wavell's motives; it was an attempt to create a 'King's party' inside his government, he thought. But with so much 'surrender' by Jinnah, he was not going to risk being labelled the wrecker of another opportunity to obtain a Congress–League coalition. So he controlled his reservations, and what could not take place in UP in 1937 took place in Delhi in 1946. A Congress–League coalition was announced on 15 October. If there had been a mistake in the press conference of July, this was more than adequate compensation.

The League ministers, however, immediately set about proving that Nehru's suspicions had been totally justified. Even before they had been sworn in, the League nominees began abusing the government they were going to join. On 19 October 1946 the Punjab leader Ghazanfar Ali Khan told a gathering of students in Lahore: 'We are going into the Interim Government to get a foothold to fight for our cherished goal of Pakistan, and I assure you that we shall achieve Pakistan.' When, on 20 October, Liaquat Ali Khan repeated the same ambition in a speech in Karachi, Nehru formally demanded a retraction. Even before the swearing-in, on 26 October, Nehru was weary and disillusioned about the coalition. Nothing happened later to change this. The League openly and tauntingly sabotaged the government. Jinnah, as Wavell found out after an hour with him on 30 October, was once again 'at his most Jinnah-ish' (diaries). When they were not in a coalition with the Congress, the League screamed betrayal and demanded Pakistan. Now that they had been given their share of power, the League screamed 'impossible' and demanded Pakistan.

On 15 November 1946 the Muslim League newspaper *Dawn* had a large headline on its front page: 'Absolute Pakistan the only solution'. It was a quotation from an interview with Quaid-e-Azam Muhammad Ali Jinnah, who also added that he did not approve of the 'present arrangement' – the Interim Government his party had joined hardly a fortnight before. There was nothing even the hated Jawaharlal could have done to ensure such quicksilver changes of Jinnah's mind. Pethick-Lawrence tried to bring some peace through a London summit in December. Some unnecessary last-minute drama apart, it aroused little interest, for everyone knew it would solve nothing, and it didn't. On his way back from the summit, Jinnah stopped at Cairo to tell a pan-Islamic gathering that India would create a Hindu imperialist Raj which would spread its tentacles into the Muslim Arab world if they did not have a Muslim buffer called Pakistan in between.

Gandhi had said before the war that the British would become like the victorious Arjuna of the *Mahabharata*: so weak that a petty robber could loot the man who conquered the Kauravas. Their strength gone, the British decided it was time to scuttle. In a few weeks Clement Attlee would formally call curtains. The most piquant story about the prelude is one of those minor happenings which illuminate major events. Nehru had started a practice of informal discussions among his ministers over tea. It was not necessarily held in his room, but naturally as Vice-President of the Council he was most frequently the host. Nehru had a good political reason for this practice. The formal meetings of the Cabinet included the Viceroy, and he wanted to build a consensus so that they could deal with problems in one voice and gradually sideline the Viceroy into becoming a constitutional rather than an executive head of government. The invitations for tea would go through Nehru's private secretary. When the Muslim League joined, Liaquat Ali Khan at once professed to feel insulted that a mere private secretary had come round with the invitation to tea and refused to go. Rather absurdly, he then began holding his separate tea-sessions with Muslim League ministers. This might be called the only non-co-operation movement which the Muslim League ever launched. It was all a very bitter tea-party.

There is an old superstition in India that a *kaana* (or one-eyed) king inevitably signals the end of a dynasty. Archibald Percival Wavell had only one good eye. By March of 1947 the Field Marshal would be replaced by the Admiral: the last Viceroy and the first Governor-General of free India, Louis Francis Albert Victor Nicholas Mountbatten, a son of royalty with so many Christian names that the Empire's most distinguished newspaper, *The Times*, confused the sequence when printing the news of his birth on 25 June 1900 in its issue of 18 July.

36 Friends and Lovers

The first Vicereine whom Jawaharlal Nehru charmed was Lady Eugenie Wavell, but since she was old, fat and motherly there was never any gossip. After his first long talk with Wavell, on 2 July 1945, Jawaharlal had 'stopped to tea with Q., Archie John and the staff; and they all like him' (from Wavell's *Journal*; he used to call his wife Queenie, hence the Q.). Nehru would swim in the Viceregal Palace during Wavell's time too, but a buzz was heard only when Lady Mountbatten shared the pool. Nehru was far more intimate with the Mountbattens, and enough has been said about their personal friendship for there to be little need for reiteration here. However, everyone wants to know the answer to the Great Question: was the Edwina–Jawaharlal relationship platonic or not? Mountbatten's favourite authors Larry Collins and Dominique Lapierre discreetly skirt the issue in their book tingling with revelations about others, *Freedom at Midnight* (1976), in what is certainly a deferential gesture to the Earl. Mountbatten's official biographer Philip Ziegler is delicate towards the Lady in his classic *Mountbatten* (1985): 'Her close relationship with Nehru did not begin until the Mountbattens were on the verge of leaving India.' Just enough said, and a very good point made: that the politics of the transfer of power had very little to do with the quality of *this* close relationship.

The nearest this author has come to an answer to the Great Question is this lovely story from Russi Mody (son of Sir Homi Mody, governor of Uttar Pradesh from 1949 to 1952), who has capped a brilliant executive career as the powerful chief executive of the mammoth business empire, Tata Steel. He had met, said Russi Mody, Jawaharlal thrice – and each time Nehru did not speak a word to him. The first occasion was during a visit Nehru made to the steel factory at Jamshedpur. As a junior executive, Russi Mody stood at the bottom of the receiving line and got a silent handshake before the great man continued to the next person. The second time was during the meal that day. Nehru was sitting at the VIP table, and Russi was, along with other juniors, serving. He went up to Nehru and asked if he would like more chicken. His mouth full, Nehru nodded a silent thank-you and returned to his food. The third occasion was at Nainital, where Sir Homi Mody was governor of UP between 1949 and 1952. The Prime Minister had come to the hills for a short holiday and was staying with the governor. Sir Homi was very pukka, and when the gong sounded at eight he instructed his son to go to the Prime Minister's bedroom and tell him dinner was ready. Russi Mody marched up, opened the door and saw Jawaharlal and Edwina in a clinch. Jawaharlal Nehru looked at Russi Mody and grimaced. Russi quickly shut the door and walked out. Once again, not a word was exchanged.

Be it on record that the first Prime Minister of India and the last Vicereine of India came promptly to dinner.

When the Mountbattens came to Delhi their marriage was already in trouble. The burden of this job did not help matters. Moreover, Edwina wanted to be as active a Vicereine as her husband was Viceroy, and both were determined to leave a very good impression. One of the first things they did on arrival was to cut the portions served during their meals as a gesture to the famine still stalking India, an idea that would not have occurred to Wavell. They also vastly increased the number of Indians on their guest-lists. Within a fortnight of their arrival they even had Aruna Asaf Ali for tea. Violently anti-British, she needed a prod from Gandhi to accept, but once she met Edwina the two became very good friends. The Mountbattens tried to woo Jinnah too, but the initial response was cold. In contrast, both found Nehru eloquent, warm and human. Nehru had been impressed by the political sense and personal regard the Mountbattens had shown in Singapore; in Delhi the relationship flowered into a genuine friendship that aroused all manner of suspicion. Their relationship is best caught in a photograph taken by Henri Cartier-Bresson in Delhi in 1948. Mountbatten, in full white admiral's uniform, stands at ease in front, while, a step behind him, Jawaharlal and Edwina are laughing loudly at a shared joke: Edwina's laughter circumscribed by some British reserve, but Jawaharlal laughing whole-heartedly, stooping naturally with the effort but looking still at Edwina's face.

The accusation has been too often made, however, that the personal friendship between the two influenced the course of political events. Jinnah gave currency to it first, in his private–public accusations of Mountbatten's 'favouritism' towards Nehru. From some Congress quarters the virulence was no less vicious, with allegations made of a Nehru–Mountbatten conspiracy to solve the problem quickly, using partition as the easiest recourse, so that the ageing Congressmen could get their day in power. Part of the hostility, at least on the Congress side, surely also derived from an inability to appreciate the nuances of a Western attitude to man–woman relationships. Nehru never believed in Gandhian abstinence and, as he once remarked in his *Autobiography*, was amoral about sex. Certainly after Kamala's death he had close friendships with women. His love-letters to Padmaja, in particular, are often quite touching and honestly sentimental though never soppy. (The appendix of Volume 13 of *Selected Works of Jawaharlal Nehru*, 1972, contains a good selection of such letters to 'Bebee dear'.) On 2 March 1938 Nehru wrote to Padmaja from Lucknow:

> You made me promise to write to you. Foolish one, as if a promise was needed, or as if a promise means anything. Would you have me write to you just to keep that promise even though the desire was lacking? And could you prevent me from writing, short of commanding me to do so and my believing in your command, if the desire to write to you moved me? I shall write to you, as I have written in the past, even when you have not replied. For I write, selfish and self-centred as I am, to please myself, though in my vanity I imagine that I might be giving you some pleasure also. You will not write to me, you tell me, lest you say something which might hurt. A word of yours has power to hurt, but have you thought of the pain of having no word from you? Have you thought of the loneliness that is my life, of the shell in which I live, encompassed and cut off, and from which I seek escape in activity?

Ending with 'My love to you', this billet-doux has a flourish as a postscript: 'The flowers are aflame and send you greetings.' But it is the beginning which is a true gem. It was written in reply to a rather long personal telegram from Padmaja. Nehru begins: 'My dear, your telegram has reached me. How foolish and womanlike and extravagant. Or was it a kind of *prayaschitta* or atonement for having made love to Subhas?' The two middle-aged heroes, Nehru and Bose, were obviously competitors in more than politics.

Though edging towards fifty in 1937 Nehru was quite infatuated by the daughter of the family friend, Sarojini. On 18 November 1937 he wrote to Padmaja from Allahabad:

> How terribly near you are all the time to me since the Ajanta Princess [a representation of the sculpture of the Ajanta caves] has come and taken possession of my room. Why is it that I think of you whenever I look at it? . . . How old are you now? Twenty? Oh, my dear, how infantile we are even though the years steal over us. How I long to see your dear face.

Twenty was obviously a personal joke, for Padmaja was born in 1900. On 29 September 1937 Nehru warned her to mark her letters to him 'Personal' to save them from being read by his secretary. The affair continued for many years, maturing gently with time. On 15 December 1940 Nehru wrote to Padmaja: 'It was good to see you. Keep growing younger and thus make up for those who grow older.' And on 20 June 1946 it was his 'Bebee dear' whom he remembered at Domel, the junction of two rivers, the Jhelum and Kishanganga, during a political mission to Kashmir, to help Sheikh Abdullah.

As Nehru grew older, other women entered his life – but many more claimed the honour than actually deserved the privilege. The most extravagant claim was made in the disjointed memoirs of Nehru's controversial special assistant, M. O. Mathai, who joined him in February 1946 and stayed with him (professionally and literally) till a scandal about money forced him to resign in 1959. In 1978, long after Nehru had passed away, and when his daughter Indira was briefly out of power (the circumstances are mentioned consciously; it was a time when the post-emergency environment in India encouraged much licence in the name of freedom), Mathai published *Reminiscences of the Nehru Age*. Mathai alleged that a beautiful woman from Varanasi, claiming to be a *sanyasin* and calling herself Shraddha Mata, seduced Nehru in 1948 and had an illegitimate son by him before she disappeared. In an interview with the famous novelist, journalist and historian Khushwant Singh, for the magazine *New Delhi* in 1979, this lady (now a tantric *sanyasin*) denied the charge of any sexual relationship quite vehemently; though she coyly insisted that she had met Nehru often, that he was most impressed by her, and she believed that if the thought of remarriage had ever arisen in his mind he would have married her, and not any of the other women with whom his name had been linked.

A charismatic personality's reputation is rarely safe in his lifetime; after it, any scoundrel can mock, through the well-known tactics of hint, nudge and half-suppressed smile. Since such stories have become part of the Nehru legend it is necessary for a biographer to confront them, rather than choose the easier option of evasion. Three points however do stand out. First, that Nehru was not a hypocrite: he made no secret of the fact that he lived by a value system which did not consider sex to be a moral sin. Second, Gandhi, who was sharp enough to know what was going on, never demanded *brahmacharya* from the man he nurtured as his heir. This could only be because Gandhi was convinced that Jawaharlal never allowed his private life to interfere with his public one. Third, the people of India could not care less. The propaganda about Nehru's 'affairs' was carried out by his enemies (in the Congress even more than outside) from the time of the 1937 elections onwards in the effort to poison the masses against him, but the people cheated the gossip-mongers by their indifference to such stories. Jawaharlal Nehru led the Congress in five general elections: 1937, 1945–6, 1952, 1957 and 1962. Over a quarter-century, through high drama and low, glorious achievement and stunning, dazing tragedy, he never lost the love and trust of those to whom he had given his life: the people of his country. In fact, the people fell in love even with their hero's friends – as Edwina Mountbatten would find out when the time came to say a heart-wrenching farewell to India.

37 Operation Madhouse

Field Marshal Wavell was a disaster on the battlefield (at least if Churchill, who should know, is to be believed), but this did not prevent him from giving very military captions to his political plans. One of the 'solutions' he submitted to the Cabinet on the complex question of British withdrawal was called Operation Madhouse: simply pack up and leave, province by province, women and children first, then civilians, lastly the army. Clement Attlee's response was to look for another Viceroy. The trouble with the proposed replacement was that Mountbatten did not particularly want the job of undertaker to the Empire, and he put up as many conditions as fell within reason to avoid going to India. The Labour Prime Minister simply accepted the conditions. The most crucial commitment he wanted was that London must have a firm timetable for departure; the Indians must believe he had come to quit, not to continue British rule. Mountbatten got his way on this too. The British would leave no later than 1 June 1948.

Penderel Moon repeats the well-travelled story in his introduction to Wavell's *Journal* that Nehru was so impressed by Mountbatten's air of authority during the negotiations that he asked, 'Have you by some miracle got plenipotentiary powers?'

Mountbatten replied, 'Suppose I have, what difference would it make?'

Nehru answered, 'Why, then, you will succeed where all others have failed.'

There is some dispute as to whether Mountbatten had such powers or not; the point is that he certainly behaved as if he had them. He cut his deadline arbitrarily to half, and Attlee was in no mood to argue with his Viceroy if he could deliver on such a messy mission. But this, in retrospect, is the least of the controversies. What would certainly have created a proper flap, if word had got around, was that the man who suggested Mountbatten's name to Attlee as last Viceroy was none other than Jawaharlal Nehru. This, at least, is the version which Krishna Menon gave to Collins and Lapierre for their book *Freedom at Midnight*. Menon claimed that he had a secret meeting with Sir Stafford Cripps in December 1946 where Menon conveyed Nehru's view that there would never be a solution as long as Wavell was Viceroy and then added that Nehru had suggested Mountbatten's name as replacement. The conversation obviously had to be kept secret to avoid antagonizing Jinnah. Attlee would claim publicly that Mountbatten's name had come to him as an inspiration, but dry socialists like him did not have such Gandhian qualities as conveniently transmitted inspiration.

Nehru may have got the Viceroy he wanted, but the Viceroy could not in the end deliver the India Nehru wanted. Mountbatten says he sincerely believed that partition would destroy India's future. On 10 April 1947, to give one instance, he told Jinnah (all quotations from the period are from Mansergh and Moon, eds., *The Transfer of Power*, Vol. 10, which covers 22 March to 30 May) that 'he was ruining the position of India as a great Power, and forever pulling her down to something below a second class Power'. Just after meeting the Quaid, he met the League's second-in-command (although with Jinnah around there was never much point in being second-in-command), Liaquat Ali Khan, the same day. After requesting, and getting, a pledge of secrecy, Mountbatten got down to *realpolitik*:

> I started off with Pakistan and complete partition of the Punjab and Bengal and Assam. I told him that I had no doubt that the Indian leaders and their peoples were in such an hysterical condition that they would all gladly agree to my arranging their suicide in this way. He nodded his head, and said, 'I am afraid everybody will agree to such a plan; we are all in such a state.' I told him that the worst service I could do to India, if I were her enemy or completely indifferent to her fate, would be to take advantage of this extraordinary mental condition to force the completest partition possible upon them, before going off in June 1948 and leaving the whole country in the most hopeless chaos.

Mountbatten described partition accurately as suicide – and Liaquat agreed, in private. Mountbatten concluded: 'I have an impression that Mr Liaquat Ali Khan intends to help me find a more reasonable solution than this mad Pakistan.'

But if Gandhi would not accept Pakistan, and Nehru hated it as fraud on the people, and the British Lord Mountbatten considered it suicidal and mad, and Ambedkar thought it was such a stupid idea that the Muslims would come running back to India in five years, and Azad saw it as the ultimate betrayal, and even Liaquat Ali Khan was willing to be persuaded out of going that far, then how and why did Pakistan happen? The conclusion is inescapable. The British had given Jinnah a commitment that they would not arrive at any settlement without Jinnah's concurrence, and they would not renege on that commitment unless Jinnah made it possible by withdrawing his demand. Even Mountbatten, for all his friendship with Nehru, admiration for Gandhi and conviction that Pakistan was a disastrous decision, could not step outside the confines of British commitment. In his very first meeting with Jinnah, on 5 April 1947, he made that much clear – to Jinnah's relief, and even elation. This is what the record of Viceroy's Interview No. 35, over 5 and 6 April, tells us.

When Jinnah arrived for his first meeting with Mountbatten he was hostile and 'in a most frigid, haughty and disdainful frame of mind'. Preoccupied and worried, he made a terrible gaffe when the pre-meeting photographs were being taken of the Quaid, the Viceroy and Her Excellency on the lawns of Government House. Jinnah had prepared a rather laboured joke for the occasion; assuming that Edwina would stand between him and her husband for pictures, he had decided to describe the threesome as 'a rose between two thorns'. It might have passed as a less than historic quip were it not for the fact that the Mountbattens stood on either side of Jinnah. The Quaid quite forgot to change his quip and blurted it out, to the astonishment of everyone. It was not until next evening's private dinner that the ice was broken. Jinnah said his set piece – partition – and claimed, as he had done for a decade, that when it came to Muslims he was the only one who mattered. He would not allow Congress to represent India, only Hindu India. Mountbatten responded by saying he was impartial, had not made up his mind, would hear out every side and try out ideas which might calm the situation without demanding the ultimate price. The most significant sentences are the last two in Mountbatten's record: 'I said that I would of course not recommend any solution which was patently unacceptable. He seemed pleased with these remarks.'

This, of course, was it; another Viceroy had confirmed Jinnah's veto power. No wonder he was pleased.

On 11 April, at his thirteenth staff meeting, at 10 a.m., Mountbatten informed his British colleagues Lord Ismay, Sir Eric Mieville, Sir George Abell, Captain Brockman, I. D. Scott, Alan Campbell-Johnson and Lt-Col Erskine Crum. The note of this meeting records:

> He [Mountbatten] had brought all possible arguments to bear on Mr Jinnah but it seemed that appeals to his reason did not prevail. He had pointed out to Mr Jinnah the enormous advantages of retaining an unified India – as one, India could be immensely powerful and in the front rank of world powers. He had asked Mr Jinnah why he could possibly wish to throw away such advantages. Mr Jinnah had not been able in his presence to adduce one single feasible argument in favour of Pakistan. In fact he had offered no counter arguments. He gave the impression that he was not listening. He was impossible to argue with. They had covered the whole ground time and again on every conceivable basis with no progress whatsoever. He had assured Mr Jinnah that he regarded himself as more or less the first head of the Indian state and that it was his sole intention to do whatever was best in the interests of the Indian people. Mr Jinnah was a psychopathic case . . . He added that until he had met Mr Jinnah he had not thought it possible that a man with such a complete lack of sense of responsibility could hold the power which he did.

Strong words. What a thorough condemnation of the personality and politics of Jinnah and partition.

The records of the discussions are extremely illuminating and should be read in detail by anyone interested in the psychology behind the demand for Pakistan. Ismay's own view was that 'the dominating feature in Mr Jinnah's mental structure was his loathing and contempt of the Hindus. He apparently thought that all Hindus were subhuman creatures with whom it was impossible for the Muslims to live.' Hate was the only argument. There was never any other. On 18 April, Mountbatten pointed out that if Jinnah's 'surgical operation' had to be conceded then obviously Punjab and Bengal would have to be divided. Jinnah, who wanted undivided Bengal and Punjab, immediately launched into an explanation of how division would hurt these provinces, wounding their economy and destroying the social harmony there to no purpose. Mountbatten replied that these were precisely the reasons why he did not wish to see India divided – and Jinnah could only exhibit rage in response.

It was, partly, this inability to find a persuasive rationale for Pakistan that encouraged a rash of last-minute new 'solutions'. Suhrawardy, who had done so much damage to Hindu–Muslim relations on instructions from Jinnah, now cooked up his scheme for a united and independent Bengal! He abandoned the concept of Pakistan, and asked the Congress in Bengal and the Forward Bloc (Subhas Bose's party) to join him in a coalition government so that together they could create an independent state, since all Bengalis had common economic interests and a common language and culture. There is an amazing degree of contradiction, an irrational quality, to the decisions and discussions of 1947. The question that will never go away is just this: the British could happily describe, in their private discussions, the Pakistan demand as the greatest disservice to India, and call Jinnah a psychopathic case, but they would not stop talking to him. Whatever the plan, it had to be acceptable to him.

Someone has well described the difference between Gandhi and Jinnah; if the former had a solution to every problem, then the latter had a problem for every solution. What was the legitimacy for Pakistan? Nothing, on the face of it, except a disturbed and dying man's belief that Muslim could not live beside Hindu, a conviction supported by nothing more than the power to incite violence. Nor was Jinnah giving any guarantee that the communal problem would be solved by his surgery of India. After all, the Muslims in the minority provinces would still be where they were, and Pakistan would be formed in Punjab and Bengal and Sind and Frontier where there were Muslim chief ministers or premiers already. What did Suhrawardy in Bengal or Khizr Hayat Khan in Punjab or Khan Sahib in Frontier need Pakistan for? They were already in power. All these leaders, even Suhrawardy at the end, actually *opposed* Pakistan. They were the representatives of the Muslim interest in their provinces and they could not, when the moment of truth came, accept the idea of partition. Dr Khan Sahib and his brother Khan Abdul Ghaffar Khan were Congressmen, bitterly opposed to the concept. Khizr Hayat Khan was a Unionist, successor of Sir Sikandar, and a man Wavell described as the most decent politician in India: high praise, since Wavell had little but abuse for all Indians he encountered. Suhrawardy was a flashy, power-grabbing politician on the other end of the moral scale. From different corners of India, rising out of different cultural milieux, raised on different politics, reared by diverse, even conflicting, hopes, they yet agreed that Pakistan was not in the interest of either India or the Muslims. The most moving comment on what had happened would come, in fact, from Suhrawardy, the last ruler of united Bengal, who, when he laid down office on 12 August 1947, called the partition of Bengal a calamity and hoped that God might grant this land peace 'born not by imposition of power but of the willing hearts of men'. This was the same man who, exactly 361 days before, had let loose the havoc of the Great Calcutta Killings. Only Jinnah wanted his Pakistan – a dream which would turn bitter even in the few months he ruled the country he had created with a British scalpel and the Muslim League sword.

Jawaharlal Nehru and Vallabhbhai Patel have of course been charged with, and held guilty of, loss of nerve and a breakdown of will at a decisive moment in the life of this subcontinent. Could Nehru and Patel have joined Gandhi in rejecting freedom without unity? Did they become victims of fear on one side, and the ache to enjoy office within their lifetimes on the other? Were they convinced that Jinnah would keep the British back rather than let the Congress take over the country, and therefore handed Jinnah Pakistan? They had seen League leaders tell the British that they would prefer the continuation of the Raj to Congress rule in India. Accusations are a simple matter. The truth is a more complex business.

It is not a well-advertised fact that the Congress implicitly accepted the concept of partition even before Lord Mountbatten's converted Lancaster bomber, the York MW102, touched Delhi airport on the afternoon of 22 March. On 8 March 1947 the Congress working committee concluded its deliberations by passing resolutions welcoming Attlee's announcement of freedom, demanding dominion status for the Interim Government, inviting the Muslim League for party-to-party talks and offering a way out for Punjab's 'tragic troubles'. How? 'Therefore it is necessary to find a way out which involves the least amount of compulsion. This would necessitate a division of the Punjab into two provinces, so that the predominantly Muslim part may be separated from the predominantly non-Muslim part.' The words were preceded and succeeded by a lot of brave talk about the unity of the country, but nothing could hide the fact that the Congress was making a very fundamental concession – that a secular government could not guarantee peace in a united Punjab. It had, thus, handed an important victory to Jinnah, whose armed volunteers were seeking to prove just that. Seeking to destroy the Unionist ministry which Jinnah had been unable to defeat at the polls, League thugs had set off tension and violence in city after city, a process in which they were ably helped by the counter-violence of the Rashtriya Swayamsevak Sangh (RSS). On 24 January 1947 the Punjab government under Khizr Hayat, alarmed at the arms they had collected and were using, banned both the Muslim National Guards and the RSS in the province. The League immediately raised a storm of protest: the Guard was its strike force; these were the troopers of the communal offensive who fought in the lanes and bylanes with knives and guns and cans of petrol and the lit match. The Punjab government was forced to withdraw the ban. The process of communal violence now acquired unprecedented dimensions, forcing the Congress to accept the idea of partition of the province into a Muslim-majority West Punjab and Hindu–Sikh-majority East Punjab as the only way out.

It would, however, be a gratuitous insult to the long years of sacrifice made by Nehru and Patel to suggest that their only motivation was to accept division in exchange for power. What they were convinced about now was Jinnah's ability to set a torch to the country, and their inability to control the conflagration. In his first interview with Mountbatten, on 5 April, Jinnah had made his intentions very clear to the Viceroy. To quote the record: 'Mr Jinnah claimed that there was only one solution – a "surgical operation" on India, otherwise India would perish altogether.' As they watched city after city succumb to communal frenzy, Nehru and Patel realized that Jinnah would truly destroy everything if he was not appeased. Nehru's experience in the Interim Government had further convinced him that peace, planning and development were virtually impossible in coalition with the League. The British, on their part, only helped him expand his strength through the end of 1946 and 1947.

The British governor of the Frontier, Sir Olaf Caroe, was in flagrant collusion with the League to topple the Congress government of Dr Khan Sahib. The League's violence in Punjab finally destroyed the Khizr Hayat government by 2 March, forcing the Congress resolution of 8 March. Observers were quick to note the implications. The correspondent of Calcutta's *Hindusthan Standard* sent a story on the very day the resolution was passed noting that there was now nothing to stop another partition of Bengal. With Jinnah having begun his war, and the north in flames from Rawalpindi to Sylhet, the battle for unity was clearly being lost. Pakistan was germinating in this womb of fire. As usual, only one man thought otherwise: Gandhi.

Gandhi was in Bihar on the day the Congress passed the Punjab partition resolution, 'going round with ointment', as Nehru later told Mountbatten, 'trying to heal one sore spot after another on the body of India, instead of diagnosing the cause of this eruption of sores and participating in the treatment of the body as a whole'. If Nehru was caustic, Patel was angry. The disciples had already begun to forget the Mahatma's methods of treatment. Since the start of this madness on Direct Action Day, Gandhi had walked the villages of East Bengal, where his humanism and honesty had touched even Muslim League hearts and brought calm. The Mahatma now turned to Bihar where Hindus had butchered Muslims with appalling venom. Nehru had nothing to be embarrassed about as far as his behaviour was concerned. On his initiative (which included an immediate tour of Bihar) the army was called in and dispersed rioters by firing; his personal anger against the sadists indulging in murder was quite apparent. Gandhi also wanted an inquiry into the behaviour of the Congress government in Bihar, and Congress leaders were upset that he could defame one of their own governments in this manner. But now Gandhi had only one concern: the unity of India. The fate of the Congress he left to Congressmen. He told Hindus at his prayer-meeting at Patna on 9 March: 'You must realize that by your action you have not harmed the Muslims – as you wanted to do – but you have harmed the greater interest of the country and the entire Hindu community itself.' Arson and murder raged in Lahore, Amritsar, Rawalpindi and Multan; but in Bihar, Gandhi wanted Hindus to atone for their sins by liberal donations to the Muslim relief fund. Whatever atrocities by Muslims he had seen in Noakhali, he said, he found repeated by Hindus in Bihar. 'I', said the Mahatma on 8 March, 'represent all religions and I am as true and faithful a Hindu as I am a true Muslim, a true Christian, a true Sikh, and a true Parsi.' On 10 March he argued: 'The mad fury of mob frenzy now going on in the Punjab cannot either achieve Pakistan or protect Hindusthan. It will achieve and retain our own slavery.' The next day he set off for the villages of Jehanabad and Gaya.

The leaders of India may have been lost in their different worlds, but the people of India were with their Mahatma. The *Standard*, which reported his tours each day, told a touching story of an unknown villager, a Bengali from the district of far-away Barisal, who appeared one day in the compound of Gandhi's camp in Patna. He had brought with him a dozen oranges. It was his gift of love to the Mahatma, an offering, the most he could give. The camp-followers tried to stop him from meeting the Mahatma, saying Gandhi was too busy, but he simply sat down and would not budge. When Gandhi finally was told about this villager from Barisal, he called the man to his room immediately. The villager spent a little while with his Mahatma, presented the oranges and, happy, took his long road back to Barisal. The correspondent who wrote this story forgot to ask the villager his name – or simply did not think of doing so. Wherever Gandhi went, the anonymous villager was touched and changed by a miracle. In Punjab, Muslims had been looting and killing Hindus and Sikhs; the Sikhs had rallied under Master Tara Singh to retaliate. But in Bihar, Hindu women were rushing to give money and ornaments to the Mahatma for the Muslim Sufferers Fund. UPI filed this report on 11 March from Patna:

> Notes came flying towards Gandhi from all sides and there was a regular rush among the crowd to reach Gandhiji to give their contribution in his hand. Many ladies gave Gandhiji their gold ornaments including rings, ear rings and bangles. After collecting money for twenty minutes Gandhiji said he would again begin collecting tomorrow. As he was about to come out, a tumultuous crowd of men who waited outside the ladies' barricade rushed towards the pandal shouting 'Mahatmaji ki jai'. Gandhiji had again to sit to collect funds from the crowd. The rush was terrible and many caught hold of Gandhiji's hands which made it rather difficult for Gandhiji to collect.

The sheer humanity of Gandhi, his love for his people, was never more evident than in this hour of hatred.

Congress leaders argued that their Punjab resolution was the only way to prevent Pakistan. But the man who mattered did not see things this way. On 12 March, Gandhi told a meeting of more than 50,000 at Mangles Tank in Patna that the Congress resolution was wrong: 'Division of the Punjab, Bengal or of any other province will

mean creation of provinces on religious basis. I do not like partition
or division of provinces like this. This may ultimately lead to the
creation of Brahministan, Dravidistan and other Stans.'

On 30 March, Gandhi interrupted his Bihar tour after twenty-five
days and left for the capital by a third-class bogie specially attached
to the Delhi Express. He had received an invitation to talk to
Mountbatten, who had become Viceroy barely a week before. Now
it was the Mahatma who gave time to the Viceroy, not the other way
round: two hours a day, for a week. He came on 31 March at five in
the evening and, after the pictures for the press, sat down to chat
with the couple. Lady Mountbatten left after an hour so that the two
men could get down to business, but that day Gandhi wanted only to
establish a personal rapport. By 7.15, when he left, they had 'pro-
gressed along the path of friendship'. Soon Mountbatten was calling
Gandhi 'an old poppet', which may not have been the English
synonym for Mahatma but was a distinct improvement on 'charlatan'
and 'old humbug', which were Wavell's private opinion of Gandhi.
The next morning Gandhi arrived half an hour before his appointment, to take a walk in the beautiful gardens of the palace. At 9.30
they drew up chairs in the garden, and now Gandhi began talking
politics. Hindu–Muslim enmity preceded the British, he agreed, but
the imperialists had divided further to rule, deliberately keeping the
tensions alive. He wanted Mountbatten to 'have the courage to see
the truth and act by it, even though the correct solution might mean
grievous loss of life on our departure on an unprecedented scale'.
Then he dropped his bombshell. His solution was: invite Jinnah to
form a central Interim Government at once, on whatever terms he
wished. He would ensure that the Congress and India co-operated.
Mountbatten was staggered.

'What would Mr Jinnah say to such a proposal?' he asked.

'If you tell him I am the author he will reply, "Wily Gandhi",' the
Mahatma responded. It was wily enough as an observation.

'And I presume Mr Jinnah will be right?' the Viceroy asked.

'No,' said Gandhi with great fervour. 'I am entirely sincere in my
suggestion.'

That afternoon, 1 April, at three o'clock Mountbatten met Nehru
and told him about Gandhi's suggestion. Nehru coolly shot it down
as impracticable, and they moved on to other topics. Nehru left at
4.20 p.m. Sardar Patel came at seven, and Mountbatten did not even

mention Gandhi's idea to Patel. The next day Mountbatten sounded out Azad to check Congress Muslim reaction to the idea. Now Azad staggered the Viceroy even more by saying it was a perfectly feasible option, particularly since Gandhi would be able to bring the Congress into line. Patel's thinking, however, was adequately expressed by Rao Bahadur V. P. Menon when he blasted the idea apart as unrealistic if not naïve. The theme of his criticism was summed up thus (*Transfer of Power*, Volume 10, p. 122): 'It is Gandhi's habit to make propositions, leaving many of their implications unsaid, and this method of negotiating has put him and the Congress in difficult positions in the past.' Menon thought that neither Jinnah nor the Congress would accept such a plan. At their ninth staff meeting on 5 April 1947 the Viceroy's top advisers agreed that it was too improbable, and no one mentioned the idea seriously again. On the same day V. P. Menon sent Sir Eric Mieville four copies each of two notes. The first was headed 'Tactics to be adopted with Gandhi as regards his scheme'. The message of this note lay in the last sentence: 'In other words, we must, while keeping Gandhi in good humour, play for time.' The second note was on 'Transfer of Power – possible alternatives'. The crux of this one lay in this sentence: 'If all our efforts to induce the parties to work together on the basis of the Cabinet Delegation Plan fail, it seems inevitable that we shall have to consider some form of Pakistan.' With this rejection of his 'mad' plan, Mahatma Gandhi slipped out of India's politics; but who could take him away from India's heart?

Nehru lulled himself with a convenient illusion. It might be necessary to accept partition now, but India would be certainly reunited later. On 29 April 1947 he wrote to his ambassador in China, K. P. S. Menon: 'I have no doubt whatever that sooner or later India will have to function as a unified country. Perhaps the best way to reach that stage is to go through some kind of a partition now.' Nehru felt drained by the shambles around him as riots tore apart city after city, and soon his chief aim was to rid the country of the man he held responsible for this terrible violence, Jinnah. Then, suddenly, a new and terrible problem loomed ahead – one, moreover, on which he had to maintain total silence.

On the night of 10 May a shocked Jawaharlal Nehru learned of Plan Balkan.

38 Plan Balkan

Sardar Vallabhbhai Patel, the strong man of India, had accepted the idea of partition even before Pandit Jawaharlal Nehru, the romantic. Rao Bahadur Vapal Pangunni Menon's (1894–1966) memory fails him just a little in his book, *Transfer of Power*, as to whether it was in December 1946 or January 1947 that he convinced his favourite minister, Patel, that a united India was impossible, that Jinnah would never agree to anything except Pakistan and that it was better to save what could be saved of India rather than 'gravitate towards civil war'. Menon's view: keep the predominantly non-Muslim parts of Punjab, Bengal and Assam, accept dominion status in the transition phase before a Constituent Assembly could produce the basis for full freedom, deal with the princes without British interference and take over full power as soon as feasible. This, in fact, was what partition was all about, a scheme which Menon calls his plan. After Patel's broad concurrence Menon forwarded it that winter to Pethick-Lawrence with Wavell's permission. Mountbatten saw this plan before he left London for India. But the British were not going to leave without one last stab at something infinitely worse.

The Mountbattens took a short trip to the hills of Simla as another fierce summer descended in the first week of May. Nehru, along with Indira and Krishna Menon, joined them as their personal guests on 8 May and were put up at the Viceregal Lodge. It was an ugly and uncertain time; no one knew quite what was happening, or what would happen. In the chaos of competing ambitions, everyone kept their demands high, their expectations low, and tried to bridge the gap with clamour. Some of the stronger princes thought they could get away with independence in the confusion – and the feudal desire cut across religious lines. The Rajputs of Kashmir or Jodhpur were as keen to keep their states as the Nawabs of Bhopal or Hyderabad. Voices on the extreme wings of the Akali movement had been raised in favour of an independent Sikh state – Khalistan. Trapped between the League's Pakistan and a withering Congress, the Pathans of the Frontier sought independence in preference to merger with Pakistan. Suhrawardy set up a momentum for an independent Bengal, an idea which Jinnah did not mind much because it meant another part of India was lost to Gandhi and Nehru. He told Suhrawardy that he would prefer the Balkanization of India after he got his Pakistan in the north-west; Suhrawardy could keep his Bengal. Jinnah's doctor, J. A. L. Patel, who kept those X-rays in his office safe to protect the dangerous secret, had told him after a seizure in May 1946 that he had only two years left before the lungs gave up. Now only one year remained, and Jinnah wanted his dream before he died. One of the most extraordinary suggestions of that time, however, was made by Brigadier (later General) K. M. Cariappa, who on 9 May called on Lord Ismay and suggested that the British hand over power to the Indian Army in June 1948, with either Nehru or Jinnah as the commander-in-chief (Lord Ismay reported to Viscount Mountbatten, 10 May 1947: 'Cariappa came to see me yesterday and volunteered the amazing suggestion that Indian Army with either Nehru or Jinnah as commander-in-chief should take over power when we left in June 1948. I at once said that proposal was not wholly impracticable but highly dangerous, that throughout history the rule of an army had always proved tyrannical and incompetent, and that army must always be servants and not masters. I added that Indian Army, by remaining united and refusing to take sides, could wield a tremendous influence for good in disturbed days that lie ahead but that they must always be subservient to civil power. I concluded by begging him to put the idea right out of his mind and never to mention it again even in the strictest secrecy.' Ismay adds: 'It is hard to know whether Cariappa in putting forward this idea was ingenuous and ignorant or ingenuous and dangerous.')

On 2 May, Lord Ismay and Sir George Abell flew to London with what is known as Mountbatten's First Draft Plan for the transfer of power to obtain the final approval of the British Cabinet. Mountbatten wanted this by 10 May, so that he could put in a week's preparation; he had marked out 17 May for separate meetings with the princes and the leaders of the political parties, when he would reveal his plan. The princes could be pressured to accept. But if the politicians did not agree, and could not offer an alternative, Mountbatten had decided he would simply hand over power on the basis of this plan and quit. By 10 May word came from London that the Cabinet had approved the plan, with some minor modifications.

On the evening of 10 May, Mountbatten and Nehru retired to the Viceroy's study after dinner for a convivial chat over a glass of port, quite the normal thing to do in British etiquette. They were alone. Mountbatten says that he decided to show Nehru a copy of this secret plan on a 'hunch'. He was not supposed to, of course. On 11 May in a secret telegram to Lord Ismay he explained: 'Last night, having made real friends with Nehru during his stay here, I asked him whether he would look at the London draft, as an act of friend-ship and on the understanding that he would not utilize his prior knowledge or mention to his colleagues that he had seen it'. It was so obviously a sincere gesture from a man of goodwill, who was still perhaps unaware of the extraordinary dimensions of all the decisions waiting to be taken. His staff were strongly opposed to showing the plan to Nehru; they argued that it would be a 'breach of faith' to reveal it to Nehru in advance without showing it to Jinnah too. But perhaps they understood how Nehru would react.

According to this plan, the provinces would initially become successor states; and inevitably this would influence the negotiating powers of particularly the larger princely states, which in any case would have the right to strike deals with the Centre before inte-gration into the Union. The government in Delhi would be weak; with uncertain power being transferred to so many different points in the country, it was difficult to see how an ineffectual and con-tradiction-ridden central government could prevent the civil wars and chaos that would break India into chunks, large and small. (We need to remember that, even after the partition that came, Hyderabad, Kashmir and Junagadh remained outside Delhi's con-trol.) At least a dozen confused nations would emerge, at the very minimum, through this plan. Kashmir, Bhopal and Hyderabad could quite easily have become independent, not to mention Travan-core. There could have been an independent Bengal, and there cer-tainly would have been two Punjabs. The fissiparous tendencies that this in turn would generate can only be imagined. All this was going to be unveiled on 17 May. The ifs of history sometimes stagger one. What if there had been another Viceroy, hostile to Nehru? What if Mountbatten himself had not been sympathetic to the idea of Indian unity? One must appreciate that even he, the most pro-Congress Viceroy of all, had become persuaded that there was no other way to quit India; what if it had been an im-perialist like Wavell still in charge? And the biggest if of all: if Mountbatten had not followed his 'hunch'? But Mountbatten went against the advice of his administration to break this historic secret to his friend, at the cost, no doubt, of what many saw as the long-term British interest.

Nehru did not have the remotest suspicion about what he was going to see when he took the file Mountbatten proffered. They continued their conversation, and he began reading it only when he had returned to his bedroom. He was horrified. Shaking with rage, he stormed into Krishna Menon's room, unable to compose himself. He felt cheated, betrayed. So far the only plan the British had discussed with him had been V. P. Menon's, which course had Patel's approval too. On 8 and 9 May they had formally discussed these proposals at meetings which included V. P. Menon. But even this Indian ICS officer did not breathe a word about the alternative scheme which was certain to Balkanize India, because he was under strict instructions not to. Theories of conspiracy are no longer fashionable, but if the reader has another word for it, he or she is welcome to use it. As recently as that very morning, on 10 May, details were being discussed formally between Nehru, Mountbatten, Mieville, V. P. Menon and Crum at the Viceregal Lodge. The minutes of the Viceroy's eleventh miscellaneous meeting, which started at 11 a.m., begin:

> His Excellency the Viceroy explained that Rao Bahadur Menon had been working on a scheme for the early transfer of power on a Dominion status basis long before he (His Excellency) arrived in India. He said that he would like to give Rao Bahadur Menon an opportunity of explaining the outline of his scheme to himself and Pandit Nehru together. Rao Bahadur Menon said that he had mentioned the scheme to Pandit Nehru the day before; and also about four months previously to Sardar Patel. Both had appeared extremely anxious for the early transfer of power.

At that meeting Nehru accepted transfer of power on the basis of dominion status, and though he claimed that the only real difficulty would be in regard to Pakistan, he said it was now clear Pakistan would have to be conceded. Menon said power would broadly be handed over to two central governments, with their own governors-general, with government on the basis of a suitably amended Government of India Act 1935, till the Constituent Assemblies could work out their own Constitutions. Mountbatten remarked that this process should not be too difficult.

Mountbatten then wrote officially to Nehru:

I have now reached certain conclusions, with which I have reason to believe H. M. G. will agree. I should like to have a final talk about these conclusions before they are announced and I am therefore inviting the following in addition to yourself, to meet me round the table in Delhi at 10.30 a.m. on 17th May. Sardar Patel, Mr Jinnah, Mr Liaquat Ali Khan and Sardar Baldev Singh.

The States Negotiating Committee got a differently styled invitation: at 10.30 Saturday 17 May the Viceroy proposed to start the timetable, and end it with an announcement in Parliament at 16.00 hours Tuesday 20 May. A delay of forty-eight hours might be conceded, but no further, as Parliament would rise for the Whitsuntide recess on 23 May.

When V. P. Menon saw Nehru on the morning of 11 May, he recalls in his memoirs, 'I found that his usual charm and smile had deserted him and that he was obviously upset.' It was a civil servant's understatement. But Nehru was in no mood to talk to a civil servant. He rushed a 'Personal and Secret' letter to Mountbatten. The proposals, he said, had 'produced a devastating effect upon me . . . The whole approach was completely different from what ours had been and the picture of India that emerged frightened me . . . a picture of fragmentation and conflict and disorder, and, unhappily also, of a worsening of relations between India and Britain.' Nehru could not wait to 'give you some indication of how upset I have been by these proposals which, I am convinced, will be resented and bitterly disliked all over the country' (*Transfer of Power*, Vol. 10, pp. 756–7). He sent a long note later, in which he charged London with completely abandoning every previous decision and pledge, of virtually scrapping the Constituent Assembly, of vitiating the central authority which could protect the nation and of engineering the Balkanization of India through successor states which would conclude treaties with Delhi on one side and His Majesty's Government on the other, breeding a rash of Ulsters on Indian soil.

Nehru's violent opposition shook Mountbatten. However, he was now, as he told V. P. Menon, glad he had shown the draft to Nehru and admitted that it would have been disastrous if he had not done so. Menon advised that the best course now was to return and proceed according to his plan. At 11.30 on 11 May a meeting was called by the Viceroy – Jenkins, Mieville and Erskine Crum attending – to discuss Nehru's 'most disturbing' response. (Incidentally, item 3 of this meeting reveals how the Muslim League used power and why it so desperately wanted it. I quote from the Minutes of Viceroy's Twelfth Miscellaneous Meeting: 'His Excellency the Viceroy asked Sir Evan Jenkins why the Nawab of Mamdot had asked to form a Ministry in the Punjab. Sir Evan Jenkins explained that the Nawab of Mamdot was a very stupid man. He was under the influence of some younger men, who were in a fanatical mood. They evidently thought if the Muslim League could take power, they would be able to withdraw the proceedings which were being taken against Muslims and to use the Police force, which [was] 70% Muslim, to suppress the Sikhs.')

Mountbatten then met Nehru alone and agreed that Jinnah would get his Pakistan, with Punjab and Bengal truncated. But power in the rest of the country would be handed to only one central successor government. At 2.15 p.m. there was a formal meeting (where, when the details were being discussed, Nehru introduced the problem of Gurdaspur, with its evenly divided population, and virtually ensured that this critical land-link with Kashmir remained in India). Given that so much would have to be changed, the 17 May deadline would now be too much of a rush. The meeting with the leaders was postponed to 2 June. After a short break, they met again at four; now Nehru's longer note was discussed. Nehru outlined how the plan should be reframed. That night at 9.30 Mountbatten sent Ismay a telegram saying he should stay on in London 'to help with the redrafting of the plan and to pilot through my proposals on dominion status'.

It sounds one of those very dramatic things to say which immediately arouse suspicion, but the record proves beyond doubt that Jawaharlal Nehru, with the help of his friend Krishna Menon, performed a unique and immeasurable service to his country, a service which has not been sufficiently recognized. Nehru had gone to Simla for a pleasant break, not a crisis. It came upon him suddenly. In fact, he was lucky to be there; in Delhi the environment may not have existed for such an exchange of confidence. Only one other man knew what was happening that day, and he too did not disclose the details to a soul: Vallabhbhai Patel, who was being secretly informed through the telephone by his mole, V. P. Menon. That night Menon dined with Mountbatten and found that the Viceroy 'had completely regained his buoyant spirits and good cheer'. There were of course numerous details to be finalized, but in essence a settlement had been reached. Nehru and Patel gave their commitment that they would bring the Congress round; the only trouble was now to force Jinnah to accept a divided Punjab and Bengal. Mountbatten returned to Delhi on 14 May and found an invitation from Attlee to come to London to clear this new plan. The Viceroy consulted Jinnah, Liaquat Ali Khan, Baldev Singh and, for the sake of public consumption, Nehru and Patel. Jinnah and Liaquat were willing to accept the general principles but would guarantee nothing in writing. On 18 May, Mountbatten left for London. The Cabinet approved. The Viceroy and his party returned to India on 31 May. Lord Mountbatten formally presented the plan to the leaders on 2 June 1947. Nehru sat on Mountbatten's right, Jinnah on his left; the rest, clockwise, were Liaquat Ali Khan, Abdur Rab Nashtar, Baldev Singh, Acharya Kripalani and Sardar Patel. This time the deadline was kept.

Seven men came to sit at the Viceroy's round table at ten in the morning. There were still problems to be resolved, in particular regarding the Sikhs, but this was the best consensus anyone could find. Nehru accepted it with the caveat that Congress could never completely approve of it. Jinnah took the same line, leaving the final decision to his working committee. The Viceroy announced that he would make a broadcast the following evening; Nehru, Jinnah and (at Nehru's request) Baldev Singh would follow. The Viceroy had got everyone's agreement. Only one man was left to be persuaded, the man they had all forgotten: Mohandas Karamchand Gandhi.

The leaders' conference ended at five past twelve. Barely were they out when Mountbatten made an urgent phone call to a hut in the untouchables' colony in Delhi. At 12.30, in response, the Mahatma met the Viceroy. Nehru, Patel and Kripalani were at that moment at Patel's residence, planning out their moves for the marathon working committee session that afternoon. The committee had, actually, been in session since 31 May, meeting at the Bhangi Colony where Gandhi was staying, but Gandhi was in an uncompromising mood – he would not accept the division of his motherland. This was his message to those who came to his prayer-meetings, and this is what he told the Congress leaders, now going their own way, leaving, for the first time in their lives, Gandhi behind. Now Mountbatten tried to persuade Gandhi. The Mahatma stayed with the Viceroy till twenty past one, listening, uttering not a word; it was his day of silence.

That long session of the working committee was full of pain, of anguish, of doubt, of reluctance to admit reality and of anger – as younger socialists like Ram Manohar Lohia and Jaya Prakash Narain (specially invited) lashed out at the older men for betraying India and the symbol of Indian unity, Mahatma Gandhi. Gandhi at one point mildly reproved Nehru and Patel for not keeping him fully informed of all the details of the scheme they were accepting, and Nehru tried to claim unconvincingly that he *had* written, broadly, all the details to him. But, aware of Gandhi's total commitment against partition, they had deliberately kept such communication vague. In any case, how was Nehru going to convey to either the Mahatma or the hot-heads, whose fire could not compensate for their ignorance of the details, what he had saved India from? How could he argue, without disclosing truths that might still unsettle events, the shambles and Balkanization he had averted, and convince them that partition into only two countries was perhaps the smallest price of all? The Congress Muslims felt betrayed. Azad, in deep pain, sat morosely and chain-smoked, rarely entering the discussions. Dr Khan Sahib remonstrated. Khan Abdul Ghaffar Khan kept his grief chained to brief sentences, rarely uttered. The Muslim Congressmen felt the tragedy to perhaps a greater degree; it was they in particular who had been destroyed by the steel will of a despot. Kripalani looked weary. Eventually, as party president, he sent the necessary letter of acceptance to the Viceroy.

Jinnah met Mountbatten for an hour from eleven to the midnight of 2 June. As Mountbatten reported to the Secretary of State for India, Listowell: 'Jinnah's delight was unconcealed.' On 3 June, Attlee announced the acceptance of partition in the House of Commons. Nehru, in his broadcast over All-India Radio, said that there was no joy in his heart and still hoped 'that in this way we shall reach that united India sooner than otherwise and that she will have a stronger and more secure foundation'. There was joy in Jinnah's heart, however. He closed his speech on 3 June with 'Pakistan Zindabad!' ('Victory to Pakistan!') but his Urdu accent was so poor that many startled listeners, noted Campbell-Johnson, thought he had said, 'Pakistan's in the bag!' The next day Mountbatten gave a press conference: the first ever by a Viceroy. And also, of course, the last. He now revealed the date of freedom – 'about the 15th of August'. That evening a sad Mahatma met the Viceroy at six, amid strong rumours that he was to break with the Congress. They spent an hour together. 'You and your magic tricks,' Gandhi told Mountbatten; it was a tribute. That evening, at his prayer-meeting,

Gandhi finally ended the doubts about where he stood on partition. Accept Mountbatten's plan, he told the country, but do not blame the Viceroy: 'It was the act of the Congress and the League.' Gandhi wanted united India but was now powerless in the face of Congress acceptance. He too accepted defeat. The next day he repeated his stand: he had his differences with the Congress, but his loyalty to the party was unquestioned. The only forces now opposing partition were the extremists: the Hindu Mahasabha and the RSS, who wanted a Hindu Rashtra from Assam to the border of Afghanistan, and the Muslim extremists, the Khaksars, who wanted Pakistan from Karachi to Chittagong. A Sikh conference in Lahore, even while welcoming division, left an ominous warning – it would accept no partition which did not preserve the solidarity and integrity of the Sikh community.

On 14 June the All-India Congress Committee met to ratify the 3 June plan. Pant moved the resolution; Azad seconded it but could not refrain from touching on the lost dream: 'the division is only of the map of the country and not in the hearts of the people, and I am sure it is going to be a short-lived partition'. Patel, aware, like Nehru, of Plan Balkan, came nearer the truth; if they had not accepted partition, he said, India would have been shattered. Nehru pointed out the prevailing madness of violence, as did Kripalani. Gandhi settled the issue. He had opposed Pakistan, he said, but now he would urge the AICC to accept the plan. The resolution was carried by 157 votes to 29, with 32 abstaining. For the sake of history, Congress, the party of India's freedom, included these lines in its resolution out of what might be called the Nehru thesis:

Geography and the mountains and the seas fashioned India as she is, and no human agency can change that shape or come in the way of her final destiny . . . The picture of India we have learnt to cherish will remain in our minds and our hearts. The AICC earnestly trusts that when the present passions have subsided, India's problems will be viewed in their proper perspective and the false doctrine of two nations in India will be discredited and discarded by all.

It was all over, bar the shouting. Except that the shouting would become an eerie, horrifying wail as the decision to part began to torment and destroy millions of unsuspecting lives. Nehru had clearly lulled himself into believing that the price would be acceptable, that India would muddle through somehow towards 15 August, par-

ticularly now that Pakistan had been conceded. Gopal, in his biography, attributes this to Nehru's faith in the essential nobility of his
countrymen, an unwillingness to believe that they could rape women
and kill men and hack babies on the savage scale they did. But
perhaps there was an element of conscious self-delusion too, a resistance to reality born out of guilt. If it is of any solace, no leader
would suffer more anguish than the emotionally vulnerable Jawaharlal when the subcontinent became a map of horror. Nehru
remained convinced that somehow this partition would be reversed;
the absurdity of it all was simply too difficult to absorb.

What irony, then, that before his death in the autumn of 1948 the
man who had created Pakistan would begin to rail at his blunder! In
the summer of 1947, however, Jinnah was at his most aggressive,
even demanding something as extraordinary as a corridor through
India to connect the two wings of Pakistan; but, well, if you could
demand a country split by a thousand miles of foreign territory then
you could demand anything. Jinnah's corridor was dismissed out of
hand. But the confusion of those months of 1947 would generate a
Pandora's box of ill-fated hopes. The plebiscite in the Frontier, for
instance, would directly influence later Kashmiri ambitions. Despite
the frenzied exploitation of religious passions (Hodson, the British
assistant political agent in South Waziristan, recalls burnt pages of
the Quran being displayed at public meetings as an example of Hindu
violence in Calcutta) only 50.49 per cent of the Frontier voted in
favour of Pakistan. Even so, the concept of plebiscite was given
legitimacy and would haunt Nehru all through his seventeen years as
Prime Minister.

The dominant thought in the minds of Indian leaders was the
desire to restore unity. Gandhi was worried that the specific wording
of the Independence Act would give permanent legitimacy to the
two-nation theory; he had accepted partition as a compromise, not
as a principle. Nehru shared this position. This was one good reason
why he wanted Mountbatten as the common Governor-General of
both nations even after freedom. On 17 May 1947 Nehru and Patel
met Mountbatten at 4.30 p.m. Nehru argued that the Interim
Government should be treated as the Dominion Government, and
the Governor-General should exercise overriding powers on the
treatment of minorities and Pakistan. Jinnah would have none of it,
wisely from his point of view, and took the Governor-General's
position himself, nominating Liaquat Ali Khan as the new country's

first Prime Minister. Nehru, however, needed Mountbatten in Delhi for at least three reasons: as an arbiter in relations with Pakistan; as an authoritative symbol of impartiality during communal tensions; and as a helpful presence in the difficult negotiations regarding the integration of the princely states. Events bore out the wisdom of the decision to ask Mountbatten to stay on as Governor-General after freedom. Mountbatten's influence on the course of the first Indo-Pak War was substantial; his work as head of the Emergency Committee when the long caravans began to trail a gruesome path across Punjab was exceptional; and he was deeply involved in persuading the princes to see reason and accede to India with the minimum fuss.

The last was perhaps the only political problem then which was not communal. In Kashmir a Hindu maharaja wanted to retain his rule over a Muslim majority; in Bhopal and Hyderabad the obverse was the case; and in Travancore a Hindu king of a Hindu-majority state even sent an ambassador-in-waiting to Pakistan. Helped actively by the British Residents and political agents, the princes surrendered only after substantial arm-twisting. Major or minor, these tinpot feudals, whom Nehru generally treated with contempt, did not give up power as easily as their successors might pretend. Many wept openly, and the tough Patel had to send a few threats before some of them signed on the dotted line. There was even conspiracy. Ranged on the border, Jodhpur and Jaisalmer, for instance, began secret negotiations with Jinnah to see if they could get a better deal for themselves in Pakistan. Jinnah was delighted; he handed these princes a blank sheet of paper saying they could write down their conditions. He was willing to offer Karachi as a free port to Jodhpur and independence if it did not accede to India. The prince finally caved in to Delhi after much end-of-empire drama, getting drunk and drawing a gun on V. P. Menon after signing his accession to India. Mountbatten intervened often, and successfully, on behalf of India. V. P. Menon, the Reforms Commissioner, was the operational man, collecting the apples for Patel's bag. By the time 15 August came around, only Hyderabad, Kashmir and Junagadh (infamous for a nawab who cared infinitely more for his pet dogs than for human beings, including the wives in his harem) had not signed the Instrument of Accession and the Standstill Agreement. As Menon says, with legitimate satisfaction, in his book *Transfer of Power in India* (1979), the essential unity and integrity of India had been assured. Of the remaining three, Patel settled the problem easily enough in the smaller state. On 1 November

1947 the Indian Army walked into Junagadh, allowing the capricious nawab just enough time to escape to Pakistan (with his dogs) in his private aeroplane. The other two were a different matter.

The seventh Nizam of Hyderabad had ten titles, the last being the most useful one: Most Faithful Ally of the British Crown. Addicted to opium at night and betel leaves through the day, owner of a fabulous treasure and yet an utter miser, he could not reconcile himself to the fact that the British Crown had fallen. His army was not insubstantial, including heavy artillery and aircraft; and Delhi had to move with some caution. On 21 November 1947 India and the Nizam entered into an agreement similar to that between the British and Hyderabad. The Nizam, Mir Usman Ali Khan, might have his strange foibles (collecting pornography on the one hand and hoarding cash in mice-infested cellars on the other) but he was no fool. He began a crash programme to improve his defence, spending Rs 22 crores in one year (the state's normal annual revenue was Rs 20 crores). He banned Indian currency, stopped the export of bullion and precious metals and began promoting relations with Pakistan, while pleading with the British to make Hyderabad a full member of the Commonwealth. Delhi, on its side, kept up the pressure, demanding full accession or a plebiscite which it would obviously win. Pakistan, in its turn, took out the Muslim card yet again. On 1 June 1948 Jinnah announced on behalf of Muslims 'all over the world' that they would defend the Nizam's right to rule. For all the kudos that Patel would acquire later, he actually conceded a great deal of latitude to the Nizam, including a promise to confer near-sovereign status. On the other hand, till Mountbatten finally left in June 1948 the Nizam also had someone in Delhi who could keep a restraining hand, however mild, over the Government of India. With the last Viceroy's departure, though, all Delhi needed was an excuse. That came with reports of the terror unleashed by the Nizam's private force, the Razakars, on the Hindus. On 13 September 1948 the Indian Army, under the command of Major-General J. N. Chaudhuri, entered the state; by 18 September the last feudal charade, as also the first phase of integration, was over. Nehru would nevertheless be greatly troubled by the second phase, when the demands of identity, language and religion kept threatening to poison the slow evolution of a modern political consciousness.

Much has been made of the tensions between Nehru and his stern and puritanical deputy, Sardar Vallabhbhai Patel. Their differences were hardly new; they had represented different streams within the movement through the 1930s. Patel was the archetypal right-wing Congressman, suspicious of socialism, happier with capitalists and free enterprise and with a propensity for playing the Hindu card. On the communal question, even Gandhi had to rebuke him frequently, particularly during the post-partition riots, even charging him with the ultimate sin – provoking violence. Patel, on his part, made little secret of his view that Gandhi and Nehru appeased Muslims at the cost of Hindus. Patel's sharpest conflict with Gandhi came during the Mahatma's last days. Nehru was very much an emotional Gandhian in communal matters. But the two were totally at one in the central cause: commitment to Indian nationalism. And experience had taught them to respect each other's strength, even while temptation often provoked them to snipe at each other's weaknesses. They were complementary and they knew it. The Sardar did resent Gandhi's nomination of Jawaharlal as the heir but he also understood why Gandhi had done so: Nehru had the confidence of all Indians, rather than of just the Hindus. Nehru was a leader with an international view; he could see as far into the future as into the past, and had the physical strength and sheer will to bear the awesome burden of being the first Prime Minister of modern India. Neither was a child; Nehru and Patel were men in their late fifties and sixties when freedom came. They had not sacrificed their youth in British gaols to squander freedom through immaturity. Yet such was the extent of this belief that even Mountbatten heard that Jawaharlal would, vindictively, drop Patel from his first government.

On 4 August 1947 Nehru sent Mountbatten his first list of ministers. Not only was Patel's name there, but Nehru wanted him named Deputy Prime Minister. Nehru had already written to Patel, on 1 August, describing the latter as 'the strongest pillar of the Cabinet'. Patel replied: 'My services will be at your disposal, I hope, for the rest of my life and you will have unquestioned loyalty and devotion from me in the cause for which no man in India has sacrificed as much as you have done. Our combination is unbreakable and therein lies our strength.' The last sentence is certainly the best commentary on their relationship. Nehru was conscious that his first government should have an all-party rather than just a Congress character. So even the leader of the Hindu Mahasabha, Dr Shyama Prasad Mookerjee, found a place (he was number eleven on the list of thirteen). In order of precedence, as defined by Nehru himself, the list read: Patel, Azad, Rajendra Prasad, Dr John Matthai, Jagjivan Ram, Baldev Singh, C. H. Bhaba, Rajkumari Amrit Kaur, Rafi Ahmed Kidwai, B. R. Ambedkar, S. P. Mookerjee, Shanmukhan Chetty and Narhari Vishnu Gadgil. Rajagopalachari was sent as governor to Bengal, a province which might so easily explode again without firm administration.

On the same day, 4 August, the governor of Punjab, Sir Evan Jenkins, sent an unusual messenger to Delhi: Gerald R. Savage, a police officer in the CID. Savage first told his story to George Abell over breakfast on the 4th. When Mountbatten heard it later, he kept back Jinnah, Liaquat and Patel after a Partition Council meeting and asked them to listen to what Savage had to relate. On 4 June the Punjab CID had arrested a man called Pritam Singh, ex-member of the Indian National Army, for causing disturbances. Pritam Singh revealed under interrogation how the Rashtriya Swayamsevak Sangh, in co-operation with Sikh groups under Master Tara Singh, was organizing the violence against Muslims, producing bombs and even planning to attack headworks of canals. This led to the arrest of Kuldip Singh, an RSS member since February, for planting the bomb which exploded in Lahore's Crown Talkies. Kuldip Singh spilled the name of another man in the chain: Gopal Rai Khosla, a clerk in the Lahore secretariat. Khosla was a middleman for purchasing rifles and grenades and kept in contact with Master Tara Singh directly. Tara Singh, he said, was collecting arms with the help of the Raja of Faridkot and was planning to blow up trains carrying Muslim refugees to Pakistan. His most important plan, however, was not the murder of refugees but the assassination of Jinnah during the festive ceremonies in Pakistan's new capital, Karachi, on 15 August.

Punjab was not the only place where an assassination conspiracy was being hatched.

The front page of most newspapers in India on 15 August echoed with triumph. But one newspaper had a blank space where a front-page editorial usually appeared; the white was enclosed by black bands of sorrow. The name of the paper was *Hindu Rashtra* (*Hindu Nation*). Its editor was a 37-year-old bachelor, Nathuram Godse. On the morning of 15 August he was in Pune, addressing a band of about 500 followers. The flag that they saluted on the first day of freedom was not the tricolour but a saffron triangle with a swastika on it: the standard of the RSS. They vowed that day to give their lives to their Motherland and swore hatred against the Congress, which had allowed the Motherland to be divided, and Gandhi, the man who appeased these treacherous Muslims.

Mountbatten had to play midwife to two nations. As he wrote in his secret personal report on 16 August: 'This last week of British rule in India has been the most hectic of any.' On the 13th Mountbatten was in Karachi. The Viceroy's programme had to be changed at the last minute because Jinnah (whose knowledge of Islam matched his knowledge of Urdu), quite forgetting that it was the month of Ramzan, had suggested a formal lunch party to honour the Viceroy. This was hurriedly changed to a state banquet for sixty at night, followed by a reception for some 1,500 leading citizens, including, Mountbatten recalls in his 16 August report, 'some very queer looking "jungly" men'. The Viceroy was placed between Fatima Jinnah and Begum Liaquat at the banquet, and they teased him about India's decision to celebrate freedom at midnight on the advice of astrologers. The next day Mountbatten addressed the Pakistan Constituent Assembly, drove in an open car with the state procession and then went to the airport to leave for Delhi. For once, he remembers, 'even the austere Jinnah himself showed some emotion on bidding us farewell'. But this was nothing compared to the joyous scenes the next day in Delhi. At midnight came the appointed hour: the Constituent Assembly met to usher in India's freedom.

One horizon had been reached, and Jawaharlal Nehru was looking at the next. At the midnight hour he spoke to the Constituent Assembly. It was a speech that can emerge only from a lifetime's pursuit of man's ultimate dream, independence. It was all Nehru: a harmony of belief, endeavour and promise strung together in a superb selection of words. After the conch shells launched a new period in the world's history, the leader of the first nation to defeat colonialism in the twentieth century began:

> Long years ago we made a tryst with destiny, and now the time comes when we shall redeem our pledge, not wholly or in full measure, but very substantially. At the stroke of the midnight hour, when the world sleeps, India will awake to life and freedom. A moment comes, which comes but rarely in history, when we step out from the old to the new, when an age

ends and when the soul of a nation long suppressed finds utterance. It is fitting that at this solemn moment we take the pledge of dedication to the service of India and her people and to the still larger cause of humanity.

Which nation could ask for a nobler guide?

'The 15th August', wrote Mountbatten, 'has certainly turned out to be the most remarkable and inspiring day of my life.' His first day as Governor-General of India began at 8.30 with the swearing-in at the Durbar Hall in front of an audience of freedom fighters, princes and ambassadors. They drove the short distance from Government House (it was no longer a Viceroy's House) to the Council Chamber for the formal ceremony. The crowds on the spacious roads outside were extraordinary. The press was so great that the 400-strong Guard of Honour was unable to clear the way for the Viceroy to his coach after the ceremony. But one man that day could turn every wish into a command. Nehru went to the roof and waved to the crowds to go back and let Mountbatten return to his coach. It took the Mountbattens half an hour to cover a distance of five minutes. Slogans of joy followed their own staccato rhythm: 'Jai Hind!' 'Mahatma Gandhi ki jai!' 'Pandit Nehru ki jai!' And, most affectionately, 'Pandit Mountbatten ki jai!'

The event of the day was scheduled for six in the evening: the salute to the new flag of a new country at India Gate. In December 1929 Jawaharlal Nehru had danced around the flagpole on the banks of the Ravi as the Congress, under his presidentship for the first time, demanded *purna swaraj* – freedom. Today, independence had finally come, and Nehru was again the voice of freedom. He did not want the least hint of bitterness. The programme included the formal lowering of the Union Jack and the raising of the tricolour; but Nehru dropped the first when he learned that the sentiments of some British officials still in government service might be hurt. The crowd at India Gate that evening was beyond counting. Bands had been arranged, as well as an elaborate ceremony, but everything was swamped by the crowds. Mountbatten, Nehru and Major-General Rajendra Singh, the Delhi area commander, held a quick consultation and decided that the only thing left to do was to forget the ceremonial and go ahead with the gun salute and the raising of the flag. The people of India were pouring out their long-fettered emotions in a great and beautiful roar of spontaneous rejoicing. As the flag broke against the evening sky, a glorious rainbow suddenly appeared behind it, and to every Indian that rainbow seemed to have just three colours: saffron, white and green. The gods had sent a sign. It was the kind of day of which the dreams of countless generations are made.

One man was missing. And who more than Nehru could miss the man who reduced the day by his absence? Mohandas Karamchand Gandhi had made 15 August possible but he was far away from the pomp and circumstance of Delhi. In his moving message to the nation, Nehru's thoughts were divided between the country he would lead and the man who had been the soul of the freedom movement:

> The appointed day has come – the day appointed by destiny – and India stands forth again after long slumber and struggle, awake, vital, free and independent . . . On this day, our first thoughts go to the architect of freedom, the Father of our Nation who, embodying the old spirit of India, held aloft the torch of freedom and lighted up the darkness that surrounds us. We have often been unworthy followers of his, and we have strayed from his message, but not only we, but the succeeding generations, will remember his message and bear the imprint in their hearts of this great son of India, magnificent in his faith and strength and courage and humility.

This man was sitting in a Muslim's house in Calcutta on the day of freedom, his heart heavy with grief. An official of the Government of India approached him for a message. His reply was cold; he had 'run dry', he said. When the government servant insisted, the Mahatma replied, 'There is no message at all. If it is bad, let it be so.' When the BBC turned up, he said, 'You must forget that I know English.' As he spent 15 August fasting and praying, did he feel that three decades of work had been destroyed by this savage violence, this senseless partition?

And yet there was hope. He himself was the hope. Wherever he went, by some great act of Providence, the seas of violence parted; wherever he stood, a magic circle of peace descended upon the most tortured land. This old man had still one last miracle left in him.

39 A Life That Was the Message

The authorized version of his post-prayer speech at Sodepur ashram, Calcutta, on 9 August said:

> Some Muslim friends and even some Hindus complained that the Hindus seemed to have gone mad; not that the Muslims had become any wiser. But now that the Muslim police and officials were almost withdrawn and replaced by Hindus, the Hindus had begun to believe that they were now free to do what they liked, as the Muslims were reported to have done under the League ministry.

It was so audacious an idea that it would have occurred only to a Mahatma. Gandhi announced on 6 August that he wanted to spend the rest of his life in Pakistan. And meant it. He was in Lahore that day, on his way back from Kashmir. 'The rest of my life is going to be spent in Pakistan, maybe in East Bengal or Western Punjab, or perhaps the North-West Frontier Province,' he told Congress workers. 'My present place is Noakhali, and I would go there even if I have to die. But as soon as I am free from Noakhali I will come to Punjab.' It was not a politician's artifice. He took the cross-country Punjab Mail to Patna, where he planned to check on relief operations being provided for Muslims, before setting off for Calcutta and Noakhali.

He had spent the first week in Kashmir, where he spurned the Maharaja's offer of hospitality and met the people – an astute move on the eve of freedom. The Delhi Express brought him from Patna to Calcutta on the morning of Saturday 9 August, to find that the city was burning. Now the Hindus had begun to take revenge. The Muslims of Calcutta clung to him, pleading all through that Saturday that only he could save them; if he left Calcutta they would be butchered. They came singly and in delegations, common folk and ex-mayors like S. M. Osman, secretary of the Calcutta District Muslim League. It was the leaders of the great Muslim League who were now pleading with Gandhi to save them. And of course he did.

Gandhi agreed to postpone his visit to Noakhali, but told the reporter of the *Hindusthan Standard* that he would definitely be in Noakhali before 15 August. On Tuesday 13 August he cancelled this plan, shifted to a ramshackle residence called Hydari House, open on all sides, in Beliaghata, where Muslims were worst affected, and launched yet another non-violent war for peace. There was one thing very strange in this mission. His latest ally was none other than the swashbuckling leader of the Muslim League who had directed the anti-Hindu massacres of a year before, Shaheed Suhrawardy. The sheer need for survival had forced even this man to come to Gandhi. Before proceeding, one cannot but wonder at the symbolism of what might have been: Jinnah in Karachi on 15 August, Nehru in Delhi and Gandhi in Noakhali; both the ageing antagonists, so different in every way, in the same country, one exulting, the other bowed by defeat but heroic in his determination never to surrender to communal violence. But no matter: what this one man achieved in Calcutta was something that humanity can never afford to forget.

The first reaction was anger: Hindu anger. Young Hindus demonstrated in front of that house, demanding to know where Gandhi was on Direct Action Day. But his presence brought some calm; there was no incident on 14 August. Excess is Calcutta's style. When the city celebrated freedom on Friday the 15th there were quite unbelievable displays of friendship; on this day of freedom, everything that was good surfaced. Hindus and Muslims sought and embraced each other. His face beamed as the Mahatma drove through Calcutta's streets that night, savouring these scenes, accompanied by Manu and Abha Gandhi, Osman and Suhrawardy, who drove the car. Id came on 18 August and was celebrated with a joy that Bengal had not known for some while. By the end of the month Gandhi thought Calcutta had been saved and he could go to Noakhali. Two things made him pause. Suddenly on 31 August the peace in Calcutta was shattered by organized attacks against Muslims. And from the north Nehru sent a frantic message that Gandhi should come to Punjab.

Words are inadequate to portray the madness which had already seized that land of five rivers, all five now flowing with blood. If Patel had reconciled himself to an inevitable and brutal transfer of population, Nehru had not. The trains were coming in from Pakistan full not of refugees but of corpses and scattered, barely stirring bodies of survivors, forgiven by some unbelievable quirk of an arbitrary destiny. The trains going towards Pakistan had their own horror stories to tell, and each day was more proof that no cruelty was beyond the human imagination. Nehru would get nearly physically ill; nothing could have prepared him for this misery which he saw in Lahore and Amritsar. At one moment he would weep with a victim, at another threaten an assailant. He heard in one village he was visiting that a group was planning to attack the Muslims of a neighbouring village the next day. He ordered his bodyguards to personally shoot these men if they dared do any such thing. Such stories about Nehru in these months have become legendary. His home became a sanctuary for terrified Muslims, particularly during the Delhi riots in September; or for young refugees who had lost everything, but still retained some small touch of hope that this man living at 17 York Road might be the difference between disaster and survival. (Two people who joined Nehru's personal secretariat, Vimla Sindhi and Mohan, were refugees from Punjab who had lost everything and come to him for help.)

At about ten on the night of 31 August a group of young men gathered outside Hydari House. They had brought a bandaged man, who they said had been attacked by Muslims. Gandhi was sleeping on his straw mat between Abha and Manu. The young men began to shout abuse, and a sense of impending danger seized the room. Gandhi woke up but lay quietly on his mat. The girls went out and tried to pacify the crowd. The old Muslim lady who owned the house, Bi Amman, and a young relative of hers came out and stood next to the Mahatma. Outside, the crowd swelled. The anger rose. A few stones were hurled, and the window panes were smashed. Gandhi stood up, his hands folded, and walked towards this crowd. Policemen had arrived by now and appealed to Gandhi to leave Hydari House for his safety. They did not know how much longer they would be able to check the crowd. The Mahatma, his hands folded, stood his ground, as did those around him. Someone heaved a lathi at him, which missed. A brick was thrown; it missed Gandhi and hurt the Muslim youth standing bravely next to him. The police redoubled their energies, and very slowly this violent crowd was finally pushed back. The next day the 78-year-old Gandhi announced that he would begin his fifteenth fast. He had undertaken his fasts for major and minor reasons, for long and short durations. This one would end either with peace in Calcutta or with his death, whichever came first.

Rajagopalachari, now governor of Bengal, tried to argue him out of this punishment on a tired body. 'Can you fast against *goondas* [thugs]?' he asked. Tendulkar says Gandhi answered, 'The conflagration has been caused not by the *goondas*, but by those who have become *goondas*. It is we who make them *goondas*. Without our sympathy and passive support *goondas* would have no legs to stand upon. I want to touch the hearts of those who are behind the *goondas*.' And he did. The fast began on the night of Monday 1 September. Gandhi decided that he would forsake even the sour lemon juice in his water which he added to dull the nausea arising from drinking water on an empty stomach. As news of the fast spread, first the leaders came, from every party; then the people, in trickles. They pleaded with him to give up his fast. No. Peace, or his life. Stop killing the Muslims, or he would kill himself, slowly, in a fast of penitence. By dawn on Thursday his pulse was weak, his voice a murmur, and a rumour ripped through Calcutta that he was about to die. That day, it was as if a dam of love had burst. Processions of Hindus and Muslims, separately and together, came to him, begging his forgiveness, pleading with him to save himself. Knives, spears, pistols, crude and sophisticated weapons, were thrown in surrender at his feet. In a barely audible voice Gandhi would tell the Hindus that they must go to Muslim areas and pledge protection. Forget the past, he said, the future was difficult enough. Finally, that evening the governor of Bengal, Rajagopalachari announced that peace had come. No incident had been reported that day. At fifteen minutes past nine Mahatma Gandhi broke his fast with a few sips of orange juice. He would now, he said wearily, go to Punjab. A Muslim League paper, the *Morning News*, commented in wonder: 'He was ready to die so they might live peacefully.' Rajagopalachari thought that not even independence had been as great a triumph as this victory over evil in Calcutta. And Mountbatten sent a grateful message: 'In the Punjab we have 55,000 soldiers and large-scale rioting on our hands. In Bengal our forces consist of one man, and there is no rioting. As a serving officer, as well as an administrator, may I be allowed to pay my tribute to the one-man boundary force!'

When Gandhi was strong enough to leave for Delhi on 7 September he was approached for a message. He wrote down one sentence: 'My life is my message.' He would not return to Calcutta; he was entering the last phase of his life.

The Boundary Commission mapped out the realities of partition. The 95 million Muslims in a total population of 300 million suddenly cracked into three: 60 million in the two wings of Pakistan and a huge 35 million in India. The more frightening statistic came from Punjab: 5 million Muslims were left on the Indian side, and an equal number of Hindus and Sikhs on the Pakistan side. As each survivor relived his searing memories, revenge became the sole rationale. When Gandhi left for Delhi on 7 September the capital was quiet. When he arrived on the morning of 9 September he found a grim Sardar Patel at the station; the familiar quips Gandhi had heard so often from him were missing. He had come to take Gandhi to Birla House instead of to the Bhangi Colony where Gandhi now usually stayed when in Delhi. Reason: Bhangi Colony was being occupied by refugees. Riots had suddenly seized every corner of Delhi. Gandhi was shocked. From this day till he died, Gandhi's life was nothing but a constant tour to refugee camps, to the homes of the ravaged and terrorized: to the Muslim Jamia Milia and the Meo Refuge Camp near Humayun's Tomb one day; and to the Dewan Hall, Wavell Canteen Camp and Kingsway on another to hear the woes of Sikhs and Hindus. On 12 September, for instance, he went to Jumma Masjid where 30,000 Muslims had found a modicum of safety in numbers, and Purana Qila where 50,000 were crowded together. The air was tense as news came that the largest caravan in human history, of some 800,000 people, had left west Punjab on foot for the safety of India. Even the gods were in a bitter mood; the monsoon rains were exceptionally heavy, adding to the misery and filth of a beleaguered city. Nehru and Patel had persuaded Mountbatten on Saturday 6 September to head an Emergency Committee with special powers to restore some order, to bring some sense of management to this awesome task. What the Mountbattens achieved in this period – he in an executive role and she as a tireless organizer of civil and medical services – is enough to earn them a unique place on India's roll of honour. When Mountbatten had left for India barely six months before, his mother had wondered if he would return without an Indian bullet in his back. Now in the first weeks of their freedom the only people safe in the north were the British. The orchestra at

Faletti's Hotel in Lahore, which catered to a British clientele, never stopped playing on any evening, while on the streets there was havoc. Within weeks the toll reached up to 500,000 dead in Punjab, if numbers have any meaning in such a situation. In Bengal, however, a million people crossed the border in comparative peace: thanks to Gandhi.

Nehru worked without pause, sleeping five or less hours each night. Indira bravely entered Muslim areas where no Hindus ventured, alone or with Dr Sushila Nayar, to organize relief. But outside Gandhi's residence each day RSS-inspired groups gathered to chant hostile slogans: 'Gandhi murdabad' ('Death to Gandhi'). The weeks passed, and other enormous problems seized the first government of free India. Gandhi concentrated on his one-point mission – to bring peace. But for once the Mahatma's crusade did not seem to be working. The circulation of the Urdu edition of his paper, *The Harijan*, aimed at the Punjabi Hindu as much as the Urdu-speaking Muslim, had dwindled to a point where he wanted to stop it. On 12 January he told a friend (quoted in Tendulkar, Vol. 8): 'We are steadily losing hold on Delhi. If it goes, India goes, and with that goes the last hope of world peace.' He had made up his mind to resort once more to a saint's blackmail: do or die. A few hours before his prayer-meeting on 12 January 1948 he met Nehru and Patel but gave them no inkling of what he wanted to do. He disclosed his intentions at his prayer-meeting that evening; as in Calcutta, he would fast, and to his death, unless brother stopped killing brother. 'No man, if he is pure, has anything more precious to give than his life,' he said. Today he had no answer to give to his Muslim friends. 'My impotence is gnawing at me of late. It will go immediately the fast is undertaken.'

That same day, four men met in Pune: Madanlal Pahwa, aged twenty, a refugee from Punjab whose horoscope said he would be famous one day throughout India; Vishnu Karkare, thirty-seven, owner of the run-down Deccan Guest House and leader of the local RSS; Narayan Apte, thirty-four, handsome, flashy, charming, the well-groomed chairman of *Hindu Rashtra*; and Nathuram Godse, thirty-seven, homosexual, fanatic, ascetic (addicted only to coffee), follower of Veer Savarkar, editor of *Hindu Rashtra* and a tailor by craft. Their decision: to kill Gandhi.

That was the voice of the extremist, but there was not much

comfort from other quarters either. Sardar Patel was angry when he heard of the fast, because he felt that by doing so Gandhi was deliberately painting Hindus as killers in front of the world. Of course the now predictable stream of people came to persuade Gandhi to give up his fast, but it was no longer unanimous. Another slogan began to be heard too, particularly from refugees: Let Gandhi die. Naturally, Nehru was worried. On the 14th he spent more than three hours at Birla House, in two spells, in the morning and the evening. Sardar Patel and Azad were with him in the evening. As the three stalwarts emerged together in the gathering darkness they saw a group of about thirty refugees chanting 'Let Gandhi die!' Nehru suddenly flared up. As the *Hindusthan Standard* reported on 15 January, Nehru 'brought his car to a halt near the gate and dashed towards the demonstrators shouting, "How dare you say these words! Come and kill me first!" The demonstrators immediately ran away in different directions.'

Nor was the Mahatma's body able to take such punishment easily any more. By the morning of 15 January he had entered the danger zone. There was acid in his urine, and his kidneys were not functioning. In the meantime Gandhi had raised fanatic anger even higher by insisting that the government of India pay the Rs 55 crores it owed to Pakistan by the terms of the settlement at once. Even the liberal Nehru had no wish to pay this sum while there were hostilities in Kashmir, but he was forced to give in.

In Bombay two men bought one-way Air India tickets to Delhi: D. N. Karmarkar and S. Marathe. These were the aliases used by Godse and Apte.

As his condition deteriorated, All-India Radio began to broadcast hourly bulletins about Gandhi's health. Once again, as in Calcutta, as a tear-rimmed nation suddenly began to realize that the old man might actually die, another miracle began. Gandhi was so weak by the 15th that he could barely stir. The brutal pain of hunger had placed an eerie mask on his face. For Nehru it was an impossible situation. The debate on Kashmir had just opened in the Security Council; in domestic politics, Dr B. C. Roy had successfully manoeuvred out Dr P. C. Ghosh from the leadership of Bengal. Muslim distrust of home minister Patel had reached bitter proportions, and he had to go to peace rallies each day himself. The Nizam of Hyderabad's troops were on a rampage, creating fresh bursts of tension in the still peaceful south. By Friday the 16th Gandhi's voice had sunk to a whisper – and that whisper was still saying that he had no wish to live unless there was total peace in India and Pakistan. A bedside microphone carried that whisper to the now huge crowds on the lawns for his prayer-meeting. On the fifth day of the fast Nehru left his prime ministerial problems aside and stayed at the Mahatma's bedside; now and then, when he could no longer hold back his tears, he went to a corner and wept. The Mountbattens came; Edwina was composed during the meeting but broke down as she left. Gandhi's doctors, B. C. Roy, Jivraj Mehta and Sushila Nayyar, issued a bulletin of bad news in the evening. Dr B. C. Roy gave Gandhi a maximum of thirty-six hours to live. A frantic Azad finally extracted specific demands out of Gandhi, on the fulfilment of which he would break his fast: that Hindus would allow the Urs of Khwaja Bakhtyar Kaki, a revered saint of Delhi, to be held peacefully; 117 mosques would be returned to Muslims; Muslims must be able to move about freely, anywhere, even those who had gone to Pakistan and wanted to come back; there should be no economic boycott of Muslims; people should live wherever they wanted. To ask so much for the Muslims on that day was an awesome display of faith. But the people of India loved their Bapu too much to let him down. A Peace Committee of 130 leaders signed a pledge to fulfil the conditions, and 200,000 citizens took a written oath to do everything humanly possible to protect Muslims.

On Sunday, finally, Gandhi relented. Verses were recited from the Quran, *Gita* and Bible, and at 12.40 in the afternoon Maulana Azad extended a small glass of lemon juice mixed with glucose to Bapu. Nehru sat silently beside the Mahatma. Gandhi took a sip, and those in the room raised an old, old cheer: 'Gandhiji ki jai!'

The words emerged only in a whisper. Everyone was too drained.

Peace came to Delhi, but not to the hearts of fanatics. On Friday, Clement Attlee had sent a message to Jinnah requesting him also to try to help break Gandhi's fast. Jinnah had not responded. Nor could the Hindu fanatics forgive this man who sabotaged them each time by rising above hate, and taking the people with him. Each day Gandhi's message went to the people through the unique institution he had created, the all-faith prayer-meetings which anyone could attend – anyone, including killers.

Their first attempt on the life of the Mahatma came within a little more than forty-eight hours after Gandhi's fast: at five in the evening of Tuesday, when very punctually he mingled with the crowds on the lawns of Birla House. The planning was meticulous. Madanlal Pahwa would set off a bomb in front of the Mahatma, an accomplice called Digambar Badge would simultaneously shoot from a window in the servants' quarters about ten feet away from the pavilion where Gandhi sat, and Gopal Godse (Nathuram's brother; Nathuram was down with migraine) would deliver the *coup de grâce* from the same place with a grenade. There were only four policemen on duty at Birla House, but the assassins bungled it. Madanlal was caught after the bomb went off. Gandhi was unperturbed. Nehru came rushing to Birla House when he heard of the incident. The guard was expanded to sixteen policemen. Unfortunately, home minister Sardar Patel's department did not pursue the clues provided by Madanlal Pahwa during his interrogation. He told them that it was a plot involving at least seven Hindu Mahasabha, RSS and refugee elements; by Friday, Madanlal had even given them the names of Nathuram Godse and Apte. But the CID and police still could not prevent the second attempt. Their lack of zeal in pursuing this information would become a scandal.

The day of the remaining jackals came on 30 January, a Friday. Gandhi was a little late because of a long meeting with Patel and decided to walk straight to the prayer ground, across the lawns. As he climbed the four steps to the mound where he sat, he heard a voice say, 'Bapuji, Bapuji' ('Father, Father'). He turned. A young man in a khaki dress faced him. The man bowed his head in a respectful *namaskar* and then shot the Mahatma three times, point blank, with a black Beretta. A stain coloured the livery of India's freedom, as the blood spread across the hand-spun cloth around Gandhi's bare body. 'Hey, Ram!' the Mahatma said, and collapsed. At forty minutes past five Mohandas Karamchand Gandhi was dead. Nathuram Godse had fulfilled his mission. At five minutes to six, in two sentences, All-India Radio told the world that Mahatma Gandhi had passed away. The first sentence informed the world that the father was dead. The second sentence informed India that the assassin was a Hindu.

He had always wanted to live to be 125. On his seventy-fifth birthday the inmates of Sevagram decided to cheer up the place. Tricolour flags flew over every hut, and festoons filled the normally austere ashram. The telegrams came flooding in. When Gandhi got Malaviya's cable of congratulations he complained, smiling widely, 'I want to live for 125 years. But Malaviyaji cut it down by twenty-five years, when he wired to me that I must live for a hundred years.' This wish was, interestingly, based on his deep study of religion, as Gandhi told Dr Zakir Husain and other members of the Talimi Sangh on 16 February 1946: 'The basis for my wish is the third mantra from Ishopanishad which, literally rendered, means that one should desire to live for 100 years while serving with detachment. One commentary says that 100 really means 125.' Service. Detachment. The escape from the burden of hate. A volume of tributes, titled *Gandhiji*, was presented to him on his seventy-fifth birthday. Albert Einstein wrote in his contribution:

> A leader of his people, unsupported by any outward authority, a politician whose success rests not upon craft, not mastery of technical devices, but simply on the convincing power of his personality; a victorious fighter, who has always scorned the use of force; a man of wisdom and humility, armed with resolve and inflexible consistency, who has devoted all his strength to the uplifting of his people and the betterment of their lot; a man who has confronted the brutality of Europe with the dignity of the simple human being, and thus at all times risen superior.

The force was inside, in his convictions, in his faith in non-violence. All through human history, power and violence have been natural partners. Rulers have survived on the strength of armies, and revolutionaries have challenged them through new strategies of counter-violence. Suddenly history produced a man who believed that he could change the rules, that he could transfer power from the most mighty imperial authority the world had ever known to the starving, ill-led, divided masses of his country, and do it with the mantra of non-violence, a message whose embodiment became his own life.

Destiny pitted him against an exact opposite: a fellow Gujarati, a fellow-lawyer and a man equally determined about his goal, Muhammad Ali Jinnah. The paradoxes were both personal and philosophical. Gandhi the Hindu did not drink. Jinnah the Muslim did. Gandhi read the Quran. Jinnah barely knew whether it was

Ramzan or not. Yet these are minor compared to the elemental differences of political philosophy. Gandhi's life was a dedication to unity, Jinnah's to partition, and surely nothing revealed their lives better than the manner in which they died. The world bowed in awe on 30 January 1948. When Jinnah died at twenty minutes past ten on the night of 11 September that same year, he was a lonely and wasted man, with only his faithful sister Fatima at his side. Jinnah's personal physician in his last days, Colonel Ilahi Bakhsh, has recorded that once Jinnah, on his death-bed, blew up at Liaquat Ali Khan, who had come to see him and described Pakistan as 'the biggest blunder of my life'. The story was printed in Peshawar's *Frontier Post* in November 1987 and quotes Jinnah as saying, 'If now I get an opportunity I will go to Delhi and tell Jawaharlal to forget about the follies of the past and become friends again.' It might be only fancy, but one cannot help feeling that if the Mahatma had survived the bullets of the Hindu fanatics he might have brought off one last miracle by melting hearts in the country created by Muslim fanatics. He had begun saying, after all, that he was now ready to go to Pakistan, when they shot him. Einstein wrote in wonder: 'Generations to come, it may be, will scarce believe that such a one as this ever in flesh and blood walked upon this earth.'

In his emotional broadcast to the country, in the deep and silent grief which stilled into calm a nation trembling on the edge of hysteria, Jawaharlal Nehru's words caught the mood of helpless sorrow. He said that 30 January night:

> Friends and comrades, the light has gone out of our lives and there is darkness everywhere. I do not know what to tell you and how to say it. Our beloved leader, Bapu as we called him, the father of the nation, is no more. The light has gone out, I said, and yet I was wrong . . . For that light represented something more than the immediate present; it represented the living truth, the eternal truths, reminding us of the right path, drawing us from error, taking this ancient country to freedom.

Mahatma Gandhi had appointed Jawaharlal Nehru the guardian of this freedom. Nehru was fifty-nine years old in 1948 – not a young age, though his passionate temperament always seemed more appropriate to a younger man. But perhaps a man is never old until he loses his father. Jawaharlal Nehru lost the man he had followed for three decades, from his earliest days in politics. Whether he agreed with his Bapu or not, the light was always there, a comfort, a crutch, taken for granted. Suddenly three bullets had snuffed the light out. Jawaharlal Nehru was left alone in the growing darkness.

40 The First War

One of the happiest holidays that Jawaharlal Nehru ever took was twelve days' respite in the first fortnight of June 1940. The last time the Kashmiri had visited this motherland of beautiful hills, valleys, lakes and glaciers was in the summer of 1917, three months after his marriage. The world was at war in 1917 too, but at least the young Jawaharlal was at reasonable peace with himself. Time had brought fame, but along with it also a whole catalogue of demands. Prison had eaten away so many of those twenty-three years; what was left was devoured by an even more avaricious monster called politics. It was not as if Nehru did not want to holiday in Kashmir; but each time he arranged it something more important always cropped up. In 1939 he had planned a trip with Gandhi; the Mahatma, in fact, had never visited Kashmir, and the disciple was quite anxious to flaunt the glories of his motherland to his Gujarati Bapu. But at the very last minute plans had to be changed, and he flew off instead towards the southernmost tip of the subcontinent, Ceylon.

As the date of this visit neared, great events stirred the world once again. The fate of France was being decided on Europe's battlefields, and the architect of Congress war policy was apprehensive that yet another visit to Kashmir might have to be aborted. He nevertheless decided to forget the fate of nations for a while and carry on. When Paris fell on 14 June, Nehru was in Kashmir, in the company not of Gandhi but of the Frontier Gandhi, Khan Abdul Ghaffar Khan. The two made a fine contrast: Nehru short and dapper in his Western attire (boots, jodhpurs, coat) and the tall Khan ranging through his familiar mountains in the traditional Pathan *shalwar-kameez*. They enjoyed themselves hugely. Nehru delighted in the exquisite beauty of the Amarnath and Liddar valleys and the glaciers he loved to tramp. His descriptions of his holiday on his return (published in the *National Herald* between 24 and 31 July) are a wonderful example of Nehru's English prose, a truly authentic style, in complete harmony with his emotional nature; the prose style was also the man. A famous passage goes:

I wandered about like one possessed and drunk with beauty, and the intoxication of it filled my mind. Like some supremely beautiful woman, whose beauty is almost impersonal and above human desire, such was Kashmir in all its feminine beauty of river and valley and lake and graceful trees. And then another aspect of this magic beauty would come to view, a masculine one, of hard mountains and precipices, and snow-capped peaks and glaciers, and cruel and fierce torrents rushing down to the valleys below. It had a hundred faces and innumerable aspects, ever-changing, sometimes smiling, sometimes sad and full of sorrow. The mist would creep up from Dal Lake and, like a transparent veil, give glimpses of what was behind. The clouds would throw out their arms to embrace a mountaintop, or creep down stealthily like children at play. I watched this ever-changing spectacle, and sometimes the sheer loveliness of it was overpowering and I felt almost faint. As I gazed at it, it seemed to me dream-like and unreal, like the hopes and desires that fill us and so seldom find fulfilment. It was like the face of the beloved that one sees in a dream and that fades away on awakening.

His host and constant companion during those twelve days was a man who had become a good friend: Sheikh Muhammad Abdullah (1905–82), a leader whose courage and sacrifice had already earned him the admiring title of *Sher-e-Kashmir* (Lion of Kashmir) from the people. He had burst into prominence during a popular insurrection against the oppressive rule of Hari Singh, the Dogra Maharaja of Kashmir, in July 1931 and was soon the dominant leader of the major local political party, the Muslim Conference. Mrs Indira Gandhi recalled that she saw him leading a procession on the streets in 1934 during one of her visits to Kashmir. If in those days protest needed courage in British India, it needed heroism in the despotic dictatorships that littered the subcontinent: the fiefdoms ruled by princes and legitimized by the British prop. As Gandhi wrote in his article on Travancore in *The Harijan* of October 1939: 'every Indian prince is a Hitler in his own state. He can shoot his people without coming under any law. Hitler enjoys no greater powers.' Hari Singh, who once in the 1920s had the misfortune of being blackmailed by a common London tart, and acquired a reputation for upstart ex-travagance thanks to parties in which champagne flowed from fountains, was a particularly poor specimen of this feudal breed. Sheikh Abdullah's true achievement was not that he stood up to this tyranny, but that he did so on a nationalist platform. He started the 1930s as a leader of the Muslim Conference, but in that crucial decade when Muslim leaders began to edge towards the temptations of separatist politics the Sheikh travelled in the other direction. Nehru was most impressed by this and befriended the younger man, inviting him over to stay at Anand Bhavan and giving him letters of introduction so that he could meet idols like Rabindranath Tagore at Shantiniketan. Nehru publicly supported Abdullah's politics. In June 1936, for instance, he sent a message to Abdullah (printed in the *Hindusthan Times* of 30 June 1936) which said:

> I am very glad that you and other friends are trying to bring about unity amongst the Hindus and Mussalmans of Kashmir and spreading nationalistic ideas among them as well as the message of political, economic and social reform . . . I wish you success in the work you are doing and through you I wish to convey my hearty greetings to the people of my homeland.

Abdullah's contribution needs to be contrasted with Jinnah's. In Hari Singh, Abdullah had just the foe who could have been played up as a 'Hindu' oppressor of 'Muslims'. Hari Singh, in a sense, was the kind of stereotype Jinnah would have loved to hate. Instead, Abdullah built a united front of Muslims, Hindus and Sikhs and targeted Hari Singh as a feudal despot who was the common enemy of all the people. In 1939 Sheikh Abdullah dropped the Muslim label and changed the name of his party to the All-India Jammu and Kashmir National Conference. As Nehru noted in his articles for the *Herald* after his Kashmir holiday:

> Sheikh Muhammad Abdullah was a real leader of the people, beloved of them, and with vision which looked ahead and did not lose itself in the petty conflicts of the moment. He was the founder and initiator of the movement. At first it began on communal lines and became entangled in many unfortunate occurrences. But Sheikh Abdullah pulled it out of these ruts and had the courage and statesmanship to steer it out of the narrow waters of communalism into the broad sea of nationalism . . . It was a remarkable feat for any person to have brought about this political awakening among the poverty-stricken and helpless people of Kashmir.

Nehru was prescient enough to appreciate that the future would not necessarily be easy: 'Dangers and difficulties still remain – which one of us is free from them? – and he will have to steer carefully and to overcome them.' The words were more prophetic than Nehru then realized.

On 17 May 1947, when they were discussing last-minute touches to the draft announcement on the transfer of power, the father of Pakistan repeated that old Rahmat Ali anagram to the Viceroy. The K in PAKSTAN stood for Kashmir, he explained. The original scheme for PAKSTAN, in other words, never included the half of Bengal which Pakistan did get but it did include the whole of Kashmir, which it didn't. Gandhi and Nehru were not willing to surrender Kashmir to the Muslim League so easily. Both believed that the accession of an overwhelmingly Muslim state to India would destroy the politics of the Muslim League and bring the subcontinent back to the politics of secularism. Technically, of course, this could happen if the Hindu Maharaja of Kashmir signed for India, but that was not the point. As Gandhi put it during his first – and last – visit to Kashmir in the first week of August, he wanted the *ryot* (peasant) to decide the future of the state, not the ruler. Kashmir must join India because the people wanted to do so. The key, then, was in Abdullah's hands. But while the Maharaja dithered and deceived in his effort to maintain his rule into the post-British future, the man who wanted to bring Kashmir to secular India, Sheikh Abdullah, lay rotting in Hari Singh's gaol. It was this more than anything else which frustrated Nehru in the critical months of June, July, August and September. As we shall see, not only was Nehru's mind extremely clear about Kashmir, but he had the foresight to plan far ahead. This foresight kept Kashmir in India.

During the discussions in Simla in May, Nehru insisted (and got his way) that whatever the eventual nature of the post-partition boundaries might be, the road link to the Kashmir valley through Gurdaspur would have to be kept in Delhi's control. Gurdaspur was a district with an evenly divided population which could easily have been awarded to Pakistan, but Nehru insisted to Mountbatten that doing so in effect meant giving Kashmir to Pakistan, for it would put all the land routes in Pakistani territory. Nehru was also worried that the Maharaja might make some pre-emptive announcement and declare independence. He was in touch with Abdullah and knew that the Sheikh would declare for India if given the necessary concessions; a rash move by the Maharaja might upset this applecart. And so, on Nehru's and Gandhi's urging, Mountbatten sent instructions to the

British Resident in Kashmir on 9 June 1947 to use his 'verbal influence' to ensure that Hari Singh did not say or do anything until Mountbatten had met him. Using the pretext of a long-standing personal invitation, the Mountbattens reached Srinagar on 18 June for a working holiday scheduled to last till the morning of 23 June. Mountbatten's advice to Hari Singh was: say nothing, sign the standstill agreement with both India and Pakistan and then join one of the two at least for the purposes of defence, communications and external affairs, basing this final choice upon the will of the people. Gandhi and Nehru repeatedly urged this last aspect, both because it was right and because they knew that Abdullah, as the undisputed voice of the people, would opt for India. If, however, a decision could not be delayed then they made it clear to Mountbatten that Hari Singh should be made to declare for India. On 27 June, in his personal report to London, Mountbatten said as much, adding that Nehru was 'pathological' on the subject. Nehru wanted Abdullah freed immediately so that he could be a party to the discussions, and he had to be restrained from starting a popular movement in Srinagar demanding Abdullah's freedom. Instead, Gandhi went in the first week of August and pointedly spurned Hari Singh's offer of hospitality while accepting Begum Abdullah's welcome. He was garlanded by the Begum on his arrival and stayed as the guest of the National Conference. In the meanwhile Hari Singh kept his word given to Mountbatten and signed standstill agreements with both India and Pakistan – and when freedom came to the rest of the country, Kashmir was independent.

As the weeks passed, Abdullah still remained in gaol, and the question of Kashmir's accession seemed to stagnate, Nehru became increasingly apprehensive. Only Pakistan, he was convinced, could gain by this stalemate created by Hari Singh – for obviously this Maharaja had no clue of the trap he was walking into and the damage he was doing to the Indian cause by his obstinacy. There is a remarkable letter written by Nehru to Sardar Patel on 27 September 1947 (Patel, *Correspondence*, edited by Durga Das, 1971, Vol. 1) which deserves to be quoted at length. The letter proves just how accurate Nehru was about what was going to happen, and about the precise nature of the war-plans being made by Pakistan while Hari Singh lived out his fantasies of independence.

'It is obvious to me', Nehru wrote to Patel,

from the many reports I have received that the situation there is a dangerous and deteriorating one. The Muslim League in the Punjab and the NWFP are making preparations to enter Kashmir in considerable numbers. The approach of winter is going to cut off Kashmir from the rest of India. The only normal route then is via the Jhelum valley. The Jammu route can hardly be used during winter and air traffic is also suspended. Therefore it is important that something should be done before these winter conditions set in. This means practically by the end of October or, at the latest, the beginning of November. Indeed, air traffic will be difficult even before that.

I understand that the Pakistan strategy is to infiltrate into Kashmir now and to take some big action as soon as Kashmir is more or less isolated because of the coming winter.

Whether this strategy succeeds or not depends upon the forces opposed to it. I rather doubt if the Maharaja and his state forces can meet the situation by themselves and without popular help . . . Obviously the only major group that can side with them is the National Conference under Sheikh Abdullah's leadership. If by any chance that is hostile or even passive, then the Maharaja and his Government become isolated and the Pakistani people will have a relatively free field.

Nehru wanted Patel to pressure Hari Singh and get Abdullah released:

I hope you will be able to take some action in this matter to force the pace and to turn events in the right direction. We have definitely a great asset in the National Conference provided it is properly handled. It would be a pity to lose this. Sheikh Abdullah has repeatedly given assurances of wishing to co-operate and of being opposed to Pakistan; also to abide by my advice. I would again add that time is [of] the essence of the business and things must be done in a way so as to bring about the accession of Kashmir to the Indian Union as rapidly as possible with the co-operation of Sheikh Abdullah.

Nehru was right on every point. However, while Patel did manage to pressure Hari Singh into releasing Abdullah, Hari Singh still refused to sign the accession treaty with India. If, after Abdullah's release, he had done so, the whole of Kashmir province would certainly have remained in India, since Nehru would have certainly posted the Indian Army on its borders. But greed and dreams of independent power caused Hari Singh to do the greatest disservice possible to

India. As far as the Sheikh was concerned, he left no doubts about where he stood. In his first public meeting after his release, on 4 October 1947 in Srinagar, he said: 'I never believed in the Pakistan slogan. It has been my firm conviction that this slogan will bring misery . . . what have the four and half crore [45 million] Muslims in India gained through it? . . . Pandit Jawaharlal Nehru is my best friend and I hold Gandhiji in real reverence.' Kashmir wanted a people's government, he said, of Muslims, Hindus and Sikhs.

The Sheikh in fact was staying at the home of this best friend, at 17 York Road, New Delhi, when Pakistan did exactly what Nehru had foretold in his letter written four weeks before to Patel. Before partition, Jinnah's Muslim League saboteurs were backed only by the apparatus of a political party; now they were armed by the might of a state. On the night of 21 October some 6,000 well-armed and ably led raiders slipped through the Jhelum valley and headed towards Srinagar, about 140 miles down a good, motorable road with nothing to stop them except their own mistakes. It was fortunate for India that they made plenty of them. Equally fortunately, Nehru understood what was happening as soon as he got first wind of it, since he had been expecting it, and he wasted not a moment in his response. As it turned out, if Nehru had dithered even for a couple of hours, Srinagar would have fallen, and all would have been lost.

Hari Singh was celebrating the Mahesasura festival in his palace on the night of 24 October when suddenly the lights went off. He learned why soon enough; the powerhouse at Mahura which supplied electricity to the valley had fallen to the raiders. The glorious Maharaja instantly started preparations to flee, leaving the people behind, vulnerable and defenceless.

Delhi learned of the attack through the army. British officers still serving in the Pakistan Army had passed on the news of the raid to their counterparts on the Indian side. Later, during the talks, Pakistan's official position was that it came to know about this 'spontaneous' raid into Kashmir only after the tribesmen had crossed the border and therefore could do nothing to stop it. But this lie was exposed even before it had been uttered. As H. V. Hodson has written in *The Great Divide* (1969), General Sir Frank Messervey, commander-in-chief in Pakistan, was aware of the preparations for this invasion and advised Liaquat Ali Khan against it. He also told other Britishers like Sir George Cunningham that such moves should not be supported. Nevertheless, after a final conference in Lahore between Jinnah, Liaquat and Khan Quaiyum Khan, Pakistan decided to go ahead with this plan.

Nehru got news of this invasion before Mountbatten. He was hosting a dinner for the Governor-General and Foreign Minister of Siam (now Thailand) on the evening of Friday 24 October when he took Mountbatten aside for a moment and told him. Mountbatten summoned a meeting of the Defence Committee for eleven o'clock the next morning. Mountbatten had an additional worry. There were a couple of hundred Britishers living in the valley, and the British officers were convinced that they would be massacred if Indian troops did not fly in immediately.

The chief of the Indian Army, General R. M. M. Lockhart, prepared a report for the Defence Committee which outlined the basic facts about what had happened so far. (The General had been put in the picture even before the invasion by Sir George Cunningham, governor of the NWFP, who had added a postscript in a private letter saying: 'Some people up here have been acting very foolishly. You will know what I mean by the time this letter reaches you.') He now knew. The main incursion had taken place along the Kohala–Srinagar road. Muzaffarabad was sacked on the 22nd. Hari Singh's army of about 8,000 troops collapsed; those who were not defeated either dispersed or deserted. It was in no position to take on the raiders, who had mortars, bren-guns, mines, grenades and anti-tank rifles and were led by able officers. The raiders could have easily established control over the valley before the winter snows closed the passes. India should have been defeated by winter.

The emergency meeting of the Defence Committee did not waste any time. Two historic decisions were taken that day. First, orders were issued to prepare an immediate airlift of Indian troops to Srinagar. Aircraft were requisitioned from the Indian civilian fleet, while BOAC planes brought to help fetch refugees from Punjab were drafted to keep the normal air services through India going. On the political side, Nehru said, the immediate requirement was co-operation between Hari Singh and Abdullah and the creation of a common resistance. Mountbatten suggested an immediate temporary accession to India to legitimize the presence of the army in Kashmir; this would be ratified later by ascertaining the will of the people.

Nehru and Patel were both firm that they would send the army into Kashmir whether the dithering Hari Singh formally requested it or not. No final decision on accession was taken, but V. P. Menon was directed to fly to Kashmir and talk to Hari Singh. Nehru had the full support of Abdullah in all these moves, most particularly over sending troops.

When Menon reached Srinagar that same day, Saturday the 25th, he found the airport deserted but for a few supporters of Sheikh Abdullah bravely maintaining a motley presence. The raiders were now less than a day away from the airport and in fact could easily have taken it already if they had not been tempted by loot and the morbid pleasures of rape and abduction along the way. When Menon reached the palace he found a panic-stricken Hari Singh preparing to flee. Hari Singh told Menon he would now do anything Delhi asked to save his family and his throne. When Menon left for Delhi at dawn the next day he found the airport besieged with terrified Hindus, waiting for some miracle.

On Sunday morning the Defence Committee took stock of the military and the political situation. The commanders were worried about the price the troops would have to pay if the local population, which was Muslim, proved to be hostile. Nehru guaranteed that the troops would find them on their side, because the Sheikh was on their side. In the meanwhile, the British officers had begun to pressure Mountbatten to send, if necessary, the British troops in the army to save British lives in the valley. He vetoed this. He was also in two minds about flying troops to Srinagar, but then was confronted with the determined resolve of Nehru and Patel. The two Congressmen were further reassured by the backing they received from Gandhi, who made it clear that his non-violence did not extend to submission under evil, as was happening in Kashmir. Gandhi compared the small force that was the first to reach Kashmir to the Spartans, and said they would become symbolic of the unity and common interests of all communities in India.

At first light on the morning of Monday 27 October, Operation JAK commenced. One after another more than a hundred aeroplanes, both civilian and of the Royal Indian Air Force, droned out of Delhi airport, ferrying equipment, six days of rations and troops of the 1st Battalion of the Sikh Regiment, which had been posted near Delhi at Gurgaon. By nightfall 329 men were in Srinagar under the command of Lieutenant-Colonel Ranjit Rai. Their orders: secure the airport and keep the raiders out of the city. If they needed transport they should find it locally. When the troops landed, the tardy and sated raiders were about two hours away. Two companies, led by Lieutenant-Colonel Rai himself, set off immediately towards Baramulla to hold them, while the rest set up the defences at the airport. The commanding officer was one of the first to give his life in the war; but he achieved the first and most important objective. The Indians established a bridgehead on the road about seventeen miles from the city, which halted the invasion and eventually saved Srinagar. In the meantime, a force of armoured cars raced up through the Gurdaspur road, crossed the Ravi by a pontoon bridge, sped through the Banihal pass and linked up with Rai's units in remarkable time. By the end of October three more battalions had reached Srinagar. The initiative shifted; the raiders were now falling back.

Officially Jinnah maintained the fiction that Pakistan had nothing to do with the fighting, but of course there was no satisfactory explanation for the many contradictions in his stand. To name but one: he complained that India should have informed Pakistan and sought its co-operation in stopping the invasion, rather than unilaterally sending troops, but he had no answer when asked why he or Liaquat did not send Delhi information about the more than 300 trucks rolling through Pakistan carrying the raiders towards Kashmir. His unofficial offensive having been checked, Jinnah made one more try at forcing the issue. On hearing that Indian troops had landed at Srinagar, he ordered General Gracey, acting chief of the Pakistan Army, to move troops into Kashmir, seize the pass on the Rawalpindi–Srinagar road, move towards the Banihal pass and cut off Kashmir from Jammu and the rest of India. General Gracey refused. He and the British officers still serving had accepted the transfer of power – but clearly only nominally. Although Jinnah was the Governor-General and Mountbatten had no *locus standi* in Pakistan, they made it clear that they would not involve any Britishers in the fighting without orders from London through the man they still considered their Supreme Commander, Mountbatten. Suddenly the advantages of having Mountbatten as Governor-General in Delhi became apparent. The British generals in India, it is certain from Gracey's example, would not have taken orders from Nehru without

Mountbatten's nod, and the Indian Army was still not in a position to dispense with the British generals. (The complete Indianization of the army command would be possible only on 15 January 1949 when Lieutenant-General K. M. Cariappa took over as commander-in-chief; this date is celebrated as Army Day each year.)

Late on the morning of Sunday 26 October, Menon flew to Hindu-majority Jammu, where the fleeing Hari Singh had taken shelter. Menon was carrying a draft letter by which Hari Singh would sign a conditional acceptance of the Instrument of Accession, with the proviso that the will of the people be ascertained when conditions became normal. Menon had to wake up the Maharaja, who had escaped through the night. Hari Singh was ready to sign anything by now. That evening the Defence Committee accepted the accession of Kashmir – with the sting in its tail, plebiscite. However, it was a subconditional sting. It stipulated that this plebiscite would be held only when the law-and-order situation allowed a free election, that is, when the raiders and foreign troops had left Kashmiri soil. Since Pakistani troops are still, at the moment of writing, in possession of a part of Kashmir, this final condition has become a most useful alibi for India in the international diplomatic war over Kashmir, some of whose excesses would put to shame anything done on the military battlefield.

The man who first turned down the idea of a plebiscite was Jinnah, not Nehru. As H. V. Hodson tells the story in *The Great Divide*, when Mountbatten met Jinnah for the first time after the outbreak of hostilities, on 1 November (Nehru was asked to join the talks but refused to go after Pakistan issued a statement accusing India of 'fraud and violence' in Kashmir), the Viceroy offered an immediate plebiscite as the solution, and Jinnah turned it down. With Indian troops there, and Sheikh Abdullah in power, Pakistan would never get the people's vote, he said. Mountbatten then suggested that the plebiscite be held under the supervision of the United Nations – and Jinnah rejected that too! He wanted the plebiscite to be held under joint Indo-Pak control, and not with him and Nehru in charge but with Jinnah and Mountbatten as the two Governors-General in control. This was the first time that a reference to the United Nations was mentioned. As we will see, Mountbatten became totally convinced that only the United Nations could find a solution to the dispute.

Having helped India put the troops into Srinagar, Mountbatten now anxiously wanted to bring the fighting to an end, because he was afraid that a larger war at this stage could destroy the very existence of Pakistan. He told Jinnah that his proposal that the two Governors-General take charge of the plebiscite was unreal because, very simply, they were not equals. He was only a ceremonial head of state whose influence was always subject to the will of his ministers, whereas there was nothing ceremonial about Jinnah's powers. Mountbatten had no illusions about Pakistan's involvement in the Kashmir incursions. At that meeting on 1 November he caught Jinnah out more than once. To give an instance: when Jinnah protested that Pakistan had not been informed of India's unilateral action in sending troops to Kashmir, he reminded Jinnah that Nehru had in fact sent a telegram on 26 October. Jinnah then proposed that both sides should now withdraw at once and simultaneously. Mountbatten countered by asking how Jinnah could guarantee the withdrawal of the tribesmen when so far the official Pakistan position had been that they had no control over this 'spontaneous' uprising. Jinnah rather lamely replied that he could 'call the whole thing off' by cutting off the lines of communication. However, it was not in Britain's or Mountbatten's interest that Pakistan should pay a larger price for this foolishness. Mountbatten clearly became convinced that the *via media* between Jinnah's position on plebiscite and Nehru's position was an independent authority whom both sides could trust. Mountbatten had a sound rationale for pursuing this line, because, when he made the suggestion, all the sides involved – India and Pakistan as the claimants and Kashmir as the prize – had in principle accepted the idea of plebiscite; the only dispute was over how it should be conducted, not whether it should be conducted. The accession to India had very clearly indicated that it would have to be ratified by the will of the people. Gandhi, in fact, at prayer-meeting after prayer-meeting, said that the people of Kashmir must be the final arbiters of Kashmir's destiny. On 26 October, for example, he told his prayer-meeting that he would humbly put it to the rajahs and maharajas that they were not the real rulers of their states, but merely puppets of British imperialism. British power had now gone, and the people had become the real rulers. The people of Kashmir, therefore, must decide, without any coercion, to which dominion they belonged.

The Indian leaders were not aware that the Governor-General of India had introduced the idea of a reference to the United Nations in his talks with Jinnah on 1 November. When Nehru later learned about this he asked all the right questions: under which article of the UN Charter would such a reference be possible? How did, in fact, Pakistan formally enter this dispute at all? All that India was concerned with was driving out the raiders. Patel, of course, was vehemently opposed to the very thought. Their confidence was bolstered by good news from the battlefield. By 8 November, Baramulla had been taken, and the Sheikh had inspired stunning popular resistance to the invaders. The Sheikh was so angry that he asked Nehru to send Pakistan an ultimatum: if it did not withdraw the invaders, India would launch a full-scale war. This was precisely what Mountbatten had feared. He successfully sabotaged any possibility of such action by threatening to resign if India escalated hostilities into a war across the international borders. On 4 November, Nehru turned down the Sheikh's suggestion. But the same Nehru who had achieved such a dramatic victory in the first battle now got bogged down in the war. After having saved most of Kashmir for his country, he could not show the capacity to pursue this will to a logical end. It was not the soldiers who let him down. Morale was high, despite the heavy involvement of regular Pak troops in 1948. (More than two Pak divisions would take part in the fighting.) Lieutenant-General E. A. Vas, who saw action with the Jammu Division (later 26 Division), recalls the courage and commitment of the men and officers in his account of the war, *Without Baggage* (Nataraj, Dehra Dun, 1987). Vas is particularly proud of Brigadier Muhammad Usman, a Muslim officer of the Indian Army, who had to face abuse from Pakistan and suspicion in India, but died a hero on the evening of 3 July 1948 when the enemy shelled Jhangar with 3.7-inch howitzers and 25-pounders. (He was awarded the Maha Vir Chakra, General Vas recalls in his book, a song popular with the serving forces at the time. Two stanzas are reproduced:

> If you're working to excess,
> If you find you're sleeping less,
> If another tot of rum
> Doesn't glow within your tum,
> Please don't crib. It's JAK DIV.

> If you cannot buy a fag,
> If the women won't play tag,
> If the houseboat that you're in
> Won't encourage you to sin,
> Please don't crib. It's J A K D I V.)

Mountbatten intensified his efforts to bring peace in November and December. On 26 November, Liaquat came to Delhi for a Joint Defence Council meeting, creating an opportunity to see Nehru for the first time since 30 September. On the morning of his arrival Nehru received two telegrams sent by Liaquat from Pakistan, in which he accused Abdullah of being a quisling and India of trying to mislead and lie to the world over Kashmir. Nehru was livid. Mountbatten, however, managed to placate him, and a meeting of the Prime Ministers took place at four. Nothing came out of it except a decision that more meetings should take place at lower levels. The pattern of fractious, inconclusive dialogue over Kashmir was set. Public anger, as much as the ire of leaders, was in the meanwhile fuelled by stories emerging from Kashmir of the rape, abduction and pillage which the raiders were indulging in. Mountbatten now became even more convinced that the only way to achieve his single goal – an immediate stop to the fighting – was to make the UN an arbiter. He kept up incessant pressure on Nehru. Eventually, the latter succumbed. On 20 December 1947 the Indian Cabinet finally decided to appeal to the United Nations to force Pakistan to withdraw the raiders. Patel was against doing so, and wisely too. Gandhi did his heir one last service by amending the draft which Nehru showed him and deleting a clause which could be open to misinterpretation, since it suggested that independence was an option India was willing to consider for Kashmir. That was an extremely sensible change, at least from India's point of view, for the moment the matter reached the UN on the first day of the new year the quality and content of the dispute totally changed. The British delegate, Philip Noel-Baker, seized the opportunity, equated India and Pakistan as equal claimants to Kashmir and convinced the Security Council that Pakistan, being a Muslim country, had the moral edge in the dispute. This became the prevalent view all over the world, and nothing that Nehru or Abdullah could now say would do much to alter this perception. By referring to the United Nations, Nehru allowed what was legally a domestic Indian problem to become an international issue. If there was any argument over the ratification of the accession by Hari Singh, then the only parties to the argument could be Nehru and Abdullah; how did Pakistan have any *locus standi*? The reference to the UN gave Pakistan a place in the argument. It was perhaps the most serious error of judgement which Nehru made, and he had no one to blame but himself.

One cannot contain one's surprise at the error, for Nehru had an extremely clear understanding of the Kashmir issue, in both its national and international ramifications. On 3 December 1947 Nehru wrote to Sheikh Abdullah: 'Kashmir has become a symbol of the basic conflict in India. On the decision in Kashmir, one might almost say, depends not only the future of Kashmir, but the future of Pakistan and to a considerable extent the future of India. Thus we are playing for much higher stakes than might appear on the surface.' He was also aware that British neutrality was conditional to British self-interest. On 20 February 1948 he wrote to Krishna Menon pointing out how Britain and the United States were trying to win back the Western influence in the Islamic world, particularly the Arab countries, which had been lost by their Palestine policy. He knew that Ernest Bevin had approached Liaquat to become the West's advocate with the Arabs. It did not take too large a leap of the imagination to appreciate that the quid pro quo would be a pro-Pakistan bias over Kashmir. The mistake was made, however, and its consequences stretched far into the future, to trouble generations long after Nehru's departure from the India he had so lovingly built.

Distrustful of the West, Nehru nominated a country from the Eastern bloc, Czechoslovakia, to the UN Commission on Kashmir. On 13 August 1948 the commission announced its award: an immediate ceasefire; withdrawal of Pak troops and tribesmen; after which India should withdraw the bulk of its troops; and the status of Kashmir would then be determined by plebiscite. The ceasefire came eventually on 31 December, exactly one year after Nehru had referred Kashmir to the UN. But the second condition of the UN solution was never met in Pakistan, so there was never any question of the third and fourth.

The Nehru–Abdullah partnership, once seen as the hope of Kashmir and the promise of India, began to crumble under the acid strain of suspicion in Delhi and shifting ambitions in Srinagar. By the terms of Hari Singh's conditional accession, Kashmir had granted Delhi rights only over defence, external affairs and communications. Abdullah began to make it clear that he would abide solely by the letter of this pact. For instance, he did not want to extend the Supreme Court's jurisdiction over Kashmir. Nehru reacted with distress at what he considered to be deliberate attempts to distance Kashmir from India, but Abdullah furrowed the difference between accession and occupation. He found another reason to complain after the death of the Mahatma: that the Hindu right wing was becoming dominant, and that Nehru was unable or unwilling to challenge it. On 10 July 1950 Abdullah wrote to Nehru:

> While I feel I can willingly go down and sacrifice myself for you, I am afraid as custodian of the destinies of 40 lacs [*sic*] of Kashmiris, I cannot barter away their cherished rights and privileges. I have several times stated that we acceded to India because we saw there two bright stars of hope and aspiration, namely Gandhiji and yourself, and despite our having so many affinities with Pakistan we did not join it, because we thought our programme will not fit their policy. If, however, we are driven to the conclusion that we cannot build our state on our own lines, suited to our genius, what answer can I give to my people and how am I to face them?

The Sheikh had also started to believe that Nehru had begun to compromise with communal forces within his party. He had no illusions about either their strength or their intentions. But instead of co-operating with Nehru and trying to help him, he was encouraged to believe that the time had come to raise the independence bogy.

Nehru, for his part, was stuck in an uncomfortable cleft. On the one side, a lobby bayed that India's national interest demanded action against Abdullah, who had become a closet secessionist. On the other, Abdullah made life difficult by the liberal use of the *double entendre*. With partition such a powerful recent memory, suspicions were easily aroused. Nehru had also begun to suspect that the Americans were encouraging talk of an independent Kashmir, and privately accused Dulles and Adlai Stevenson of egging Abdullah on. Stevenson denied this, and Nehru accepted his word; but the same credit rating could hardly be extended to Dulles. A look at the map will easily show how valuable a military base Kashmir would make in the West's confrontation with communism.

On top of this, Hindu communal forces, which had been routed by Nehru in the 1952 general elections, attempted to resuscitate themselves through a popular movement. Shyama Prasad Mookerjee had formed a new party, the Jana Sangh, and with the help of the RSS, the Hindu Mahasabha, the Akali Dal and the local Jammu Praja Parishad he launched an agitation demanding the 'security' of Kashmir, the rehabilitation of Bengali refugees and a ban on cow slaughter. Master Tara Singh's rhetoric was not a whit less violent now than in his partition phase; he virtually demanded the assassination of Nehru. Nehru thought that old comrades like J.P. and Kripalani would rally to his side in what was fast becoming a national, rather than a government's problem. But they kept to the sidelines. Men like Mookerjee were now of course near-paranoid in their dislike of Nehru, claiming that he was taking India to the edge of disaster by his appeasement of Muslim communalism in its latest incarnation – that of Abdullah.

A web built by many spiders was beginning to demand a victim. Abdullah hid his confusion with inaction, even as he incited more fury with a carefully careless phrase. Faced with the gathering crisis, Nehru tried to cut through the tangle. Tara Singh was arrested. Mookerjee courted arrest. But Nehru's own home minister Kailas Nath Katju proved weak and incompetent – which begs the question as to why Nehru should have given him the job at all. Nehru asked Katju to ban the Jana Sangh if necessary. Released on technical grounds by the Supreme Court, Mookerjee (aided, astonishingly, by government officials) decided to walk illegally into Jammu. Abdullah promptly arrested him and sprinkled fuel on the angry fires by upping his demand to 'full autonomy' for Kashmir. Now misfortune compounded the crisis. Mookerjee, an ill man, died on 23 June 1953 while in Abdullah's gaol. (Nehru was in Cairo, on his way back from a round of international diplomacy, when this happened. Abdullah would later say that he was going to hand over Mookerjee to Delhi on Nehru's return.) Mookerjee's death sharpened emotions on either side. If his supporters now wanted nothing short of Abdullah's scalp, and if possible Nehru's too, for the first time slogans were heard in Kashmir against the Indian Army. Nehru described the situation in a letter to B. C. Roy on 29 June 1953: 'it is for me almost a personal tragedy'. Nehru pleaded with Abdullah to remain the man he was in 1947, and Azad assured him that Kashmir would be guaranteed its special status; but Abdullah was now convinced that even Nehru would not be able to subdue the communal forces in India, and therefore the only option left for Kashmir was to seek some other course. There was no question of Nehru allowing this. Delhi responded by manipulating a split in the National Conference along 'nationalist' and 'secessionist' lines. This duly took place. On 9 August 1953 the government of Sheikh Muhammad Abdullah was dismissed. One of his favourite lieutenants, Bakshi Ghulam Muhammad, became the new Delhi-approved premier of Kashmir. His first decision was to place Sheikh Abdullah under arrest.

Nehru was bitterly disappointed that the man he had pulled out from Hari Singh's gaol in September 1947 should now have to be incarcerated in free and secular India's prisons. Abdullah would in fact remain in prison (except for a brief spell in January 1958) almost till the last days of Nehru's life. The only consolation that Nehru had in 1953 was that a larger tragedy had been averted; his intelligence agencies had told him that Abdullah was on the point of demanding that the Indian Army leave the soil of Kashmir. Nehru had kept Kashmir within India, but the regret that Abdullah had to suffer gaol was a burden he was never able to shake off. This, however, was no longer the Nehru who kept flicking out a letter of resignation when a bout of depression seized him, or whenever reality seemed at odds with the dream. This was a man still filled with ideals but also tempered by a new will that accepted the imperfections of life; the cross was now nothing more than a regular part of a Prime Minister's baggage. The mission of building a new India was too big a challenge to permit the luxury of remorse, or the comfort of retreat.

The Nehru of 1953 was a far harder man, one who had been steeled by many challenges. Perhaps the most serious of them was a revolt against him by the Patel–Prasad forces – one which almost cost him the prime ministership.

Two people outside Jawaharlal Nehru's immediate family called him 'Bhai' ('Brother'). One was the scientist Homi Bhabha, and the other Nehru's young socialist comrade Jaya Prakash Narayan. But while the personal affection lasted, the politics of the two 'brothers' went in separate directions. Freedom released the Socialists from the obligation of supporting the Congress. On 21 March 1948 a special convention of Congress Socialist Party delegates, under the leadership of their general secretary, Jaya Prakash Narayan, resolved at Nasik to resign their primary membership of the Indian National Congress at latest by 15 April and work, alone, for a socialist India. The 1,000-word resolution was passed without a murmur, without even a debate, so strong was the common conviction that the Congress had outlived its utility. The resolution claimed: 'The Congress is in danger because it has an authoritarian bias of being overwhelmed by anti-secular, anti-democratic forces of the Right.' The Socialists, said one of the leaders, Asoka Mehta, were not leaving the Congress because they could not capture it, but because the Congress was no longer worth capturing; it was no longer a liberating instrument, but a limiting force.

Jawaharlal would have happily agreed with much of the diagnosis, but he was totally opposed to the cure. He was convinced that the only way towards socialism was through the Congress, and deeply regretted that honest socialists should rush towards self-destruction with their premature leftism. On 1 July 1948 Nehru wrote to Govind Ballabh Pant: 'He [Jaya Prakash] is one of the straightest and finest men I have known, and if character counts, as it does, he counts for a great deal. It seems to me a tragedy that a man like him should be thrust, by circumstances, into the wilderness.' The Socialists were nothing if not totally convinced about their destiny, about the righteousness of their morality and the rightness of their political line. On 10 December 1948, for instance, Jaya Prakash lectured Nehru in a letter: 'You want to build socialism with the help of capitalism. You are bound to fail in that.' Jaya Prakash was soon accusing

Nehru of imposing fascism in India, particularly after the ban on strikes in essential services. But Nehru was hardly a dictator; in those early days he could not even dictate to his own party. He had a strong right wing to contend with and was irritated by the high moral tone of the Socialists, who seemed to have little understanding of the complexities of reality. Given a chance, Patel would have banned all trade unions. Jawaharlal was in the thankless role of a bridge between the two strong lobbies. While he performed a vital service, he also got trampled on by both. Often his anger showed. As he said in a letter to Patel on 30 June 1949: 'As for the Socialists, they continue to show an amazing lack of responsibility and constructive bent of mind. They seem to be all frustrated and going mentally to pieces.' With little sympathy available from either the Left or the Right, Jawaharlal was drawn to men like Rajagopalachari in this phase; the Chakravarti was the kind of intellectual Nehru could communicate with, well read and unweighed by mental blocks of any 'ism' – including that vicious north Indian disease, communalism.

The mood of the Congress Party after partition was weighted far more towards Patel than Nehru, and Patel's inclinations were hardly secret. In one of his more important speeches, made on 6 January 1948 at Lucknow, Patel said:

> I am a true friend of the Muslims although I have been described as their greatest enemy. I believe in plain speaking. I do not know how to mince words. I want to tell them frankly that mere declarations of loyalty to the Indian Union will not help them at this critical juncture. They must give practical proof of their declarations ... I invite the RSS to join the Congress and not to weaken the administration by creating unrest in the country. I realize that they [the RSS] are not actuated by selfish motives but the situation warrants that they should strengthen the hands of the government and assist in maintaining peace ... In the Congress those who are in power feel that by virtue of authority they will be able to crush the RSS. By *danda* [the stick] you cannot suppress an organization. Moreover, *danda* is meant for thieves and *dakus*. Using of *danda* will not help much. After all, the RSS men are not thieves and dacoits. They are patriots. They love their country. Only their trend of thought is diverted. They are to be won over by Congressmen with love.

Patel was, of course, accusing the Nehru brand of Congressmen of wanting to beat the RSS with a stick, while he, on the other hand, wanted to 'strengthen' the Congress by wooing the RSS into the fold with love. Little wonder that the police under Patel would be accused of being soft towards the RSS.

The views of a leader like Rajendra Prasad were even more extreme. On 17 September 1947 Prasad actually wrote to Nehru saying that there was no use deploying the army to save Muslims, since this was making the government unpopular. Nehru gave a spirited reply to his senior minister on 19 September:

> There was a time when under Bapu's guidance and insistence we used to condemn terroristic acts even when by normal standards they might have been justified in the cause of national freedom. Now open murder committed in the most brutal way stalks everywhere and we hesitate to say much about it lest we may lose our hold on the people. I must confess I have no stomach for this leadership. Unless we keep to some standards, freedom has little meaning, and certainly India will not become the great nation we have dreamt of for so long.

As S. Gopal puts it in the second volume of his biography of Nehru:

> The old stalwarts of the Congress, however, such as Patel and Rajendra Prasad, with the backing of the leader of the Hindu Mahasabha, Syama Prasad Mookerjee, believed not so much in a theocratic state as in a state which symbolized the interests of the Hindu majority. Patel assumed that Muslim officials, even if they had opted for India, were bound to be disloyal and should be dismissed; and to him the Muslims in India were hostages to be held as security for the fair treatment of Hindus in Pakistan. He, therefore, resisted Nehru's efforts to reserve certain residential areas in Delhi for Muslims and to employ Muslims to deal with Muslim refugees. Even more non-secular in outlook than Patel was Rajendra Prasad, the meek follower of Gandhi but untouched in any real sense by the spirit of Gandhi's teachings.

These forces were checked for a while by the sheer enormity of the tragedy of Gandhi's assassination. The resultant anger against the RSS at least stopped Patel from wooing the RSS with love any more. (In fact, he had to ban the RSS; he managed to get his own ban lifted in July 1949.) But as the woes of refugees inflamed the headlines, tensions mounted, and leaders like Bidhan Roy lined up behind Patel; the two even wanted Nehru to threaten Pakistan and say bluntly that Muslims from India would be forced out in equal proportion to the number of Hindu refugees coming in from Pakistan. Nehru would have none of this. Yet even a good friend like Mohanlal Saxena, then Union minister of rehabilitation and a friend from the old days in Lucknow and Allahabad, succumbed to this vengeful infection and ordered Muslim shops in Delhi and UP to be sealed. In despair Nehru wrote to him on 10 September 1949:

> As I see things happening in India, in the Constituent Assembly, in the Congress, among young men and women, which take us away step by step from those ideals, unhappiness seizes me. Gandhiji's face comes up before me, gentle but reproaching. His words ring in my ears. Sometimes I read his writings and how he asked us to stick to this or that to the death, whatever others said or did. And yet those very things we were asked to stick to slip away from our grasp. Is that to be the end of our lives' labour? . . . All of us seem to be getting infected with the refugee mentality or, worse still, the RSS mentality. That is the curious finale to our careers.

The mentality had seized the Congress and was evident in ways both major and minor. One of the first disputes Nehru had to face was over cow slaughter. The lobbying to ban cow slaughter immediately after freedom began much before 15 August. Predictably Rajendra Prasad championed the cause. On 7 August 1947 Nehru wrote to Prasad: 'Nobody can possibly doubt the widespread Hindu sentiment in favour of cow protection. At the same time there is something slightly spurious about the present agitation. Indeed the number of telegrams and postcards, though impressive, is itself a sign of artificiality to some extent. Dalmia's money is flowing and Dalmia is not exactly a desirable person.' (Seth Ram Krishna Dalmia was a polygamous industrialist who later tripped up on his misdemeanours. In the 1940s he was one of the main financiers of Hindu revivalism.)

Nehru alone would have been a poor advocate for beef, for he was already suspect as a Westernized, meat-eating Muslim lover, but in this case he had the support of Gandhi. In the same letter he added: 'You know how strong an advocate of cow protection Bapu is. Nevertheless, so far as I am aware, he is opposed to any compulsory stoppage of cow slaughter. His chief reason, I believe, is that we must not function as a Hindu state but as a composite state in which

Hindus no doubt predominate.' But Nehru was too weak to be able to take on this lobby, particularly after Gandhi's death. Nehru, in fact, was on a losing spree. Patel got his way on privy purses for the dethroned princes, for instance. It had been agreed that the princes would be given tax-free money for their expenses after the loss of their states, work being alien to their nature. (In 1949 this amounted to Rs 4.66 crores annually.) Patel wanted this commitment to feed the feudals out of the public purse to be guaranteed by the Constitution. Nehru, with support from many Cabinet colleagues, was against binding the government down to a permanent disbursement. Patel got his way. It was the same during the battles over the right to property. Nehru did not want property to be listed as a fundamental right. He was keen to abolish zemindari and was in search of ways to reduce the influence of the courts in holding up land reforms. Yet it was only in 1951, after Patel's death, that he got the Constitution amended to ensure that estates could be acquired irrespective of any conflict with the fundamental right to property. The courts, however, proved dogged, and in 1955 Nehru had the Constitution amended again to prevent the courts from examining the adequacy of the compensation. But of course by 1955 he was the dominant authority within the government and the party – a far cry from 1950, when he could not even get his candidate elected president of the Congress.

The differences between Patel and Nehru were open enough, and the party tended to divide along these lines. On 23 December 1947 Patel even wanted to resign over the question of a Prime Minister's powers. He thought Nehru was interfering in his department and resented it. Nehru, in turn, insisted that every minister had to accept, in principle, the overriding authority of a Prime Minister. The dispute went to Gandhi, who reminded both that the national interest demanded they learn to work together. They did for a while, particularly after Gandhi's death, but the differences soon surfaced again, as they were bound to, for they were ideological. Nehru was wary about the Patel-school ministers hijacking government policy; witness the letter he wrote to Mookerjee on 5 March 1948 complaining that the industrial policy statement that was being prepared by him as industry minister was against the spirit and stated policy of the Congress economic programme subcommittee and would shock public opinion if it were to be adopted. Patel's advantage lay in the fact that his supporters remained in the Congress while Nehru's kept dribbling away for one reason or another – ideology, personality clashes, ego, miscalculation. Patel suffered a heart attack less than two months after Gandhi's death – Azad suggests in *India Wins Freedom* that this was caused by the shock and humiliation of hearing people accuse him of neglect in protecting Gandhi's life. Patel recovered but he was an ill man for the three remaining years of his life. Perhaps these intimations of mortality drove him to try and protect his legacy by placing his men in the two most powerful chairs after the prime ministership.

On 21 June 1948 Lord Mountbatten finally bade goodbye after fifteen historic months in which he had seen India touch the highest pinnacles of joy and sink to the lowest depths of despair. The most powerful memory that he took back, he said in his farewell message, was of people: 'I myself saw the most stupendous crowds in my life in India – on Independence Day, at Gandhiji's funeral, at the *mela* [fair] in Allahabad and on other historic occasions. The good nature and friendliness of these vast masses were unforgettable; I realized then that I was seeing before me the raw material of India's future greatness.' At 7.15 in the morning Lord Mountbatten, accompanied by Lady Mountbatten and Lady Pamela Mountbatten (his daughter), descended the red-carpeted steps of Government House, accompanied by Nehru and Mountbatten's successor, the first Indian Governor-General, Rajagopalachari. Mountbatten took the salute from the 65th Gurkha Rifles and the Central Reserve Police. The band played 'God Save the King' followed by Tagore's 'Jana Gana Mana' (which would soon become India's national anthem). Lady Mountbatten now bade farewell to the staff; it was an emotional moment, and from every door and window men, women and children peeped out for a last look at the last Angrez. There were cheering crowds in the forecourt. Lord and Lady Mountbatten waved back in response to the affectionate goodbye. All along the eleven-mile drive to Palam airport, the Mountbattens saw crowds, as Delhi turned out to give them a spontaneous, warm send-off. Troops of the Indian Army lined either side of the road for a mile before Palam airport, and a combined services guard of honour saluted them as their favourite York aircraft which had brought them fifteen months before stood ready for the final journey home. The last person to say goodbye was Nehru. He shook hands with his friends, then bent and kissed Lady Pamela. The York opened its engines, and a flight of

Royal Indian Air Force fighters dipped in salute overhead. At precisely 8.30 in the morning the York took off. Thirty-one guns fired a salvo. The last Viceroy had left India.

Nehru wanted the interim head of state Rajagopalachari to continue as President of India after the proclamation of the Republic on 26 January 1950 and he was confident that there would be no problem. Overconfident, in fact. Working behind Nehru's back, Patel organized a majority in the Congress parliamentary party for his nominee, Rajendra Prasad. Taken by surprise, Nehru suggested to Prasad that he should withdraw and himself propose Rajaji's name. Prasad lobbed the ball back neatly, saying that if Nehru and Patel agreed over Rajaji they could easily keep him out. Realizing that Patel was behind Prasad, Nehru accepted defeat. Prasad became the first President of India and gave full rein to what Gopal calls his 'inferior intellectual quality' and 'a social outlook which belonged to the eighteenth century'. Nehru got an immediate taste of what was to come. Prasad wanted the day fixed for the declaration of the Republic, 26 January, changed because his astrologers had told him that it was not an auspicious day. Nehru did not lose the opportunity to tell his President that India would not be run by astrologers at least as long as he was around. Prasad's insensitivity is appalling, for 26 January commemorated a major event in the political history of India; it was the anniversary of the national celebration which Gandhi organized after the *purna swaraj* resolution exactly two decades before, and the Congress used to celebrate that as freedom day each year.

The second defeat was even more galling, coming in the struggle for control of the party. The last date for nominations for the elections for Congress president in 1950 was 8 August. Nehru's name was on top of the list of seven candidates, the others being Kripalani, Shankar Rao Deo, N. G. Ranga, Seth Gobind Das, S. K. Patil and Purushottam Das Tandon. Nehru withdrew, explaining in a statement that 'It would not be proper for me to stand for election as president of the Congress so long as I am the Prime Minister of India.' It was the last time in his life he would display such qualms. By 17 August, the last date for withdrawals, only the three serious candidates were left: Kripalani, Tandon and Deo, with the first two being the main contenders.

Nehru was not overly fond of Kripalani but he was certain about

one thing – that Tandon had to be stopped; and so he supported
Kripalani. We have met Tandon before in our story. He was the man
who could not become chairman of the Allahabad municipality in
1923 because the Muslims would not support him, and Jawaharlal
had to be drafted into the job at the last minute. An associate of
Malaviya, and a member of Lala Lajpat Rai's Servants of the People
society, Tandon became an articulate member of the pro-Hindu
lobby within the Congress. By the 1940s he had become a 'pure
Hindi' enthusiast, even demanding that numerals be written in
Devanagari rather than in Roman as was the norm. But that was the
least of Tandon's passions. As chief of the Congress in UP at that
sensitive time, he kept making speech after speech demanding that
Muslims must adopt a 'Hindu culture' if they wanted to live in India.
On 17 April 1950 Nehru protested in writing to the chief minister of
UP, Pant: 'Purushottam Das Tandon, for whom I have the greatest
affection and respect, is continually delivering speeches which seem
to me to be opposed to the basic principles of the Congress . . .
Communalism has invaded the minds and hearts of those who were
pillars of the Congress in the past. It is a creeping paralysis and the
patient does not even realize it.'

Nehru protested publicly against Tandon's candidature, saying
that he had become a symbol of Hindu revivalism. On 8 August 1950
he wrote to Tandon urging him to withdraw, pointedly saying that if
he became party president his own position as Prime Minister would
become untenable. The reply came the next day – from Patel, who
advised Nehru not to oppose Tandon. Nehru shot off his answer to
Patel the same day. There was nothing personal, he said; it was a
matter of principle. Nehru told Patel that he would find it difficult to
serve in Tandon's working committee.

The nexus of Patel and important chief ministers (like K.
Hanumanthaiya of Karnataka and Bidhan Roy of Bengal) proved too
strong for Nehru. Patel's own strength within the organization was
formidable enough; to this he added the influence and power which
his position as minister in charge of the states gave him. (Nehru
learned the value of having pliant home ministers after Patel's death.)
On 29 August 1950, 2,618 of the 2,800 delegates to the All-India
Congress Committee voted to elect the Congress president for the
year. At 2.40 on the afternoon of 2 September the general secretary of
the AICC, Kala Venkata Rao, announced the results. Tandon had

got 1,306 votes against Kripalani's 1,092, with Deo mustering just 202. Tandon had got 60 per cent or more of the votes from UP, Bengal, PEPSU (Patiala and East Punjab States Union), Bombay and Nagpur.

Far from congratulating the winner, Nehru declared how disappointed he was at the results. His statement of 12 September, printed in the newspapers the next day, was a severe indictment of Tandon. He said: 'Communal and reactionary forces openly expressed their joy at the result.' He also made it clear that he would not brook any influence on government policies by the new party chief. The Congress, at its forthcoming session in Nasik, would have to support his line on international affairs, economic policy and communalism. He also demanded that the Congress reaffirm support to this drive to end *jagirdari* and zemindari (Prasad, incidentally, was already obstructing the Bihar Land Bill) and declared: 'I am clearly of the opinion that we must aim at what has been given the name of the Welfare State.' This, in Nehru's view, was possible only through planning and a controlled economy.

When the subjects committee met on 19 September 1950 Nehru moved a resolution (seconded by P. C. Ghosh) reaffirming that the Congress would not deviate from Gandhi's path on communalism. It was passed by a huge majority, with only four hands raised against. Nehru bulldozed his way through the Nasik session. The outgoing president, Dr Pattabhi Sitaramayya, had drawn much laughter by paraphrasing the Duke of Windsor and saying, in jest, that the Congress 'presidentship is a position of responsibility without authority, expectation without opportunity, prestige without power'. Nehru spent the next year ensuring this was precisely how Tandon would feel. After having snubbed Tandon implicitly throughout the session, Nehru decided to snub him explicitly afterwards. As he had warned Patel much earlier, he refused to join Tandon's working committee. Obviously taking his cues from how Gandhi had sabotaged Bose after Tripuri, Nehru launched an open war against his own party president. For a while that year the familiar depression seems to have gripped him, and his thoughts wandered predictably towards resignation. But when he realized that he was being eased out by this Hindu right-wing element in the Congress, and that his opponents were waiting for his temperament to defeat him and drive him towards resignation, Nehru suddenly showed that he could fight, that he could counter-attack with skill not unmixed with that basic instinct for the jugular. After Nasik, he wanted to follow up by taking the states ministry away from Patel; he did not do so only because he realized that Patel was on his death-bed. But there was little mercy now towards the other leaders. When he finally agreed to join Tandon's working committee he made it clear, in a letter to Tandon on 16 October 1950, that 'I feel as if I had done something ... approaching disloyalty to myself.' The one thing, however, that Nehru would never contemplate was leaving the Congress. He understood better than others its strengths. He would never go so far as to do anything which would break the party; he wanted only to rescue it from those opposed to the Gandhian commitment. He refused to make Jaya Prakash's mistake; the Socialists underestimated the place of the Congress in the country. As Nehru once said, the Congress was the central fact about India.

The conservatives were not ready to give in so easily, even after they lost the great Sardar Patel in December 1950. Prasad took on the Patel mantle and consciously made pro-Hindu gestures, like going to inaugurate the rebuilt Somnath temple, long a source of Hindu–Muslim tension because of Mahmud of Ghazni's raids nine centuries before. Nehru advised Prasad against going to Somnath and then disassociated his government from Prasad's visit when the president did not change his mind. But Nehru was on less confident ground here; one of his own Cabinet ministers, K. M. Munshi, was the chief organizer of the Somnath function and dared Nehru to do his worst. The next battle was fought over the Hindu Code Bill, seeking to rid Hindu social law of its medieval elements. Tandon accused Nehru of driving the Hindu vote away from the Congress by such provocative legislation, but Nehru countered that he was no longer in the mood for compromise. He wanted to rid the party of its Tandon-type tendencies and recapture its Gandhian soul.

Nehru was not helped by the behaviour of some of those who should have been fighting alongside him. B. R. Ambedkar resigned because he felt that Nehru was weakening over the Hindu Code Bill. Kripalani, with encouragement from Nehru through his close aides like Rafi Ahmed Kidwai, had set up a Congress Democratic Front to pursue similar goals. Instead of fighting from within, however, this group in May seriously contemplated leaving the Congress. Nehru appealed to them to stay on, but on 17 May 1951 Kripalani announced that he was resigning from the Congress. Nehru personally urged Kripalani to stay back and asked Tandon not to accept the resignations. As he wrote to Mountbatten on 24 June 1951: 'I am a good fighter, provided I have something worthwhile to fight for.' In an attempt to put pressure on Tandon, Nehru now resigned from the parliamentary board (ostensibly because the chief minister of Punjab had defied the board). He also demanded that Tandon reconstitute the working committee and the central election committee (an important body, given the fact that elections were due soon). Tandon refused and said he would rather give up his presidentship than surrender a president's rights. The confrontation was once again heading towards a climax, but this time the initiative was in the hands of Nehru. In June the Kripalani–Kidwai Congressmen announced the formation of the Kisan Mazdoor Praja Party. Nehru was livid. Kidwai resigned from government, along with Ajit Prasad Jain. Nehru tried to retain them in his ministry, but Tandon pointed out that they could not be both members of the ruling government and senior leaders of an opposition party. Point.

Now playing his final card, Nehru resigned from Tandon's working committee and the central election committee. The time had come for the party to choose between him and Tandon. Rejecting all midway solutions, Nehru explained to mediators like B. C. Roy that he and Tandon could not coexist, there would be bitter conflicts every month. Put so starkly, there was hardly any question of the consequences being any different from what they were. The party surrendered to Nehru. On 8 and 9 September 1951 the AICC met and elected Nehru president in place of Tandon, who offered his resignation.

Tandon quickly returned to footnote status, but Prasad would not yet give in. That very month he wanted to send a message to Parliament stating his objections to the Hindu Code Bill, which was a blatantly unconstitutional move by the President, since it sought to bypass the government. A strengthened Nehru called Prasad's bluff easily. He made it clear to the President that he would resign if Prasad insisted. Prasad backed off. As Nehru wrote to N. G. Ayyangar on 22 September 1951: 'I regret to say that the President attached more importance to his astrologers than to the advice of his Cabinet on some matters. I have no intention of submitting to the astrologers.' It was the confidence of a man who had won a tough round of a bitter slugging match. What little hope his foes might have had of revenge were snuffed out by the elections, in which Nehru led Congress to a massive victory. The first general elections of India, in three stages and spread over six months, began on 25 October 1951, in the distant villages of Himachal Pradesh. When the polling of 176 million voters was over and counted, Jawaharlal Nehru was the undisputed leader of the nation. More than 17,000 candidates contested on behalf of nearly 75 political parties to fill 489 seats in Parliament and 3,283 seats in the Assemblies. The Congress won absolute majority at the Centre and in 18 out of the 22 states; in the other 4 (Madras, Travancore–Cochin, PEPSU and Orissa) it was the largest single party. The Socialists, so confident before the polls, were routed. And the communal parties were demolished. The only parties to do reasonably well in that context were the Communists and the pro-feudal groups in these former princely states where the grip of feudalism still held the peasant's mind. (Candidates who lost their deposits contributed Rs 22 lakhs to the state exchequer.) The biggest victory of the Congress came in Nehru's home state, Uttar Pradesh. A sadhu, Prabhudutt Brahmachari, had been put up by the opposition against Nehru in the Phulpur constituency to symbolize Hindu anger against the man who appeased Muslims; the Hindu electorate swept aside the sadhu and returned Jawaharlal by an overwhelming margin of 233,571 votes to 56,718. Nehru had once told Tandon that he did not want a Congress victory in the elections at the cost of Congress's soul. Jawaharlal proved he could preserve both the power and the principle.

It was a referendum, and Jawaharlal Nehru once again proved that he retained a unique legitimacy, the only true one in a democracy, the vote of the masses. Nehru was now keen to bring his friends and comrades back into a purged Congress and get on with his dreams. He wanted nothing less than to change the destiny of India. This, he was certain, would affect the fate of the world.

42 *Khadi* Socialism

The older members might have muttered, but the enthusiastic young men and women clustered around their hero were off and running, devising innovative techniques to promote their party president's campaign for the 1937 elections. One of the brightest of them, Minoo R. Masani, took a long step towards modern advertising by preparing a campaign film called *Pandit Jawaharlal's Message*. On 19 May 1936 Nehru sat before the cameras to record, in carefully simple words, the core of his political philosophy:

> At present there are two groups of people in the world. On one side, there are people who want to advance the world further and free the people from the chains of imperialism and capitalism. On the other side, there are a handful of people who are deriving benefit from . . . the present state of things. There is a conflict going on between these two groups. The question is, on which side our country, our people, are going to stand. Out of these two groups I have no doubt that our country will side with that group which stands for independence and socialism. If there is any country in the world which stands most in need of this, that is, independence and socialism, it is our own poverty-stricken country where unemployment prevails.

Nehru was not only a preacher. He could say with some pride during that election campaign, as for instance at Bombay on 20 May 1936:

> If the Congress has grown stronger, it is because I raised the issue of socialism. Today the masses in the country have come nearer to the Congress and to that extent the position of Congress has strengthened. I myself have derived strength for what little I do because I have seen the sufferings and poverty of the peasants and the workers.

Nehru's convictions were born of his passionate concern for the poor; from Marx and the Soviet Union he took some guidance on the process. His faith in Gandhi, and his belief that no one understood India better than the Mahatma, stood between him and communism. But while Gandhi kept him away from Marx he could not keep Nehru away from socialism with a scientific face. Nehru did not join M. N. Roy or the Communists, who dismissed Gandhi as a petty-bourgeois reactionary; he used the Gandhian umbrella. While Bose went in search of liberation through Berlin and Tokyo, and the Communists sought liberation through Moscow, Nehru stuck to liberation through *khadi* (homespun). If what materialized was an ungainly mongrel, it was largely because the complex Indian reality could not afford to breed anything else.

The plank on which Nehru's strategies rested was planning. Economic planning at a national level began for the first time in the USSR in 1927. That was the year during which Nehru attended the Brussels conference, visited the Soviet Union and returned to India so full of the fire of revolutionary change that Gandhi had to snub him for being immature. If Congress could not accept the pace, it did accept the idea; as early as in May 1929 an All-India Congress Committee resolution had affirmed that 'in order to remove the poverty and misery of the Indian people and to ameliorate the condition of the masses, it is essential to make revolutionary changes in the present economic and social structure of society and to remove gross inequalities'. When Nehru became president at the Lahore session in December 1929 he declared his bona fides:

> I must frankly confess that I am a socialist and a republican and am no believer in kings and princes, or in the order which produces the modern kings of industry, who have greater power over the lives and fortunes of men than even the kings of old, and whose methods are as predatory as those of the old feudal aristocracy.

The Congress was many steps behind, however. Nehru's insistent pressure finally led to a historic resolution at the Karachi Congress in March 1931, the forty-fifth session of the party. The twenty-point resolution on Fundamental Rights was moved by Gandhi on 31 March – although it had been drafted by Nehru. Some of the changes made by Gandhi were quite apparent, for instance, the insistence on reduction of military expenditure to half its current level, a salary peg for bureaucrats at Rs 500 per month and prohibition. But Nehru's point was equally in evidence, whether in demanding religious neutrality on the part of the state, the right to trade unions, better working conditions or, most significantly, clause 19: 'Control by the state, of the key industries and mineral resources'. Moving the resolution, Gandhi said:

This Congress is of opinion that to enable the masses to appreciate what *swaraj*, as conceived by the Congress, will mean to them, it is desirable to state the position of the Congress in a manner easily understood by them. In order to end the exploitation of the masses, political freedom must include real economic freedom of the starving millions.

The socialist lobby incorporated itself in May 1934, with a nudge from Nehru, and formed the Congress Socialist Party. It was a ginger group which quickly created a distinct identity of its own; very soon it was charting its own future. At its second session, in Meerut, on 20 June 1936 it resolved: 'Marxism alone can guide the anti-imperialist forces to their ultimate destiny. Party members must, therefore, fully understand the technique of revolution, the theory and practice of class struggle, the nature of the state and processes leading to a socialist society.' It was an invitation, and the Communists accepted it gratefully. The Communist Party of India had been banned since the Meerut conspiracy case; so now Communists joined the CSP without calling themselves Communists. The attempt was, in part, to build a left-wing united front within the Congress and take over the nationalist struggle. But Gandhi was too immovable an object, the Left quite resistible as a force. (By March 1940 the differences between the Socialists and Communists had become so acute that the latter were expelled from the CSP, and by 1941 the split was complete in the Kisan Sabha too.) Nehru was an indefatigable promoter of the CSP. The Andhra leader N. G. Ranga, who had set up a Kisan Sabha in his province in 1923, joined hands with Narayan and established the All-India Kisan Sabha in 1936. The first meeting of the expanded forum was held simultaneously with the Congress session at Lucknow. Nehru tried to get the Congress to accept Ranga's programme but failed both at the open session and in the AICC.

He was nevertheless able to push through an idea even closer to his heart. In October 1938, with Congress ministries now in power, the then party president, fellow-leftist Bose, called a conference of the party's ministers of industries. The conference agreed that industrialization was essential to economic regeneration. On its recommendation a National Planning Committee was set up with Nehru as its chairman. Nehru was apprehensive. As he wrote in *The Discovery of India*: 'It was a strange assortment of different types and it was not clear how such an odd mixture would work. I accepted the chairmanship of the committee not without hesitation and misgiving; the work was after my own heart and I could not keep out of it.' The work was meant to be preparatory to a more comprehensive National Planning Commission. It created twenty-nine subcommittees working in seven main areas: agriculture, industry, demography, transport and communication, finance and commerce, public welfare, education. Its professed aim: to create an adequate standard of living within ten years. Professor K. T. Shah was appointed honorary general secretary and Rs 50,000 sanctioned as expenses. Between December 1938, when it first met, and September 1940 Nehru presided over seventy-one meetings, missing only one. This was in addition to a host of informal discussions and related work. In his very first note, sent on 21 December 1938, Nehru underlined his bias towards the need for heavy industries: 'There can be no planning if such planning does not include big industries, but in making our plans we have to remember the basic Congress policy of encouraging cottage industries.' The qualification only underlines Nehru's dilemma, for he was straining at the Gandhian leash, even while making room to keep Gandhi content. He sometimes wondered (as during a conversation with the brilliant statistician who was to work with him very closely, P. C. Mahalanobis) whether the committee had been set up only to humour him. In any case, he was not going to ignore such a gift-horse. It concluded its work only after the Quit India resolution and years of gaol, in Bombay on 10 November 1945. The committee reaffirmed the Karachi Resolution's call for state ownership of key industries and added services. However, there was no programme for large-scale nationalization, and adequate compensation was promised in lieu of take-overs.

Gandhi suddenly seemed to wake up to what was happening. So far he had watched his heir's work with a benign and sometimes bantering eye. In his speech after the Quit India resolution, for instance, Gandhi had said: 'In Jawaharlal's scheme of free India, no privileges or privileged classes have a place. Jawaharlal considers all property to be state-owned. He wants planned economy. He wants to reconstruct India according to plan. He likes to fly; I don't. I have kept a place for the princes and the zemindars in the India that I envisage.' But now that freedom and self-rule seemed imminent, Gandhi decided to take issue (although confidentially) with his heir. On 5 October 1945 he wrote to Nehru (the letters were given by Nehru to D. G. Tendulkar and form part of the appendix of the biography of Gandhi):

> The first thing I want to write about is the difference of outlook between us. If the difference is fundamental then I feel the public should also be made aware of it ... I have said that I still stand by the system of government envisaged in *Hind Swaraj*. These are not mere words. All the experience gained by me since 1909 when I wrote the booklet has confirmed the truth of my belief ... I am convinced that if India is to attain true freedom, and through India the world also, then sooner or later the fact must be recognized that people will have to live in villages, not in towns; in huts, not in palaces. Crores of people will never be able to live at peace with each other in towns and palaces. They will then have no recourse but to resort to both violence and untruth ... While I admire modern science, I find that it is the old looked at in the true light of modern science which should be reclothed and refashioned aright ... I want our position vis-à-vis each other to be clearly understood by us for two reasons. Firstly the bond that unites us is not only political work. It is immeasurably deeper and quite unbreakable ... I want to live to 125 for the service of India but I must admit that I am now an old man. You are much younger in comparison and I have, therefore, named you as my heir. I must, therefore, understand my heir and my heir should understand me. Then alone shall I be content.

The heir decided that he could not fudge any more. He replied from Anand Bhavan on 9 October:

> Briefly put, my view is that the question before us is not one of truth versus untruth or non-violence versus violence ... The whole question is how to achieve this [equitable] society and what its contents should be. I do not understand why a village should necessarily embody truth and non-violence. A village, normally speaking, is backward intellectually and culturally and no progress can be made from a backward environment. Narrow-minded people are much more likely to be untruthful and violent ...
>   It is many years since I read *Hind Swaraj* and I have only a vague picture in my mind. But even when I read it twenty or more years ago it

seemed to me completely unreal. In your writings and speeches since then I have found much that seemed to me an advance on that old position and an appreciation of modern trends. I was, therefore, surprised when you told us that the old picture still remains intact in your mind. As you know, the Congress has never considered that picture, much less adopted it . . . It is 38 years since *Hind Swaraj* was written. The world has completely changed since then possibly in the wrong direction. In any event any consideration of these questions must keep present facts, forces and the human material we have today in view, otherwise it will be divorced from reality.

It was a sharp snub from the heir. Gandhi did not take issue with Nehru after this last effort to recreate India around his idyllic village full of self-disciplined, caring and co-operative villagers, and Nehru got on with his own idyllic plans for heavy industries spawning a new India bursting with science and technology and fragrant with the secular culture of smiling socialism. That was the romance, at any rate.

As soon as he joined the Interim Government, Nehru set up a planning advisory board. It submitted its report in December, but the more demanding problems of pre-partition India overshadowed it. (Among the reasons Nehru would later use to explain the 'inevitability' of partition was that a compulsory union with a Muslim League bent on sabotage – as happened in the Interim Government phase – would make progress, and particularly planning, impossible.) The year of the Interim Government was one of crisis and chaos. As soon as freedom came, Nehru took up his favourite cause again. Riots were threatening the very survival of India, the government barely existed, but the AICC did not forget planning. In November 1947 it set up the Constitution and Economic Programme Committee, with Nehru, Azad, Ranga, Jaya Prakash, Gulzarilal Nanda, Achyut Patwardhan, Shanker Rao Deo and J. C. Kumarappa as members. Its report came on 25 January 1948 and recommended, among other things, the setting up of a permanent Planning Commission. Patel tried to stall it; he was worried once again, on behalf of the business community. The government published its first Industrial Policy Resolution on 6 April 1948, by which state monopoly was established over the manufacture of defence equipment, atomic energy and railways, and it reserved rights over any new enterprise in coal, steel, minerals, shipbuilding, communications and aircraft. Even this was far less than Nehru would have sought, for the policy assured business houses that there would be no nationalization, and that foreign firms could continue as before.

On 26 November 1949 the Constituent Assembly adopted the Constitution. The goals of the Karachi Resolution were given constitutional status in Part Four, which enumerated the 'Directive Principles of State Policy', though the sting was withdrawn by making it non-enforceable by a court of law. In 1950 the Planning Commission was set up, with Nehru as its chairman and Gulzarilal Nanda as deputy chairman. In July 1951 a draft outline was presented, and the final version of the First Five-Year Plan appeared in December 1952. It was only a reconstruction effort, with the emphasis on projects which were already on the drawing-board, or on which work had already begun, like the Chittaranjan Locomotive Factory and the Damodar Valley Corporation. But the seeds of the Nehru philosophy – of peaceful social change – were scattered through the document. The plan was limited by its aims, which were principally to rescue the economy from the effects of the war and partition; to solve the food crisis (Nehru had to tell rice-eaters like Tamils that they would have to learn to eat wheat); to check inflation (prices had shot up tremendously); and then to begin creating the infrastructure for a genuine leap forward, both in agriculture and in industry. The limitations were a sensible concession to realism. The Nehru line was evident in the outline of the future rather than the definition of present goals. Notice was clearly given that the public sector would be made the pre-eminent agency of development. Witness this assertion in the plan:

Whether one thinks of the problems of capital formation or the introduction of new techniques or the extension of social services, or the overall realignment of productive forces and class relationships within society, one comes inevitably to the conclusion that a rapid expansion of the economic and social responsibilities of the State will alone be capable of satisfying the legitimate expectations of the people. This need not involve complete nationalization of the means of production or elimination of private agencies in agriculture or business or industry. It does mean, however, a progressive widening of the public sector and a reorientation of the private sector to the needs of a planned economy.

The private sector learned that it would now have to operate under the Industries (Development and Regulation) Act of 1951, which meant that all growth would be only by permission from the government through a licence. C. Rajagopalachari would condemn Nehru's years in power when he launched his Swatantra Party at the end of the decade as the 'licence and permit Raj'; this Bill was the father of the system. And when the government found that the allocation to industry could be raised from Rs 101 crores to Rs 173 crores between the Draft Plan and the Final Plan, the bulk of the additional money went to basic industries.

The First Plan's most striking achievement lay in agriculture. It analysed the problem in terms not of inadequate technology but of the exploitative social and economic relationships that had throttled the dynamism of village India. 'The problem,' said the plan, 'therefore, is not one of merely rechannelling economic activity within the existing framework; that framework itself has to be remodelled.' The answer lay in providing small farmers and agricultural labourers with the necessary incentives, both technological and social, to raise production. Irrigation had to be expanded, of course, and production techniques updated; but equally vital was land reform, ending the extreme inequality in ownership. (Twenty-two per cent owned no land at all; 25 per cent owned less than an acre; another 14 per cent were marginal farmers with between 1 and 2.5 acres; more than 60 per cent consequently owned less than 8 per cent of the total land.) The traditional Congress failure or weakness – compromise – effectively reduced the mandate for change, but the land reforms that followed were still a major achievement. Moreover, making the village panchayat the centre of rural development was an exceptionally sound fusion of economics and community. Change did come, not to the extent Nehru wanted, nor as effectively, but it came on this side of conflict. And there were results. Foodgrain production increased by 20 per cent, as targets were reached and exceeded. Irrigation went to 16 million more acres. Overall the national income rose by 18 per cent, per capita income by 11 per cent and per capita consumption by 9 per cent. The co-operative movement was taken to about a quarter of the rural population, while the abolition of zemindari and the reform of tenancy created a new environment. The plan succeeded despite its obvious weaknesses (hurry, insufficient data *et al.*); perhaps everyone had the sense to keep ambitions within limits.

The Second Five-Year Plan would be far grander, more Nehruvian and far more bitterly controversial. As a first step, Nehru, simply by being so closely associated with it, turned the Planning Commission into something far more than just a high-status advisory body. In 1952 the National Development Council had been created to involve the chief ministers in the planning process; but with the party in power in all the states, and with Nehru a virtual emperor of the party, planning became largely a Nehru-run show. No chief minister dared interfere with this Prime Minister's pet passion. Among the key advisers he selected for the Second Plan was the professor he had met in the 1930s during visits to Shantiniketan and with whom he had spent a long evening talking about planning in 1940: P. C. Mahalanobis. As statistical adviser between 1955 and 1958 and member of the Planning Commission from 1959 he was one of the main engineers giving a practical construct to Nehru's dreams. Another key member of the Nehru team was Tarlok Singh, an ICS officer who had won fame with his book *Poverty and Social Change* (published in 1945). Singh was associated with planning from the beginning, as additional secretary from 1950 to 1962 and then member till 1966. Whatever their names or designations, all those working in this department had one thing in common: a commitment to Nehruvian socialism – a peaceful revolution, without turmoil or 'the breaking of heads'.

Having proved in the first general elections that he had the people's trust, Jawaharlal now attempted to rescue socialism from the Socialists. He saw no reason why Jaya Prakash and his comrades should plough a separate furrow in the name of an ideology which he was only too happy to describe as his own. His generosity was not shared by other Congressmen, who sneered at the Socialists as Nehru's Second Eleven. The Second Eleven, on its part, had thorough contempt for the First; and defeat only seemed to make the ideologues more bitter. Jaya Prakash was convinced that Nehru would never be unequivocal in his commitment to socialism, that the pressures from within the Congress would force Nehru to compromise. He was right, too. When talks of a merger between the Congress and the Socialists seemed to be moving in a positive direction, in February and March 1953, Jaya Prakash laid down very specific conditions: constitutional amendments, land reforms and nationalization of banks, insurance and natural assets like mines. Nehru replied candidly that he agreed with everything in principle but with little in practice. On 17 March 1953 he wrote to Jaya Prakash: 'It is fairly easy to make a list of what we would like to have. It is more difficult to get that done in the proper order of priority. To attempt to do many things at the same time sometimes results in nothing being done.' That marked the end of the search for co-operation, to the great relief of the Congress satraps. Nehru himself was irritated by the very patronizing attitude of the Socialists towards the Congress; whatever the faults of the party, he was proud of its place in the history of the nation and convinced of its role in the political and economic development of the country. And he was incensed by the behaviour of some Socialist leaders, even those whom he liked personally like Jaya Prakash. As he wrote to V. N. Sharma on 7 October 1956: 'Privately, of course, we meet many of them [Socialists] often. But what is one to do when Jaya Prakash Narayan talks the most unmitigated nonsense and hates the Congress so much as to prefer the devil to it?' By this time Nehru had done what he had to do: commit the Congress to a socialist grid and launch his Second Five-Year Plan, which he described to his chief ministers in his regular letter to them as an 'adventure worthy of this country'.

Fifteen years after his last visit, the air route from China was still the same: with stops at Saigon, Rangoon and Calcutta. On his way back from what was billed as a historic journey, Nehru was asked at Rangoon airport on 2 November 1954 whether he was now contemplating retirement – he would, after all, be sixty-five years old in a fortnight's time. Fit, and in excellent humour, Nehru told the airport press conference: 'I am seriously considering to work as hard as I can. I am not trying to run away from politics ... If I may say so, I am not the retiring type.' That same afternoon he addressed a rally of several hundred thousand people at the Calcutta *maidan*, organized to welcome him back. He began with a sad tribute to one of his dearest friends, who had passed away during his twelve-day stay abroad: Rafi Ahmed Kidwai. The next day Nehru left for Darjeeling to lay the foundation-stone of a project very close to his heart: the Himalayan Mountaineering Institute. Speaking to Congress workers on 4 November, at the Durbar Hall in the Raj Bhavan, Nehru said Mao Tse-tung had told him China would take about twenty years to lay the foundations of socialism. He too, he said, wanted to evolve plans for India so that this country might prosper.

On 8 November the Congress working committee met at the Prime Minister's residence at nine in the morning to consider who to name party president for the two-year term beginning with the next session in January. Nehru had indicated that he no longer wanted to be both party president and Prime Minister. Ucharangai Navaishanker Dhebar, another lawyer-Congressman from Gujarat, was chosen to succeed Nehru; this, incidentally was the first time the selection was done by the working committee, rather than a ballot. This was a reversal to the Gandhian days, when Gandhi made the decision and the party 'voted' his nominee in. But Nehru was now the king of the Congress. The dates of the coming session were also finalized: between 17 and 23 January, at Avadi, near Madras. Avadi would enter the history books. Nehru gave an indication at a meeting of the National Development Council the very next day, on 9 November:

> The picture I have in mind is definitely and absolutely a socialistic picture of society. I am not using the word in a dogmatic sense at all. I mean largely that the means of production should be socially owned and controlled for the benefit of society as a whole. There is plenty of room for private enterprise provided the main aim is kept clear.

What India needed was import substitution to create a strong domestic, self-reliant economy with an indigenous ability to produce 'basic things' (steel, power, heavy machinery). Consumer demands should be met by expanding rural and small-scale industry. The government committed itself to 'a socialistic pattern of society' in the Lok Sabha in December. On 8 January 1955 the Congress steering committee met in Delhi and decided that an official resolution on economic policy be placed before the sixtieth session of the party at Avadi. Predictably it was Jawaharlal Nehru who moved the resolution.

More than 300,000 people were gathered at the Avadi session to hear Nehru; the surge was so great that the dais looked like a small island in a vast sea. The history of the country, he told them, was the history of the Congress: 'We grew with the people and the people grew with us.' The Congress, he said, was not an adventurist party; neither were Congressmen either schoolboys or mere academic debaters. With Gandhi, the party had moved to the grass roots, becoming the voice of the peasantry. Now the Congress was once again taking a turn, representing another stage of development and growth. But though the word 'socialism' had come from the West, 'I want to tell you that, whatever it is going to be, it has to be in keeping with India's genius.' In Europe, socialism was connected with class war, 'but it is not necessary we should go through the troubles of Europe to achieve our brand of socialist pattern'. Of course there was bound to be conflict in any society, particularly at a time of change. 'But the point is how you meet that conflict. There was a major conflict between British imperialism and Indian nationalism. How did we meet it? By peaceful methods which proved to be effective.' Everything, Nehru said, 'that we now do should be governed by the ideal of a socialistic society'. But 'we are not going to get socialism by resolutions, even by a decree, or by saying that there is socialism. We can only get it by hard work, by increasing our production and distributing it equally.' 'I put this resolution', he concluded, 'because I think it represents the hopes and aspirations of the Indian people, and much more than that. It is a pledge which you and I take – not a pledge, but a challenge to the future that we are determined to conquer.'

That future may not have been conquered as fully as Nehru wished, but there was no doubt that he was, on the day, the man in whom reposed the dreams of his people. A woman, fifty-year-old Bolinayana Gangamamba, walked up to him on the second day of the session and thrust a golden crown on his head, calling Nehru the real Lord Krishna of modern India. (Lord Krishna passed on the crown to Dhebar to be auctioned off for party funds.) The Congress resolution on socialism and the new Industrial Policy Resolution of 30 April 1956 (which grew out of the first) were watersheds in the history of free India. Till 1919 the Congress was Hume's party. Till January 1955 it was Gandhi's party. After 1955 it became a Gandhi–Nehru party. Of course Nehru's socialism too was diluted by the Gandhian principle of co-operation rather than coercion. The Planning Commission might totally reject the private sector's thesis that the state was meant only to create capital for the expansion of free enterprise, but the private sector was guaranteed 'the opportunity to develop and expand' by the Industrial Policy Resolution. The resolution, however, certainly created the base for India's economic regeneration and kept control of this base in the hands of the state. All new units in seventeen 'basic and strategic' industries and utilities (arms; atomic energy; iron and steel; heavy castings and forgings of iron and steel; heavy plant and machinery for this sector; mining and machine tools; heavy electrical plants; coal and lignite; mineral oils; mining and processing of specified ores, metals and minerals; aircraft, air and railway transport; shipbuilding; electricity; public communications) were reserved only for the state sector. Another twelve were meant to be predominantly within the public sector. The rest was open to both sectors. The Second Plan reflected the new priorities. Public sector investment went up to Rs 3,800 crores, or two and a half times the First Plan level. And the private sector investment by plan-end was placed at only Rs 2,400 crores, or about 50 per cent higher. The Second Plan totally reversed the importance of the private and public sectors; it was the state which was now in charge of rapid industrialization.

There was a price, of course. The total outlay on agriculture and irrigation went down from 34.6 per cent in the First Plan to 17.5 per cent in the Second. And though total expenditure on agriculture did rise, the expenditure on agricultural production programmes in fact declined from Rs 197 crores to Rs 170 crores. Irrigation got only 7.9 per cent of the outlay against 16.3 per cent. Nor were these cuts, and the new taxes, in any way sufficient to fill the resource gap. While the planners accepted that the combined impact of increase in population, higher standards of per capita consumption and higher demands resulting from higher purchasing power and redistribution of income would require a doubling of food production by 1965, they had provided direct investments for only a 15 per cent rise in total production between 1955–6 and 1960–1 (from 65 million to 75 million tons). The planners hoped to meet this deficit through greater mobilization of local labour and resources. The hope was belied. By the summer of 1956 Nehru himself was admitting that 15 per cent growth 'manifestly is too little'. The agriculture lobby demanded more money; the Planning Commission wanted higher targets without more funds. If China could get 35 to 40 per cent growth through surplus labour power, it argued, why not India? The reality on the Indian ground exposed the planners. By the summer of 1957 agricultural production went below the level of 1953–4. In just August, September and October food prices jumped 50 per cent. The government was forced to import two million tons of foodgrain. The summer crop of 1957 was damaged in the north by the failure of the monsoon; food production was down to 63 million tons in 1957–8. Hoarding lent an evil dimension to the crisis, and the government responded by talking of a progressive take-over of wholesale trade in foodgrains. The Congress politicians, who had suffered the armchair authority of the Planning Commission long enough, now reminded the economists that life was about human beings, not arithmetic. India was not Stalin's or Mao's country; any quick comparisons would be self-defeating. Rather than take over the foodgrains trade, the food ministry signed the first PL480 agreement with the USA in August 1956 for the import of foodgrains and bought commercially from Australia, Burma, Cambodia and Thailand. Fair-price shops were opened, and this food was released to ease the miseries of the people. This, in turn, further depleted the foreign exchange reserves. With commercial imports dwindling, the government turned to selective procurement from surplus areas; but no effort was made to replace the private trader. The government, wisely, kept to a supplementary – and therefore regulatory – role.

Time only pushed up costs, even as it ate away foreign exchange reserves. Inflation forced reallocation of plan outlays, but the core sectors were protected. The failures of implementation could fill – and indeed have done – a book on their own. But this enormous task of social reconstruction which Nehru embarked on (without 'the breaking of heads') was hardly ever going to be easy. India had to be its own role model, so at least some of the confusion was probably inevitable. The concepts which motivated Nehru's thinking were his major contribution to the creation of the economy of modern India. It was, if you like, a greater psychological victory than an economic one, but then Nehru had spent decades of his life watching his countrymen being defeated simply because they could not summon the will to win. He had become leader of a defeated nation. He wanted to leave behind one strong enough never to be defeated again. That achievement his worst critics will now grant him. He dreamed of independence in all its facets; he wanted an independent foreign policy as much as an independent domestic economy, and he knew that one was not possible without the other.

One of the finest assessments made of the man was by the socialist intellectual Asoka Mehta in *A Study of Nehru* (edited by Rafiq

Zakaria, 1959): 'In the case of all leaders of men there is an angle of refraction between ideas and achievement. In Nehru the angle has grown with the unfolding of his ideas. In their very acceptance has disenchantment grown. That is at once the glory and tragedy of Jawaharlal Nehru.' The brilliant use of the geometric image illuminates the Nehru contradiction superbly. 'He has been a socialist,' writes Mehta:

> and against heavy odds he has striven to push the Congress and the country towards socialism. His understanding of political and cultural forces has been immense, but in economic matters he has generally been unsure of himself. While he has been leading the country towards socialist policies, his understanding of the economic implications of such policies has grown more or less *pari passu* with their unfolding. Socialism, therefore, has come to India under his leadership more as a grand idea than as a strategy for social change.

Perhaps the truest statement Nehru made at Avadi was that his socialism would be an Indian socialism. That day at Avadi was a pinnacle of the Nehru era; he always launched his dreams magnificently, from the mountaintops. It might be downhill the rest of the way, but great men inspire their generations with the nobility of their ideas, their hopes. Avadi was the session of the 'Nehru dollar': a gold disc with Nehru's picture on one side and the Congress flag on the reverse. India wore Nehru on its heart. One of those watching this magical chemistry between Jawaharlal and India from the dais at Avadi was a friend from abroad, a revolutionary guest of the Congress from Yugoslavia: Marshal Josip Broz Tito.

43 The Realism of Tomorrow

Born the seventh of fifteen children in the home of a poor peasant near Zagreb, Croatia, on 25 May 1892, the 62-year-old Josip Broz Tito was already a world-famous hero when his yacht, the *Galeb*, brought him to the Gateway of India on 16 December 1954 to start an eighteen-day state visit, his first to the land of Jawaharlal Nehru.

An early communist, and a soldier who left the Austro-Hungarian forces to join the Red Army after the October Revolution, Tito became secretary-general of the Yugoslav party in 1937 after Stalin's purges left him the only ranking member to claim the post. His genius flowered in the war. The brilliant successes of Marshal Tito's National Liberation Army forced a royalist like Churchill to ditch the government-in-exile of King Peter in December 1943 and declare support for the partisans instead. Tito entered Belgrade on 20 October 1944. The man who had defeated Hitler now did something which seemed to require even more courage; he challenged Stalin. When Tito refused to join the East European bloc, Stalin expelled him from the Cominform. Tito proclaimed neutrality and equidistance from the superpowers as his policy. He was precisely the kind of statesman Nehru was in search of. Nehru had begun his quest for a trellis to hold the nations emerging from the long sleep, a new coalition outside the clutch of the great powers. The first linkages were bilateral; by the turn of the decade he would, in co-operation with Tito and Nasser, give this idea a more permanent structure which would be one of his outstanding contributions to an ideal very dear to his heart: world peace.

The post-war world was crowded with heroes. At the helm of free nations were men who had led their people through cataclysmic events, wars of either liberation or survival which defined the shape of events as nothing had done in many centuries. If Gandhi had delivered India back to Indians, Jawaharlal Nehru now brought this emerging world to India's doorstep. They all came, and each Indian's heart swelled as he saw his Nehru walk the world's stage in a leading role, his advice and involvement influencing all the great affairs that occupied this post-war environment in which colonialism was cracking up. The people lined the streets and cheered those who came calling on Nehru. 'Viva Marshal Tito!' they shouted, and the more natural 'Marshal Tito ki jai!' as he stepped off a launch on 16 December at 9.25 in the morning. Liberators of the Indian Air Force dipped their wings, and the shore batteries boomed a 21-gun salute; the naval guard of honour presented arms, and for the very first time the President of India's colours were paraded and dipped in honour of a visiting head of state. This was no ordinary visitor in Nehru's scheme of things, and he made sure that not a detail was missed. When Marshal Tito left Bombay for Delhi at four that afternoon, the special train carrying him was equipped with a library, a cinema theatre and a bar. (Nehru's penchant for worrying about every detail was well caricatured by that superb cartoonist of *The Times of India*, Laxman, on the eve of the Krushchev–Bulganin visit in 1955. The cartoon showed him in a series of sketches, scrubbing the floor, getting the flowers ready, fixing the decorations, teaching crowds how to cheer (spontaneously!), preparing children to sing, touching up culture by showing a dancer how to dance, spreading the red carpet – and then, finally a proper Prime Minister, receiving the dignitaries.)

The joint Indo-Yugoslav declaration on 22 December 1954 outlined the Nehruvian recipe for peace:

The President and the Prime Minister desire to proclaim that the policy of non-alignment adopted and pursued by their respective countries is not 'neutrality' or 'neutralism' and therefore passivity, as sometimes alleged, but is a positive, active and constructive policy seeking to lead to collective peace, on which alone collective security can really rest . . . The President and the Prime Minister desire to state, as their considered view, that the relations of their two countries and governments are, and must continue to be, based on principles of recognition of each other's sovereignty, independence and integrity, of non-aggression, of equality, of mutual respect and non-interference in the domestic affairs of each other or of other countries, and on the promotion, both for themselves and for the world, of the approach and conditions of peaceful coexistence.

This was the Pancha Sheela (Five Principles) which were the ideological heart of Nehru's vision of the world: Sovereignty, non-aggression, non-interference, equality, peaceful coexistence –

non-interference of every kind, political, ideological, military and economic. It was a thesis which challenged both the superpowers: those who had replaced colonialism with neo-colonialism, and those who thought that their ideology, Marxism, could and should be exported. As Nehru often pointed out, the Pancha Sheela may not have been a 'new' truth – he himself traced the concept to Ashoka at the very least – but never had their application been more necessary than at this delicate moment in history when the world, without even recovering from one great war, was hovering on the brink of another (and far worse, since the atomic age had arrived). Nehru's India would not join any camp no matter what the provocation (there was enough of that from a Pakistan happily signing US-sponsored pacts) and it invited other nations to escape the pincer and assert their right to genuine independence.

Unlike his socialism, Nehru's world view did not succumb to the temptations of compromise. It might have failed, as it did in relations with China, but Nehru would never renege on it. He had a deeply moral view of history: of conflicts at two levels, between oppressor and oppressed within a society, and the concurrent struggle between those states which became powerful through mastery over others, and those struggling to escape this enslavement. Having spent fifty-eight years of his life before he saw his own country escape the second fate, his experience influenced his self-taught knowledge of the past. His socialism and his foreign policy were, consequently, of a piece. The first was continuation of the internal struggle, the second part of the international confrontation. His idealism – which he described beautifully (as usual) as 'the realism of tomorrow' – remained steadfast: from the time he was writing letters to his daughter from gaol in 1932, through the tensions of war, through the awful confusion of a new nation's birth, through the lures of the 1950s when he was wooed on every side and, most nobly, through the defeat of 1962.

Nehru – and Gandhi – saw the liberation of India as the beginning of a new age in the world's history. To progress from simply seeing it that way to making it happen needed courage and will as much as vision. There was no foreign service in the Indian bureaucracy for the good reason that the Raj did not need one. When Nehru decided to set it up, the material available to him was not encouraging. On the one hand there was the British-trained bureaucrat, whose mind-set was conditioned by service to the Raj. It was not very easy to inculcate in him overnight the philosophy of a foreign policy which had been nurtured by the freedom movement. Nehru's first secretary-general was the polished, sophisticated and brilliant Sir Girja Shankar Bajpai – the same man who had argued Churchill's case in Washington on a question as volatile as the Bengal famine. A Mao would have punished Bajpai, not promoted him. Nehru did not hold the past against his bureaucrats, although his contempt for their behaviour during the Raj is obvious enough from his autobiography. What he demanded in return was a new commitment, and this he got in fair measure, not because the Savile Row bureaucrats had suddenly seen the light, but because his personal leadership inspired a new response in them. Jawaharlal Nehru's idealism was infectious. There were some rough moments, particularly in the relations between the new Prime Minister and the old bureaucrat. Nehru's violent temper was famous, and the first lesson seniors tended to pass on to juniors in the department was never to argue with the boss, for fear of reprisal. This was unfair. Nehru was impetuous and prone to fits of temper, but he had too large a heart to be petty. He did not suffer the occasional foolishness of otherwise sensible men gladly or easily, but that was a minor foible. Those same bureaucrats grew to hero-worship him no less than the masses. Inevitably in his lifetime his weaknesses were exaggerated and his greatness taken for granted. Even so, all those who worked with him soon understood what he was trying to do: create, after a long history of subservience, the culture of true independence.

Although Nehru's natural sympathies were with the Socialist bloc, he neatly side-stepped the powerful arguments of international solidarity and Marxist equality that made so many smaller nations *de facto* satellites of the Soviet Union. If he or Krishna Menon could fulminate against Washington, Nehru could also give Tito the grandest of welcomes. Tito would later recall that when he met Nehru for the first time that December in 1954 it seemed to him that he was meeting someone he long knew. It was because Tito, like others, had heard the constancy in his voice and seen the unwavering timbre of Nehru's ideals for so many years that even the face seemed familiar on a first meeting. In the same volume where Tito's memoir is published (Zakaria, ed., *A Study of Nehru*, 1959) Nasser describes Nehru as 'the expression of human conscience'; it was a phrase which caught the truth about Nehru.

In its special centenary volume in 1987 the Paris-based *International Herald Tribune* took a poll of what a select group of respondents thought were the ten most important news stories of the century. The freedom of India was one of them – obvious enough now, but this is a judgement of hindsight. On 15 August 1947 this was not all so easily obvious. No matter what illusions of generosity and maturity they might currently colour history with, the colonizing powers were in no mood to surrender their power without a bitter effort to hold on to their possessions. Indonesia, Indo-China, Africa: nothing came easily. By the demands of precedence, and by virtue of his own stature, Nehru was in the van of the oppressed world's struggle. He fought proudly and without fear. No one was surprised when he made himself Member for External Affairs and Commonwealth Relations in the Interim Government of September 1946. The British were still in power, and freedom was still a long and tortured year away, but Nehru was in no doubt about the foreign policy of his government:

> We propose, as far as possible, to keep away from the power politics of groups, aligned against one another, which have led in the past to world war and which may again lead to disasters on an even vaster scale. We believe that peace and freedom are indivisible and the denial of freedom anywhere must endanger freedom elsewhere and lead to conflict and war. We are particularly interested in the emancipation of colonial and dependent countries and peoples, and in the recognition in theory and practice of equal opportunities for all races. We repudiate utterly the Nazi doctrine of racialism, wheresoever and in whatever form it may be practised. We seek no dominion over others and we claim no privileged position over other peoples. But we do claim equal and honourable treatment for our people wherever they may go, and we cannot accept any discrimination against them.

Lord Wavell undoubtedly squirmed when Nehru broadcast these thoughts over All-India Radio on 7 September 1946, but Nehru was beyond caring about the sentiments of imperialists. He had a mission and he was going to fulfil it. All the principles of the Nehru doctrine were contained in this first speech: non-alignment, freedom, equality of people and nations, honour and non-interference.

The very first decision he took was a dramatic one: to hold an Asian Relations Conference. Invitations were sent in September itself. By early March nearly everyone had accepted, while the Hebrew University, the Arab League, the United Nations, Britain, the Soviet Union and the USA sent observers. There were 243 delegates from twenty-eight Asian countries. At 5 p.m. on Sunday 23 March 1947 an audience of more than 10,000 gathered at the specially constructed *pandal* in the fort built by the emperor Sher Shah in 1540, Purana Qila (the Old Fort). The rostrum was a hundred feet long with flights of steps on either side; behind the president's pillow (everyone sat cross-legged) was a huge map of the continent, with Asia written in neon lights. Mrs Sarojini Naidu was in the chair. Nehru inaugurated the conference, speaking first in Hindustani and then in English. They were meeting, he said, because 'Asia is once again finding herself' after two hundred years of European imperialism which had sucked the continent's wealth and emasculated it. The 'entire economy [of Asian countries] was bound up with some European imperialism or other; even culturally they looked towards Europe and not to their own friends and neighbours from whom they had derived so much in the past'. The revival of land routes and air travel was once again making co-operation possible. India had a special role to play: 'Apart from the fact that India herself is emerging into freedom and independence, she is the natural centre and focal point of the many forces at work in Asia. Geography is a compelling factor, and geographically she is so situated as to be the meeting point of Western and Northern and Eastern and South-East Asia.' This new spirit, Nehru said, was not directed against anyone, but he could hardly resist throwing a direct challenge to imperialists: 'For too long we of Asia have been petitioners in Western courts and chancelleries. That story must now belong to the past. We propose to stand on our own feet and to co-operate with all others who are prepared to co-operate with us. We do not intend to be the playthings of others.'

Exactly eleven days before this speech President Harry Truman had addressed a joint session of the Congress and enunciated the doctrine that has become the most famous symbol of his presidency. A Pax Americana was announced; the United States would replace Britain and defend the free world against communism. Stalin had to be confronted, or weak nations would fall into his basket like rotten apples, argued Dean Acheson. The world was being divided into black and white, and Nehru's refusal to become one or the other infuriated Washington's ideologues. The *New York Herald Tribune* of 18 January 1947 reported John Foster Dulles as saying: 'In India, Soviet communism exercises a strong influence through the Interim Government.' The irony was that the Communists were as hostile to Nehru. Stalin and Mao both decided that India was an imperialist stooge, citing its continued membership of the Commonwealth as evidence. The sentiment was reciprocated. Nehru had lost much of his initial admiration for the Soviet Union after Stalin's purges, the partition of Poland, the invasion of Finland and, worst of all, the Stalin–Hitler pact. (In an article in the *National Herald* on 16 January 1940 he openly condemned Stalin.)

It was perfectly true that Nehru had rejected his own campaign of twenty years when he accepted dominion status after transfer of power, but he had good reasons. First, he saw this as ensuring a smooth transition during the time it took to fully Indianize the services. Second, it would calm the suspicions of the princely states as full integration went its course. The British connection was also useful as a third party in the bitter tangle of Indo-Pak relations with their horrible over- and undertones. He saw an international value too in keeping India within the Commonwealth even after becoming a republic. As he reminisced to one of his favourite journalists, R. K. Karanjia, in an interview more than a decade later (*The Philosophy of Mr Nehru*, 1966): 'Then, also, from the Commonwealth link, or new pattern of relationship between India and her erstwhile enemy, Britain, emerges a unique and constructive synthesis which has opened the gates of freedom and free association to so many former British colonies belonging to different races, nationalities and colours.' It was also a very valuable link to the Western powers, which Nehru used with consummate skill. He would not woo them but he did not want to alienate them either. He wanted bipolar friendship, not bipolar hostility. Certainly, without him the Commonwealth would have remained a white man's club and lost much of its relevance. But his most important reason for remaining in the Commonwealth was worry about a US–Pakistan axis; Nehru wanted leverage with the West to prevent the conversion of Pakistan into a US fortress. A most interesting conversation took place between Nehru's most important adviser on foreign affairs, Menon, and Mountbatten on 22 April 1947 (the record is in *Transfer of Power*,

Vol. 10). Menon argued that the US objective in free India would be 'to capture all the markets, to step in and take the place of the British, and finally . . . to get bases in India for ultimate use against Russia'. Mountbatten did not refute this; he only reminded Menon that Pakistan was not only eager to join the Commonwealth but would happily be such a client state of the USA. In return, its armed forces would become 'immensely superior' to those of India, and Karachi would become a big air and naval base within the Commonwealth. It was, consequently, in India's interest for Patel and Nehru to seek dominion status. Nehru and Patel saw the point and quickly gave up their 'firm' commitment to 'full' freedom.

The British link certainly played its part in the early Indo-Pak equation. War over Kashmir, as we have seen, broke out soon enough, but even after the ceasefire the fever did not die down. Officials on both sides, with much help from fire-breathing journalists, promoted varying levels of hysteria. This by itself might not have been as dangerous were it not for the fact that outbreaks of communal violence set passions on either side screaming. There was always talk of war; and if there was one thing Nehru did not want, it was a ruinous war, which he knew would unleash another vicious spell of Hindu–Muslim rioting in India. His plea for peace was not very popular, either with many of his colleagues or with the influential middle class, but he stuck, although often teetering, to his resolve.

India became a republic on 26 January 1950, but the joy of bugles was soon overtaken by the familiar wail. Bengal had been saved in 1947 by the miracle of the one-man boundary force, but that saint was dead for two years; and blood rose to men's eyes again. A great massacre of Hindus began in East Pakistan, leading to another massive wave of migration. Patel wanted the Indian Army to intervene and take over the administration of East Pakistan to save Hindu lives. Nehru wanted to bring peace the Gandhian way. He suggested to Liaquat Ali Khan that the two Prime Ministers should tour the affected areas together. When silence was the only response, he expressed his wish to go to East Pakistan alone. It was an unreal thought. There was little likelihood of a sovereign Pakistan allowing a foreign Prime Minister to go traipsing through its countryside to see Muslims butcher Hindus. However, Delhi's moral superiority was severely dampened by the counter-riots that broke out in Calcutta in which – as usual – Muslims were killed with matching ferocity. Under pressure, Nehru kept the military option open; the army was redeployed, and London was formally informed so that Pakistan would get the message about the seriousness of India's intentions. Nehru wrote to Attlee hoping Britain would lean on Pakistan to force it to negotiate. High Commissioner Krishna Menon even suggested that Lord Addison come out to mediate at these talks, but Nehru rejected the thought.

Depressed by Liaquat's non-co-operation, Nehru seriously contemplated resignation and a unilateral walk into East Pakistan, in the manner in which Gandhi had wanted to go to Karachi in his last days. On 20 March 1950 Nehru wrote to the President, Rajendra Prasad: 'It is my intention, soon after the Budget is passed, to offer you my resignation, and, together with it, the resignation of the present Cabinet. Thereupon a new Council of Ministers will have to be formed. I would beg of you then not to charge me with this responsibility.' Patel, who was still hoping for a decisive war with Pakistan, began publicly to dissociate himself from Nehru's soft line. He called a meeting of Congressmen at his house where he attacked Nehru. Typically, when pushed, Nehru fought back instead of surrendering. The man who just days before was quite willing to resign now challenged Patel to face a full discussion on what should be the party's policy towards Pakistan, either at an emergency meeting of the AICC or at a full session of the Congress. He was so keen for a decisive confrontation that he even wrote to Patel on 26 March doubting whether it was now good for the country that the two should work together any more. Patel retreated before this frontal challenge, protesting that he was still loyal to Nehru. Nehru pushed his point further. On 29 March he again wrote to Patel, saying: 'I see every ideal that I have held fading away and conditions emerging in India which not only distress me but indicate to me that my life's work has been a failure.' He boldly authorized the imposition of martial law in Bengal if necessary to save Muslim lives. Simultaneously, he sent a telegram to Liaquat, on 26 March, inviting him to Delhi for talks to find a peaceful and rational method by which the life and identity of the minorities could be safeguarded. On 1 April, Nehru wrote in his regular letter to the chief ministers: 'For my part my mind is clear in this matter and, so long as I am Prime Minister, I shall not allow communalism to shape our policy, nor am I prepared to tolerate barbarous and uncivilized behaviour.'

Fortunately, Liaquat was in no mood for war either. His Viking landed at 11.35 on the morning of 2 April; as a gesture of goodwill it was flying both the Indian and Pakistani colours. One of the first things he did was to go to Gandhi's *samadhi* and lay a wreath. After a week of talks and eleven drafts, the Nehru–Liaquat pact was finally signed, in which both governments committed themselves to complete equality in citizenship for minorities. Nehru was relieved and happy at what had been achieved. After he had seen Liaquat's plane taxi off on 9 April he stood for a while on the runway in silent contemplation. He later described the pact as a new turn in life's journey. The Hindu Mahasabha leader in his Cabinet, Syama Prasad Mookerjee, revolted, and his fellow Bengali K. C. Neogy resigned along with him. But Patel now stood by Nehru. India had signed an international agreement, and it had to be honoured, he said. He personally went to Bengal to calm passions, and Nehru was publicly grateful for the support he received from Patel. For a while the atmosphere on the subcontinent improved visibly. A delegation of Pakistani journalists came to Delhi, and there was a sentimental reunion with their old colleagues, which the Prime Minister attended. On 8 May 1950 Nehru wrote to Menon: 'Literally these fire-eaters wept on each other's shoulders and became quite soppy. How extraordinarily emotional our people are.' Nehru addressed the Pakistan Newspaper Editors' Conference on 4 May, saying: 'We should try to develop a common policy in regard to international matters, in regard possibly to defence matters and in many cases in economic matters. That should be the natural course.' However, on the very day he was advocating co-operation in defence, something very different was happening in Washington.

Liaquat Ali Khan had reached Washington on his first US visit on 3 May. His address to Congress the next day, far from being objectionable, contained sentiments which Nehru would have welcomed. 'There is', said Liaquat about his country, 'no room here for theocracy, for Islam stands for freedom of conscience, condemns coercion, has no priesthood and abhors the caste system.' But the real motivation for the US trip was soon evident. In answer to a question at a press conference, Liaquat said quite candidly that he had come shopping for arms. On 5 May, speaking at the lunch in his honour at the National Press Club, he said Pakistan would welcome a US guarantee of its 'territorial integrity'. That was also the day the US senate passed the Global Aid Bill and the Marshall Plan; the new US resolve was voiced by Dean Acheson, who called on the nations of the West to meet the global challenge of communism with 'utmost vigour'. Ex-President Hoover even demanded a reorganization of the UN without the Soviet Union and the Communist countries – an idea which Nehru openly condemned in an interview with the United Nations radio department. On 7 May, Liaquat made it very clear, at a press conference in New York, why, in his view, Pakistan needed both territorial guarantees and arms – he feared an attack from India. The tone of his anti-Indian remarks, and the support he got from a Washington establishment irritated by Nehru's unwillingness to fan the anti-communist momentum, soured the mood in Delhi. Patel described it as a 'diabolical breach' of the Nehru–Liaquat pact. The brief sunshine on the subcontinent was lost once again.

Within a month the United States had finally some reason to be pleased with Nehru. The Korean War broke out in June, and India voted for the US resolution in the UN declaring North Korea the aggressor. Nehru repeated the charge in an interview with the *US News and World Report*, published on 15 September. But Washington soon realized that this did not mean that Nehru had joined Dean Acheson's 'vigorous' struggle against global communism. India's stand was that there should be a political solution through an agreement between the powers concerned, a position Nehru took as early as 14 July 1950. In October, Chou En-lai woke up India's ambassador in Beijing at midnight and conveyed a message through him to the Western powers: China would intervene if General MacArthur's troops crossed the 38th Parallel. India passed on the warning. Washington ignored it, to its later regret; by the end of the war the USA had lost 50,000 dead, and not much had been achieved beyond MacArthur's original victories in South Korea. The perils of being in the non-aligned middle were soon apparent. Nehru was vilified as a communist fellow-traveller in the war-inflamed USA and snubbed by China and North Korea. Yet there was some vindication at the end, when India played the leading role in the formula which led to the exchange of prisoners, and an Indian Custodian Force under General Thimayya was made responsible for the exchange of POWs. Nehru's and India's standing in world affairs touched an astonishing high in the mid-1950s. Nehru and Menon were active in virtually all the efforts to put out the fires that raged through Indo-China and Africa. Even when India was not a party, as at the Geneva Conference on Indo-China in the summer of 1954, it was Krishna Menon who, from behind the scenes, helped construct a formula acceptable to the nations concerned.

The United States did not view all this with any sympathy, and Nehru's advocacy of a place for Mao's government at the United Nations only enraged US opinion further. Nehru expected as much. As early as 8 March 1948 he had told the Constituent Assembly: 'The policy of standing up ... for the weak and the oppressed in various continents is not a policy which is to the liking of the Great Powers who directly or indirectly share in that exploitation. It is that, that puts us in the wrong with them.' But true opportunism, he argued, lay in being moral rather than in seeking short-term gains, because from morality came strength, and strength was a nation's most important asset. He was now practising what he had preached, against heavy odds. The USA made sure that the International Control Commission for Indo-China, with India as the unanimously selected chairman, was sniped into impotence. Simultaneously, Washington sponsored the South-East Asia Treaty Organization and the Baghdad Pact with Pakistan in tow.

It is an interesting point that India and the USA could not create a friendship that would have been eminently logical, given their common commitment to democracy, not because of any direct conflict of interest, but because of different perceptions of third-party problems: communism, Korea and, from there, China, Indo-China and of course Pakistan – for Pakistan was ever ready to declare itself a trooper in the Western crusades. Perhaps if Roosevelt had been a President of the 1950s the world might have evolved differently. For Nehru admired Roosevelt, and the latter had the vision to understand a Nehru. But Truman and then Eisenhower were in charge; they belonged to different parties, but the foreign-policy establishment was the same under both. Nehru's first two visits to the USA, in 1949 and 1956, were ruined by the anti-communist hysteria and pro-Pakistan diplomacy of John Foster Dulles and company, and of course by the backlash against Krishna Menon's acerbic, and garrulous, speeches. When the USA did get a President who admired Nehru, John Kennedy, Nehru himself spoiled the opportunity by lecturing the younger man rather than turning his sympathy to advantage. Nehru did take time off in New York to see *Camelot*, but he had a far better meeting with Richard Burton than with the political star of the New Camelot. Kennedy, ready to be sympathetic, even admiring, was to later call the Nehru visit the worst state visit he had endured.

No cause which Nehru took up proved more thankless than China. When Dulles was warning China (as on 8 March 1955) not to underestimate US willingness to go to war, and the Pentagon had even selected targets on the mainland to be hit, Nehru was promoting Chou En-lai, most notably at Bandung in the second half of April. Nehru gave a great deal to befriend China. In return he got hostility from the USA, exploitation from Beijing and, eventually, war in 1962. (In the strangest irony of all, Nixon and Kissinger eloped with Mao and Chou by the end of the 1960s; and overnight China stopped being the murderous, slit-eyed 'yellow peril' in the US press.)

However, Nehru was always ready to pay what price was required for independence, and he conducted his foreign policy with a conscious display of national pride. Yezdezard Dinshaw Gundevia, who began his career in the Indian foreign service in 1948 as a junior joint secretary under Nehru, and ended it as Nehru's last Foreign Secretary, recalls a story which is relevant in this context in his book *Outside the Archives* (1984). The year was 1949, and one of the government's top priorities was to create a million-ton food reserve as an insurance against crop failure. The USA was approached, but Washington kept stalling. When Nehru was about to leave for his first state visit to the USA, the food ministry suggested that this subject be included in the Prime Minister's brief for the talks with Truman. When Nehru saw this paragraph during the discussions on the brief, he pushed his chair back, stood up and shouted at his secretary-general, Sir Girja: 'What do you want me to do? Am I going to America with a begging-bowl in my hand?!' Sir Girja, who had once argued against food aid to India on behalf of Churchill, now saw nothing wrong in Nehru asking for food. In his mellifluous Urdu he said it was not a question of a begging-bowl but of realities. Nehru sat down and put a pencil sharply across the paragraph. A calm Sir Girja waited a moment, then did precisely the same in his draft of the brief, and the meeting continued. It was food, however, which finally created a thaw in Indo-Soviet relations and set them on to greater things.

The first ruler of Delhi to send an elephant to his counterpart in Russia was Emperor Aurangzeb, who sent this symbolic gift all the way to St Petersburg for Peter the Great. The second was Nehru, who sent two baby elephants, Ravi and Shashi, to entrance Soviet children. The ambassador in Moscow then was K. P. S. Menon, and he recalls the letter Nehru sent, in his essay 'India and the Soviet Union' (in B. R. Nanda, ed., *Indian Foreign Policy: The Nehru Years*, 1976): 'These are two Ambassadors of India to the Soviet Union, apart, of course from yourself: only they will be specially accredited to the children of the Soviet Union.'

Nehru was keen on establishing diplomatic relations with the Soviet Union as soon as he formed the Interim Government in 1946. It was partly a way of displaying his independence from the Viceroy; and Moscow responded with great alacrity. Nehru was already putting his ideas into operation. When K. P. S. Menon left for China in January 1947 as India's ambassador, he received a note from Nehru, dated 2 January 1947, in which the new foreign policy was spelt out:

> Our general policy is to avoid entanglement in power politics and not to join any group of powers as against any other group. The two leading groups today are the Russian bloc and the Anglo-American bloc. We must be friendly to both and yet not join either. Both America and Russia are extraordinarily suspicious of each other as well as of other countries. This makes our path difficult and we may well be suspected by each of leaning towards the other. This cannot be helped.

Every Soviet suspicion seemed to be confirmed when India announced it would remain in the Commonwealth. This was proof to Stalin that he was right about the nature of the Indian freedom movement. Lenin, the wisest of them all, had accepted Gandhi as a revolutionary and a genuine leader of the masses; but under Stalin, *The Great Soviet Encyclopaedia* described Gandhi as 'A reactionary who hails from the Bania caste – betrayed the people and helped the imperialists against them; aped the ascetics; pretended, in a demagogic way, to be a supporter of Indian independence and an enemy of the British and widely exploited religious prejudices'. India's non-partisan role in the Korean conflict led to the first reassessment in Moscow, although Vishinsky, then Soviet representative at the UN, denounced Menon's formula on Korea which had been accepted by the rest of the General Assembly.

The Soviets took the opportunity provided by the US stonewalling over food supplies to make their first conciliatory gesture. With arguments still continuing in the USA, the Soviet embassy offered to send foodgrains in March 1951, on barter: jute, rubber, cotton and shellac in exchange for wheat. By the first week of May four ships left Odessa with foodgrains for India. The Indian ambassador then, Radhakrishnan (who later became India's first Vice-President), was so enthused that he suggested that a treaty of friendship be signed between the Soviet Union and India, but Nehru cooled such ardour. (It was left to Nehru's daughter to do this twenty years and two months later.) Yet Radhakrishnan did achieve a signal success in persuading Moscow to support India over Kashmir when he gently indicated in a conversation with Vishinsky in September 1951 that the Soviet Union would do well to take a careful look at what Western control of Kashmir would mean for Soviet defences. Thus far, Moscow had kept away from the Kashmir issue, preferring silence even when a very pro-Pakistan UN resolution was introduced by the USA and Britain on 30 March 1951. But on 17 January 1952 its permanent representative Yakov Alexandrovich Malik finally lashed out during a Security Council debate:

> The United States of America and the United Kingdom are continuing as before to interfere in the settlement of the Kashmir question, putting forward one plan after another ... These plans in connection with Kashmir are of an 'annexionist', imperialist nature, because they are not based on the effort to achieve a real settlement. The purpose of these plans is interference ... and the conversion of Kashmir into a protectorate of the United States of America and the United Kingdom under the pretext of rendering assistance through the United Nations. Eventually the purpose of these plans in connection with Kashmir is to secure the introduction of Anglo-American troops into the territory of Kashmir, and convert Kashmir into an Anglo-American colony and a military and strategic base.

Moscow was undoubtedly stirred by its own worries, but this was still music to Indian ears.

The significant change in the Soviet attitude came only after Stalin's death. Gandhi was reconverted, at the twentieth congress of the Communist Party of the Soviet Union in 1956, into one of the great liberators of mankind. History being of easy virtue, *The Great*

Soviet Encyclopaedia was suitably amended to reflect the new thinking. The process of wooing was stepped up in 1953 and 1954, and several cultural delegations arrived in Delhi. Nehru's visit to the Soviet Union between 11 and 23 June 1955 was a huge success. He saw hydroelectric dams at Volga and the tombs of Muslim saints at Tashkent; in Leningrad, the welcoming crowds lined up for miles; there was a speech at the Dynamo Stadium and, naturally, a visit to the Bolshoi. On 22 June, Nehru and Bulganin signed a joint declaration committing their countries to Pancha Sheela. Bulganin and Krushchev returned the visit on 18 November, and (as Laxman's cartoon indicated) Nehru spared nothing to make this visit a magnificent success. The most intelligent thing that the Soviets did was to build Indo-Soviet relations on the basis of Nehru's perceptions as much as on their own – unlike the Americans, who kept seeking to change Nehru into a champion of free enterprise. Nehru's socialism was as far from Soviet socialism as it was from US capitalism, but the Soviets were not in the least bothered. They bought their influence with the steel factories that Nehru wanted for his country. After Britain, the USA and West Germany had refused to help India build another steel plant, Delhi approached Moscow. The Soviets said yes quickly, and Bhilai emerged on the industrial map of the country. This, in fact, opened Western eyes, and Britain put up the Durgapur plant while West Germany created one in Rourkela. The Americans, however, were still unwilling to help the Bokaro project, and the Soviets came in again. The Soviets were now even ready to (and did) distance themselves from the Indian Communists in order to please Nehru.

By the time Nehru visited the Soviet Union his contribution to world peace was being hailed as one of the great successes of the age. Pancha Sheela became, to mix a metaphor, the battle-cry of peace. He was in demand at every deliberation. Take 1955, which was arguably the finest year of his prime ministership. On 3 January 1955 he received the UN Secretary-General in India; on the 28th he left for the Commonwealth Conference, returning mid-February. On 25 February, in a major policy speech, he called on the UN to recognize China and its claim on Formosa. On 17 March he welcomed Sihanouk; Kampuchea joined the Pancha Sheela club the next day. On 25 March he welcomed U Nu. On 1 April he met Anwar Sadat. On 8 April the Vietnamese came to Delhi to sign the Pancha Sheela declaration. By 16 April he was in Bandung. On 26 April he returned and sent Krishna Menon as his emissary to Beijing on yet another diplomatic mission: to restore calm in another confrontation with the Americans and get US airmen taken prisoner by China released. (On 30 May, Dulles thanked him for his mediation.) On 5 June, Nehru left for the Soviet Union, via Cairo and Prague, reaching Moscow on 7 June. His return journey was the grand procession of a world statesman. On 23 June he was received in Warsaw. After a quick interlude to take a look at the Georgian Republic, he went to Austria, visited Auschwitz and had talks with the Chancellor. On 28 June he held a two-day conference of Indian ambassadors at Salzburg (a comparative break in the hectic schedule). On 30 June he reached Belgrade for a state visit; on 6 July he held talks with Tito at Brioni. He was in Rome on 8 July, where he achieved a vital mission: during a twenty-minute audience in his private library Pope Pius XII agreed with Nehru that the Portuguese occupation of Goa was a political problem. (There were about 200,000 Catholics in Goa, and Salazar's propaganda insisted that Portugal was there to save the Church.) The same day he flew to London for talks with Sir Anthony Eden at the invitation of the British Prime Minister. On 11 July he halted at Cairo and met Nasser, before returning to India to a hero's welcome. When the Air India Superconstellation, the Rani of Ind, landed at Bombay at 9.37 at night on 12 July there were thousands gathered at the airport to cheer the 'Leader of Peace'. And at Delhi the next afternoon crowds broke all police cordons and threw garlands and flowers at him. 'Shanti ke Doot – Vijayee Nehru!' they cried, calling him an apostle and a victor of peace. Even the cartoonists took a break and gloried in his successes.

There was no finer tribute to Nehru that year than one which came from a crusty old foe, Winston Churchill. On 21 February 1955 Churchill wrote to Nehru:

> I hope you will think of the phrase 'The Light of Asia'. It seems to me that you might be able to do what no other human being could in giving India the lead, at least in the realm of thought, throughout Asia, with the freedom and dignity of the individual as the ideal rather than the Communist Party drill book.

On 30 June, Churchill ended another letter saying: 'Yours is indeed a heavy burden and responsibility, shaping the destiny of your many millions of countrymen, and playing your outstanding part in world affairs. I wish you well in your task. Remember "The light of Asia!" With warm personal regards . . .'

On 15 July, President Rajendra Prasad held a state banquet in Nehru's honour – almost as if he was a visiting dignitary. At this banquet Nehru received the highest award the nation could offer: the Bharat Ratna. Whether it was at Avadi, Bandung or Moscow, at Beijing, Cairo or London, 1955 was Jawaharlal Nehru's and India's year. To a nation which only eight years before had been mired in the grip of communalism and imperialism, this seemed nothing less than a miracle. Nowhere did Nehru dominate more than at Bandung, where the third axis of the emerging world's great triumvirate, Gamal Abdel Nasser, entered the world scene, in the shadow of Nehru.

The reason why the subcontinent's leaders stopped over in Cairo on their inward or outward journeys was not because of any particular fascination for either the Pyramids or the political leaders of Egypt, but because Cairo was the most convenient refuelling stop. Nehru was a little sceptical about the leaders he would meet in Cairo, briefly on his way out and for a longer while on his return, when he left India on 28 May 1953 to attend the coronation of Queen Elizabeth. There had been a coup against the admittedly corrupt regime of King Farouk, but ambassador K. M. Panikkar had reported to Delhi on 27 January 1953 that the new regime of General Muhammad Neguib seemed to be a creation of the United States.

A great deal happened both in India (where Azad was Prime Minister in Nehru's absence) and the world before Nehru returned to Bombay on the rain-swept morning of 27 June. On 1 June came a news flash that Everest had fallen to Edmund Hillary and Tenzing Norgay. (It was at once followed by a controversy – with racial overtones – about who had reached the summit first. Tenzing refused to attend a British reception because he felt Hunt was denying him his due.) On the 2nd, Queen Elizabeth was crowned at Westminster Abbey after a $1\frac{1}{2}$-hour ceremony; Jawaharlal attended in his formal black *achkan* and *churidaars*. On 8 June the Korean PoW agreement was finally signed, and India was made chairman of the Neutral Nations Repatriation Commission. On 19 June the new government in Egypt abolished all royal titles and proclaimed a republic. Neguib was still the man formally in charge, but real power was in the hands of the vice-premier: Lieutenant-Colonel Gamal Abdel Nasser, an officer who had entered the limelight with his successful defence of Faludja in the war against Israel in 1948–9, one of the few exploits the Egyptians could be proud of. The 19th of June was also the day Ethel and Julius Rosenberg died on the electric chair in the USA. In the early hours of Tuesday 23 June, Shyama Prasad Mookerjee died in detention in Kashmir. Nehru was in Egypt that day.

Nehru was given a warm welcome in Cairo. The new leaders had opened the controversy concerning sovereignty over the Suez Canal. Nehru helped Churchill by persuading them not to be too violent in their language, although he agreed that they should insist on Egyptian control over the canal. A special boat ride down the Suez was organized for Nehru with all the senior members of the government on board so that he could get to know them better. He struck up an excellent rapport with Nasser (although Nasser's *The Philosophy of the Revolution* did not overly impress Nehru; he thought it shallow). By early 1954 Nasser had eased out Neguib and taken control. The West now began putting pressure on him to join the Baghdad Pact. Nehru obviously saw this as an unfriendly alliance, with Pakistan, a member, being armed by Britain under its aegis. Between the Manila treaty and the Baghdad Pact, Pakistan had effectively used the West to pressure India from both sides. Nehru was relieved when Egypt kept away from the Baghdad Pact.

Active promotion of the pact by the United States convinced Nehru that the time had come to follow up the suggestion by the Colombo powers for a conference of Asian and African countries. His hesitation so far had rested on the suspicion that it might degenerate into a slanging-match over Asian problems like Israel and Palestine, but clearly the time had come to demonstrate that there were other voices in Asia than merely the pseudo-American. (His anger against US puppets was deep and lasting. Gundevia narrates Nehru's reaction during a four-day conference of India's ambassadors to the South-East Asian countries in the summer of 1963. The former INA hero Niranjan Singh Gill was the envoy in Bangkok, and, as he churned out the predictable stuff about there being a great deal in common between Thailand and India, Nehru suddenly burst in angrily, 'Great deal in common between Thailand and India! What is there in common? The Prime Minister of Thailand is an important personality in the Coca-Cola Company!')

India, Indonesia and Burma formed the nexus of an independent Asian viewpoint; the task was to broaden this base and to create a distinctive Afro-Asian influence in world affairs. To avoid internal bickering, there was no formal agenda. And although Krishna Menon wanted Israel's presence, Nehru succumbed to Arab pressure and kept Israel out. He admitted (in his telegram to all Indian missions on 4 January 1955) that keeping Israel out was illogical, although he did nothing to correct what he himself clearly admitted was a mistake. But he put his foot down when it came to China, and kept it there. Eden conveyed to Krishna Menon that the USA and Britain would not approve of China's participation. Nehru dismissed their objections with some irritation – and a pointed hint that there was much that the USA and UK did which India did not like, but it did not prevent them from talking to each other. Pakistan, on cue from the West, initially opposed China's participation but withdrew in the face of the general pro-China sentiment. Taiwan, consequently, was automatically excluded. The mutual bitterness between the two Koreas was considered too great, and so it was decided to keep both out. Some states on the verge of independence – like the Central African Federation – were invited. South Africa was kept out, to everyone's satisfaction.

Nehru was the centre-point. All the major nations used his good offices for negotiations, and as the Bandung conference neared there were requests from all over for his personal-private intervention with nations which would be attending. He was already the conduit for negotiations with the China which the West did not recognize, whether on US prisoners in China, or the coastal islands, or Hong Kong. When UN Secretary-General Dag Hammarskjöld visited the mainland it was through Nehru's good offices. From Australia, R. G. Casey requested him to restrain Indonesia over West New Guinea, while the Dutch asked him to persuade Soekarno to ensure a quick and fair trial for the thirty-five Dutch prisoners. This is only a small sample of his individual influence. The philosophy of Bandung was Jawaharlal's Pancha Sheela. Speaking in the Lok Sabha on 31 March 1955, Nehru described Pancha Sheela as Asia's challenge to the world: 'The Asian–African conference at Bandung would throw this challenge, in all its baldness and straightness, and every country would have to answer whether it stood for non-interference, or non-intervention.' Much of the seventy-minute speech was devoted to Bandung. 'When the history of this time is written in the future, two things will stand. One is the coming of atomic energy, and the other the emergence of Asia . . . This conference', Nehru noted,

> is something historic. It is unique. Of course, no such thing has ever happened before and the fact of representatives of 1,400 million people meeting there even though they have differences amongst themselves is a matter of utmost significance. It has become a regular practice for the affairs of Asia to be determined by certain Great Powers of Europe and sometimes of America and the fact that Asia might have any views about these subjects was not considered a matter of very great importance.

Nehru set out to change this equation of so many hundred years. He was defeated not by those he sought to challenge but by those he sought to promote. On the one side there were those who wanted to whittle his stature. On the other were the many nations linked quietly to one coat-tail or another. Nehru was wary of, and constantly on the watch for, the Western tune. When a resolution condemning colonialism was being discussed, Ceylon's Sir John Kotlewala at once tagged on Soviet domination over Eastern Europe. Nehru rebuked the comparison; it was not as if everything the Soviet Union did was praiseworthy, but this was provocative and extraordinary. He attacked SEATO; the answer was not military pacts, but strength created through industrialization and self-reliance. He kept hammering away at non-alignment, defining in often simple terms what he meant. In his concluding speeches on 22 and 23 April he said: 'We do not agree with the Communist teachings, we do not agree with anti-Communist teachings, because they are both based on wrong principles.' The final communiqué was hardly as non-aligned as Nehru might have wished. It granted the principle that every nation had the right to defend itself singly or collectively, the second being a thin euphemism for military pacts. Nor was anything practical achieved in terms of building an organization of non-aligned nations. But, as Nehru noted later, the success lay in the idea, in the fact that the conference had taken place at all.

Nehru was proud of the way he had placed Chou En-lai in the heart of international diplomacy. Chou, proud inheritor of the Chinese legacy, exploited the opportunity and then, quite brilliantly, with a bearing and a display of moderation which left a great impact, he quietly, without any touch of sentiment, promoted China's interests over those of his mentor, Nehru. When deception was needed, Chou used it. There was no question, he said (to give one example) of China imposing communism in Tibet; he even invited senior leaders to come to Tibet and see the situation for themselves. His most important – in Delhi's perspective – ploy was a secret overture to Pakistan, the country which had initially opposed China's participation. Chou told the Pakistan Prime Minister Muhammad Ali that he saw no clash of interest between their two countries. But he indicated that a definite conflict of interests between India and China was likely soon. Ali responded by saying that Pakistan had no enmity towards China and would stay away from any US–China war. Nehru had no idea that the man he saw as his protégé was preparing his final humiliation. But at least he had greater reason for satisfaction over Nasser, who was on his first visit abroad (apart from a visit to Saudi Arabia for Haj).

After Bandung, the confrontation with Britain over Suez simmered slowly towards a crisis. On 18 and 19 July 1956 the three men who were to launch the non-aligned movement – Nehru, Nasser and Tito – met together for the first time, at Brioni. Nasser gave no hint of the sensational decision he was about to take. On the plane back to Cairo, however, Nasser showed Nehru a radio version of the Dulles speech withdrawing US assistance for the Aswan dam; among the options they discussed was that perhaps the whole project should be abandoned and smaller schemes created. Nehru was not prepared for the news when Nasser nationalized Suez on 26 July; he wondered if Egypt had bitten off more than it could chew. India played an active part in the negotiations which followed. (Mindful surely of his mistake over Kashmir, Nehru warned Nasser not to take Suez to the UN.) But notwithstanding any earlier reservations, Nehru was absolutely clear on where he stood after the Israeli attack on Egypt on 29 October and the Anglo-French invasion of 5 November. On 31 October he cabled Nasser: 'This is a reversal of history which none of us can tolerate.' This war showed Nehru at his best: principled, wise and courageous. No one could have supported Nasser more, and yet he privately advised Nasser after Britain had been forced to withdraw that he should be sensible and recognize that Britain had legitimate interests. At home, feelings were so high that there was even talk of India leaving the Commonwealth, but Nehru would not contemplate such an option. Suez was Eden's mistake, he argued, not the whole of Britain's. The reward to India came in the shape of its popularity in the Arab and Muslim world. The Arabs called Nehru Rasul-as-Salaam. (Rasul means 'messenger', not 'prophet', so there need be no controversy.) There was much embarrassment in Pakistan, for Nehru's role destroyed its strategy of isolating India from the Muslim world. Moreover, while the government squirmed, Pakistani poets showered encomiums. A verse written by Rais Amrohvi was published in the Karachi Urdu paper *Jung*:

> Jap raha hai aaj mala ek Hindu ki Arab
> Barhaman zade mein shaan-e dilbari aisi to ho.
> Hikmate Pandit Jawaharlal Nehru ki kassam
> Mar mite Islam jis par kafiri aisi to ho.

(A rough prose translation: 'The Arab world is singing praises today of a Hindu Brahmin's courage. Nehru is such a man that even Islam would embrace such an infidel.')

Nasser paid his dues during Nehru's confrontation with the Western powers over Goa. Sentiment apart, there was no question of allowing continued Portuguese domination over the island; it militated directly against India's defence interests. The Americans were ready to use Goa as a pawn. Angry at Bulganin and Krushchev's speeches in India in 1955, Dulles issued a joint statement with the Foreign Minister of Portugal recognizing Goa as a 'Portuguese province' in Asia. Indian anger at this stance was predictable, but there remained the bigger question of whether the USA would extend its military might in defence of Portugal. Salazar was so bitter against Nehru that Indian intelligence suspected him of financing assassination attempts. (Obviously, such things can never be proved.) The French had left their little dots in Chandannagar and Pondicherry peacefully (if messily), but Portugal had ambitions. In 1948 Portugal even offered to help the Nizam fight Delhi. Nehru had total contempt for the authorities in Lisbon but he wanted their departure through negotiations. The Congress had, in its resolution of 11 August 1946, condemned the 'fascist and authoritarian administration of Portugal' over the Indian people of Goa. But Lisbon was in no mood to relent and depart. Even Winston Churchill was convinced the Portuguese were being stupid. Writing to the chief ministers on 2 July 1953, Nehru mentioned: 'Generally it is recognized that both the Portuguese and the French possessions must come to India. Sir Winston Churchill said so to me and remarked on the extreme backwardness of the Portuguese thought.' However, the backwardness was a reality Nehru had to deal with, and for more than a decade it kept Goa, Daman and Diu outside India. Nehru could have – even should have – seized Goa just as Indian troops had secured Junagadh or Kashmir or Hyderabad, but he tarried and gave the Western powers another issue through which to pressure India. In 1954 Britain informed India that old treaties made it obligatory for her to support Portugal in case of armed conflict. Dulles indicated the US position in 1955. Nehru was reluctant to opt for a military solution not because of Western might but because it went against his whole thesis that talks and consultations, not war, must be the only basis for the conduct of international relations. His domestic opponents exploited this contradiction, and a collection of Socialist, Jana Sangh and Communist volunteers entered Goa for a mass *satyagraha*. The Portuguese opened fire on unarmed men, and passions in India shot up. Nehru still refused to change his policy of a peaceful settlement. Pakistan, equating peace with weakness, supported Portugal. Nehru was hamstrung by his own foreign policy and he gradually realized that this was becoming a particularly complicated knot.

He finally decided to cut the knot in 1961. He still argued that India must stick to its policy of peace even though the Indian Army could push Portugal out in twenty-four hours, but the argument was wearing thin. The experience of Africa showed that Portugal was nowhere prepared to surrender without the most bitter fighting. On 30 November 1961 Nehru promised military action, and skirmishing began between Portuguese and Indian forces. But so much did Nehru waver that John Kenneth Galbraith, Kennedy's envoy to Delhi, became convinced – as he notes in his *Ambassador's Journal* (1969) – that India would never use force. A meeting with Nehru changed his mind, and now he tried to persuade Nehru against the idea. Galbraith suggested going to the UN. Once bitten, many times shy. On 16 December, Kennedy, who conceded India's right to Goa, wrote urging that Nehru stop short of military action, and all the latent fears of an Anglo-American defence of Portuguese colonialism awoke. Secretary of State Dean Rusk, in active collaboration with

Portugal, came up with a last-minute proposal for a postponement of military action by six months; but, by the time Galbraith met Nehru on the evening of 17 December to press this case, matters had already gone too far. Indian troops were on the move.

It took just twenty-six hours to settle a problem which had bothered free India for fourteen years. The Governor-General of Goa, General Vassalo de Silva, ignored Lisbon's demand for martyrdom and surrendered without a fight. Kennedy, who felt peeved, shrewdly told India's ambassador, B. K. Nehru, that this should have happened fifteen years before, but drove the point home that Nehru should now deliver fewer sermons about non-violence. Nehru himself sounded guilty enough, confused about whether the ends justified such means. In his now regular interview with R. K. Karanjia, this one taken a little after Goa's freedom, he answered the accusation that India had lost its moral face:

> It's nonsense to say that we have lost face, moral or otherwise. At the same time, I will admit that there has been something lost in terms of our philosophy of finding peaceful solutions to all such problems. The military approach – that is, any kind of warlike action – is alien to our culture and tradition. In fact we want the use of force outlawed ... The means employed are as vital for us as the ends they serve. This is what Gandhiji taught us; and really this was the dilemma that held us back from any military action in Goa for 14 long years.

But it did not hold Nehru back, or Gandhi for that matter, when the raiders came to Kashmir; and Goa was always considered as much a part of India as Kashmir. However, the Soviet Union applauded (Brezhnev was visiting India then), as did Africa. And Nasser proved his friendship when on 16 December he stopped a Portuguese troopship carrying arms and ammunition at Suez – after Britain had allowed it through Gibraltar. India warmed to Nasser.

Much of the criticism Nehru faced – of hypocrisy – was self-inflicted. He had the option of 'police action' on the lines of Hyderabad; it would be a logical outcome of his contention that Goa was part of India. (General J. N. Chaudhury was, incidentally, involved in both Hyderabad and Goa.) But he allowed the image of the India he was constructing before the world to get in the way. On 1 September of that very year 1961 Nehru, Tito and Nasser had formally institutionalized their concept of non-alignment at Belgrade. Nehru had taken the lead in condemning war, particularly in this nuclear age. Their resolution on nuclear war was Nehru's last great achievement on the stage he loved so much, one which encompassed the world.

Foreign policy was Jawaharlal Nehru's love, and those who worked with him here were privileged to watch not only a brilliant mind but also the full range of his moods and passions. The finest fund of stories comes from that natural raconteur, Gundevia, and it seems a shame not to steal a few from his book. It was September 1946, just after Nehru had formed the Interim Government. Keen to meet the man of the future, but unable to find a way through protocol, Gundevia, on an impulse, sent a handwritten letter by the simplest of processes – a bearer, to Nehru's residence at 17 York Road. To the astonishment of the Foreign Office mandarins, Gundevia got a call from the Prime Minister's office inviting him to join Nehru for dinner at 8.15 p.m. K. P. S. Menon was the second guest, Indira was the hostess, and Feroze Gandhi was the other person at the table. The only conversation all through dinner was about Chiang Kai-shek, the current darling of the West. (Nehru was the Bad Boy for having kept the Congress out of the war.) Suddenly in the middle of dinner, Jawaharlal asked Indira to bring out the multi-coloured kimono Chiang had presented to him, put it on and began strutting about in the tiny drawing-room, imitating Chiang, while the audience combined their amusement with a proper degree of admiration for his histrionics, applauding on the unsuggested but understood cues. Nehru took off the kimono only after dinner, when he suddenly looked sleepy. Menon took the hint, bade goodbye and indicated to Gundevia that it was time to go. Nehru awoke suddenly and asked Gundevia to stay back. The others said goodbye, and the two began discussing Burma, where Gundevia was then posted. It was the start of yet another working night for Nehru, a schedule he would keep to the end of his life. As he was leaving, Gundevia asked, 'Are you sitting down to work again, sir?'

Nehru replied, 'Yes, there is far too much to do yet.' There would never be any less.

The same man could lose his humour quickly too. When Gundevia returned to Delhi from Burma in August 1948 to join the Indian foreign service, he brought a message from the Burmese Prime

Minister, Thakin Nu, suggesting an India–Burma defence pact, or a mutual defence treaty, which would help both in any confrontation with China. When Nehru heard the idea, he exploded. Gundevia writes: 'And then I saw the angry Nehru for the first time. "He must be crazy," he shouted at me. "Does he want to provoke China? What is China going to do to Burma? It's nonsense. It is real nonsense. I will explain it to him when he comes here," he said, cooling down.'

The mercury kept shifting even at the end of Nehru's life, when Gundevia returned to become Commonwealth and Foreign Secretary. Once Gundevia showed Nehru a Pak newspaper article describing Occupied Kashmir as the 'kept wife of Pakistan'. Nehru was extremely amused and retained the cutting with him. That evening there was an important formal dinner for a visiting dignitary. Seeing Gundevia and his wife Rokshi, Nehru walked up and, laughing loudly, said, 'Don't be angry; I have given away your "kept wife" to someone.' That someone was a British correspondent who had come to see him. Then Nehru turned to Rokshi and said, 'Don't ask your husband any questions about this.' Nehru's humour could be sardonic too. At one meeting he heard endless complaints from ambassadors about how Pakistani propaganda always managed to score over Indian because the Pak envoys were encouraged to use lies, while Indians were not. Nehru turned to Gundevia, sitting in as Commonwealth Secretary at the conference, and said with a short laugh, 'Maybe you are right. But I don't know that our Commonwealth Secretary sits in his room and spends all his time telling the truth, all twenty-four hours.'

Well, at least the sense of humour had survived the war with China.

44 Occupational Hazards

Norman Cousins was, as any good journalist should have been doing, teasing the Prime Minister – seriously. He was interviewing Nehru in 1961, when the man who used the sword so bluntly in 1947, the fire-belching Master Tara Singh, was on a Gandhian 'hunger-strike' in pursuit of his demand for a Punjabi-speaking state in India. The quotation marks are due to the fact that there were widespread rumours that he was cheating and nibbling a bit of food secretly. Be that as it may, it was a problem which Nehru had to tackle, and quite clearly a question which a journalist had to ask in an interview. How did he react to this hunger-strike? 'Frankly,' Nehru replied, 'I don't like it, I don't think this is the right way to go about persuading a government.' The irony of his answer struck him. He smiled and added, 'I think I told you that a politician has to act in a certain way. What else is there to be done? I can't give in to the man and allow India to become a mass of splinters.' Later he mused, 'But you don't have to try very hard if you want to catch me in an inconsistency. This is the occupational disease of any philosopher who finds himself in the position of an operating leader.'

Norman Cousins mentions in his essay ('Nehru: Man and Symbol', in *Profiles of Nehru*, edited by Cousins, 1966) that the evidence of fatigue was written on Nehru's face. Half a century given to his country had seeped into the eyes; the handsome man, who outshone any Eastern prince with nothing more on him than hand-spun cotton, was finally beginning to show signs of the burden he had had to carry. The country seemed to be in a carping mood. After the euphoria of the 1950s the sharp twang of criticism could now be heard. The criticism was still shrouded in affection for Nehru, and people volunteered their own excuses to defend the PM (as he was now known) they loved: if only he was not so tired all the time, if only his advisers were not so vile, and so on. Of all the burdens Nehru had to carry, none was greater than preventing India from further fragmentation. The steel came out in Jawaharlal but rarely, but this was one issue which never failed to bring it out. He had no illusions about the Akalis and in particular Master Tara Singh; 'this man' would readily turn India into splinters if he was appeased.

The greatest failure of Jawaharlal Nehru's life was the partition of India in 1947. But at least that was a responsibility he shared with others. His greatest success, perhaps, was the fact that he kept the rest of India united. It was not just Kashmir and Punjab where separatism threatened, but also in the far corner of the north-east, Nagaland, and in the south, in Tamil Nadu. Nor was his problem only a matter of minorities demanding their different homelands. Language, that most potent of loves, was at one point a far greater source of internal bitterness in the country, particularly when the south began to feel that Hindi, the official national language, was the latest incarnation of north Indian domination.

When Jinnah issued his dramatic edict declaring Friday 22 December 1939 a 'day of deliverance', to celebrate the resignation of the Congress ministries, there was at least one Hindu on his side: E. V. Ramaswami Naicker, leader of the Justice Party of 'Dravidistan' (or 'Dravida Nadu') and honoured with the title of 'Periyar' ('Man of Genius') by his followers for his leadership and his courage in going to gaol for the Dravidian cause. Periyar sat beside Jinnah on a stage dressed in green silk when the Muslim League's Madras session began on 12 April 1941 at the People's Park, a fellow secessionist in spirit. In fifteen years he went to gaol twenty-three times – all under Congress rule. The first man to send him inside was C. Rajagopalachari, in 1937. In obedience to party policy, the first Congress Premier introduced Hindi into the schools, and Naicker launched an anti-Hindi agitation. Hindi, said the father of Dravida Nadu, was the language of northern imperialism, and the Tamils would break India rather than surrender to the Aryan north. The problem, of course, was that the Congress was committed to making Hindi the national language, and some of its advocates in *khadi* could have taught Periyar a thing or two about militancy. The dilemma was a critical one when the time came to frame the Constitution; and Nehru was directly responsible for creating an exit route, both in his capacity as Prime Minister and as chairman of the committee of experts set up by the Congress in 1946. It was he who drafted and moved the objectives resolution in the Constituent Assembly in December 1946. He found a solution by retaining English as one of the official languages till 1965 – so the problem did not return in his lifetime. (When it did, within months of his death, the solution was to leave things broadly as he had left them.)

Now a more serious issue cropped up: should the internal map of India, so far drawn to facilitate imperial interests, be changed and, if so, on what principles? The Congress had long committed itself to the creation of linguistic states in the federation of free India. As far back as in 1905 Congress accepted the principle that language was the best yardstick for the geography of a province when it demanded the reunification of Bengal. In 1908 the party set up a separate Bihar unit on the same principle. In 1917 it demanded the creation of Sind and Andhra, although there was strong opposition from leaders like Annie Besant. Gandhi put his huge weight behind this view after he took over the Congress. At Nagpur in 1920 the Congress made the redemarcation of provinces on a linguistic basis into one of its principal political objectives, and the next year Gandhi reorganized the party on these lines in his new Constitution. In 1927 the Congress formally resolved that 'the time had come for the redistribution of provinces on a linguistic basis' and demanded the immediate formation of Andhra, Utkal, Sind and Karnataka. The Nehru Committee in 1928 affirmed: 'If a province has to educate itself and do its daily work through the medium of its own language, it must necessarily be a linguistic area . . . Language as a rule corresponds with a special variety of culture, of traditions and literature. In a linguistic area all these factors will help in the general progress of the province.' In 1937 at the Calcutta session the Congress demanded the immediate formation of Andhra and Karnataka. (Sind and Orissa had been conceded.) And in 1938 the working committee promised at a session in Wardha that the Congress would create Andhra, Karnataka and Kerala the moment it came to power in free India.

When freedom came, however, Jawaharlal Nehru changed his mind. Partition had so affected him that he would not be party to any decision which he felt encouraged fissiparous tendencies. As he told the Constituent Assembly on 27 November 1947: 'First things must come first, and the first thing is the security and stability of India.' Patel, who found so much to differ on with Nehru, agreed on this. The Dar Commission was appointed by the drafting committee of the Constituent Assembly and (doubtless on a nod) recommended in December 1948 that provinces should be created on the basis of administrative convenience, not language. Then a Gandhian who had participated in the Dandi march, Potti Sriramalu, decided to try an old formula on the new government; on 20 October 1952 he began a fast unto death – or unto an Andhra state. It was a fast of Gandhian proportions. Sriramalu survived till 11.20 p.m. on 15 December before passing away. As violence now shook the Telugu-speaking districts of Madras province, Nehru surrendered. On 18 December 1952 the Cabinet decided to allow the formation of what was described as the first linguistic state in India. Nehru ruefully observed to his home minister K. N. Katju on 13 February 1953, 'You will observe that we have disturbed the hornets' nest and I believe most of us are likely to be badly stung.' He tried to stress to the Andhras that they had only got a province and not a country. When he addressed the mammoth crowds at the Cole's High School grounds in Kurnool on 1 October 1953, the day the state was formed, Nehru said in Hindi: 'I am a Kashmiri. I live in Delhi. Today I have come to Andhra. I have as much right here as anyone living in Andhra . . . do not forget that the Andhra state is part and parcel of the mother country.'

But other hornets had to be appeased. On 29 December 1953 a three-member States Reorganization Commission, headed by Sayyid Fazl Ali (H. N. Kunzru and K. M. Panikkar were the other members), was set up. Its report, presented on 30 September 1955, conceded linguistic states but was not always logical. While there were a number of inconsistencies over borders, the report left two large bilingual provinces untouched: Bombay, which was an amalgam of Marathi- and Gujarati-speaking populations, with the capital Bombay itself reflecting a sophisticated, urban and cosmopolitan culture distinct from either; and Punjab, with Punjabi- and Hindi-speaking populations. There was violence and intense wrangling before Bombay was divided into Maharashtra and Gujarat in 1960 (one of the important decisions Mrs Gandhi influenced in her father's lifetime). The demand for a separate Punjabi-speaking (and consequently Sikh-majority) state was being promoted by the theocratic Akali Dal. Every memory of the 1930s and 1940s warned Nehru that theocrats could never be trusted. With time, his firmness on the question of Indian unity had only strengthened; as he made extremely clear, he was quite ready even for war with any secessionist movement in the country (in his speech at Tiruchirapalli on 9 December 1957).

He was equally certain that any concession to the Akalis would lead eventually to a secessionist problem in Punjab.

The Cabinet Mission of 1946 may or may not have been able to accede to every demand but it was certainly willing to hear one made. Master Tara Singh offered two options which in his view would satisfy the Sikhs: a united India with a national government in which representation was on the basis of communities; or, failing that, a separate Sikh state which the Khalsa could call their own. The violence of partition made Sikhs and Hindus allies against Muslims, and the idea of Khalistan got submerged. Nehru promised the Sikhs that they would 'experience the glow of freedom' in India; and when he formed his government took a Sikh on the principle of communal representation. Baldev Singh came in as a nominee of the Panthic Committee.

Punjab was first administered in two units. The princely states were merged into PEPSU (Patiala and East Punjab States Union), while the rest remained simply Punjab. Sikh–Hindu harmony was first shaken during the 1951 census when Hindus in large numbers claimed Hindi as their mother tongue. The Akalis immediately set off the alarm bells: Hindi was the first step towards Hindu domination; the Sikhs must rally and preserve their language, Punjabi, with its separate Gurmukhi script. They began to demand a smaller Punjab in which Punjabi with the Gurmukhi script could be the official state language. Instead of granting this smaller Punjab Suba, the Fazl Ali Commission made the state bigger by merging Punjab, PEPSU and Himachal Pradesh into a single integrated unit. The commission offered a disingenuous reason for doing so:

> Numerically, the Sikhs are a small community, but they are an enterprising and vigorous people. Their creative energy needs greater opportunities than those which a small unit can offer. Those amongst them who have pinned their faith to a homeland which cannot be justified on administrative grounds, and in which the political power of the Sikh community is likely to be evenly balanced by the power and influence of the other major community, seem to disregard this fact.

Nehru had no illusions that he was fighting Sikh communalism in Punjab and, unlike the commission, did not feel compelled to hide what he thought. The Akalis vilified him. 'Tyrant' and 'Goebbels' were the mildest of the epithets. Master Tara Singh fulminated in *Spokesman* of 19 October 1955: 'A decree of Sikh annihilation has been passed. We are face to face with a calamity greater than that of 1947. The catastrophe of 1947 finished thousands of Sikhs. The report of the States Reorganization Commission wipes us out from the face of the world.' One Sikh who had no such fears was the dynamic chief minister of Punjab, a graduate in political science from the University of Michigan, Pratap Singh Kairon. He tackled the communalists among both Hindus and Sikhs with such firmness that he won Nehru's unstinting admiration. Nehru even turned a quiet blind eye when he learned that Kairon's police had shot people dead although under instructions not to open fire. Kairon backed his police, and Nehru backed Kairon, albeit with a hint that such extreme action should be avoided. When local Congressmen revolted against Kairon, accusing him of both high-handedness and corruption, Nehru defended him valiantly, putting his own reputation on the line as his enemies tried to make the Kairon mud stick on the Nehru jacket. As Nehru wrote to Tara Singh on 26 May 1958, Kairon may have had his failings, 'no doubt, as all of us have. But in this land where communalism is always raising its head in some form or the other, it was a relief to have as a comrade a person who was above this failing.' After the 1962 polls, Nehru took the personal initiative to ensure that, despite all the factional anger against him, Kairon was re-elected unanimously by the legislature party as chief minister.

Corruption had become an issue by the late 1950s, as the mystique of the sacrificing, gaol-going Congressman began to wear off, and as revelations of pay-offs and deals in high places began to circulate. Nehru, of course, was never attacked himself, but he seemed to take the criticism of colleagues to heart. Increasingly he began to look upon any attack on a colleague as an indirect attack on him, in the sense that since his critics could not hurt him they went after his closest colleagues. One of his dearest friends, T. T. Krishnamachari, became victim of a charge made by Nehru's own son-in-law, Feroze Gandhi. He attacked Krishnamachari, then finance minister, for helping a particular business man by asking the government-owned Life Insurance Corporation to make dubious investments in his firm. An inquiry confirmed that malpractices had occurred; but though Nehru insisted that there was no *mala fides*, only carelessness, he also accepted Krishnamachari's resignation. Neither could he save his trusted private secretary M. O. Mathai, who had been his powerful special assistant since 1946. In the winter of 1958 the Communists launched an intense campaign against a man who probably had more access to confidential files than anyone else, the Prime Minister apart. He had begun to work for Nehru as an unpaid secretary some months before the latter joined government. Mathai said he did not need the money because he had made enough during his service with the American Red Cross on the Assam–Burma border through the sale of wartime surpluses. The charge against him was that he built a fortune through improper means, using a trust as the funnel for the generosity of the famous business house, the Birlas. Formally, all the inquiries exonerated him, and Nehru himself gave him as clean a bill of health as could be expected. Mathai none the less resigned, and Nehru accepted the resignation on 18 January 1959. On 27 January – his birthday – Mathai left the Prime Minister's house after an affectionate hug from Nehru. But the real charge against him was that he was a CIA agent, that his initial wealth had been the CIA's investment in a mole and that he had been supplying his mentors with just about every bit of valuable information for all these years. As S. Gopal, Nehru's official biographer, puts it, Cabinet Secretary Vishnu Sahay, who investigated the case, was privately convinced that Mathai had compromised just about every file since the days of the Interim Government, although he never made the slightest suggestion of this in his formal report to the government. Nehru was apparently persuaded by the private conviction of his investigating officer.

In April 1960 Master Tara Singh launched a fresh agitation for a Punjabi Suba. He went to gaol, and his second-in-command Sant Fateh Singh took over and began a fast, which ended when Kairon offered him a weak excuse to do so. On 15 August 1961 Tara Singh, aiming to recoup the heroism stakes, began his 'fast unto death'. Kairon let Tara Singh down badly; he decided to let him die of hunger. To ensure that this would be a real fast, elaborate security arrangements were made – on the face of it to guard Tara Singh, but in fact to ensure that no food was taken in surreptitiously at night. Tara Singh gave up his fast on 1 October; with it went his credibility. Sant Fateh Singh took over. But as the elections of 1962 proved, the Congress had very successfully met this challenge from the Master and the Sant. And, as the war of 1965 with Pakistan proved, the commitment of the Sikhs to India had not been affected one iota by the agitation for a Punjabi Suba. It was left to Nehru's successors to turn Punjab into a tragedy after he had kept it safe for his country.

By 1960 Nehru had also brought another strong challenge to Indian unity within reasonable control, although the violence continued intermittently till his last days. There were no guns in the Punjab; here, on exactly the opposite side of India, it became a regular guerrilla war. This was the well-armed secessionist movement on the borders of Burma, a tale which, Nehru once said, read almost like detective fiction.

The British came to Assam in the traditional way: when the ruling clan of Ahoms (a semi-Mongoloid people from Burma who conquered the region in the thirteenth century) had become so weak and corrupt that they had to seek British help in repelling an invasion by the Burmese in the first quarter of the nineteenth century. The price of support was the Treaty of Yandabo, and the British began to extract their reward. They slowly consolidated their presence, using a combination of conciliation and control to keep the tribes quiet while they concentrated on the economic exploitation of the region: first tea, and later oil, minerals and forest resources. As they expanded their sway, the toughest resistance came from a number of sects, clubbed under one name, the Nagas. It was only in 1878, after a fair cost in lives, that they managed to set up a civil and police headquarters in the picturesque Angami Naga village called Kohima.

Kohima was to become one of the most famous battlefields of the Second World War. It was from this point, now a town, that the forces of Japan and Subhas Bose's Indian National Army were turned back. One of the chief collaborators of the invading columns was a man called Zapu Phizo, who provided the Japanese with the most critical of assets: knowledge, the lie of routes and paths along the hills through which they could fulfil the ultimate Japanese dream – the invasion of India. His only condition was that, after the Japanese had won, the Nagas would be allowed complete independence as a sovereign state. The Nagas had good reasons for their antipathy towards the plainsmen, who added the insult of superiority to the injury of economic exploitation, looking down upon the Nagas as 'dog-eaters' and naked 'licentious drunkards'. It was the missionaries who had brought some change to the traditional behaviour patterns of the clans. With Christianity came education and a better life, but the Nagas still stuck proudly to their ancient culture, even if some of its excesses were whittled away by access to the nineteenth and twentieth centuries. In any case, they had nothing to thank the plainsmen for.

But the Allies, not the Japanese, won. Just before freedom, the Nagas signed a nine-point agreement with the British by which the existing administrative arrangements would continue for ten years, after which the Nagas would have the right either to extend the agreement or to draw up a new one. Phizo, now the unchallenged leader of Naga nationalism, had no doubt in his mind that this piece of paper signified independence by 1957. He instructed the Nagas not to participate in the first elections under the Indian Constitution, and the boycott was successful. Equally, however, the first Prime Minister of India had no doubt in his mind that the Nagas might want anything but the one thing they would never get was independence. They would be offered equality and development instead.

The first major programme was launched in the Naga hills on the day India adopted its new Constitution: 26 January 1950, when construction began on the 128-mile Aizwal–Lungleh road. Three years and three months later the Prime Minister of India himself came to declare it open. He had made his views on the status of Nagaland known from the very beginning; the maximum he would consider was autonomy, but there was no question of independence. On 2 February 1951 he wrote to Jairamdas Daulatram, the governor of Assam, and Bishnu Ram Medhi, the chief minister, about the policy to be followed: while no violence would be tolerated, the administration should concentrate on winning the support of the people. He wanted to visit the area himself soon. He was willing to meet Phizo but not to discuss Naga freedom. On 7 August 1951 Phizo was formally informed that independence was not possible. When Phizo met Nehru in March 1952 he heard the same thing.

The chance to visit Nagaland came in March and April 1953 when Nehru went to Burma. From there he flew with the Burmese Prime Minister U Nu to the Naga areas in Burma, and they crossed into the Indian Naga hills together. The organized receptions were colourful, if not always enthusiastic. One of the songs prepared for Nehru went:

> The morning stars are fading,
> The moonlight is becoming dim,
> Birds chirp; the eastern sky is getting red.
> From over the hills our own great man Nehru comes.
> Oh, Lushai maidens, get ready your welcome;
> Our own great man comes.

The sentiment was hardly as generous everywhere. Nehru was visibly angry when at a meeting a group of Nagas walked off while U Nu was talking; he thought it a deliberate insult to a guest. When inaugurating the new road on 3 April he attacked 'outsiders' for misleading the Naga people and left little doubt about who he meant when he added that, during the British days, officials and missionaries had worked in tandem. Since 1947 there had been an additional influx of American missionaries into the region.

What Nehru saw of the situation during his visit left him in no doubt that tough action was required. He told the governor not to hesitate if there was any provocation from Phizo. But he was careful not to antagonize Christian sentiment in the country, through any selective harshness towards missionaries. He did not want Christians to feel any sense of persecution. So while he would not encourage such activity, he refused to ban evangelical work either. There was cause for provocation, though. When a letter was discovered in circulation to pastors urging them to celebrate 5 April as Independence Day, Nehru made it quickly clear that any pastor doing so would find himself out of the country. Orders were issued to check the antecedents and activities of missionaries, and fresh recruitment was stopped. Even so, when his ministers – and his President, Rajendra Prasad – made statements that sounded hurtful to missionaries, Nehru asked them not to do so. As he impressed on others, he was against foreign missionaries only when they behaved like foreigners, not when they behaved like missionaries. His chief adviser on tribal affairs was in fact a British missionary totally committed to India, Verrier Elwin.

The political solution that Nehru envisaged was the gradual and careful creation of an autonomous area for the Nagas while the Assam Rifles would deal with the hostiles. His message to Phizo remained the same: give up arms, accept India; only then would a compromise be possible. Phizo responded by stepping up violence.

Nehru ordered an all-out hunt for Phizo. In March 1956 Phizo's Naga National Council declared the formation of a federal government. This was clear rebellion, and Nehru decided that it would have to be dealt with as a military rather than a political problem. The politics could resume only once the resistance was truly broken. But Nehru vetoed suggestions that hostiles be machine-gunned from the air. The army was now increasingly being accused of brutality. Nehru was worried both about international propaganda and about the effect such methods would have on Nagas. He asked his most distinguished commander, General Thimayya, to go and take charge at once. That had immediate impact, and by the end of the year a feeling began to grow that Phizo's men were on the run. Of course with the jungles of Burma offering sanctuary, they could always hit, even when on the run.

Following an inspired 'demand' by the moderate Naga People's Convention, Nehru felt confident enough to announce an amnesty on 25 September 1957. The government also said it would amend the Constitution to separate the Naga areas from Assam and put them under central administration. The hostiles made better use of the amnesty than the government. They used the opportunity to recoup and re-arm themselves (Pakistan was generous), and slowly the initiative went back to them, while public perception grew that Nehru was being weak. Delhi engaged in a carrot-and-stick approach: the civilian commissioner set about winning hearts, while the armed forces concentrated on breaking heads. It was a messy deadlock. Nehru upped the ante. The Naga People's Convention was now asked to demand a separate state of Nagaland, within the Indian union. It was not, on paper, a very good idea; with a population of just 400,000 and only half a million rupees in revenue, Nagaland was simply too small to become a state. This would, moreover, set in motion similar demands elsewhere in the hills of the north-east, as indeed it did.

Phizo meanwhile turned his rebellion into an international campaign. Purchasing an illegal passport under a false name, he reached Britain. Two influential men, David Astor, owner of *The Observer*, and the Reverend Michael Scott, whose work in Africa had made him a hero, took up his cause with a vigour that angered Nehru, particularly as Phizo's claims about army atrocities in Naga areas were totally believed by his British lobbyists. Scott asked Nehru for a meeting to discuss Nagaland. Nehru refused. The next day, 16 July 1960, Nehru wrote to Vijaylakshmi Pandit:

> This whole story, ever since Michael Scott appeared on the scene and produced Phizo, has been quite extraordinary. It almost sounds like some detective fiction. Why Michael Scott or David Astor should have proceeded in this particular way is beyond me . . . When the famous day comes when these charges are made public, we shall look into them and deal with them . . . Astor and Scott can go ahead and do just what they like.

The suspicion that British intelligence might be involved in Phizo's sudden arrival in London was being voiced. In any case Nehru had made up his mind that he would not settle with Phizo any more. He refused to talk to Phizo and/or Scott in Delhi in August 1960. The maximum he would allow was a conversation with an official in the High Commission in London. Then he put the rest of his political plan into operation and granted statehood to Nagaland – with the governor of Assam also overseeing the new state as a small sop to Assamese opinion. The army continued its work. Scott was allowed to visit Nagaland to measure for himself the strength of Phizo's accusation, but Nehru was not going to pull up his army in any way. He assured Parliament that the army would continue its campaign. The Chinese war produced a lull in this particular battle, but hostilities resumed in early 1963. Phizo, still in exile in Britain, seems to have felt outflanked by this time, particularly since desertions from his camp to the government side had begun. On 12 February 1963 Bertrand Russell conveyed a message from Phizo to Nehru saying he was now willing to negotiate; and Scott brought Phizo's proposal for a ceasefire. But now the Nagas who had been loyal to Nehru and India discouraged a settlement, and Nehru agreed with them. They had no desire to see Phizo back. In desperation Phizo appealed to Pakistan for help, but time was running out on him. The first elections in Nagaland were due in the spring of 1964 and, despite the attempts of the rebels at disruption, they went through. Delhi now told Phizo that if he wanted peace he could talk to the elected government in Nagaland; obviously this would destroy Phizo's claim to be the only legitimate voice of the Nagas, and he could only turn down the suggestion. That was, in fact, the end of the road for Phizo. In 1964 a last attempt to come to terms was made – with Nehru's consent –

when Jaya Prakash Narayan, Michael Scott and B. P. Chaliha went to Nagaland and signed an agreement with the hostiles. But the success, such as it was, remained purely psychological. It was the government brought into power through the democratic process of the Indian Constitution which remained in charge. Instead of power in a free country, Zapu Phizo received nothing but a small house in the British countryside and the loneliness of self-imposed exile as gradually the Astors and Scotts wearied of him. The India that Jawaharlal Nehru left behind for his successors had the same geography that obtained at the moment of ceasefire on 1 January 1949; all that had been lost was the portion of Kashmir occupied by Pakistan. Perhaps if destiny had given him a little more time he might have just about settled that problem too, for in the last four weeks of his life he made one final lunge for a peaceful solution to Kashmir. But if one error of judgement had defeated him in the fourth month of his prime ministership, then time ran out in the last.

45 What Present Can I Send You?

The first time that Jawaharlal Nehru made a serious effort to resign was on 29 April 1958. In 1946 Lord Wavell had ignored the frequent flip-flop threats of a man unaccustomed to power. In 1950 Patel and Tandon almost goaded him into giving up power. This time there was a great outcry against the suggestion, not just in India, but from all corners of the world.

The newspapers, but naturally, had eight-column headlines. The *Hindusthan Standard* published the full text of the prepared statement Nehru read out that day at the Congress parliamentary party meeting. 'Some weeks ago I said', it went, 'that I felt rather tired and stale and would like a change. Since then many friends and colleagues have asked what I meant and there have been speculations in the press. I had no desire to come to a decision in a hurry or without consulting the Party which has done me the honour of electing me its leader.' He said he had earlier written to the President and was now formally approaching the party. Why did he want to quit? Fatigue. These forty years of public life, and the intimate relationship that had grown with the Indian people in this time, had been the source of great exhilaration, but he now wanted some respite from the sheer burden and staleness of office:

> The work of a Prime Minister allows no respite, it is continuous and unceasing, much of it is routine, and much requires important decisions. There is little time for quiet thinking. I feel now that I must have a period when I can free myself from this daily burden and can think of myself as an individual citizen of India and not as Prime Minister.

The absence of two close colleagues in February had deepened Nehru's depression. Krishnamachari was forced to resign (Nehru, though, brought him back in the 1960s), and his beloved comrade of so many decades, Azad, died on 22 February. Nehru was not putting on an act; it was a genuine desire to take a break, even if only a temporary one. In retrospect, it would both have been an excellent precedent to set and have settled the contentious question of succession. But the eventual successor, Lal Bahadur Shastri, immediately organized an emergency meeting of Congress MPs and leaders, who predictably decided that there was no question of allowing the Prime Minister to resign. One Congress MP at the parliamentary party meeting piquantly complained that Nehru wanted time off to think about how to save the world from hydrogen bombs (a declared aim in the statement) but he had no hesitation in dropping a hydrogen bomb on the Congress Party. Equally reassuring – and doubtless uplifting – were the messages he received from abroad. Washington and Moscow might agree on nothing else, but they agreed that there was no question of Nehru leaving the scene. Eisenhower, with whom Nehru got on very well, wrote immediately, on 1 May, saying it would be a misfortune. And when the Congress pressure forced Nehru to stay on, Krushchev wrote on 8 May 1958 to say how delighted he was. The only concession Nehru extracted from his party was a long holiday in the hill station of Manali in the Himalayan foothills. (At the age of sixty-eight he still could not resist his glaciers and wanted to go across the Rohtang pass into Lahaul and Spiti. His doctors finally managed to stop him at the 13,600-foot-high pass.)

As his daughter and constant companion, Indira, would complain, however, a holiday in India was never much of a holiday. Wherever Nehru might be, the phone would ring and people queue up to see him. The only 'full' holidays that Jawaharlal managed to eke out were brief days during a long foreign tour, when an excuse (as for instance an ambassadors' conference in a picturesque Alpine village) would cover a day or two of relaxation. Perhaps the most famous of these holidays was the one in Burgenstock in the summer of 1953. The mandarins gathered from all over the world to give Nehru a chance to dangle his feet from cable-cars: Secretary-General N. R. Pillai, Foreign Secretary Subimal Dutt, Commonwealth Secretary M. J. Desai from South Block in New Delhi, K. P. S. Menon from Moscow, H. S. Malik from Paris, B. N. Chakraborty from London, Prem Krishen from Czechoslovakia and Jagat Mehta and Gundevia from Berne. There was work, of course – the conference itself. And there were calls: from Dr Karl Gruber, Foreign Minister of Austria, then under four-power occupation, who had come over to ask for advice on how to placate the Russians. After two afternoons of talks, Nehru's message was that Austria would get nowhere by ganging up with either side. Nor would the Russians leave if they believed Austria would become pro-West. Try neutrality, Nehru advised; in any case, he doubted if Austria could try anything else.

The man who made this holiday famous was someone Nehru was keen on meeting, an exile from McCarthy's United States: Charlie Chaplin. Nehru invited him to dinner on the last day of the conference. The programme was that Chaplin would stay overnight and then motor down with Nehru to his estate at Corsier for lunch before Nehru flew off to London. Nehru was enchanted by this genius, and the genius by his equal in the world of politics. In *My Autobiography* (1964), Chaplin remembers the morning's drive to Corsier:

> Nehru talked brilliantly through the journey, while his chauffeur must have been going at 70 miles an hour or more, speeding along precipitous narrow roads, and coming suddenly upon sharp turns. Nehru was engrossed in explaining India's politics, but I must confess I missed half of what he was saying, so occupied was I with backseat driving. As the brakes screeched Nehru continued unperturbed.

He continued his lectures in Chaplin's apple orchard and on the lawn as they walked through the fabulous 37-acre estate, Manoir de Ban, at Corsier, above Vevey on Lake Geneva. When they finally sat on the veranda for pre-lunch drinks, trays appeared with Chaplin's finest champagne. Nehru protested that he did not drink. But Chaplin, all hands and gestures, insisted that the very best wine in his cellar had been brought out. Nehru took a sip and kept the glass with him for the rest of the sumptuous meal. Lunch over, it was off to the Air India Constellation and work once again, this time in London.

Indira went to the USSR from Switzerland for a month's private holiday, and she discovered that the government had kept a plane at her disposal to enable her to go wherever she wanted. It may have been one of the best investments in a human relationship made by Moscow. Indira was alone; Feroze Gandhi had not come with her. After a brief spell as a dutiful wife Indira Gandhi had returned to being what she preferred to be: her father's daughter, rather than someone else's wife. It was not as if the marriage had broken up; they still met frequently, and Feroze was a very good father to his two sons. But Indira had already chosen a different life; she had moved into her father's orbit and outside her husband's.

The ambivalence of the twin-culture Anand Bhavan found expression in a hundred minor ways. Despite all the Westernization, Indira's birthday was celebrated by the Hindu Samvat calendar rather than the Gregorian. Thus it was on 26 October 1930 rather than 19 November that Jawaharlal had written 'A Birthday Letter' from his cell in the Central Prison at Naini to his thirteen-year-old daughter, now on the threshold of another phase of her life as she became a teenager. 'On your birthday you have been in the habit of receiving presents and good wishes,' father wrote to daughter in the letter with which *Glimpses of World History* opens. (This epistle, however, is not one of the 196 letters which add to a massive romp through the history of civilization.) 'Good wishes', said Jawaharlal, 'you will still have in full measure, but what present can I send you from Naini Prison? My presents cannot be very material or solid. They can only be of the air and of the mind and spirit, such as a good fairy might have bestowed on you – things that even the high walls of prison cannot stop.' But Indira breathed that gift of the air with gratitude. Life with such a father was not easy. Her early loneliness is well known; all her fantasies and games of childhood were political. She would, in her games, get one set of dolls arrested by another; she started a Vanar Sena (Monkey Brigade) to challenge the British; she dreamt of herself as a Joan of Arc. She became fiercely protective and loyal to her tubercular mother, particularly as Kamala had to suffer the taunts of sisters-in-law. She remained in Europe after Kamala's death, but there were days when she did not even have enough money for a proper meal. Her father's prime ministership may have brought power, but there was not all that much of comfort, at least initially. When her second son, Sanjay, was born in December 1946, Nehru's house was so crowded with visitors that Feroze had briefly to camp on the lawn in a tent. (Indira had been hoping for a daughter and did not have a male name ready when Sanjay was born.)

Feroze was working on the *National Herald* in Lucknow in 1946, and he made his home there. But Nehru's need for someone to organize the social side of his life made him increasingly dependent on his daughter, whom he summoned frequently to Delhi. After Feroze joined the Constituent Assembly and shifted to Delhi, matters became a little easier, but eventually Indira felt she had no choice but to live with her father. As she explained in the nearest equivalent of an autobiography, a series of interviews published as *My Truth* (1980): 'When I went to live with my father at Teen Murti House, the residence of the Prime Minister, it wasn't really a choice. My father asked me to come and to set up the house for him. There was nobody else to do it.' There was no shortage of problems when it came to looking after guests. Oriental eating habits, conditioned by religion, run the gamut of possibilities. On top of this was the burden of a VIP's unpredictable tastes. (Indira discovered, for instance, that 'one distinguished guest, who declared himself a vegetarian, ended up eating everything but chicken'.) And then there were Nehru's own quirks. After his first meal at Buckingham Palace he changed the rules in his own house, and milk and sugar began to be passed around before the coffee (à la British royalty), to the constant bewilderment of guests who wondered if they had missed the coffee. Breakfast also was served country-house style with the food on hot plates – except that often guests who did not understand buffet breakfast would expect you to serve them at the table. There were guests every single day, ranging from close friends like Edwina, who came to live with them once a year, to the endless procession of VIPs and official invitees.

Life at Teen Murti was enriched by the traditional Nehru fondness for animals. There were dogs both of sophisticated pedigree and others rescued off the streets. Parrots, pigeons, squirrels, peacocks, deer: it was an informal zoo. On a visit to Assam they were presented with a baby catbear, or the red Himalayan panda, whom the boys named Bhimsa (or, like the warrior of the *Mahabharata*, Bhim). Bhimsa came as a small ball of fur and was given a corner in the children's bathroom before a home was made for him in an enclosure surrounded by wire netting. When Bhimsa got a mate they named her Pema – which means 'lotus' in Sikkimese. (The fondness for 'lotus' can hardly be missed.) Their cubs were the first born in captivity. The panda family doted on Jawaharlal and missed him when he was away. In 1955 came tiger cubs: Bhim, Bhairav and Hidimba. (Bhimsa was jealous.) Indira Gandhi recalls in *My Truth* that they were soon 'too big to be kept loose in a house with so much *va-et-viens*'. (Having studied on the Continent, Indira knew French well, although a purist might sniff that she spoke it with a

Swiss accent.) Bhim and Hidimba went off to the Lucknow zoo, while Bhairav had a more glamorous fate in store – Tito took him to Belgrade.

Entertaining the visiting VIPs, not to mention their wives, was an obvious strain. Yet for Indira it was also a splendid education in the nuances of power. Indira was chairman of the committee in charge of all the arrangements for the visit of Bulganin and Krushchev. When the two equals came to India, they made every effort to be seen as perfectly equal, in what was their first trip abroad; even their cars had to be abreast if they were travelling in separate vehicles. Indira recalled: 'When they arrived, they were equal but, by the time they left, Krushchev was already walking ahead. In lots of small ways you could see that Krushchev was putting Bulganin in his place, and that the latter didn't answer back. In the beginning, you couldn't take them through a small door because they had to walk side by side.' Like her formal education, this political tuition too was staccato and scattered, but utterly unique. If Jawaharlal Nehru had consciously been creating an heir, there was no better way to do it.

Well: did he? This is, of course, one of the great question marks about him. The best answer, one is afraid, will have to be the most boring one: yes and no. He never promoted her in politics himself; but he never restrained anyone else from promoting her. The point perhaps is that the second might never have been possible but for the fact that Indira took very naturally to politics and soon showed she was very good at it.

Just after freedom, when Gandhi was still alive, Govind Ballabh Pant, who had in 1937 inducted Nehru's sister Vijaylakshmi into the first Congress ministry in Uttar Pradesh, asked Indira to join UP politics or at least enter the Assembly. Unlike her aunt, Indira turned down the suggestion. An irritated Pant complained to Gandhi, implying that this slip of a girl had been rude to him. Indira repeated her answer to Gandhi; she claimed she was not cut out for politics. Gandhi laughed and let the matter pass. But she began accompanying her father on his election tours from the very first campaign. There were appeals to her to contest in 1952 from a constituency in Himachal Pradesh, Chamba. She refused and suggested Rajkumari Amrit Kaur's name instead, since they wanted a woman in any case. Indira promised however that she would visit the constituency during the campaign. She assumed, of course, that she would come with her father, and a visit was put in his itinerary. But in Himachal a rather possessive Rajkumari changed Nehru's schedule to suit the needs of just her own constituency, and he had no time to visit Chamba – to the bitter disappointment of the people who had built such expectations. To console them, Nehru arranged a visit by Indira to Chamba. That was the first meeting which Indira addressed alone. It was a great success. Spurred, she became deeply involved in Feroze's election, taking charge of one-half of Rae Bareli while Feroze concentrated on the other; it was a constituency from which she would later win and, in 1977, also lose. The area from Allahabad to Lucknow serves as a kind of Nehru borough in Indian politics.

In 1953 Indira was given the responsibility of organizing the women's wing of the Congress. Jawaharlal may have been careful about not being seen to take any initiative personally, but he quite evidently used trusted lieutenants from Allahabad like Lal Bahadur Shastri to nudge his daughter's political career along. She soon occupied all the chairs her father once did. In 1956 she became president of the Allahabad Congress Committee. Then, in 1957, she was elected to the powerful Central Election Committee, a critical job in an election year. The party president, U. N. Dhebar, put her name for election without consulting her, but it is inconceivable that he would have done so without consulting Jawaharlal. If there were only a paltry four votes against her, it was largely because she was Nehru's daughter. (Opposition from even just four people bothered Indira, and she tried to find out their names. She could get only one name.) She campaigned like a seasoned veteran all over the country in the 1957 elections, of which Shastri was placed in overall charge. She and Shastri worked closely together, and the Congress did even better than in 1952. Except for one shock: in the southern state of Kerala, for the first time in history, a Communist government came to power in a free vote.

With the communal violence of the north barely under control after independence, the crackle of another war began to be heard in the south. In March 1948 the Communist Party of India, with the approval of Stalin (they did very little then without approval), launched a militant movement in search of the revolution which the bourgeois lackeys of Anglo-American imperialism, Gandhi and Nehru, had thwarted. To varying degrees, the movement sparked off in Hyderabad, Andhra, Travancore-Cochin and Malabar in the south; in Tripura and Manipur in the north-east; in parts of Bengal, Bihar and Uttar Pradesh in the east; and in some corners of Maharashtra in the west. A key day in the revolutionary calendar was 9 March 1949; a railway strike was meant to choke the government, while an insurrection paralysed it. The Communists could find nothing right with the Congress government, not even the take-over of Hyderabad. One of their ideologues, G. M. Adhikari, argued (*What Is Happening in Hyderabad?*, 1949): 'Sardar Patel's army went to Hyderabad to stop the onward march of history, to save the Nizam and the oppressive feudal order, to save the bourgeois-feudal rule from the rising tide of the forces of the democratic revolution.' But Nehru refused to be hustled into banning the Communist Party. As he put it in a speech at Calcutta on 14 July 1949, the greatest enemy of communism in India was the Communist Party of India. They would destroy themselves by their own tactics. The crowds cheered.

He was even sharper at a press conference on 5 August the same year. Asked which was the lesser evil between communism and communalism, he retorted: 'An extraordinary question to ask, which do you prefer, death by drowning or falling from a precipice?' And when a journalist wondered whether Nehru would seek the help of the RSS to fight the Communists, he replied that although the RSS and the Communists were in a sense poles apart, nevertheless, in another sense, they were very near, because of their common love for violence and authoritarianism. When Bidhan Roy banned the CPI in Bengal in May, Nehru warned him that this would prove counterproductive. Yet Nehru had no doubt in his mind that the Communists did not have India's interests at heart. The violent war launched by the CPI in Telengana only confirmed his view that they would destroy this newly won freedom by their distorted leftism. When the CPI finally changed its policy, renounced violence and accepted parliamentary democracy, Nehru was relieved – if still acerbic about their propaganda. By the late 1950s he was confident that communism was no longer a threat to India, in some measure because of how he had handled the situation. Moscow too had given up hoping for an Indian revolution, leaving the ultra-loyal CPI wondering about how much use their loyalty had been. Nehru complained to Krushchev and Bulganin during their talks in India that Moscow was sending the CPI both instructions and money. Krushchev denied any abnormal help; it was only party-to-party fraternity and nothing more. Nehru, however, had made his point and was satisfied that Krushchev would keep Indo-Soviet interests above his concern about the fate of Indian communism.

In 1957 Nehru campaigned for the Congress as ardently in Kerala as anywhere else. If anything, he had become even more scathing about the Communists. He questioned both their patriotism and their intelligence. Speaking at Ernakulam on 24 February 1957 he said: 'The clock of the world has moved on while the clock of communist minds in India stopped long ago.' But the voters of Kerala preferred local time; the Communists won and formed their first government under one of their most brilliant leaders, a veteran of the Congress Socialist Party, E. M. S. Namboodiripad. Nehru's dismay was tempered with pleasure that India had provided such a triumphant display of democracy, and he was happy to let the CPI have its chance in authority.

Indira Gandhi had done heroic work in the 1957 elections, particularly in mobilizing women. Her nomination to the working committee of the Congress therefore was a perfectly legitimate reward. But the whispers were inevitable when in January 1959 the Congress unanimously named her to succeed Dhebar as the party president: the third Nehru and fourth woman to do so (Annie Besant, Nellie Sengupta and Sarojini Naidu being the others). She was on a *padayatra* (a walk) in Uttar Pradesh villages when she learned of the honour on 2 February 1959. The powerful chief of the Tamil Nadu Congress, K. Kamaraj, who had to talk to other Indians through an interpreter because he had absolutely no English, was among the main enthusiasts behind the move. (In 1966 he would make Indira Gandhi Prime Minister and regret his decision soon after.) Nehru kept studiously away from the whole process. Indira was sensible enough to appreciate that the honour was being devalued by the charge of nepotism, and she protested that she had not wanted the job. Observers could hardly not draw the parallel that Nehru had become party president in his fortieth year – thanks to *his* father. (Rajiv Gandhi became president of the Congress in 1984, in his fortieth year too; but only after the tragedy of Mrs Gandhi's assassination. The whole Nehru family had its tryst with destiny.) Even in *My Truth* the touchiness is apparent:

In February 1959 I was elected president of the Indian National Congress at the Nagpur session. This was a most important event in my political life. A few questions were asked at that time by political observers: had my father deliberately groomed me as his political heir? Or was he averse to the idea? Did he compromise my independence of thought or action? Could I remain in the public eye without attracting adverse comment? Was I able to stand for myself in Indian politics without compromising my independence as a woman? Finally, would my role have been easier if I had been my father's son rather than his daughter? These questions are not really for me to answer. All I can say is how I tried to fulfil what I considered to be my task.

Indira fulfilled the task well enough to earn the admiration of her party, if not its foes. Buffeted by factionalism and charges of corruption, the Congress was in a state of severe demoralization. Her remedy was a mixture of self-criticism within party circles and a counter-offensive against other parties in public. The party, she said, must keep pace with the times, involve more people in its activities, pick itself up. Despite a painful kidney ailment she worked tirelessly during her term. Simultaneously, she personally intervened in the 'direct action' which had been launched against the Communist government in Kerala. Nehru, keen to preserve his reputation as a democrat, was determined not to seem partisan; but she was party chief, not Prime Minister, and raised a national outcry against the Communists. She visited Kerala early in 1959 and told reporters on her return, 'Everything the Communists are doing is wrong.' You cannot get more definitive than that. E. M. S. Namboodiripad believed firmly that she played a major role in getting his government dismissed on 31 July 1959 under Article 356, which enables the President to take charge of a state if he is satisfied that constitutional governance has become impossible. Indira Gandhi later tried to play down her role, pointing out that most Congress leaders – even Feroze, who was an acknowledged dissident liberal – agreed with her assessment of the situation in Kerala. She certainly led from the front when going to the President, Rajendra Prasad, to argue why the Communists should go. No bleeding heart himself, Prasad was happy to concur, but of course it had to be a Cabinet decision. Congressmen believed that Nehru would not have been persuaded but for Indira's influence.

That she had influence is accepted. She was widely believed, for instance, to have played a major part in convincing her father to drop Krishna Menon after the Chinese débâcle and thereby deflect the mounting anger within the party towards Menon and the left-wingers. Equally undeniable is the fact that her stature in the country after her term as Congress president was now much higher than that of a Prime Minister's daughter. Success is its own virtue. Indira's politics in Kerala paid off when the Congress, in alliance with the Praja Socialist Party and the Muslim League, swept the polls in the special elections held in February 1960, winning 93 seats against the CPI's 29. She justified the alliance with the League thus: 'I don't believe the Muslim League is any more communal than anyone else in Kerala. Everything there is communal. Everything is run by the Nairs, the Nestorians, the Namboodiris, or some other sect. You have to deal with communal parties unless you want to forget about Kerala entirely.' (See Welles Hangen's *After Nehru, Who?*, 1963.)

Success in politics coincided with personal unhappiness for Indira. The drift in the marriage had taken Feroze far away by 1958. The separation was common knowledge. That was also the year Feroze suffered his first stroke. In September 1960 Feroze felt a pain in his chest while sitting in Parliament, and ignored it. Indira was on a visit to Kerala then. Only two days later did Feroze go to hospital, where the pain was found to be a stroke. Indira reached Delhi at eleven that night and rushed straight to hospital. Early next morning Feroze passed away. Zareer Masani quotes Indira (in his biography, *Indira Gandhi*, 1975) as saying: 'I was actually physically ill. It upset my whole being for years, which is strange, because after all he was very, very ill and I should have expected that he would die. However, it was not just mental shock, but it was as though somebody had cut me into two.' Averse to the Parsi method of disposing of corpses (being eaten by vultures), Feroze had wanted to be immolated. His teenage son Rajiv lit the funeral pyre. In the eyes of the common man, Nehru's son-in-law died a Hindu.

Indira now sought activity. 'I felt I had to be occupied,' she says in *My Truth*. She was nominated to the UNESCO executive board by the new President, Dr Radhakrishnan, and was active politically as chairman of the Congress National Integration Council. Her work after the communal riots in Jabalpur in 1961 was reminiscent of what she had done in 1947, and once again she was a star campaigner for the party in the 1962 general elections. The question of her succeeding her father, consequently, kept recurring. There was talk of giving her Cabinet experience, but Nehru never went to that extent. Her claim, though, was recognized by the man who wrote the famous book on the subject, Hangen. Morarji Desai headed his list of potential successors in *After Nehru, Who?*, followed by V. K. Krishna Menon, Lal Bahadur Shastri, Y. B. Chavan, Indira Gandhi, Jaya Prakash Narayan, S. K. Patil and – tendentiously, on the assumption that army rule was a real possibility in India – General Brij Mohan Kaul. Hangen may, however, be forgiven his last choice for he finished his book in November 1962, just before Kaul's humiliation in the war with China. Kaul apart, there is a degree of political logic in all the names. Nehru had seen Narayan as a potential Prime Minister from the very beginning. Morarji was a self-declared chairman and had made his intentions clear during the struggle for the deputy leadership of the Congress parliamentary party in 1961. (Indira Gandhi backed Jagjivan Ram, put up by Menon, against Morarji; it was, in effect, a struggle for the succession, and Morarji believed he would have won if Nehru had not called off the election.) Menon was a brilliant heir to the Nehru philosophy. Shastri had Nehru's affection, trust and the thoroughly important merit of coming from the right state, Uttar Pradesh. Chavan and Patil were dark horses, but not so dark as to be invisible. Why was Indira Gandhi there? Hangen believed that Nehru would promote her claim actively. He agreed with Frank Moraes that Nehru was too big a man to think in terms of dynasty, but yet felt that 'Nehru will do everything in his power to thwart the ambitions of the Congress Right Wing. He may well persuade himself that only his daughter could provide the essential continuity of policy after he leaves office. She is, after all, his only child and the only member of the family capable of holding the torch aloft after he goes.' But this logic demanded that Nehru organize the succession when still alive, for after him even her aunts would oppose Indira: 'Mrs Pandit says that India would not accept another Nehru as prime minister.' Hangen ended his chapter on Indira most perceptively:

Even now, as Nehru declines in health and strength, his grip on Congress is loosening. How much weaker will it be by the time he goes? Indira Gandhi will cast a shorter shadow when she leaves the Prime Minister's house. It is her misfortune that she will lose her most precious key to power the moment she needs it most – when her father's passing has left an empty room at the top. Without the key, I doubt that Indira Gandhi can open the door to that room unless, of course, it were battered down for her by as yet unseen forces dedicated to the Nehru legend and its political trappings.

The unseen forces did batter the door down.

Nehru took care to avoid making any suggestions. His standard answer was that the country's democracy was now good enough to find a successor from among 400 million people. He told Norman Cousins (*Saturday Review*, 27 May 1961):

> This business of picking an individual successor is something I find quite alien to my way of thinking. I am not trying to start a dynasty. I am not capable of ruling from the grave. How terrible it would be if I, after all I have said about the processes of democratic government, were to attempt to handpick a successor. The best I can do for India is to help our people as a whole to generate new leadership as it may be needed.

The one person who seemed to know who would succeed Jawaharlal Nehru – perhaps because she knew her father's mind – was Indira Gandhi. She recalls in *My Truth*: 'some time before my father's death, an American called Welles Hangen had asked who would succeed him. Without hesitation I had said: Mr Shastri. Hangen said that no one else mentioned that name and that his hot favourite was S. K. Patil.'

Hangen should have believed Indira Gandhi. He could have then dispensed with the question mark at the end of his book's title.

46 China: a Stab from the Front

Krishna Menon was only the sacrifice. The humiliation of 1962 was primarily the fault of Jawaharlal Nehru. It was, certainly, the kind of fault which only a visionary with trust could have made – a mistake which, in a very elemental sense, only a good man could have committed. But it was his failure, nevertheless; it was an intellectual mistake for which India had to pay such a heavy price that for a while it seemed as if all Nehru's own achievements of fifteen years would be undone. When it was all over, Nehru described the China war as a stab in the back. He was wrong. It was a stab from the front. He had only closed his eyes. Nehru should have understood the Chinese leaders, Mao and Chou, better. They had their visions too, they dreamt great dreams for their country also, but they did not become victims of a sentimentality which placed the idealism of peace over their perception of national interest. Chou signed the Pancha Sheela with India in 1954 – and, after using Nehru as the chaperone at Bandung in 1955, quietly and secretly established the first bridgehead with Pakistan in preparation for a war which was still seven long years of argument, accusation, nibbling, haggling, deceit and perfidy away. China replaced India as the most influential voice from Afro-Asia after that war. Yet surprisingly India gained too. In defeat, in tragedy, in desolate adversity, it discovered itself, finding deep roots of a nationalism which many thought never existed because no one had ever bothered to check. All good things come to an end, and so did the glorious years of Jawaharlal's leadership, when the magic of his genius created industry in the barren plains of central India, built dams in the hills from which rivers tumbled into the fields, brought presidents and prime ministers to Delhi's door, from Khrushchev to Eisenhower, and sent the armies of India to keep the peace in lands as distant as Korea and Congo and Gaza.

Even in defeat, then, there was consolation after the debris had slowly drifted into the vast desert of the historic memory. It became evident that Gandhi and Nehru had built into this India a sense of nationalism, a pride and an intense willingness to protect modern

India. Indian unity, the cynics said, was an artificial accident kept alive by the abilities of a singular man sent to societies only occasionally by history. The Selig Harrisons condemned India to Balkanization even within Nehru's time. After Nehru, who? was a very good question in 1961 because of the widespread conviction that Indian unity was unlikely to survive the appalling centrifugal pulls once this hub or, to alter the metaphor, this superb centre of Indian gravity was gone. But Jawaharlal saw in his own lifetime that Gandhi's freedom movement and his prime ministership had rebuilt India, had rejuvenated an old culture after so many centuries of dismay and fratricide and a series of defeats which had sapped Indian self-confidence. The war was lost, but India would survive. That was achievement enough.

The power of Jawaharlal Nehru's voice quickly returned when he saw that there was so much to be proud of; he became Churchill after Dunkirk. He told Russy Karanjia two months after the war (*The Philosophy of Mr Nehru*):

> You don't find me weeping or whining, do you? Greater nations than ours, big military powers like America, Russia, Britain and France, have had to recoil and retreat before similar massive and treacherous aggressions. You have heard of Dunkirk, Stalingrad, Yalu and other similar occasions. We are grateful that our army, though outnumbered, fought so courageously. In some places, the entire force allowed itself to be wiped out rather than surrender. We are proud of the patriotic response of our people also. I am, therefore, disinclined to treat what happened as humiliation or degradation. Of course, the lessons of the war must be learnt over and over again, and we must remain vigilant, prepared and strong, but I have nothing to regret so far as our people or soldiers are concerned.

If there was a mistake, it was his, and he was great enough to accept it: 'Maybe, we pinned overmuch faith in Chinese friendship, and our policy in relation to them misfired.'

Jawaharlal Nehru's love affair with China had begun in the 1920s when he first began applying his mind seriously to world affairs. In his speech at Brussels in 1927 he said:

> I do submit that the exploitation of India by the British is a barrier for other countries that are being oppressed and exploited (*applause*). It is

an urgent necessity for you that we gain our freedom. The noble example of the Chinese nationalists has filled us with hope, and we earnestly want as soon as we can to be able to emulate them and follow in their footsteps (*long applause*).

In his report to the All-India Congress Committee after Brussels, sent on 19 February 1927, he commented: 'The chief planks of the congress, as the organizers wrote to me at the time, were going to be China and India, and partly Mexico.' India and China would lead the battle against British imperialism. Writing out 'A Foreign Policy for India' (AICC File No. 8, 1927), Nehru said: 'In developing our foreign policy we shall naturally first cultivate friendly relations with the countries of the East which have so much in common with us. Nepal will be our neighbour and friend; with China and Japan, Indonesia, Annam, and Central Asia we shall have the closest contact.'

There was more to the China angle than routine good relations. The common experience of imperialism and the sheer strength of size provided these two countries with a unique opportunity to join hands in a viable fight first to destroy imperialism and then – equally difficult – preserve the freedom. His initial enthusiasm for the Soviet Union was sharply diminished by his dismay at Stalin's excesses in the 1930s; what was left was further diluted by Stalin's support to the violent war launched by the Communists in 1948. The warm reception he received during his trip to China in 1939 – aborted by the start of the war – fuelled hopes of a friendly future. We have seen how Nehru's anger flared when Gundevia passed on the verbal message he brought from Burma about a potential defence treaty implicitly aimed at China. The change of government in Beijing did not worry him; his relations with the Communists were by no means antagonistic, and he had in fact been on his way to see Mao when he had to cut short his China visit. Foreign policy interests would survive changes in domestic ideology. But the Burmese proved to be far wiser. Spurned by Nehru, they approached China and hammered out a border settlement, in writing. U Nu signed his pact with Chou in October 1960. Minor differences apart, the essence of the agreement lay in the fact that China had accepted as the border a line drawn by a certain Henry McMahon in red ink at a conference started in Simla in October 1913 – which was why it was also known as the Red Line.

Sir Henry McMahon, Foreign Secretary of the Government of India, had a self-acknowledged love for drawing boundaries. Twenty years before, he had been part of the mission which demarcated the Durand Line. Now, in 1913, he set out at the summer capital of the British Indian Empire to settle a problem involving Russia, China, Tibet and India. (There was not all that much of Asia left after this.) By the 1907 Anglo-Russian Convention, Tibet had become the buffer between the London- and Moscow-controlled empires. Now, after the collapse of Chinese domination over Tibet, Britain primarily wanted to ensure that Tibet served as a buffer between the Raj and China too, though the formal objective of the conference was a settlement of relations between Tibet and China, between whom fighting had begun. Britain wanted the creation of an Outer and Inner Tibet (on the lines of Mongolia), with China having no administrative power over Outer Tibet, although its suzerainty over Tibet would be recognized. This would keep China away from the borders of the Raj; for the Tibetan border in the Himalayan foothills reached Tawang.

The Chinese delegate to Simla was Chen I-fan, an experienced diplomat who had served in London and (as happened to so many Orientals) seen his name Anglicized to Ivan Chen. Whatever may have been the Chinese sentiment, Chen did not dispute the division itself but only where the line should run. After the predictable harangues, McMahon was able to get Chen to initial the draft treaty as well as its illustrative map, along with himself and the Tibetan representative Lonchen Shatra. But Beijing repudiated Chen's action the moment it heard of it. And so on 3 July 1914 McMahon signed (after an amendment) the eleven-article draft treaty only with Tibet, despite London's instructions not to sign bilaterally. It was a thorough mess; three sides had initialled the map and a draft convention, but only two had signed an amended draft.

In 1921 Britain informed China that it was recognizing Tibet as an autonomous state, though under the suzerainty of China, and would deal with it on that basis. Tibet now conducted itself as an independent nation, and it did not join China as an ally in the Second World War; it declared neutrality, and in 1947 its trade mission travelled abroad on Tibetan and not Chinese passports. There is absolutely no doubt that at least between 1912 and 1950, when the Chinese Army returned to conquer Lhasa, there was absolutely no trace of any

Chinese authority in Tibet. There was, however, a well-documented Beijing claim that Tibet was a part of China and not just a territory ruled by Beijing through conquest. These details were grist to the diplomatic mill. There was enough for generations to dispute, particularly when one remembers the largely uncharted terrain they were talking about. The British admitted the weakness of the 1914 Simla agreement when they did not publish any map for twenty-two years; the Survey of India's maps of 1917 show Tibet's borders at Tawang. It was largely at Sir Olaf Caroe's initiative in the 1930s that in 1937 the *Collection Engagements, Treaties, and Sanads*, edited by C. U. Aitchison, formally recorded a detailed, pro-British version of the agreement; the 1929 entry had been only one brief paragraph.

The dispute between India and China, however, had much less to do with the technicalities of the McMahon Line, or the boundaries on the western sector, at Aksai Chin, than with politics. In any case, if rejecting the 'imperialist' McMahon Line was so sacrosanct to the Chinese, why did Sir Henry's exertions become the principle on which the settlement with Burma was reached? The truth lies rather in Liu Xiao-qi's conclusions, in conversation with Felix Bandarnaike (which Gopal quotes in the third volume of his biography of Nehru): that a chief purpose of the 1962 war had been to demolish India's 'arrogance' and 'illusions of grandeur', and that China 'had taught India a lesson and, if necessary, they would teach her a lesson again and again'. Gopal also notes Mao's taunt (from S. Schram, ed., *Mao Tse-tung Unrehearsed*, 1974): 'It's no fun being a running dog. Nehru is in bad shape; imperialism and revisionism have robbed him blind.' China's ambition to become the pre-eminent power of Asia, a dream which Nehru had usurped on behalf of India, was back on course after 1962.

Mao Tse-tung's People's Republic of China was established on 1 October 1949. Almost immediately Beijing announced that it would shortly march into Tibet. India protested at once. Delhi had inherited some rights in Tibet; its trade agents in Tibet, for instance, could have their own military escort, deal with crimes committed by their subjects according to Indian (and not Tibetan) law and operate telegraph and telephone lines from Gangtok to Yatung and Gyantse, and the post and telegraph offices at Yatung, Gyantse and Phari. India owned eleven rest-houses in Tibet. New Delhi warned the new government that military action in Tibet would jeopardize India's efforts to get recognition for Mao's government, and its entry into the United Nations. Beijing ignored the warning and walked into Tibet, claiming it was an integral part of China and entirely a domestic problem. One interesting feature of the exchange of notes is that, in the version released in Delhi, India uses the term 'suzerainty', while in the version of the same note released in Beijing, the term had been changed to 'sovereignty'. Who did the mischief? Since it was India's note, the Delhi version should be accepted as the definitive one. At that time, India was willing to accede to China a relationship with Tibet akin to India's with Bhutan, but no more. The Chinese responded by wondering whether India was preparing to make Tibet a second Bhutan – an action, incidentally, which would have earned the applause of Harry Truman, for it would mean a second front for China, with the situation tense in Korea. Nehru believed that this region could see the beginning of a third world war and decided to handle the issue with the utmost care.

The week beginning 7 October 1950 was marked by much drama. At Flushing Meadow the United Nations General Assembly gave General Douglas MacArthur the go-ahead to cross the 38th Parallel by 47 votes to 5. Only the Soviet Union and its allies were against the decision. India was among the seven nations which abstained; its delegate, B. N. Rau, said that India viewed this plan which authorized the occupation of North Korea with grave misgivings. Within India, the familiar concerns of communalism, communism and black-marketing were absorbing the headlines. Patel was lecturing Muslims in Hyderabad on 7 October on how to prove their loyalty to India and warning the Communists that there was no way they could produce a Chinese-style revolution here. On 8 October, Pakistan's law and labour minister Jogendra Nath Mandal, an untouchable Hindu who had been the Muslim League's 'showboy' Hindu since 1943 (Jinnah's answer to Gandhi's Azad, as it were), finally resigned, saying: 'After anxious and prolonged struggle I have come to the conclusion that Pakistan is no place for Hindus to live in, and that their future is darkened by the ominous shadow of conversion or liquidation.' The practical Mr Mandal took the precaution of sending his 8,000-word resignation letter to Prime Minister Liaquat Ali Khan from Calcutta. On 11 October, China warned the world that it was not going to 'stand by idly' after the 'US invasion' of Korea. But it was only on 12 October that first reports came filtering through about what had been happening in the highest plateau in the world: that the Chinese Army had marched into Tibet on 7 October.

A Tibetan trade delegation then in Delhi denied any knowledge of this action, while official circles in Delhi called it a 'hotchpotch story'. (The term may have wandered out of use now, but one notices its merits.) The officials were quiet in Beijing, yet it was apparent that something was going on from the heightened tempo of the 'Liberate Tibet' campaign in the press. On 13 October the Press Trust of India reported from Beijing that a Foreign Ministry spokesman had said, 'No comment', when asked whether troops of the People's Liberation Army had entered Tibet. The official *People's Daily*, however, reported from Chinghai province that Tibetan women of the frontier region had been singing 'Mao is the rising sun of Tibet' – always an ominous sign. It was not till 24 October that a New China News Agency dispatch from Beijing reported that the Chinese Army had been ordered 'to free three million Tibetans from imperialist oppression and to consolidate the national defences of China's western corner'. Very clearly the second consideration outweighed the first. The leader of the Tibetan trade delegation in India, Kungho Surkhang Depon, dismissed even this report as propaganda, saying it was highly unlikely. Finally, on 27 October, India sent its first protest; its ambassador Sardar K. M. Pannikar asked for full details and conveyed 'Delhi's surprise and regret' at the move into Tibet, adding that this would also make it difficult for India to support the Mao government's admission into the United Nations. China's reply was firm: 'Tibet is an integral part of China, and the problem of Tibet is entirely a domestic problem of China. The Chinese People's Liberation Army must enter Tibet, liberate the Tibetan people, and defend the frontiers of China.' For good measure, China warned India that no foreign interference would be tolerated.

Sardar Patel wanted a strong Indian reaction. A letter he sent on 7 November 1950 to Nehru was to sound very perceptive in the hindsight of the post-1962 debate. Patel wrote: 'We can, therefore, safely assume that very soon they [the Chinese] will disown all the stipulations which Tibet has entered into with us in the past ... the undefined state of the frontier and the existence on our side of a population with its affinities to Tibetans or Chinese have all the elements of potential trouble between China and ourselves.' Patel wanted the Indian government immediately to set out a definite policy, particularly 'in regard to the McMahon Line'. But Nehru's thinking was motivated by larger considerations, and before we join the bandwagon of accusations, of describing Nehru's world-view as 'unrealistic' when compared to Patel's 'practical toughness', it must be remembered that if poverty-stricken and newly independent India strode the world as a near-equal of the major powers for more than a decade it was because of this particular world-view of Nehru – an understanding which even Eisenhower and Krushchev publicly acknowledged by the end of the 1950s as having done as much as anything else to preserve the peace of the 1950s. Those were days of the Korean War and McCarthyism, of Stalin and an aggressive China, of colonialism's last-ditch battles in South-East Asia and Africa and of wars in the Middle East over the creation of Israel. It was a volatile, unstable world, barely recovering from the horrors of the 1940s. All the ingredients of another conflagration, with Afro-Asia as the new central battleground rather than Europe, were there.

Nehru's thinking, then, is best understood from a long conversation he had with the American writer Marquis Childs in the second week of October. Childs wrote in the *Washington Post* (quoted in the *Hindusthan Standard*, 22 October 1950):

> Wearing handspun garments and leading a life of almost Spartan austerity in his vast official residence, one of the leading figures of the world stage talks eloquently and movingly of the world's despairing need for peace. Prime Minister Jawaharlal Nehru in a four-hour talk with me expounded the philosophy behind India's foreign policy. That policy has confused some and seemed to resemble appeasement. It is not due to any wavering of Nehru's mind. He sees the supreme tragedy of a third world conflict overshadowing humanity and his deepest convictions are that everything must be done to avert it.

It was, in fact, Nehru's desire to protect India, as much as the philosophy of non-violence, which made him a champion of peace. He feared that the world could slip back into the barbarism it had seen in the 1940s. And who would be the first victims of a fascist resurgence other than the newly independent nations which still had not had time to consolidate their strength and restructure their societies? His perceptions, as Childs noted, were remarkable; he believed, contrary to current United States wisdom, that 'In the long run China can never become a satellite of Russia or a communist state in the Russian pattern.' China's peasantry, he said, would be a restraining factor on the theoretical Communists in the cities. While Tibet was an element in the new nationalism in both China and India, it could not be seen in isolation from other realities. Finally:

> Nehru makes plain in almost everything he says the influence on him of Gandhi, who was like a father and brother to him. Gandhi's non-violence, which deeply swayed the Indian masses, lives on in the hearts and minds of those who are trying to establish democratic self-government in this land, torn by religious strifes and burdened by ancient tradition.

Nehru may not have agreed that the ancient tradition was necessarily a burden, but he would have gone along with the rest of the assessment.

So on 18 November 1950, in his reply to Patel, Nehru tried to broaden the issue: 'If we lose our sense of perspective and world strategy and give way to unreasoning fears, then any policy that we have is likely to fail.' But two days later in Parliament, Nehru was extremely firm about what might be called the cut-off point, as far as India was concerned, for Chinese expansionism:

> Tibet is contiguous to India from the region of Ladakh to the boundary of Nepal and from Bhutan to Irrawady-Salween defile in Assam. The frontier from Bhutan eastwards has been clearly defined by the McMahon Line which was fixed by the Simla Convention of 1914 ... Our maps show that the McMahon Line is our boundary and that is our boundary – map or no map. The fact remains there and we stand by our boundary and we will not allow anybody to come across that boundary.

Hear, hear, said the Honourable Members of Parliament. Nehru now adopted a pragmatic line. He would not be hustled by the Congress Right into an anti-China policy, although they accused him of appeasement. He continued to champion China's cause at the United Nations. But simultaneously he did all that was necessary to establish India's claims: pickets were moved up, and the Indian administration was extended all through the North-East Frontier

Agency (NEFA), as the area was named, up to the McMahon Line. Twenty additional posts were set up, and by February 1951 the Indian government was running the administration from Tawang, which so far had been claimed by Tibet. If in fact China had not accepted the McMahon Line as the boundary with India, then it should have protested. Beijing was quick enough to retort when India accused it of invasion in Tibet.

Beijing kept totally quiet when Nehru established India's *de facto* control of an area which till 1949 and 1950 had been under Tibet's claimed jurisdiction. Neville Maxwell, who can hardly be accused of being soft towards Delhi, admits as much (*India's China War*, 1970, p. 73): 'In the event, the Chinese Government made no comment at all on the Indian move, so far as the record shows. This otherwise puzzling silence can be construed only as China's acquiescence in India's filling out to the McMahon Line.' Chinese apologists have had to gloss over such uncomfortable facts; but, to his credit, Maxwell does not, irrespective of his conclusions about who was more, or less, guilty in 1962.

Nehru, then, had reason to believe that his China policy was working. He did not want to commit India to the defence of Tibetan independence, as Truman desired; but he would not relent on the McMahon Line being accepted as the border. The geopolitics of the region would demand nothing less. Any withdrawal from this line would expose the plains of the north-east and the valley of the Brahmaputra to the mercy of the Chinese troops. McMahon's considerations were certainly practical in terms of the defence of India. This was Nehru's consistent position all through, from the beginning of the crisis to the end; he did not ever waver on this. By allowing Indian control up to the McMahon Line without any protest for so many years, the Chinese acknowledged *de facto* acceptance of this boundary.

In September 1951 Chou En-lai clearly and formally stated, while suggesting that border issues be resolved between China, India and Nepal, that 'there was no territorial dispute or controversy between India and China'. To quote Maxwell again, this was 'further confirmation that China had decided to accept the McMahon alignment as India's north-east boundary'. India replied that it would welcome negotiations, but the Chinese now went cold. Neither did India follow up. Later, Nehru explained this by saying: 'It was our belief that since our frontier was clear, there was no question of raising this issue by us' (*Prime Minister on Sino-Indian Relations*, 1961). This, however, turned out to be one of Nehru's most critical mistakes. The alarm bells certainly began ringing as far as Sir Girja Shankar Bajpai, Nehru's first Secretary-General in External Affairs, was concerned. But he had retired from the ministry and become governor of Bombay by 1952. Even so, he wrote to his old ministry pointing out that the Chinese might activate frontier disputes later, when it might not be to either India's liking or its interest. Nehru considered the advice and discussed it with Panikkar, before rejecting it on two considerations. First, if India raised it rather than the Chinese, China would have to take one of two positions. Either China would have to accept the Indo-Tibetan treaty as valid, or it would have to ask for a renegotiation. Since no Chinese government had accepted the Simla Convention as binding on China, there was little hope of Mao's government doing so either. In other words, if India raised the issue, China would be forced to the second position, renegotiation, which did not suit India, since India was quite content with China's admitted position, through Chou's statement, that there was no border dispute. Moreover, Chou was making this statement despite the presence of Indian administration in NEFA. Second, if China raised the issue on its own, India could always take the position that the territory this side of the line was India's, and so there was nothing to discuss. The sensible Bajpai was less trusting. The Chinese had never in principle accepted the McMahon Line, he argued, and would raise the issue when it suited them. But Nehru had made up his mind, and that was that.

There is no harsher judge than hindsight, and it is obvious enough that this was a mistake. But was there something else which led Nehru to this mistake? Would it be right to say that, unlike the more (and rightly) sceptical Bajpai, Nehru did not want to believe that the Chinese would ever want to deceive him? There is much evidence that he was very irritated by the propensity of the West to treat every position taken by the Chinese as deceitful or meaning something other than what they were stating. Did he suspect an underlying racism in this Western attitude, an easy assumption that the Orientals from the winding lanes of their bazaars must be wily – an old stereotype which he himself had encountered during the Raj? Nehru's temperament must have reacted against the traditional stereotypes: West equals straight-from-the-shoulder public-schoolboy honesty; East equals labyrinthine minds, where what is said is rarely what is meant. Talking to Marquis Childs about Korea and China, and the messages transmitted by China to the USA and UK through India, Nehru challenged the assumption that these messages contained an element of deceit. 'But how', Nehru asked, 'could anyone assume that those statements were bluffs? They had to be taken at face value unless one presumed to know the inner workings of the minds of the men now governing China.' Well, whatever the reason, Nehru took Chou at face value. And the cost was heavy.

In what seems an even more astonishing display of generosity, India simply surrendered all its treaty rights and privileges in Tibet on 29 April 1954 and formally recognized Tibet as a part of China – without getting any written commitment from the Chinese on either the McMahon Line or the western borders at Aksai Chin. All that the Maoists, who had lived by war and believed in war, did in return was sign the Five Principles of the Pancha Sheela: mutual respect for territorial integrity, non-aggression, non-interference, equality and peaceful coexistence. The men who gave the world the slogan that power grows out of the barrel of a gun happily signed a commitment to peaceful coexistence with Nehru. The Indians did not even try to raise the boundary question, still certain that it would be counter-productive to do so. Chou came to India on 25 June 1954 on a state visit, and Nehru put the chant of 'Hindi–Chini bhai bhai' ('Indian–Chinese brotherhood') on every Indian lip. The Chinese must have been laughing all the way to their strategy sessions. (Indira Gandhi, incidentally, says in *My Truth* that India learned only much later that Mao himself had wanted to be invited, and comments on how differently everything might have gone if that had been done. One wonders.)

Within exactly nineteen days – just nineteen, not more – of the end of Chou's state visit to India, after yet another affirmation of the Pancha Sheela, the government of China protested against the presence of Indian troops at a place called Barahoti, south of the Niti pass, along the Himalayan fringe of Uttar Pradesh. On 17 July 1954 China told India that this place, which it called Wuje, was part of Tibet–China. This was the first time that China had laid claim to any Indian territory – just seventy-nine days after India had voluntarily surrendered all its rights over Tibet, rights which even China did not dispute existed. Once again, however, Nehru did not want to believe that there could be anything more than ignorance behind China's claim to Barahoti; this, in fact, was the formal conclusion of the ministry which Nehru headed. The Chinese provoked Delhi again when their officials tried to enter Barahoti. On 27 August 1954 India sent a note protesting that there had never been any dispute about Barahoti's status as Indian territory. Both sides claimed the other had violated the spirit of Pancha Sheela.

Barahoti was nevertheless too small a matter to interfere in the larger perspectives. On 18 October 1954 Nehru went on his first state visit to China. Now, for the first time, he raised the border question – after he had handed over to China all the diplomatic trump-cards. (The military trump-card was always with China; even in 1950 China was assessed to be at least ten times as strong militarily as India, and defence spending in the Nehru years was the minimum possible.) Nehru pointed out that recent maps published in China had usurped some 50,000 squares miles of Indian territory. Chou bluffed his way through. These maps were of little significance, he said; they were merely reproductions of Kuomintang maps and would be revised when the government had time. Nehru, in the meanwhile, had directed that India publish maps declaring where its boundaries lay. The Survey of India, consequently, produced new maps in 1954; in the east the McMahon Line was shown as the international border, and a clear line was also now drawn with Nepal and Afghanistan. (British maps had left the specific borders shaded.) To the east of the Karokaram pass, on the northern crown of India, the new maps followed the British claim (known as the Johnson–Ardagh Line) to include the Aksai Chin area. But Indian administration stopped far short of this line, the most advanced post being at Chushul in Ladakh; only a patrol had shown the flag in 1952 and 1954 at Lanak pass. The Chinese did not make any immediate protest, although their embassy in Delhi could hardly have missed the maps. The very reasonable and suave Chou told the Bandung Afro-Asian conference:

With some of these countries [neighbours] we have not yet finally fixed our borderline and we are ready to do so ... [but] we are ready to restrain our Government and people from crossing even one step across our border. If such things do happen, we should like to admit our mistake.

As to the determination of common borders which we are going to undertake with our neighbouring countries, we shall use only peaceful means and we shall not permit any other kinds of method. In no case shall we change this.

It was all very noble, and Jawaharlal joined the applause. The Barahoti incident, which directly contradicted what Chou had said, was ignored. Nor did Nehru know of the secret talks between Chou and the Pakistan Prime Minister Muhammad Ali (as Gopal notes in his biography). But the key to Chou's behaviour lies in his answer to a later question as to why the Chinese did not bring up the border issues earlier – in 1951 or 1954 – or complain about Aksai Chin in 1956 when Chou had talks with Nehru in Delhi. Chou's reply: 'the time was not ripe'.

The Chinese ripened it slowly. On 5 November 1955 India protested Chinese intrusions into Damzan. On 28 April 1956 an armed Chinese party camped half a mile east of Nilang in Uttar Pradesh; India protested on 2 May. On 26 July, China claimed Barahoti and denied that Tunjun La was a border pass. On 1 September, Chinese soldiers crossed the Shipki pass into India, repeating the crossing on 10 and 20 September; there nearly was an armed clash with an Indian patrol. On 28 November 1956 Chou came again for talks to Delhi and once again deceived Nehru. These were only petty disputes, he said, and could be amicably settled at the lower levels. He reconfirmed China's stance that there were no disputes regarding the border, and added that China had accepted the 1914 demarcation (that is, the McMahon Line) in the case of Burma, and the same principle could be applied with India in the eastern sector.

Seven months before, in March 1956, the Chinese had quietly begun laying a 750-mile motorable road from Yarkand to Gartok through Aksai Chin. They finished it in the remarkable time of nineteen months. About 112 miles of this road lay in territory claimed by India. Delhi, which did not administer Aksai Chin, learned of this road only after China announced its completion. Delhi's apprehension came a little too late. China's time was now reaching the 'ripe' stage. After only one altercation in 1957 (the first in NEFA), the summer of 1958 was crowded with incidents. In Ladakh, the Khurnak fort was occupied, leading to an Indian protest on 2 July. In

September the Chinese came to Barahoti with building materials. On 18 October, after making its belated checks, India protested against the Aksai Chin road and, for the first time, claimed Aksai Chin in a note to China. On 27 October aircraft from Tibet flew over the Spiti valley in the first incursion of air space; two days later there were similar flights over Chini in Himachal. An Indian patrol party was caught by the Chinese in Ladakh and, India claimed, ill-treated. On 10 December, India asked China to withdraw its personnel from Barahoti, Lapthal and Sangchamalla. And on 14 December, Nehru wrote to Chou drawing attention to what he called wrong boundaries; such incorrect maps could cause grave misunderstanding, he said. The letter was written in a friendly tone, but Nehru made it a point to stress that India had been 'under the impression that there were no border disputes between our respective countries'. He stated India's view that 'There can be no question of these large parts of India being anything but India and there is no dispute about them.'

On 23 January 1959, for the first time since the Communists had seized power, China admitted that there were border disputes. Said Chou: 'First of all, I wish to point out that the Sino-Indian boundary has never been formally delimited. Historically no treaty or agreement on the Sino-Indian boundary has ever been concluded between the Chinese central government and the Indian government.' In two sentences, the very crux of Nehru's China policy – that there were no boundary disputes, as admitted by both sides, and relations could be built on that premiss – was knocked hollow. As for the McMahon Line, which, far more than Aksai Chin, India was determined to hold, Chou said: 'As you are aware, the "McMahon Line" was a product of the British policy of aggression against the Tibet Region of China and aroused the great indignation of the Chinese people. Judicially, too, it cannot be considered legal. I have told you that it has never been recognized by the Chinese central government.' This letter included the famous phrase: if the issue had not been raised in 1954, it was because 'the time was not ripe for a settlement'.

The Chinese were finally saying they were strong enough to ensure a settlement on their terms. It was not that they were saying they would never settle, or that war was inevitable; they were only saying, as politely as such things can be said, that now only a settlement on their terms would be possible. They might yet concede on the

McMahon Line (or at least over large parts of it), but you would have to talk it out. The old commitment that there were no boundary disputes had bought them the time they needed. Chou suggested in his letter that pending an agreement both sides agree to a status quo. Nehru accepted the idea of a standstill, to preclude hostilities, but could not accept the principle of the status quo since this might be construed as sanction of the Chinese presence in Aksai Chin. So he added a rider. Detailing India's historical claims over the disputed areas, he added that India would be the 'last country to make any encroachments beyond its well-established frontiers'. But: 'I agree that the position as it was before the recent disputes arose should be respected by both sides and that neither should try to take unilateral action in exercise of what it conceives to be its right. *Further, if any possession has been secured recently, the position should be rectified*' (italics added). Nehru would not compromise on India's frontiers.

By the time the next round of letters were exchanged six months later the whole environment had changed. 'Bhai bhai' was dead in January; by the end of 1959 relations were bitter. In spring that year the Khampa rebellion became an insurrection, and the Dalai Lama, who was head of the Tibet government, proclaimed independence. The rebellion was put down, and the Dalai Lama had to escape across the McMahon Line, reaching Tawang on 31 March 1959. Thousands of refugees came in his wake. For Nehru this was another blow – because public sentiment in India turned pro-Dalai Lama, and questions were raised about why India had accepted China's sovereignty over Tibet in 1954. The Dalai Lama was now himself claiming independence, pointing out that the very presence of Tibet as an equal at the 1913–14 Simla talks was proof of its sovereignty. India's ability to help was sabotaged by the 1954 agreement with China. Nehru tried a balancing act – giving the Dalai Lama political asylum while refusing to condemn China – and received thanks from neither side.

The deteriorating climate inevitably affected the border. The most serious incident took place at the hamlet of Longju, where the Indians had established a disputed border picket. On 25 August the Chinese cleared the small Indian garrison from this disputed post. India called this 'deliberate aggression'. This was the first of the shooting battles. Then, on 20 October 1959, came the incident at Leh. An Indian border patrol of about seventy men came in contact with the Chinese, forty miles within India's claimed territory. The next day, fire was exchanged; nine Indians lost their lives and ten were captured (three on the 20th, seven on the 21st). Obviously in both incidents Delhi and Beijing offered self-serving versions. That was not as important as the new conviction spreading through India that China was itching for a war, and a brutal one. Nehru himself was now convinced that the period of friendship with China was over. By the end of 1959 he had much to be happy about as far as his foreign policy was concerned. Even Eisenhower had dropped the criticism of India's 'immoral neutralism', and told India's Parliament during his December 1959 visit: '[India] speaks to other nations of the world with greatness of conviction, and is heard with greatness of respect . . . India is a triumph that offsets any world failure of the past decade.' But Nehru's China policy was in clear reverse gear, and perhaps that is why Eisenhower's India policy was in forward momentum.

With a threat so obvious nibbling away at its borders, what was India doing in military terms to defend them? Bickering, that's what. Nehru's wrong assessment of China's intentions on the border was now compounded by a failure either to arm the country's troops sufficiently or, more seriously, to judge China's military intentions correctly. Till the very end, Nehru believed that China would never go so far as to launch full-scale war.

In the 1950s the only country with which war seemed possible was Pakistan. There was a year-long war over Kashmir in 1947–8; in 1950 a second war almost erupted, and the two neighbours were on the brink again in 1951. By the mid-1950s John Foster Dulles had secured Pakistan's defence by pacts and military supplies, and gradually the balance shifted as simultaneously the Indian Army's abilities declined in the decade of peace that Nehru wrought. In fact, by the end of the 1950s it seemed more likely that Pakistan would attack in Kashmir than India. One indication of the shifting balance is the fact that, while India rejected a no-war pact early on, it was Pakistan which kept tripping up the idea later. What little attention Nehru's government paid to the army's requirements was concentrated on the needs of the western front. Any serious attempt even to consider a possible strategy against a Chinese attack in the mountains found little support in the defence ministry.

Nehru's indifference to this ministry was evident from his choice of ministers. The first was the Sikh nominee to the central government,

Sardar Baldev Singh; whatever political considerations may have put him there, defence was beyond his ken. The ministry was in effect run by an ICS officer, H. M. Patel, who later became finance minister of India under Morarji Desai's Janata government. The Indianization of the army brought K. M. Cariappa as army chief; the first tragedy was not Baldev Singh's inabilities but the personality clash between Patel and Cariappa, which began a process of confusion, overlapping of responsibilities and mismanagement arising from jealousy. Strategic thinking about China should have begun with China's take-over of Tibet in 1950. There was none. The ministry was fortunate when Baldev Singh was succeeded by the brilliant Gopalaswami Ayyangar and then doubly unfortunate when he died soon after. Now entered Kailash Nath Katju, who had sent Sheikh Abdullah to gaol as home minister; he lumbered on till 1957, totally unaware and unconcerned about the army's needs. And so when Nehru's old friend V. K. Krishna Menon was made defence minister in 1957 there was elation in both the officer corps and the ranks; it seemed a signal that Nehru wanted to restore the importance of this portfolio, to rebuild morale and to find the resources for it once again which had been diverted to planning and the creation of an industrial base for the country. A great political career seemed ahead of Menon, and of course he had Nehru's ear.

Menon had been a minister without portfolio since 1956 and was thoroughly dissatisfied at what he considered a lack of confidence in him. He wanted an 'important' portfolio. He was however already viewed with great suspicion in Congress circles, and Azad was known to be strongly against the idea of increasing Menon's importance. Yet Menon had sufficient powers of emotional blackmail, and Nehru gave him the defence portfolio in 1957. There was good news for the army elsewhere too. In March 1957 the new army chief was named – a man who was not only the best but also the best loved: General Thimayya, popularly called Timmy. To their utter despair the defence services were soon to be totally disillusioned with Menon. Menon himself thought that defence was too minor a charge for a man of his talents. (Ego was never a problem with Menon.) Within two months of getting the portfolio he wanted to resign because 'You do not need me . . . I can make no impact on your mind and your collective Prime Ministerial self or function to any purpose' (Menon to Nehru, 10 June 1957). He wanted to be a sort of deputy prime minister, with special attention to external affairs. Nehru made a grievous mistake by succumbing to Menon's tactics. Kashmir, Indo-China and the UN became Menon's preserve in addition to defence. Twice more Menon offered to resign: in May 1958 over the jeep scandal, and then November 1958 over what he called the influence of the Congress Right on Nehru. Nehru held back his protégé.

Tragically for the defence ministry, Menon tried out his leftism in the ministry least suited to it. He introduced measures of economy in spending and defence production – not a bad thing in principle, but absurd when the ideologue in Menon put it into practice. The excellent author and journalist T. J. S. George, in his biography of Menon, reveals that he carried self-reliance in defence production so far that the factories were making hairclips and pressure-cookers and preparing to make mechanical toys when the Chinese interfered with their dream world. Nor did Menon make any defence purchases from abroad. It was pathetic neglect, and Nehru allowed it. Menon kept repeating to his own troops that the Chinese would never attack. Why? His political wisdom told him so. The army was convinced that Menon was more concerned about promoting himself abroad than defending his country at home, and there was good reason for such a view. Even Nehru was perturbed at Menon's foreign tours. When the Chinese advanced into Ladakh in 1959 the defence minister was in New York and showed no desire to return till Nehru rebuked him. Army officers were shocked when Menon allowed a Chinese military mission to tour India's major defence establishments as late as in 1958. The Chinese were led by Marshal Yeh Chiang-ying, who commented when being given a token gift of a silver owl at the Wellington Staff College that the owl was a bird of ill omen in China. Among other things this mission did was watch a display of firepower by 4 Division – then under the command of a man who would become quickly famous and then infamous, Major-General B. M. Kaul. Even if Menon had tried harder to get more money for his ministry, he might have found it difficult. He was soon openly feuding with the finance minister Morarji Desai, who found a special joy in fighting any Menon proposal. Moreover, while the opposition was strident enough when it came to criticizing Nehru on China, it seemed to become equally strident when any attempt was made to raise defence expenditure. Wanting success without paying for it is, unfortunately, an old weakness of the Indian middle class which produces so many of India's politicians.

The incidents at Longju and Kongka pass stirred the defence establishment, though, with Menon in charge, it could never be accused of fully waking up. Till 1956 the deployment had been mainly on the Pak border. Three of the six infantry divisions were in Kashmir, with even the battalion in Leh facing south (Pakistan-wards) rather than north (China-wards). A two-division strike force was kept in Punjab to counter-attack at Lahore in case Kashmir was threatened. The one armoured division of the army was stationed at Jhansi. After 1956 (particularly because of the Naga problem) forces began to be siphoned off to the north-east and were replaced by fresh recruitment. After the 1959 incidents 4 Division was shifted from Punjab to the north-east (without adequate equipment), and a new division, the 17th, was raised. But the infrastructure of defence was still abysmal, in arms, in clothing, in roads, in armour. General Thimayya did not hide the problems, and he officially warned the government about the weaknesses the army was suffering from in 1959. Menon saw this as an affront, took offence and accused Thimayya of being pro-West. Thimayya returned the compliment and called Menon a communist. (Both were right, to a point.) Thimayya resigned. Nehru intervened and promised to use his personal authority and see that Thimayya's note was given due consideration. But once Thimayya had withdrawn his resignation, Nehru publicly supported Menon. It was a volte-face which the soldiers never forgave; but, more important, it cost the nation badly. Menon now began to promote Kaul, and soon, although a junior, Kaul was perceived as the most powerful general with direct access to Nehru. Kaul was made Lieutenant-General in July 1959, and the Menon–Kaul combination became the decisive clique in India's defence. Thimayya retired in April 1961 but had already been reduced in importance. He had the last, if bitter, laugh when Nehru was forced to recall him and put him in the National Defence Council after the defeat in NEFA. In one of his farewell speeches, recalls Brigadier J. P. Dalvi, one of the defeated warriors of 1962, in his book *Himalayan Blunder* (1969), Thimayya sadly told his audience: 'I hope that I am not leaving you as cannon-fodder for the Chinese. God bless you all.' But that was precisely to be their fate.

In January 1961 the chiefs of staff of the Indian defence forces made it clear to the government that, given its condition, the Indian Army was not in a position to fight more than a limited war against China. Around this time, Chou stepped up his international campaign to paint India as a potential aggressor. In his interview to Edgar Snow (*Look*, 31 January 1961) he said that India had two objectives: to turn Tibet into a buffer state (the old imperialist objective) and to use the confrontation with China as the excuse to secure foreign aid which would then be used to crush 'progressive forces' within India. Nehru's problems were further complicated by the 'coup from above' in Nepal.

For more than a century Nepal had been ruled by a toothless monarchy. In 1848 the King lost the power struggle to the feudal barons, and Jang Bahadur Rana assumed the office of Prime Minister. A *sanad* was signed by the King making the Rana prime ministership hereditary; and the Ranas consolidated their hold and remained unchallenged. But the ideas released by the freedom movement in India were bound to have their influence on this nation tucked between UP/Bihar and Tibet. One of the younger men arrested by the British for his role in the Quit India movement of 1942 was Biseswar Prasad Koirala, leader of the Nepalese Congress. After 1947 it was the turn of the Nepalese Congress to seek the overthrow of both the Ranas and the King, and they looked to Delhi for help. It came, but indirectly. India allowed a young socialist, Bhola Chatterjee, to visit Burma and pick up a plane-load of arms from the Socialist government in power there; U Nu was the Prime Minister and Ne Win the army chief. The plane landed in Bihar, and the arms went to Nepali Congress partisans across the border. On 6 November 1950 King Tribhuvan, along with his two queens, Crown Prince Mahendra and the latter's eldest son Birendra, suddenly sought asylum in the Indian embassy at Kathmandu. The King was obviously in the know about what was to happen and did not want to end up in the Rana gaol when the fighting broke out. On 10 November 1950 the Nepali Congress, using these Burmese weapons (plus 400 guns from the police arsenal in Bihar, gifted by the state government), launched an armed struggle against the Rana government to establish democracy in Nepal. On 11 November an Indian Air Force plane picked up the royal family from the Indian embassy in Kathmandu and flew them to Delhi.

Nehru now proceeded to organize a peace, and in January 1951 a coalition was patched together. The King got back his throne, and power was shared between the Ranas and the Nepali Congress. Mohun Shumsher became Prime Minister and B. P. Koirala home minister. (He was later replaced by his brother M. P. Koirala in the coalition.) When elections were held in 1959 the Nepali Congress swept the polls, and B. P. Koirala became Prime Minister. On 15 December 1960 the King turned the tables. With the support of the army, he dismissed the elected government, gaoled Koirala and most of his Cabinet and dissolved Parliament. For the first time since 1848 a king of Nepal had power; and the credit for that went to Mahendra. Nehru was furious, but there was little he could do. This was not 1951, and Nepal now had the support of a powerful neighbour which it could play off against Delhi. In April 1960 Nepal had signed a treaty of peace and friendship with China. A loyal Kathmandu press launched a tirade against India. Nehru wrote to Mahendra, who coolly justified his action. China gained substantially from this rift; yet another patient move had worked out successfully on Chou's chessboard.

In February 1961 the reports prepared by Indian and Chinese officials were published (separately, in one volume). There was more disturbing news for India; China had also begun to question the legitimacy of Kashmir as a part of India, while its territorial claims were generalized rather than specific. On the ground, the incursions and reinforcements continued. By summer the Chinese had advanced about seventy miles south-west of their positions in 1958. As for Indian defence, even Menon's own man, General Kaul, officiating as Chief of General Staff, wrote to the ministry: 'As things stand today, it has to be accepted that, should the Chinese wish to carry out strong incursions into our territory at selected points, we are not in a position to prevent them from doing so.' By June the army was saying that, unless the air force could treble supplies to Ladakh that month, several of the new posts would have to be evacuated.

Publicly, Nehru maintained that there was nothing so radically wrong on the border as to talk of war; in any case, India would not compromise on its declared border. On 22 August 1961, initiating a debate on foreign policy in the Rajya Sabha, he maintained that India was not thinking in terms of settling the dispute through a long war in the high Himalayas. War was an event which would affect generations, so they had to move with both 'wisdom and strength' and 'not in a huff'. He believed that the officials' report would persuade the Chinese that their claims were wrong, and although externally their position might not have changed, he did not see how the Chinese could, after reading the report, continue to believe their case was strong. (The report, incidentally, was made public only in Delhi and not in Beijing.) Nehru took a far tougher line with domestic communists than with foreign ones, accusing the CPI of being 'anti-national' because of its equivocations on the border dispute. But with elections due in six months, and political temperatures rising, members were not going to let Nehru get away with such bland assertions. Dr H. N. Kunzru warned about China's military preparations and condemned Nehru for giving the impression that India was imploring the Chinese for a settlement. 'Our national self-respect should not be lost sight of in the quest of peace,' he said. As for Nehru's 'unbounded faith' in China – he called it unrealistic.

The pressure of public opinion, particularly with elections approaching, must have played its part in the next steps taken by Nehru. For the Congress Party certainly wanted – even more than the opposition – to hear him say that the Chinese would be thrown out from the positions they had advanced to. On more than one occasion Nehru had asserted that the Himalayas were not going to be gifted away to China; they were part of India's culture. The Hindu veneration for the Himalayas, and their emotional place in the Hindu psyche, can hardly be underestimated. This made their defence a doubly sensitive political issue. In a sense, the trap had partly been created by the strength of India's protests to China; if the Chinese were doing what the Indian notes were saying they were doing, then why wasn't the army throwing the Chinese out of Indian territory? No one, of course, had the courage to tell the people the truth – that the Indian Army, by the sensible assessment of its own generals, was in no position to do so. Those officers within the army who wanted to speak up were silenced. The most infamous case, apart from the well-known Thimayya–Menon dispute, was that of General S. D. Verma, corps commander of the western sector which looked after Aksai Chin, Leh and Ladakh. Reading, in early 1961, Nehru's claim in Parliament that the situation was changing in India's favour in that sector, he wrote to his superior, General P. N. Thapar, pointing out that what Nehru was saying had nothing to do with the facts. He wanted the letter to be placed on record, because he did not want to be associated with what was nothing but a distortion of reality. Thapar asked him to withdraw the letter; Verma did not. He was superseded. Soon Lieutenant-General Daulat Singh became GOC-in-C Western Command, Lieutenant-General Sen GOC-in-C Eastern Command. Verma resigned and was victimized; only a personal appeal to Nehru more than a year later saved even his pension. And so, though the Indian roads had not even reached Leh (only in October 1961 did a convoy finally replace mules), while the Chinese had excellent supply lines in Aksai Chin, and though the troops' strength was hopelessly unbalanced, the bravado continued in Delhi.

During the last round of talks, in April 1960, all the friendship had disappeared, and there was a visible chill as Nehru and Chou went through the formal courtesies in public. The talks were inconclusive, leading only to the agreement that officials from both sides should sit down and thrash out the details which obviously men like Nehru and Chou had no time for. It was after these talks that Nehru decided that China's one-sided provocations would have to be countered. India would show the flag up to its claimed borders. India's case was strengthened by the fact that China as yet had not been able to produce any precise delineation of its claims. (The officials' report of February 1961 at least exposed this much thoroughly.) China charged that India was adopting a 'forward policy' – a term made popular by Chinese propagandists – and called this a provocation which justified the strengthening of its own forces. As Krishna Menon pointed out, the term was meaningless, for no country can have a 'forward policy' on its own territory.

On 2 November 1961, with public opinion against China building up, Indian strategy on the border entered a further dimension. The meeting was attended by Nehru, Menon, Foreign Secretary M. J. Desai, army chief General Thapar, Kaul and, most crucially, the director of the Intelligence Bureau, B. N. Mullick. Mullick persuaded his colleagues about two things: that the Chinese were getting ready to move up to the points they claimed; but that they would do so only in untenanted land, and stay away if they found that Indians had already manned a point. Nehru did not question the credentials of this advice. It was never explained why, for instance, the Chinese would stop advancing just because as few as a dozen Indian soldiers were at a particular post. But Nehru had developed an extraordinary confidence in some men over the years – in this case, Menon and

Mullick. So he sent out detailed instructions to the army to advance as far as possible towards the international border, but not to clash anywhere with the Chinese. To give the direct quote:

> So far as Ladakh is concerned, we are to patrol as far forward as possible from our present positions towards the international border. This will be done with a view to establishing our posts which should prevent the Chinese from advancing any further and also dominating from any posts which they may have already established in our territory. This must be done without getting involved in a clash with the Chinese, unless this becomes necessary in self-defence.

There was a sound military reservation added in Nehru's instructions. Paragraph (C) said: 'In view of the numerous operational and administrative difficulties, efforts should be made to position major concentrations of forces along our borders in places conveniently situated behind the forward posts from where they could be maintained logistically and from where they can restore a border situation at short notice.'

With this condition, the order to patrol at the border makes military sense. Without it, it turns soldiers into the cannon-fodder Thimayya was so apprehensive about. Nehru had kept the reservation in his directives. Now the defence ministry and the army brass – Menon, Thapar, Kaul – which had already weakened India so substantially by their neglect, gave the order to patrol *without* including the last condition. On 5 December, Thapar sent a letter to the western and eastern commands ordering the patrols but amending the directive to build up behind the patrols. Nehru had no knowledge of this change. Speaking in the Lok Sabha, he said specifically that strong, armed groups would establish positions with strong bases behind to support them. On 5 December 1961 he amplified the concept, saying that he would not allow the troops to become adventurist and therefore self-defeating. They must have a support base before they went forward. Anything else 'is not fair to our men. They are brave and fine men, but it is not fair to put them in that position and not fair to the nation to take some action which cannot be supported and therefore which ends abruptly.' Prophetic words. Nehru believed that he had ordered a sound policy, and in fact no one can fault his instructions. But that is not what happened on the ground.

How does one explain this? One answer lies in Menon's complete conviction that the Chinese would never launch an all-out war, so the risk of unsupported patrolling was an acceptable one. Just border clashes, after all, would never reveal the lack of depth behind the small groups at the front lines. Nehru had given those instructions after having been led to believe that they could be implemented. Any failure to carry out those patrols would reveal Menon's mismanagement of defence planning, and he was not a person given to admitting mistakes. Menon's arrogance is hardly a secret, and he backed it up with a sharp tongue and a brilliant mind – which, by now, were winning more enemies than admirers. A typical Menon story is repeated by Gopal, who got it from General J. N. Chaudhuri's note to Y. B. Chavan, then defence minister, on 1 July 1963. In the summer of 1961 Menon told an audience of junior officers: 'Seventy-five per cent of our difficulties come from Chiefs of Staff. I am not saying they have not made up their minds, because they haven't got minds to make up.' And Menon was talking of his friends! But Nehru had by now convinced himself about Menon's genius and took personal umbrage at any attack on Menon. Nehru actually praised Menon in a public speech at Delhi on 20 February 1962 for bringing about a 'complete reawakening' in the army. He saw the third consecutive success of the Congress, in the 1962 general elections, and in particular Menon's spectacular victory in Bombay, as the people's endorsement of his policies and of his decision to stick by his friend against the Congress Right. The relative quiet on the border also seemed to augur well.

Mullick's Intelligence Bureau, however, was by now picking up some other signals. In *My Years with Nehru: The Chinese Betrayal* (1972), Mullick claims to have discovered that the Chinese consulate in Calcutta was informing friends that military action had now become necessary. But no one in Delhi was in a mood to listen to such predictions. A clash on the borders on 21 July was ignored; Delhi soft-pedalled it. Nehru, in fact, now stepped up talk of a peaceful settlement. On the borders, the Chinese increased their preparations; a road was built in the Qara Qash valley in the western sector and thirty-three new posts established. Meanwhile the Indian border patrols were out, thinly spread on the front, without any back-up.

The Chinese chose their moment well. The world was engrossed by the Cuban crisis, and Krushchev (as his initial pro-Chinese stance indicates) had no desire to buy enmity from his largest neighbour. By the time Moscow decided to tell India's ambassador T. N. Kaul on 9 November 1962 that he had no sincerer friend than the Soviet Union, China's war was virtually over.

Nehru was at a Commonwealth summit when the first spark was lit on 8 September 1962, as Chinese troops crossed the McMahon Line at several points. They stopped when they met stiff resistance. China's propaganda machinery – which Nehru called Goebbelsian in his interview to Karanjia – mounted a chant that India had begun an offensive, obviously in order to mould international opinion. If Nehru had wanted war he would hardly have been in London that month talking to leaders of the Commonwealth. As if to confirm India's innocence of any martial intentions, Menon went out of the country too. Nehru and Menon returned only in early October. Nehru was totally convinced that this was just 'normal' border trouble, and he asked the army to be firm and take what decisions were necessary to protect India's positions. However, when, on 12 October, Nehru left for Colombo, he began to sense that this might be building up to more than a skirmish. Kaul had now brought reports of the size and depth of the Chinese mobilization. The Chinese had already seized some 12,000 square miles of Indian territory. On 20 October, at five in the morning, battle-hardened Chinese troops, well acclimatized to high altitude by their service in Tibet and massed in great numbers, launched their famous invasion.

In a way, the progress of the war itself is not so relevant, because Nehru had lost the war by the time it started. The formalities were conducted on the field, where the proud Indian Army suffered the greatest humiliation in its history. A short, sharp, bitter description of the war by one who fought it nobly, Brigadier J. P. Dalvi, sums it up: 'The Sino-Indian conflict of 1962 was restricted to a small fraction of the opposing armies, was fought in a small, remote corner of the border and lasted a mere month – with only ten actual days of fighting – and yet it is a fact that it did initiate profound changes in our international standing, domestic politics and economic progress.' India reacted with a fine show of unity and courage, but there was no escaping a creeping sense of panic as defeat followed defeat. Shastri thought the Chinese would reach Bengal, and who was to say he was wrong? Kuldip Nayar, the journalist who was to become a celebrity with his scoops, visited Assam then as press officer to Shastri and recorded the utter confusion and demoralization there. There were hurried plans to blow up the oilfields at Digboi (fortunately never carried out), and one evening at Tezpur he suddenly heard an announcement over loudspeakers that the government was no longer responsible for citizens' lives and property. But elsewhere there was a national outpouring of patriotic sentiment; men, women and children threw their all into a determined effort to mobilize all the nation's resources in its defence. The worst had suddenly brought out the best in Indians.

Nehru kept his nerve, forgot his non-alignment for a while and appealed to anyone who could to help. The non-aligned leaders, incidentally, with the valuable exceptions of Tito and Nasser, decided to be non-aligned in this conflict too. The USA and Britain rallied to Delhi's aid, and Dalvi notes that the Chinese unilaterally ordered a ceasefire two days after President Kennedy said that if the Chinese advanced any further 'they would be forcing the hand of the President of the United States'. The Chinese also doubtless took note that the naval blockade of Cuba had been lifted on 20 November, leaving Kennedy brimming with confidence to fight communism elsewhere. On 21 November, China announced the ceasefire and ten days later withdrew north of the McMahon Line and the 'line of actual control' elsewhere. China retained 2,500 square miles of Indian territory in the western sector but gave up about 6,000 square miles there too. There was much appreciative puzzling over why China stopped at its moment of victory, quite forgetting that Mao was one of the shrewdest strategists in military history. The reasons are obvious: he knew India might lose in the short term, but it would never surrender, that it would recoup and fight at some point, while Chinese supply lines would be overstretched; the West would intervene more heavily on India's side in a longer war; and, finally, China's goals had been achieved in the limited war. To do any more would risk what had already been gained. Had Mao himself not once turned a retreat into victory?

Indian public opinion took its anger out on Krishna Menon. Nehru's resignation was unthinkable, but not even a Nehru could now save Menon. Nehru's own bewilderment and anguish at Menon's failure is visible in his letter of 28 October 1962: 'I do not know how I shall explain to Parliament why we have been found lacking in equipment. It is not much good shifting about the blame. The fact remains that we have been found lacking and there is an impression that we have approached these things in a somewhat amateurish way.' He had no answer to that essential question: why was India not prepared for this war? The answer was, of course, because Nehru did not want war, and neither he nor Menon ever expected it – despite all the evidence to the contrary. But that was not an answer he could afford to give at that moment. Defence was taken away from Menon on 31 October, but Nehru made one last effort to save his friend by keeping him as defence production minister. There followed a virtual revolt in the Congress. Menon was sacked on 7 November. Thapar resigned later on 'health grounds', and Kaul took premature retirement.

In April 1962 the Jawaharlal Nehru who took such pride in his daily yoga and his good health fell ill; a viral infection of the urinary tract caused intermittent fever and forced him to spend most of that month in bed. He changed his diet, giving up meat and milk and turning to fruit, vegetables, a little fish and eggs. But the call of age had come. A puffiness surrounded his eyes. The sag in the skin became pronounced. The causes lay in age, but the coincidence of ill health and defeat seemed interdependent. Nehru had been defeated by himself, not China, although that was not the public impression.

No epic in India is complete without an astrologer, even if the hero once threw out astrologers from his court. The men who learn from stars and sages never lose. Would you believe it? Everything about Jawaharlal Nehru's last days – the sorrow of Menon, the defeat, even the day of his death – had been written down by seers long, long ago. This was India, after all.

47 Greater than His Deeds

Caesars should die suddenly. A slow death hypnotizes them, reduces them. They stare at it, in still fascination. They cannot fight the inevitable, but will not surrender before it either. Jawaharlal Nehru was too proud to be afraid of death, but as he said so often he wanted the end to come quickly; he wanted to work on the last day of his life. The shadow of death fell across Nehru's vision on 6 January 1964. The sixty-eighth session of the Congress had just begun at Bhubaneswar with Kamaraj Nadar as president. When Nehru reached the venue of the session, named Gopabandhunagar, at 3.30 on the afternoon of 5 January he had some reason for relief: a major crisis in Kashmir had been resolved with the recovery of a strand of the Prophet Muhammad's beard, a relic which was found to be missing from the Hazratbal shrine on the night of 26–27 December. The crowds were there of course along the three-mile route from the airport to the Raj Bhavan, where he was staying, as he drove in an open car. But he was not looking well at all. There was an unhealthy puffiness in the face; the eyes had sunk; and his step was slow. It was little wonder that this session was rife with stories about the succession. The *Hindusthan Standard* reported on 6 January:

> There is a move to create the post of deputy Prime Minister of India. The move has been made by a very powerful section of the Congress High Command. This group has even [*sic*] their choice for this office. Mrs Indira Gandhi appears to be the first choice for this post. Other names mentioned in this connection include Mr Lal Bahadur Shastri and Mr Morarji Desai.

(Indira Gandhi's popularity in the party was borne out when she got the highest number of votes in the elections for Kamaraj's working committee, but the two senior men were far ahead of her in the prime ministerial stakes.)

They first kept the news secret, but it was no use. Too many people had seen Nehru being helped up by Indira and an aide as he suddenly left the meeting of the subjects committee. The *Standard* carried a photograph of the incident, which was destined to become famous. On 7 January an official communiqué at seven in the evening again tried to hide the truth, saying it was only high blood pressure due to strain; he had been advised complete rest. No one was fooled. Jawaharlal Nehru had suffered a stroke. He did not participate in the rest of the session, and his ministerial work was temporarily divided between Gulzari Lal Nanda and T. T. Krishnamachari (who took charge of external affairs). The country sensed what had happened, though Indira Gandhi kept a brave and cheerful face in public. The photograph in the *Hindusthan Standard* had revealed too much. Telegrams and messages came in their thousands, and when Nehru was fit enough to be flown to Delhi his arrival was kept secret both to stop the crowds and to prevent journalists from taking pictures. Yet the complete rest that the doctors had advised was simply beyond Nehru's temperament.

As soon as he reached Delhi, Nehru asked for a situation report on the horrible riots taking place in Calcutta, with Muslims being killed and driven out of their *bustees* as had not been done since 1950. Communalism: this cancer which had wasted so much of his life, this awful plague which had swept Delhi at the beginning of his prime ministership, was still consuming him in his last months. Nehru would not rest because he could not rest. Ambassador T. N. Kaul remembers him saying angrily when he heard that Soviet doctors had advised a longer convalescence, 'Let them go to hell. If I lie down in bed for even a week, I know I will not get up!' He began, as it were, to clean his table; he knew that the last phase had begun and did not want to leave loose ends for the successor he would not anoint by naming. In his last weeks he even tried to find a way out of the miserably tangled Kashmir thicket by releasing the Sheikh, involving Jaya Prakash and setting in motion a round of talks which seemed to promise a dramatic denouement. (Pakistan, however, was only playing along, waiting for the moment to strike and seize Kashmir by force from an India weakened by China.)

One day in May – no one knows which – Jawaharlal had, as was his habit of so many years, jotted down lines of poetry which appealed to his mood. These were four famous lines from Robert Frost, lines which would become many times more famous when they were found on Nehru's table after he died:

> The woods are lovely, dark and deep,
> But I have promises to keep,
> And miles to go before I sleep.
> And miles to go before I sleep.

It was too late.

An astrologer had predicted the precise day on which he would die. Gulzari Lal Nanda, who became interim Prime Minister after Nehru's death, was fond of the tribe and introduced a well-known seer, living in Daryaganj in Delhi, Haveli Ram Joshi, to Jawaharlal 'about five years before Nehru's death' (in Nanda's words). Haveli Ram belonged to a family of astrologers from the Gujranwala district of Punjab, which went to Pakistan after partition. There are two familiar methods which astrologers use to predict. One is by measuring the planetary positions at the precise moment of an individual's birth and then making their deductions. The second is by referring to a *samhita*: manuscripts written by *rishis* countless centuries ago in which, they believe, the whole future of mankind has been put down, with detailed reference to India. Several such *samhitas* exist, the most famous of them being the *Bhrigu Samhita*. If an astrologer has a genuine *samhita* with him, he can (at least he claims he can) decipher the reference to you and tell you about yourself. Haveli Ram had, in his early days, come across some people in Wazirabad who were selling off some old papers in their possession as junk. He recognized these papers as the *Arun Samhita*, which concentrated on India's national politics, and bought it from them. Nanda would listen to Haveli Ram's predictions based on his analysis of these papers and was amazed at their accuracy. When Nehru finally was persuaded to hear out Haveli Ram one day, he too was amazed and asked him to come again – not, recalls Nanda, to learn about his personal future, but to find out what Haveli Ram thought would happen politically. The defeat in the China war and the betrayal by a close friend (Menon, obviously) were apparently all predicted. But this only proves that, while Nehru may have enjoyed being entertained by predictions, he clearly did not alter his politics because of them, for he did nothing about either China or Menon before the tragedies took place. The one thing he could do nothing about even if he wanted to was Haveli Ram's prediction of when he would die: 27 May 1964.

Jawaharlal, writes Mathai in *My Days with Nehru* (1978), was in a particularly good mood one morning at breakfast in 1958 and told his secretary that he was not going to live beyond the age of seventy-four. Astrologers, Mathai tut-tutted. Not at all, replied Nehru. All he had done was added the ages of all the male members of his family and divided them by the number to get the average, which was seventy-four. Jawaharlal lived exactly 74 years, 6 months and 13 days. This was the real Jawaharlal: rational even in his whimsy and fun, a child of intellect, a man whose personality, erudition and nationalism won the admiration of the world – including the most cynical of the world's tribes, journalists.

Delhi was a prized posting in the 1950s, and the city saw a procession of journalists who were to build great reputations in their profession (generally, may it be said, justifiably). One of the very best to cover the most glorious years of the Nehru era was the brilliant correspondent of the *New York Times*, Abe Rosenthal. Not surprisingly, one of the most illuminating descriptions of Nehru is in a short piece Rosenthal contributed to Cousins's *Profiles of Nehru*:

> But the great irony of his [Nehru's] role in world affairs was that so many of the Asian and African leaders who fawned on him seemed to miss the point of his life. That point, most simply, was that it was possible for a country economically degraded to raise itself, give its people rice and a roof and a book, and still maintain political freedom at home.

Put wonderfully well: rice, a roof and a book – and freedom and respect. Nehru would have been pleased by these words. This was what he wanted to achieve for his beloved India in his lifetime – and he redeemed that pledge, not wholly or in full measure, but very substantially. Democracy was a deeply personal commitment, and nothing embodied the new culture he was creating more than his own behaviour. On a policy level, he totally rejected the option of using inexperience, or the enormous problems that faced him, as an excuse for postponing or aborting democracy. He faulted communism because he considered it anti-democratic. On the table in his office two things were always present: a gold statuette of Gandhi and a bronze hand of Lincoln. It was an instructive combination. For occasionally statecraft demanded that Gandhi be kept aside and

Lincoln be produced; he had no doubt that the only time democratic rights needed to be kept aside was when they were a cover for secession. The country's unity was above democracy. And so he allowed the army what methods it desired in Nagaland. He would go a long way along the democratic road, but if anyone threatened secession it would mean war. The heart of Gandhi and the hand of Lincoln – a fair symbol of Nehru's philosophy of power.

The charge of having become a Caesar was an easy one to make. There was an imperious manner in Nehru's bearing which sprinkled salt on the scars of jealousy in the minds of his peers. It was true long before he was in power, and Nehru himself drew attention to it in his self-parody, 'The Rashtrapati' by 'Chanakya', written in October 1937:

> From the far north to Cape Comorin he has gone like some triumphant Caesar passing by, leaving a trail of glory and a legend behind him. Is all this for him just a passing fancy which amuses him, or some deep design, or the play of some force which he himself does not know? Is it his will to power, of which he speaks in his *Autobiography*, that is driving him from crowd to crowd and making him whisper to himself:
>
> > 'I drew these tides of men into my hands
> > And wrote my will across the sky in stars.'
>
> What if the fancy turn? Men like Jawaharlal, with all their capacity for great and good work, are unsafe in democracy. He calls himself a democrat and a socialist, and no doubt he does so in all earnestness, but every psychologist knows that the mind is ultimately a slave to the heart and logic can always be made to fit in with the desires and irrepressible urges of a person. A little twist and Jawaharlal might turn a dictator sweeping aside the paraphernalia of a slow-moving democracy. He might still use the language and slogans of democracy and socialism, but we all know how fascism has fattened on this language and then cast it away as useless lumber.

But that was where the parody also became too harsh, and Nehru gave himself the benefit of at least one doubt. Caesar, possibly. Fascist, no. 'He is far too much of an aristocrat for the crudity and vulgarity of fascism.'

In the 1950s his power was absolute. On the one side, Patel's death

removed the one man who could have challenged him (and did so).
On the other, his sweeping election victories and his growing international stature suffused his image with a halo. The people really
believed, as the old woman at Avadi told him in January 1955,
that he was a modern Lord Krishna. Krishna is appropriate, for
Nehru was a leader not in the pious tradition of Ram, but in the
more liberal and multifaceted tradition of Krishna; he could be
mischievous with women at one moment and a sage at the battlefields of the *Mahabharata* the next. A sage, moreover, who was
also sought all over the world. Norman Cousins remembers him
at the height of his glory, at Bandung in 1955, and compares him
with Chou:

> When Nehru spoke some time later, the contrast between the men
> couldn't have been more startling. It wasn't only that he spoke without a
> manuscript or without an interpreter. He had warmth, personal rapport.
> He became part of each individual, speaking to the best inside him. He
> was creating strength, awakening the individual's capacity and his hopes
> rather than attempting to convert a man to any large impersonal system.
> He held up no glorious certainties of historical determinism, only the
> saturating uncertainties of the human situation. But this was in the nature
> of freedom, which guaranteed nothing except a chance to do better: and
> freedom was within their reach. At Bandung, the delegates may have
> been impressed by Chou En-lai, but they believed Nehru. And even when
> they did not agree with Nehru, they believed in him ... At Bandung,
> Chou En-lai was surrounded by bodyguards, Nehru by men who wanted
> to talk to him – men from new nations who suddenly were obligated to
> make history and needed the kind of confidence that a Nehru could
> impart to them. He was Olympian but he was never aloof.

Not many of those at Bandung lasted the tough course that freedom
placed in front of them; so many slipped into a new despotism so
quickly, at the first hint of pressure, and their people found that all
that had happened was that foreign dictatorship had been replaced
by a domestic one. Jawaharlal also provided, in the same 'Chanakya'
piece, the antidote for the temptations Nehru might succumb to: 'For
it is not through Caesarism that India will attain freedom, and though
she may prosper a little under a benevolent and efficient despotism,
she will remain stunted and the day of the emancipation of her
people will be delayed.'

It is because he understood temptation so well that Nehru strove consciously to build a democratic culture through lecture, example and the word. He loved writing, which exhausted him but satisfied a deep creative urge. He had a leader's instinctive need to communicate all his thoughts, and he was not embarrassed to label himself a philosopher-politician. His books are well known, and after the superb work done by the editors (S. Gopal, H. Y. Sharada Prasad, B. R. Nanda and M. Chalapathi Rau) on behalf of the Jawaharlal Nehru Memorial Fund, so are his letters. Indira Gandhi did history a great service by handing these letters over for publication, including Jawaharlal's exquisite love-letters, which were an opportunity for his thoughts to run wild on an endless, green, dew-strewn field of affection. Padmaja (again the lotus – Padmaja means 'lotus-born') was not so much a Beatrice as a confidante in whom every trust could be reposed: the luxury of weakness, the pains of depression, the pleasures of conceit and of course the chance to indulge in sheer description of nature, or gossip. Four consecutive paragraphs of a letter sent to Padmaja on 2 January 1937 are like quicksilver cuts of four images in one sequence of a running film. Witness:

What shall I write to you about Ajanta? It seems almost vulgar and profane to use foolish words of praise which have been so cheapened in the marketplace. The joy of seeing these pictures of long ago almost becomes a pain, to see beauty of form and beauty of life that are unattainable, unrealizable. What manner of people were they who created this dream world out of a few colours and lines? What was the texture of their lives? How rich it must have been! How can one forget the Bodhisattva even after seeing a picture – and the lovely women of Ajanta. I wish one did forget, for they disturb.

During all my recent wanderings one fact has impressed me. The beauty of Indian women, especially in the villages, has surprised me. In spite of all the poverty and squalor, they stand out and one cannot pass them without looking again.

I loved the sight of the envelope that brought your letter. I read it and then a feeling of loneliness took possession of me and I have found it difficult to get rid of it. Weak-mindedness.

A strange thing happened this evening. My mother casually mentioned, but with suppressed rage, that my name was being coupled with that of Devika Rani's! She had never heard of her but somebody told her that a newspaper contained this item of news. I was rather tickled and I thought at first that this was the usual pleasant Indian way of making insinuations. Probably because the incident of her garlanding me had been shown on the screen.

Or was this pre-emptive action by Jawaharlal? His name was linked with Devika Rani, a grandniece of Rabindranath Tagore as well as a glamorous film star of the 1930s. She was the wife of Himanshu Rai, a film producer, and married the Russian artist Svetslav Roerich after Rai's death in 1940.

Nehru could be publicly indiscreet with girl-friends. A famous (with so many people watching, it had to become famous) incident took place in London in 1955, when he went to attend the Commonwealth Conference. The all too frequent dash to Broadlands to stay with the Mountbattens was in itself sufficient for the gossips. Then at a reception given in London by his sister Vijaylakshmi Pandit, who was also High Commissioner, an obviously enchanted Jawaharlal, in a rare carefree mood, ignored the guests who had come to see the great man, spent most of the time chatting to Edwina and then disappeared with her to a private dinner which the Air India manager had organized for him, leaving a lot of burning hearts, red faces and bitter scowls at the reception.

The Indian masses were quite happy to overlook this aspect of his character, assuming that they minded it at all in the first place. They loved their Panditji. And he was deeply conscious of this, wondrously overwhelmed that he should be the man who got so much love from the poor. When he spoke to them, it was not as an orator. In fact, he could not even be called a good public speaker. He was just himself in all his moods, and the poor, unclouded by the posturing and moralizing of the middle class, understood that this man was being honest with them; there was no artificiality, no humbug, no cringing for votes and no nonsense either about what was possible to do and what was not. A dip into Rosenthal brings up another valuable passage:

And yet, when Mr Nehru moved in India and talked with Indians, it was a strange thing – it was as if one person were talking to just one other person. Sometimes he talked angrily to his India and sometimes he shrieked at it and denounced it and said it was just impossible, impossible. Sometimes he courted his India, laughed with it, and was merry and delicate and understanding. But it was always as if Jawaharlal Nehru was looking into the eyes of India and India was just one soul.

Nehru did not need to be told that it was this support – freely given, in a democracy – which gave him the moral authority to stride the world. Escott Reid, who came to Delhi as Canada's ambassador in 1952, recalls a conversation with Morarji Desai in his book *Envoy to Nehru* (1981). Morarji told Reid in February 1955 that Americans never realized how akin Nehru was to them, because, like the Americans, he had never known defeat; he too had always fought his wars to virtually unconditional surrender. (The 1960s saw both Nehru and the Americans defeated.) Morarji Desai added, perceptively: 'Mr Nehru is the most powerful man in the world today. He is powerful because he is the idol of all the people of India, who love him even when he is abusing them.' It should be 'berating them'. Nehru never abused the poor. He abused the rich regularly, journalists sometimes and the middle-class professionals periodically, but never the poor.

His day – every day – began with a public audience for the poor on the lawns of his official residence at Teen Murti House: about fifty or more ordinary people who demanded the right to complain to their Panditji personally about whatever grievance they had. Most of them came simply to worship. They sat in rows as Nehru listened to them and talked to them. There would be plain-clothes men interspersed in the group; the men in charge of protecting his life were not going to take any chance of a Gandhi-style assassination attempt being repeated. But they always had to battle on two fronts, for Nehru was irritated by the very thought of protection. In his early days as Prime Minister he ended the whole paraphernalia of policemen lining the streets and the traffic being stopped while an escort blared through the streets announcing the passage of a twentieth-century emperor. A motor cycle rider in front of his car was all that he would permit. It was not that he was stupidly brave or careless of death; he wanted to live as much as any human being. What he resented was the barrier that the idea of security imposed between him and the people. His goodness, his love for his people and their love for him – these were what truly guarded his body. And this love bred faith. After partition the Intelligence Bureau wanted Nehru to change all the domestic servants who were Muslims, particularly since they were largely on the kitchen staff. The great scare was that

Nehru's food might be poisoned; after all, many of their relatives had gone over to Pakistan after the havoc of the partition riots. Nehru threw out the suggestion. Not a single Muslim was touched. All the Muslims who worked for Jawaharlal adored him to the point of worship, not because he was Prime Minister, but because of the kind of human being he was. Power, in fact, can excite hate far more easily than love, so Jawaharlal's power was not necessarily an asset in awakening the admiration of the valet.

The tailor who stitched all Nehru's clothes was a delightful man called Muhammad Umar, who had two shops in Delhi, one in the Muslim part of the old town and another in fashionable New Delhi. The latter was burnt during the riots, and Nehru helped him get it restored. Umar had a sign in his shop: 'Tailor to the Prime Minister'. That was understandable enough. But his son, who had migrated to Pakistan and set up shop in Karachi, had the same. M. O. Mathai writes he once asked Umar if Nehru's name helped in Karachi. Umar replied in his lovely not-so-broken English: 'Sahib, Panditji is best-seller anywhere.' Access to Nehru gave Umar, in turn, entrée into the wardrobes of distinguished visitors like the King of Saudi Arabia. Muhammad Yunus recalls, in his book *Persons, Passions and Politics* (1980), that when Umar once asked Nehru for a testimonial, Nehru replied with a laugh:

'What will you do with my certificate? You have got them from kings and emperors.'

Umar answered in Urdu, 'But you too are a king.'

The republican retorted, 'Don't call me a king. They are the ones who get their heads cut off.'

Umar replied, 'But those kings sit on thrones, while you rule over people's hearts. Where is the comparison?'

It was not a courtier's fawning. Nehru was, truly, a king of hearts, and if this sounds soppy – well, maybe the 1950s belonged to a more sentimental age. It would really have been the end as far as the Indian Muslims were concerned if ever Jawaharlal Nehru had lost trust in them, or they had lost trust in him. He was the hope against the conversion of India into Hindu India. If he too retreated, the fight was over.

Nehru never fought a senseless fight or made the dangerous mistake of treating life as a black-and-white battle. Better than anyone else, he understood that a new government needed to absorb and include every shade of opinion at a moment of crisis if the crisis had to be managed within the constraints of a democracy; this was Gandhi's method too. Jawaharlal compromised. It was not just a matter of accepting a Patel, though that – as he wrote in his long and sorrowing letter to Gandhi in the first week of January 1948 – was bad enough. After all, whatever his anti-Muslim stresses, Patel was a Congressman and a disciple of Gandhi and could be counted upon to stay loyal to the Gandhian idea if it ever came to an either/or situation. But Syama Prasad Mookerjee? The man was the leader of the Hindu Mahasabha, a person who left absolutely no doubt about what he would like to do with this minority, a powerful advocate of Hindu theocracy. Jawaharlal made him one of the senior ministers of his government in 1947, giving him the industry portfolio. It was not a decision which could have found any favour with an Azad. Yet Nehru did it and also found place for Mehr Chand Khanna and Mohanlal Saxena even while, on the other side, he propped up Rafi Ahmed Kidwai and Ajit Prasad Jain. Nor did Nehru drop Mookerjee; the latter resigned in a huff after the Nehru–Liaquat pact signalled a stop to the retaliatory anti-Muslim riots in West Bengal. On the other hand, he could be absolutely resolute when he thought this lobby was going too far. Prasad and company made a serious bid in the Constituent Assembly to change India's name to just Bharat, but Nehru stopped it. The country consequently is described as 'India that is Bharat' in the Constitution. (From Bangladesh to Zimbabwe, twenty-five countries have changed their names for one reason or another this century.)

Apart from Gandhi, who was a superb guru in the business of dealing with human affairs, Jawaharlal Nehru also took advice from one of the great philosopher-politicians of Indian history, a man whose name is legendary but has, because of misinterpretation, also acquired a touch of 'sleaze', like Machiavelli's. This was a Malayali scholar-soldier-statesman called Vishnugupta, more famous to the world as Chanakya Kautilya, author of a 150-chapter treatise on the art of government called the *Artha Shastra*. More than 300 years before Christ, Chanakya travelled from his native Kerala, on the southernmost tip of India, to the University of Takshila in the north of Punjab, near Afghanistan, then one of the finest schools of learning in the world. After building a great reputation as a scholar he put his learning to practical use. Disgusted at the decay and corruption of the reigning Nanda king, he organized his overthrow and placed Chandragupta on the throne of Pataliputra (today's Patna, in Bihar), from whence emerged one of the greatest dynasties – the Maurya Dynasty. When Jawaharlal Nehru sneered at himself, as we have seen, he used the pseudonym Chanakya.

Talking to Russy Karanjia on peaceful coexistence (*The Mind of Mr Nehru*, 1960), Nehru interrupted the interviewer to ask, 'Do you know the story of Chanakya?' Karanjia did not. Nehru went on:

> It appears in a very interesting Sanskrit book translated by my brother-in-law, the late Mr Pandit, who was a Sanskrit scholar. You must get the English translation and read it if it is available. It tells a story of King Chandragupta and his Prime Minister Chanakya. Chanakya was typical of the Indian genius: peace-loving, shrewd, cunning, very scholarly, proud and selfless, and reputed to be a very wise man. Now some kings and chieftains opposed Chandragupta and organized themselves into a confederation and declared war on the Kingdom. Chandragupta called Chanakya to lead the defence, and this person, who appears to have been a great statesman and superb diplomat, succeeded in confusing and defeating the enemy front without resorting to anything like a war or even a battle. Somehow the enemy was won over. Then came the test. Chandragupta asked Chanakya's advice as to what to do next. Chanakya replied that his job was done. He had dispersed the foe and won a victory for his king. All he desired now was to be relieved of his responsibility so that he may retire to the forest and attend to his reading and writing. The King was shocked. For who could substitute Chanakya as the Chief Minister? Chanakya's reply was classic and very symptomatic of Indian thought. He told the King to get the defeated leader of the enemy confederation to serve him as his Chief Executive. That was the only way to restore peace and goodwill to the Kingdom. Now that was coexistence some 2,000 years ago. Wasn't it?

Two thousand years later, coexistence failed when he tried it with China. Nehru could not woo and disperse his foe without war, and when war came the man he had entrusted to manage its preparations was found to be totally wanting. The China war illuminated a few aspects of Nehru's personality. The first was that this man, who had never known, like the Americans, anything but success, had the strength to absorb defeat and still fashion sensible options for the future. He kept his nerve, and, despite all the battering it received, the core of his foreign policy survived the crisis. But what was amazing to the country was the rather un-Chanakya-like loyalty Nehru displayed towards his friend, Krishna Menon. Indeed, if Nehru had defended the frontiers as well as he defended Krishna Menon, China's armies would have been nearer Lhasa than Calcutta. They were of totally dissimilar characters. Naresh Kumar, the tennis player who along with Ramanathan Krishnan kept India healthy on the Davis Cup circuit for two decades, recalls an experience which reveals the difference. He and Krishnan were in London. Nehru, who was also there, invited them for breakfast. The two sportsmen had made a special effort to bone up on their politics for the occasion, but Nehru, says Naresh Kumar, put them at their ease in minutes, and they had a marvellous breakfast. Krishna Menon, hearing about the breakfast, invited them too. As they entered his room they found him at his writing table. For twenty minutes he continued to write while the two waited in his room, and he then tried to impress upon them how busy he was. It was obviously the display of an insecure man. Nehru nevertheless became Menon's guardian, and the consistent opposition Menon provoked from every quarter only made Nehru more determined to push his will through. This became particularly noticeable after he finally managed to bring Menon into the Cabinet. Nehru went to the extremes of believing that Menon was innocent and was merely the victim of enemies gunning for him – something he would not allow. Menon was brilliant, but hardly a saint. In fact, he was involved in acts of gross stupidity, if not actual corruption, in at least two scandals. As High Commissioner, he had bought jeeps in Britain for the Indian Army which when they arrived proved to be reconditioned second-hand vehicles. He had also authorized excess payments in a contract to purchase ammunition. Some of the operators involved were of dubious repute, to put it mildly.

When Nehru had a blind spot, it stayed blind. He tended to attribute charges of corruption against his ministers to either anti-Nehru villainy or the propensity to gossip which was a hallmark of Indians. The compensation was that Nehru's favourites had the merit of being exceptional in their jobs. His protection of Kairon, for instance, reflected much more of the spirit of Chanakya, as did his whole Punjab policy. A central thesis of the *Artha Shastra* is that the success of a government can be measured by the exercise of its *danda-niti* (law of punishment). If a ruler is too severe, he will become repulsive to the people; if he is too mild, he will become contemptible. When *danda-niti* collapses, society becomes victim of the Matsyanyaya, the Law of the Fish, where the bigger fish swallows the smaller. Disorder prevails. Just how much to surrender in Punjab and when: that was always the question. It had to be a finely tuned policy, and Nehru and Kairon conducted it well, keeping a tight leash on the amount of rope they gave the Akalis. Conversely, Nehru had no hesitation in using the army harshly in Nagaland. He also kept aside his reservations when he felt that India's interests demanded the arrest of Sheikh Abdullah in Kashmir.

One is tempted to say that Jawaharlal Nehru saw himself as the ideal ruler portrayed in the *Artha Shastra*. Chanakya describes 'the best qualities of the king' in these words:

> Born of a high family, godly, possessed of valour, seeing through the medium of aged persons, virtuous, truthful, not of a contradictory nature, grateful, having large aims, highly enthusiastic, not addicted to procrastination, powerful to control his neighbouring kings, of resolute mind, having an assembly of ministers of no mean quality and possessed of a taste for discipline – these are the qualities of an inviting nature.

Nehru was born high enough: a Kashmiri Pandit, and wealthy to boot. He was certainly very moral, if not quite godly; he took care to include peers in the processes of decision-making; he was virtuous and truthful and, though he had the good sense to change his mind when found wrong, did not double-deal. If anything, perhaps he was too grateful; his generosity was legendary. Of course, he had large aims; his vision was broad and deep, and his enthusiasm for it substantial. Procrastination? Certainly the bureaucrats at the external affairs ministry would not accuse him of that; in fact, on occasion there would even be the famous double knock on *their* doors, as he came to check out something. But he failed in controlling his neighbours, although his resolve to do his best by his country could hardly be doubted. His ministers were of uneven quality and erratic temperament; his Cabinet always seemed worthy of lesser men, which was more his fault than that of the talent available. Discipline, of course, he had.

Nehru also fulfilled another of Chanakya's demands, though this was much lower in the pecking order: the ability to make 'jokes with no loss of dignity or secrecy'. He loved a little fun, when he could afford the time. His birthday slowly developed into a day of national celebration. The morning audience on 14 November would be exceptionally large, as people came to greet him. Dinner time was when family and close friends dropped by. But they could not just drop by; often, on Nehru's urging, this dinner became a fancy-dress party. If any guest came normally attired Nehru would bring out something from his large collection of foreign national costumes, gifts picked up on his travels, and hand over one to the guest for the evening. Family friend and devoted Congresswoman Mridula Sarabhai, who was famous for wearing utilitarian, rough hand-spun unisex clothes like the *shalwar* and *kameez*, once became a target of his sharp sense of humour. Upon receiving an invitation, she asked Jawaharlal what she should wear to the fancy-dress party. Nehru replied, 'Why don't you come dressed like a woman, for a change!' In 1957, 14 November was declared the national Children's Day, an appropriate recognition of 'Chacha' (Uncle) Nehru's special empathy with them. The intense nationalist that he was, he saw in the faces of children the future that he was working for, and it inspired him and revitalized him. As in his fancy dress, he was not in the least inhibited about playing with children in public, and visitors to his house had often seen his grandsons on his back as he played the horse. Norman Cousins was an eyewitness to this and a magic show by a visiting entertainer at which Nehru was in his element. Radhakrishnan, giving Cousins a ride back, commented:

> There is something eternally young, even boyish, about the PM. People tend to think of him as a man lost in brooding, not even knowing how to laugh. Not so; he loves to laugh, as we have seen. It is very good for the nation that he can laugh. It helps to freshen his spirits. The important thing about Nehru is that he continues to think young. A man like this can never grow old. He will never look old, no matter how old he is. But must take better care of himself. He works too hard.

He was that kind of a man. A break came but rarely from the morning-till-2-a.m. routine. He loved it when it did; seeing a comparatively easy day on his schedule on 24 June 1956, for instance, he went off to Lord's to watch Australia bat.

The good thing was that Nehru did not mind being teased when anyone thought he was taking himself too seriously. There was much teasing about a widely promoted photograph of him in what became known as a 'thinker's pose'. His ability to take serious criticism was fairly high too. He had enormous respect for the writing of one of his most exceptional journalist critics, S. Mulgaonkar, and even wanted to co-opt him into the government. (Mulgaonkar's terms were unacceptable, not to Jawaharlal, but to some of his Cabinet colleagues.) Clearly, however, no Prime Minister's relations with the media could be free from anger at examples of partisan, tendentious or maliciously inaccurate reporting. What he really minded was the attack from newspapers and journalists whom he suspected of being sympathizers of the Congress right wing, with its communal tinge: *The Times of India* when owned by Ram Krishna Dalmia, for instance. But there was never any question of being vindictive. Liberty was the watchword, and Nehru was happy to raise its torch wherever he saw it being suffused: getting Milovan Djilas released from solitary confinement (if not from confinement) in Yugoslavia; protesting against the treatment of Boris Pasternak in the Soviet Union; pleading for B. P. Koirala in Nepal even though he knew King Mahendra would not like it. This energy for liberation abroad did not always sit well with what he had to do at home, but Nehru never claimed freedom from the contradictions that afflict a ruler of men. By simple precedence he was given the opportunity to turn a European word like 'democracy' into a stable, practical, Indian system, and he achieved this.

Yes, other traditional problems, like corruption, did begin to infect Indian democracy, but Nehru himself was never touched by any substantial accusation. The aristocrat in him had a remarkable indifference to money. He went to great lengths, not merely to be honest – which he was, without anyone's advice – but also to be seen to be honest, for he knew the curative powers of example in Indian society. Thus when the Allahabad municipality assessed the wealth tax (introduced in 1957) on Anand Bhavan at a ridiculously low sum, Nehru protested and forced the finance minister, T. T. Krishnamachari, to multiply it five times. When the industrialist G. D. Birla gave him a cheque for Rs 70,000 on his seventieth birthday, the money to be spent on public causes, Jawaharlal politely returned the cheque. The only industrialist he was friendly with was J. R. D. Tata (they were on first-name terms), and the only thing he ever asked Tata to do was start a cosmetics plant post-haste when, in order to save foreign exchange, his government banned the import of cosmetics, and rich women in every Indian city rose in revolt. (Tata started Lakme; never had government clearances come so fast, or would they come again.) In fact, they scrupulously avoided discussing business affairs. Jawaharlal was certainly no help to Jamshed when the government nationalized Tata's airline despite the latter's bitter opposition. It was a common interest in aviation which brought the two together in the first place, and then Jamshed did something close to Nehru's heart by starting the Tata Institute for Fundamental Research near Bombay. The cause of Indian science – particularly atomic energy – was a passion with Nehru, and he dreamt of seeing India as one of the leaders in the world of scientific creativity and achievement. He was a proud man when he inaugurated the first atomic research reactor, Apsara, on 20 January 1957. On 21 November 1963 India's space programme began with the launching of an equatorial rocket from Thumba in Kerala. He was in the last months of his life by then, yet it must have been deeply satisfying to Nehru that his Indian Dream was beginning to unfold. Cartier-Bresson has a superb picture of the period: a man is carrying part of a rocket on the back of a bicycle. The photograph might amuse at a superficial level but it also captures the distance that Indian science and technology had to travel in the seventeen years of Jawaharlal Nehru's prime ministership: from the bicycle age to the space age, and without the first dying away before the second was born. Many lifetimes of ambition had to be compressed within a decade and a half. This was the Nehru achievement.

'My love to you. It was all done bravely. You have braver things to do. May God spare you for many a long year to come and make you His chosen instrument for freeing India from the yoke.' Mohandas Karamchand Gandhi had penned down the destiny of his heir as far back as 3 December 1928. Jawaharlal did his best. Unlike his Bapu, Jawaharlal was not, and nor did he aspire to be, a saint. Gandhi would have lived in an ashram even if there had been no independence struggle. Jawaharlal would not. He did not want to suffer the long and sometimes hopeless torture of gaol, the years of struggle, for any reason other than one. He loved his country and he wanted India and Indians to be free, free of the British and free of the worst curse of their recent history, poverty – wretched, degrading poverty which had broken the Indian, destroyed his confidence and damned his future. He dreamt of a powerful India, not the power of arms but the power of prosperity and a new confidence. If he was proud of his foreign policy, it was because it had made India the equal of those nations which had toyed with the earth's destinies for so many centuries. After the Eisenhower visit, Jawaharlal could stand in Parliament and say, proudly, that 'It has been an amazing thing ... that India's voice has counted for so much in the councils of the world in the last several years, since independence ... [despite being a country] which is poor and is struggling hard to get rid of its poverty. Why? Because "we have spoken with conviction and earnestness and sincerity about peace and our desire for peace" ... [coexistence] was not a phrase in our mouths and lips – it was a deep feeling from inside our hearts and a deep understanding of the world as it is today.' What gave a special meaning to this achievement was that coexistence, Pancha Sheela, was India's contribution to a world urgently in need of the voice of Asoka. Nehru took that message to every capital, and every leader bowed in agreement. Some paid only lip-service, but they all paid service.

Jawaharlal Nehru was not a Gandhian; he was not a Marxist. There was no orthodoxy, old or new, which could claim him. But while his mind supped from everywhere, his heart was Gandhian: committed to the good in humankind with an unshakable conviction. Yet if any name has to be given to his special mix, then it has to be called the ideology of Indian nationalism. Even when proclaiming the new creed at Avadi, he said and repeated that the socialism he was talking about was an Indian socialism, the socialism of coexistence not the socialism of conflict and class struggle. If that meant a dose of confusion in the mixture, so be it, but he was not going to deviate. As we have seen, Gandhi created a multi-class Congress, and Nehru gave it a socialist bias; for, as he had so often said so vehemently, freedom from the yoke meant not only release from the British yoke but also from the yoke of hunger.

There was, however, one yoke which still threatened Indian unity – and, implicitly, freedom, for disunity would leave a vulnerable medley of states unable to protect themselves from newer and more sophisticated forms of colonialism. This was communalism. Before partition, Nehru fought Muslim communalism with a vigour which disconcerted his colleagues and he was painted as indiscreet and impetuous when he refused to be polite about Jinnah. After partition, the focus of attention shifted, and he made it his primary concern to try to make Muslims feel equal and secure; he regarded the perennial threat of Hindu dominance as a major danger to the unity of India, a unity which could survive only through a commitment to secularism. He refused to condemn the Muslims to second-class-citizen status. What worried him even more than the official parties of Hindu revivalism – the Hindu Mahasabha or the Jana Sangh – was the possibility of Gandhi's Congress being usurped by such elements. He would not drive this element out of the Congress, for that would then only drive them straight into the Jana Sangh. But he kept them under strong check. As his own influence increased, theirs declined, and in the 1950s the communalists of the 1940s were slowly weeded out or put into limbo. In the 1960s he began to worry about what might happen after his death. A little before the Bhubaneswar session of the Congress, remembers Gundevia, Nehru had joined one of the Friday morning meetings at the Foreign Office where all the senior and junior bureaucrats gathered for a general free-for-all. Since the Prime Minister himself had come that day they dispensed with the agenda and decided to ask him questions. The topic shifted to the professed neutrality of the Indian Civil Service.

Gundevia asked, 'Well, sir, this being the case, what happens if tomorrow, shall we say, the Communists come into power? We have had a Communist government in Kerala. But what happens to the services if the Communists are elected to power, tomorrow, at the Centre, here in Delhi?'

Nehru pondered before answering, 'Communists, Communists, Communists! Why are all of you so obsessed with Communists and communism? What is it that Communists can do that we cannot do and have not done for the country? Why do you imagine the Communists will ever be voted into power at the Centre!' A pause, and then the words came slowly and deliberately: 'The danger to India, mark you, is not communism. It is Hindu right-wing communalism.' Before the meeting closed he repeated those two sentences. That was his message. Sadly, the last major problem he faced was another round of blood-letting, this time in Bengal, in January and February. Muslims were reminded once again to which class of citizenry they belonged in free India.

The press conference was originally scheduled for Wednesday 20

May 1964 but was postponed to Friday the 22nd. It was his first press conference in six months, the first since the stroke at Bhubaneswar. He seemed fine, but his voice was weak. It lasted only thirty-eight minutes, with just about half an hour for questions, the briefest ever press conference by Jawaharlal Nehru. As usual, he answered a whole range of questions, but the main concentration was on Sheikh Abdullah's efforts to settle the Kashmir problem. The last question however, was, as Nehru himself put it, a leading one. Referring to a recent television interview in which Nehru had said that he was not grooming his daughter as his successor, a correspondent asked whether it was not preferable that he settle the question in his lifetime. Reclining in his chair, a smiling Jawaharlal Nehru replied, 'My life is not going to end so soon.' There were more than 300 journalists present. They thumped their desks and cheered. Jawaharlal went off to Dehra Dun for his last holiday after that press conference.

There is a photograph of Indira Gandhi with her father taken in Dehra Dun on 26 May. He is seated in an armchair on the balcony, and she is kneeling on the floor beside him, her face towards the camera but her eyes looking down. Jawaharlal is looking back, a little surprised by the cameraman from behind. Perhaps one reads meanings into a moment which were never meant to be, but if ever a photograph could portray the last evening of one's life, this was it. And if ever the love of a father and a daughter could be recorded on mere film, then this must be it. They returned to Delhi that evening.

That night he worked as usual, clearing all the papers on his desk. The night would claim him. The time had come to go to sleep, whatever promises might be left unfulfilled, however many more miles he might have wanted to walk in his beloved India. At 6.25 on the morning of 27 May, his normal time to wake, he opened his eyes in pain. His doctors found a rupture of the abdominal aorta. He soon became unconscious. He did not open his eyes again. At two in the afternoon he was declared dead.

Millions lined the roads as Jawaharlal Nehru's cortège took three hours on one of the hottest days of the year to reach a brick-laid, five-foot-high pyre at Rajghat on the banks of the Jumna, next to his Bapu, Gandhi's, *samadhi*. A helicopter showered rose petals, and the chanting of the Vedas by Kashmiri pandits mixed with the sound of sobs. Indira Gandhi was serene and composed. She went up the steps of the pyre, sprinkled holy water and gently placed a piece of sandalwood at her father's feet. She stood there, alone, silent, for nearly eight minutes. Then she took one last glance at her Papu's face and walked down.

At thirty-eight minutes past four her son, Sanjay, lit the flames. The sky reverberated with a cry as millions of voices joined in one last homage: 'Jawaharlal Nehru amar rahe!' ('Jawaharlal Nehru is immortal!') There was a rainbow in the sky on the day he became Prime Minister. An earthquake shook Delhi on the day after he died. India believed that it was the sign of a great soul's departure.

On 12 June, as per his will, Indira Gandhi, helped by an officer of the Indian Air Force, K. N. Shastri, scattered his ashes from a Dakota over Pahalgam in the valley of his beloved motherland Kashmir and over the Himalayas. A handful was thrown into the Ganga at Allahabad, the city where he grew up, 'to be carried to the great ocean that washed India's shore', while other IAF planes took more urns to scatter the ashes in all corners of the country, 'where the peasants of India toil'.

By this time, a new Prime Minister had been elected and sworn in: Lal Bahadur Shastri. Among his Cabinet ministers was Indira Gandhi. In a sense, both democracy and the succession had been preserved.

On 31 May 1936 the poet Rabindranath Tagore had written a brief letter to the man he called Rituraj, the Prince of Spring, about the *Autobiography*, which he had just read: 'I have just finished reading your great book and I feel intensely impressed and proud of your achievement. Through all its details there runs a current of humanity which overpasses the tangles of facts and leads us to the person who is greater than his deeds and truer than his surroundings.'

Greater than his deeds: it is a beautiful obituary.

Yet by far the finest assessment of what Jawaharlal Nehru meant to India and what India meant to him was made by Nehru himself, in an extraordinary document – his last will and testament, written on 21 June 1954:

I have received so much love and affection from the Indian people that nothing I can do can repay even a small fraction of it, and indeed there can be no repayment of so precious a thing as affection. Many have been admired, some have been revered, but the affection of all classes of the Indian people has come to me in such abundant measure that I have been overwhelmed by it. I can only express the hope that, in the remaining years I may live, I shall not be unworthy of my people and their affection . . .

When I die, I should like my body to be cremated. If I die in a foreign country, my body should be cremated there and my ashes sent to Allahabad. A small handful of these ashes should be thrown in the Ganga and the major portion of them disposed of in the manner indicated below. No part of these ashes should be retained or preserved.

My desire to have a handful of my ashes thrown in the Ganga at Allahabad has no religious significance, so far as I am concerned. I have no religious sentiment in the matter. I have been attached to the Ganga and the Jumna rivers in Allahabad ever since my childhood and, as I have grown older, this attachment has also grown. I have watched their varying moods as the seasons changed, and have often thought of the history and myth and tradition and song and story that have become attached to them through the long ages and become part of their flowing waters. The Ganga, especially, is the river of India, beloved of her people, round which are intertwined her racial memories, her hopes and fears, her songs of triumph, her victories and her defeats. She has been a symbol of India's age-long culture and civilization, ever-changing, ever-flowing, and yet ever the same Ganga. She reminds me of the snow-covered peaks and the deep valleys of the Himalayas, which I have loved so much, and of the rich and vast plains below, where my life and work have been cast. Smiling and dancing in the morning sun – shadows fall: a narrow, slow and graceful stream in winter, and a vast roaring thing during the monsoon, broadbosomed almost as the sea, and with something of the sea's power to destroy, the Ganga has been to me a symbol and a memory of the past of India, running into the present, and flowing on to the great ocean of the future. And though I have discarded much of past tradition and custom, and am anxious that India should rid herself of all shackles that bind and constrain her and divide her people, and suppress vast numbers of them, and prevent the free development of the body and the spirit; though I seek all this, yet I do not wish to cut myself off from that past completely. I am proud of that great inheritance that has been, and is, ours, and I am conscious that I too, like all of us, am a link in that unbroken chain which goes back to the dawn of history in the immemorial past of India; that chain I would not break, for I treasure it and seek inspiration from it. And, as witness of this desire of mine and as my last homage to India's cultural inheritance, I am making this request that a handful of my ashes be thrown into the Ganga at Allahabad to be carried to the great ocean that washes India's shores.

The major portion of my ashes should, however, be disposed of otherwise. I want these to be carried high up into the air in an aeroplane and scattered from that height over the fields where the peasants of India toil, so that they might mingle with the dust and soil of India and become an indistinguishable part of India.

The testament was the last chapter of Jawaharlal Nehru's interrupted autobiography.

Bibliography

Works by Jawaharlal Nehru
Glimpses of World History (Allahabad: Kitabistan, 1934–35).
An Autobiography (London: John Lane, 1936).
India and the World (London: Allen & Unwin, 1936).
Letters from a Father to a Daughter (Allahabad: Kitabistan, 1938).
Eighteen Months in India (Allahabad: Kitabistan, 1938).
China, Spain and the War (Allahabad: Kitabistan, 1940).
Towards Freedom (New York: John Day & Co., 1941).
The Discovery of India (Calcutta: Signet Press, 1946).
The Unity of India: Collected Writings, 1934–40 (London: Lindsay Drummond, 1948).
Independence and After (Delhi: Ministry of Information and Broadcasting, Publications Division, 1949).
A Bunch of Old Letters (Bombay: Asia Publishing House, 1958).
India: Today and Tomorrow (Calcutta: Orient Longman, 1960).
India's Foreign Policy (Delhi: Government of India, Publications Division, 1961).
Selected Speeches, September 1946 to April 1961 (Delhi: Government of India, Publications Division, 1961).
Nehru's Letters to His Sister, ed. Krishna Hutheesingh (London: Faber, 1963).
Selected Works of Jawaharlal Nehru, (First Series), Vols 1–15, ed. M. Chalapathi Rau, H. Y. Sharada Prasad and B. R. Nanda (Delhi: Orient Longman and NMML, 1972).
Selected Works of Jawaharlal Nehru, (Second Series), Vols 1–15, ed. S. Gopal (New Delhi: NMML, 1984).
India's Independence and Social Revolution (Delhi: Vikas, 1984).
Letters to Chief Ministers, 1947–64, ed. G. Parthasarathi (Oxford and NMML, 1985).

Official publications
Asian Relations: A Report of the Proceedings and Documentation of the First ARC, New Delhi, 1947 (Delhi: Asian Relations Organization, 1948).

First Five-Year Plan (Delhi: Government of India, Publications Division, 1952).

The Indian Annual Register, ed. N. N. Mitra (Calcutta, 1919–37).

Prime Minister on Sino-Soviet Relations (Delhi: Government of India, Publications Division, 1961).

Report of the Indian Statutory Commission (London: HMSO, 1930).

Second Five-Year Plan (Delhi: Government of India, Publications Division, 1956).

States Reorganization Commission, February 1954 to September 1955 (Delhi: Government of India, Ministry of Home Affairs, 1955).

Third Five-Year Plan (Delhi: Government of India, Publications Division, 1960).

Other works

Acheson, Dean, *Present at the Creation: My Years in the State Department* (New York: Norton, 1964).

Adhikari, G. M., *What is Happening in Hyderabad* (Bombay: Communist Party of India, 1949).

Afaque, Khan Muhammad, *The Gandhian Approach to Communal Harmony* (Delhi: Ajanta, 1986).

Ahmad, Hasan S., *Iqbal, His Political Ideas at the Crossroads* (Aligarh: Printwell, 1979).

Ali, Mohammed, *My Life: A Fragment* (Lahore: Ashrat, 1966).

Allen, Charles, *A Glimpse of the Burning Plain: Leaves from the Indian Journals of Charlotte Canning* (London: Michael Joseph, 1986).

Amrita Bazar Patrika, Calcutta.

Anderson, Walter K., and Damle, Sridhar D., *The Brotherhood in Saffron: The RSS and Hindu Revivalism* (Delhi: Vistaar Publications, 1987).

Asian Recorder 1959–61, Delhi.

Azad, Abul Kalam, *India Wins Freedom* (Calcutta: Orient Longman, 1959).

Baig, M. R. A., *The Muslim Dilemma in India* (Delhi: Vikas, 1974).

Baxter, Craig, *The Jana Sangh: A Biography of a Political Party* (University of Pennsylvania, Philadelphia, 1969).

Besant, Annie, *How India Wrought Her Freedom* (Madras: Theosophical Publishing House, 1915).

Bhambri, C. P., *Foreign Policy of India* (Delhi: Sterling, 1987).

Bose, Sisir K. (ed.), *Beacon Across Asia: A Biography of Subhas Chandra Bose* (Calcutta: Orient Longman, 1973).

Bose, Subhas Chandra, *The Indian Struggle* (London: Wishart, 1935).

Bose, Subhas Chandra, *Crossroads* (Calcutta: Netaji Research Bureau, 1962).

Bose, Subhas Chandra, *An Indian Pilgrim, an Unfinished Autobiography* and Collected Letters (Calcutta: Netaji Research Bureau, 1965).

Brecher, Michael, *Nehru: A Political Biography* (London: Oxford University Press, 1959).

Brecher, Michael, *Succession in India* (London: Oxford University Press, 1966).

Bright, J. S., *The Great Nehrus* (Delhi: Tagore Memorial Publications, 1961).

Brown, Judith M., *Gandhi's Rise to Power: Indian Politics 1915–1922* (Cambridge University Press with Blackie India, 1972).

Chagla, M. C. *Roses in December* (Bombay: Bharatiya Vidya Bhavan, 1973).

Chakravarty, Sukhomoy, *Development Planning: The Indian Experience* (Oxford: Clarendon Press, 1987).

Chand, Tara, *History of the Freedom Movement in India* (Delhi: Government of India, Publications Division, 1977).

Chandra, Bipan, *Communalism in Modern India* (Delhi: Vikas, 1984).

Chaplin, Charlie, *My Autobiography* (London: Bodley Head, 1964).

Chatterjee, Bhola, *Palace, People and Politics: Nepal in Perspective* (Delhi: Ankur Publishing House, 1980).

Chattopadhyay, Gautam, *Communism and Bengal's Freedom Movement* (Delhi: People's Publishing House, 1970).

Chattopadhyay, Gautam, *Subhas Chandra Bose and the Indian Communist Movement* (Delhi: People's Publishing House, 1987).

Chattopadhyaya, Kamaladevi, *Tribalism in India* (Delhi: Vikas, 1987).

Chaube, S., *Hill Politics in Northeast India* (Calcutta: Orient Longman, 1973).

Collins, Larry, and Lapierre, Dominique, *Freedom at Midnight* (Delhi: Vikas, 1976).

Collins, Larry, and Lapierre, Dominique, *Mountbatten and Independent India* (Delhi: Vikas, 1982).

Corr, Gerald H., *The War of the Springing Tigers* (London: Osprey, 1975).

Coupland, Reginald, *The Constitutional Problem in India* (London: Oxford University Press, 1944).

Cousins, Norman (ed.), *Profiles of Nehru* (Delhi: Indian Book Company, 1966).

Cousins, Norman, *Talks with Nehru* (London: John Day, 1951).

Crocker, W. R., *Nehru* (London: Allen & Unwin, 1966).

Curran, Jean A. Jr, *Militant Hinduism in Indian Politics: A Study of the RSS* (New York: Institute of Pacific Relations, 1957).

Dalvi, J. P., *Himalayan Blunder* (Bombay: Thacker, 1969).

Dayal, R., *Mission for Hammarskjöld* (Delhi: Oxford University Press, 1976).

Desai, Morarji, *Envoy to Nehru* (Delhi: Oxford University Press, 1981).

Dove, Marguerite, *Forfeited Future: The Conflict over Congress Ministries* in British India, 1933–37 (Delhi: Chanakya Publications, 1987).

Dutt, Subimal, *With Nehru in the Foreign Office* (Calcutta: Minerva Associates, 1977).

Edwardes, Michael, *Nehru: A Political Biography* (London: Penguin, 1971).

Engineer, Asghar Ali (ed.), *The Role of Minorities in India's Freedom Struggle* (New Delhi: Ajanta Publications, 1980).

Frankel, Francine R., *India's Political Economy 1947–77* (Princeton, New Jersey: The University Press, 1978).

Frykenberg, R. E. (ed.), *Delhi through the Ages: Essays in Urban History, Culture and Society* (Delhi: Oxford University Press, 1986).

Galbraith, J. K., *Ambassador's Journal* (London: Hamish Hamilton, 1969).

Galbraith, J. K., *A Life in Our Times* (London: André Deutsch, 1981).

Gandhi, M. K., *Communal Unity* (Ahmedabad: Navjivan, 1949).

Gandhi, M. K., *An Autobiography or My Experiments with Truth* (Ahmedabad: Navjivan, 1958).

Gandhi, Indira, *My Truth*, presented by Emmanuel Ponchpadass (New York: Grove Press, 1980; Delhi: Vision Books, 1981).

Gandhi, Rajmohan, *The Rajaji Story* (Madras: Tamilnad Printers, 1984).

Gandhi, Rajmohan, *Eight Lives: A Study of Hindu–Muslim Encounter* (Albany: State University of New York Press, 1986).

Ganguli, Milada, *A Pilgrimage to the Nagas* (Delhi: Oxford/IBH, 1984).

Gardezi, H., and Rashid, J. (eds.), *Pakistan: The Roots of Dictatorship* (London: Oxford Uniiversity Press, 1983).

Ghosh, Sudhir, *Ghandi's Emissary* (Cresset Press, 1966).

Gilbert, Martin S., *Winston S. Churchill: Road to Victory 1914–45* (London: Heinemann, 1986).

Golwalkar, M. S., *We, or Our Nationhood Defined* (Nagpur: Bharat Prakashan, 1947).

Golwalkar, M. S., *A Bunch of Thoughts* (Bangalore: Vikrama Prakashana, 1966).

Gopal, Ram, *Trials of Jawaharlal Nehru* (Bombay: The Book Centre, 1962).

Gopal, S., *Jawaharlal Nehru, a Biography*, 3 vols. (Delhi: Oxford University Press, 1976).

Goyal, Des Raj, *Rashtriya Swayamsevak Sangh* (Delhi: Radha Krishna Prakashan, 1979).

Griffiths, Charles John, *A Narrative of the Siege of Delhi*, ed. by Henry John Yonge (London: John Murray, 1910).

Gundevia, Y. D., *Outside the Archives* (Hyderabad: Orient Longman, 1984).

Gupta, N. L. (ed.), *Nehru on Communalism* (New Delhi: Sampradayikta Virodhi Committee, 1965).

Guruji, Shri, *The Man and His Mission* (Delhi: Bharat Prakashan, 1957).

Hangen, Welles, *After Nehru, Who?* (London: Hart-Davis, 1963).

Haq, Mushir A., *Muslim Politics in Modern India* (Meerut: Meenakshi, 1970).

Harrison, Selig S., *India, the Most Dangerous Decade* (Madras: Oxford University Press, 1960).

Haksar, P. N. (ed)., *Nehru's Vision: Peace and Security in the Nuclear Age* (Delhi: Patriot Publishers, 1987).

Hindusthan Standard, Calcutta.

Hodson, H. V., *The Great Divide* (London: Hutchinson, 1969).

Hunter, W. W., *Indian Mussalmans: Are they Bound in Conscience to Rebel against the Queen?* (London: Trubner & Co., 1971).

Hutheesingh, Krishna (ed.), *Nehru's Letters to His Sister* (London: Faber, 1963).

Hutheesingh, Krishna, *We Nehrus* (New Delhi: India Book House, 1967).

Iqbal, Afzal, *Life and Times of Mahomed Ali* (Delhi: Idara-i-Adabiyat, 1978).

Irvine, W., *Later Mughals* (Delhi: Oriental Books, 1971).

Ispahani, M. A. H., *Qaid-e-Azam Jinnah As I Knew Him* (Karachi: Forward Publications Trust, 1967).

Iyer, Raghavan (ed.), *The Moral and Political Writings of Mahatma Gandhi* (Oxford: Clarendon Press, 1986).

Jalal, Ayesha, *The Sole Spokesman: Jinnah, the Muslim League and the Demand for Pakistan* (Cambridge University Press, 1985).

Jetley, Nancy, *India–China Relations, 1947–77* (Delhi: Radiant Publishers, 1979).

Jha, C. S., *From Bandung to Tashkent: Glimpses of Foreign Policy* (Madras: Sangam Books, 1983).

Jones, Marc Bence, *The Viceroys of India* (London: Constable, 1982).

Kabir, Humayun, *Muslim Politics* (Calcutta: Firma K L M, 1969).

Kalhan, Promilla, *Kamala Nehru: An Intimate Biography* (Delhi: Vikas, 1973).

Kamath, Hari Vishnu, *The Last Days of Jawaharlal Nehru* (Calcutta: Jayasree Prakashan, 1977).

Karaka, D. F., *Nehru – The Lotus Eater from Kashmir* (D. Verschoyle, 1953).

Karanjia, R. K., *The Mind of Mr Nehru* (London: Allen & Unwin, 1960).

Karanjia, R. K., *The Philosophy of Mr Nehru* (London: Allen & Unwin, 1966).

Kaul, B. M., *The Untold Story* (Bombay: Jaico, 1969).

Khaliquzzaman, Chaudhury, *Pathway to Pakistan* (Lahore: Longman Greens, 1961).

Khan, Ayub, *Friends, Not Masters* (London: Oxford University Press, 1967).

Khan, Wali, *Facts Are Facts: The Untold Story of India's Partition* (Delhi: Vikas, 1987).

Khera, S. S., *India's Defence Problem* (Bombay: Orient Longman, 1968).

Kulkarni, V. B., *The Indian Triumvirate* (Bombay: Bharatiya Vidya Bhavan, 1969).

Kumar, Ravinder, and Panigrahi, D. N., *Selected Works of Motilal Nehru: Nehru Memorial Museum and Library* (Delhi: Vikas, 1982).

Kumar, Kapil, *Peasants in Revolt* (Delhi: Manohar, 1984).

Lakdawala, D. T., *Lessons of Planning* (Delhi: Oxford University Press, 1987).

Limaye, Madhu, *Prime Movers: The Role of the Individual in History* (Delhi: Radiant Publishers, 1985).

Lohia, Rammanohar, *Guilty men of India's Partition* (Hyderabad: Rammanohar Lohia Samata Vidyalaya Nyas, 1970).

Madhok, Balraj, *Portrait of a Martyr: Biography of Dr Shyama Prasad Mookerjee* (Bombay: Jaico, 1969).

Majumdar, R. C. (ed.), *The History and Culture of the Indian People*; Vol. IX, *British Paramountcy and the Indian Renaissance*; Vol. X, *Struggle for Freedom* (Bombay: Bharatiya Vidya Bhavan, 1965).

Malsiani, Arsh, *Abul Kalam Azad* (Delhi: Government of India, Publications Division, 1976).

Mankekar, M. R., *Lal Bahadur, a Political Biography* (Bombay: Popular Prakashan, 1964).

Mansergh, Nicholas, and Moon, Penderel (eds.), *The Transfer of Power* (London: HMSO, 1981).

Masani, Zareer, *Indira Gandhi: A Biography* (New York: Thomas Y. Crowell Co., 1975).

Masselos, Jim, *Indian Nationalism* (Delhi: Sterling, 1985).

Masselos, Jim (ed.), *Struggling and Ruling – the Indian National Congress 1885–1985* (Bangalore: Sterling, 1987).

Mathai, M. O., *My Days with Nehru* (Delhi: Vikas, 1979).

Mathai, M. O., *Reminiscences of the Nehru Age* (Delhi: Vikas, 1978).

Maxwell, N., *India's China War* (London: Jonathan Cape, 1970).

Mehta, Asoka, and Patwardhan, Achyut, *The Communal Triangle in India* (Allahabad: Kitabistan, 1942).

Mende, Tibor, *Conversations with Nehru* (London: Secker & Warburg, 1956).

Menon, V. P., *The Story of the Integration of the Indian States* (Calcutta: Orient Longman, 1956).

Menon, V. P., *The Transfer of Power in India* (Delhi: Orient Longman, 1979).

Misra, B. B., *The Indian Political Parties* (Delhi: Oxford University Press, 1976).

Montagu, Edwin S., *An Indian Diary* (London: Heinemann, 1930).

Moore, R. J., *The Crisis of Indian Unity 1917–1940* (Delhi: Oxford University Press, 1974).

Moraes, Francis Robert, *Jawaharlal Nehru: A Biography* (New York: Macmillan, 1956).

Moraes, Francis Robert, *Nehru: Sunlight and Shadow* (Bombay: Jaico, 1964).

Moraes, Francis Robert, *Witness to an Era* (Delhi: Vikas, 1973).

Mujeeb, M., *The Indian Muslims* (London: Allen & Unwin, 1967).

Mukherjee, Hirendranath, *The Gentle Colossus: A Study of Jawaharlal Nehru* (Calcutta: Manisha, 1964).

Mukherjee, Hirendranath, *Was India's Partition Unavoidable?* (Calcutta: Manisha Granthalaya, 1987).

Mullick, B. N., *My Years with Nehru, 1948–64* (Allied Publishers, 1972).

Myrdal, Gunnar, *The Asian Drama* (New York: Pantheon, 1968).

Naidu, Sarojini (ed.), *Mohammad Ali Jinnah; His Speeches and Writings* (Madras: Ganesh, 1918).

Nanda, B. R., *The Nehrus* (London: Allen & Unwin, 1962).

Nanda, B. R. (ed.), *Socialism in India* (Delhi: Vikas, 1972).

Nanda, B. R., *Gokhale, Gandhi and the Nehrus* (London: Allen & Unwin, 1974).

Nanda, B. R. (ed.), *Indian Foreign Policy: The Nehru Years* (Delhi: Vikas, 1976).

Nanda, B. R. (ed.), *Essays in Modern Indian History* (Oxford University Press, 1980).

Nanda, B. R., *The Nehrus* (Oxford University Press, 1984).

Nanda, B. R., *Gandhi and His Critics* (Delhi: Oxford University Press, 1985).

Narayan, Shriman, *Memoirs: Window on Ghandi and Nehru* (Bombay: Popular Prakashan, 1971).

Nehru Abhinandan Granth Committee, *Nehru Abhinandan Granth, A Birthday Book* (Allahabad: Law Journal Press, 1949).

Nehru Family and Ghanshyamdas Birla (Delhi: Vision Books, 1986).

Norriter, T. J., *Communism in Kerala* (London: C. Hurst & Co., 1982).

Overstreet and Windmiller, *Communism in India* (Berkeley: University of California Press, 1959).

Page, David, *Prelude to Partition* (Delhi: Oxford University Press, 1982).

Paliwal, Om Prakash, *Rameshwari Nehru: Patriot and Internationalist* (New Delhi: National Book Trust, 1986).

Pande, B. N. (ed.), *Centenary Volume of the Indian National Congress*, 3 vols. (Delhi: AICC and Vikas, 1985)

Pannikar, K. M., *Asia and Western Dominance* (London: Allen & Unwin, 1953).

Panikkar, K. M., and Pershad, A. (eds.), *Selected Speeches of Motilal Nehru* (London: Asia Publishing House, 1961).

Park, Richard L., and Tinker, Irene, *Leadership and Political Institutions in India* (Princeton: Princeton University Press, 1959).

Patel, Sardar, *Correspondence*, ed. Durga Das (Ahmedabad: Navajivan, 1972).

Philips, C. H. (ed.), *The Evolution of India and Pakistan 1858–1947, Select Documents* (London: ELBS and Oxford University Press, 1962).

Pirzada, Syed Sharifuddin (ed.), *Foundations of Pakistan: All-India Muslim League Documents* (Karachi: National Publishing House, 1969).

Prasad, Rajendra, *India Divided* (Delhi: Anmol Publications, 1986).

Rai, Lajpat, *Autobiographical Writings* (Delhi University Publications, 1965).

Range, Willard, *Jawaharlal Nehru's Worldview* (University of Georgia Press, 1961).

Rao, V. K. R. V., *The Nehru Legacy* (Bombay: Popular Prakashan, 1971).

Rao, Amiya, and Rao, B. G., *Six Thousand Days – Jawaharlal Nehru, Prime Minister* (Delhi: Sterling, 1974).

Rau, Chalapathi M., *Ghandi and Nehru* (New Delhi: Allied Publishers, 1967).

Rau, Chalapathi M. *Journalism and Politics* (Delhi: Vikas, 1984).

Reid, Escott, *Envoy to Nehru* (Oxford University Press, 1981).

Roy, M. N., *Jawaharlal Nehru* (Delhi: Radical Democratic Party, 1945).

Roy, Samaren, *M. N. Roy and Mahatma Gandhi* (Calcutta: Minerva Associates, 1987).

Russell, William Howard, *My Indian Mutiny Diary* (London: Cassell, 1957).

Rustomji, Nari, *Imperilled Frontiers: India's Northeast Borderlands* (Delhi: Oxford University Press, 1983).

Sahgal, Nayantara, *Indira Gandhi – Her Road to Power* (New York: Ungar, 1978).

Saraswati, Swami Dayanand, *The Light of Truth* (Allahabad: Arya Pratinidhi Sabha, 1915).

Scarfe, A., and Scarfe, W., *JP: His Biography* (Delhi: Orient Longman, 1975).

Schlesinger, A. M., *A Thousand Days: John F. Kennedy in the White House* (London: André Deutsch, 1965).

Schram, S. (ed.), *Mao Tse-Tung Unrehearsed* (Harmondsworth: Penguin, 1974).

Sen, A. K., *Poverty and Famines: An Essay on Entitlement and Deprivation* (Oxford University Press, 1981).

Sen, S. P., (ed.), *National Biography* (Calcutta: Institute of Historical Studies, 1972).

Sen, Surendranath, *Eighteen Fifty-Seven* (Delhi: Government of India, Ministry of Information and Broadcasting, Publications Division, 1957).

Seton, Marie, *Panditji: A Portrait of Jawaharlal Nehru* (London: Dennis Dobson, 1967).

Shakir, Moin, *Politics of Minorities* (Delhi: Ajanta Publications, 1980).

Shamasastry, R. (trans.), *Chanakya: Kautilya's Arthashastra* (London: Wesleyan Mission Press, 1923).

Shankar, *Dont Spare Me, Shankar* (New Delhi: Children's Book Trust, 1983).

Shirodkar, P. P., *Goa's Struggle for Freedom* (Delhi: Ajanta Publications, 1988).

Singh, Anita Inder, *The Origins of the Partition of India, 1936–1947* (Delhi: Oxford University Press, 1987).

Singh, B. P., *The Problem of Change – a Study of Northeast India* (Delhi: Oxford University Press, 1987).

Singh, Charan, *India's Economic Policy* (Delhi: Vikas, 1978).

Singh, K. Natwar (ed.), *Legacy of Nehru* (Delhi: Vikas, 1984).

Singh, Karan, *Sadar-i-Riyasat, an Autobiography,* 2 vols. (Delhi: Oxford University Press, 1985).

Sitaramayya, B. Pattabhi, *The History of the Indian National Congress* (Bombay: Padma Publications, 1946).

Tandon, P. D., *The Human Nehru* (Allahabad: Law Journal Press, 1957).

Tendulkar, D. G., *Mahatma: The Life of Mohandas Karamchand Gandhi,* 8 vols. (Delhi: Government of India, Publications Division, 1951).

Trench, Charles Chenevix, *Viceroy's Agent* (London: Cape, 1987).

Tripathi, Amales, *The Extremist Challenge* (Calcutta: Orient Longman, 1967).

Tuker, F. I. S., *While Memory Serves* (London: Vassett, 1950).

Vas, E. A., *Without Baggage* (Dehra Dun: Natraj, 1987).

Wavell, Lord, *The Viceroy's Journal,* ed. Penderel Moon (London: Oxford University Press, 1973).

Wolpert, Stanley, *Jinnah of Pakistan* (New York: Oxford University Press, 1984).

Yunus, Muhammad, *Persons, Passions and Politics* (Delhi: Vikas, 1980).

Yunus, Muhammad, *Letters from Prison* (Delhi: Vikas, 1986).

Zaidi, A. M. (ed.), *Congress, Nehru and the Second World War* (Delhi: Document Press, 1985).

Zaidi, A. M. (ed.), *The Jinnah–Ispahani Correspondence* (Karachi, 1976).

Zakaria, Rafiq (ed.), *A Study of Nehru* (Bombay: Times of India Publications, 1959).

Zakaria, Rafiq, *The Rise of Muslims in Indian Politics* (Somaiya Publications, 1970).

Ziegler, Philip, *Mountbatten* (London: Collins/Fontana, 1955).

Index